Cisco® ASA
Configuration

ABOUT THE AUTHOR

For over ten years, **Richard Deal** has operated his own company, The Deal Group Inc., in Oviedo, Florida, east of Orlando. Richard has over 20 years of experience in the computing and networking industry including networking, training, systems administration, and programming. In addition to a BS in Mathematics from Grove City College, he holds many certifications from Cisco and has taught many beginning and advanced Cisco classes. This book replaces Richard's *Cisco PIX Firewalls* (2002), an in-depth book on Cisco's PIX firewalls and their implementation, published by McGraw-Hill Professional. Richard has also written two revisions for the CCNA certification for McGraw-Hill, *CCNA Cisco Certified Network Associate Study Guide* (2008) and will be finishing his book for the CCNA Security certification in mid-2009: *CCNA Cisco Certified Network Associate Security Study Guide*. Richard is also the author of two books with Cisco Press: *The Complete Cisco VPN Configuration Guide* (2005) and *Cisco Router Firewall Security* (2004), named a Cisco CCIE Security recommended reading. In all, Richard has more than ten books under his belt.

Richard also periodically holds boot-camp classes on the CCNA and CCSP, which provide hands-on configuration of Cisco routers, switches, and security devices.

About the Technical Editor

Ryan Lindfield has worked in IT since 1996 and is currently teaching Cisco certification courses at Boson Training and consulting for Westchase Technologies. Ryan holds several certifications including CCSP, CISSP, CEH, GCFA, CCSI, and MCSE and enjoys vulnerability research and exploring the latest trends in security technologies. He lives in Tampa, Florida, with his wife, Desiree, and his dog, Logan.

Cisco® ASA Configuration

RICHARD A. **DEAL**

New York   Chicago   San Francisco
Lisbon   London   Madrid   Mexico City   Milan
New Delhi   San Juan   Seoul   Singapore   Sydney   Toronto

The *McGraw·Hill* Companies

Cataloging-in-Publication Data is on file with the Library of Congress

McGraw-Hill books are available at special quantity discounts to use as premiums and sales promotions, or for use in corporate training programs. To contact a representative, please e-mail us at bulksales@mcgraw-hill.com.

Cisco® ASA Configuration

1234567890   DOC DOC   019

ISBN   978-0-07-162269-1
MHID   0-07-162269-1

Sponsoring Editor
Jane K. Brownlow

Editorial Supervisor
Janet Walden

Project Manager
Vipra Fauzdar,
International Typesetting
and Composition

Acquisitions Coordinators
Carly Stapleton
and Joya Anthony

Technical Editor
Ryan Lindfield

Copy Editor
Jan Jue

Proofreader
Claire Splan

Indexer
Claire Splan

Production Supervisor
Jean Bodeaux

Composition
International Typesetting
and Composition

Illustration
International Typesetting
and Composition

Art Director, Cover
Jeff Weeks

I dedicate this book to my two daughters, the loves of my life: Alina and Nika. May life bring you love, health, and happiness.

AT A GLANCE

Part I	**Introduction to ASA Security Appliances and Basic Configuration Tasks**	
▼ 1	ASA Product Family	3
▼ 2	CLI Basics	33
▼ 3	Basic ASA Configuration	45
▼ 4	Routing and Multicasting	75

Part II	**Controlling Traffic Through the ASA**	
▼ 5	Address Translation	105
▼ 6	Access Control	151
▼ 7	Web Content	189
▼ 8	CTP	207
▼ 9	IPv6	233

Part III   Policy Implementation

▼ 10   Modular Policy Framework   247
▼ 11   Protocols and Policies   277
▼ 12   Data Applications and Policies   295
▼ 13   Voice and Policies   327
▼ 14   Multimedia and Policies   347

Part IV   Virtual Private Networks (VPNs)

▼ 15   IPSec Phase 1   371
▼ 16   IPSec Site-to-Site   395
▼ 17   IPSec Remote Access Server   409
▼ 18   IPSec Remote Access Client   441
▼ 19   SSL VPNs: Clientless   451
▼ 20   SSL VPNs: AnyConnect Client   487

Part V   Advanced Features of the ASA

▼ 21   Transparent Firewall   509
▼ 22   Contexts   523
▼ 23   Failover   541
▼ 24   Network Attack Prevention   577
▼ 25   SSM Cards   597

Part VI   Management of the ASA

▼ 26   Basic Management from the CLI   619
▼ 27   ASDM   647

▼   Index   703

CONTENTS

Foreword xxiii

Preface xxv

Acknowledgments xxvii

Introduction xxix

Part I

Introduction to ASA Security Appliances and Basic Configuration Tasks

▼ 1 ASA Product Family 3

ASA Features 4
    Operating System 5
    Security Algorithm 7
    Redundancy 15
    Advanced Features of the Operating System 18

ASA Hardware 23
    ASA Models 23
    Hardware Modules 28
    Licensing 30

▼ 2   CLI Basics 33

Access to the Appliance 34
    Console Access 34
    Other Access Methods 35
CLI 36
    ASA Bootup Sequence 36
    CLI Modes 38
    ASA and Router IOS CLI Comparison 41

▼ 3   Basic ASA Configuration 45

Setup Script 46
Basic Management Commands 48
    Viewing Configurations 48
    Copy Commands 49
    Write Commands 51
    Clear Commands 51
Basic Configuration Commands 52
    Host and Domain Names 52
    Device Names 53
    Passwords 53
    Login Banner 54
    Interfaces 55
    Dynamic Addressing 62
Management 65
    Remote Access 65
    Connectivity Testing 68
Hardware and Software Information 70
    Version Information 71
    Memory Usage 72
    CPU Utilization 72
ASA Configuration Example 73

▼ 4   Routing and Multicasting 75

Routing Features 76
    Routing Recommendations 76
    Administrative Distance 76
    Static Routes 77
    RIP 82
    OSPF 84
    EIGRP 91
Multicast Features 95
    Multicast Traffic and the Appliances 95
    Multicast Usage 96

Stub Multicast Routing 96
PIM Multicast Routing 100

Part II

Controlling Traffic Through the ASA

▼ 5 Address Translation 105

Protocol Overview 106
    TCP Overview 106
    UDP Overview 108
    ICMP Overview 109
    Other Protocols 110
    Protocol and Application Issues 110
Translations and Connections 113
    Connections 113
    Translations 115
    TCP Connection Example 115
Address Translation Overview 119
    Private Addresses 119
    Needs for Address Translation 120
    Examples of Address Translation 122
Address Translation Configuration 128
    Requiring Address Translation 128
    Configuring Dynamic Address Translation 129
    Configuring Static NAT Translation 138
    Configuring Static PAT Translation 140
    Finding a Matching Translation Policy 141
TCP SYN Flood Attacks 143
    The Original TCP Intercept 143
    TCP Intercept with SYN Cookies 143
Translation and Connection Verification 144
    Viewing Active Translations 144
    Viewing Active Connections 146
    Viewing Local Host Information 147
    Clearing Entries in the Xlate and Conn Tables 148

▼ 6 Access Control 151

Access Control Lists (ACLs) 152
    Introduction to ACLs 152
    Creating and Activating ACLs 155
    ACL Activation 160
    ACL Verification 160

ACL Maintenance 161
ACL Configuration Examples 163
Object Groups 171
Advantages of Object Groups 171
Creating Object Groups 171
Examining Your Object Groups 174
Deleting Object Groups 174
Using Object Groups 175
Object Group Configuration Example 176
ICMP Filtering 177
ICMP Traffic Through the Appliances 178
ICMP Traffic Directed at the Appliances 179
Connection Troubleshooting 181
Packet Tracer Feature 181
Packet Capture Feature 184

▼ 7   Web Content 189
Java and ActiveX Filtering 190
Java and ActiveX Issues 190
Java and ActiveX Filtering Solutions 191
Configuring Java Filters 191
Configuring ActiveX Filters 192
Web Content Filtering 192
Web Filtering Process 193
URL Filtering Server 195
URL Filtering Verification 200
URL Filtering Example 202
Web Caching 203
WCCP Process 203
WCCP Configuration 204
WCCP Verification 205
WCCP Configuration Example 206

▼ 8   CTP 207
AAA Overview 208
AAA Components 208
AAA Example 208
AAA Protocols 209
AAA Servers 211
AAA Server Configuration 211
CTP Authentication 213
CTP Overview 214
Appliance Configuration of CTP Authentication 215
Verifying CTP Authentication 222

CTP Authorization 224
CTP Authorization Options 225
Classic Authorization Configuration 226
Downloadable ACL Configuration 228
CTP Accounting 230
Appliance Configuration for Accounting 230
Cisco Secure ACS Reports 231

▼ 9   IPv6 233

IPv6 Overview 234
IPv6 Capabilities of the Appliances 234
IPv6 Limitations of the Appliances 235
IPv6 Interface Configuration 236
Stateless Autoconfiguration 236
Link-Local Address Configuration 237
Global Address Configuration 237
IPv6 Interface Configuration Verification 238
IPv6 Routing 238
IPv6 Neighbors 239
Neighbor Solicitation Messages 240
Router Advertisement Messages 241
IPv6 ACLs 242
IPv6 ACL Configuration 242
IPv6 ACL Example 244

Part III

Policy Implementation

▼ 10 Modular Policy Framework 247

MPF Overview 248
MPF Policies 248
Why MPF Is Necessary 249
MPF Components 252
Class Maps 252
Layer 3/4 Class Maps 253
Application Layer Class Maps 256
Policy Maps 260
Layer 3/4 Policy Map 261
Layer 7 Policy Map 271
Service Policies 274
Activating a Layer 3/4 Policy Map 274
Service Policy Verification 275

▼ 11 Protocols and Policies 277

ICMP Inspection Policies 278
   ICMP Issues 278
   ICMP Inspection Configuration 279
DCE/RPC Inspection Policies 280
   DCE/RPC Policy Configuration 280
   DCE/RPC Example Configuration 281
Sun RPC Inspection Policies 281
   Sun RPC Policy Configuration 282
   Sun RPC Example Configuration 283
ILS/LDAP Inspection Policies 284
   Mechanics of ILS/LDAP Connections 284
   ILS/LDAP Policy Configuration 285
   ILS/LDAP Example Configuration 285
NetBIOS Inspection Policies 285
   NetBIOS Policy Configuration 286
   NetBIOS Example Configuration 286
IPSec Pass-Thru Inspection Policies 287
   IPSec Pass-Thru Policy Configuration 287
   IPSec Pass-Thru Example Configuration 288
PPTP Inspection Policies 288
   PPTP Policy Configuration 289
   PPTP Example Configuration 289
XDMCP Inspection Policies 289
   Mechanics of XDMCP Connections 290
   XDMCP Policy Configuration 291
   Established Command Configuration 291
   XDMCP Example Configuration 293

▼ 12 Data Applications and Policies 295

DNS Inspection 296
   DNS Inspection Features 296
   DNS Policy Configuration 299
   DNS Example Configuration 301
SMTP and ESMTP Inspection 302
   SMTP and ESMTP Inspection Features 302
   SMTP and ESMTP Policy Configuration 303
   SMTP and ESMTP Example Configuration 305
FTP Inspection 306
   FTP Operation 306
   FTP Inspection Features 309
   FTP Policy Configuration 309
   FTP Example Configuration 311

TFTP Inspection 312
   TFTP Operation 312
   TFTP Policy Configuration 313
HTTP Inspection 313
   HTTP Inspection Features 313
   HTTP Policy Configuration 314
   HTTP Example Configuration 317
Instant Messaging Inspection 318
   IM Policy Configuration 318
   IM Example Configuration 320
RSH Inspection 321
   Mechanics of RSH Connections 321
   RSH Policy Configuration 322
SNMP Inspection 322
   SNMP Policy Configuration 322
   SNMP Example Configuration 323
SQL*Net Inspection 323
   Mechanics of SQL*Net Connections 323
   SQL*Net Policy Configuration 325

▼ 13 Voice and Policies 327
SIP Inspection 328
   SIP Connections and Application Inspection 328
   SIP Policy Configuration 331
   SIP Example Configuration 334
SCCP Inspection 335
   SCCP Connections and Application Inspection 335
   SCCP Policy Configuration 337
   SCCP Example Configuration 339
CTIQBE Inspection 340
   CTIQBE Connections and Application Inspection 340
   CTIQBE Policy Configuration 341
MGCP Inspection 342
   MGCP Connections and Application Inspection 343
   MGCP Policy Configuration 344
   MGCP Example Configuration 345

▼ 14 Multimedia and Policies 347
Multimedia Overview 348
   Common Problems with Multimedia
      Applications and Firewalls 348
   Firewall Solutions for Multimedia Applications 348

RTSP Inspection 349
   RTSP Connections and Application Inspection 350
   RTSP Policy Configuration 353
   RTSP Example Configuration 355
H.323 Inspection 355
   H.323 Overview 356
   H.323 Connections and Application Inspection 357
   H.323 Policy Configuration 364
   H.323 Example Configuration 366

Part IV

Virtual Private Networks (VPNs)

▼ 15 IPSec Phase 1 371
IPSec Introduction 372
   IPSec Preparations 372
   Same Interface Traffic 373
ISAKMP Configuration 373
   Global ISAKMP Properties 373
   ISAKMP Policies 375
   NAT Traversal and IPSec over TCP 375
   VPN Traffic and ACLs 377
Tunnel Groups 378
   Tunnel Group Creation 378
   General Tunnel Group Attributes 379
   VPN-Specific Tunnel Group Attributes 380
Certificate Authorities 380
   Introducing Certificates 381
   Obtaining Certificates 381
   Using Certificates 392

▼ 16 IPSec Site-to-Site 395
Site-to-Site Preparation 396
   ISAKMP Phase 1 Configuration 397
   Tunnel Group Configuration 397
   VPN Traffic and Address Translation 398
ISAKMP Phase 2 Configuration 399
   Crypto ACLs 400
   Transform Sets 400
   Connection Lifetimes 401
   Crypto Maps 402

Site-to-Site Verification 404
    Viewing and Clearing Connections 405
    Troubleshooting Connections 407
Site-to-Site Example 407

▼ 17 IPSec Remote Access Server 409

Easy VPN Overview 410
    Easy VPN Products 411
    Easy VPN Features 412
    Easy VPN Connectivity 413
Remote Access Preparation 414
    VPN Traffic 415
    VPN Traffic and Address Translation 415
    Tunnel Limits 415
ISAKMP Phase 1 Configuration 416
    ISAKMP Phase 1 Commands 416
    Group Policy Configuration 417
    Tunnel Group Configuration 425
    Auto Update 428
ISAKMP Phase 2 Configuration 430
    Dynamic Crypto Maps 430
    Static Crypto Maps 431
Remote Access Verification 432
    Viewing Remote Access Connections 432
    Disconnecting Remote Access Users 434
IPSec Remote Access Server Example 434
VPN Load Balancing 436
    Clustering Overview 437
    Clustering Configuration 438
    Clustering Example 439

▼ 18 IPSec Remote Access Client 441

Connection Modes 442
    Client Mode 442
    Network Extension Mode 444
    Network Extension Plus Mode 445
ASA 5505 Remote Client 445
    Hardware Client XAUTH Authentication Methods 445
    User Authentication 446
    Basic Client Configuration 447
    Tunnel Maintenance 448
Easy VPN Configuration Example with a Hardware Remote . . . 449
    ASA 5505 Configuration Example 449
    Example Easy VPN Server Configuration 449

▼ 19   SSL VPNs: Clientless   451

    Introduction to SSL VPNs   452
       Connection Modes   453
       WebVPN Restrictions   454
    Basic WebVPN Configuration   455
       Implementing SSL Policies   455
       Enabling WebVPN   456
       Supporting Both WebVPN and ASDM   456
       Performing DNS Lookups   457
       Implementing Web Proxying   458
       Defining General WebVPN Properties   460
    WebVPN Group Policies   460
       Configuring Group Policies   460
       Overriding Group Policies on a Per-User Basis   465
    Tunnel Groups   467
       Tunnel Group General Attributes   467
       Tunnel Group WebVPN Attributes   468
       Group Matching Methods   469
    WebVPN Clientless Home Portal   470
       Login Screen   471
       Home Portal Overview   472
       Home Portal Tabs   473
    Non-Web Traffic   475
       Port Forwarding   476
       Web Browser Plug-Ins   480
       Smart Tunneling   481
    WebVPN Verification and Troubleshooting   485
       show Commands   485
       debug Commands   485

▼ 20   SSL VPNs: AnyConnect Client   487

    AnyConnect Client Overview   488
       WebVPN Network Clients   488
       AnyConnect Client Implementation   489
       AnyConnect Client Connections   489
    AnyConnect Client Preparation and Installation   490
       ASA Preparation for the AnyConnect Client   491
       AnyConnect Policies   493
       WebVPN Tunnel Groups   497
       Client Profiles   499
    Managing and Troubleshooting AnyConnect Sessions   501
       Connecting to a WebVPN Server   501
       Viewing and Managing Connected Users   504

Part V

Advanced Features of the ASA

▼ 21 Transparent Firewall 509

Layer 2 Processing of Traffic 510

    Routed vs. Transparent Mode 510

    Bridges vs. Transparent Mode 511

    Supported and Unsupported Features 513

    Traffic Flow and ACLs 515

Configuring Transparent Mode 515

    Switching to Transparent Mode 516

    Management IP Address 516

    MAC Address Table and Learning 517

Additional Layer 2 Features 518

    Non-IP Traffic and Ether-Type ACLs 518

    ARP Inspection 519

Transparent Firewall Example Configuration 520

▼ 22 Contexts 523

Context Overview 524

    Licensing 524

    Context Uses 524

    Context Restrictions 525

    Context Implementation 526

    Traffic Classification 527

Context Mode 528

    Switching to Multiple Mode 528

    System Area Configuration 529

    Designating the Administrative Context 529

    Creating Contexts 530

    Managing Resources 532

Context Management 535

    Switching Between Contexts 535

    Saving Configurations 535

    Removing Contexts 536

Context Example 536

    Example: Changing to Multiple Mode 537

    Example: Setting Up the Interfaces 537

    Example: Creating the Contexts 538

    Example: Configuring the Admin Context 538

    Example: Configuring the ctx Context 539

    Example: Saving the Appliance Configuration 540

▼ **23 Failover** **541**

Failover Introduction 542
  Failover Types 542
  Failover Requirements 543
  Failover Restrictions 545
  Software Upgrades 545
Failover Implementations 545
  Active/Standby Failover 546
  Addressing and Failover 546
  Active/Active Failover 547
Failover Cabling 548
  Failover Link 548
  Stateful Link 549
  PIX Cabling 550
  ASA Cabling 550
Failover Operation 551
  Failover Communications 551
  Failover Triggers 552
  Switch Connections 554
Active/Standby Configuration 555
  Active/Standby: PIXs and the Serial Cable 555
  Active/Standby: LBF 558
  Active/Standby: Optional Commands 560
  Active/Standby: Example Configuration 561
Active/Active Configuration 566
  Active/Active: LBF Configuration 566
  Active/Active: Optional Commands 569
  Active/Active: Example Configuration 570

▼ **24 Network Attack Prevention** **577**

Threat Detection 578
  Basic Threat Detection 578
  Scanning Threat Detection 582
  Threat Detection Statistics 584
IP Audit 587
  IP Audit Signatures 587
  IP Audit Configuration 590
Additional Features 590
  TCP Normalization 590
  Reverse Path Forwarding 593
  Fragmentation Limits 594

▼ 25 SSM Cards   597
      AIP-SSM Card   598
            AIP-SSM Card Modes and Failure Options   598
            Traffic and the AIP-SSM Card   599
            Traffic Forwarding to the AIP-SSM Card   600
            AIP-SSM Basic Configuration   601
      CSC-SSM Card   606
            Traffic and the CSC Card   606
            Forwarding Traffic to the CSC-SSM Card   607
            Setting Up the CSC-SSM Card   609
      SSM Card Management   612
            Verifying an SSM Card Operational Status   612
            Hardware Module Commands   614
            Re-Imaging an SSM Card   615

Part VI

Management of the ASA

▼ 26 Basic Management from the CLI   619
      DHCP Services   620
            DHCP Server   620
            DHCP Relay   622
      Remote Management Features   623
            Date and Time   623
            Logging   625
            SNMP   629
      File Management   630
            Files and Flash   630
            OS Upgrades   631
            Controlling the Bootup Process   633
            License Keys   634
      Password Recovery   635
            Restricting the Password Recovery Process   635
            Performing the PIX Password Recovery Process   636
            Performing the ASA Password Recovery Process   638
      AAA   639
            Restricting CLI Access   639
            Command Authorization   642
            Management Accounting   645

▼ **27 ASDM** 647

    ASDM Overview 648
       ASDM Requirements 648
       ASDM Restrictions 649
    ASDM Configuration Preparations 650
       Setup Script 650
       Basic Configuration Commands 651
    ASDM Access 651
       Web Browser Access 652
       Startup Wizard 653
    ASDM Home Screen 654
       Menu Items 655
       Toolbar Buttons 661
       Home Screen Elements 662
    ASDM Configuration Screens 663
       Device Setup Tab 663
       Firewall Tab 664
       Remote Access VPN Tab 668
       Cisco Secure Desktop 678
       Site-to-Site VPN Tab 690
       Device Management Tab 691
    ASDM Monitoring Screens 692
       Interfaces Tab 693
       VPN Tab 694
       Routing Tab 694
       Properties Tab 695
       Logging Tab 695
    ASDM and Contexts 697
       Initial Access and Context Manipulation 698
       Failover 700

▼   Index 703

FOREWORD

Over the past decade computer networks as well as the attacks against them have become increasingly complex. As information technology professionals we are faced with overcoming challenges every day, and learning new security concepts should not be one of them. I have known Richard, the author of this book, during this same time, and his gift of making difficult technology concepts understandable has remained constant. Whether he is presenting to a room of information technology professionals or writing books, Richard's communication skills are unsurpassed.

As the importance of networks continues to grow, security becomes ever more vital. The Cisco Adaptive Security Appliances intelligent threat defense offers the needed protection for businesses today as well as for the future. Technologies and devices based on Internet protocol continually touch every aspect of our lives—we need to be confident that our data is safe. *Cisco ASA Configuration* is a great reference and tool for answering our challenges.

Steve Marcinek, CCIE 7225
Systems Engineer, Cisco Systems

PREFACE

Over the last several years we have seen a rise in the number of attacks launched against our networks. These attacks are not only more plentiful, but also becoming more sophisticated. The complexities of our networks grow at an equal rate, while IT departments and budgets shrink. The number of protocols on our networks is also rising, and the number of clients is increasing. Meanwhile there is the demand to keep services available and to keep data from being leaked.

While there is no single technology that can guarantee a secure network, one of the most critical components in your infrastructure is the firewall. Possessing a solid understanding of firewall capabilities is a critical prerequisite to fortify your defenses.

The Cisco ASA 5500 series products and the latest revisions of Cisco's firewall software have introduced some awesome new features. Topics discussed within this book include Modular Policy Framework, transparent firewalls, deep packet inspection, contexts, failover, WebVPN, and more. A plethora of capabilities on your firewalls is waiting to be unleashed; the key is knowing what these features are, understanding how the technology works, and then how to configure them. Richard has put together an excellent reference with over 20 chapters of technologies, explanations, and configuration examples.

Richard has been recognized as an expert on the Cisco firewall for many years, and this book is an excellent follow-up to his *Cisco PIX Firewalls* book from 2002. This book does a great job of walking you step-by-step through the technologies and configuration behind the ASA 5500. *Cisco ASA Configuration* is an excellent resource for both the novice and seasoned Cisco PIX administrator.

Ryan Lindfield
Senior Technical Instructor
Boson Training

ACKNOWLEDGMENTS

would like to thank the following people:

▼ This book would not have been possible without the support of family. A book of this size is very time-consuming, especially when you have to balance a book, a job, and, most importantly, a family. My two girls are the love of my life.

■ A special thanks to Ryan Lindfield for providing excellent feedback and encouragement on the technical content of this book. I've worked with Ryan for quite some years, and I've always been impressed with his security and, especially, his hacking skills. And congratulations to him for getting married!

▲ The team at McGraw-Hill, especially Jane Brownlow, Joya Anthony, Carly Stapleton, Vipra Fauzdar, Janet Walden, and Jan Jue. I owe a debt of gratitude to this team, especially in pulling all of the pieces together for the final proofing—thanks for your help!

Best wishes to all! And cheers!

INTRODUCTION

For those of you who have kept asking me when the replacement for my PIX book would be out, I appreciate your long patience. Over the past five years I have focused my business solely on security, spending most of my time with Cisco's security products like the ASAs and PIXs, and with VPN technologies.

Firewalls, as a technology, have been around for over a decade. However, it wasn't until the explosion of the Internet that the use of firewalls has become commonplace in corporate and small offices, and even in home environments. (I use an ASA 5505 for my home office and Eset on my laptop.) I'm continually amazed at the number of times curious people and hackers on the Internet have attempted to scan and probe my home office network.

Because of the large number of products available, I have limited the focus of this book primarily to Cisco's ASA security appliance family. Most of what I discuss in this book also applies to Cisco's end-of-sale PIX security appliances, and where there are differences I point them out. Many of the readers of my previous book on the PIXs have constantly asked me to update it; having a family life has slowed down my writing, but I'm back in the groove. So many critical changes have occurred since version 6 of the security appliances that I have finally succumbed to my faithful readers. Most medium-to-enterprise companies I've consulted for use Cisco's security appliances, so having a good background in understanding their capabilities and configuring their features makes you more marketable as a consultant and more valuable as an employee. I have written this book for the following reasons:

▼ To bring you up to date on the large number of very important changes in the security appliance operating system since version 6 of the PIXs.

■ To explore network security, a hot topic because of increasing levels of threats and damage, as well as the explosive growth of Internet services.

■ To familiarize you with ASA and PIX security appliances. You are likely to run into them in your job because Cisco is the market share leader in enterprise networking solutions.

■ To fill the need for a really good, focused book on Cisco's security appliance products.

▲ To make you more aware of the product technology and intelligence Cisco brings to the security arena, because I have never seen a networking company offer a better set of enterprise products and top-notch technical support.

THE INTENDED AUDIENCE

The concepts and configurations provided in this book are not for people thinking about a career in computer networking, but for people who are using ASAs (and PIXs) to secure their internal networks. This book can easily be read by not only network administrators, engineers, and technicians, but also by networking salespersons and managers. The objective of this book is to provide you with an understanding of the functions of a firewall; an overview of Cisco's ASA security appliance family; the features available on the ASAs, including those in the most recent operating system versions (version 8.0); and the configuration of the ASAs.

WHAT THIS BOOK COVERS

I make no assumptions about your skill level with ASAs, and I have attempted to present every subject in a clear and easy-to-understand layout. I've separated the book into different sections in order to make the presentation of the material easier to understand, and to provide a step-by-step progression in setting up your security appliance. This book contains six parts, with a total of 27 chapters. I assume that you have never seen the command-line interface (CLI) or graphical-user interface (GUI) of a Cisco security appliance.

Part I introduces you to the ASA product family, the CLI interface, and basic configuration tasks, like setting up interfaces and routing. Part II discusses controlling traffic through the security appliances, including address translation, access control lists (ACLs), object groups, filtering web content, filtering connections using AAA (called Cut-through Proxy), and IPv6. Part III covers the implementation of policies for protocols, data applications, voice, and multimedia through the use of the Modular Policy Framework (MPF). Part IV introduces the configuration of VPN implementations, including IPSec site-to-site, IPSec remote access, and Cisco's implementation of SSL VPNs, called WebVPN. Part V introduces the advanced features of the security appliances, including the layer 2 transparent firewall, security contexts, failover, network attack prevention features, and the AIP-SSM and CSC-SSM cards for the ASAs. The end of the book, Part VI, introduces you to the management of the appliances, including basic administrative tasks you perform from the CLI and Cisco's GUI-based product to manage the appliances: Adaptive Security Device Manager (ASDM).

FINAL WORDS

Even though I discuss many of the components and configurations of the security appliances, it is impossible to cover every type of configuration and network scenario in a single book. I highly recommend that you use Cisco's web site (http://www.cisco.com) as well as various Usenet newsgroups as additional resources. I cannot begin to count the number of times that I have found the answer to a question in either of these two places. Because of the value of this information, I've rarely had to call TAC (Technical Assistance Center) at Cisco for help with a security appliance configuration issue, except for the occasional bugs that I've discovered.

I wish you the best in your networking endeavors and hope that this book helps make your job easier when it comes to using Cisco's security appliances, especially the ASAs. I love to hear from my readers, so any and all feedback is appreciated!

Cheers!

PART I

Introduction to ASA Security Appliances and Basic Configuration Tasks

CHAPTER 1

ASA Product Family

T his chapter introduces the features and hardware of Cisco's Adaptive Security Appliance (ASA) product line. The topics include

▼ Features of the ASA, including the operating system, security algorithm, redundancy, and others

▲ The hardware of the ASA product line, including the models, supported hardware modules (cards), and licensing

ASA FEATURES

Cisco's ASA is a set of stateful security appliances ranging from the model 5505, which is designed for Small Office, Home Office (SOHO) environments, to the 5580, which is designed for large enterprise networks and ISP sites. All of these products use the same operating system and management tools, easing your implementation and monitoring tasks. Because all the security appliances use the same operating system, the major differences between the models primarily concern scalability and performance.

The ASA family of products (and their older siblings, the PIX products) can best be described as hybrid firewalls. Cisco, however, does not like to use the term "firewall" to describe the ASA and PIX product family. Instead, Cisco prefers using the term "security appliance," mainly because the ASA products and the products they replaced, the PIX products, are not just stateful firewalls; they also support many other security features, including

▼ Secure, real-time, proprietary operating system

■ Stateful firewall using the Cisco Security Algorithm (SA)

■ Sequence Number Randomization (SNR) to secure TCP connections

■ Cut-through Proxy (CTP) for authenticating telnet, HTTP, and FTP connections

■ Default security policies to ensure maximum protection, as well as the ability to customize these policies and build your own policies

■ Virtual private network (VPN) abilities: IPSec, SSL, and L2TP

■ Intrusion detection and prevention systems (IDS and IPS)

■ Address translation using dynamic and static network and port address translation

■ Stateful redundancy of connections and VPNs between two security appliances

▲ Virtualization of policies using contexts

This is just a small list of some major features of the security appliances. The following sections provide an overview of some of these features. The features that I don't briefly cover in this chapter are covered in subsequent chapters.

NOTE   Throughout the book, whenever the terms "security appliance" or "appliance" are used, they refer to both the ASA and PIX products unless otherwise noted.

Operating System

The operating system (version 7 and later) you currently see on the ASA appliances and on the PIX 515 and higher appliances is based on the PIX Finesse Operating System (FOS). The FOS is a proprietary, stand-alone operating system. It implements the actual security functions that the security appliance hardware performs. In this sense, it is somewhat similar to the Internetwork Operating System (IOS) of Cisco routers and switches, or what the Microsoft Windows XP or Linux operating systems are to PCs. Cisco no longer uses the term FOS to describe the operating system, though. Starting in version 7 and later, Cisco refers to the security appliance operating system as just the "operating system."

NOTE   Even though Cisco's PIX appliances are no longer for sale, which Cisco denotes as end-of-sale (EOS), the PIX 515s and higher support the same operating system as the ASAs. The main difference between the PIXs and ASAs is that the lower-end PIX 501 and 506E do not support version 7 and later of the OS, and none of the PIXs supports SSL VPNs. This book focuses on the use of the ASAs; however, the topics discussed can be equally applied to the PIXs in most situations.

Firewall Applications

Some firewall products run on top of an operating system; these solutions are commonly called *firewall applications*. One disadvantage that firewall applications have compared with a proprietary operating system is that the firewall vendor must deal with two software products in creating a firewall: the operating system and the firewall application. This process can often lead to a less secure system. This is especially true when you consider all the security threats that have been directed specifically at UNIX and Microsoft operating systems.

An example of a firewall product that uses firewall applications is Check Point. This is not to say that Check Point's firewall is a worse solution than a firewall product that uses a proprietary operating system. However, a firewall vendor like Check Point will have to do many more things to ensure that the firewall application and operating system provide a secure solution. (Note that Check Point's next-generation product, SecurePlatform 1, is moving away from this approach and moving toward an integrated solution.)

The main problem with a firewall application solution is that the vendor not only has to provide a secure firewall application, but must also secure the operating system it runs on. However, firewall applications do provide two advantages:

- ▼ They tend to be easy to install and maintain.
- ▲ They run on a wide variety of PC/server platforms.

Proprietary Operating System

Proprietary operating systems provide a security advantage over firewall applications—a proprietary operating system vendor has to be concerned about only one system, instead of two, in providing a secure firewall solution. Another huge advantage of proprietary operating systems is scalability. Because a proprietary operating system can be customized to a specific hardware platform, this firewall system can provide extremely fast packet filtering abilities and security capabilities.

Off-the-shelf operating systems like UNIX and Microsoft Windows are general-purpose operating systems that were developed to perform many tasks, not all of which are performed at an optimal level. Using a general operating system decreases the performance of the packet filtering and firewall functions of the firewall application. To provide for scalability, you must load your firewall application on very expensive server platforms.

Using a proprietary operating system in a firewall solution also makes it much more difficult for hackers to penetrate the firewall. Attackers are familiar with the functions of common operating systems like UNIX and Microsoft products, which makes it a little bit easier for them to attack the firewall application. However, when vendors use a proprietary operating system to implement their firewall solution, an attacker will have little or no knowledge about the functions and processes of the operating system, making it very difficult for the attacker to compromise the firewall solution.

Using a proprietary operating system has some disadvantages. First, because the operating system is proprietary, your security personnel will have to learn the new system. Many of your personnel will already have experience with UNIX or Microsoft Windows, and thus their learning curve in implementing the solution will be shortened.

NOTE   When you are using an underlying proprietary operating system such as Cisco's security appliances, the administrator is unable to interact with the underlying OS.

Also, because firewall applications are developed for a specific operating system platform like UNIX or Microsoft Windows, your security personnel will already be familiar with the interface that is employed by the firewall. A good example of this is Check Point's firewall solution—it has a very good, intuitive GUI interface, which makes configuration easy and also reduces the likelihood of making mistakes and opening up unintended holes in your firewall system.

Here are some of the main advantages of using proprietary OSs for firewalls:

▼   They tend to be more secure than firewall applications.

▲   They provide for better scalability and packet filtering speeds because the operating system is customized directly to work with specific hardware.

ASA Management

Because the security appliances use the same operating system, the configuration of Cisco's ASAs and PIXs is simplified. You have a choice of three methods to configure your security appliance:

▼   Command-line interface (CLI)

■   Adaptive or Appliance Security Device Manager (ASDM)

▲   Cisco Secure Manager (CSM), which is the replacement for the Cisco Works product

The CLI implemented on the security appliances is somewhat similar to Cisco's IOS-based router CLI. As you will see in later chapters, however, the CLIs of both platforms differ in many ways. The ASDM interface is a Java-based graphical user interface (GUI) tool that allows you to remotely manage a security appliance with a web browser. CSM is a complete management package that allows you to manage the security policies and configurations for Cisco firewalls (ASAs, PIXs, and IOS-based routers), Cisco IPS devices (4200s, AIP-SSM cards, IDMS2 cards, and AIM-IPS cards), Cisco VPN devices (ASAs, PIXs, IOS-based routers, and the 3000 concentrators), and Cisco host IPS implementations (Cisco Security Agent [CSA]).

As you can see, you have many options available to configure your security appliance and to implement your security policies. This book primarily focuses on using the CLI, but Chapter 27 covers the ASDM GUI.

Security Algorithm

One main function the security appliances perform is a *stateful* firewall. A stateful firewall adds and maintains information about a user's connection(s). In version 6 and earlier of the operating system, the Adaptive Security Algorithm (ASA) implemented the stateful function of the PIX firewall by maintaining connection information in a state table, referred to as a *conn table.* When Cisco introduced the ASA hardware platform in version 7, it dropped the term "adaptive" and now just refers to the process that handles the security functions as the "security algorithm." The security appliances use the conn table to enforce the security policies for users' connections.

Here is some of the information that a stateful firewall keeps in its state table:

▼   Source IP address

■   Destination IP address

■   IP protocol (like TCP or UDP)

▲   IP protocol information, such as TCP/UDP port numbers, TCP sequence numbers, and TCP flags

NOTE   The security appliances provide a stateful process for TCP and UDP traffic only, by default. Starting in version 7, ICMP can also be treated statefully, but this is disabled by default.

Stateful Firewall Explanation

Figure 1-1 is a simple example that illustrates the stateful process performed by a stateful firewall. These are the steps shown in Figure 1-1:

1.   A user (PC-A) inside your network performs an HTML request to a web server outside your network.

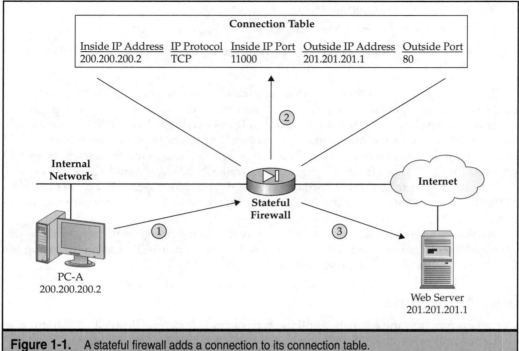

Figure 1-1.   A stateful firewall adds a connection to its connection table.

2. As the request reaches the stateful firewall, the firewall takes the user's information, for example, the source and destination address, the IP protocol, and any protocol information (such as the source and destination port numbers for TCP), and places this data in the state or connection table.

3. The firewall forwards the user's HTTP request to the destination web server.

Figure 1-2 shows the returning traffic from the HTTP server. These are the steps as the traffic returns from the web server:

1. The destination web server sends the corresponding web page back to the user.

2. The firewall intercepts the connection response and compares it with the entries that it has in its state table.

    ■ If a match is found in the connection table, the returning packet(s) are permitted.

    ■ If a match is not found in the connection table, the returning packet(s) are dropped.

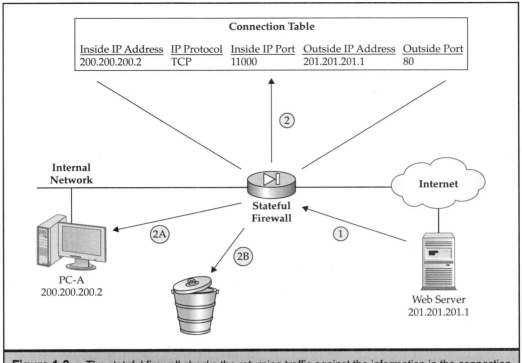

Connection Table

Inside IP Address	IP Protocol	Inside IP Port	Outside IP Address	Outside Port
200.200.200.2	TCP	11000	201.201.201.1	80

Figure 1-2. The stateful firewall checks the returning traffic against the information in the connection table.

A stateful firewall maintains this connection table. If it sees a connection teardown request between the source and destination, the stateful firewall removes the corresponding connection entry. If a connection entry is idle for a period, the entry will time out, and the stateful firewall will remove the connection entry.

Stateful vs. Packet Filtering Firewalls

The example in the previous section shows the difference between a stateful firewall and a packet firewall. A stateful firewall is *aware* of the connections that pass through it. Packet firewalls, on the other hand, don't look at the state of connections, but just at the packets themselves.

A good example of a packet filtering firewall is the extended access control lists (ACLs) that Cisco IOS routers use. With these ACLs, the router will look only at the following information in each *individual* packet:

▼   Source IP address

■   Destination IP address

- IP protocol
▲ IP protocol information, like TCP/UDP port numbers or ICMP message types

At first glance, because the information is the same that a stateful firewall examines, it looks like a packet filtering firewall performs the same functions as a stateful firewall. However, a Cisco IOS router using ACLs doesn't look at whether this is a connection setup request, an existing connection, or a connection teardown request—it just filters individual packets as they flow through the interface.

NOTE Cisco IOS routers, however, do support two features that implement stateful firewall functions like the security appliances: Context-Based Access Control (CBAC) and its replacement, Zone-Based Firewalls (ZBF).

Some people might argue that the `established` keyword with Cisco's extended ACLs implements the stateful function found in a stateful firewall; however, this keyword only looks for certain TCP flags like FIN, ACK, RST, and others in the TCP segment headers and allows them through. Again, the router is *not* looking at the state of the connection itself when using extended ACLs, just information found inside the layer 3 and layer 4 headers.

Sequence Number Randomization

The security appliances include a security feature called *Sequence Number Randomization* (SNR), which is implemented by the security algorithm. SNR is used to protect you against reconnaissance and TCP session hijacking attacks by hackers. One problem with the TCP protocol is that most TCP/IP protocol stacks use a fairly predictable method when using sequence numbers—a sequence number in a TCP segment indicates the number of bytes sent. With many connection types, a hacker can use this information to make predictions concerning the next set of data to be sent, and thus the correct sequence number. Sophisticated hackers will then use this information to hijack the session.

The security appliance's SNR feature addresses this problem by randomizing the TCP sequence numbers that the TCP/IP application places in the TCP segment header. The security appliance will place the old sequence number as well as the new sequence number in its conn table. As traffic is returned from the destination, through the appliance, back to the source, the appliance looks for this information and changes it back for acknowledgment purposes.

For example, a TCP segment might pass through the security appliance where the sequence number is 578 in the segment, as shown in Figure 1-3. The SNR changes this sequence number to a random number and places it in the state table (992 in this case), and forwards the segment to the destination. The destination is unaware of this change and acknowledges to the source the receipt of the segment, using an acknowledgment number of 993. The appliance, upon receiving the reply, undoes the SNR process by changing the 993 value to 579, so that the source device is not confused. Remember that the TCP acknowledgement process has the destination increase the sequence number by one and uses this as the acknowledgment number.

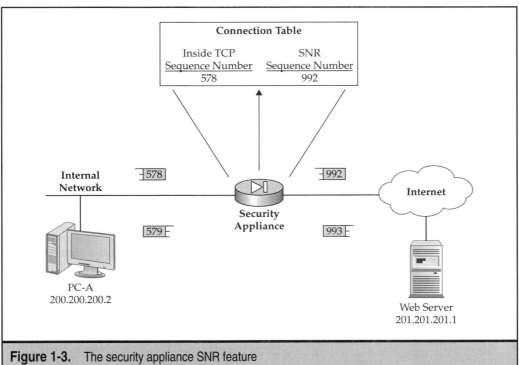

Figure 1-3.   The security appliance SNR feature

SECURITY ALERT!   To both the source and destination devices, the SNR process is transparent. Cisco highly recommends that you do *not* disable this feature. Disabling SNR opens your network to TCP session hijacking attacks. However, in certain situations, like the use of MD5 for packet signatures, having the security appliance change the sequence number would corrupt the signature. As you will see later in this book, you can disable SNR globally or be very specific about when it is disabled (like between two BGP routers using MD5 signatures).

Cut-through Proxy

As you saw in the previous section, the security algorithm implements many security features of the operating system besides the stateful firewall functions of the appliances. Another security algorithm enhancement is the Cut-through Proxy (CTP) feature. CTP allows the appliances to intercept incoming and/or outgoing connections and authenticate them before they are permitted. CTP is typically used in situations where the end-server the user is connecting to can't perform authentication itself.

The user connections are not typically authenticated by the appliance itself, but by an external security server, such as the Cisco Secure Access Control Server (CSACS).

Cisco supports both the TACACS+ and RADIUS protocols for authentication. The CTP feature on an appliance can authenticate the following connection types:

▼ FTP

■ HTTP and HTTPS

▲ Telnet

When the security algorithm is configured for CTP, it first authenticates connections before permitting them through the firewall. Figure 1-4 illustrates the steps that occur for CTP:

1. User *Pong* initiates an FTP to 200.200.200.2.

2. The appliance intercepts the connection and checks for an entry in its conn table—if the entry exists, the appliance permits the connection (step 4A). In this case, the user has previously been authenticated.

3. If the appliance does not find an entry in the conn table, it will prompt the user *Pong* for a username and a password, and forward this information to the security server for authentication.

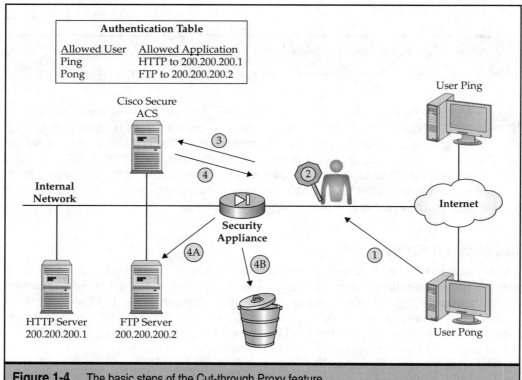

Figure 1-4. The basic steps of the Cut-through Proxy feature

4. The security server examines its internal authentication table for the username and password and what service this user is allowed access to—the security server sends either an *allow* or *deny* message to the appliance.

- If the appliance receives an *allow* message, it adds the user's connection information to the conn table and permits the connection.

- If the appliance receives a *deny* message, it drops the user's connection, or, possibly, reprompts the user for another username/password combination.

Once the user has been authenticated, all traffic will be processed by the appliance primarily at layers 3 and 4 of the OSI Reference Model, since the user's connection is placed in the conn table. This is different from your traditional Application layer proxy, where all traffic, from the authentication phase to the user's actual data traffic, is processed at layer 7 of the OSI Reference Model. With CTP, the authentication phase is processed at layer 7, but data traffic is, for the most part, processed at layers 3 and 4.

NOTE Cut-through Proxy authenticates the connection at the application layer, but processes the subsequent data stream at layers 3 and 4.

The CTP feature is susceptible to eavesdropping because the username and password are sent across the network in clear text; this can be alleviated by using HTTPS instead of telnet, FTP, or HTTP, since HTTPS uses SSL for encryption. If a hacker happened to be eavesdropping on a clear-text connection while the username and password were being transferred to the appliance, the hacker could use this information to gain unauthorized access to your internal network. You could remove this weakness either by using one-time passwords (OTPs) or by using a smartcard system where the smartcard-generated key is only valid once. Another problem with the CTP process is that the user might have to authenticate twice: once via CTP, and then again at the actual end-server the user is attempting to access. CTP is discussed in Chapter 8.

Policy Implementation

The security algorithm is responsible for implementing and enforcing your security policies. The algorithm uses a tiered hierarchy that allows you to implement multiple levels of security. To accomplish this, each interface on the appliance is assigned a security level number from 0 to 100, where 0 is the least secure and 100 is the most secure. The algorithm uses these security levels to enforce its default policies. For example, the interface connected to the public network should have the lowest security level, whereas the interface connected to the inside network should have the highest security level. Here are the four default security policy rules for traffic as it flows through the appliance:

- ▼ Traffic flowing from a higher-level security interface to a lower one is permitted by default.

- Traffic flowing from a lower-level security interface to a higher one is denied by default.

■ Traffic flowing from one interface to another with the same security level is denied by default.

▲ Traffic flowing into and then out of the same interface is denied by default.

Figure 1-5 shows a simple example of what is and is not allowed. In this example, the internal user who initiates a connection to a web server on the Internet is permitted out. Also, the security algorithm adds a connection in its conn table so that the returning traffic from the external web server will be permitted back to the user. Once the user terminates the connection, the entry will be removed from the conn table. At the bottom of Figure 1-5, a user on the Internet is trying to access a web server on the inside of the network. The algorithm rules on the appliance automatically drop this traffic by default.

The rules in the previous list are the default rules. You can create exceptions to these rules for the security algorithm, which generally fall into two categories:

▼ Allowing access based on a user account

▲ Allowing access based on a filter

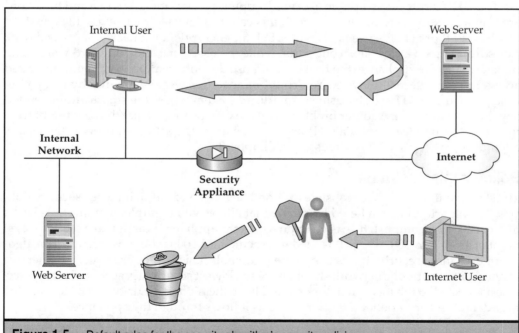

Figure 1-5. Default rules for the security algorithm's security policies

For example, a user from the Internet who is trying to access an FTP server on the inside of your network is by default denied the connection. You could use a couple of methods to open a small hole in the firewall to allow this connection:

▼ Set up CTP to allow the user's connection.

▲ Use an access control list (ACL) to open a temporary hole.

If only a handful of outside users need access to the FTP server, CTP is an excellent method to use. However, if this is a public FTP server where people from the Internet are constantly accessing files in the server, and these people could be anyone in the world, CTP doesn't provide a scalable solution.

Instead, you can use an ACL to open a temporary hole in the security algorithm to allow FTP traffic to the specific FTP server inside your network. In this sense, you are creating an *exception* to the appliance's default security policy, which is to deny all inbound traffic by default. Both of these exception rules are discussed in Chapters 6 (ACLs) and 8 (CTP).

NOTE Conduits and outbound filters are Cisco's older implementation on the PIXs to filter traffic between interfaces. Both methods have been supplanted on security appliances by ACLs. Starting in version 7, conduits and outbound filters are no longer supported.

Redundancy

Cisco's security appliances support two forms of redundancy:

▼ **Type** Hardware and stateful failover

▲ **Implementation** Active/standby and active/active

Not all appliances support failover. For failover to function properly, you need to meet the following requirements:

▼ For the PIXs, use a model 515/515E, 525, or 535. For the ASAs, use the ASA 5505 or higher.

■ Use identical hardware models and cards running the same version of software.

▲ Connect the security appliances together with a failover cable.

The following sections will briefly introduce the two types and two implementations of failover. Chapter 23 will cover failover in more depth.

Failover Types

This section will introduce the two types of failover: hardware and stateful failover.

Hardware Failover   With hardware failover, only chassis redundancy is provided: if the primary security appliance in the failover configuration fails, the standby appliance will begin processing traffic. The only item replicated between the two appliances is the configuration used. This type of failover is disruptive for communications that were being transported by the primary appliance because the necessary table information to maintain connections, like the state table, the translation table, and the VPN tables, is not synchronized between the primary and standby appliances. Therefore, this type of failover is not stateful—users have to reestablish their connections when a failover occurs. The top part of Figure 1-6 shows an example of a non-stateful (chassis) failover setup.

Stateful Failover   A stateful failover configuration performs the same functions as a hardware failover—the two main differences are that a stateful failover setup requires a dedicated Fast or Gigabit Ethernet connection between the primary and standby unit, and the state information on the primary is synchronized with the standby across this connection. A LAN connection is used to synchronize the primary's state, translation, and VPN tables with the standby unit.

As with a chassis failover, the standby unit monitors the primary unit, and when it sees that the primary is not functioning correctly, the standby unit promotes itself to the

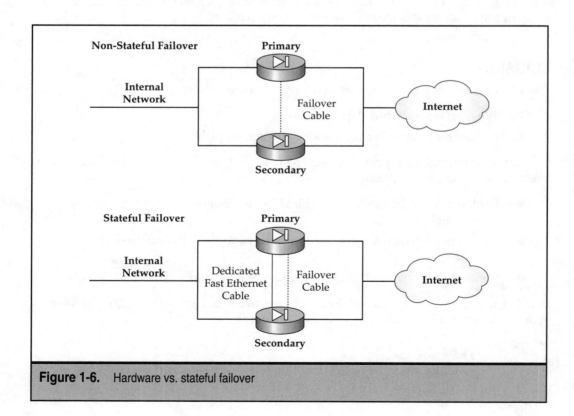

Figure 1-6.   Hardware vs. stateful failover

primary role. When it does this, the cutover should be completely transparent to the users and their connections because the state table on the standby is the same as that on the primary. An example of a stateful failover setup is shown in the bottom part of Figure 1-6.

> **NOTE**   Starting in version 7.0 of the OS, VPN sessions are also replicated between the failover appliances.

Failover Implementations

This section will introduce the two failover implementations: active/standby and active/active.

Active/Standby Failover   Up through version 6 of the operating system, only active/standby failover was supported. Both hardware and stateful failover are supported in this configuration. With the active/standby failover implementation, the primary security appliance assumes the active role, and the secondary appliance assumes the standby role. When an appliance is in an active state, it forwards traffic between interfaces; this is not true of the standby unit. An appliance in a standby state only monitors the active unit, waiting for a failover to take place and then cutting over to an active role. These two roles are shown in Figure 1-7.

Active/Active Failover   Starting in version 7 of the operating system, Cisco added a new failover implementation called *active/active failover*. Both hardware and stateful failover are supported in this configuration. With active/active failover, both security appliances can be processing traffic, basically taking advantage of the money you spent on both appliances as well as the bandwidth of the Ethernet cables connected to them.

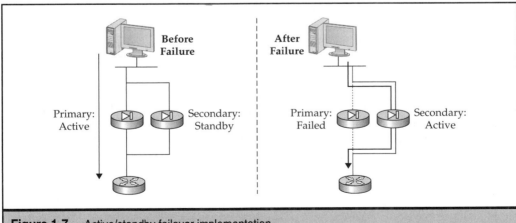

Figure 1-7.   Active/standby failover implementation

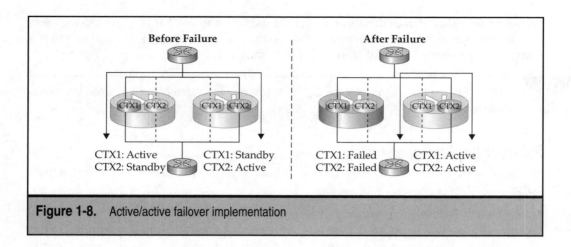

Figure 1-8.   Active/active failover implementation

Active/active failover is demonstrated in Figure 1-8. Use of active/active failover requires the use of two contexts, commonly called *virtual firewalls* (contexts are discussed in the "Advanced Features of the Operating System" section). On a security appliance, for one context the appliance will perform the active role, and for the other context the standby role. On the other security appliance, the roles for the two contexts are reversed. Of the appliances that supported failover, only the ASA 5505 doesn't support the active/active failover implementation, since it doesn't support contexts.

NOTE   The ASA 5505 does not support active/active failover.

Advanced Features of the Operating System

As I mentioned earlier, Cisco doesn't use the term "firewall" when referring to the ASAs and PIXs since these products are multifunction security devices. This section will introduce some of the advanced features that will be discussed throughout the book.

Address Translation

Few people realize the importance of the next statement, but the PIX was originally designed as an address translation solution: PIX actually stands for "Private Internet Exchange." Only later were security features built into the product. Therefore, one of security appliance's main strengths is its address translation abilities. It can perform the following types of address translation:

▼   Dynamic network address translation (NAT) and port address translation (PAT)

■   Static NAT and PAT

■   Identity address translation: commonly referred to as translation exemption or NAT 0

▲   Policy address translation: controlling when translation should take place based on the source and destination addresses involved

Address translation is discussed in Chapter 5.

Traffic Filtering

ACLs are the most common method of allowing traffic to travel from a lower to higher interface, as well as restricting traffic from a higher to a lower interface. ACLs are made up of two components: creating a list of filtering statements and applying the statements to an interface. To help with the implementation of ACLs, in version 6.2 of the operating system, Cisco introduced a concept called *object groups*. Basically an object group is a group of objects of a similar type, like IP addresses and network numbers, TCP and/or UDP port numbers, IP protocols, and ICMP message types. You can create an object group and then reference it in a single ACL statement.

For example, if you need to allow web traffic to three different servers, without object groups, you would need three individual ACL statements. Instead, you can create an object group that contains the three addresses, and in a single ACL statement, reference the object group. Object groups thus greatly simplify the maintenance and understanding of ACL policies. ACLs and object groups are discussed in Chapter 6.

Cisco also supports the filtering of HTTP and FTP content, including ActiveX scripts, Java applets, and web URLs. The last is only supported when used in combination with a web proxy server. Currently only Websense and Smartfilter are supported as proxy servers. With a traditional proxy, the user establishes a connection to the proxy, and the proxy connects to the actual destination, requiring the proxy to maintain two connections to transmit the data. With Cisco's solution, the security appliance passes the URL to the proxy server, the proxy determines whether it is allowed, and the result is passed back to the appliance, which implements the policy. This approach greatly increases throughput and supports more connections since the user's connection isn't being proxied in the traditional sense.

Routing and Multicasting

Originally the appliances supported static routing. Starting in version 6 of the operating system, passive RIP and then OSPF were added. With passive RIP, the appliance can learn routes from neighboring RIP routers, but can only pass a default router to other RIP routers. With OSPF, the security appliance is a full functioning OSPF router, having almost all the same abilities as a Cisco IOS router running OSPF.

Starting in version 8 of the operating system, Cisco enhanced the appliance's RIP implementation to include a full functioning RIP routing process. Cisco also added the support for their proprietary TCP/IP routing protocol, EIGRP.

Prior to version 6.2, the security appliances could not process multicast traffic: only unicast traffic would be transmitted between interfaces. Originally, to solve this problem, a router was placed on each side of the security appliance, and the multicast traffic was tunneled using the GRE TCP/IP protocol, which uses unicasts. The problem with using GRE is that it adds overhead to the transmission process: longer packets and increased delay. Starting in version 6.2, Cisco added some multicast capabilities to the appliances: they can proxy IGMP messages from user devices to an IGMP router, and they can route multicast traffic using static multicast routes or Cisco's proprietary PIM routing protocol. Routing and multicasting are discussed in more depth in Chapter 4.

IPv6 Traffic

Starting in version 7 of the operating system, IPv6 support was added. Today, you can process both IPv4 and IPv6 on the same interfaces. IPv6 support includes the following features, which are discussed in Chapter 9:

▼ IPv6 addressing, including dual stacking of IPv4 and IPv6 addresses on interfaces

■ Default and static IPv6 routes

■ Filtering IPv6 packets

▲ IPv6 neighbor discovery: static and dynamic

Contexts

Contexts, commonly called *virtual firewalls,* are a new feature introduced in version 7 of the operating system. Contexts are not the same as a product like VMware, where multiple operating systems and their applications can be running on one device. Instead, contexts allow you to have multiple policies for different groups of people or traffic. When you're using contexts, all contexts use the same operating system and share the resources of the appliance; however, each context can have its own security policies and its own dedicated or shared resources (RAM, interfaces, and so on). Two common examples where contexts are used include

▼ Active/active failover implementation: two contexts are needed on the appliance to implement active/active failover.

▲ Two firewalls, geographically close to each other, with different policies: instead of purchasing two firewalls, purchase a security appliance with two contexts, reducing your overall equipment costs.

Contexts are discussed in more depth in Chapter 22.

Transparent Firewall

Another featured added in version 7 is the transparent firewall feature. Up through version 6, the security appliances were layer 3, or routed, devices; you had to assign IP addresses on the interfaces and route between them. Now you have the option of running your appliance in transparent mode, where it can behave similarly to a layer 2 or transparent bridge or switch. As you will see in Chapter 21, when running in transparent mode, the security appliance will not behave exactly as a true transparent bridge. For example, you can still apply policies on your appliance that allow you to examine the payloads of packets (layer 7 of the OSI Reference Model). Two advantages that transparent mode provides include

▼ You can insert a security device into an existing LAN segment or VLAN without having to readdress the devices.

▲ The appliance transparently bridged interfaces don't have IP addresses on them, thus restricting access to the appliance, which greatly reduces the likelihood of an access attack.

Virtual Private Networks (VPNs)

Cisco has supported VPN functionality on the security appliances since version 5 of the operating system. Originally the only VPN solution supported was IPSec, with PPTP and L2TP added later. When version 7 was rolled out, PPTP and L2TP support were discontinued; however, because of customer demand, L2TP support was added back starting in version 7.2. Another major add-on for VPNs in version 7 was SSL VPNs. Cisco's SSL VPN implementation is WebVPN and supports clientless, thin client, and network client connection methods. Currently only the ASAs support SSL VPNs.

Implementing IPSec is discussed in these chapters:

▼ Chapter 15: Configuring IPSec Phase 1 policies and parameters

■ Chapter 16: Configuring IPSec site-to-site connections

■ Chapter 17: Configuring an IPSec remote access (Easy VPN) server

■ Chapter 18: Configuring an ASA 5505 as a remote access client

WebVPN is discussed in these chapters:

■ Chapter 19: Implementing clientless mode with WebVPN

▲ Chapter 20: Implementing network mode with WebVPN

The configuration of L2TP is not discussed in this book.

Anti-X Capabilities

The Cisco ASA 5500 Series Content Security Edition is provided by the Content Security and Control (CSC) Security Services Modules (SSM), or CSC-SSM for short. The CSC-SSM is technology developed by Trend Micro and integrated into Cisco's ASA hardware platform. Trend Micro's technology includes antivirus, antispyware, URL filtering, antiphishing, and antispam. Because of the term "anti" in many of its features, the card is commonly called the *Anti-X* card. Basically this card allows you to centralize these capabilities and policies on the ASA for small companies that don't want to manage these technologies on individual user desktops. These cards are managed through the use of ASDM and are not supported on the PIX appliances. The cards are discussed in more depth in Chapter 25.

Intrusion Detection and Prevention Systems

All the security appliances implement a very basic form of intrusion detection and prevention systems (IDS and IPS respectively). The ASAs, however, support a full-blown implementation of IDS/IPS with the add-on Advanced Inspection and Prevention (AIP) SSM modules (AIP-SSM for short). These cards support the full functionality of Cisco's 4200 series sensors, including the detection and prevention of the following:

▼ Application and operating system attacks, including web, e-mail, and DNS attacks

■ External attacks from hackers

■ Internal attacks from disgruntled employees

■ Zero-day exploits

▲ Internet worms (through the use of anomaly detection techniques)

The AIP-SSM cards are discussed in more depth in Chapter 25.

Network Attack Prevention

The security appliances support a handful of network attack prevention features:

▼ Threat detection

■ TCP normalization

■ Connection limits and timeouts

▲ IP spoofing prevention

With threat detection, the appliance monitors the rate of dropped packets and security events, which can be caused by matches on ACL deny statements, receiving invalid packets, exceeding connection limits (total connections and TCP connections that don't complete the initial three-way handshake), detecting denial of service attacks, receiving suspicious ICMP packets, overloading interfaces, detecting a reconnaissance scan, and many other factors. When a threat is detected, a log message is generated.

The TCP normalization feature lets you specify matching criteria that identify abnormal TCP packets, which the security appliance drops when detected. TCP normalization is implemented using the Modular Policy Framework (MPF, discussed in Chapter 10). TCP normalization can identify and prevent inconsistent TCP retransmissions by validating TCP checksums, allowing or dropping TCP segments that exceed the maximum segment size (MSS), limiting the number of out-of-order packets for a connection, dropping SYN segments with data, and handling many other abnormalities with TCP transmissions.

Cisco supports a TCP Intercept feature that allows you to place limits on the number of complete and/or half-open connections. A *half-open connection* is one that has not completed the initial three-way handshake: SYN, SYN/ACK, and ACK. This feature can be used to defeat or greatly limit the effect of a TCP SYN flood attack.

IP spoofing, where the source address has been changed, can be detected and prevented using ACLs. However, Cisco supports a feature called Reverse Path Forwarding (RPF) that provides a more efficient process, where the appliance does a reverse-route lookup— examines the source address and compares it with the routing table entries—to determine if the source address is coming from an interface it is expected to be connected to.

Network attack prevention features are discussed in more depth in Chapter 24.

ASA HARDWARE

The ASAs are one of Cisco's newer security products, introduced in May 2005 along with the version 7.0 operating system update. The ASA 5510, 5520, and 5540 were the first ASAs. Since then, three new models were added to the product line—the 5505, 5550, and 5580—and four revisions of the software have been introduced—version 7.1, 7.2, 8.0, and 8.1. The following sections will discuss the ASA models you can purchase as well as the licensing method Cisco uses to control the features that are activated on the security appliances.

NOTE   As of the writing of this book, the ASA 5580s support 8.1—the remainder of the ASA and PIX security appliances support up to 8.0.

ASA Models

Unlike the PIX security appliances, which were originally designed on a PC-/server-based Intel architecture, the ASAs are designed on a proprietary hardware architecture. A few reasons are behind this change in philosophy:

▼   Because the PIXs are based on an Intel PC/server architecture, it is possible to build your own box and run Cisco's software on this (even though this is illegal). Cisco wants to make sure that you run only their software on their hardware; therefore, the ASAs hardware has been customized to address this and other issues.

▲   Using a generic motherboard limits the capabilities of the appliances. By custom designing the ASAs, Cisco has created a much more flexible, faster, and more capable product.

The remainder of this section will provide an overview of the ASA models.

NOTE   Since the PIXs are end-of-sale (EOS), their architecture and capabilities are not discussed in this book. Suffice it to say, however, that the ASAs by far outperform the PIXs and have more capacity than the PIXs. Likewise, the ASAs are the replacement of the Cisco VPN 3000 concentrators, which are also EOS.

ASA 5505

The ASA 5505 is one of the newer ASAs and replaces the PIX 501. It is meant as a small office, home office (SOHO) device; however, its throughput and capabilities put it almost in parallel with Cisco's older PIX 515, which targeted medium-size companies. The 5505 runs version 7.2 and later of the operating system. Table 1-1 has an overview of the features and capabilities of the ASA 5505. Unlike the other ASAs, the 5505 can be purchased with a 10-user, 50-user, or unlimited user license. (The other ASAs place no restriction on the number of users, or unique IP addresses, they can process.)

Figure 1-9 displays the front and rear of the ASA 5505 chassis. The front only has LEDs on it, while the rear has the connectors. The power supply is external to the chassis. Above this is a slot that is not currently used: Cisco plans on producing a smaller version of the CSC-SSM card for the ASA 5505; however, as of the writing of this book, the card is still unavailable. There are eight "10/100" autosensing Ethernet ports. The two on the left support PoE. To gain initial CLI access to the unit, a proprietary Cisco rollover cable is used: pins 1–8 on one side are reversed on the other (8–1). The console cable is also used with the other ASAs with the exception of the 5580s. The two USB ports can be used to offload encryption/signature keying information. There is a lockdown connector that you can attach a lockdown cable to so that someone doesn't walk off with the unit: it's about 1/8th of the size of a 1U (one unit high) chassis like the ASA 5510. Below the lockdown connector is a reset button: when it's pressed, a hard reset is performed.

NOTE   It's also rumored that the USB ports will eventually be able to be used for additional flash storage.

Characteristic	Value
RAM	256 MB
Flash	64 MB
Included interfaces	8 switch ports, including 2 Power-over-Ethernet (PoE)
Throughput	150 Mbps
Connections	10,000–25,000
IPSec/L2TP connections	10–25
SSL VPN connections	2–25
VPN throughput	100 Mbps
VLANs	3 (trunking disabled) to 20 (trunking enabled)

Table 1-1.   ASA 5505 Features

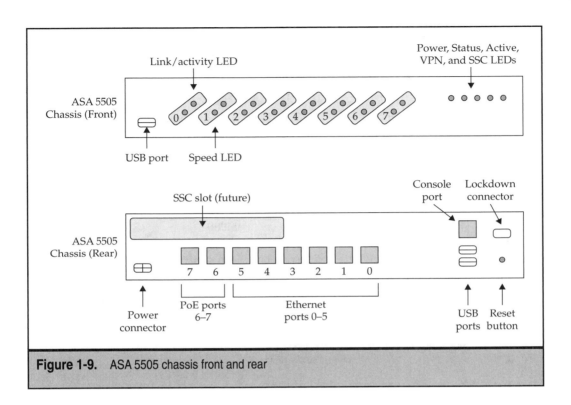

Figure 1-9.   ASA 5505 chassis front and rear

ASA 5510, 5520, 5540, and 5550

The ASA 5510, 5520, 5540, and 5550 all use the same physical chassis: the main differences between them are the CPU and RAM used on the motherboard. These units were primarily targeted at branch office to smaller enterprise customers. The 5510, 5520, and 5540 were the first ASAs introduced by Cisco. The ASA 5550 was introduced about the same time as the ASA 5505. Table 1-2 has an overview of the features and capabilities of these ASAs.

Figure 1-10 displays the front and rear of the ASA 5510, 5520, 5540, and 5550 chassis. The unit is rack-mountable and is a 1U chassis. The front only has LEDs on it, while the rear has the connectors. On the left is an SSM slot for an optional SSM card: AIP-SSM, CSC-SSM, and the 4-port GE cards. To the right of this is a 10/100 Fast Ethernet management port. The management port is meant to be used for out-of-band management of the appliance when using things like ASDM, SSH, telnet, FTP, and other IP management protocols or applications. Below this are two USB ports. To the right of these are four Ethernet ports. On the 5520s and higher these are autosensing 10/100/1000. For the 5510, these are locked down, in software, to 10/100. To the right of these ports is a compact flash card slot. These ASAs have built-in flash on the motherboard (see Table 1-2); you can add additional flash by inserting a compact flash card. To the right of the flash slot

Characteristic	5510	5520	5540	5550
RAM	256 MB	512 MB	1 GB	4 GB
Flash	64 MB	64 MB	64 MB	64 MB
Included interfaces	5 FE and optional 4 GE	1 FE, 4 GE, and optional 4 GE	1 FE, 4 GE, and optional 4 GE	1 FE and 8 GE
Throughput	300 Mbps	450 Mbps	650 Mbps	1.2 Gbps
Connections	50,000–130,000	280,000	400,000	650,000
IPSec/L2TP connections	250	750	5,000	5,000
SSL VPN connections	2–250	2–750	2–2,500	2–5,000
VPN throughput	170 Mbps	250 Mbps	325 Mbps	425 Mbps
VLANs	50–100	150	200	250

Table 1-2. ASA 5510, 5520, 5540, and 5550 Features

are the console (CON) and auxiliary (AUX) ports—they use the same rollover cable as the 5505 uses. To the right of these are the on/off switch and the power receptacle. (The power supply is built into these chassis, and only a power cord is necessary.)

ASA 5580

The ASA 5580s are the newest ASAs in the ASA lineup. Architecturally, they are very different from the other ASAs and are the most scalable of all the ASAs. There are two models: the ASA 5580-20 and 5580-40. These units primarily target large data center and campus environments. The 5580s require at least version 8.1 of the operating system. Table 1-3 has an overview of the features and capabilities of these ASAs. Unlike the other ASAs, no data interfaces are included (only two management interfaces)—you buy the cards you need. The Ethernet frame sizes used (normal versus jumbo) will affect the throughput for your model.

Figure 1-11 displays the front and rear of the ASA 5580 chassis. The unit is rack-mountable and is a 4U chassis. The front has LEDs on it, along with a power button, while the rear has the connectors and slots. Unlike the other ASAs, the 5580s have two power supplies for redundant power (the top left and right of the chassis). On the bottom left are two USB connectors that perform the same role as on the other ASAs. To the right

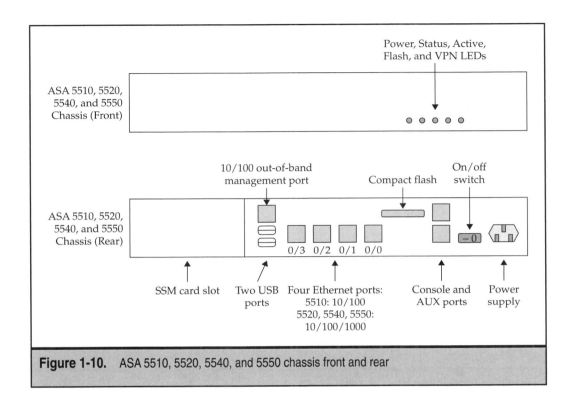

Figure 1-10.   ASA 5510, 5520, 5540, and 5550 chassis front and rear

Characteristic	5580-20	5580-40
RAM	8 GB	12 GB
Flash	1 GB	1 GB
Included interfaces	None	None
Throughput	5–10 Gbps	10–20 Gbps
Connections	1,000,000	2,000,000
IPSec/L2TP connections	10,000	10,000
SSL VPN connections	2–10,000	2–10,000
VPN throughput	1 Gbps	1 Gbps
VLANs	100–250	100–250

Table 1-3.   ASA 5580 Features

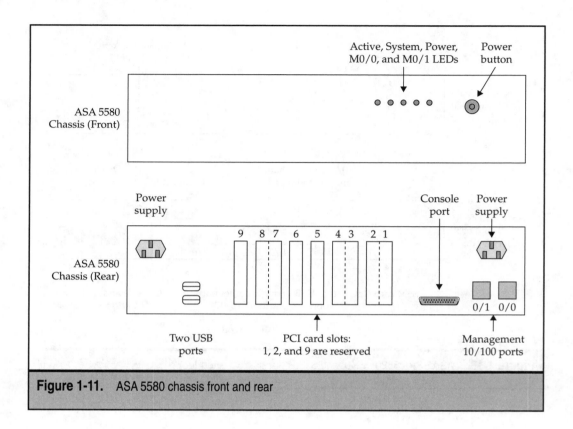

Figure 1-11.   ASA 5580 chassis front and rear

of these are nine PCI slots for Gigabit Ethernet (GE) cards. Some slots are "dual" slots, meaning that some cards take up two slots: these are slots 1 and 2, 3 and 4, and 7 and 8. The other slots are single-card slots. Slots 1, 2, and 9 are currently reserved and cannot be used for GE cards. To the right of the PCI slots is a DB-9 console port. And to the right of this port are two 10/100 Fast Ethernet management ports.

Hardware Modules

All of the ASAs support at least one modular card slot. The ASA 5505 has no current cards available for it, but the other ASAs do. This section will briefly cover the cards available for the ASA 5510s and higher.

Gigabit Ethernet Modules

The ASA 5510 through the 5550 support one Gigabit Ethernet module, called the Cisco ASA 4-Port Gigabit Ethernet Security Services Module (4GE SSM). It has four 10/100/1000 RJ-45 ports and four small form-factor pluggable (SFP) ports that support both copper and fiber connections. Even though the card has a total of eight ports, you can only use a total of four between the two sets. If you use the first copper RJ-45 port, then you cannot use the first SFP port. With the ASA 5550, this card automatically ships with the unit.

The ASA 5580s support a handful of cards that you can plug into their PCI slots:

▼ Cisco ASA 5580 4-Port Gigabit Ethernet Copper

■ Cisco ASA 5580 4-Port Gigabit Ethernet Fiber

▲ Cisco ASA 5580 2-Port 10 Gigabit Ethernet Fiber

AIP-SSM Modules

The AIP-SSM modules provide the same functionality as the 4200 IPS sensors for the ASA 5510, 5520, and 5540 appliances. Having the AIP-SSM cards is like having a box inside a box: they have their own RAM, a flash-based drive, their own processor, and their own operating system. They have one Gigabit Ethernet port for out-of-band management using IP, like CLI access using SSH or GUI access using IPS Device Manager (IDM). To get traffic to the card so that the card can examine it for attacks, you must set up policies in the ASA operating system to have traffic either copied to the card (the card acts as an IDS) and/or redirected through the card (the card acts as an IPS). The three models of the card are AIP-SSM-10, AIP-SSM-20, and AIP-SSM-40. Table 1-4 compares the cards.

NOTE Minimally, you must be running version 5 of the IPS software on these cards. If you want to run version IPS 6.0 or later, Cisco recommends that the appliances be running version 8.0 or later. Also, to obtain signature updates of new attacks from Cisco, you must purchase a separate license for the card itself.

CSC-SSM Modules

The CSC-SSM cards are fairly new and provide Anti-X features to the security appliances. Cisco and Trend Micro have worked together to design these cards: Cisco primarily designed the hardware, and Trend Micro provided the technology behind the software.

Characteristic	AIP-SSM-10	AIP-SSM-20	AIP-SSM-40
Model support and throughput	5510: 150 Mbps 5520: 225 Mbps	5510: 300 Mbps 5520: 375 Mbps 5540: 500 Mbps	5520: 450 Mbps 5540: 650 Mbps
RAM	1 GB	2 GB	4 GB
Flash	256 MB	256 MB	2 GB

Table 1-4. AIP-SSM Features

Characteristic	CSC-SSM-10	CSC-SSM-20
Model support	5510 5520 5540	5520 5540
RAM	1 GB	2 GB
Flash	256 MB	256 MB
Standard user license	50 users	500 users
User upgrade licenses	100 users 250 users 500 users	750 users 1,000 users

Table 1-5. CSC-SSM Features

Like the AIP-SSM cards, the CSC-SSM cards have their own CPU, RAM, flash drive, and operating system. The "Anti-X Capabilities" section previously introduced the capabilities of these cards. This section will focus primarily on the two different cards that you can purchase.

The cards come with one of two licenses: Base and Plus. The Base license supports antivirus, antispyware, and file blocking. The Plus license adds these features to the Base license: antispam, antiphishing, URL blocking and filtering, and content control. When you purchase one of these cards, it includes a one-year subscription for updates; after that period, you must purchase an extension to your license to continue receiving updates for viruses, spyware, and so on. Table 1-5 compares the two cards.

Licensing

The security appliances, both PIXs and ASAs, are unusual compared with many of Cisco's other products: they use a license scheme to lock down the features that can be used by the product. More and more of Cisco's products are moving in this direction. A *license key*, which is partly based on the serial number of the appliance, is used to unlock features of the operating system. Since the serial number of the appliance is used for the license key, you cannot take a key from one appliance and use it on a different appliance.

License keys can be used to unlock the following features on some of the appliances:

▼ Number of connections allowed in the state table

■ Number of interfaces that can be used

■ Amount of RAM that can be used

■ Encryption algorithms that can be used: DES, 3DES, and/or AES

- Number of IPSec/L2TP VPN sessions supported
- Number of SSL VPN sessions supported
- Number of users that the appliance supports
- Number of VLANs that can be used
- Whether failover is supported
▲ Number of contexts supported

As mentioned in the "ASA 5505" section, per-user licensing is implemented. The ASA 5505 and 5510 have a Base and Security Plus license: these licenses restrict the number of interfaces you can use, the number of entries allowed in the state table, and whether failover can be implemented. On all the ASAs, you get two SSL VPN licenses for WebVPN. If you want more than two, you have to purchase the appropriate license to unlock additional WebVPN sessions. This is also true of contexts: on the ASA 5510, you minimally need the Security Plus license to use contexts, but this is not true for the other higher-end ASAs. Assuming your ASA supports contexts, you get two contexts for free: for additional contexts, you purchase the appropriate license for the number of contexts you need. Upgrading your license key to unlock features is discussed in more depth in Chapter 26.

CHAPTER 2

CLI Basics

The last chapter focused on the features of the Cisco ASA security appliances and the various ASA models in the Cisco product lineup. Starting with this chapter and continuing through the remainder of this book, I will focus on how to configure your security appliance to meet the requirements outlined in your security policy. This chapter will focus on the following two items:

▼ Accessing the appliance

▲ Becoming familiar with the command-line interface (CLI) of the appliance

The next chapter will focus on creating a very basic configuration for your appliance.

ACCESS TO THE APPLIANCE

Cisco offers three main methods for configuring your security appliance:

▼ Command-Line Interface (CLI)

■ Adaptive Security Device Manager (ASDM)

▲ Cisco Security Manager (CSM)

The following sections provide an overview of these access methods.

Console Access

The most popular method of configuring the security appliance, and your initial access to it, is by using the CLI. The CLI is similar to that used by Cisco's IOS-based routers and switches. If you have configured Cisco routers and/or switches before, becoming accustomed to the appliance's CLI and configuring and managing the appliance will be fairly easy. To gain access to the CLI, you can use one of the following access methods: console port, auxiliary port (on certain ASA models), telnet, and secure shell (SSH).

For console access, you need to connect one end of Cisco's ribbon serial cable to the console interface of the appliance, and the other end to an RJ-45-to-DB9 terminal adapter that you'll attach to the serial port of your PC. On your PC, you'll need to run a software package like HyperTerm, Putty, TeraTerm, or some other program that performs terminal emulation. In your terminal emulation program, you'll need to use the settings shown in Table 2-1 for access to the security appliance's console port.

You can also access the CLI of the security appliance via telnet and SSH. For security reasons, Cisco denies both of these types of remote access—you must perform some configuration tasks to allow these access methods. Of these two methods, SSH is more secure because SSH encrypts information between your PC and the appliance. I will discuss the configurations of these two modes of access to the appliance in the next chapter.

Setting	Configuration
Baud Rate	9600 bps
Data Bits	8
Stop Bits	1
Parity	None
Flow Control	None

Table 2-1. Terminal Emulation Settings for the Appliance's Console Access

Other Access Methods

Cisco supports two GUI-based products that allow you to configure and manage your security appliance. The Adaptive Security Device Manager (ASDM) is used as an alternative to the CLI. Many administrators are very familiar with GUI-based interfaces and don't feel comfortable working with the OS-style CLI. For them, Cisco offers the ASDM software. ASDM offers an easy-to-use web/Java-based GUI that lets you not only configure your appliance, but also manage it. With ASDM, you can perform complex configuration tasks and gather important statistics. Chapter 27 covers the use of the ASDM.

NOTE ASDM replaces the PIX Device Manager (PDM) starting in version 7 of the operating system. If you are running version 6 or earlier on a PIX, then you'll need to use PDM for a GUI-based tool.

Cisco also offers an alternative GUI product called the Cisco Security Manager (CSM). CSM is more of a management tool than a configuration tool. One problem that larger internetworks face is the management of policies, especially security policies, across a broad range of devices. If you have 50 perimeter routers and 20 ASAs, ensuring that all of these security devices have the appropriate security policies applied to them can become a daunting task. CSM allows you to create your security policies from a single management platform and then have these policies applied to the appropriate device or group of devices. With CSM, you can create separate sets of policies based on the location and the traffic flowing through these devices. CSM even supports change management tools to ensure that an extra set of eyes can view and approve the changes before they are applied to devices in your network.

NOTE In this sense, CSM is not a tool you'd use to configure an individual security appliance, but rather a tool you'd use to manage the security policies on multiple security appliances.

CLI

Most of this book will focus on the CLI of the ASA operating system (OS). As you will see throughout this book, the CLI that the OS uses is very similar to that of Cisco's IOS-based routers and switches. Be forewarned that there *are* differences between the CLIs of these operating systems. In other words, you will see many of the same commands used on both products; however, just as many commands as well as other items make the two CLIs distinctly unique.

> **NOTE** Understand that the security appliances *do not run the IOS*—Cisco routers and switches use the IOS operating system. Cisco has designed the OS of the security appliances, especially starting in version 7 and later, to highly mimic that of the IOS CLI. However, the guts of the operating system (the code to implement the security algorithm and many of the appliance's features) are *different* from the IOS.

ASA Bootup Sequence

The security appliance bootup sequence is similar to the bootup of any networking device. The appliance first loads its BIOS, performs some diagnostic checks on its hardware components, and then loads the OS, as shown in Listing 2-1.

Listing 2-1. The bootup sequence of an ASA 5505

```
CISCO SYSTEMS
Embedded BIOS Version 1.0(12)6 08/21/06 17:26:53.43

Low Memory: 632 KB
High Memory: 251 MB
PCI Device Table.
Bus Dev Func VendID DevID Class              Irq
 00  01  00   1022   2080  Host Bridge
 00  01  02   1022   2082  Chipset En/Decrypt 11
 00  0C  00   1148   4320  Ethernet           11
<--output omitted-->
Cisco Systems ROMMON Version (1.0(12)6) #0: Mon Aug 21 19:34:06
     PDT 2006
Platform ASA5505

Use BREAK or ESC to interrupt boot
Use SPACE to begin boot immediately.
Launching BootLoader...
Default configuration file contains 1 entry.
Searching / for images to boot.
Loading /asa803-k8.bin... Booting...
```

```
Loading...
Processor memory 188010496, Reserved memory: 20971520 (DSOs: 0 +
    kernel: 20971520)
<--output omitted-->
Total SSMs found: 0
Total NICs found: 10
88E6095 rev 2 Gigabit Ethernet @ index 09 MAC: 0000.0003.0002
88E6095 rev 2 Ethernet @ index 08 MAC: 001f.9e2e.e519
88E6095 rev 2 Ethernet @ index 07 MAC: 001f.9e2e.e518
88E6095 rev 2 Ethernet @ index 06 MAC: 001f.9e2e.e517
<--output omitted-->
Licensed features for this platform:
Maximum Physical Interfaces  : 8
VLANs                        : 20, DMZ Unrestricted
Inside Hosts                 : 10
Failover                     : Active/Standby
VPN-DES                      : Enabled
VPN-3DES-AES                 : Enabled
VPN Peers                    : 25
WebVPN Peers                 : 2
Dual ISPs                    : Enabled
VLAN Trunk Ports             : 8
AnyConnect for Mobile        : Disabled
AnyConnect for Linksys phone : Disabled
Advanced Endpoint Assessment : Disabled

This platform has an ASA 5505 Security Plus license.
<--output omitted-->
Cisco Adaptive Security Appliance Software Version 8.0(3)
<--output omitted-->
Cryptochecksum (unchanged): 5e355bee 9afd42b6 c4dc6f57 fb869c8e
Type help or '?' for a list of available commands.
ciscoasa>
```

Listing 2-1 is an example of the bootup sequence from an ASA 5505. I've omitted some output information from Listing 2-1, focusing on some of the more important information. You can see some basic information about your ASA, like the version of its BIOS, the version of the OS, and the features enabled for your appliance.

The ASA 5505 in Listing 2-1 has the following features enabled: 10 inside hosts (users); 25 VPN peers; 2 WebVPN peers; DES, 3DES, and AES encryption algorithms; active/standby failover; and an unrestricted DMZ.

Once the appliance has completed booting, the CLI prompt appears. For a PIX, this would be pixfirewall>; for an ASA, this would be ciscoasa>, as shown at the bottom of Listing 2-1.

CLI Modes

The security appliances support different levels of access to the OS. These levels, and the user prompts that go with them, are shown in Table 2-2.

Looking at the levels of access and user prompts listed in Table 2-2, you would think that you were dealing with a Cisco IOS device. Like a Cisco IOS device, the security appliances have three main levels of access: User EXEC, Privilege EXEC, and Configuration modes.

User EXEC Mode

User EXEC mode is the first mode that you are presented with once you log into a security appliance. You can tell that you are at this mode by examining the prompt: the prompt will contain the name of the appliance, which defaults to `pixfirewall` for a PIX or `ciscoasa` for an ASA, and is followed by the > symbol. The following is an example of gaining access to User EXEC mode:

```
Type help or '?' for a list of available commands.
ciscoasa>
```

Within any of the access modes of the appliance CLI, you can pull up context-sensitive help by either typing in the **help** command or entering a **?**, like this:

```
ciscoasa> ?
  clear       Reset functions
  enable      Turn on privileged commands
  exit        Exit from the EXEC
  help        Interactive help for commands
  login       Log in as a particular user
  logout      Exit from the EXEC
  ping        Send echo messages
  quit        Exit from the EXEC
  show        Show running system information
  traceroute  Trace route to destination
ciscoasa>
```

Level of Access	User Prompt
User EXEC mode	`ciscoasa>`
Privilege EXEC mode	`ciscoasa#`
Configuration mode	`ciscoasa(config)#`
Monitor or ROMMON mode	`> or rommon>`

Table 2-2. The Levels of Access to the Appliance

On a Cisco IOS device, User EXEC mode allows you to execute a limited number of basic management and troubleshooting commands. However, from User EXEC mode on an appliance, your only real options are to enter Privilege EXEC mode, log out of the appliance, perform basic IP connectivity troubleshooting, and to execute only a handful of **show** commands. To log out of the appliance while in User EXEC mode, use the **exit** or **quit** commands.

Privilege EXEC Mode

Privilege EXEC mode is a level of access one step above User EXEC mode. Access to this mode gives you complete access to your appliance. To gain access to this mode, you first must access User EXEC mode and then type in the **enable** command, as shown here:

```
ciscoasa> enable
Password:
ciscoasa#
```

You will *always* be prompted for the Privilege EXEC password, even if one is not configured. As you can see in this example, the CLI prompt changes from ciscoasa> to ciscoasa#, indicating that you are now at Privilege EXEC mode. To view the commands that you can use in Privilege EXEC mode, either type in the **help** command or enter a **?**. Because you are in Privilege EXEC mode, you will see a couple of screens with commands that you can execute—many more than in User EXEC mode.

To go back to User EXEC mode, use the **disable** command. When you execute this command, the prompt will change from a # to a >. If you want to log out of the appliance, from either User or Privilege EXEC mode, use the **exit** or **quit** command.

Configuration Mode

Configuration mode is used to enter most of your appliance's configuration implementations and changes. To enter Configuration mode, you'll need to execute the **configure terminal** command from Privilege EXEC mode, as shown here:

```
ciscoasa# configure terminal
ciscoasa(config)#
```

Notice that the prompt changed from # to (config)# when you entered the **configure terminal** command, indicating that you are now in Configuration mode. To view the commands that you can execute in Configuration mode, enter the **help** command or **?**.

If the message <--More--> shows up at the bottom of the screen, there is more information than can fit into one screen. Pressing ENTER will scroll down through the output one line at a time; pressing the SPACEBAR will scroll the information down one screen at a time.

TIP Interestingly, unlike with Cisco's IOS devices, you *can* execute Privilege EXEC commands in Configuration mode on a security appliance.

To exit Configuration mode, either enter the **exit** or **end** command, or press CTRL-Z, which will return you to Privilege EXEC mode.

NOTE   Like Cisco IOS devices, the appliances support various subconfiguration or subcommand modes to configure various components such as interfaces and routing protocols.

ROM Monitor (ROMMON) Mode

ROMMON mode is similar to ROMMON on a Cisco IOS device like a router—it is typically used to perform password recovery, low-level troubleshooting, and to recover from a lost or corrupt operating system. The PIXs support a similar mode called *Monitor* mode that performs these functions.

To access ROMMON mode, you'll first need to reboot your appliance to have access to the appliance's console port. As the appliance boots up, you'll see a message that states Use BREAK or ESC to interrupt flash boot. Press one of these keys within 10 seconds of seeing this message, and you'll be taken into ROMMON mode, as shown in Listing 2-2.

Listing 2-2: Accessing Monitor mode on your PIX

```
CISCO SYSTEMS
Embedded BIOS Version 1.0(12)6 08/21/06 17:26:53.43
<--output omitted-->
Evaluating BIOS Options ...
Launch BIOS Extension to setup ROMMON

Cisco Systems ROMMON Version (1.0(12)6) #0: Mon Aug 21 19:34:06
     PDT 2006
Platform ASA5505

Use BREAK or ESC to interrupt boot.
Use SPACE to begin boot immediately.
Boot interrupted.

Ethernet0/0
MAC Address: 001f.9e2e.e51a
Link is DOWN

Use ? for help.
rommon #0>
```

Notice that at the end of Listing 2-2, the prompt now reads rommon #0>. To see the commands that you can execute at ROMMON mode, enter the **help** command or **?**. To have the ASA load the OS and continue with the bootup process, either repower the ASA, or execute the **reload** command. I will discuss ROMMON mode in more depth when I cover the password recovery procedure in Chapter 26.

> ***NOTE*** While you're in ROMMON or Monitor mode, the security appliances will not pass any traffic between interfaces; you must have the appliance load the OS to accomplish this.

ASA and Router IOS CLI Comparison

So far in this chapter, the CLI that appliances use appears to be very similar to what Cisco's IOS devices use. Here are some of the differences between the appliance and IOS CLI:

▼ With the appliances, you can execute **show** commands in both Privilege EXEC *and* Configuration mode.

▲ User EXEC mode on an appliance has a very limited set of commands that you can execute compared with the commands for IOS devices.

Given these differences, however, these two products have many CLI features in common:

▼ Context-sensitive help

■ Command abbreviation

■ History recall

▲ CLI editing features

The following sections cover the basics of these PIX CLI features.

Context-Sensitive Help

I have already covered the **help** and **?** commands to pull up help at each access level. In addition to seeing a list of commands available to you at each access level, you can also access help for a specific command. Cisco refers to this help as *context-sensitive* help. The context-sensitive help available to you was radically changed from version 6 of the OS to version 7. In version 6 and earlier, the CLI help of the PIX was not as feature-rich as that of IOS-based devices. Starting in version 7, the CLI help mimics what is found on IOS devices.

You can pull up help for a command by typing in the command and following it by a space and a **?**, like this:

```
ciscoasa(config)# clock ?
configure mode commands/options:
  summer-time   Configure summer (daylight savings) time
  timezone      Configure time zone

exec mode commands/options:
  set   Set the time and date
ciscoasa(config)# clock
```

In this example, I was in Configuration mode when I used help for the **clock** command. The help can be broken into two or more sections. In the preceding example, Configuration and EXEC mode parameters can be executed from the mode I'm currently in. The Configuration mode commands are **clock summer-time** and **clock timezone**, and the EXEC mode command is `clock set`. Also notice that after the help output is displayed, the command that you typed is redisplayed on the command line; in this case, it's the `clock` command.

Command Abbreviation

Another nice feature of the appliance CLI is that you can abbreviate commands and command parameters to their most unique characters. For example, to go from User EXEC to Privilege EXEC mode, you use the `enable` command. The `enable` command can be abbreviated to `en`. When you enter a `?` at a User EXEC prompt, you'll notice that there are two commands in User EXEC mode that start with the letter *e*: `enable` and `exit`. Therefore, you cannot abbreviate the `enable` command to the letter *e*. If you were to attempt to, the appliance would give you an `ambiguous command` error message.

The command abbreviation feature is not just restricted to appliance commands, but also applies to the parameters for these commands. As an example, to access Configuration mode, you can enter `con t`, which is short for `configure terminal`. You can use another useful abbreviation when you are entering a wildcard for an IP address: `0.0.0.0` can be abbreviated to just the number `0`.

If you are not sure how to spell a command, you can start typing in some of the characters and press TAB to autocomplete the command—if you don't type in enough characters to make the command unique, nothing will be displayed. However, if you type in enough characters to make the command unique, you'll see something like the following listing:

```
ciscoasa> en<TAB>
ciscoasa> enable
```

History Recall

Each access level of the appliance stores the commands that you previously executed in a history buffer—these commands can be recalled, edited, and then executed. The history recall feature works the same as that on IOS devices. Table 2-3 lists the control sequences to recall commands.

Control Sequence	Explanation
CTRL-P	Recall the last command.
UP ARROW	Recall the last command.
CTRL-N	From a previous command in the history list, recall a more recent one.
DOWN ARROW	From a previous command in the history list, recall a more recent one.

Table 2-3.   Control Sequences for the History Feature

To view the commands that you have executed at an access level, move to that access level, and execute the **show history** command, like this:

```
ciscoasa(config)# show history
  en
  con t
  exi
  con t
  show history
ciscoasa(config)#
```

One interesting point about this example is that from Configuration mode, you can see commands that you executed in both Configuration mode and Privilege EXEC mode.

Editing Features

When you use the history recall feature, you may want to edit the contents of a recalled command. The control sequences used by the security appliances are almost the same as those used by IOS devices. These sequences are listed in Table 2-4.

If you see a $ sign at the beginning of a command line when you are performing your editing functions, this indicates that the complete command cannot fit in the display and that more letters are to the left of the $. By default, you can have up to 512 characters on a command line—any extra characters are ignored.

Control Sequence	Description
CTRL-A	Takes you to the beginning of the command line
CTRL-E	Takes you to the end of the command line
CTRL-B	Takes you back one character at a time
LEFT ARROW	Takes you back one character at a time
CTRL-F	Takes you forward one character at a time
RIGHT ARROW	Takes you forward one character at a time
CTRL-D	Deletes the character that the cursor is on
BACKSPACE	Deletes the character that is to the left of the cursor
CTRL-L	Redisplays the current line
CTRL-U	Erases the current line and puts the cursor at the beginning
CTRL-W	Erases the characters to the left of the cursor until the next space is reached

Table 2-4. Control Sequences for Editing

CHAPTER 3

Basic ASA Configuration

The last chapter focused on introducing you to the command-line interface (CLI) of the security appliances. Starting with this chapter and continuing through the remainder of this book, I will focus on how to configure your appliance to meet the requirements outlined in your security policy. This chapter will focus on creating a very basic configuration for your appliance. If you have configured Cisco IOS devices like routers and switches, the configuration of the appliances, as you will see, is somewhat similar. The topics in this chapter include

▼   Using the setup script to place an initial, and very basic, configuration on an appliance

■   Using basic management commands to view, back up, and restore your appliance configuration

■   Entering commands to place a basic configuration on your appliance, including a name, passwords, a login banner, and interface parameters

■   Allowing remote access to your appliance using telnet and SSH, and testing connectivity with ping and traceroute

■   Viewing information about your appliance, including hardware and version information and CPU and memory utilization

▲   Using a simple configuration example to pull together the information discussed in the chapter

SETUP SCRIPT

The appliances support a short scripting utility that enables you to create a very basic configuration on the appliance and to store that configuration in flash. When you boot up a new security appliance, or if you erase the configuration file with the `write erase` command and reboot the security appliance, the appliance will start the setup script utility automatically before presenting you with the User EXEC CLI.

With the setup script, you can basically configure the following:

▼   Whether the appliance is running in routed or transparent mode (routed is the default)

■   The enable password (Privilege EXEC access)

■   The password recovery process (discussed in Chapter 26)

■   The current date and time

■   The IP address and subnet mask of the inside interface

■   A name and domain name for the appliance

▲   The management station or PC that can access the appliance on the inside interface using ASDM (discussed in Chapter 27)

You can also start the script manually by entering Configuration mode and executing the **setup** command, as shown here:

```
ciscoasa(config)# setup
Pre-configure Firewall now through interactive prompts [yes]?
Firewall Mode [Routed]:
Enable password [<use current password>]:
Allow password recovery [yes]?
Clock (UTC):
  Year [2008]:
  Month [Jul]:
  Day [17]:
  Time [09:46:57]:
Inside IP address: 10.0.1.1
Inside network mask: 255.255.255.0
Host name: bigdog
Domain name: dealgroup.com
IP address of host running Device Manager: 10.0.1.11

The following configuration will be used:
Enable password: <current password>
Allow password recovery: yes
Clock (UTC): 09:46:57 Jul 17 2008
Firewall Mode: Routed
Inside IP address: 10.0.1.1
Inside network mask: 255.255.255.0
Host name: bigdog
Domain name: dealgroup.com
IP address of host running Device Manager: 10.0.1.11

Use this configuration and write to flash? yes
INFO: Security level for "inside" set to 100 by default.
WARNING: http server is not yet enabled to allow ASDM access.
Cryptochecksum: 411b6025 26142b6f cff4a911 51351c72
1409 bytes copied in 1.860 secs (1409 bytes/sec)
Type help or '?' for a list of available commands.
bigdog(config)#
```

The script prompts you for your configuration parameters. If an entry appears in brackets ([]), you can press ENTER to accept this default value. If a default value is not listed, you must enter a parameter. One limitation of the script is that if you make a mistake, you have no way of going back to the previous question; however, you can press CTRL-Z to abort the script and its changes. Of course, once you are done answering these questions, you can answer "no" to the question "Use this configuration and write to flash?" and restart the script. As you will see throughout this book, most configuration tasks require you to enter the actual command (because the script lacks most configuration tasks). Because of this, most security appliance veterans never bother using the **setup** command, but manually perform this process by entering the appropriate appliance commands in Configuration mode.

NOTE If you are executing the setup script from Configuration mode, one interface must be labeled as "inside," have a security level assigned to it, and enabled.

BASIC MANAGEMENT COMMANDS

The security appliances use flash memory to store the OS, the ASDM image, and the appliance configuration file. As with IOS devices, whenever you make configuration changes, these changes affect only the configuration that is running in RAM—the configuration that the appliance is actively using (commonly called the *running configuration*, or *running-config* for short). You must manually enter a command to copy the configuration to flash in order to save it. This section covers the commands that you can use to manipulate your configuration files. Manipulating other files in flash is discussed in Chapter 26.

Viewing Configurations

On the security appliances, you have two locations for a configuration file:

▼ **RAM**   Commonly called the *running-config*
▲ **Flash**   Commonly called the *startup-config*

Viewing the Running-Config File

To view the configuration running in RAM, use the **show running-config** command, which requires you to be in either Privilege EXEC or Configuration mode to execute it:

```
bigdog# show running-config
: Saved
:
ASA Version 8.0(3)
!
hostname bigdog
domain-name dealgroup.com
enable password 8Ry2YjIyt7RRXU24 encrypted
names
<--output omitted-->
```

Viewing the Startup-Config File

To view the startup-config file in flash, use the **show startup-config** command:

```
bigdog# show startup-config
: Saved
: Written by enable_1 at 09:47:01.816 UTC Thu Jul 17 2008
!
ASA Version 8.0(3)
!
hostname bigdog
domain-name dealgroup.com
enable password 8Ry2YjIyt7RRXU24 encrypted
names
<--output omitted-->
```

You can store more than one configuration file in flash; however, the default file that is loaded on bootup is the startup-config file, unless you override this behavior. More on this topic is discussed in Chapter 26.

Viewing Partial Configurations

You also have the ability to view partial configurations or commands from the running-config file by using the **show** command:

```
ciscoasa# show {running-config | startup-config} command
```

Here's an example of viewing the interface configurations in the running-config:

```
ciscoasa# show running-config interface
!
interface Vlan1
 nameif inside
 security-level 100
 ip address 10.0.1.1 255.255.255.0
!
interface Ethernet0/0
 shutdown
!
interface Ethernet0/1
!
<--output omitted-->
```

Copy Commands

The **copy** and **write** commands (covered in the next section) work in either Privilege EXEC or Configuration mode. The **copy** command works the same way it does on

IOS devices: you need to specify a source and a destination. This command can be used to do the following:

▼ Back up the running-config configuration to flash

■ Merge a configuration file with the running configuration

■ Restore the startup configuration file in flash from a remote server

■ Back up the running-config or startup-config to a remote server

■ Copy an ASDM image to flash (discussed in Chapter 26)

▲ Copy an operating system to flash (discussed in Chapter 26)

Table 3-1 lists the **copy** commands for configuration files. When specifying a URL, use the following syntax:

```
file_type://destination_IP_or_name/[directory_name/]file_name
```

Supported file types include

▼ **disk0** or **flash**   Flash on the motherboard

■ **disk1**   The compact flash card on the ASA

■ **ftp**   FTP server

■ **smb**   Windows server

▲ **tftp**   TFTP server

Command	Explanation
copy running-config startup-config	Saves your active configuration file in RAM to flash
copy startup-config running-config	Merges the startup-config file in flash with the running-config in RAM
copy {running-config | startup-config} *URL*	Saves your running or startup configuration to the destination specified in the URL
copy *URL* **{running-config | startup-config}**	Copies the file from the URL to the running or startup configuration (merges with the running-config, but replaces the startup-config)

Table 3-1.   The copy Commands for Configuration Files

Write Commands

The **write** commands are used to save, view, or remove your configuration file and were the commands used, along with the **configure** command, to perform these functions before the introduction of the **copy** command.

NOTE With the exception of the **configure terminal** command, the other **configure** commands have been deprecated. You must use the **copy** command instead; however, this is not true of the **write** commands, which still work.

Table 3-2 lists the **write** commands.

TIP A quick way of saving your running-config to the startup config is to use the abbreviated form of the **write memory** command (**copy running-config startup-config**): **wr**.

One miscellaneous command that you should remember is the **reload** command. Use this command in either Privilege EXEC or Configuration mode to reboot your appliance. When rebooting, if you've made changes to your running-config and haven't saved them, the appliance will prompt you to save or discard these changes to the startup-config file in flash.

Clear Commands

The **clear** command performs two functions on the appliance:

▼ Resets the statistics for the specified process

▲ Removes a configuration command or commands to the referenced process

Command	Explanation
write memory	Saves your active configuration file in RAM to flash
write terminal	Views your configuration file in RAM (was used before the **show running-config** command was introduced, but is still supported)
write net *URL*	Saves your configuration file in RAM to a remote server
write erase	Erases your saved configuration file (startup-config) in flash
write standby	Copies the configuration file from RAM on this appliance to the RAM of the standby appliance when failover has been configured (discussed in Chapter 23)

Table 3-2. The write Commands

For example, if you wanted to reset the statistics counters for an interface, you would use the following syntax:

```
ciscoasa# clear interface physical_if_name
```

If you wanted to remove or undo a configuration from your appliance, use the **clear configure** command (you must be in Configuration mode):

```
ciscoasa(config)# clear configure command
```

Use care when executing this command. For example, if you were to enter **clear configure access-list**, this would delete *every* access control list (ACL) on your appliance! You can qualify the command with which item you want to clear. For example, with an ACL, you could enter **clear configure access-list** *ACL_ID*, specifying the exact ACL you wish to delete. To reset the appliance configuration back to its factory defaults, use the **clear configure all** command.

NOTE   Be very careful about using the **clear configure** command. The appliance does *not* prompt you to verify if you want to actually perform the action: the appliance just performs the action. If you want to delete a specific command such as an entry in an ACL, preface the command with the **no** parameter, which is the same way of doing it on an IOS device.

BASIC CONFIGURATION COMMANDS

This section covers some of the commands that you use to create a basic configuration for your security appliance. Some of these commands are the same or similar to those found on an IOS device; other commands, however, are quite different. In most situations, if you need to undo a configuration command, you will either preface the command with the **no** (which is what you would do on an IOS-based router) or use the **clear configure** command (delete all the referenced commands).

Host and Domain Names

The name of your appliance defaults to either `ciscoasa` if it is an ASA or `pixfirewall` if it is a PIX. You can change the appliance name with the **hostname** Configuration mode command:

```
ciscoasa(config)# hostname name_of_your_appliance
```

The name that you give your appliance only has local significance. The only visible effect of executing this command is that your prompt will include the new name, like this:

```
ciscoasa(config)# hostname alina
alina(config)#
```

To assign a domain name to your appliance, use the **domain-name** command:

```
ciscoasa(config)# domain-name your_appliance's_domain_name
```

Domain names are required when you generate RSA encryption keys for functions like SSH or digital certificates.

Device Names

One handy feature of the appliance is that you can use the **name** command to build a static Domain Name Service (DNS) resolution table:

```
ciscoasa(config)# name IP_address device_name
ciscoasa(config)# names
```

The **name** command performs a similar function as the **ip host** command does on IOS devices: it maps an IP address to a particular name. However, one major difference between the appliance and IOS devices is that when you're using names on the appliances, any configuration command that references an IP address used by a **name** command will be replaced with the name in the **name** command. To enable the use of the **name** commands, execute the **names** command.

TIP   When using names on the appliances, since they will appear in configuration commands with the corresponding IP address, you'll want to give the devices descriptive names. For example, "inside_PC" or "web_server" as names are not very descriptive; however, "nikas_PC" or "DMZ_web_server" are more meaningful. Once you execute the **names** command, any static IP address in your configuration that has a corresponding name will be displayed with the name instead of the IP address.

Passwords

The appliances support two levels of passwords: one for access to User EXEC mode via telnet and SSH, and one for access to Privilege EXEC. These passwords are automatically encrypted when stored in RAM or flash to protect them from eavesdropping attacks.

User EXEC Password

To configure the User EXEC password, use the **passwd** command:

```
ciscoasa# passwd password
```

Note that this command is really spelled with the letters *"or"* missing, like the corresponding UNIX command. The password is case-sensitive and can be any combination of characters and numbers. The limit to the length of the password is 16 characters. The default password is *cisco* for User EXEC access.

Privilege EXEC Password

To set the Privilege EXEC password, use the **enable password** command:

```
ciscoasa# enable password password
```

It is highly recommended that you configure a Privilege EXEC password because there is no default password. This command is somewhat similar to the one for IOS devices, except that this command automatically encrypts the password. The password is case-sensitive and can be any combination of characters and numbers. The length of the password is limited to 16 characters. Remember that when you access Privilege EXEC mode, you'll always be prompted for a password, even if one hasn't been configured.

Login Banner

You can create login banners that are displayed during the login process to the appliance by using the **banner** command:

```
bigdog(config)# banner banner_type banner_description
```

Table 3-3 lists the banner types you can create.

Banner Type	Explanation
asdm	Displays a post-login banner for ASDM access
exec	Displays a banner before the CLI prompt is displayed
login	Displays a banner before the username and password prompts
motd	Displays a message of the day (MOTD) banner

Table 3-3.   The Banner Types

Interfaces

Now that you have configured the name, passwords, and login banner on your appliance, you are ready to proceed with the configuration of the appliance interfaces. Before I discuss the configuration of the interfaces, I'll first discuss the nomenclature used for interfaces.

Interface Nomenclature

Interfaces on your appliances have two names to distinguish them:

▼ Physical name, commonly called a hardware name

▲ Logical name

The following sections will discuss the differences between the two.

Physical Names   The physical name is used whenever you need to configure the physical properties of an interface, like its speed, duplexing, or IP address. The appliance you have will affect the physical names you use. On the PIX, all the names of the physical interfaces begin with "ethernet," which can be abbreviated to the letter *e* and is followed with the interface number, which begins with *0*. For example, the first interface on a PIX is **ethernet0**, or **e0** for short.

The ASAs are different with their nomenclature:

▼ The 5505 physical interface names are **ethernet0/**number, where the numbers range from 0 to 7. An example would be **ethernet0/0**, or **e0/0** for short.

■ The 5510 physical interface names are **ethernet**slot/number, where the slot number of 0 is the four fixed interfaces on the chassis, and slot 1 refers to the interfaces on the SSM card if it's installed. For example, **ethernet0/0**, or **e0/0** for short, would refer to the rightmost data interface on the chassis.

▲ The 5520s and higher use a physical name of "gigabitethernet": **gigabitethernet**slot/number. For example, **gigabitethernet0/0**, or **g0/0** for short, would refer to the rightmost data interface on the chassis.

The 5510s and higher support a management interface (the 5580s support two management interfaces). The nomenclature of this interface is **management0/0**. The management interface, by default, will not pass traffic through it: only traffic to it or from it. Cisco designed this interface primarily for out-of-band management of the appliance using IP. However, you can override this behavior and use the management interface as a data interface. To use the management interface as a data interface, configure the following:

```
ciscoasa(config)# interface management0/0
ciscoasa(config-if)# no management-only
```

Once you have done this, you can treat the management interface as a physical interface and reference it in your policy commands, like ACLs and address translation commands.

NOTE   On the 5510s, you need the Security Plus license in order to use the management interface as a data interface because of the restriction on the number of physical interfaces that can be used with the 5510 Base license.

Logical Names   Logical names are used in most other commands, like applying an ACL to an interface, or specifying an interface for an address translation policy. Logical names should be descriptive about what the interface is connected to. Two common names used are "inside" (connected to your internal network) and "outside" (connected to the external or public network).

Security Levels

Each interface has a security level assigned to it that can range from 0 to 100. The least secure is 0 and the most secure is 100. Assuming you are using the name of "inside" for an interface, the security level defaults to 100. All other interface names have the security level default to 0 (the least secure). The security algorithm uses the security levels to enforce its security policies. Here are the rules that the algorithm uses:

▼   Traffic from a higher to a lower security level is permitted by default, unless you have restricted traffic with an ACL. This is called an *outbound* connection.

■   Traffic from a lower to a higher level is denied, by default, unless you explicitly permit it by configuring access control lists (ACLs), discussed in Chapter 6, and/or configure Cut-through Proxy (CTP) authentication, discussed in Chapter 8. This is called an *inbound* connection.

▲   Traffic from the same security level to the same level is denied by default.

To allow traffic between interfaces with the same security level, use the following command:

```
ciscoasa(config)# same-security-traffic permit inter-interface
```

Once you execute this command, all traffic is permitted between interfaces with the same level number; if you want to restrict this traffic, use ACLs, which are discussed in Chapter 6.

SECURITY ALERT!   By default, outbound traffic on your appliance is permitted. However, inbound traffic is automatically dropped when it's going to any other interface, unless you explicitly permit it.

Let's look at an example to illustrate the use of security levels. Figure 3-1 shows a network that I use throughout the rest of this chapter. In this example, the appliance has three interfaces: an external (connected to the perimeter router and the Internet),

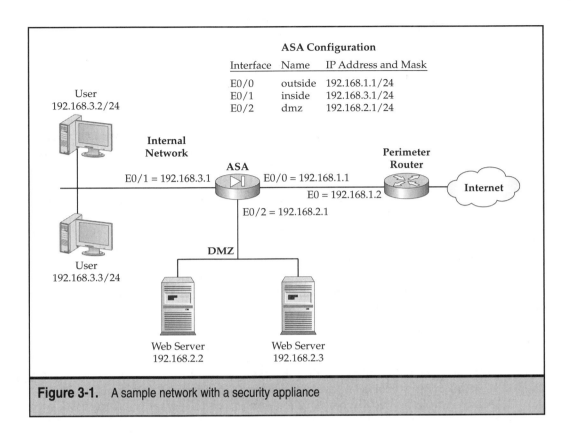

Figure 3-1. A sample network with a security appliance

an internal, and a DMZ interface. With the appliance security algorithm in action, here are the data connections that are, by default, permitted:

▼ Traffic from the inside interface to the DMZ

■ Traffic from the inside interface to the outside

▲ Traffic from the DMZ interface to the outside

If the traffic originates from any source other than the ones listed here and is going to any other destination through the security appliance, the appliance will automatically deny it.

Physical Interface Configuration

To configure the properties of a physical interface, access the interface using the **interface** command, referencing its physical interface name. (This will take you into a subcommand mode where the commands you enter affect only the specified interface.)

```
ciscoasa(config)# interface physical_if_name
ciscoasa(config-if)# nameif logical_if_name
```

```
ciscoasa(config-if)# ip address IP_address [subnet_mask]
ciscoasa(config-if)# security-level number
ciscoasa(config-if)# speed {10|100|1000|auto|nonegotiate}
ciscoasa(config-if)# duplex {auto|full|half}
ciscoasa(config-if)# [no] shutdown
```

In version 7.0, Cisco introduced an Interface subcommand mode; in prior versions, global commands were used to configure interface properties. The **interface** command specifies the name of the physical interface and the interface identifier (slot and port). The **nameif** command assigns a logical name to the interface. If you assign a name of "inside" to the interface, the security level defaults to 100. Any other logical name defaults the security level to 0. The **ip address** command assigns a static IP address to the interface; omitting the subnet mask will cause the mask to default to the configured class of the IP address. You can also assign a dynamic address to the interface using DHCP or PPPoE—this is discussed later in the chapter in the "Dynamic Addressing" section. The **security-level** command assigns a security level to the interface: this can range from 0 (least trusted) to 100 (most trusted). The **speed** and **duplex** commands set the speed and duplexing of the interface. By default, interfaces are disabled and need to be enabled with the **no shutdown** command.

VLAN Configuration

Starting in version 6.3, the security appliance operating system supports trunk connections. Of all the appliances, only the PIX 501 lacks support for trunks and VLANs. Only the 802.1Q trunking protocol is supported: Cisco's proprietary ISL is not.

VLANs are implemented by creating a subinterface (a logical interface associated with a physical interface) and by associating the VLAN identifier (the VLAN number) that the subinterface should process. For the physical interface the subinterfaces are associated with, typically only hardware characteristics (speed, duplexing, bringing it up) are configured. IP addresses, security levels, and logical names are configured on the subinterfaces. The one exception to this rule is if you need to use the native VLAN in 802.1Q; in this instance, you configure the IP address, security level, and logical name on the physical interface (the physical interface handles untagged frames).

Creating a VLAN interface is done the same as it's done on a Cisco IOS router; however, associating the VLAN tag to the subinterface is different from that on a Cisco router. Here is the configuration to create the subinterface and to identify the VLAN for the subinterface:

```
ciscoasa(config)# interface physical_name slot_#/port_#.subid_#
ciscoasa(config-subif)# vlan vlan_#
```

The *subid_#* is the number of the subinterface. The number you specify here doesn't have to match the VLAN number the interface will process; however, it is common practice.

TIP To make it easier to determine what subinterfaces are processing which VLANs, I typically prefer to match the VLAN number on the subinterface with the subinterface number. Remember that by default there is no correlation between these two numbers, however.

Here is a simple example illustrating the use of VLANs on a physical interface:

```
ciscoasa(config)# interface ethernet0/0
ciscoasa(config-if)# no shutdown
ciscoasa(config-if)# exit
ciscoasa(config)# interface ethernet0/0.1
ciscoasa(config-subif)# vlan 10
ciscoasa(config-subif)# ip address 192.168.10.1 255.255.255.0
ciscoasa(config-subif)# nameif dmz1
ciscoasa(config-subif)# security-level 51
ciscoasa(config-subif)# exit
ciscoasa(config)# interface ethernet0/0.2
ciscoasa(config-subif)# vlan 20
ciscoasa(config-subif)# ip address 192.168.20.1 255.255.255.0
ciscoasa(config-subif)# nameif dmz1
ciscoasa(config-subif)# security-level 50
ciscoasa(config-subif)# exit
```

Notice that the only thing done on the physical interface is to enable it, since in this example the appliance doesn't need to process traffic for the native VLAN.

ASA 5505 Interface Configuration

The model 5505 use of interfaces differs from all the other ASAs: the eight interfaces (e0/0 through e0/7) are layer 2 switch ports. Unlike the other ASAs, the 5505 doesn't use subinterfaces to associate interfaces with VLANs. Instead, a logical layer 3 interface called a VLAN interface is used. As you will see shortly, the configuration is somewhat similar to Cisco's IOS switches. With a Base license installed, three VLAN interfaces are supported. With the Security Plus license, three VLAN interfaces are supported using the local interfaces, and one interface can be set up as a trunk, supporting a total of 20 VLANs across the physical interfaces and the trunk.

By default, two VLAN interfaces are configured on the ASA 5505. Table 3-4 displays the properties of these two logical interfaces.

Property	VLAN 1	VLAN 2
Logical name	inside	outside
Security level	100	0
IP address	192.168.1.1/24	DHCP client
Physical interfaces associated with it	All except e0/0	e0/0

Table 3-4. Default ASA 5505 Logical Interfaces

To change the properties of the two logical VLAN interfaces, or to create a new logical VLAN interface, use the following configuration:

```
ciscoasa(config)# interface vlan vlan_#
ciscoasa(config-if)# nameif logical_name
ciscoasa(config-if)# ip address IP_address [subnet_mask]
ciscoasa(config-if)# security-level number
```

To associate a physical interface with a logical VLAN interface, use the following configuration:

```
ciscoasa(config)# interface physical_name
ciscoasa(config-if)# switchport access vlan vlan_#
```

Here's an example configuration with three logical interfaces: inside, outside, and dmz:

```
ciscoasa(config)# interface vlan 1
ciscoasa(config-if)# nameif inside
ciscoasa(config-if)# ip address 192.168.1.1 255.255.255.0
ciscoasa(config-if)# security-level 100
ciscoasa(config-if)# exit
ciscoasa(config)# interface vlan 2
ciscoasa(config-if)# nameif outside
ciscoasa(config-if)# ip address 200.1.1.1 255.255.255.248
ciscoasa(config-if)# security-level 0
ciscoasa(config-if)# exit
ciscoasa(config)# interface vlan 3
ciscoasa(config-if)# nameif dmz
ciscoasa(config-if)# ip address 192.168.2.1 255.255.255.0
ciscoasa(config-if)# security-level 50
ciscoasa(config-if)# exit
ciscoasa(config)# interface ethernet0/0
ciscoasa(config-if)# switchport access vlan 2
ciscoasa(config-if)# no shutdown
ciscoasa(config-if)# exit
ciscoasa(config)# interface ethernet0/1
ciscoasa(config-if)# switchport access vlan 1
ciscoasa(config-if)# no shutdown
ciscoasa(config-if)# exit
ciscoasa(config)# interface ethernet0/2
ciscoasa(config-if)# switchport access vlan 3
ciscoasa(config-if)# no shutdown
ciscoasa(config-if)# exit
```

Use the **show switch vlan** command to verify your VLAN configuration on the ASA 5505 (from the preceding configuration):

```
ciscoasa# show switch vlan
VLAN Name              Status    Ports
---- ----------------- --------- ------------------------------
1    inside            up        Et0/1, Et0/3, Et0/4, Et0/5,
                                 Et0/6, Et0/7
2    outside           up        Et0/0
3    dmz               up        Et0/2
```

Interface Verification

Now that you have set up your physical and/or logical interfaces, you are ready to verify your settings by using **show** commands. To examine an interface, use the **show interface** command:

```
ciscoasa# show interface
Interface Ethernet0/0 "", is administratively down,
     line protocol is down
  Hardware is 88E6095, BW 100 Mbps, DLY 100 usec
        Auto-Duplex, Auto-Speed
        Available but not configured via nameif
        MAC address 001f.9e2e.e512, MTU not set
        IP address unassigned
        0 packets input, 0 bytes, 0 no buffer
        Received 0 broadcasts, 0 runts, 0 giants
        0 input errors, 0 CRC, 0 frame, 0 overrun, 0 ignored, 0 abort
<--output omitted-->
```

The format of the output of this command is very similar to the same command used on IOS devices. One important item to point out is the first line of output, where the status is shown for both the physical and data link layers respectively. In this example, the interface is disabled. Here are the status values of the interface:

▼ If you see up and up, both the physical and data link layers are functioning correctly.

■ If you see up and down, there is a data link layer problem.

■ If you see down and down, there is a physical layer problem.

▲ If you see administratively down and down, the interface has been manually disabled.

The **show interface** command displays all of the interfaces on the appliance. If you are only interested in seeing the status of a single interface, enter the **show interface** command followed by the physical name of the interface, like **ethernet0/0**. You can also display just the status of a subinterface, like **ethernet0/0.1**, or a VLAN interface on a 5505, like **vlan 1**.

You can use either the **show interface** or **show ip** [**address**] command to view the IP configuration of your appliance interfaces:

```
ciscoasa(config)# show ip
System IP Addresses:
        ip address outside 192.168.1.1 255.255.255.0
        ip address inside 192.168.3.1 255.255.255.0
        ip address dmz 192.168.2.1 255.255.255.0
Current IP Addresses:
        ip address outside 192.168.1.1 255.255.255.0
        ip address inside 192.168.3.1 255.255.255.0
        ip address dmz 192.168.2.1 255.255.255.0
```

The System IP Addresses are the IP addresses assigned to the active appliance when you have failover configured. If this appliance were the standby unit, it would assume these addresses on the interface when a failover occurred. The Current IP Addresses are the IP addresses currently being used on the interface. Failover is discussed in Chapter 23.

TIP   Remember that **show** commands can be executed in either Privilege EXEC or Configuration mode.

Dynamic Addressing

Besides specifying a static IP address, you can also acquire addressing dynamically by using DHCP (Dynamic Host Configuration Protocol) or PPP over Ethernet (PPPoE). The following two sections will discuss these approaches.

DHCP Client

Your appliance can be a DHCP client and obtain its addressing information on interface(s) dynamically from a DHCP server. Here's the interface syntax for an interface using DHCP to acquire its addressing information:

```
ciscoasa(config)# interface physical_name
ciscoasa(config-if)# ip address dhcp [setroute] [retry retry_count]
```

The **setroute** parameter causes the appliance to accept the default route from the DHCP server—this is typically done when your outside interface is acquiring its addressing dynamically from the ISP. If you omit this parameter, you'll need to configure a default route on your appliance (this is discussed in Chapter 4). You can also specify the number of times the appliance should attempt to obtain its addressing.

NOTE By default, the ASA 5505 is preconfigured from Cisco to include `ethernet0/0` in VLAN 2 (the outside interface), and this interface is set up as a DHCP client.

To verify your addressing information, use the **show ip address dhcp** command:

```
ciscoasa# show ip address outside dhcp lease
Temp IP Addr:200.200.200.2 for peer on interface:outside
Temp sub net mask:255.255.255.0
DHCP Lease server:200.200.199.2, state:3 Bound
DHCP Transaction id:0x4123
Lease:7200 secs, Renewal:1505 secs, Rebind:7000 secs
Temp default-gateway addr:200.200.200.1
Next timer fires after:6809 secs
Retry count:0, Client-ID:cisco-0000.0000.0000-outside
```

To perform detailed troubleshooting, the appliances support debug capabilities similar to IOS-based devices. Cisco also supports **debug** commands for troubleshooting the DHCP client on the appliance. Here are the **debug** commands that you can use:

▼ **debug dhcpc packet** Displays the partial contents of DHCP client packets

■ **debug dhcpc error** Displays DHCP client error information

▲ **debug dhcpc detail** Displays all information related to DHCP client packets

TIP To disable all debug functions, use the **no debug all** or **undebug all** command.

PPP over Ethernet (PPPoE)

PPPoE is typically used on broadband DSL connections to an ISP. Configuring PPPoE involves these tasks:

▼ Creating a PPPoE group

■ Specifying the PPP authentication method: PAP, CHAP, or MS-CHAP

■ Associating a username to the PPPoE group

■ Creating a local username account and password assigned by the ISP

▲ Enabling PPPoE on the interface

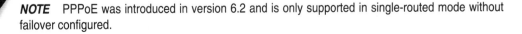

NOTE PPPoE was introduced in version 6.2 and is only supported in single-routed mode without failover configured.

Here is the syntax to accomplish the preceding tasks:

```
ciscoasa(config)# vpdn group group_name request dialout pppoe
ciscoasa(config)# vpdn group group_name ppp authentication
                         {chap | mschap | pap}
ciscoasa(config)# vpdn group group_name localname username
ciscoasa(config)# vpdn username username password password [store-local]
ciscoasa(config)# interface physical_if_name
ciscoasa(config-if)# ip address pppoe [setroute]
```

The first **vpdn group** command specifies a locally significant group name that groups together the appliance PPPoE commands for an interface. The second **vpdn group** command specifies the PPP authentication method to use. The third **vpdn group** command specifies the local user account the ISP assigned. The **vpdn username** command specifies the username and password assigned by the ISP; the **store-local** parameter causes the appliance to store the username and password in a special place in flash so that a **clear configure** command will not erase it. Once you have configured your PPPoE parameters, enable PPPoE on the interface with the **ip address pppoe** command; the **setroute** parameter performs the same function as with the **ip address dhcp** command from the previous section.

Once you have configured PPPoE, use these **show** commands for verification:

▼ **show ip address** *logical_if_name* **pppoe**   Displays the IP addressing for the outside interface

▲ **show vpdn** [**session pppoe**]   Displays the PPPoE session information

The first **show** command displays the appliance PPPoE client configuration information. Its output is similar to that of the **show ip address dhcp** command. The **show vpdn** command shows a brief overview of the PPPoE sessions:

```
ciscoasa# show vpdn
Tunnel id 0, 1 active sessions
     time since change 1209 secs
   Remote Internet Address 192.168.1.1
   Local Internet Address 200.200.200.1
   12 packets sent, 12 received, 168 bytes sent, 0 received
Remote Internet Address is 192.168.1.1
     Session state is SESSION_UP
<--output omitted-->
```

This example has one active PPPoE session. You can restrict the output of this command by adding the **session pppoe** parameters—this will only display PPPoE information, and no VPN information.

For detailed troubleshooting of PPPoE, use the **debug** command:

```
ciscoasa(config)#  debug pppoe {event | error | packet}
```

The **event** parameter displays protocol event information concerning PPPoE. The **error** parameter displays any PPPoE error messages. The **packet** parameter displays the partial contents of PPPoE packets.

Dynamic DNS

Dynamic DNS is a feature where the appliance, acting as a DHCP client, obtains its IP address dynamically from a DHCP server. The appliance can then update a DNS server with its name and the dynamic address. Therefore, no matter what dynamic IP address is assigned to the appliance, you can always use the same name to reach it.

To configure this process, use the following commands:

```
ciscoasa(config)# dhcp-client update dns server none
ciscoasa(config)# ddns update method ddns-2
ciscoasa(DDNS-update-method)# ddns both
ciscoasa(DDNS-update-method)# exit
ciscoasa(config)# interface physical_if_name
ciscoasa(if-config)# ddns update ddns-2
ciscoasa(if-config)# ddns update hostname appliance's_FQDN
```

The **dhcp-client update** command specifies that the client (the appliance itself), rather than the DHCP server, will update the DNS server with the dynamic addressing information. The **ddns update** and **ddns both** commands specify that the appliance will update both the A and PTR DNS records on the DNS server.

Once you have done this, you need to enable dynamic DNS on the physical or VLAN interface with the **ddns update ddns-2** command and to specify the fully qualified domain name (FQDN) being passed to the DNS server with the **ddns update hostname** command, like "appliance.dealgroup.com".

MANAGEMENT

This section rounds out the basic security appliance configuration commands. In the following sections, I cover how to allow remote CLI access to the appliance for management purposes and some basic testing and monitoring tools that you can use on your appliance.

Remote Access

By default, the only access that the appliance allows is on the console port—HTTP (ASDM), telnet, and SSH access are denied. The following sections show you how to enable the latter two types of access to the appliance; ASDM access is discussed in Chapter 27.

Telnet

To allow telnet access to your appliance, you need to configure two commands. First, you should assign a telnet password with the **passwd** command discussed in the "User EXEC Password" section of this chapter. Second, you must specify the IP addresses that are allowed access to the appliance with the **telnet** Configuration mode command:

```
ciscoasa(config)# telnet IP_address subnet_mask [logical_if_name]
```

If you omit the name of the logical interface, it defaults to *inside*. You can list up to 16 hosts or networks with multiple **telnet** commands.

If you want to allow telnet access from all internal machines, use the following syntax:

```
ciscoasa(config)# telnet 0 0 inside
```

Remember that you can abbreviate **0.0.0.0** as **0**.

To allow access from only a specific internal network segment, use this syntax:

```
ciscoasa(config)# telnet 192.168.4.0 255.255.255.0 inside
```

If you want to allow telnet access from only a specific machine, use this configuration:

```
ciscoasa(config)# telnet 192.168.5.2 255.255.255.255 inside
```

Note that you can enter the **telnet** command multiple times to set your telnet access policies. To see your telnet access policies, use the **show run telnet** command.

The default timeout for idle telnet sessions is 5 minutes. You can change this with the **telnet timeout** command:

```
ciscoasa(config)# telnet timeout number_of_minutes
```

The time can range from 1 to 60 minutes.

To see who is currently logged into the appliance via telnet, use the **who** command:

```
ciscoasa# who
1: From 192.168.1.7
2: From 192.168.1.2
```

The first number is the session ID and is unique for each logged-in user. You can terminate a telnet connection by using the **kill** command:

```
ciscoasa# kill session_ID
```

You can view the session IDs by using the **who** command. When you're terminating a session, the appliance allows the telnet user to permit any currently executing command and then, without warning, terminates the user's telnet connection.

SSH

Secure shell (SSH) allows a user to establish a pseudo-console connection via a remote secure shell. SSH basically provides an encrypted CLI connection between the client and the appliance by using the RSA encryption algorithm. One limitation of using telnet is that you cannot telnet to the appliance from the *outside* interface; SSH does not have this limitation.

To allow SSH access, you must configure the following on your appliance:

▼ Define a hostname and domain name.

■ Generate a public/private RSA key combination.

▲ Specify the addresses allowed to access the appliance via SSH.

I have already talked about assigning a hostname and domain name to the appliance in the "Host and Domain Names" section. A public/private RSA key combination is used to secure the connection for the secure shell. To create your keying information, use the **crypto key generate rsa** command:

```
ciscoasa(config)# crypto key generate rsa [modulus_size]
```

To execute the preceding command, you must first install either a DES or 3DES/AES license key if one has not already been installed. The modulus size can be 512, 768, 1024, or 2048 bits; if you omit it, the modulus defaults to 1024 bits. The larger the size, the more secure the connection will be.

Here is an example of generating an RSA key pair for SSH:

```
bigdog(config)# crypto key generate rsa
WARNING: You have a RSA keypair already defined named
    <Default-RSA-Key>.
Do you really want to replace them? [yes/no]: yes
Keypair generation process begin. Please wait...
bigdog(config)#
```

You can have multiple RSA key pairs on your appliance, which are discussed in Chapter 15. By default, SSH uses the "Default-RSA-Key" pair; so if it already exists, you'll be prompted to overwrite it.

To see the public key created by the **crypto key generate rsa** command, use the **show crypto key mypubkey rsa** command like this:

```
ciscoasa(config)# show crypto key mypubkey rsa
Key pair was generated at: 13:27:25 UTC Jul 18 2008
Key name: <Default-RSA-Key>
 Usage: General Purpose Key
 Modulus Size (bits): 1024
 Key Data:
  30819f30 0d06092a 864886f7 0d010101 05000381 8d003081 89028181
  00b27da4 3243ec84 e8b44059 1c8393f6 92b3db8c fa641f39 ee0c3775
  afe8bb24 792f2691 0cace31d 619183d9 f7efdaa1 52ba98fe 79152d66
```

```
a71b7e7e 8969e9af d256bbfe f0d14ed0 44ea416b 0becbd5c eb4ec25d
74b6049e 5ea4a064 ee12550b 3b4d989f 5e9205a1 0092c033 2119641f
770a62d3 8ee7c9db c560185d f7f7aabd ff020301 0001
```

Use the **write memory** command to store RSA key pairs in flash memory. I discuss RSA and public/private keys in more depth in Chapters 15 and 16.

Once you have created your RSA key pair, you can now specify the addresses permitted to establish SSH connections to the appliance. Use the **ssh** command to specify permitted addresses:

```
ciscoasa(config)# ssh ip_address subnet_mask [logical_if_name]
```

The default idle timeout for SSH sessions is 5 minutes. To alter this value, use the **ssh timeout** command:

```
ciscoasa(config)# ssh timeout minutes
```

To see your SSH commands, use the **show run ssh** command.

To see what users have current SSH connections to the appliance, use the **show ssh sessions** command:

```
ciscoasa# show ssh sessions
Session ID    Client IP     Version Encryption  State    Username
   0          192.168.1.2   1.5     DES         6        pix
```

To disconnect a session, use the **ssh disconnect** command:

```
ciscoasa# ssh disconnect session_ID
```

The session ID number is shown with the **show ssh sessions** command.

NOTE If you're logging into the appliance using SSH when you are not using AAA, the username you enter is "pix" (for both the PIX *and* ASA), and the password is the password from the **passwd** command.

Connectivity Testing

To verify that you have IP connectivity, you can use three basic troubleshooting commands: **ping**, **traceroute**, and **show arp**. The following two sections cover these appliance commands.

Ping

To test whether you have a connection with other IP devices, you can execute the **ping** command:

```
ciscoasa# ping [logical_if_name] destination_IP_address
          [data pattern] [repeat count] [size bytes]
          [timeout seconds] [validate]
```

The *logical_if_name* parameter allows you to specify which interface IP address to use as the source of the ping. If you omit the name, it will default to the IP address of the interface that the appliance will use to reach the destination. You can include a data pattern in the ICMP payload, specify the number of pings to perform (four by default), the size of the pings (100 bytes by default), the timeout when waiting for echo replies (2 seconds by default), and validation of the payload.

If you cannot ping a destination, verify that the appliance's interface(s) are up and that you have the correct IP addresses assigned to them. You can use the **show interfaces** or **show ip** command to verify this. You can also use the **debug icmp trace** command to see the actual ICMP packets. Once you have assigned an IP address to an interface on the appliance, you can verify its accessibility by pinging it from another machine in the same subnet. On the appliance, first enter the **debug icmp trace** command to enable debugging for ICMP traffic. Then go to another machine on the same subnet, and ping the appliance's interface. Your output will look something like this:

```
ciscoasa# debug icmp trace
ICMP trace on
Warning: this may cause problems on busy networks
ciscoasa#
1: ICMP echo request (len 32 id 2 seq 256) 192.168.1.2 > 192.168.1.1
2: ICMP echo reply (len 32 id 2 seq 256) 192.168.1.1 > 192.168.1.2
<--output omitted-->
```

The output of the command is fairly readable: there were four echo requests from the machine and four replies from the appliance (the last two sets were omitted from the output). To turn off the debug for ICMP, preface the preceding command with the **no** parameter: **no debug icmp trace**; or you could use the **undebug all** or **no debug all** commands.

Traceroute

Starting in version 7.2, the security appliances support the **traceroute** command, which allows you to trace the layer 3 hops that packets go through to reach a destination. Here is the syntax of the command:

```
ciscoasa# traceroute dst_ip_address [source src_ip_addr |
          logical_src_if_name] [numeric] [timeout timeout_value]
          [probe probe_num] [ttl min_ttl max_ttl]
          [port port_value] [use-icmp]
```

The only required parameter is the destination IP address. Optionally, you can specify a different source IP address on the appliance than the one it will use when exiting the destination interface. Also, you can disable the reverse-DNS lookup with the **numeric** parameter. The default timeout for replies is 3 seconds and can be changed with the **timeout** parameter. The default number of probes for each layer 3 hop is 3, but can be changed with the **probe** parameter. You can control the number of hops with the `ttl` parameter. By default, traceroute uses UDP port 33,434, but can be changed with the `port` parameter. And instead of using UDP, you can specify the use of ICMP when performing the traceroute with the `use-icmp` parameter.

Address Resolution Protocol (ARP)

The TCP/IP ARP protocol resolves an IP address (layer 3) to a MAC address (layer 2). MAC addresses are used for communications between devices on the same segment or subnet, that is, the same LAN medium. Anytime the appliance initiates connections or receives requests for connections to itself, it will add the connected device's IP and MAC addresses to its local ARP table. To view the appliance ARP table, use the `show arp` command, as shown here:

```
ciscoasa# show arp
        inside 192.168.7.200 00e0.9871.b91e
```

Currently one entry is in the appliance ARP table: a device with an IP address of 192.168.7.200 that is off of the *inside* interface. You can clear the entries in the ARP table with the `clear arp` [*logical_if_name*] command.

By default, the appliance keeps addresses in the ARP table for 4 hours (14,400 seconds). You can modify the timeout for ARP entries with the `arp timeout` command:

```
ciscoasa(config)# arp timeout seconds
```

To view the timeout that you have configured, use the `show run arp timeout` command.

You can manually add or remove an entry from the ARP table by using the appliance Configuration mode commands shown here:

```
ciscoasa(config)# arp logical_if_name IP_address MAC_address [alias]
ciscoasa(config)# no arp logical_if_name IP_address
```

You need to specify the name of the interface that the device is off of, as well as the device IP and MAC addresses. If you add the `alias` parameter, the entry will become a permanent entry in the ARP table; if you save the appliance's configuration, then the static ARP entry is saved, even upon a reboot of the appliance. If you omit the `alias` parameter, any rebooting of the appliance will cause the appliance to lose the static ARP configuration.

HARDWARE AND SOFTWARE INFORMATION

The security appliances support a multitude of `show` commands. Many of these commands are the same commands that you would execute on an IOS-based device to see the same kinds of information. The following sections will cover some common `show` commands, including `show version`, `show memory`, and `show cpu usage`.

Version Information

To display the hardware and software characteristics of your security appliance, use the **show version** command. The information that you can see from this command is similar to the **show version** command on an IOS-based device. With this command, you can see the following information about your appliance: OS software and ASDM versions, uptime since last reboot, type of processor, amount of RAM and flash, interfaces, licensed features, serial number, activation key, and the timestamp showing when configuration was last changed.

The following is an example of the show version command on an ASA 5505 running version 8.0(3):

```
bigdog# show version
Cisco Adaptive Security Appliance Software Version 8.0(3)
Device Manager Version 6.1(1)

Compiled on Tue 06-Nov-07 22:59 by builders
System image file is "disk0:/asa803-k8.bin"
Config file at boot was "startup-config"
bigdog up 2 hours 39 mins

Hardware:   ASA5505, 256 MB RAM, CPU Geode 500 MHz
Internal ATA Compact Flash, 128MB
BIOS Flash M50FW080 @ 0xffe00000, 1024KB

Encryption hardware device : Cisco ASA-5505 on-board accelerator
     (revision 0x0)
                      Boot microcode   : CN1000-MC-BOOT-2.00
                      SSL/IKE microcode: CNLite-MC-SSLm-PLUS-2.01
                      IPSec microcode  : CNlite-MC-IPSECm-MAIN-2.04
 0: Int: Internal-Data0/0    : address is 001f.9e2e.e51a, irq 11
 1: Ext: Ethernet0/0         : address is 001f.9e2e.e512, irq 255
 2: Ext: Ethernet0/1         : address is 001f.9e2e.e513, irq 255
 3: Ext: Ethernet0/2         : address is 001f.9e2e.e514, irq 255
 4: Ext: Ethernet0/3         : address is 001f.9e2e.e515, irq 255
 5: Ext: Ethernet0/4         : address is 001f.9e2e.e516, irq 255
 6: Ext: Ethernet0/5         : address is 001f.9e2e.e517, irq 255
 7: Ext: Ethernet0/6         : address is 001f.9e2e.e518, irq 255
 8: Ext: Ethernet0/7         : address is 001f.9e2e.e519, irq 255
 9: Int: Internal-Data0/1    : address is 0000.0003.0002, irq 255
10: Int: Not used            : irq 255
11: Int: Not used            : irq 255

Licensed features for this platform:
```

```
Maximum Physical Interfaces : 8
VLANs                       : 20, DMZ Unrestricted
Inside Hosts                : 10
Failover                    : Active/Standby
VPN-DES                     : Enabled
VPN-3DES-AES                : Enabled
VPN Peers                   : 25
WebVPN Peers                : 2
Dual ISPs                   : Enabled
VLAN Trunk Ports            : 8
AnyConnect for Mobile       : Disabled
AnyConnect for Linksys phone : Disabled
Advanced Endpoint Assessment : Disabled

This platform has an ASA 5505 Security Plus license.
Serial Number: JMX1209Z0CM
Running Activation Key: 0x84016a7e 0x0c293f62 0x9c7201c8 0x85641c50
                       0x882de4ab
Configuration register is 0x1
Configuration last modified by enable_15 at 14:33:47.385
  UTC Fri Jul 18 2008
bigdog#
```

Notice that the license installed on the ASA 5505 is the Security Plus license, which allows for failover (active/standby), more VLANs, and an unrestricted DMZ.

Memory Usage

The security appliances use RAM to store many of their components, including their active configuration, the translation table, the state (conn) table, the ARP table, a routing table, and many other tables. Because RAM is an important resource that the appliances use to enforce their security policies, you should periodically check how much RAM is free on the appliance. To view this information, use the **show memory** Privilege EXEC command:

```
ciscoasa# show memory
Free memory:       141399240 bytes (53%)
Used memory:       127036216 bytes (47%)
-------------      ----------------
Total memory:      268435456 bytes (100%)
```

CPU Utilization

To see the process CPU utilization of your security appliance, use the **show cpu usage** Privilege EXEC command, as shown here:

```
ciscoasa# show cpu usage
CPU utilization for 5 seconds = 20%; 1 minute: 14%; 5 minutes: 14%
```

You can see the CPU utilization over the last 5 seconds, 1 minute, and 5 minutes. Again, periodically you should check this to ensure that your appliance CPU can handle the load that goes through it; if not, you'll need to replace your appliance with a higher model.

ASA CONFIGURATION EXAMPLE

In this section, I will go over a basic appliance configuration using an ASA 5510 by using the network shown in Figure 3-1. Listing 3-1 shows the basic configuration for the appliance shown in Figure 3-1.

Listing 3-1. A sample ASA configuration for Figure 3-1

```
ciscoasa# configure terminal
ciscoasa(config)# hostname asa
asa(config)# domain-name dealgroup.com
asa(config)# enable password OpenSaysMe
asa(config)# interface ethernet0/0
asa(config-if)# nameif outside
asa(config-if)# security-level 0
asa(config-if)# ip address 192.168.1.1 255.255.255.0
asa(config-if)# no shutdown
asa(config-if)# exit
asa(config)# interface ethernet0/1
asa(config-if)# nameif inside
asa(config-if)# security-level 100
asa(config-if)# ip address 192.168.3.1 255.255.255.0
asa(config-if)# no shutdown
asa(config-if)# exit
asa(config)# interface ethernet0/2
asa(config-if)# nameif dmz
asa(config-if)# security-level 50
asa(config-if)# ip address 192.168.2.1 255.255.255.0
asa(config-if)# no shutdown
asa(config-if)# exit
asa(config)# passwd NoEntry
bigdog(config)# crypto key generate rsa
WARNING: You have a RSA keypair already defined named
     <Default-RSA-Key>.
Do you really want to replace them? [yes/no]: yes
Keypair generation process begin. Please wait...
asa(config)# ssh 192.168.3.0 255.255.255.0 inside
asa(config)# exit
asa# write memory
```

```
Building configuration...
Cryptochecksum: 21657c19 e04a2a24 e502173c 8626e76d
[OK]
asa#
```

The first command that I executed in Listing 3-1 was to change the hostname of the appliance to *asa* and a domain name of *dealgroup.com*. Following this, I configured a Privilege EXEC password of *OpenSaysMe*. I then configured the three interfaces, assigning them logical names, security levels, and IP addresses, and enabling them. Once IP was configured, I wanted to be able to SSH on this appliance, so I assigned a User EXEC password of *NoEntry*, generating the public and private RSA keys and allowing any internal computer SSH access. Finally, I saved the appliance configuration—remember that you can execute the **write memory** command at either Privilege EXEC or Configuration mode.

You will actually need to do quite a few more things to pass traffic through your appliance, like setting up routing, configuring translation policies (if necessary), setting up ACLs, and many other policy configurations. This chapter, as well as this example, only focused on the basics—preparing your appliance so that you can implement your security policies. The following chapters will deal with traffic as it flows through the appliance.

CHAPTER 4

Routing and Multicasting

This chapter will introduce you to the routing and multicasting capabilities of the security appliances. Appliances support static routing and dynamic routing protocols, including RIP, OSPF, and EIGRP, the newest edition. The appliances also have limited multicast capabilities, including support for interaction with multicast clients using the IGMP protocol and routing of multicast traffic. The topics in this chapter include

▼ Routing features

▲ Multicast features

ROUTING FEATURES

You can use two methods to get routing information into your appliance: static routes and a dynamic routing protocol. The three dynamic routing protocols supported include RIP, OSPF, and EIGRP. The appliances need some basic routing information to take incoming packets and forward them out of an appropriate interface to reach a destination that is more than one hop away. The following sections cover the implementation, configuration, and verification of routing on your appliance.

Routing Recommendations

It is important to point out that your appliance is *not* a full-functioning router. This was very apparent up through version 6.2 of the operating system. With the introduction of version 6.3, OSPF was added as a routing protocol. As you will see later in the "OSPF" section, the appliances have most of the OSPF capabilities of Cisco IOS routers; however, they don't have all the same capabilities.

You can use two common practices for routing on the appliances, depending on whether the appliance is at the perimeter of your network, or located inside the campus or data center. For small networks, it is common to use a default route pointing to the router connected to the *outside* interface and to use static routes pointing to your networks connected to your remaining appliance interfaces. For large networks, it is common to use static routing on the perimeter appliances, but to use a dynamic routing protocol for appliances located within the campus or data center.

TIP   The most preferred routing method on a perimeter appliance is to have a default route pointing to the outside interface and to have a specific route(s) pointing to the internal interface(s).

Administrative Distance

If you have multiple paths to reach the same destination within a routing protocol, the appliance uses the lowest metric value when choosing a route and places the lowest metric route in the routing table. However, if more than one routing protocol is learning

Routing Protocol	Administrative Distance
Connected interface	0
Static route	1
EIGRP summarized route	5
Internal EIGRP route (within an autonomous system or AS)	90
OSPF	110
RIP	120
External EIGRP route (different AS)	170
Unknown	255

Table 4-1.   Administrative Distances of Routing Protocols

a route, Cisco uses a proprietary feature called *administrative distance* to rank the routing protocols. The routing protocol with the lowest administrative distance value will have its route placed in the routing table. Table 4-1 lists the administrative distances of the routing protocols. Note that Cisco uses the same administrative distance values to rank routing protocols on their IOS routers.

Static Routes

The three kinds of static routes are

▼   Connected route

■   Static route

▲   Default route

Once you configure an IP address on your appliance's interface, the appliance automatically creates a static route for the specified network number and associates it with the configured interface. This is referred to as a *connected route.* When you're determining what route to use to reach a destination, connected routes have the highest preference (lowest administrative distance). Once you are done configuring your interface IP addresses, the appliance will know about all of the directly connected networks. However, the appliance doesn't know about networks more than one hop away from itself. To solve this problem, one option is to configure static, or default, routes. This topic is discussed in the next section.

Static Route Configuration

To create a static or default route, use the **route** command, as shown here:

```
ciscoasa(config)# route logical_if_name network_number subnet_mask
                    next_hop_IP_address [metric] [tunneled]
```

As you can see from the syntax, the configuration of this command is not too different from configuring a static route on an IOS router. The first parameter you must enter for the **route** command is the logical name of the interface where the destination route exists. If you examine Figure 4-1, for 192.168.4.0/24 and 192.168.5.0/24, this would be the **inside** interface. Next, you follow it with the network number and the subnet mask. For a default route, enter **0.0.0.0** for the network number, or **0** for short, and **0.0.0.0** for the subnet mask, which can also be abbreviated to **0**.

After you've entered the network number and subnet mask, specify the router's IP address that the appliance will forward the traffic to in order to get the traffic to the correct destination. Again, for the 192.168.4.0/24 and 192.168.5.0/24 networks, the next-hop address is 192.168.3.2.

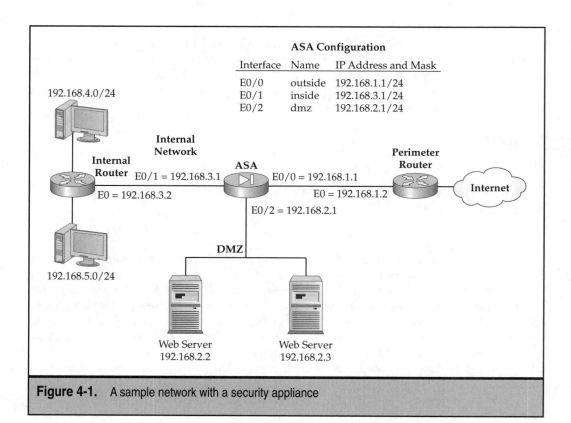

Figure 4-1.   A sample network with a security appliance

You can optionally add a hop count to rank static routes when your appliance is connected to more than one router and you want the appliance to know about both routing paths—this is configured with the **metric** parameter. This parameter weights the static routes, giving preference to the one with a lower metric value.

When you create a default route with the **tunneled** parameter, all encrypted traffic that arrives on the appliance which cannot be routed using a dynamically learned route or a static route is sent to this route. Otherwise, if the traffic is not encrypted, the appliance's standard default route is used. Two restrictions apply when you're using the **tunneled** option:

▼   You cannot define more than one default route with this option.

▲   ICMP for tunneled traffic is not supported with this option.

NOTE   The security appliances will *not* load-balance between multiple paths—they will only use one path. If the metric is different, the appliance will use the path with the lower metric value. If the metric value is the same, the appliance will use the *first* **route** command that you configured.

Route Verification

To view the routes in your appliance's routing table, use the following command:

```
ciscoasa# show route [logical_if_name [ip_address [netmask [static]]]]
```

Here is an example of the use of the **show route** command:

Listing 4-1. A static route configuration for Figure 4-1

```
ciscoasa(config)# show route
S    0.0.0.0 0.0.0.0 [1/0] via 192.168.1.2, outside
C    192.168.3.0 255.255.255.0 is directly connected, inside
C*   127.0.0.0 255.255.0.0 is directly connected, cplane
C    192.168.2.0 255.255.255.0 is directly connected, dmz
C    192.168.1.0 255.255.255.0 is directly connected, outside
S    192.168.4.0 255.255.255.0 [1/0] via 192.168.3.2, inside
S    192.168.5.0 255.255.255.0 [1/0] via 192.168.3.2, inside
```

A static route is represented by an S in the routing table. A directly connected route is represented by C. If you see a 127.0.0.0 route, it indicates that you are on an ASA—this address is used to access the pseudo-console port of an installed IPS or CSC card. For nonconnected routes, as with static routes, you'll see two numbers in brackets (" [] "). The first number is the administrative distance of the routing protocol, and the second number is the metric of the route.

Static Route Configuration Example

To illustrate the configuration of static routes, I'll use the network shown previously in Figure 4-1. Here is the configuration to accomplish the routing table output shown previously in Listing 4-1:

```
ciscoasa(config)# route outside 0 0 192.168.1.2
ciscoasa(config)# route inside 192.168.4.0 255.255.255.0 192.168.3.2
ciscoasa(config)# route inside 192.168.5.0 255.255.255.0 192.168.3.2
```

Static Route Tracking

One problem with static routes is that the appliance, by default, has no way of knowing if the path to the destination is available unless the interface on the appliance associated with the static route were to go down. However, if the next-hop neighbor were to go down, the appliance would still forward traffic to this destination.

Static route tracking is a new feature, introduced in version 7.2, to deal with this problem when using static routes. This feature allows an appliance to detect that a configured static route that is currently in the routing table is no longer reachable and to use a backup static route that you've configured. ICMP is used by the appliance to test connectivity for the static route currently in the appliance routing table. If ICMP echo replies are not received for a preconfigured period from the monitored device associated with the current static route, the appliance can then remove the associated static route from its routing table, and use a configured backup static route.

NOTE   One restriction with the static route tracking feature is that it cannot be used with a static route that has the **tunneled** option enabled.

Static Route Tracking Configuration   Use the following commands to configure static route tracking:

```
ciscoasa(config)# sla monitor SLA_ID
ciscoasa(config-sla-monitor)# type echo protocol ipIcmpEcho
                    monitor_device_IP interface logical_if_name
ciscoasa(config-sla-monitor-echo)# timeout milliseconds
ciscoasa(config-sla-monitor-echo)# frequency #_missed_echo_replies
ciscoasa(config)# sla monitor schedule SLA_ID life forever
                    start-time now
ciscoasa(config)# track track_ID rtr SLA_ID reachability
ciscoasa(config)# route logical_if_name network_number subnet_mask
                    next_hop_IP_address [metric] track track_ID
```

The **sla monitor** command specifies how the tracking should be done. The *SLA_ID* associates an identification value to the tracking process. The **type** subcommand mode command specifies the protocol to use when performing the test, the device to test access to, and the interface the monitored device is connected to. Currently the only protocol supported for testing is ICMP (**ipIcmpEcho**). The **timeout** command specifies the number of milliseconds to wait for the echo reply. The **frequency** command specifies the number of echo replies that must be missed before the tracked static route is considered bad. The **sla monitor schedule** command specifies when monitoring should start and for how long. Normally you want the tracking to start right now and continue forever, but you can change these values. The **track** command associates the *SLA_ID* for monitoring with the tracking ID specified in the **route** command(s).

Static Route Tracking Configuration Example   To illustrate how static route tracking is used, examine Figure 4-2. In this example, the perimeter appliance is connected to two ISPs via two different perimeter routers, where ISP1 is the default path and ISP2 is the backup. However, if either of these two ISP links were to go down, the appliance, since it is not connected to them, would not know this. Here is the configuration for static route tracking for this example:

```
ciscoasa(config)# sla monitor 100
ciscoasa(config-sla-monitor)# type echo protocol ipIcmpEcho
            200.1.1.1 interface outside
ciscoasa(config-sla-monitor-echo)# timeout 1000
ciscoasa(config-sla-monitor-echo)# frequency 3
ciscoasa(config-sla-monitor-echo)# exit
ciscoasa(config)# sla monitor schedule 100 life forever start-time now
ciscoasa(config)# track 1 rtr 100 reachability
ciscoasa(config)# route 0 0 outside1 192.168.1.1 1 track 1
ciscoasa(config)# route 0 0 outside2 192.168.2.1 2 track 1
```

In the preceding configuration, the appliance is tracking a device, probably a router, in the ISP1 network (200.1.1.1). If an echo reply is not received when tracking within 1 second (1,000 milliseconds) and this process is repeated three times, the primary default

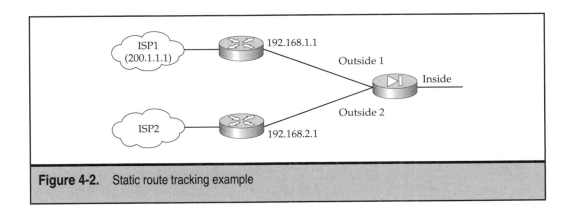

Figure 4-2.   Static route tracking example

route is considered bad (the 192.168.1.1 neighbor with a metric of 1), and the backup default route for the outside2 interface will be used.

RIP

Until version 8 of the operating system, the appliances were restricted in how they ran RIP: they could only accept RIP routes and optionally advertise a default route; they could not take routes learned from one RIP neighbor and advertise these routes on another interface. Starting in version 8, the appliance is a full-functioning RIP router. If more than one routing process is running on the appliance, you can even redistribute routes from one process, like RIP, into another routing process.

Both RIPv1 and RIPv2 are supported. With RIPv2, you can authenticate routing updates from neighboring RIPv2 routers. You can also control, on an interface-by-interface basis, what RIP version is run on an interface.

RIP Configuration

The configuration of RIP is performed globally, with some features controlled on an interface-by-interface basis. The following two sections will cover the configuration of RIP.

RIP Global Configuration   Configuring RIP on an appliance is similar to configuring RIP on a Cisco router. To enable RIP, use the **router rip** global Configuration mode command:

```
ciscoasa(config)# router rip
ciscoasa(config-router)# network network_address
ciscoasa(config-router)# version [1 | 2]
ciscoasa(config-router)# default-information originate
ciscoasa(config-router)# passive-interface [default | logical_if_name]
ciscoasa(config-router)# no auto-summarize
```

The **router rip** command takes you into the RIP routing process. The **network** command specifies the networks that the appliance is connected to that should be included in the RIP process. The **version** command specifies, globally, the RIP version the appliance should run. (This can be overridden on an interface-by-interface basis.) The **default-information** command allows a default route to propagate into and through the RIP routing process on the appliance. The **passive-interface** command specifies whether all interfaces or just the specified interface is allowed to propagate RIP routes to other neighbors (the interface is operating in passive mode).

By default, the RIP routing process will automatically summarize Class A, B, and C network numbers at their class boundary. The **no auto-summarize** command works only for RIPv2: it disables automatic summarization of subnets back to their Class A, B, and/or C network numbers when advertising networks across a network boundary, like 172.16.0.0/16 to 10.0.0.0/8.

RIP Interface Configuration   You have two configuration options for RIP on an appliance's interface: controlling the RIP version(s) that run on the interface and the authentication of routing updates. Here are the commands to configure these options:

```
ciscoasa(config)# interface physical_if_name
ciscoasa(config-if)# rip {receive | send} version {[1] [2]}
ciscoasa(config-if)# rip authentication mode {text | md5}
ciscoasa(config-if)# rip authentication key key_# key-id key_ID
```

You can run both version 1 and 2 of RIP on an interface if you have RIP routers speaking both versions. You can control this in both the send and receive directions on the interface with the **rip send** and **rip receive** commands. To run RIP in compatibility mode, make sure both versions of RIP are enabled on the interface in the appropriate direction(s).

Assuming you are running RIPv2 on an interface, you can also authenticate routing updates with RIPv2 peers connected to the interface. The **rip authentication** command allows you to set up authentication for RIPv2. You have two choices for validating a peer:

▼ Send the authentication information in clear text (**text**) in the routing update.

▲ Digitally sign the routing update using MD5 authentication (**md5**).

It is highly recommended to use the MD5 hash function and not clear text for authentication. When specifying MD5, you need to specify the encryption key, which can be up to 16 characters long, as well as the key identification number, which can be a number between 1 and 255. Note that on your peer RIPv2 neighbors, you'll need to match these values. I discuss MD5 in more depth in Chapter 15.

SECURITY ALERT!   RIP version 1 has no security mechanism built into it and thus can be easily spoofed. Therefore, you should use RIP version 2 on your appliance, with MD5 authentication configured, and the routers connected to your appliance. This also applies to the appliance if you are using OSPF or EIGRP: use MD5 authentication to greatly reduce the likelihood that your appliance would accept a spoofed route from a rogue router.

RIP Verification

To view the routing table that has RIP routes, use the **show route** command:

```
ciscoasa(config)# show route
S     0.0.0.0 0.0.0.0 [1/0] via 192.168.1.2, outside
C     192.168.3.0 255.255.255.0 is directly connected, inside
C*    127.0.0.0 255.255.0.0 is directly connected, cplane
C     192.168.2.0 255.255.255.0 is directly connected, dmz
C     192.168.1.0 255.255.255.0 is directly connected, outside
R     192.168.4.0 255.255.255.0 [120/1] via 192.168.3.2, inside
R     192.168.5.0 255.255.255.0 [120/1] via 192.168.3.2, inside
```

In this example, you can see the connected routes, as well as a default route that was statically configured. At the bottom, you can see the two RIP routes, designated by an R, learned from the 192.168.3.2 RIP neighbor.

TIP The **clear route** [*logical_if_name*] command clears dynamic routes—RIP, OSPF, and EIGRP—from the local routing table.

For further troubleshooting of RIP, you can use the **debug rip** command. Here's an example:

```
RIP: broadcasting general request on Ethernet0/1
RIP: Received update from 192.168.3.2 on 0/1
 192.168.4.0 in 1 hops
 192.168.5.0 in 1 hops
RIP: Sending update to 255.255.255.255 via Ethernet0/1 (192.168.3.1)
 subnet 192.168.1.0, metric 1
 subnet 192.168.2.0, metric 1
```

You can qualify the output of the preceding command by using the **debug rip events** command to see information that is being shared between RIP devices. Use the **debug rip database** command to see how the local RIP database and routing table are updated with RIP routes.

RIP Configuration Example

To illustrate the configuration of RIP, I'll use the network shown previously in Figure 4-1. I'll assume that Internal Router understands RIPv2 and that a default route is used to reach networks beyond the External Router. In this example, the e0/1 interface (inside) is included in RIP, and MD5 authentication is used.

```
ciscoasa(config)# route outside 0 0 192.168.1.2
ciscoasa(config)# router rip
ciscoasa(config-router)# network 192.168.3.0
ciscoasa(config-router)# version 2
ciscoasa(config-router)# default-information originate
ciscoasa(config-router)# exit
ciscoasa(config)# interface ethernet0/1
ciscoasa(config-if)# rip authentication mode md5
ciscoasa(config-if)# rip authentication key peekabooiseeu key-id 100
```

OSPF

OSPF support, with the exception of the Firewall Services Module (FWSM), is new to the appliances in version 6.3. The exception to this is the PIX 501, which doesn't support OSPF. The appliances share most of the features that Cisco IOS routers support for OSPF. For example, the appliances support *intra*-area routing, *inter*-area routing, and external type-1 and type-2 routing. The appliances can play the role of a designated router (DR) and backup DR (BDR) in an area, an area border router (ABR), and an autonomous system boundary router (ASBR). The appliances support advanced OSPF features like route authentication with MD5, stubby and NSSA areas, ABR link state advertisement (LSA) type-3 filtering, virtual links, and route redistribution, providing you with a lot of flexibility in setting up OSPF on your appliance to provide a scalable OSPF network design.

NOTE   The OSPF discussion in this book is kept somewhat brief, covering about 70 percent of the actual OSPF capabilities of the appliances. The topics that are discussed are the ones most commonly implemented by administrators.

Basic OSPF Configuration

Enabling OSPF is a two-step process:

1. Create your OSPF process.

2. Specify the interfaces that are associated with a particular area.

The basic configuration of OSPF is similar to that done on a Cisco router:

```
ciscoasa(config)# router ospf process_ID
ciscoasa(config-router)# network IP_address subnet_mask area area_#
ciscoasa(config-router)# timers spf spf_delay spf_holdtime
```

First, create your OSPF process with the **router ospf** command, giving the OSPF a process ID—you can have only *two* OSPF processes running simultaneously on your appliance. Notice that this command takes you into a subcommand mode for the OSPF routing process.

Second, you use the **network** command to specify which interface is in which area. This is almost like the router's OSPF **network** command…with one exception: you don't specify a wildcard mask; instead, you specify a *subnet* mask. To put a specific interface into a specific area, use the interface's IP address and a subnet mask of 255.255.255.255.

Optionally, you can change the shortest-path first (SPF) delay and hold-down time with the **timers spf** command. The delay is the number of seconds the appliance will wait upon receiving a topology change and running the SPF algorithm; this defaults to 5 seconds. If you specify 0, then the appliance doesn't wait when a change is received. The hold-down period is the number of seconds the appliance waits between two SPF calculations; by default this is 10 seconds. These timers are used to prevent a flapping route from causing CPU issues on an appliance by delaying the SPF calculation when a change is received.

Here is a simple example of a single-process configuration of OSPF on an appliance, based on the network shown in Figure 4-3:

```
ciscoasa(config)# router ospf  1
ciscoasa(config-router)# network 10.0.0.0 255.0.0.0 area 0
ciscoasa(config-router)# network 192.168.1.0 255.255.255.0 area 1
ciscoasa(config-router)# network 192.168.2.0 255.255.255.0 area 1
```

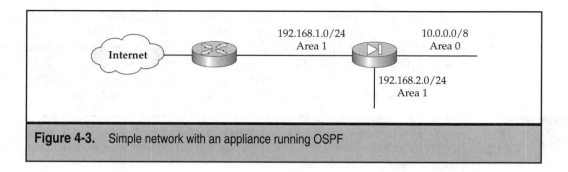

Figure 4-3. Simple network with an appliance running OSPF

In the preceding example, any interface beginning with *10* is placed in area 0; any interface beginning with *192.168.1* or *192.168.2* is in area 1.

OSPF Interface Parameters

You can tune many interface-specific OSPF parameters, but this is typically unnecessary. Here are some of the interface-specific OSPF commands on an appliance:

```
ciscoasa(config)# interface physical_if_name
ciscoasa(config-interface)# ospf cost cost
ciscoasa(config-interface)# ospf priority priority
ciscoasa(config-interface)# ospf hello-interval seconds
ciscoasa(config-interface)# ospf dead-interval seconds
```

The `ospf cost` command hard-codes the cost of an interface, overriding the default calculation that is used. The cost needs to match what the neighbors use, or inadvertent SPF calculations can occur. The `ospf priority` command is used to elect the DR and BDR—the default priority is 1; setting it to 0 causes the interface to not participate in the election process.

The `ospf hello-interval` command specifies how often LSA messages are generated. The `ospf dead-interval` command specifies the number of seconds after which if a neighbor's hello messages aren't seen, the neighbor is declared dead. The hello and dead interval timers default to 10 and 40 seconds, respectively, and must match up with the value configured on OSPF neighbors connected to the interface, or the appliance won't form an adjacency with them.

OSPF Authentication

OSPF and the appliances support authentication of routing updates by using a clear-text password or the MD5 function. If you want to authenticate OSPF routing updates, you must enable authentication for each area you will be doing this within the OSPF routing process. Here are the commands to accomplish this:

```
ciscoasa(config)# router ospf process_ID
ciscoasa(config-router)# area area_# authentication [message-digest]
```

For MD5, you need the **message-digest** parameter. Without it, clear-text keys are used for authentication instead of MD5 signatures.

After enabling authentication for an area or areas, you'll need to configure authentication on the interface(s) that will be using it:

```
ciscoasa(config)# interface interface_name
ciscoasa(config-if)# ospf authentication [message-digest | null]
ciscoasa(config-if)# ospf authentication-key key
ciscoasa(config-if)# ospf message-digest-key key_# md5 key
```

On the interface, if you're using clear-text authentication, use the **ospf authentication** and **ospf authentication-key** commands. For authentication using MD5, use the **ospf authentication message-digest** and **ospf message-digest-key** commands.

Here's an example of using MD5 authentication for an area:

```
ciscoasa(config)# router ospf 1
ciscoasa(config-router)# area 0 authentication message-digest
ciscoasa(config-router)# exit
ciscoasa(config)# interface e0/1
ciscoasa(config-if)# ospf authentication message-digest
ciscoasa(config-if)# ospf message-digest-key 500 md5 cisco123abc
```

In this example, MD5 authentication is used in area 0, which includes the e0/1 interface. The key number used is *500,* and the actual signature key is *cisco123abc.*

NOTE To protect against routing attacks, it is highly recommended to configure your appliance with OSPF authentication, which supports MD5 signatures for authentication of routing updates.

OSPF Area Stubs

Stubs are used to limit the number of routes in an area. A stub has type-1 and type-2 intra-area LSAs, type-3 and type-4 inter-area LSAs, and a default route injected into them by the ABR for external routes from a different autonomous system. If your appliance is an ABR and you want to designate an area as a stub, use the following configuration:

```
ciscoasa(config)# router ospf process_ID
ciscoasa(config-router)# area area_# stub [no-summary]
ciscoasa(config-router)# area area_# default-cost cost
```

To configure an area as a stub, use the **area stub** command. Any type-5 LSAs (external routes type 1 and type 2) will not be forwarded into the specified area; instead a default route is forwarded. The stub function must be configured on all OSPF devices in the area, including the ABR. On the ABR, if you specify the **no-summary** parameter, you are making the area "totally stubby." This is a Cisco proprietary feature: external routes from ASBRs and routes from other areas are not injected into a totally stubby area: only a default route is injected. The **area default-cost** command allows you to assign a cost metric to the injected default route that will be advertised into a stub area.

NSSA stands for "not-so-stubby area." Suppose your appliance is an ASBR and it is not connected to area 0, but to a different area, and that area is a stub. To get the external routes to the backbone through the stubby area, the ASBR must advertise the external routes as type 7; this is referred to as a not-so-stubby area (NSSA). Again, all OSPF devices in the area must be configured as NSSA. When configured as such, the devices in the area will forward type-7 LSAs to the backbone (area 0), but will not incorporate them into their local OSPF database. To configure your ABR appliance for NSSA, use the following configuration:

```
ciscoasa(config)# router ospf process_ID
ciscoasa(config-router)# area area_# nssa
                         [default-information originate]
ciscoasa(config-router)# area area_# default-cost cost
```

On the ASBR that's NSSA, the **area nssa** command makes the device understand about this issue. Adding the **default-information originate** parameter causes the appliance, when it is an ASBR, to inject a default route into the NSSA area. The **area default-cost** command allows you to change the default cost of the default route.

OSPF Summarization

If your appliance is an ABR, it can summarize routes between areas with the **area range** command:

```
ciscoasa(config)# router ospf process_ID
ciscoasa(config-router)# area area_# range network_# subnet_mask
                         [advertise | not-advertise]
```

This command only summarizes routes located in the area specified. The **advertise** parameter is the default—it advertises the summarized route. The **not-advertise** parameter will not advertise any routes matching the network/subnet mask specified for the area to any other connected areas (type-3 and type-4 LSAs).

Here are the commands necessary to perform summarization on an appliance that is an ASBR:

```
ciscoasa(config)# router ospf process_ID
ciscoasa(config-router)# default-information originate
                  [always] [metric metric-value]
                  [metric-type {1 | 2}] [route-map map-name]
ciscoasa(config-router)# summary address network_# subnet_mask
                  [not-advertise] [tag tag]
```

You can inject a default route into your OSPF process with the **default-information originate** command. The **always** parameter causes the appliance to always inject a default route into the OSPF process, even if one doesn't exist in the local routing table.

When injecting a default route, you can assign a metric to it with the **metric** parameter, specify the type of external route with the **metric-type** parameter, and apply a route map to the process, which can be used to change properties of the route. Route maps are beyond the scope of this book.

You can also summarize external routes using the **summary address** command. As in the previous configuration, the **not-advertise** parameter will not advertise external routes that match the network number and subnet mask values configured into the local OSPF process. The tag value is a 32-bit number that OSPF itself doesn't use, but that other routing protocols like BGP can use.

> **NOTE** You cannot create a summary route of 0.0.0.0/0; instead you need to use the **default-information originate** command.

OSPF Route Filtering

The appliances support filtering of type-3 LSAs; this might be necessary if you are using private network numbers on certain interfaces and do not want to pass these as routes via OSPF. Configuring prefix filtering (filtering of type-3 LSAs) is a two-step process:

```
ciscoasa(config)# prefix-list prefix_list_name {permit | deny}
                     network_#/prefix_length
ciscoasa(config)# router ospf process_ID
ciscoasa(config-router)# area area_# filter-list
                     {prefix_list_name in | out}
```

Configure your list of prefix routes that will or will not be filtered with the **prefix-list** command. The order you enter the prefix list is important, since the appliance processes the list top-down. The **permit** statements allow the route, while **deny** statements filter the route. To specify a prefix, enter the network number, followed by a slash ("/") and the number of network bits, like 10.0.0.0/8.

You then apply the prefix list to an area in an OSPF routing process with the **area filter-list** command. You can filter routing updates entering an area (**in** parameter) or leaving an area (**out** parameter).

OSPF Route Redistribution

You can take routes from an external source on your appliance, assuming it's acting as an ASBR, and inject them into OSPF, and vice versa. The configuration of redistribution on the appliances is similar to how it is configured on Cisco IOS routers. Redistribution is accomplished by using the **redistribute** command.

```
ciscoasa(config)# router ospf process_ID
ciscoasa(config-router)# redistribute {connected | static}
                     [[metric metric_value] [metric-type
                     {type-1 | type-2}] [tag tag_value]
                     [subnets] [route-map route_map_name]
```

```
ciscoasa(config-router)# redistribute ospf process_ID
                         [match {internal | external [1 | 2] |
                         nssa-external [1 | 2]}] [metric metric_value]
                         [metric-type {type-1 | type-2}] [tag tag_value]
                         [subnets] [route-map route_map_name]
ciscoasa(config-router)# redistribute rip [metric metric_value]
                         [metric-type {type-1 | type-2}] [tag tag_value]
                         [subnets] [route-map route_map_name]
ciscoasa(config-router)# redistribute eigrp AS_# [metric metric_value]
                         [metric-type {type-1 | type-2}] [tag tag_value]
                         [subnets] [route-map route_map_name]
```

The **redistribute** command takes routes from an external routing process and redistributes them into the current OSPF process. The **metric** parameter allows you to associate a cost to the redistributed routes. The **metric-type** parameter allows you to specify if the redistributed routes are type-1 or type-2 external routes—the default is type-2 if omitted. You can also tag the route with a number with the **tag** parameter: OSPF doesn't process this information, but an ASBR speaking BGP can use this information. If you omit the **subnets** parameter, only classful routes are redistributed into OSPF—not the subnets of a network number. The **match** parameter is used when taking routes from another OSPF process—you can control if you'll take the other process' internal and/or external type-1 or type-2 routes into the local OSPF process. With each of the preceding **redistribute** commands, you can use the **route-map** parameter and change information related to the matching routes, like their metrics. Route maps are beyond the scope of this book.

To illustrate the simplicity of configuring route redistribution, examine the network shown in Figure 4-4. In this network, the appliance will redistribute routes from autonomous system (AS) 100 into AS 200. Here's the redistribution configuration to accomplish this:

```
ciscoasa(config)# router ospf 100
ciscoasa(config)# router ospf 200
ciscoasa(config-router)# redistribute ospf 100 match internal
```

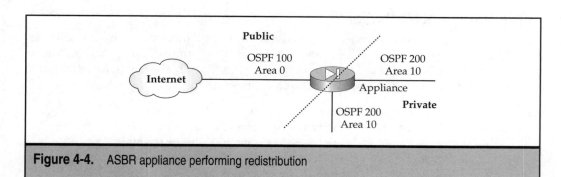

Figure 4-4.   ASBR appliance performing redistribution

NOTE If there are overlapping network numbers in the two routing processes when you're performing redistribution, you'll need to filter them using LSA type-3 filtering, or you will create reachability issues with your routing processes.

OSPF Verification

When running OSPF, use the **show route** command to view the routes in your routing table: OSPF routes show up as an O in the routing table. This command was discussed earlier in the chapter. Other commands you can use include the ones shown in Table 4-2.

EIGRP

Support for Cisco's proprietary EIGRP routing protocol was added to the appliances in version 8.0. Very similar EIGRP capabilities are on the appliances that you may have used on the Cisco IOS routers for many years. Some supported features include the following:

▼ Neighbor authentication

■ Route summarization

■ Route filtering

■ Redistribution with other routing protocols (very similar to redistribution discussed in the "OSPF Route Redistribution" section and therefore omitted from this section)

▲ Stub routing

NOTE The EIGRP discussion in this book is kept somewhat brief, covering about 70 percent of the actual EIGRP capabilities of the appliances. The topics that are discussed are the ones most commonly implemented by administrators.

OSPF Command	Explanation
show ospf [*process_ID* [*area_#*]]	Viewing information about the OSPF routing process
show ospf [*process_ID* [*area_#*]] **database**	Displaying the OSPF database
show ospf interface [*logical_if_name*]	Displaying the OSPF interface information
show ospf neighbor [*logical_if_name*] [*neighbor_ID*] [**detail**]	Displaying the OSPF neighbor table

Table 4-2. Commands to Verify Your OSPF Configuration

Basic EIGRP Configuration

Setting up EIGRP routing on an appliance is very similar to setting it up on a Cisco IOS router. Here are the basic commands to enable EIGRP routing:

```
ciscoasa(config)# router eigrp AS_#
ciscoasa(config-router)# network IP_address [subnet_mask]
ciscoasa(config-router)# [no] passive-interface {default |
                         logical_if_name}
```

To enable the EIGRP routing process, you need to assign it an AS number. Within the routing process, for every network you list (with the **network** command) that matches an interface on the appliance, that interface is included in the EIGRP routing process. If you omit the subnet mask, it defaults to the network class mask (A, B, C).

The **passive-interface** command places a specified interface in a passive mode: the appliance will not process any EIGRP updates on the interface. The **default** parameter disables EIGRP on all interfaces: then to enable for specific interfaces, use the **no passive-interface** command, referencing the specific logical interface names. Here's a simple example, based on Figure 4-3, of enabling EIGRP on all the appliance interfaces:

```
ciscoasa(config)# router eigrp 1
ciscoasa(config-router)# network 192.168.1.0 255.255.255.0
ciscoasa(config-router)# network 192.168.2.0 255.255.255.0
ciscoasa(config-router)# network 10.0.0.0 255.0.0.0
```

In this example, all three interfaces are in autonomous system 1.

EIGRP Authentication

Setting up authentication of EIGRP routing updates is easy. Enter the interface the EIGRP neighbor(s) are connected to, and for the AS, specify that MD5 is used with the **authentication mode** command. Then configure the key and key number used within the AS on that interface with the **authentication key** command:

```
ciscoasa(config)# interface physical_if_name
ciscoasa(config-if)# authentication mode eigrp AS_# md5
ciscoasa(config-if)# authentication key eigrp AS_# key key-id key_#
```

Note that all EIGRP routers connected to the interface need to have the same AS number along with the same key value and key number. Here's a simple example based on the code listing in the previous example:

```
ciscoasa(config)# interface e0/1
ciscoasa(config-if)# authentication mode eigrp 1 md5
ciscoasa(config-if)# authentication key eigrp 1 cisco123abc key-id 100
```

EIGRP Summarization

By default, EIGRP behaves, in many instances, like a distance vector protocol. One example of this process is when EIGRP advertises subnets across network boundaries: before advertising any subnets across a different network number, EIGRP automatically summarizes the subnets back to the network class boundary (A, B, or C) and advertises the network class address instead. You can disable this automatic summarization with the **no auto-summary** command in the EIGRP routing process:

```
ciscoasa(config)# router eigrp AS_#
ciscoasa(config-router)# [no] auto-summary
```

Executing the preceding disables all summarization.

To perform manual summarization, enter the interface the summarization should be performed on, and use the **summary-address** command to summarize the contiguous networks or subnets:

```
ciscoasa(config)# interface physical_if _name
ciscoasa(config-if)# summary-address eigrp AS_# network_# subnet_mask
                    [administrative_distance]
```

When your appliance is at the edge of the network, like a WAN link or the access layer in the campus network, it is typically not necessary to share an entire network's list of EIGRP routes to edge devices. EIGRP supports a process similar to OSPF called *stubs*. Here is the configuration to set up stub routing for EIGRP on your appliance:

```
ciscoasa(config)# router eigrp AS_#
ciscoasa(config-router)# eigrp stub [receive-only | [connected]
                    [redistributed] [static] [summary]]
```

You need to specify which network types will be advertised by the stub routing process on the appliance to any connected EIGRP distribution layer routers with the **eigrp stub** command; you can configure more than one option on a line.

The **receive-only** parameter will receive routes from neighbors, but will not advertise routes. Static and connected networks are not automatically redistributed into the stub routing process; if you want to include them, specify the **connected** and **static** parameters respectively. The **redistributed** parameter causes the appliance to advertise routes that were redistributed from other routing protocols on the appliance. The **summary** parameter allows the appliance to advertise summarized routes.

Here are some examples of the use of the **eigrp stub** command:

▼   **eigrp stub connected summary**   Advertises connected and summarized routes

■   **eigrp stub connected static**   Advertises connected and static routes

▲   **eigrp stub redistributed**   Advertises routes redistributed into EIGRP from other routing protocols

EIGRP Route Filtering

You also have the ability to filter EIGRP routes entering or leaving the EIGRP process or a particular interface. This is accomplished using access control lists (ACLs) and distribution lists, as it is done on Cisco IOS routers:

```
ciscoasa(config)# access-list ACL_ID standard [line line_#]
                       {deny | permit} {any | host IP_address |
                       IP_address subnet_mask}

ciscoasa(config)# router eigrp AS_#
ciscoasa(config-router)# distribute-list ACL_ID {in | out}
                       [interface logical_if_name]
```

First, you need to define a standard ACL (**access-list** command) that will list the EIGRP routes that are permitted and/or denied; note that you are entering network numbers for routes—you are not using the standard ACL to filter data traffic. ACLs and their syntax are discussed in more depth in Chapter 6. One important item to point out about ACLs, though, is that ACLs on the appliances, unlike IOS routers, use subnet masks, not wildcard masks, to match on ranges of addresses.

Within the EIGRP routing process, use the **distribute-list** command. You can filter traffic in or out of the EIGRP process itself or for a particularly named interface.

EIGRP Verification

When running EIGRP, use the **show route** command to view the routes in your routing table: EIGRP routes show up as a D in the routing table. This command was discussed earlier in the chapter. Other EIGRP commands you can use include the ones shown in Table 4-3.

OSPF Command	Explanation
show eigrp [AS_#] **interfaces** [logical_if_name] [**detail**]	View the EIGRP operation on the interfaces.
show eigrp [AS_#] **neighbors** [logical_if_name]	Display the EIGRP neighbor table.
show eigrp [AS_#] **topology**	Display the EIGRP topology table.
show eigrp [AS_#] **traffic**	View EIGRP traffic statistics.

Table 4-3.   Commands to Verify Your EIGRP Configuration

MULTICAST FEATURES

TCP/IPv4 has three kinds of addresses: unicast, broadcast, and multicast. Multicast traffic is data sent to one or more devices comprising a multicast group, where membership of the group is dynamic. A unique multicast address is used to represent membership in the group, where multicast addresses range from 224.0.0.0 through 239.255.255.255.

Multicast Traffic and the Appliances

Before version 6.2, the PIXs would only forward *unicast* packets between interfaces: multicast traffic between interfaces would be dropped. To solve this problem, administrators originally would place a router on each side of the PIX and build a GRE tunnel between the two, and then would encapsulate the multicast packets in GRE unicast packets. GRE is a layer 3 IP protocol that the appliance can switch between interfaces (see the top part of Figure 4-5). The problem with this solution is that it introduces delay in the multicast data streams and creates more overhead, since the original multicast packets must have an outer IP and GRE header added to them.

Starting in version 6.2, Cisco introduced the ability for the PIXs to move multicast traffic between interfaces. The appliances support both stub multicast routing (SMR) and PIM multicast routing; however, you can only enable one or the other on the appliance at a time. SMR was introduced in version 6.2 and PIM in version 7.0.

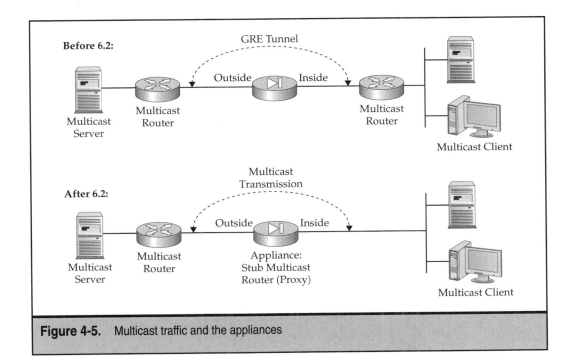

Figure 4-5. Multicast traffic and the appliances

Multicast Usage

Whether you are using PIM or SMR, you must first enable multicast routing on your appliance:

```
ciscoasa(config)# multicast-routing
```

The **multicast-routing** command allows the appliance to process and forward multicast packets. Once you configure the command, PIM and IGMP are automatically enabled on all the appliance's interfaces. IGMP version 2 (IGMPv2) is enabled by default, whereas IGMPv1 is disabled. This shouldn't be an issue since no applications today use the older protocol; however, the appliance does support both. The amount of RAM your appliance has will affect the size of the multicast tables the appliance maintains. Table 4-4 lists the table limits.

NOTE Enabling multicasting on a perimeter appliance is very rare; normally this is done on appliances in a data center or within a campus network.

Stub Multicast Routing

Stub multicast routing (SMR) allows end stations, like user PCs, to register for the multicast streams they want to receive via the IGMP protocol and allow for multicast routing. When the appliance uses SMR, it acts as an IGMP proxy, where it doesn't fully participate in the multicast process.

IGMP Protocol and IGMP Proxying

When acting as an IGMP proxy, the appliance takes IGMP queries from fully functional multicast routers and forwards them to the end-user stations. IGMP queries allow a multicast router to learn the end stations that wish to receive or continue receiving a multicast stream. For a multicast stream where no response is received, the multicast router assumes that no end stations wish to receive the stream and stops forwarding the stream to the associated network segment.

Table Limitations	16 MB	128 MB	128+ MB
Number of Multicast Forwarding Information Base (MFIB) entries	1,000	3,000	5,000
Number of IGMP groups	1,000	3,000	5,000
Number of PIM routes	3,000	7,000	12,000

Table 4-4. Multicast Table Size Limitations

The appliance also takes IGMP reports from end stations and forwards them to fully functional multicast routers. Reports include the multicast data stream or streams an end station wants to receive. In IGMP version 2 (IGMPv2), end stations can also generate join and leave messages, respectively, to speed up the process of alerting a multicast router that a stream needs to be forwarded to the segment and/or that a stream is no longer desired by the end station.

The appliance's role in this process is to proxy the IGMP messages between the multicast router and the end stations as well as to forward the multicast data streams between its interfaces.

Interface Configuration for IGMP

This section will discuss some of the IGMP properties you can manage on your appliance's interfaces. Here are the commands you can configure for IGMP:

```
ciscoasa(config)# interface physical_if_name
ciscoasa(config-if)# igmp forward interface logical_if_name
ciscoasa(config-if)# igmp join-group multicast_group_address
ciscoasa(config-if)# igmp static-group multicast_group_address
ciscoasa(config-if)# igmp query-timeout seconds
ciscoasa(config-if)# igmp query-interval seconds
ciscoasa(config-if)# igmp query-max-response-time seconds
ciscoasa(config-if)# igmp version {1 | 2}
```

The only required command for SMR (besides enabling multicast routing) is the **igmp forward interface** command. This command is configured on the interface where the end stations are connected and specifies the logical interface name where the fully functional multicast router resides. The rest of the commands discussed in this and the next section are optional for SMR.

The **igmp join-group** command configures the appliance to act like an end station and will advertise, by an IGMP report message to a multicast server, that the appliance wants the configured multicast data stream (multicast IP address) to be forwarded to the appliance.

NOTE   Normally this command is configured to test the appliance's multicast configuration to ensure that multicast data streams are forwarded through the appliance—once you have this working, make sure you disable the command. Otherwise every time a multicast router generates an IGMP query, the appliance will always respond back with an IGMP report with the configured multicast group address. Therefore, the configured multicast data stream will always be forwarded to the appliance, whether or not any connected end stations want to view multicast data.

The **igmp static-group** command performs a similar function as does the **igmp join-group** command. Where the latter command causes the appliance to accept, process, and forward multicast packets, the former command causes the appliance to forward only the multicast packets out the configured interface. The **igmp static-group** command is used when either you have an end station that has an IGMP compatibility issue with the multicast router and the end station needs to receive the specified multicast stream, or you always want the specified multicast traffic to be forwarded out the configured interface whether or not a connected end station wishes to receive it.

By default, it is the responsibility of the fully functional IGMP router to periodically generate the IGMP query messages, which the appliance will proxy. If there is a failure in this process, the appliance can generate the query messages itself. By default, if the appliance doesn't receive a query message from the IGMP router within 225 seconds, the appliance promotes itself to this role. You can change the timeout with the `igmp query-timeout` command. When acting as an IGMP router, the appliance will generate queries every 125 seconds to the end stations; you can change this with the `igmp query-interval` command. Also, when acting as an IGMP router and when the appliance generates a query, it expects a report message back within 10 seconds; otherwise the specified multicast data stream will no longer be forwarded out the end stations. You can change this interval with the `igmp query-max-response-time` command.

NOTE The `igmp query-timeout` and `igmp query-interval` commands are only applicable to IGMPv2.

As I mentioned in the "Multicast Usage" section, when multicast routing is enabled on the appliance, all the interfaces use IGMPv2. You can change this on an interface-by-interface basis with the `igmp version` command.

NOTE Since I was first introduced to multicasting in the late 1990s, I have yet to run into an implementation that only uses IGMPv1; therefore, you will probably never use the `igmp version` command. On top of this, an interface only supports one version of IGMP on an interface at a time. However, connected end stations should support both protocols.

Limiting the IGMP Proxy Process

This section will discuss how you can limit the proxying role the appliance plays when it is configured as an SMR. Here are the commands you can configure:

```
ciscoasa(config)# interface physical_if_name
ciscoasa(config-if)# [no] igmp
ciscoasa(config-if)# igmp limit number
```

As mentioned earlier in the "Multicast Usage" section, when you execute the `multicast-routing` command, IGMP is enabled on all the appliance interfaces. You can override this on an interface-by-interface basis with the `no igmp` command.

The `igmp limit` command allows you to limit the number of multicast groups (addresses) the appliance will accept on an interface and thus controls the number of multicast data streams forwarded out the interface. This number can range from 0 to 500; if you configure 0, then only those multicast groups defined with the `igmp join-group` and/or `igmp static-group` commands are forwarded.

Another option you have available to limit multicast traffic forwarded to a segment is to specifically control which multicast groups the appliance can process by filtering IGMP join and report messages from end stations with an ACL:

```
ciscoasa(config)# access-list ACL_ID standard {permit | deny}
                        IP_addr mask
ciscoasa(config)# access-list ACL_ID extended {permit | deny} udp
                        src_IP_addr src_mask dst_IP_addr dst_mask
ciscoasa(config)# interface physical_if_name
ciscoasa(config-if)# igmp access-group ACL_ID
```

You can either use a standard or extended ACL to list the multicast addresses that should be forwarded (ACLs are discussed in Chapter 6). With a standard ACL, specify the multicast IP address in the source field, along with a 32-bit subnet mask (255.255.255.255). With an extended ACL, the source IP address is the address of the requester (if you want to be specific about what user requests which stream), and the destination address is the actual multicast address of the multicast data stream. The use of standard ACLs is the most common implementation.

SMR Configuration Example

Examine the network shown in Figure 4-6. The following configuration illustrates how to set up the appliance as an SMR:

```
ciscoasa(config)# multicast-routing
ciscoasa(config)# interface ethernet0/1
ciscoasa(config-if)# igmp forward interface dmz
```

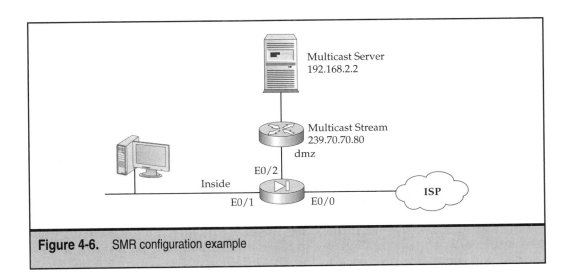

Figure 4-6.   SMR configuration example

In this example, the IGMP end stations are connected to the inside interface. Once multicast routing has been enabled on the appliance, the inside interface is set up to proxy the IGMP messages from the inside interface to the dmz interface.

PIM Multicast Routing

Dynamic routing of multicast traffic can occur in two modes:

▼ Dense mode (DM)

▲ Sparse mode (SM)

Use DM when you have lots of bandwidth, and most people need to see a multicast stream or streams. With DM, the network floods with the multicast streams; then, using IGMP, the multicast routers learn which devices don't wish to receive a stream and prune back the flooding.

Use SM when you're concerned about bandwidth usage and only want multicast traffic traversing your network when people have a need to see it. With SM, no flooding initially takes place. Instead, IGMP is used to learn which devices want to receive multicast streams, and then the streams are intelligently routed down to these segments. SM requires the use of a rendezvous point (RP), which is a multicast router responsible for disseminating and routing the multicast streams. You can have more than one RP to split up the forwarding of the multicast streams in order to reduce the multicast load on the RP: different RPs can be responsible for different multicast streams.

NOTE You can actually use both DM and SM modes in a network: some streams can be routed using dense mode and some using sparse mode.

PIM Routing Protocol

The Protocol Independent Multicast (PIM) routing protocol was originally designed by Cisco to handle dynamic and intelligent routing of multicast traffic. PIM is now defined in a handful of different Requests for Comments (RFCs). Other multicast routing protocols exist; however, the appliances only support static routing and PIM. Their support of PIM includes PIM-SM (sparse mode) and bi-directional PIM.

NOTE Cisco's IOS routers also support Distance Vector Multicast Routing Protocol (DVMRP) to connect to other multicast networks, but primarily rely on the use of PIM within a network of Cisco devices.

PIM-SM is a subset of PIM that deals with routing of multicast traffic using SM. It builds unidirectional trees with the root being an RP. Only one RP is responsible for a particular multicast stream. Through the use of IGMP, edge multicast routers learn which streams wish to be received by end stations and build a branch (link), using a shortest-path-first approach, back to the RP. Once this is done, the RP intelligently forwards the multicast stream to the segment the end stations are connected to.

Bi-directional PIM is similar to PIM-SM except that bi-directional trees are built. End stations use join messages to signify they wish to participate in a particular multicast group. Multicast streams are then forwarded from the multicast servers to the RP and then down the tree to the end stations. Bi-directional PIM was primarily designed for many-to-many applications in order to reduce the overhead of adding new sources and receivers. PIM-SM is primarily used when the multicast servers (the disseminators of multicast streams) are static.

NOTE PIM is a layer 3 TCP/IP routing protocol and will not work with any type of PAT translation (PAT is discussed in Chapter 5).

PIM Configuration

The following sections will discuss how to set up PIM on your appliance.

NOTE The security appliances support many multicast features, including mixing bi-directional and SM PIM, controlling the propagation of PIM messages by defining a multicast boundary, and others. However, because of space constraints, this section only discusses the more commonly configured PIM features.

PIM and Interfaces When you enable multicast routing with the `multicast-routing` command, both IGMP and PIM are automatically enabled on all interfaces. To disable or enable PIM on an interface, use the following configuration:

```
ciscoasa(config)# interface physical_if_name
ciscoasa(config-if)# [no] pim
```

Static RPs When using PIM SM, you need to define one or more RPs that will disseminate the multicast stream down to the segments. Unfortunately, the appliances currently do not support auto-RP, like Cisco routers, where the RPs in the network can be dynamically learned. On the appliance, use the `pim rp-address` command to statically define the RP:

```
ciscoasa(config)# pim rp-address ip_address [ACL_ID] [bidir]
```

The `ip_address` parameter defines a unicast IP address associated with the RP. Optionally, you can create a standard or extended ACL that defines the multicast streams that the RP is responsible for—this allows you to have more than one RP in your network, where different RPs are responsible for different multicast streams. If you don't specify an ACL, then the defined RP is responsible for all multicast streams (224.0.0.0/4). If you omit the `bidir` command, then the multicast streams operate using only SM; specifying the parameter enables bi-directional SM.

NOTE The appliances always advertise bi-directional capabilities in their PIM routing messages regardless of whether you configured the `bidir` parameter in the static RP definition.

Designated Routers (DR)   When using PIM, a designated router (DR) is elected for each network segment. The DR is responsible for sending PIM join, register, and prune messages to the RP. The election of the DR is based on a priority value: the one with the highest priority is elected as the DR. By default, the priority is 1; therefore, if you don't change the defaults on your PIM routers, the one with the highest IP address is elected. To change the DR priority of a segment the appliance is connected to, use the following configuration:

```
ciscoasa(config)# interface physical_if_name
ciscoasa(config-if)# pim dr-priority priority_#
```

The DR is responsible for sending router query messages on a segment to participating end stations; by default, these are sent every 30 seconds. You can change this period with the following command, where the range is from 1 to 3,600 seconds:

```
ciscoasa(config)# interface physical_if_name
ciscoasa(config-if)# pim hello-interval seconds
```

Likewise, the DR sends join and prune messages to end stations every 60 seconds; this can be changed with the following command, where the range is from 10 to 600 seconds:

```
ciscoasa(config)# interface physical_if_name
ciscoasa(config-if)# pim join-prune-interval seconds
```

PART II

Controlling Traffic Through the ASA

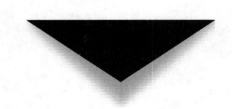

CHAPTER 5

Address Translation

In Chapter 3, I talked about some of the security appliance commands to create a basic configuration for your appliance; and in Chapter 4, I discussed how to set up routing to reach remote networks. Many factors, however, can restrict traffic flow through the appliance. For example, you will have to configure certain settings on the appliance to allow traffic to flow from lower-security-level interfaces to higher ones and vice versa. In addition, when NAT control is enabled, no traffic is allowed through the appliance unless translation policies are configured. This chapter focuses on address translation, while the next chapter covers access control lists (ACLs), which you can use to filter the traffic flow through your appliance.

This chapter will introduce you to address translation and the capabilities of the appliances. The topics include

▼ An overview of protocols and the effect appliances have on the protocols

■ An introduction to translations and connections

■ An overview of address translation

■ Configuration of dynamic and static address translation policies

■ How the appliances deal with TCP SYN flood attacks

▲ Verifying information in the translation and state tables

PROTOCOL OVERVIEW

Before I begin discussing the commands that allow traffic to flow through the appliances, you first need to have a good understanding of the mechanics of the three most-used protocols: TCP, UDP, and ICMP. This is important because the appliance treats these traffic streams differently in its stateful packet-filtering process implemented by the appliance security algorithm.

TCP Overview

TCP, the Transmission Control Protocol, is a *connection-oriented* protocol. This means that before any transfer of data can take place, certain connection parameters will have to be negotiated in order to establish the connection. To perform this negotiation, TCP will go through a three-way handshake:

1. In the first part of the three-way handshake, the source sends a TCP SYN segment, indicating the desire to open a connection (SYN is short for "synchronize"). Each TCP segment sent contains a sequence number.

2. When the destination receives the TCP SYN, it acknowledges this with its own SYN as well as an ACK (short for "acknowledgment"). This response is commonly called a *SYN/ACK*. The ACK portion indicates to the source that the destination received the source SYN.

3. The source then sends an ACK segment to the destination, indicating that the connection setup is complete.

Of course, during this three-way handshake, the devices are negotiating parameters like the window size, which restricts how many segments a device can send before waiting for an acknowledgment from the destination. Also during the transmission of actual data, the source and destination acknowledge the receipt of received segments from the other device.

The TCP setup process is often referred to as a *defined state machine* because a connection is opened first, data is sent, and the connection is torn down upon completion of the data transaction.

Outgoing Connection Requests

You may be asking what this has to do with a stateful firewall like the security appliances. First, understand that when connections are being set up, traffic flows in two directions through the appliance. Assume that you have a user on the inside of your network who initiates a TCP connection to a device on the outside of your network. Because TCP has a defined set of rules for setting up a connection, it is easy for the appliance to understand what is happening in the connection setup process. In other words, it is easy for the appliance to inspect this traffic. As I discussed in Chapter 1, a stateful firewall keeps track of the *state* of a connection.

In this example, the appliance sees the outgoing SYN and realizes that this is a setup request from an inside user. Because it is a stateful firewall, the appliance will add an entry in its connection (state) table so that the SYN/ACK from the destination will be permitted back in, and the inside user will be able to complete the connection with the final ACK. The appliance will then permit traffic to flow back and forth between these two machines for only this connection (unless the inside user opens another connection to this destination).

Likewise, TCP goes through a well-defined process when tearing down a connection. When the appliance sees the tear-down process (the FIN and FIN/ACK or an RST), the appliance knows that the connection is being terminated and will remove the connection from its state table. Therefore, once the entry is removed from the appliance state table, if the outside destination device tries to send traffic through the appliance using the old connection parameters, the appliance will drop the traffic.

Incoming Connection Requests

Because it is a stateful firewall, the appliance drops, by default, all new inbound TCP connections that try to enter your network. To allow this traffic, you will have to explicitly permit the TCP connection types that you want.

SECURITY ALERT!   By default the appliances deny all traffic flows that originate from a lower-security-level interface and that are trying to reach a higher-security-level interface.

One problem that TCP has, however, is that it is very predictable, which sometimes plays into the hands of attackers. For instance, an attacker might attempt to send a flood of TCP SYNs to an internal device, pretending to try to set up TCP connections. The real intention of the attacker, however, is not to complete the three-way handshake for each of these TCP SYNs, but to keep on sending SYNs to tie up resources on the internal machine. As I discuss later in this chapter and in Chapter 10, the appliances have capabilities that you can configure to deal with these kinds of attacks.

UDP Overview

UDP, the User Datagram Protocol, is a connectionless protocol and, unlike TCP, has no defined state machine. This means that there is no preliminary transport layer negotiation between the two devices that will be communicating. Instead, a device just starts sending UDP segments when it wishes to communicate with another device: there is no defined process, at layer 4, as to how this should occur. Likewise, there is no signal at the transport layer indicating the end of the actual UDP transmission. UDP itself also has no built-in flow control to regulate the flow of traffic between two machines. Because of these limitations, UDP is typically used only to send a small amount of information between devices.

A good example of this is the DNS protocol—used when a device needs to resolve a hostname to an IP address. The device sends a DNS query (UDP segment) to a DNS server, and the server responds with a single reply. In this example, using UDP is a more efficient process than TCP because only two segments need to be sent.

Outgoing Connection Requests

Let's look at another example to illustrate one of the problems that the appliances have with its stateful nature and UDP traffic. In this example, assume that the user is performing a TFTP to a device outside of your network. When the user initiates the TFTP connection, the appliance performs its stateful process and adds a temporary connection in its connection table to allow any UDP segments from the destination TFTP server to return through the appliance.

The problem is that once the user has completed the TFTP file transfer, the appliance has no idea that the connection has completed. Of course, you don't want the appliance to keep this temporary entry in the connection table after the transmission has completed. To solve this problem, the appliance uses a less-than-elegant solution: it keeps track of the idle time for the UDP connection. Once the appliance sees no traffic for the idle period, it will remove the connection. For UDP, the idle timer defaults to 2 minutes; however, you can customize this. Using an idle timer is not a very clean solution because a valid idle period might occur while the two UDP devices are performing other processes and will resume their communication shortly. In this example, the appliance might remove the temporary connection from its state table; when the device on the outside of your network resumes its transmission, the appliance will drop the traffic because it assumed the connection was over, and thus the connection is no longer found in the state table.

Note that some UDP applications, like DNS, are more predictable than TFTP. In a DNS example, where a user is initiating a DNS query, one and only one response should be coming back from the DNS server. In this situation, it makes sense to remove the connection from the connection table once the appliance sees the returning DNS reply.

The appliance does this by default. This feature is called *DNS Guard* and is discussed in Chapter 12.

> **SECURITY ALERT!** The appliances treat UDP as a stateful connection, like TCP. However, because there is no defined connection teardown process, the appliances will examine the idle period of a UDP connection to determine when it should be removed from the connection table. This process makes inbound UDP sessions more susceptible to IP spoofing and session replay attacks.

Incoming Connection Requests

As I mentioned earlier, because the appliance is a stateful firewall, it will not allow any traffic into your network if the source of the traffic is located on the outside of your network (inbound connections). You will have to explicitly permit this traffic to allow the UDP connection. Since UDP is connectionless, dealing with incoming connections opens you to more of a security risk. When a UDP connection is terminated, the appliance might not know this and thus would keep the connection in the connection table. A sophisticated attacker could exploit an IP spoofing attack, which uses a source address of the outside device of the original UDP connection. The appliance would be unable to identify the intrusion and would then reset its idle timer and allow the spoofed traffic through.

Also, because UDP doesn't use any type of connection setup when initiating a traffic stream, the appliances have problems differentiating between the start, continuation, and ending of a UDP connection. Therefore, an attacker could be performing a session replay attack, which replays some of the same UDP segments that the hacker saw in an earlier transmission. From the perspective of the appliance, this could appear to be the continuation of the original UDP data stream.

ICMP Overview

ICMP, the Internet Control Management Protocol, is a connectionless protocol and, like UDP, has no real defined state machine. ICMP is used for many purposes, including testing connectivity and sharing error, control, and configuration information. ICMP has some characteristics that are very similar to UDP: it's connectionless, and it has no flow control. Therefore, the appliances have the same problems dealing with ICMP connections as they do when dealing with UDP.

By default, the appliances do not add outbound ICMP messages to their state table. Therefore, you either must use an access control list (ACL) to allow the returning ICMP packets, or enable state tracking for ICMP. State tracking for ICMP is new in version 7, but is disabled by default. Once you enable stateful tracking for ICMP, when an ICMP message is sent, it contains a sequence number in the ICMP header that is included in the state table. The appliance then looks at returning ICMP traffic and the contained sequence number to determine if it is part of an existing connection. Prior to version 7, the only way to allow ICMP inbound through a PIX was to use ACLs.

Other Protocols

All other TCP/IP protocols and their associated connections are not tracked by the appliances; in other words, the appliances never add these connections to the state table. For example, if you have a GRE tunnel between two routers (GRE is a layer 3 TCP/IP protocol), and an appliance sits between them, the GRE tunnel will break by default. To allow GRE to function correctly through the appliance, you must have an ACL rule inbound on the lower-level interface to allow it.

NOTE   Remember that the appliances by default will only add TCP and UDP connections to the state table. Starting in version 7, you can optionally enable state tracking for ICMP, which is discussed in Chapter 11. For all other inbound connections, you must use ACLs, discussed in Chapter 6, to allow them to go from a lower- to higher-level interface on the appliance.

Protocol and Application Issues

The three main problems that stateful firewalls face include

- ▼ Applications that have multiple connections
- ■ Applications and protocols that embed addressing and connection information in the application layer payloads
- ▲ Applications and protocols that have security issues

This section provides an introduction to issues with protocols and applications, and how stateful firewalls, like Cisco's security appliances, can deal with them.

Applications with Multiple Connections

One problem firewalls have is dealing with applications that involve more than one connection, like FTP, multimedia, voice, database connectivity, and so on. Some form of protocol and application inspection is necessary to securely allow the additional connections through the firewall.

Let's look at an example, shown in Figure 5-1, to illustrate this issue and provide a solution to the problem. In this network, a client is opening a standard mode, sometimes called an *active mode*, FTP connection. With this type of connection, the client opens a TCP control connection to port 21 on the FTP server. Whenever the user sends an FTP command, like a `get` or a `put`, across this connection, the client includes the local port number the server should use. The server then opens a second connection, commonly called a *data connection*, with a source port number of 20 and a destination port number included in the client command request. So in this example, the client is opening the control connection to the server, and the server is opening the data connection to the client.

Assume that the firewall is a Cisco security appliance and that the user is connected to the higher-security-level interface, like the inside. The user's outbound control connection (port 21) is allowed by default, since the connection is going from a higher to

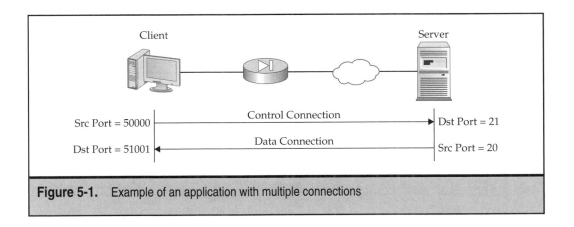

Figure 5-1. Example of an application with multiple connections

a lower security level. However, the second connection (port 20 data connection) is denied by default, since it is going from a lower to a higher security level.

The solution to this problem is to have the security appliance examine the application layer payload of the FTP control connection to determine the mode (active/standard), the command being executed, and the port number the client wants to use for the data connection. Then have the security appliance add this second connection to the state table to allow it, even before the second connection has been built. This process is discussed in much more depth in Part III of the book.

Without this approach, you would have to have an ACL that would allow the inbound data connection; and if you didn't know the IP address of the FTP servers, you would have to allow all source addresses for FTP. The problem with this approach is that the ACL is opening a permanent hole in the firewall—with the application inspection process of the appliances, the data connection is only opened when needed and torn down when done.

Applications and Embedded Addressing Information

Some applications embed addressing information in the payload of connections, expecting the destination to use this information for additional connections that might be opened; however, this addressing information might already be in the translation table of a firewall for another connection, creating an addressing conflict. Examine Figure 5-2, where I'll use FTP active mode to illustrate this problem. For the data connection that needs to be opened, the client wants to use a local port number of 51,001; however, there is already a connection with this port number in the translation table on the firewall. If the firewall doesn't fix the problem, then any traffic on the data connection would be incorrectly translated and sent to a different internal device.

A good firewall should change the payload addressing information to something different and should create a new translation in the translation table for this connection, a feature the Cisco appliances support for many protocols and applications. This is illustrated in Figure 5-2, where the appliance notices the conflict, translates the data connection port

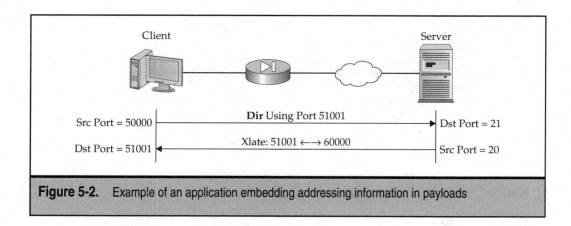

Figure 5-2. Example of an application embedding addressing information in payloads

of the client to 60,000, and adds this to the translation table. The appliance also updates the payload of the FTP control connection with port 60,000. So when the server receives the connection request on the control connection, it will use port 60,000 for the data connection to connect back to the client, which the appliance will translate correctly to 51,001. This process is discussed in more depth later in the "Disadvantages of Address Translation" section.

Applications and Security Issues

Certain behaviors by applications or their users can be malicious, creating security issues. I'll use Figure 5-3 to illustrate this problem, where an FTP active mode connection is being used. In this example, the server might not have been properly configured, and a user has the ability to upload files on the FTP server, possibly even overwriting existing files, when the user should only be able to download files.

A good firewall solution should look for security issues and malicious behavior in protocols and application payloads, and prevent them from occurring. In this example,

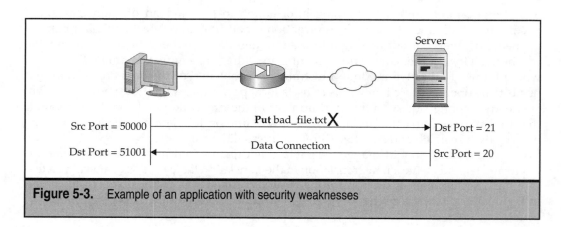

Figure 5-3. Example of an application with security weaknesses

the firewall is examining the commands that are being executed on the FTP control connection and comparing them against a list of allowed commands in the FTP policy. If the command isn't listed in the policy, it is not allowed by the firewall. As you will see in Part III of this book, Cisco's security appliances have this capability for many applications and protocols.

TRANSLATIONS AND CONNECTIONS

Before I continue, I want to differentiate between two terms commonly used when dealing with traffic that flows through Cisco security appliances: *translations* and *connections.*

A *translation* is an IP-address-to-IP-address (and possibly port) mapping. The appliances use translations to perform Network Address Translation (NAT) and Port Address Translation (PAT). You use NAT and PAT when you have deployed private addresses in your internal network, and you need to translate these addresses to a public address space before they leave your network. (I'll be discussing these terms in more depth, along with other address translation terms, later in the "Address Translation Overview" section.) Translations are stored in a translation table on the appliances, commonly called an *xlate* table.

A *connection,* on the other hand, is basically a TCP, UDP, or ICMP session between two devices. A connection specifies all of the parameters used to send traffic to a device, like the source and destination IP addresses, the TCP/IP protocol, the application port numbers (TCP and UDP), sequence numbers (TCP and ICMP), acknowledgment numbers (TCP), the state of the connection (TCP control flags), and other information. Connections are stored in a state table on the appliances, commonly called a connection or *conn* table.

The following two sections will further define these two terms and how they apply to the appliances. The third section gives an example of how a TCP connection is handled through an appliance when address translation is enabled.

Connections

As I mentioned earlier, the appliances refer to a connection as a TCP, UDP, and possibly, ICMP session. The number of sessions supported by an appliance depends on the model as well as the license that you currently have installed on the appliance.

Connection Limits

Table 5-1 states the license limits, which were discussed in Chapter 1.

As I mentioned in Chapter 1, the ASA 5505 also uses a user license scheme, along with a connection license scheme. With user licensing, the 5505 only allows the first set of users, up to the license limit, through the 5505; any additional users are not permitted, even if any of the first set of users is not sending any traffic. There are three user licenses for the 5505: 10, 50, and unlimited users.

ASA Model	License Limits
5505	10,000–25,000
5510	50,000–130,000
5520	280,000
5540	400,000
5550	650,000
5580-20	1,000,000
5580-40	2,000,000

Table 5-1.   The License Limits of the Various ASA Models

For keeping track of connections, when an end-user device starts a connection, the appliance counts the connection against the license limit, and the appliance subtracts this connection from the total available connections. Once the connection has been terminated, the appliance adds 1 to its count of available connections.

Removing Connections

As I already mentioned in the last section, the appliance can only keep track of TCP, UDP, and possibly ICMP connections in the state table. To determine when a connection is over and to remove it from the state table depends on the protocol that the connection uses: TCP, UDP, or ICMP.

For TCP, the following criteria are used:

▼   A FIN and FIN/ACK are in the TCP header control field.

■   An RST is in the TCP header control field.

■   The TCP connection is idle for more than 3,600 seconds (1 hour) by default.

▲   The connection is removed from the appliances tables with the `clear xlate` command (discussed in the "Clearing Entries in the Xlate and Conn Tables" section at the end of the chapter).

For UDP, the following criteria are used to remove entries from the state table:

▼   The UDP connection is idle for more than 120 seconds (two minutes) by default.

■   For a DNS query, the associated DNS reply is seen.

▲   The connection is removed from the appliances tables with the `clear xlate` command.

For ICMP, the following criteria are used to remove entries from the state table:

▼   The ICMP connection is idle for more than 2 seconds by default.

▲   The connection is removed from the appliances tables with the `clear xlate` command.

Translations

Up through version 6 of the operating system, the PIXs required you to define address translation policies to move traffic through the appliance: inbound *and* outbound. The primary reason for this behavior is based on the very beginnings of the PIX operating system: it was designed as an address translation device. And this was very apparent through version 6 of the OS.

Starting in version 7, address translation is optional and disabled by default. However, once you require address translation, you must define a translation policy for all traffic that will flow through the appliance—inbound or outbound—otherwise the appliance will drop the traffic. The one exception to this rule is if two interfaces have the same security level, and address translation is enabled; in this instance, you can optionally define translation policies for the two interfaces, or just have traffic moved between the interfaces without address translation.

When you enable address translation, the translations that represent a device or a connection are stored in a separate table, called a *translation* or, more commonly, an *xlate* table. Entries are removed from this table when any of the following occur:

▼   Network Address Translation (NAT) entries are removed from the table once they are idle for a time (by default 3 hours). You can control this with the `timeout xlate` command.

■   Port Address Translation (PAT) entries are removed from the translation table when the corresponding connection in the state table expires.

▲   NAT and PAT entries are both removed from the table when they match criteria in the `clear xlate` command.

TCP Connection Example

To illustrate how the appliance deals with translations and connections, examine Figures 5-3 and 5-5. I'll use telnet, which uses the TCP protocol, as an example, and I'll assume that address translation is required on the appliance. Also, I'll assume the source (10.0.1.11) is connected to the inside interface and that the destination (172.26.26.50) is beyond the outside interface. In this example, I'll only focus on the things that occur during the TCP three-way handshake.

Parts 1 and 2

Examine Figure 5-4: The first thing that happens is that the source opens a telnet connection to the destination, setting the SYN flag in the TCP header. The other connection

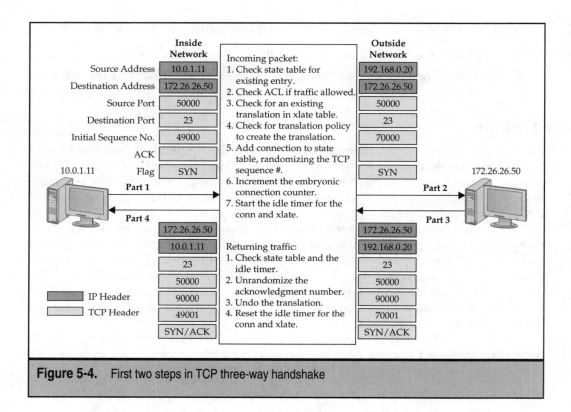

Figure 5-4. First two steps in TCP three-way handshake

parameters in the IP and TCP header are shown in part 1 under the Inside Network column.

The appliance compares packet information against the existing connections to the state table to determine if the packet is new or part of an existing connection. Since it is a new connection, it won't be found. The appliance then looks for an ACL applied inbound in the interface. If one exists, the packet must match a `permit` statement in the list of statements to be allowed.

If the packet is allowed, the appliance then compares the packet header information with the existing translation entries in the translation table to see if an existing translation can be used, or if a new one needs to be created. For the former, this is commonly referred to as looking for a "matching translation slot entry." As you will see in the "Address Translation Overview" section, for NAT translations, multiple connections from the same source can have the same NAT translation. So in this example, if the source has existing connections open, the table might have a NAT translation the appliance can use. I'll assume, however, that this is the first time the source has sent a packet through the appliance, so no existing translation entries in the xlate table will match.

Next the appliance compares the information in the packet header with the configured translation policies—static and dynamic—for a match. If a match is not found, then the packet is dropped. If a match is found, a translation entry is built and added to the xlate table, the TCP sequence number is randomized, and the TCP connection is added to the conn table.

The appliance then increments the embryonic connection counter. An *embryonic* connection is a half-open connection: it hasn't gone through the three-way handshake. The appliance keeps track of this kind of information to limit the effectiveness of TCP SYN flood attacks. If the limit is exceeded, the appliance will implement its TCP Intercept feature, discussed later in the chapter. The two idle timers are then started for the connection in the conn and xlate tables respectively.

If you examine the Outside Network column above part 2, this shows the packet header as it leaves the appliance. Notice that the source address was changed because of a match on the configured translation policy, and the TCP sequence number was randomized. Also notice that the source port number was not changed.

Parts 3 and 4

Once the destination receives the packet, it responds back with a TCP SYN/ACK response in part 3 of Figure 5-4. Upon receiving the packet, the appliance compares the header information with the conn table to find a match; in this case, since the source initiated the connection in part 1, the connection is in the table. The appliance then validates the idle timer to ensure that the entry in the state table hasn't expired: If the entry has expired, it is removed from the conn table and the packet is dropped. If there wasn't a match in the conn table or the entry had timed out, then the ACL on the interface would be used to validate whether the packet was allowed inbound to the inside interface.

Originally the source used a sequence number of 49,000, which was randomized by the appliance to 70,000. The destination acknowledges back one greater than the randomized sequence number: 70,001. However, the source is expecting 49,001: therefore, the appliance then undoes the randomization of the acknowledgment number. This is the sequence number randomization (SNR) feature at work, which is used to defeat session hijacking attacks.

The appliance then undoes the translation, changing the destination IP address from 192.168.0.20 to 10.0.1.11. After this, the appliance resets the idle timers for the entries in the xlate and conn tables. Lastly, the appliance forwards the packet out the inside interface, shown in part 4.

Parts 5 and 6

In part 5, the source completes the three-way handshake by sending a TCP ACK, shown in Figure 5-5. The appliance first compares packet information to the existing connections to the state table to determine if the packet is a new or part of an existing connection. Since it is an existing connection, it should be in the state table. The appliance then compares the packet header information with the existing translation entries in the translation table to see if an existing translation can be used or if a new one needs to be created. Again, this packet information should be there, and the appliance uses the existing translation to translate the source address from 10.0.1.11 to 192.168.0.20. The appliance then randomizes

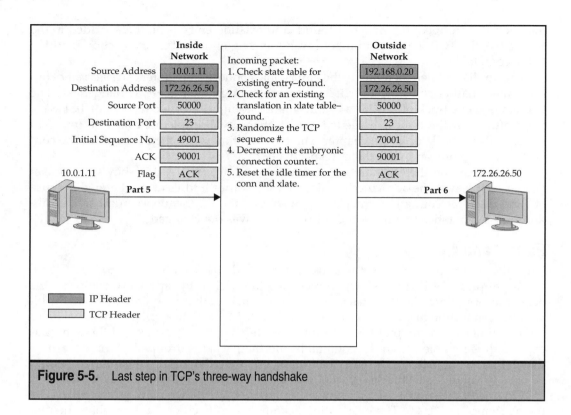

Figure 5-5. Last step in TCP's three-way handshake

the TCP sequence number and updates the conn table with this information. Since the connection has completed the three-way handshake, the appliance decrements the embryonic connection counter.

If you examine the Outside Network column above part 2, this shows the packet header as it leaves the appliance. Notice that the source address was changed because of a match on the configured translation policy, and the TCP sequence number was randomized. The corresponding idle timers in the conn and state tables are reset, and the packet is forwarded to the destination, shown in part 6.

Again, the appliance keeps track of the packets for the connection and updates the conn table appropriately. If no packets are seen for the duration of the idle timer or the connection is torn down by the source or destination, the entry is removed from the conn table.

NOTE You will see in later chapters that a lot more is going on than what was described in this section to handle a connection through the appliance. Other chapters add to this, but Chapter 10 covers it more thoroughly.

ADDRESS TRANSLATION OVERVIEW

One of the many issues that you will have to deal with in your network is the assignment of addresses to all of your networking devices. Because of the shortage of public IPv4 addresses, in many cases you will have to use private addresses for your internal devices. As you will see in the following sections, however, private addresses, even though they allow all of your devices to communicate via TCP/IP, also create problems. I will first provide an overview of private addresses and outline the pros and cons of using private addresses; then I will discuss how the appliances deal with the translation of IP addresses.

Private Addresses

To address the shortage of addresses, and to accommodate the growing need for connecting companies to the Internet, the Internet Engineering Task Force (IETF) developed RFC 1918. Table 5-2 lists the private addresses assigned in RFC 1918 for IPv4.

As you can see from the addresses listed in Table 5-2, you should have more than enough addresses to meet the internal address needs of any company. Each of the devices in your network can be given a unique address. RFC 1918, however, defines one restriction: a packet containing a private address in either the source or destination IP address fields cannot be forwarded to a public network.

Imagine two companies, Company A and Company B, that both use 10.0.0.0/8 for their internal addressing and for communicating with each other, as shown in Figure 5-6. Obviously, this will create many problems because both companies may have overlapping network issues—each company might be using the same subnet numbers. In this situation, the overlapping subnets would not be able to communicate with each other. For example, both companies might have a 10.1.1.0/24 subnet, as shown in Figure 5-6. Within their own companies no connectivity issues arise, but as soon as these two subnets need to reach each other, they will be unable to. The boundary router between these two networks will have a dilemma when trying to reach 10.1.1.0/24—does it forward traffic to Company A or to Company B?

Address Class	Addresses
A	10.0.0.0–10.255.255.255
B	172.16.0.0–172.31.255.255
C	192.168.0.0–192.168.255.255

Table 5-2. The Private Addresses Specified by RFC 1918

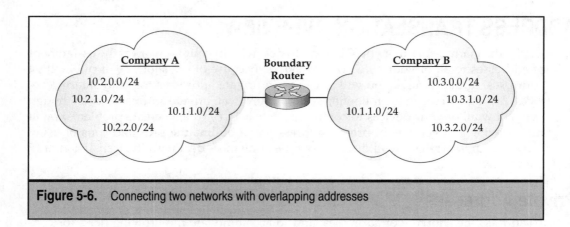

Figure 5-6.   Connecting two networks with overlapping addresses

Needs for Address Translation

To solve the problem of overlapping addresses, as well as to address the problem of using private addresses and accessing a public network, the IETF developed RFC 1631, which defines the process of address translation. This allows you to translate a private address in an IP packet header to another address—either public or private. Here are some common examples where you might need to deploy address translation:

▼   You are merging two networks that have an overlapping address space. You need to make it appear that the overlapping network numbers are unique to the two different sides.

■   Your ISP has assigned you a very small number of public addresses, and you need to provide many of your devices access to the Internet.

■   You were assigned a public address space by your ISP, and when you change ISPs, your new ISP will not support your currently assigned address space.

▲   You have critical services on a single device, and you need to duplicate these resources across many devices. However, you need to make it appear that all of the devices that contain these resources appear as a single entity.

As you will see in the next few sections, using address translation to solve these problems has both advantages and disadvantages.

Advantages of Address Translation

One of the main advantages of address translation is that you have an almost inexhaustible number of private addresses at your disposal: over 17 million. This includes 1 class A network number, 16 class B network numbers, and 256 class C network numbers. When you use private addresses and if you change ISPs, you will not have to re-address your network—you only have to change your translation rules on your translation device to match up with the new public addresses.

Because all traffic must pass through your translation device to reach your devices with private addresses, you have strict control over the following:

▼ What resources the Internet accesses on the inside of your network

▲ Which users on the inside of your network are allowed access to the Internet

Disadvantages of Address Translation

As you have seen, address translation solves many addressing problems, but not all of them. In fact, it actually introduces some new problems. First, when address translation is performed by your address translation device (like the Cisco security appliances), it will have to change the IP addresses in the IP packet header and possibly even the port numbers in TCP or UDP segment headers. Because of this, the address translation device will have to perform additional processing not only to handle the translation process, but also to compute new checksums for the packets, putting an additional burden on the translation device.

Another problem that address translation introduces deals with troubleshooting network problems. Because address translation changes the source and/or destination IP addresses in the packet headers, it becomes more difficult to troubleshoot network problems. When you examine the addresses in the packet header, you don't know whether you are dealing with the addresses that these machines have assigned on them, or with the addresses that they have been translated to by an address translation device. This also makes it easier for attackers to hide their identity.

Not all applications work with address translation. Most translation devices only perform address translation for addresses in the IP packet header. Some applications embed IP addresses in the data payload, which an address translation device cannot catch. If a receiving device uses the IP address in the data payload, it won't be able to reach the transmitter of the packet. Figure 5-7 shows an example of this process. In this example, a device on the right (172.16.1.1) sends a packet to a machine on the left (200.200.200.1). Inside the payload, the 172.16.1.1 device embeds its own IP address. When this IP packet reaches the address translation device, the device translates the addressing information in the packet header based on the rules defined in the device translation table. However, the translation device is not smart enough to figure out that an IP address is also embedded in the payload—172.16.1.1's own IP address. When the half-translated packet reaches the destination (192.168.1.1), if the destination tries to use 172.16.1.1 to return a reply instead of 201.201.201.1, the translation device will be confused and be unable to forward the packet correctly.

NOTE As you will see in Part III of the book, the appliances have the ability to examine the application layer payloads of many types of connections for embedded addressing information and to fix these issues.

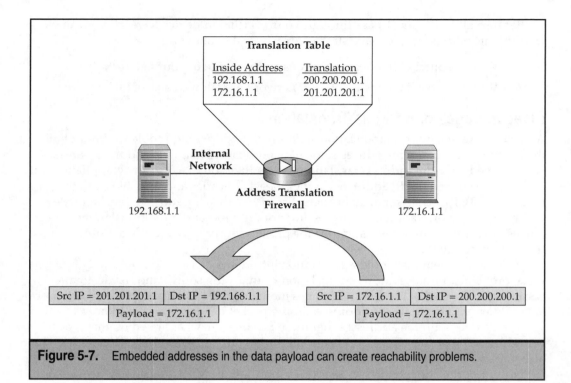

Figure 5-7.   Embedded addresses in the data payload can create reachability problems.

Address Translation Terms and Definitions

A device that performs address translation can take on many forms. This device can be a firewall, a router, a proxy gateway, or even a file server. Cisco's routers as of IOS 11.2 and the appliances both support address translation. For a better understanding of the commands used on the appliance to configure address translation, you must first understand some of the terms that are commonly used in address translation, shown in Table 5-3. Note that many of the terms can be combined, like "static inside global address": this would be a manually translated address that represents an internal device.

Examples of Address Translation

As you can see from Table 5-3, different types of address translation can be performed by an address translation device. In this section, you'll look at two examples: one that uses NAT and one that uses PAT.

NAT Translation Type	Definition of Translation Type
Local or real address	An IP address assigned to an internal device either statically or dynamically via DHCP, which can be either a private or public address.
Global address	An IP that represents the source that the destination devices see: this could be the local address or a translated address, and either a private or public address.
Inside address	An IP address of a device located inside a company's network.
Outside address	An IP address of a device located outside a company's network.
Static translation	The address translation is manually configured by an administrator.
Dynamic translation	The address translation is performed dynamically by an address translation device.
Network Address Translation (NAT)	A single IP address is mapped to another IP address; this can be done statically or dynamically.
Port Address Translation (PAT)	Each device that has its address translated is translated to the same IP address. To keep each of these connections unique, the source port number of the connection is also changed; this can be done statically or dynamically.

Table 5-3.   Different Types of Address Translation

NAT Example

NAT, as I mentioned earlier, performs a one-to-one address translation. Typically you use static translation when you have a server that you want external users to reach from the Internet. For your internal users, however, you will typically create a pool of IP addresses and let the translation device randomly assign an unused global address to the device (dynamic NAT). In this example, a user on the inside of your network is going to access resources on the outside of your network (the user on 192.168.1.5 is trying to access 201.201.201.2.). Figure 5-8 illustrates this example.

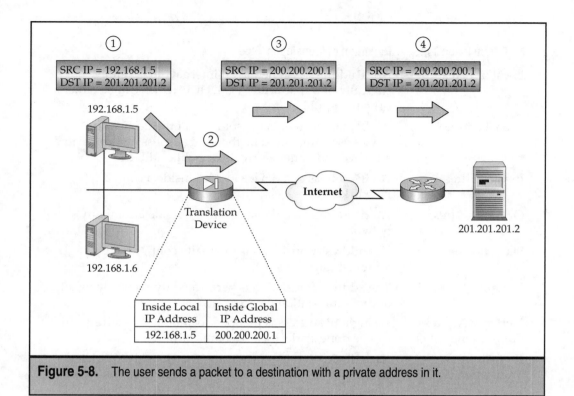

Figure 5-8. The user sends a packet to a destination with a private address in it.

In Figure 5-8, you can see the actual transmission from 192.168.1.5 (step 1). The translation device receives the packet from 192.168.1.5, determines if it needs to perform translation (and does it if necessary), and forwards the packet to the destination.

As you can see in step 2, the address translation device sees the incoming packet and compares it against its address translation rules. Because the packet matches a rule in its address translation policies, the address translation device translates the source IP address in the packet from 192.168.1.5 to 200.200.200.1, which is a global IP address. This process can be seen in step 3 of Figure 5-8. Note that if you have configured a static translation for the internal user, the address translation device will know exactly how to translate the source address. However, if you are using dynamic translation, the address translation device will pick an unused address from its address translation pool, assign the address to the user, and then add this entry to the address translation table.

In step 4 of Figure 5-8, you can see that the destination (201.201.201.2) has received the packet. From the perspective of the destination, the source appears to have an address of 200.200.200.1. This is transparent both to the local user and to the destination.

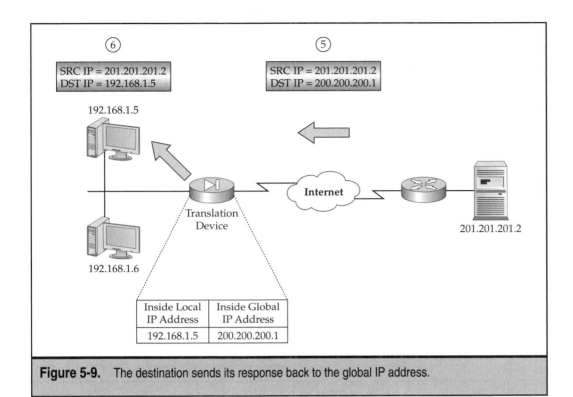

Figure 5-9.   The destination sends its response back to the global IP address.

When the destination sends the response back to the user, it uses the global IP address that it saw in the translated packet: 200.200.200.1, which can be seen in step 5 of Figure 5-9.

In step 6, the address translation device receives the packet and examines its address translation policy. After determining that it needs to translate the packet, it examines its address translation table to see how to perform the translation. It sees the entry for 200.200.200.1, changes this global destination IP address to a local address of 192.168.1.5, and forwards the packet to the inside user.

NOTE   The address translation process is transparent to the source and destination devices.

PAT Example

With PAT, an address translation device will possibly change both the packet IP address and the TCP or UDP segment port number. This example examines a situation in which

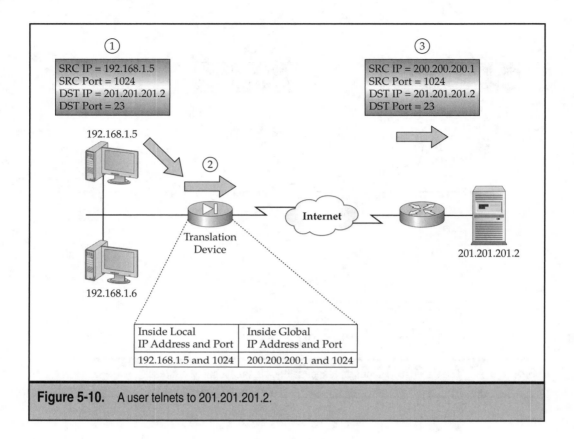

Figure 5-10. A user telnets to 201.201.201.2.

your ISP assigned you a single IP address, and you need to use this one address for all of your users' connections to the Internet. In this example, the user at the 192.168.1.5 device telnets to 201.201.201.2, as shown in step 1 of Figure 5-10.

In step 2 of Figure 5-10, the address translation device receives the packet. It compares the packet information with its internal address translation policies and determines whether it needs to perform address translation on the packet. This example has a policy match, so the translation device performs its address translation and changes the local address of 192.168.1.5 to 200.200.200.1. In this instance, the source port number of 1024 is unused in the address table, so the address translation device leaves it as is. Note that the address translation device adds an entry to its address translation table so that it can handle the returning traffic for this device. In step 3 of Figure 5-10, the destination receives the translated packet. Again, the translation process is transparent to both the source and destination devices.

When the destination device sends its reply, it uses a destination IP address of 200.200.200.1 and a destination port of 1024. When the translation device receives the

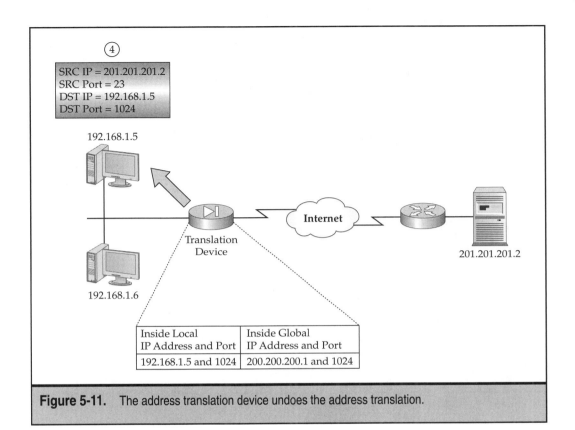

Figure 5-11.   The address translation device undoes the address translation.

inbound packet, it determines that address translation should be performed, and then looks for a match in its address translation table. It sees a match, changes the destination IP address to 192.168.1.5, and leaves the destination port number the same. This process is shown in Figure 5-11.

To illustrate the implementation of PAT, assume that 192.168.1.6 also telnets to 201.201.201.2 with a source port of 1024, as shown in step 5 of Figure 5-12. The address translation device receives the packet, determines that there is an address translation policy match, and then creates an entry in its address translation table for the user's connection. In this instance, the same global IP address is used for the translation of the source IP address. However, because the source port 1024 is already in the address translation table, the address translation device assigns a source port of 1025 for the user's connection, as shown in step 6 of Figure 5-12. The translation of the source port number allows the destination device to differentiate between the connections from 192.168.1.5 and 192.168.1.6, and also allows the address translation device to undo its translation for returning traffic from 201.201.201.2.

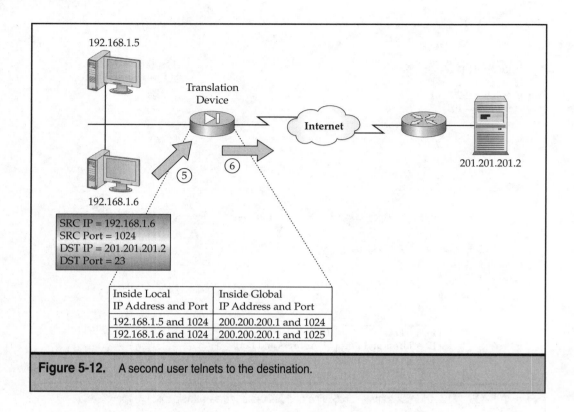

Figure 5-12.   A second user telnets to the destination.

ADDRESS TRANSLATION CONFIGURATION

The remainder of this chapter will focus on configuring address translation policies to translate traffic going through your appliance. I'll discuss how to configure dynamic NAT and PAT, static NAT and PAT, limiting the number of embryonic TCP connections to prevent TCP SYN flood attacks, and verifying your translation configuration.

Requiring Address Translation

In version 6 of the OS and earlier, you always had to configure a translation rule for a packet; otherwise, if the packet couldn't be matched against existing translation rules, it was dropped. This rule applied whether the traffic was inbound or outbound.

Starting in version 7, translation is optional and not required. To *require* address translation, use the following command:

```
asa(config)# nat-control
```

Once you require address translation with the **nat-control** command, the same rules apply as they did in version 6: if there is no matching translation policy for inbound or outbound traffic, and address translation is enabled, the packet is dropped. There is one exception to this policy: if the two interfaces involved in the communication have the same security level, then you don't need an address translation rule to move packets between them.

NOTE If you don't configure the **nat-control** command, then address translation is optional. The appliance will use any address translation policies you've configured, and if a packet doesn't match a translation policy, it isn't translated, but forwarded as is.

Configuring Dynamic Address Translation

Configuring dynamic address translation (NAT or PAT) involves a two-step process:

▼ Identifying the local addresses that will be translated

▲ Creating global address pools that local addresses can be translated to

The order in which you configure these two items doesn't matter. The following sections will discuss how to set up dynamic NAT and PAT translation rules, as well as cover many different examples of dynamic translation examples.

Identifying Local Addresses for Translation

To identify the local addresses that can be translated, use the **nat** command:

```
ciscoasa(config)# nat (logical_if_name) NAT_ID
                      local_IP_addr subnet_mask
                      [tcp] max_TCP_conns [embryonic_conn_limit]
                      [udp max_UDP_conns] [dns] [norandomseq]
```

The **nat** command specifies which local addresses will be translated to the pool specified in the **global** command. The logical name of the interface where the local devices are located appears in parentheses ("( )"), like **(inside)**, for example.

The *NAT_ID* ties the **nat** and **global** commands together, creating a policy. With one exception, the number you use for the *NAT_ID* (the policy number) doesn't matter. There is a special instance of using a *NAT_ID* number: if you enter **0**, you are telling the appliance that the addresses that follow this in the **nat** command should *not* be translated. Cisco refers to this feature as *Identity NAT*, which was introduced in version 6.2. You might want to use Identity NAT if you have a mixture of public and private addresses being used on the inside of your network—for the machines with public addresses, you can disable NAT by using the **nat 0** command and specifying the address or addresses of those devices.

If you specify a network number for the *local_IP_addr*, also specify the appropriate subnet mask. By entering a network number and a subnet mask, you are specifying a range of addresses to be translated. To translate all addresses on the inside interface, use the following syntax:

```
ciscoasa(config)# nat (inside) 1 0.0.0.0  0.0.0.0
```

Then tie the pool/NAT ID "1" to the corresponding **global** command. Note that you can abbreviate **0.0.0.0 0.0.0.0** to just **0 0**.

You can also limit the total number of TCP connections (*max_TCP_conns*) as well as the number of half-open/embryonic TCP connections (*embryonic_conn_limit*). Starting in version 7.0, you can also limit the maximum number of UDP connections. If you don't configure connection limits for devices that match a translation policy, then whatever the conn table supports is what the appliance will allow. I'll discuss the use of these parameters in more depth later in the "TCP SYN Flood Attacks" section.

It is highly recommended that you do not turn off the TCP Sequence Number Randomization feature of the appliance. You should only do this if this feature is causing a problem with a particular application, or if digital signatures are used on the packet and changing the sequence number would corrupt the digital signature, like a BGP session between two routers using MD5. The **dns** parameter enables the DNS doctoring feature, discussed in Chapter 12.

To display your **nat** commands, use the **show run nat** command.

Creating Global Address Pools

Translation policies are always configured between pairs of interfaces, like inside and outside, or dmz and outside. The **nat** command defines the local or source interface of addresses you want to translate. To define the destination or exit interface that contains the global address pool (the address or addresses you can use for a translation policy), use the **global** command:

```
ciscoasa(config)# global (logical_if_name) NAT_ID
                  {first_global_IP_addr[-last_global_IP_addr]
                  [netmask subnet_mask] | interface}
```

The *logical_if_name* parameter specifies the name of the logical interface that traffic will exit and have translation performed on it. The *NAT_ID* parameter basically specifies for which **nat** commands the global pool of addresses can be used. For example, all **nat** commands that have a *NAT_ID* of **1** can use **global** commands with a *NAT_ID* of **1** when matching packets travel between these interfaces.

NOTE Once the pool of addresses is used up, no further translations can take place for additional internal devices matching the same policy—their traffic is dropped.

If you specify a range of addresses in the pool, along with an appropriate subnet mask, then the appliance performs dynamic NAT; once the addresses are used up in the pool or pools, additional translations are denied. To overcome this issue, PAT is commonly used. To implement PAT, enter a single IP address in the pool with a subnet mask of 255.255.255.255. Optionally, you can use the **interface** parameter instead of entering a single IP address; this causes the appliance to perform PAT using the appliance IP address on the associated interface.

NOTE Cisco recommends that if you want to perform PAT using an IP address on the appliance interface, always use the **interface** parameter instead of hard-coding the IP address in the **global** command. This is obvious, of course, if the appliance interface is acquiring the interface address via DHCP or PPPoE.

PAT translations are removed from the translation table when the corresponding connection in the conn table expires. Idle NAT translations are eventually aged out of the translation table by using an idle timer. The **timeout xlate** command controls the idle timeout, which by default is 3 hours.

To view your **global** commands, use the **show run global** command.

NOTE The one exception where you don't need a corresponding **global** command for a **nat** command is if you are performing Identity NAT (**nat 0**).

Using ACLs with Address Translation Policies

One problem with the **nat** command is that, by default, translation can only be controlled based on the local addresses sending packets; you cannot control address translation based on the source *and* destination addresses given the syntax I discussed in the "Identifying Local Addresses for Translation" section.

To overcome this problem, Cisco allows you to associate an access control list (ACL) with your translation policy. If traffic matches a **permit** statement in the ACL, the corresponding translation policy is used. This feature can be used with Identity NAT (exempting traffic from translation) or Policy NAT (controlling when translation takes place based on both the source and destination information).

Here is the syntax of the **nat** command to control translation policies with an ACL:

```
ciscoasa(config)# nat [(logical_if_name)] NAT_ID
                   access-list ACL_ID
                   [tcp] max_TCP_conns [embryonic_conn_limit]
                   [udp max_UDP_conns] [dns] [norandomseq]
```

Even though I haven't covered ACLs yet (coming in Chapter 6), if you've worked with Cisco IOS ACLs before, then understanding what's happening with translations using ACLs isn't that difficult. In the preceding syntax, traffic must match a **permit** statement in the ACL in order for the translation policy to be used. I have two examples that use ACLs in the next section.

SECURITY ALERT! ACLs on an appliance use a *subnet* mask—not a wildcard mask like Cisco IOS routers use!

Address Translation Examples

Now that you have an understanding of the syntax of the **nat** and **global** commands, let's look at a few examples so that you better understand how to configure dynamic address translation policies on the appliances.

Simple NAT Example I'll first take a look at a simple NAT example, using the network shown in Figure 5-13. In this network, the appliance will perform NAT for any internal address (192.168.3.0/24 and 192.168.4.0/24). Here's the NAT policy configuration for this example:

```
ciscoasa(config)# nat-control
ciscoasa(config)# nat (inside) 1 0.0.0.0 0.0.0.0
ciscoasa(config)# global (outside) 1 200.200.200.10-200.200.200.254
                       netmask 255.255.255.0
```

In this example, address translation is required (**nat-control** command). All of the devices off of the inside interface will have their source addresses translated to an address in the 200.200.200.0 subnet when exiting the outside interface. The addresses are dynamically assigned by the appliance by choosing unused ones in the pool.

NOTE One important point to make about the network in Figure 5-13 and the configuration shown earlier is that the connection between the appliance and the perimeter router is using the 192.168.1.0/24 subnet, and the appliance is translating packets to the 200.200.200.0 subnet. By default the perimeter router doesn't know about this network. The easiest solution to this problem is to create a static route on the perimeter router pointing to 192.168.1.1 to reach the 200.200.200.0 subnet.

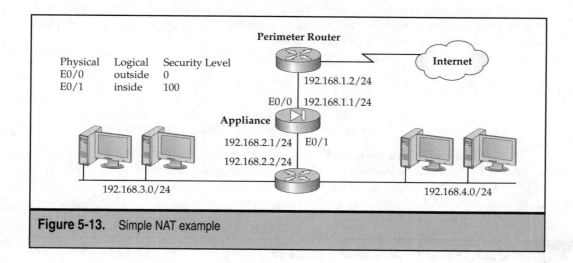

Figure 5-13. Simple NAT example

Interface PAT Example   I'll use the network in Figure 5-14 to illustrate the configuration of a PAT policy using the appliance outside interface. Here's the configuration:

```
ciscoasa(config)# nat-control
ciscoasa(config)# nat (inside) 1 0 0
ciscoasa(config)# global (outside) 1 interface
```

This is a special example of PAT, where the appliance is using the outside interface IP address for the PAT address pool. This could be a static IP address on the interface or one dynamically assigned to the appliance using DHCP or PPPoE. In this example, the appliance is directly connected to the ISP and gets the outside interface address dynamically.

NAT and PAT Example   To illustrate the use of both NAT and PAT policies on an appliance, I'll use the network shown previously in Figure 5-13. Here is the configuration:

```
ciscoasa(config)# nat-control
ciscoasa(config)# nat (inside) 1 192.168.3.0 255.255.255.0
ciscoasa(config)# global (outside) 1 200.200.200.1-200.200.200.125
                     netmask 255.255.255.128
ciscoasa(config)# nat (inside) 2 192.168.4.0 255.255.255.0
ciscoasa(config)# global (outside) 2 200.200.200.126
                     netmask 255.255.255.255
```

In this example, a combination of NAT and PAT is used for the internal devices: the two internal subnets are each assigned their own pool of public addresses:

▼   For policy 1, 192.168.3.0/24 is translated to 200.200.200.1–125 (this uses NAT)

▲   For policy 2, 192.168.4.0/24 is translated to 200.200.200.126 (this uses PAT)

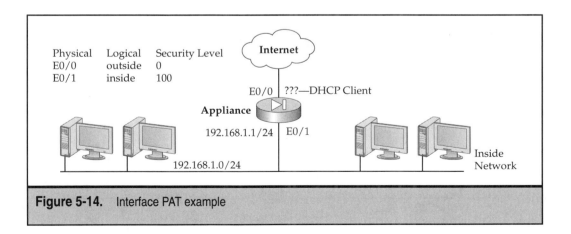

Figure 5-14.   Interface PAT example

PAT Example with Two Global Pools To illustrate the use of two global address pools on an appliance for one group of devices, I'll use the network shown previously in Figure 5-13. Here is the configuration:

```
ciscoasa(config)# nat-control
ciscoasa(config)# nat (inside) 1 0.0.0.0 0.0.0.0
ciscoasa(config)# global (outside) 1 200.200.200.1
                      netmask 255.255.255.255
ciscoasa(config)# global (outside) 1 200.200.200.2
                      netmask 255.255.255.255
```

This configuration performs PAT on all inside-to-outside connections by using the two addresses in the two **global** commands.

NOTE The second **global** command doesn't overwrite the first one: it creates a second address to use with PAT, supporting more connections in the translation table. Each PAT address can handle about 64,000 connections; so if you have an appliance that supports 130,000 connections, you would realistically need three **global** commands with a single IP address in each.

PAT and Identity NAT Example To illustrate the use of PAT and Identity NAT on an appliance, I'll use the network shown in Figure 5-15. In this example, I want to perform PAT for 192.168.3.0/24, but to perform no address translation on machines with an address from 200.200.200.128/25—the latter devices already have a public IP address. Here is the configuration:

```
ciscoasa(config)# nat-control
ciscoasa(config)# nat (inside) 0 200.200.200.128 255.255.255.128
ciscoasa(config)# nat (inside) 1 192.168.3.0 255.255.255.0 50 25
ciscoasa(config)# global (outside) 1 200.200.200.1
                      netmask 255.255.255.255
```

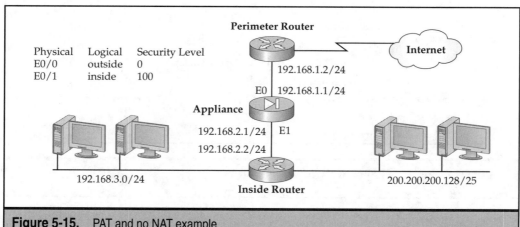

Figure 5-15. PAT and no NAT example

In this example, the 192.168.3.0/24 subnet is translated to 200.200.200.1 using PAT when going from the inside interface to the outside, along with connection restrictions (50 complete and 25 embryonic connections). The 200.200.200.128/25 is excluded from translation between any interfaces.

Three-Interface NAT Example   With two interfaces, configuring translation policies is straightforward; adding interfaces complicates matters. Let's look at an example to illustrate the complexity that three interfaces add to the situation. I'll use the network shown in Figure 5-16. Here's the configuration for the appliance:

```
ciscoasa(config)# nat-control
ciscoasa(config)# nat (inside) 1 0.0.0.0 0.0.0.0
ciscoasa(config)# nat (dmz) 1 192.168.5.0 255.255.255.0
ciscoasa(config)# global (outside) 1 200.200.200.10-200.200.200.254
                    netmask 255.255.255.0
ciscoasa(config)# global (dmz) 1 192.168.5.10-192.168.5.254
                    netmask 255.255.255.0
```

TIP   When looking for a translation match, always look for the same NAT ID value in both the **nat** and **global** commands for the two interfaces involved with the traffic.

In this example, three interfaces are involved with address translation: inside, outside, and dmz. Here's a breakdown of the address translation policies:

▼   **inside-to-dmz**   This translation policy uses the **nat** command on the inside and the **global** command on the dmz interface (they both have a NAT ID of 1). Any traffic going from the inside interface to the dmz interface will be translated with NAT using the 192.168.5.10–192.168.5.254 range of addresses. Notice something interesting about the address pool for the DMZ segment:

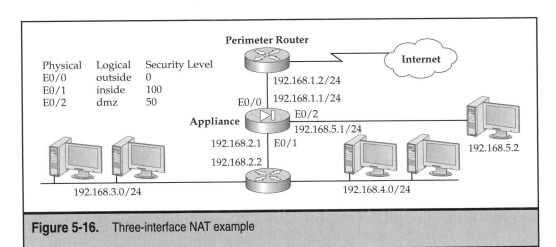

Figure 5-16.   Three-interface NAT example

it has unused addresses from the 192.168.5.0/24 network. From the DMZ server perspective, the inside devices will look like they are physically connected to the DMZ, when in reality they are being translated. In the DMZ server ARP cache, the appliance MAC address for E0/2 would appear for the translated IP addresses, which means that if a DMZ server would ARP for a translated inside device, the appliance would respond back with its own MAC address on E0/2 (this process is referred to as *proxy ARP*).

■ **inside-to-outside** This translation policy uses the **nat** command on the inside and the **global** command on the outside interface (they both have a NAT ID of 1). Any traffic going from the inside interface to the outside interface will be translated with NAT using the 200.200.200.10–200.200.200.254 range of addresses.

▲ **dmz-to-outside** This translation policy uses the **nat** command on the dmz and the **global** command on the outside interfaces (they both have a NAT ID of 1). Any traffic going from the inside interface to the outside interface will be translated with NAT using the 200.200.200.10–200.200.200.254 range of addresses. Notice that both the inside and dmz interfaces use the *same* global pool when accessing the outside network. This is a valid configuration; the only problem you might experience is that two sets of networks are sharing a limited pool of addresses.

TIP Whenever I add a new service or device, and traffic is not flowing through the appliance for the new addition, I typically first look at address translation policies, assuming **nat-control** has been configured and thus address translation is required. From my experience, most connectivity problems are related to first, misconfigured translation policies, and second, misconfigured ACLs.

Policy NAT Example The next example will show a simple configuration using Policy NAT, where the translation is controlled based on the destination the source is trying to reach. ACLs (discussed in Chapter 6) must be used in this situation. Here's the configuration example, based on the network shown in Figure 5-17:

```
ciscoasa(config)# access-list Site_A permit tcp 10.0.1.0 255.255.255.0
                  host 172.16.10.1
ciscoasa(config)# nat (inside) 100 access-list Site_A
ciscoasa(config)# global (outside) 100 172.16.1.100
                  netmask 255.255.255.255
ciscoasa(config)# access-list Site_B permit tcp 10.0.1.0 255.255.255.0
                  host 172.17.10.2
ciscoasa(config)# nat (inside) 101 access-list Site_B
ciscoasa(config)# global (outside) 101 172.17.1.88
                  netmask 255.255.255.255
```

In the preceding example, any packets from 10.0.1.0/24 being sent to 172.16.10.1 are translated using PAT to an IP address of 172.16.1.100. If any packets from 10.0.1.0/24 are

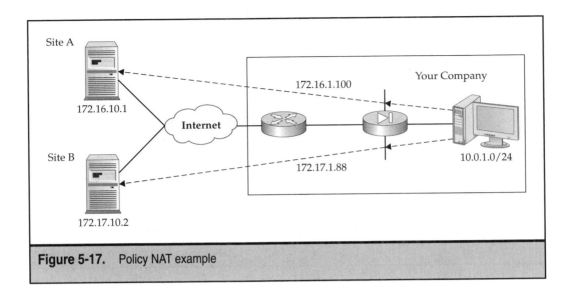

Figure 5-17. Policy NAT example

being sent to 172.17.10.2, however, they are translated, using PAT, to a different global address, 172.17.1.88. In this example, an ACL is used to control when address translation takes place: the source *and* destination involved in the connection.

Policy Identity NAT Example   The last dynamic translation policy I'll show is based on the network in Figure 5-18. In this example, I'm configuring the appliance at the SOHO site, where traffic traversing the VPN to the Corporate site should be exempted from address translation (Identity NAT), and traffic going to the Internet should be translated using PAT. Here's the configuration for the appliance:

```
SOHO(config)# access-list VPN-EXEMPT-NAT permit ip
                   10.100.10.0 255.255.255.0
                   10.10.0.0 255.255.0.0
SOHO(config)# nat-control
SOHO(config)# nat (inside) 0 access-list VPN-EXEMPT-NAT
SOHO(config)# nat (inside) 1 10.100.0.0 255.255.0.0
SOHO(config)# global (outside) 1 interface
```

In the preceding example, the following translation policies are configured:

▼ When traffic goes across the site-to-site VPN tunnel to the Corporate office, it should not be translated: the **access-list** and **nat (inside) 0** commands implement this policy.

▲ When traffic goes from the SOHO to the Internet locations, it will be translated using PAT: the **nat (inside) 1** and **global (outside) 1** commands implement this policy.

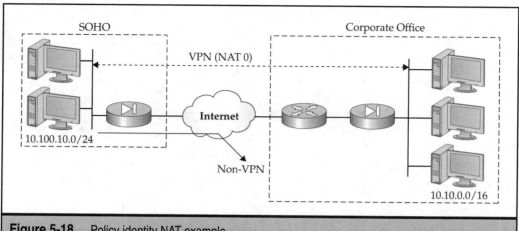

Figure 5-18. Policy identity NAT example

Configuring Static NAT Translation

Static NAT translations are commonly used for inbound connections: you have a server on a higher-level interface that you want lower-level interface users to access, like Internet users accessing DMZ web, e-mail, and DNS servers. This section will discuss how to create a static NAT translation, and show a simple example of its usage.

Static NAT Syntax

To create a static NAT translation, use the following command:

```
ciscoasa(config)# static (local_if_name,global_if_name)
                  global_IP_addr local_IP_addr
                  [netmask subnet_mask]
                  [tcp [max_conns [embryonic_conn_limit]]
                  [udp max_conns [dns] [norandomseq]
```

Of all the commands I've worked with on Cisco devices, the **static** command is the one I've most commonly seen misconfigured because of the order of the parameters: local interface, global interface, global IP address, and local IP address—notice that the local and global values *don't* match up in a logical order!

NOTE The interface names and the addresses listed in the **static** command are reversed, which has created a lot of confusion for network administrators setting up static translations!

Remember that translation policies always involve a pair of interfaces, as can be seen from the preceding syntax. The interface names are separated by a comma with no space.

For *outbound* access, traffic entering the local interface with the specified local IP address (in the source IP address field of the IP packet) will be translated when leaving the global interface to the specified global IP address. For *inbound* access, traffic entering the global interface with a destination address that matches the global IP address in the `static` command will be translated to the local IP address and forwarded out the specified local interface.

When configuring a static NAT translation, you can translate a single IP address, specifying a single local and global address with a 255.255.255.255 subnet mask value (this is the default), or you can configure what Cisco refers to as a *net static*, mapping one range of addresses in a network to a second network with the same range of addresses, like mapping 10.0.1.0/24 to 192.1.1.0/24, where 10.0.1.1 would map to 192.1.1.1, 10.0.1.2 would map to 192.1.1.2, and so on. With a net static, you need to configure the appropriate subnet mask value. The advantage of using a net static is that the appliance can now distinguish between host, network, and directed broadcast addresses for a network number, of which the appliance will not translate or forward the latter two.

The other parameters were discussed previously in the "Identifying Local Addresses for Translation" section.

TIP I recommend against using net statics, but instead recommend using individual statics. The problem with a network static is that all the mappings you create use the same parameters in the `static` command, like total TCP connections or total embryonic connections. For example, I would assume that an e-mail server and web server would probably have different connection characteristics, and to represent these, I would need separate `static` statements. You can overcome this issue by using the Modular Policy Framework (MPF) feature discussed in Chapter 10, but this assumes you have version 7 or later on your appliance.

Static NAT Example

To illustrate the configuration of static NAT translation policies, I'll use the network shown in Figure 5-19. The following configuration shows the appliance configuration for both static NAT and dynamic NAT translation policies:

```
ciscoasa(config)# nat-control
ciscoasa(config)# static (dmz,outside) 200.200.200.1 192.168.5.2
                        netmask 255.255.255.255
ciscoasa(config)# static (dmz,outside) 200.200.200.2 192.168.5.3
                        netmask 255.255.255.255
ciscoasa(config)# static (inside,outside) 200.200.200.3 192.168.4.1
                        netmask 255.255.255.255
ciscoasa(config)# nat (inside) 1 0.0.0.0 0.0.0.0
ciscoasa(config)# global (outside) 1 200.200.200.10-200.200.200.254
                        netmask 255.255.255.0
ciscoasa(config)# global (dmz) 1 192.168.5.10-192.168.5.254
                        netmask 255.255.255.0
```

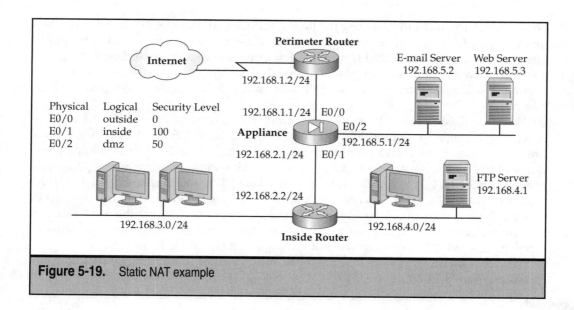

Figure 5-19. Static NAT example

In this example, the appliance has three interfaces: inside, outside, and dmz. The first **static** command creates a static NAT translation policy for the DMZ public e-mail server: outside users send traffic to 200.200.200.1, which will be translated to 192.168.5.2 and forwarded to the dmz interface. The second **static** command creates a static NAT translation policy for the DMZ public web server: outside users send traffic to 200.200.200.2, which will be translated to 192.168.5.3 and forwarded to the dmz interface. The third **static** command creates a static NAT translation policy for the inside public FTP server: outside users send traffic to 200.200.200.3, which will be translated to 192.168.4.1 and forwarded to the inside interface.

NOTE Even though the **static** commands set up the static NAT translations, traffic will not be allowed to go from the outside to the dmz, or from outside to inside interfaces until you configure ACL entries, which is discussed in the next chapter.

There are two additional translation policies for outbound access. When inside users send traffic to the outside, the addresses will be translated, using NAT, to the address pool ranging from 200.200.200.10 to 200.200.200.254. Also, when inside users access the DMZ segment, the addresses will be translated to the address pool ranging from 192.168.5.10 to 192.168.5.254.

Configuring Static PAT Translation

The appliances support static PAT, sometimes referred to as *port address redirection* (PAR). PAR is sometimes necessary when your ISP assigns you a single public IP address that you need to put on the outside interface of your appliance, but you want Internet users to access servers behind your appliance, like a web, DNS, and/or e-mail servers. Basically, PAR redirects traffic sent to one IP address and port number to a different IP address and, possibly, to a different port number. The following two sections will show you the syntax for configuring PAR as well as a simple example.

Static PAT Syntax

The **static** command is used to redirect traffic from one destination address and destination port to a different internal machine (and possibly to a different destination port number). Here is the syntax of the command:

```
ciscoasa(config)# static (local_if_name,global_if_name) {tcp | udp}
                  {global_IP_addr | interface}
                  global_dest_port_# local_IP_addr local_port_#
                  [netmask subnet_mask]
                  [tcp [max_TCP_conns [embryonic_conn_limit]]
                  [udp max_UDP_conns [dns] [norandomseq]
```

For port redirection, specify the IP protocol: **tcp** or **udp**. The *global_IP_addr* is the global/public IP address that the outside world sends traffic to. Instead of using this address, you can specify the **interface** parameter, which will have the appliance use the address assigned to the *global_if_name* interface. The global port number is the port number of the application that the external device is trying to reach, like 21 for FTP.

The *local_IP_address* is the actual IP address assigned to the internal device, and the *local_port_#* is the port number the application is listening to on the internal device. The other parameters were discussed previously in the "Identifying Local Addresses for Translation" section.

Static PAT Example

To illustrate the configuration of static PAT or PAR translation policies, I'll use the network shown in Figure 5-20. The following configuration shows the appliance configuration for PAR:

```
ciscoasa(config)# static (inside,outside) tcp interface 80
                  192.168.1.20 80 netmask 255.255.255.255
```

In this example, web traffic sent to port 80 to the IP address on the outside interface of the appliance will be redirected to 192.168.1.20 on port 80 of the inside interface.

Finding a Matching Translation Policy

An address translation is configured for every source and destination interface pair: this allows the appliance to translate a source address to something different depending on the destination interface the source is trying to reach. When address translation is required (NAT control is enabled), there must be an existing entry in the xlate table, or the

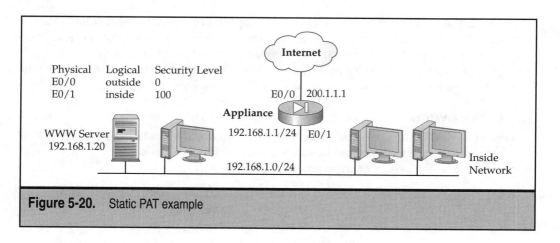

Figure 5-20. Static PAT example

appliance must be able to build an entry before the appliance will switch a packet between interfaces: Building translation policies can be done dynamically (**nat** and **global** commands) or statically (**static** command). The exceptions to this rule are the **nat 0** commands, which create exemptions to the address translation process.

However, when multiple translation policies are configured, the question is which translation policy should be used by the appliance. When looking for a matching translation policy, the appliance goes through the following steps:

1. The appliance looks for an existing translation in the translation table; sometimes Cisco will refer to this as trying to find a "matching xlate slot" in the translation table.

2. If no entry exists in the translation table, the appliance looks for address translation exceptions in the **nat 0** commands on a best-match basis.

3. If there are no matches on the Identity NAT commands, the appliance will try to find a match against the configured **static** NAT commands based on a best-match basis.

4. If there are no matches on the **static** NAT commands, the appliance will try to find a match against the configured static PAT (PAR) policies on a best-match basis.

5. If no match is found within the PAR translation policies, the appliance then looks for a match in its policy **nat** and **global** commands with a corresponding ACL.

6. If there is not a match on a policy translation configuration, the appliance then looks for a match in its normal **nat** and **global** commands.

7. If a translation or translation policy doesn't exist for the packet, the appliance will *drop* the packet if NAT control is enabled; if NAT control is not enabled, then the packet is not translated, but can flow through the appliance, assuming other appliance policies allow it.

TCP SYN FLOOD ATTACKS

Some types of traffic are malicious. One example is the weakness that TCP has during the three-way handshake when establishing a connection: the destination assumes that when it receives a SYN, it is a legitimate connection attempt. However, attackers could use this to their advantage and spoof thousands of TCP SYNs, making it look like there are thousands of legitimate connection requests.

The issue the destination has is that since the destination assumes the connection requests are valid, it must maintain them for a period before determining that they aren't going to complete the three-way handshake and removing them from the local connection table. This can have a devastating impact on the destination, since most operating systems will keep the connection in their local table from 30 to 60 seconds, and the connection table has finite resources to store connections. So an attacker could easily fill up the connection table and deny legitimate connection attempts while the attack is ongoing.

The Original TCP Intercept

Cisco introduced the TCP Intercept feature on the PIXs back in version 5.2 to limit the effectiveness of these kinds of attacks. In the original implementation, you would define embryonic connection limits in the **static** and/or **nat** commands. Once these limits were reached, the appliance would intercept the TCP SYNs and proxy the connection, sending back a SYN/ACK, pretending to be the destination. The appliances would maintain this connection in their conn table. If an ACK was not received in 30 seconds, the half-open connection was removed from the conn table. If it was received within 30 seconds, the appliance would perform a three-way handshake to the real destination, bind the two connections—source and destination—and place the single bound connection in the conn table.

NOTE 　Besides specifying connection limits with the **static** and **nat** commands, you can also set up policies using the Cisco Modular Policy Framework (MPF) starting with version 7.0. The advantage of MPF is that it is more granular and will work with or without address translation. MPF is discussed in Chapter 10.

TCP Intercept with SYN Cookies

To prevent an attacker from filling the conn table with half-open TCP connections, Cisco enhanced the TCP Intercept feature with TCP SYN cookies in version 6.2. Instead of proxying the half-open TCP connections and maintaining them in the conn table, the appliance generates a cookie by hashing certain parts of the TCP header—this is then included in the SYN/ACK sent back to the source. Nothing about the original TCP SYN connection is maintained in the state table by the appliance. If a connection attempt is legitimate, the source will respond with the TCP ACK, which should contain the cookie information in the TCP header. At this point, the appliance itself will proxy the connection to the destination and add the new connection to the state table. With the SYN cookie feature, the appliance doesn't have to maintain any connection information for the initial SYN connection attempt, greatly reducing the overhead involved when dealing with a TCP SYN flood attack.

NOTE This is not to say that TCP Intercept with SYN cookies is the best feature at dealing with TCP SYN flood attacks, but it is much better than what Cisco IOS routers support and better than the original TCP Intercept implementation on the appliances. Cisco has two products, the Guard and Traffic Anomaly Detector, which were designed specifically for flood attacks. These can be purchased as stand-alone appliances or as cards for the 6500 switches or 7600 routers.

TRANSLATION AND CONNECTION VERIFICATION

Once you have configured your address translation policies with the **global**, **nat**, and **static** commands, you are now ready to use **show** commands to verify your configuration. The following sections cover these commands.

Viewing Active Translations

One of the more important commands that you will use when troubleshooting problems with connections is the **show xlate** command. This command shows the translations that are in the translation or xlate table. The syntax of the **show xlate** command is

```
ciscoasa# show xlate [detail] [{global | local}
                        IP_address1[-IP_address2]
                        [netmask subnet_mask]]
                        {gport | lport} port[-port]]
                        [interface interface_name_1 [,interface_name_X]
                        [state state_information]
```

Typing **show xlate** by itself lists the entire translation table. Table 5-4 explains the rest of the parameters for this command.

An example of the output of the **show xlate** command is shown here:

```
ciscoasa# show xlate
Global 200.200.200.10 Local 172.16.7.80 nconns 1 econns 0
Global 200.200.200.11 Local 172.16.7.81 nconns 3 econns 0
```

In this example, the global address is the address that external devices use to access the internal device, displayed as the local address. For example, if someone from the outside world wanted to access 172.16.7.80, he would use a destination address of 200.200.200.10. Two other items in this display are of interest: nconns refers to the number of connections that are currently open to this address, and econns refers to the number of half-open (embryonic) connections.

Parameter	Explanation
`detail`	Displays the translation type as well as the interfaces the connection traverses.
`global` | `local`	Displays only the global or local addresses in the output.
`gport` | `lport`	Displays translations for the specified `global` or `local` port number(s).
`interface`	Displays only the translations for the specified interfaces.
`state`	Displays the connections by their state. You can also limit the output of the display by specifying the state(s) that you are interested in: translations configured by the `static` command (`static`); translations being removed (`dump`); translations configured with PAT by `global` command (`portmap`); translations defined by the `nat` or `static` command with the `norandomseq` parameter (`norandomseq`); or translations defined with the `nat 0` configuration (`identity`).

Table 5-4. The Parameters for the `show xlate` Command

The following is an example using the **detail** parameter:

```
ciscoasa# show xlate detail
3 in use, 3 most used
Flags: D - DNS, d - dump, I - identity, i - inside, n - no random,
       o - outside, r - portmap, s – static
TCP PAT from inside:172.16.7.80/1026 to outside:200.200.200.1/1024
     flags ri
UDP PAT from inside:172.16.7.80/1028 to outside:200.200.200.1/1024
     flags ri
ICMP PAT from inside:172.16.7.80/21505 to outside:200.200.200.1/0
     flags ri
```

This example has three PAT connections. Notice the flags listed at the end. The r indicates that this is a port map (PAT) connection, and the i indicates an inside address. Also notice that you can see the interfaces involved in the translation—all three are between the inside and outside interfaces.

Viewing Active Connections

The appliances keep track of the connections going through them by placing connection information in a state/connection table, called a *conn* table. Remember that the appliances are only stateful for TCP and UDP connections by default, but can also be stateful for ICMP. The appliances allow traffic from a lower-level-security interface to a higher-level one if there is a corresponding entry in the connection table. An entry is placed in the connection table in two basic ways:

▼ A connection is added when a TCP or UDP connection is initiated from a higher-level interface to a lower one—this allows the returning inbound traffic to the source.

▲ A connection is added when inbound traffic is allowed by an ACL and a connection matches a **permit** statement—this allows the returning outbound traffic to the source.

To see the connections in the connection table, use the **show conn** command:

```
ciscoasa# show conn [detail] [count] [{foreign | local}
                      IP_address_1[-IP_address_2]]
                     [netmask subnet_mask]
                     [protocol {tcp | udp | protocol}]
                     [fport | lport port_1[-port_2]]
                     [state state_information]
```

Typing **show conn** by itself lists the entire state table. Table 5-5 explains the rest of the parameters for this command.

An example of the output of the **show conn** command is shown here:

```
ciscoasaa# show conn
6 in use, 6 most used
TCP out 202.202.202.1:80 in 192.168.1.5:1404 idle 0:00:00 Bytes 11391
TCP out 202.202.202.1:80 in 192.168.1.5:1405 idle 0:00:00 Bytes 3709
TCP out 202.202.202.1:80 in 192.168.1.5:1406 idle 0:00:01 Bytes 2685
TCP out 202.202.202.1:80 in 192.168.1.5:1407 idle 0:00:01 Bytes 2683
```

In this output, the internal host (in) 192.168.1.5 accessed an external web server (out) at 202.202.202.1.

An example of the output of the **show conn detail** command is shown here:

```
ciscoasa(config)# show conn detail
1 in use, 2 most used
Flags: A - awaiting inside ACK to SYN, a - awaiting outside ACK to SYN,
       B - initial SYN from outside, D - DNS, d - dump,
       E - outside back connection, f - inside FIN, F - outside FIN,
       G - group, H - H.323, I - inbound data, M - SMTP data,
```

Parameter	Explanation
`detail`	Displays the translation type as well as the interfaces the connection traverses.
`count`	Displays only the number of connections in the table—this can help you figure out if you have purchased the right connection license and/or security appliance.
`foreign | local`	Displays only the specified foreign or local addresses.
`protocol`	Displays only the specified IP protocol.
`fport | lport`	Displays translations for the specified foreign or local port number(s).
`state`	Displays the connections by their state. You can also limit the output of the display by specifying the state(s) that you are interested in.

Table 5-5.   The Parameters for the `show conn` Command

```
        O - outbound data, P - inside back connection,
        q - SQL*Net data, R - outside acknowledged FIN,
        R - UDP RPC, r - inside acknowledged FIN,
        S - awaiting inside SYN,
        s - awaiting outside SYN, U - up
TCP outside:202.202.202.32/23 inside:192.168.1.10/1026 flags UIO
```

In this example, at the top of the display is a table explaining the flags that you may see at the end of a connection entry. Below this table is a TCP telnet connection that was initiated by 192.168.1.10 (`inside`) to 202.202.202.32 (`outside`). Its flags indicate that it is active and that it allows both inbound and outbound transfer of data.

Viewing Local Host Information

Starting in version 7.0, you can view and clear the translations and connections of local hosts in one command: **show local-host** or **clear local-host**. These commands allow you to view the conn and xlate entries for all hosts associated with an interface or interfaces, or a particular host, making it easier to understand what traffic is going through the appliance. The full syntax of these commands is as follows:

```
ciscoasa# show local-host [IP_address] [detail]
ciscoasa# clear local-host [IP_address] [all]
```

Here's an example of viewing a summary of the host information:

```
ciscoasa# show local-host
Licensed host limit: Unlimited
Interface inside: 1 active, 5 maximum active, 0 denied
Interface outside: 0 active, 0 maximum active, 0 denied
```

In this example, no per-host licensing is on the appliance, and currently one connection is in the state table associated with the inside interface. This command gives you a quick idea as to the number of entries in the state table per interface, and the maximum that was seen for each interface.

Here's another example of this command, but specifying a single host and using the **detail** parameter:

```
ciscoasa# show local-host 10.1.1.1 detail
Interface third: 0 active, 0 maximum active, 0 denied
Interface inside: 1 active, 1 maximum active, 0 denied
local host: <10.1.1.1>,
TCP flow count/limit = 1/unlimited
TCP embryonic count to (from) host = 0 (0)
TCP intercept watermark = unlimited
UDP flow count/limit = 0/unlimited

Xlate:
TCP PAT from inside:10.1.1.1/4984 to outside:192.1.1.1/1024 flags ri

Conn:
TCP outside:192.1.1.1/21 inside:10.1.1.1/4984 flags UI Interface
  outside: 1 active, 1
maximum active, 0 denied
```

In this example, you can see one PAT translation in the xlate table and one connection in the conn table for 10.1.1.1.

Clearing Entries in the Xlate and Conn Tables

Anytime that you make policy changes (as with the **nat**, **global**, **static**, **access-list**, and many other commands) that affect existing entries in the translation and/or conn tables, you should execute the **clear xlate** command to remove the existing entries so that the new policy changes will apply to the users: executing this command will enforce the new changes.

The syntax of the **clear xlate** command is shown here:

```
ciscoasa# clear xlate [global ip1[-ip2] [netmask mask]]
                      [local ip1[-ip2] [netmask mask]]
                      [gport port1[-port2]] [lport port1[-port2]]
                      [interface logical_if_name] [state state]
```

If you don't specify any parameters, *all* translations will be cleared from the xlate table and *all* connections will be cleared from the conn table. Most people assume that since the command has "xlate" in it, that the command only affects the xlate table: this is not true! Of course, you can be specific about which entry (or entries) is to be cleared. Refer to Table 5-4 for an explanation of these parameters.

SECURITY ALERT!   Anytime you add, change, or delete a translation policy, you should clear the translation table with the `clear xlate` command in order for your changes to take effect on existing traffic and connections. Also, when using the `clear xlate` command, *always* qualify it: without any parameters to qualify the command, the entire conn and xlate tables are cleared, breaking any existing connections in the state table, which might upset quite a few administrators and users!

CHAPTER 6

Access Control

In the previous chapter, I talked about some of the security appliance commands to perform address translation, like **global**, **nat**, and **static**. This chapter will expand on the topic of controlling traffic through the appliance, discussing these topics:

▼ Using access control lists (ACLs) to filter traffic through the appliance

■ Using object groups to simplify the management of ACLs

■ Filtering ICMP packets destined to an appliance

▲ Troubleshooting connections using the packet tracer and packet capture features

ACCESS CONTROL LISTS (ACLs)

Beginning with version 5.3, Cisco introduced ACLs to standardize the implementation of filters on the appliances. The term "ACLs," even though it is an acronym, is sometimes pronounced as a word: "ackles." Before ACLs, Cisco PIXs used conduits and outbound filters. Conduits were used to allow inbound connections, and outbound filters were used to restrict outbound connections. Conduits and filters had some major limitations in their filtering abilities. Therefore, Cisco ported their ACL technology from the IOS-based routers to the PIX platform. All three filtering features—ACLs, conduits, and outbound filters—were supported through version 6. Starting in version 7, conduits and outbound filters are no longer supported: you must use ACLs to filter traffic through your appliances.

As you will see throughout this section of the book, ACLs have many components in common with the implementation of ACLs on Cisco IOS routers. For example, you'll have to go through two steps to set up and activate your ACLs—create the ACL and apply it to an interface. However, differences exist in the configuration *and* operation of ACLs on the appliances when compared with IOS routers.

Introduction to ACLs

ACLs on Cisco IOS-based routers and on the appliances are very similar in their function, processing, and configuration. Since conduits and outbound filters are no longer supported on the appliances, you must use ACLs to exempt inbound connections and to control outbound connections.

Appliance and IOS Router ACL Comparison

Cisco is attempting to move to a more uniform command-line interface across its networking products, which you can see with the ACL commands on the appliances. This section will cover both the many similarities and a few differences between ACLs on the appliances and ACLs on IOS routers.

If you've configured ACLs on IOS routers in the past, learning to use ACLs on the appliances will be easy. Here are some of the ACL features the two products have in common:

▼ A grouping of ACLs is labeled with a group identifier.

■ Both standard and extended ACLs are supported (standard ACLs are new in version 7.0).

■ ACLs are activated on an interface in either an inbound or outbound direction.

■ The general syntax of the statements is the same.

■ Each statement has a counter that keeps track of the number of matches on the statement.

■ Each statement can have logging enabled, displaying a summary of the packet that matched on the statement.

■ Statements are processed in a top-down order, starting with the first statement, until a match is found.

■ An invisible statement, called the *implicit deny* statement, is at the end of the list and will drop traffic if it doesn't match any other statement in the list.

■ When adding statements to a list, statements are added at the end of the list by default.

■ When editing ACLs, you can delete specific statements and insert statements into the list.

■ You can have multiple remarks in your ACLs.

■ ACL statements can be enabled or disabled based on the current date and time (referred to as a *timed* ACL entry).

▲ ACLs can be used for functions other than filtering, such as classifying traffic for other features like address translation, VPNs, and so on.

Table 6-1 covers some of the differences between ACLs on appliances and IOS routers.

SECURITY ALERT! There are two main differences between ACLs on appliances and those on IOS routers. First, remember that appliance ACLs use *subnet masks,* not wildcard masks, when matching on packet addressing contents. Second, appliance ACLs filter traffic flowing through the appliance, not to it. Other commands on the appliance filter traffic sent to an IP address on the appliance.

Processing of ACLs

In Chapter 5, I went through a simple example of TCP traffic flowing through the appliance in the "TCP Connection Example" section. I'll build on this topic to give you a better understanding of what the appliance is doing to packets as they enter and

Component	Appliances	IOS Routers
ACL identification	ACLs can be identified with a name or number.	Named ACLs must use names, and numbered ACLs must use numbers.
Activating ACLs	A global command is used to activate an ACL.	ACLs are activated in an interface subcommand mode.
Matching on a range of addresses	*Subnet* masks are used.	*Wildcard* masks are used.
Logging of statement matches	When the same source is continually matching on a statement, you can control the period that a message should be regenerated as well as controlling the number of log messages generated by a statement within a period, no matter how many sources are matching on it.	When the same source is continually matching on a statement, a message is generated either every 5 minutes or every *x* packets that match.
Inserting ACL statements	ACL statements are numbered sequentially from 1 (1, 2, 3, 4…); to insert a statement, specify the exact line number the statement should be placed in.	ACL statements are numbered in increments (like 10, 20, 30, 40…); to insert a statement, use a line number that doesn't currently exist in the ACL.
Filtering traffic	ACLs applied to interfaces filter traffic flowing through the appliance, *not to the appliance.*	ACLs applied to interfaces filter traffic *to and through* the router.

Table 6-1.   Comparing ACLs on Appliances and IOS Routers

leave its interfaces. Here are the steps that a packet will go through upon entering an interface:

1. The appliance compares the packet information to the existing connections to the state table to determine if the packet is a new, or is part of an existing, connection. If it's an existing connection, the packet is allowed through, and the remainder of the ACL checks listed here are bypassed.

2. Assuming address translation is enabled, this step is performed. For inbound connections, the destination address is compared with the translation policies to make sure that it can be translated. For outbound connections, the destination address is compared with the translation policies to make sure that it can be translated. If there is no matching translation policy, the packet is dropped. Note that translation doesn't actually occur at this step.

3. If this is an inbound packet, the packet must match a permit ACL statement applied inbound on the incoming interface; otherwise the packet is dropped. If this is an outbound packet and no ACL exists, traffic is allowed to go from a higher to a lower security level by default; otherwise, if an ACL exists inbound on the interface, the packet must match a permit ACL statement or it is dropped.

4. The appliance then does a route lookup to determine the exit interface the appliance should use. This is necessary to determine the ACLs to process and to perform address translation, if enabled.

5. Assuming that address translation has been configured, the destination addressing information is untranslated with a **static** command or translated with the **nat** and **global** commands.

6. If an ACL exists outbound on the exit interface, then this is processed.

7. At this point the connection is added to the conn table and is tracked.

The appliance might perform additional steps on the packet, but I'll discuss these in Part III of the book concerning the implementation of policies.

Creating and Activating ACLs

The configuration of ACLs on your appliance is very similar to configuring ACLs on an IOS-based router. The configuration process involves two steps: create your filtering rules with the **access-list** commands, and activate your filtering rules on an interface with the **access-group** command. The following sections cover the configuration of standard and extended ACLs, as well as some ACL features like timed ACL entries, logging matches on ACLs, and updating ACLs.

Standard ACLs

Like IOS routers, appliances support standard ACLs, which filter packets based on only an address or addresses. However, standard ACLs on appliances cannot be used to filter traffic entering or leaving an interface; instead, standard ACLs are used with other features, like split tunneling with remote access VPNs, or filtering routes when performing redistribution, and many others. Only extended and EtherType ACLs can be used on the appliances to filter traffic through the appliance interfaces.

Here is the syntax for creating a standard ACL:

```
ciscoasa(config)# access-list ACL_ID standard [line line_#]
                        {deny | permit} {any | host IP_addr |
                        IP_addr subnet_mask}
```

On the appliance, each ACL is differentiated from other ACLs by a unique identifier (`ACL_ID`): this can be a name, number, or mixture of characters and numbers. You must use the **standard** parameter; otherwise the ACL type defaults to an extended ACL. If you don't tell the appliance what line number to use for the statement, the statement is added at the *end* of the existing ACL statements. Next you need to specify what should happen when there is a match on the condition: allow (**permit**) or drop (**deny**) the packet. Last, you specify the address you want to match on:

▼ **any** Any packet matches.

■ **host** `IP_addr` Only that particular IP address matches.

▲ `IP_addr subnet_mask` Only the specified range of addresses matches.

Remember that you need to configure a *subnet* mask, not a wildcard mask, when matching on a range of addresses.

Extended ACLs

The primary use of extended ACLs is to filter traffic, but they can be used for other features on the appliances. Here is the syntax for configuring an extended ACL:

```
ciscoasa(config)# access-list ACL_ID [extended] {deny | permit}
                      IP_protocol
                      {src_addr subnet_mask | host src_addr | any}
                          [protocol_info]
                      {dst_addr subnet_mask | host dst_addr | any}
                          [protocol_info]
                      [disable | default]
```

The first part of the ACL syntax is similar to a standard ACL. If you omit the **extended** parameter, the ACL defaults to an extended ACL. Unlike with a standard ACL, you must specify either the name or number of the TCP/IP protocol you want to filter, like **tcp**, **udp**, **icmp**, and others. If Cisco doesn't have a name for a particular protocol, you can enter a number instead. To match on any TCP/IP packet, use a protocol name of **ip**. For a complete listing of IP protocol numbers, visit http://www.iana.org/assignments/protocol-numbers.

Following the IP protocol designation, you need to specify the source IP addressing information that you want to match on. The syntax for this was discussed previously in the "Standard ACLs" section. If you are filtering on TCP or UDP traffic, you can also specify the source port or ports you are interested in matching on. Following this is the destination address and, optionally, destination protocol information.

If you are filtering TCP or UDP traffic, you can specify an operator and a port number or name to be specific about the traffic that is to be filtered. You can specify an operator and the port name or number, or a range of numbers. Operators include **eq** (equal to),

neq (not equal to), **lt** (less than), **gt** (greater than), and **range**. To specify a range of port numbers or names, enter the beginning and ending port numbers or names, and separate them with a hyphen with no spaces between the hyphens and the ports. If you omit the port information, the appliance assumes that you are talking about all ports for the specified protocol and address. For information about valid port numbers, visit http://www.iana.org/assignments/port-numbers.

TIP Remember that the appliances process filter functions like ACLs before any address translation is performed, so you should place the source address in the ACL that the appliance will see in the actual packet header. For example, if a server has a private address of 192.168.1.1, but is represented by a public address of 200.1.1.1, and the appliance is doing translation, then your ACL needs to permit traffic to 200.1.1.1. Here would be the static configuration: `static (inside,outside) 200.1.1.1 192.168.1.1`. In this example, when traffic enters the outside interface, the appliance is looking at a destination address of 200.1.1.1. Once passed the ACL check, the appliance will translate it to the server local address, 192.168.1.1.

For ICMP traffic, you can specify an ICMP message type (either by name or number) following the destination address. If you omit the message information, the appliance assumes that you are talking about all ICMP messages. Remember that for ICMP traffic, the appliance is not stateful by default; in version 6 and earlier, the PIXs were never stateful for ICMP. Therefore, if you want ICMP replies to your users' traffic and tests, and stateful processing of ICMP is disabled or unavailable, then you need to explicitly permit ICMP traffic with an ACL applied on the interface where the returning replies are received. Typically you'll want to allow echo reply, unreachable, time exceeded, and TTL exceeded messages. For information about ICMP message types, visit http://www.iana.org/assignments/icmp-parameters.

The **disable** parameter allows you to disable the specified ACL statement while still keeping it in the ACL—this is handy if you want to temporarily disable a statement to allow (or deny) certain connections, but then want to re-enable the statement once the connection(s) complete. The **default** parameter sets the ACL statement back to its default configuration.

You can configure other parameters with an extended ACL statement, but I'll be covering these in later sections.

ACL Remarks

One handy feature of ACLs is that you can include remarks with this command:

```
ciscoasa(config)# access-list ACL_ID [line line_#] remark text
```

There is no real limit to the number of remarks in an ACL, and it is recommended, especially in large ACLs, to copiously use remarks to help yourself and other administrators understand what different lines or sections of the ACL are accomplishing.

ACL Logging

You can have the appliance generate a 106100 log message when there is a match on an ACL command by adding the **log** parameter to your ACL statement:

```
ciscoasa(config)# access-list ACL_name [extended] {deny | permit}
                        ACL_parameters [log [[disable | default] |
                             [level]]] [interval seconds]
```

If you don't configure a logging level (*level* parameter), it defaults to informational (level 6). The **interval** parameter specifies the amount of time between 106100 log messages, preventing an overrun of log messages, which might create a denial of service (DoS) attack. The default interval is 300 seconds. The interval function works as follows:

▼ The first match in the matching flow is cached, and subsequent matches increment the hit counter on the ACL statement. (Hit counts are discussed later in the "ACL Verification" section.)

▲ New 106100 messages are generated at the end of the interval value.

With the interval function, if it is the same source matching on the statement, then a log message is generated only once every *x* seconds, depending on the configured interval. However, the appliance still keeps track of the number of matches on the statement (the hit count), but doesn't generate a log message for these additional matches.

Other ACL Logging Issues   One problem with the preceding solution and interval logging is that it works great with one attacker, but with a thousand attackers, you would see one log message from each attacker for each ACL statement they matched on in the defined interval, resulting in at least 1,000 log messages every *x* seconds. To solve this problem, Cisco allows you to control the maximum number of concurrent deny log messages that the appliance will create with this command:

```
ciscoasa(config)# access-list deny-flow number
```

The default is 4,096 unique sources for ACL logging: when this limit is reached, a message is generated with an ID of 106101. Any packet matches above this limit are not logged, but they are still dropped, and the hit counter is still incremented.

By default, the appliance generates the 106101 log message every 300 seconds while the deny flow limit is exceeded, reminding you that sources are being dropped by the ACL statement, but that you're not seeing some of these log messages because the deny flow limit was exceeded. You can change how often you see this reminder message with this command:

```
ciscoasa(config)# access-list alert-interval seconds
```

ACL Log Message   Here is the syntax of the 106100 log message:

```
%ASA-6-106100: access-list ACL_ID {permitted | denied | est-allowed}
    protocol interface_name/source_address(source_port) ->
```

```
      interface_name/dest_address(dest_port) hit-cnt number
      ({first hit | number-second interval})
```

Here's an example of a log message resulting from a match on an ACL statement:

```
%ASA-6-106100: access-list OUTSIDE denied tcp outside/192.1.1.1(51588)
    -> inside/200.1.1.1(23) hit-cnt 1 first hit [0x22e8ca12, 0x0]
```

> **TIP**   Cisco recommends that you log ACL matches to the appliance internal buffer or to an external syslog server. Logging is discussed in more depth in Chapter 27.

Timed ACL Entries

Timed ACL entries are new in version 7.0 and are configured the same as they are on IOS routers. Timed ACL entries can be toggled on or off depending on the date and time of day. For example, you might have a contractor who needs access to a server from 8:00 in the morning to 6:00 at night from May 23, 2009, to November 1, 2009. With a timed ACL entry, you can have the ACL statement active during this time, allowing the access; outside this time, the ACL statement would be inactive and would not be used by the appliance, thereby denying the contractor's access to the server.

Creating timed ACL entries is a two-step process: creating a time range, and then associating it with one or more ACL statements. The following two sections will discuss how to create a time range and how to associate it with an ACL statement or statements.

Creating Time Ranges   The function of a time range on the appliance is to specify a date and time range that you want to associate with an ACL entry or entries. Creating a time range is basically done the same as it is done on a Cisco IOS router, by using the **time-range** command:

```
ciscoasa(config)# time-range range_name
ciscoasa(config-time-range)# absolute [start hh:mm date]
                                       [end hh:mm date]
ciscoasa(config-time-range)# periodic days_of_week hh:mm to
                                       [days_of_week] hh:mm
```

The time range must be assigned a unique name. When you execute the **time-range** command, you are taken into a subcommand mode where you enter your actual date and time range.

The **absolute** command specifies an exact time range, like August 1, 2008, through August 31, 2008.With the **absolute** command, if you don't specify a start date and time, then the current date and time are used. If you don't specify an ending period, then it defaults to indefinite. Only one **absolute** command is supported per time range.

The **periodic** command specifies a recurring period, like every day or weekdays. The *days_of_week* value can be **monday**, **tuesday**, **wednesday**, **thursday**, **friday**, **saturday**, **sunday**, **daily** (Monday through Sunday), **weekdays** (Monday through Friday), and **weekend** (Saturday and Sunday).

If you are using both **absolute** and **periodic** commands in a time range, the **periodic** command qualifies the absolute time in the **absolute** command. You can have multiple **periodic** commands in a time range.

Associating Time Ranges to ACL Statements   Once you have created your time range, you then activate it by associating the time range to one or more ACL statements using the following syntax:

```
ciscoasa(config)# access-list ACL_ID [extended] {deny | permit}
                   ACL_parameters [time-range range_name]
```

To add a time range to an existing ACL command, reenter the ACL command along with the time range parameters.

ACL Activation

Once you have created your ACL, you need to activate it on an interface. The following is the syntax of the **access-group** command that you need to use to activate your ACL:

```
ciscoasa(config)# access-group ACL_ID {in | out}
                   interface logical_if_name
                   [per-user-override | control-plane]
```

The *ACL_ID* specifies which ACL you are activating. Before version 7.0, you could only activate an ACL inbound on an interface (**in** parameter). Starting in version 7.0, you can activate an ACL inbound (**in**—as traffic enters the interface) and/or outbound (**out**—before traffic leaves the interface). After the **interface** parameter, you need to specify the logical name of the interface where this ACL is to be activated. To remove an ACL applied to an interface, precede the **access-group** command with the **no** parameter.

The **per-user-override** parameter is used with downloadable ACLs (discussed in Chapter 8). The **control-plane** parameter is used to restrict traffic to the appliance itself: the latter is new in version 8.0.

ACL Verification

To list the statements in your ACL, you have two viewing choices. First, the **show run access-list** and **show run access-group** commands display those respective commands in the running-config in RAM. The downside of these commands is that they don't display any information about the operation of your ACL(s) on your appliance.

Your second option is the **show access-list** command:

```
ciscoasa(config)# show access-list [ACL_ID]
```

If you don't specify a specific ACL, all ACLs are shown on the appliance.

Here's an example of the use of this command:

```
ciscoasa(config)# show access-list
access-list cached ACL log flows: total 0, denied 0
```

```
      (deny-flow-max 4096)
   alert-interval 300
access-list ACLOUT; 4 elements
access-list ACLOUT line 1 extended permit tcp
     192.168.10.0 255.255.255.0 host 192.168.11.11 eq www
     (hitcnt=4)0x954ebd70
access-list ACLOUT line 2 extended permit tcp host 192.168.10.10
     host 192.168.11.11 eq ftp (hitcnt=1) 0x33490ecd
access-list ACLOUT line 3 extended permit tcp any host 192.168.11.9
     eq www (hitcnt=8) 0x83af39ba
access-list ACLOUT line 4 extended deny ip any any (hitcnt=4)
     0x2ca31385
<--output omitted-->
```

When displaying an ACL, you see the hit counts that show the matches on the statements (the `hitcnt` parameter). At the end of each ACL statement, you can also see a hexadecimal number, which is used to uniquely identify each entry in the ACL.

TIP   At the end of every ACL on the appliance is an implicit deny statement—this *drops* all traffic that is not matched on a previous statement. This statement is *invisible* when you look at the ACL with a `show access-list` command. Therefore, I recommend that you include a `deny ip any any` command at the end of every extended ACL so that you can see the hit count of dropped packets.

ACL Maintenance

The following two sections will discuss how to insert statements into existing ACLs, delete statements from ACLs, and delete an entire ACL.

Updating ACLs

Starting in version 6.3, the appliances support a feature called *sequenced ACLs*, where you can insert an ACL statement into an already existing ACL. This is accomplished by using the `line` parameter in the `access-list` command:

```
ciscoasa(config)# access-list ACL_ID [extended] line line_#
                        {deny | permit} ACL_parameters
```

When specifying a line number, use the number of the line where you want to insert this statement. For example, if you want a new statement to be the third line in an ACL, use **3** as the line number. If there is an existing line 3, it and the entries below it are pushed down in the ACL and are renumbered starting at 4.

NOTE   If you execute the `show running-config` command, ACL line numbers are not seen; nor are they saved in flash when you execute the `write memory` command. However, you can see the line numbers with the `show access-list` command.

To illustrate how to insert statements, let's look at an example ACL:

```
ciscoasa(config)# show access-list
access-list aclex line 1 permit tcp any host 192.168.1.1
    eq www (hitcnt=0)
access-list aclex line 2 permit tcp any host 192.168.1.3
    eq www (hitcnt=0)
```

In this example, the ACL has two statements.

I'll now insert a statement between the two ACLs:

```
ciscoasa(config)# access-list aclex line 2 permit tcp any
                    host 192.168.1.2 eq www
```

Here is the result of this configuration change:

```
ciscoasa(config)# show access-list
access-list aclex line 1 permit tcp any host 192.168.1.1
    eq www (hitcnt=0)
access-list aclex line 2 permit tcp any host 192.168.1.2
    eq www (hitcnt=0)
access-list aclex line 3 permit tcp any host 192.168.1.3
    eq www (hitcnt=0)
```

Notice that the **access-list** command inserted a new ACL entry as line 2, and the old line 2 became line 3.

NOTE Anytime you make a change to an ACL, it doesn't affect existing connections in the conn table. To ensure that all traffic uses your policy changes, clear any related translations in the xlate table and connections in the conn table by executing the **clear xlate** command. Remember to always qualify this command with the addresses that are affected by the policy change—not all IP addresses. The use of this command was discussed in the Chapter 5.

ACL Removal

To delete a single ACL statement, preface the statement with the **no** parameter; note that you must include the *entire* ACL command when deleting it. To delete an entire ACL or multiple ACLs, use the following command:

```
ciscoasa(config)# clear configure access-list [ACL_ID]
```

SECURITY ALERT! If you don't specify an *ACL_ID*, all the ACLs on your appliance are deleted... without any warning! It's amazing that Cisco would have the appliance do something so dramatic without prompting you. So be very careful when executing this command. Also, when you delete an ACL or ACLs with the preceding command, the associated **access-group** command(s) are also deleted.

ACL Configuration Examples

To help illustrate the use of ACLs, let's take a look at some examples. I'll start easy with an example of an appliance that has two interfaces and proceed to an example with an appliance that has three interfaces.

Appliance with Two Interfaces: Example 1

This simple example involves an appliance that has only two interfaces. Take a look at the network shown in Figure 6-1. In this example, the internal network is using a private class address (192.168.1.0/24) and has been assigned the following public address space: 200.200.200.0/29. Here are the security policies that you need to set up with ACLs:

▼   Allow all outbound traffic (this is the default).

▲   Restrict inbound traffic to only the internal servers.

Listing 6-1 shows the address translation and ACL configuration of the appliance.

Listing 6-1. Configuring ACLs for the appliance in Figure 6-1

```
ciscoasa(config)# global (outside) 1 200.200.200.1
ciscoasa(config)# nat (inside) 1 0.0.0.0 0.0.0.0
ciscoasa(config)# static (inside,outside) 200.200.200.2 192.168.1.2
ciscoasa(config)# static (inside,outside) 200.200.200.3 192.168.1.3
ciscoasa(config)# static (inside,outside) 200.200.200.4 192.168.1.4
ciscoasa(config)#
ciscoasa(config)# access-list PERMIT_IN permit tcp
                        any host 200.200.200.2 eq 80
ciscoasa(config)# access-list PERMIT_IN permit tcp
                        any host 200.200.200.3 eq 25
ciscoasa(config)# access-list PERMIT_IN permit udp
                        any host 200.200.200.4 eq 53
ciscoasa(config)# access-list PERMIT_IN deny ip any any
ciscoasa(config)#
ciscoasa(config)# access-group PERMIT_IN in interface outside
```

Before I discuss the ACL configuration in Listing 6-1, notice that the appliance is performing PAT (using 200.200.200.1) when users' traffic heads out to the Internet. Also, there are three `static` commands to perform the address translation for the three internal servers.

Look at the ACL named PERMIT_IN in Listing 6-1; the first line allows TCP traffic from any source if it is headed to 200.200.200.2 and only if this traffic is for port 80, the web server process running on the web server. Notice that I used the public address as the destination address. Remember that ACLs are processed before address translation is performed (the `static` and `nat`/`global` commands). One other thing to point out about the ACL is that I have added a **deny ip any any** statement at the end of the

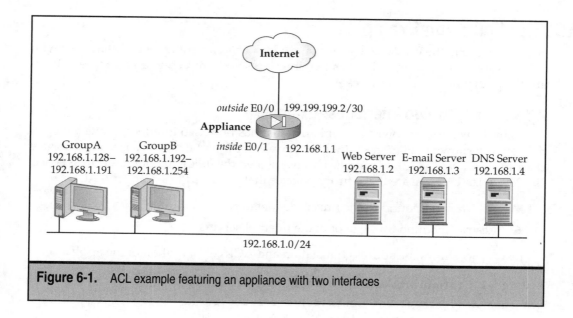

Figure 6-1. ACL example featuring an appliance with two interfaces

ACL—this is unnecessary because there is an implicit deny at the end of every ACL; however, I want to see the hit counts for each dropped packet, which this statement accomplishes. The last thing that was configured in this configuration is the activation of the PERMIT_IN ACL on the outside interface, which filters traffic as it comes inbound from the Internet.

Appliance with Two Interfaces: Example 2

In this example, I want to expand on the example in Figure 6-1 and Listing 6-1. Assume that you have two groups of internal devices, as is depicted in Figure 6-1: GroupA (192.168.1.128–192.168.1.191) and GroupB (192.168.1.192–192.168.1.254). Here are the filtering rules that will be set up for GroupA:

▼ Deny access to all devices on network 131.108.0.0/16.

■ Deny access to the following web servers: 210.210.210.0/24.

▲ Allow access to all other Internet sites.

Here are the filtering rules to set up for GroupB:

▼ Allow access to all devices in network 140.140.0.0/16.

■ Allow access to the following web servers: 210.210.210.5/32 and 211.211.211.3/32.

▲ Deny access to all other Internet networks.

I'll assume that the inbound policies remain the same; therefore I can build upon the example in Listing 6-1. Listing 6-2 shows the commands to accomplish the additional policy restrictions.

Listing 6-2. This example filters outbound traffic.

```
ciscoasa(config)# access-list PERMIT_OUT deny ip
                  192.168.1.128 255.255.255.192
                  131.108.0.0 255.255.0.0
ciscoasa(config)# access-list PERMIT_OUT deny tcp
                  192.168.1.128 255.255.255.192
                  210.210.210.0 255.255.255.0 eq 80
ciscoasa(config)# access-list PERMIT_OUT permit ip
                  192.168.1.128 255.255.255.192 any
ciscoasa(config)#
ciscoasa(config)# access-list PERMIT_OUT permit ip
                  192.168.1.192 255.255.255.192
                  140.140.0.0 255.255.0.0
ciscoasa(config)# access-list PERMIT_OUT permit tcp
                  192.168.1.192 255.255.255.192
                  host 210.210.210.5 eq 80
ciscoasa(config)# access-list PERMIT_OUT permit tcp
                  192.168.1.192 255.255.255.192
                  host 211.211.211.3 eq 80
ciscoasa(config)# access-list PERMIT_OUT deny ip
                  192.168.1.192 255.255.255.192 any
ciscoasa(config)#
ciscoasa(config)# access-group PERMIT_OUT in interface inside
```

In Listing 6-2, I've broken the ACL called PERMIT_OUT into two sections—one for GroupA and one for GroupB. Remember that ACLs are processed top-down, and the order of your statements does matter. One other item to point out is that the source IP addresses listed in the ACL statements are the addresses before translation, because the appliance processes ACLs before any address translation policies.

Take a look at the GroupA statements first. The very first entry in the ACL denies all IP traffic from 192.168.1.128/26 if it is destined for 131.108.0.0/16. The second statement denies all traffic from 192.168.1.128/26 if it is destined for TCP port 80 on any web server in network 210.210.210.0/24. The third statement allows any other IP traffic from 192.168.1.128/26 to go anywhere else on the Internet.

In the GroupB configuration (the second half of the ACL), the first **permit** statement (after the GroupA statements) allows any IP traffic from 192.168.1.192/26 to 140.140.0.0/16. The second and third statements allow all traffic from 192.168.1.192/26 to reach the two web servers: 210.210.210.5 and 211.211.211.3. The last statement in the ACL denies any other traffic from 192.168.1.192/26. The last part of the configuration in Listing 6-2 shows the application of the ACL (PERMIT_OUT) to the inside interface as traffic comes into this interface.

Appliance with Three Interfaces

To help you understand how flexible ACLs are, I'll show a more complicated example: you have an appliance that has three interfaces, and you want to control traffic between these interfaces, as shown in Figure 6-2.

Listing 6-3 shows just the address translation configuration on this appliance.

Listing 6-3. The basic configuration of the PIX with three interfaces

```
ciscoasa(config)# access-list NONAT deny ip 192.168.1.0 0.0.0.255
                    192.168.5.0 0.0.0.255
ciscoasa(config)# access-list NONAT permit ip 192.168.0.0 0.0.255.255
                    192.168.5.0 0.0.0.255
ciscoasa(config)# nat (inside) 0 access-list NONAT
ciscoasa(config)# nat (inside) 1 0.0.0.0 0.0.0.0
ciscoasa(config)# nat (dmz) 1 0.0.0.0 0.0.0.0
ciscoasa(config)# global (outside) 1 200.200.200.10-200.200.200.253
                    netmask 255.255.255.0
ciscoasa(config)# static (dmz,outside) 200.200.200.1 192.168.5.5
ciscoasa(config)# static (dmz,outside) 200.200.200.2 192.168.5.6
ciscoasa(config)# static (inside,dmz) 192.168.5.0 192.168.5.0
                    netmask 255.255.255.0
```

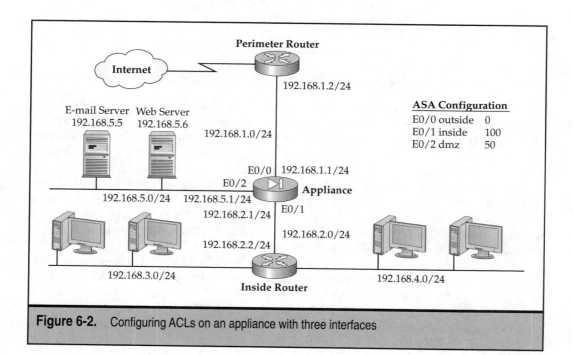

Figure 6-2. Configuring ACLs on an appliance with three interfaces

Explanation of the Basic Configuration   Before I go into the configuration of the ACLs, I will first discuss what the network in Figure 6-2 and the configuration shown in Listing 6-3 are doing. As you can see from this example, you are dealing with an appliance that has three interfaces—*outside, dmz,* and *inside.* The *outside* interface is connected to the perimeter router, which, in turn, is connected to the ISP. A default route points to the router's inside interface. The *dmz* interface has some user devices, as well as two servers: an e-mail server and a web server. The *inside* interface is connected to an inside router, which, in turn, is connected to two subnets: 192.168.3.0/24 and 192.168.4.0/24. I'll assume that two static routes are already configured for these two subnets.

Listing 6-3 has one `global` command and three `nat` commands. I'll look at these from the perspectives of both the *inside* interface and the *dmz* interface. If a device from the *inside* interface tries to access a device on the *dmz* interface, it will not have its address translated—this is based on the `static` and `access-list NONAT` commands in the configuration. With the exception of the 192.168.1.0/24 subnet, any other 192.168.0.0/16 subnet that sends traffic to 192.168.5.0/24 is exempted from translation. If a device on the *inside* interface tries to access the Internet, its address is translated to a public address: 200.200.200.10 through 200.200.200.253.

If a device on the *dmz* interface tries to access a device on the *outside* interface, its addresses will be translated to the same public address space as the devices on the *inside* interface. The exceptions to this translation are the two Internet servers. Two `static` commands perform the address translation statically. These `static` commands change the e-mail server source address from 192.168.5.5 to 200.200.200.1, and the web server address from 192.168.5.6 to 200.200.200.2. The reverse process takes place when Internet users send traffic to the servers: they use destination addresses of 200.200.200.1 and 200.200.200.2, which are translated to 192.168.5.5 and 192.168.5.6 respectively.

Configuring Filtering Policies   Now that I have discussed the basic configuration of the appliance shown in Listing 6-3, I'll talk about configuring some filtering policies for this appliance. As I mentioned in the previous section, the two servers located on the *dmz* interface need to access the internal network. Here's a list of all the policies that need to be implemented for users/servers on the DMZ segment:

▼   Users should not be allowed to access anything on 192.168.1.0/24.

■   Device 192.168.5.5 and 192.168.5.6 should be allowed access to 192.168.2.0/24.

▲   Devices on the DMZ segment should be allowed to access any destination on the Internet.

Here's a list of the policies that need to be implemented for internal users:

▼   Users should be allowed access to the e-mail and web server on 192.168.5.0/24, but not to other devices on this segment.

■   Users should not be allowed access to 192.168.1.0/24.

■   Devices on 192.168.2.0/24 and 192.168.3.0/24 should be allowed access to any destination on the Internet.

▲ Devices on 192.168.4.0/24 should only be allowed access to 131.108.0.0/16, 140.140.0.0.16, and 210.210.210.0/24 out on the Internet.

Here's a list of all of the policies that need to be implemented for external users trying to access resources in your network:

▼ Users should be allowed access specifically to the e-mail server.

■ Users should be allowed access specifically to the web server.

▲ All other types of access should be denied.

To enforce these policies, you need to create three ACLs and to apply them to the three respective interfaces of the appliances. Listing 6-4 shows the configuration of the policies for the DMZ.

Listing 6-4. The configuration for security policies for the DMZ segment

```
ciscoasa(config)# access-list DMZ deny ip any
                    192.168.1.0 255.255.255.0
ciscoasa(config)# access-list DMZ permit ip host 192.168.5.5
                    192.168.2.0 255.255.255.0
ciscoasa(config)# access-list DMZ permit ip host 192.168.5.6
                    192.168.2.0 255.255.255.0
ciscoasa(config)# access-list DMZ deny ip any
                    192.168.2.0 255.255.255.0
ciscoasa(config)# access-list DMZ deny ip any
                    192.168.3.0 255.255.255.0
ciscoasa(config)# access-list DMZ deny ip any
                    192.168.4.0 255.255.255.0
ciscoasa(config)# access-list DMZ permit ip
                    192.168.5.0 255.255.255.0  any
ciscoasa(config)# access-list DMZ deny ip any any
ciscoasa(config)#
ciscoasa(config)# access-group DMZ in interface dmz
```

Listing 6-4 is fairly straightforward. The first ACL statement denies access to the 192.168.1.0/24 segment. The second and third ACL statements allow all IP traffic from 192.168.5.5 and 192.168.5.6 to travel to 192.168.2.0/24—this is denied by default because of the security levels of the two interfaces involved. The fourth, fifth, and sixth ACLs deny any traffic from the DMZ headed to the three internal subnets. This prevents other devices on the *dmz* interface from accessing resources on 192.168.2.0/24 and also prevents any device on this segment from accessing the two networks on the internal router: 192.168.3.0/24 and 192.168.4.0/24. These statements are needed because of the statement that follows this (the seventh statement), which allows traffic from any device on 192.168.5.0/24 to go anywhere—you need to deny the specifics before you permit everything. The second to the last statement in the configuration drops all packets. I've added this so that I can see a hit count of all dropped packets—this greatly facilitates the troubleshooting of connectivity problems when the appliance is dropping packets based on its filter(s). The last command in this configuration is activation of the ACL on the *dmz* interface.

 TIP   Remember that you can use subnet masks to match on any range of addresses. For example, instead of having an individual ACL statement for denying access to each C class network, you can have one statement and the appropriate subnet mask value: `access-list DMZ deny ip any 192.168.2.0 255.255.254.0`. This statement would deny access to the 192.168.2.0/24 and 192.168.3.0/24 subnets.

Here is an interesting question: based on the ACL in Listing 6-4, if a device from 192.168.3.0/24 accesses the web server and the web server responds, is the return permitted through the firewall? One important point about these filtering policies is that the appliance will be performing two tasks to determine if the traffic is allowed or dropped. The appliance first looks into its conn table to see if there is a connection already there. In this situation, the device from 192.168.3.0/24 initiated the connection, and because the DMZ is a lower-security-level interface, and no ACL is configured on the inside interface, the appliance permits the connection and adds the temporary connection to its conn table. Thus, when the return comes back through the appliance, the appliance examines its conn table, sees the entry that was just created, and allows the response back to the 192.168.3.0/24 network. The only time the ACL is used is when there is no entry in the conn table—then the appliance examines the ACL to determine whether a hole in the firewall should be opened to allow the traffic. If you wanted to deny this traffic, you would need to create an ACL and apply it to the inside interface.

Look at the configuration for the filtering policies for the internal users, shown in Listing 6-5.

Listing 6-5. The configuration of security policies for the internal segments

```
ciscoasa(config)# access-list INTERNAL permit tcp any
                  host 192.168.5.5 eq 25
ciscoasa(config)# access-list INTERNAL permit tcp any
                  host 192.168.5.6 eq 80
ciscoasa(config)# access-list INTERNAL deny ip any
                  192.168.5.0 255.255.255.0
ciscoasa(config)# access-list INTERNAL deny ip any
                  192.168.1.0 255.255.255.0
ciscoasa(config)# access-list INTERNAL permit ip
                  192.168.2.0 255.255.255.0 any
ciscoasa(config)# access-list INTERNAL permit ip
                  192.168.3.0 255.255.255.0 any
```

```
ciscoasa(config)# access-list INTERNAL permit ip
                  192.168.4.0 255.255.255.0
                  131.108.0.0 255.255.0.0
ciscoasa(config)# access-list INTERNAL permit ip
                  192.168.4.0 255.255.255.0
                  210.210.210.0 255.255.255.0
ciscoasa(config)# access-list INTERNAL deny ip any any
ciscoasa(config)#
ciscoasa(config)# access-group INTERNAL in interface inside
```

The first and second commands allow all users on the *inside* interface to access the web and e-mail server on 192.168.5.0/24, and the third statement denies all other internal traffic to this network. The fourth statement denies all internal traffic destined to 192.168.1.0/24. The fifth and sixth statements allow 192.168.2.0/24 and 192.168.3.0/24 to access any other network. The seventh and eighth statements allow devices from 192.168.4.0/24 to 131.108.0.0/16 and 210.210.210.0/24. Any other traffic not matching any of the **permit** statements in this list will be dropped (including access to 192.168.1.0/24). The last statement in the configuration activates the ACL on the *inside* interface.

Listing 6-6 shows the configuration for the filtering policies that affect the external users (the ones on the Internet, or located on 192.168.1.0/24).

Listing 6-6. The configuration of security policies for external users

```
ciscoasa(config)# access-list EXTERNAL permit tcp any
                  200.200.200.1 eq 25
ciscoasa(config)# access-list EXTERNAL permit tcp any
                  200.200.200.2 eq 80
ciscoasa(config)# access-list EXTERNAL deny ip any any
ciscoasa(config)# access-group EXTERNAL in interface outside
```

Of the three ACLs, the one for the external users is the simplest. The first and second statements allow internal users access to the e-mail and web servers on 192.168.5.0/24—notice that the destination addresses are the public addresses, because this is what the appliance sees. The third statement drops all traffic, and the last statement activates the ACL on the *outside* interface.

As you can see from this example, the configuration of ACLs can be a very complex process. You should *always* test any changes you make to your ACLs to ensure that you are not inadvertently opening any unnecessary holes in your appliance.

TIP   I highly recommend you read a chapter in my Cisco Press book, *Cisco Router Firewall Security* (Cisco Press, 2004), on basic ACLs—you should be filtering many, many addresses, connections, applications, and protocols from untrusted sources. For example, the ACL in Listing 6-6 will have dozens or hundreds of statements before the specific **permit** statements for the DMZ servers, dropping all kinds of undesirable traffic that you don't want your servers to see.

OBJECT GROUPS

In version 6.2, Cisco introduced a feature that simplifies the management of ACLs, called *object groups*. Object groups allow you to create groups of related information that you apply to your filtering policies, thereby reducing the number of filtering commands that you have to enter. This eases your ACL implementation and maintenance, and also ensures that you apply the same policy to every device when a policy needs to be applied across a group of devices.

Object groups allow you to create the following object types:

▼ **Protocols**   TCP/IP protocols, like TCP, UDP, GRE, and others

■ **Services**   Types of TCP and UDP services (port names and/or numbers)

■ **ICMP**   Types of ICMP messages

▲ **Networks**   Network numbers and host addresses

Once you have created your various groups of objects, you can include them in your ACL commands to permit or deny packets based on matches in the object groups.

Advantages of Object Groups

I'll outline some situations where object groups do and do not make sense. For example, if you need to define a filtering policy that denies telnet traffic from 192.168.1.1 to 192.168.2.2, you could easily accomplish this with a single ACL command. However, if you have a list of ten clients trying to access three servers for both telnet and e-mail, the filtering configuration becomes very complex when using ACLs alone. Alternatively, you could use object groups to create a network group for the ten clients, a network group for the three servers, and a service group for telnet and e-mail, and then use these groupings in a *single* ACL command.

Another nice feature of object groups is that you can embed an object group within another object group; this is called *nesting*. As an example, you might have two network object groups, and want to create a filter that includes both groups. Originally, this would require two ACL statements. To solve this problem, you can create a third object group and can include the first two network object groups within this new group. Then create a single ACL statement that references the object group that includes the nesting of the two specific object groups.

Creating Object Groups

The general syntax for creating an object group is very simple, as shown here:

```
ciscoasa(config)# object-group type_of_object group_ID [protocol_name]
```

You can specify four different object types for the *type_of_object* parameter. Table 6-2 lists the valid object types.

Object Type	Explanation
`icmp-type`	Specifies a grouping of ICMP messages
`network`	Specifies a grouping of hosts and/or subnets/networks
`protocol`	Specifies a group of IP protocols, like IP, ICMP, TCP, UDP, or other IP protocols
`service`	Specifies a group of TCP or UDP applications, or both

Table 6-2.   Available Object Types for Object Groups

Once you have specified an object type, you need to follow it with an ID for the group—this is a name that groups together the various object types that you will create. If you specified **service** as the type of object, you need to tell the appliance which protocols to include in the list of applications, where your options are **tcp**, **udp**, or **tcp-udp** (for both).

Descriptions

When you execute the **object-group** command, you are taken into a Subconfiguration mode (commonly called a *subcommand mode*), where the appliance prompt changes to reflect the type of object group you are configuring. Some commands are specific to one type of object group, and others can be used in any type of object group. For example, the **description** command can be used in any object group. The **description** command allows you to enter up to 200 characters as a description for an object group. The syntax of the **description** command is

```
ciscoasa(config-protocol)# description descriptive_text
```

In this example, I'm in Protocol Subconfiguration mode; however, this command works in all Subconfiguration modes for object groups.

Nesting Object Groups

Another command common to all object groups is the **group-object** command. The **group-object** command allows you to add a previously created group to a group of the same type. This process is referred to as *nesting*. The syntax of this command is

```
ciscoasa(config-protocol)# group-object group_ID
```

To use the **group-object** command, you need to create an object group with your included services, protocols, networks, or ICMP message types. You can then create a new object group of the same type, and use the **group-object** command to reference your already created object group. You need to use the *group_ID* number of the previous group when using the **group-object** command.

NOTE   Nesting is restricted to including objects of the same type. For example, you could not include a network object group in a service object group, since the types are different.

Network Object Groups

You can create an object group to specify host addresses and/or network numbers that you use in your ACL commands. To create a network object group, use the commands shown here:

```
ciscoasa(config)# object-group network group_ID
ciscoasa(config-network)# network-object host host_address
ciscoasa(config-network)# network-object network_address subnet_mask
```

The first command, **object-group network**, creates a network object group and takes you into the Network Subconfiguration mode. The second and third commands allow you to specify the devices in the object group—the first is for a specific host, and the second is for a network or subnet number. You can use a combination of networks and hosts in an object group.

Protocol Object Groups

You can create an object group for IP protocols that you use in your ACL commands. To create a protocol object group, use these commands:

```
ciscoasa(config)# object-group protocol group_ID
ciscoasa(config-protocol)# protocol-object protocol_name_or_number
```

The first command, **object-group protocol**, creates a protocol object group and takes you into the Protocol Subconfiguration mode. The second command allows you to specify the TCP/IP protocol name or number in the object group. You can specify a protocol name, like **tcp**, **udp**, or **icmp**, or you can give the IP protocol number instead, like **6** for TCP or **17** for UDP.

Service Object Groups

You can create an object group for TCP and UDP applications that you use in your ACL commands. To create a service object group, use these commands:

```
ciscoasa(config)# object-group service group_ID {tcp | udp | tcp-udp}
ciscoasa(config-service)# port-object eq port_name_or_number
ciscoasa(config-service)# port-object range first_port last_port
```

The first command, **object-group service**, creates a services object group and takes you into the Service Subconfiguration mode. You need to specify either TCP, UDP, or both protocols—this refers to the types of ports within this object group. The second command, the one with the **eq** parameter, specifies a specific port number (or name) in the object group. You can also specify a **range** of port names and/or numbers—you need to use the keyword **range** followed by the first number in the list and the last number.

ICMP Object Groups

You can create an object group for ICMP messages that you use in your ACL commands. To create an ICMP object group, use these commands:

```
ciscoasa(config)# object-group icmp-type group_ID
ciscoasa(config-icmp-type)# icmp-object ICMP_message
```

The first command, **object-group icmp-type**, creates an ICMP message type object group and takes you into the ICMP Subconfiguration mode. The second command specifies the ICMP message type (like the ICMP name or number) in the object group.

Examining Your Object Groups

Once you have configured your object groups, you can display them with the **show object-group** command. The following is the syntax of this command:

```
ciscoasa# show run object-group {[protocol | network | service |
                    icmp-type] | [group_ID]}
```

If you only type in the **show run object-group** command and do not specify any parameters, the appliance will display all of your object groups. You can limit this by specifying a specific type of object group, or a specific object group. Here's an example of this command:

```
ciscoasa# show run object-group
object-group network web_servers
  description: This is a list of Web servers
  network-object host 200.200.200.2
  network-object host 200.200.200.9
object-group network trusted_web_servers
  network-object host 192.199.1.7
  network-object 201.201.201.0 255.255.255.0
  group-object web_servers
```

This example has two object groups. The first one is called web_servers and contains two hosts: 200.200.200.2 and 200.200.200.9. The second object group is called trusted_web_servers and contains one host (192.199.1.7), one network (201.201.201.0/24), and one embedded, or nested, object group called web_servers.

Deleting Object Groups

To remove all object groups on your appliance, use the **clear configure object-group** command. Optionally, you can remove all of the object groups of a specific type by adding the type to the end of the **clear configure object-group** command. The following is the syntax of this command:

```
ciscoasa(config)# clear configure object-group [protocol | network |
                    services | icmp-type]
```

If you only want to remove a specific object group, use this syntax:

```
ciscoasa(config)# no object-group group_ID
```

 NOTE   You cannot delete an object group that is currently being referenced by another appliance command, such as a nested reference or the `access-list` command.

Using Object Groups

To help you understand how object groups are used by ACL commands, I'll now examine how they are used in the `access-list` command. The following is the syntax for the two variations of using object groups, where the first is for ICMP and the second for anything else:

```
ciscoasa(config)# access-list ACL_ID {deny | permit} icmp
                    {source_address_and_mask |
                        object-group network_object_group_ID}
                    {destination_address_and_mask |
                        object-group network_object_group_ID}
                    [{icmp_type |
                        object-group icmp_type_object_group_ID}]
ciscoasa(config)# access-list ACL_ID {deny | permit}
                    {IP_protocol |
                        object-group protocol_object_group_ID}
                    {source_address_and_mask |
                        object-group network_object_group_ID}
                        [{operator source_port |
                            object-group service_object_group_ID}]
                    {destination_address_and_mask |
                        object-group network_object_group_ID}
                        [{operator destination_port |
                            object-group service_object_group_ID}]
```

As you can see, you can use object groups where they suit you. For example, you could list a network object group for the source address information, but list a specific host address for the destination—you can mix and match object groups and specific ACL protocol information based on your configuration needs.

Once you have referenced your object groups in ACL commands, you can see the commands you entered and the expansion of the object group references:

```
ciscoasa(config)# show access-list
<--output omitted-->
access-list ACLOUT; 9 elements
access-list ACLOUT line 1 extended permit tcp any
  object-group DMZ_HOSTS object-group DMZ_PORTS 0x959c5b39
```

```
access-list ACLOUT line 1 permit tcp any host 192.168.1.1
    eq 80 (hitcnt=0)
access-list ACLOUT line 1 permit tcp any host 192.168.1.1
    eq 443 (hitcnt=0)
access-list ACLOUT line 1 permit tcp any host 192.168.1.1
    eq 21 (hitcnt=0)
<--output omitted-->
```

Notice that in the preceding example, the first listing of line 1 is the command I typed in. The second, third, and fourth appearance of line 1 is the expansion of the object group references that the appliance created. Note that when you execute the **write memory** command, the expanded statements are not saved to flash: only the commands you physically entered are saved to flash.

NOTE   If you use the **show access-list** command to display your ACL configuration, the appliance will display the object group configuration and the ACLs that are created to enforce these policies. The appliance will replace the object references with the actual IP protocols, addresses/ network numbers, and services in real ACL commands.

Object Group Configuration Example

To help illustrate the use of object groups with ACLs, I'll use the network shown in Figure 6-3. In this example, I will allow outside access to the internal servers, but only for web and FTP access to the specific servers.

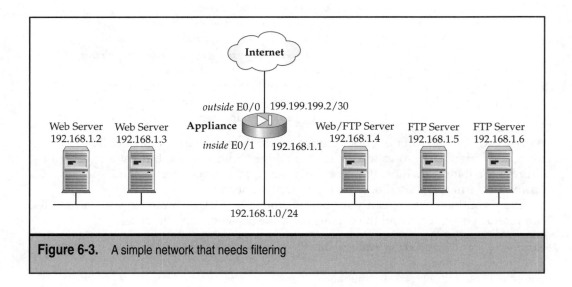

Figure 6-3.   A simple network that needs filtering

Listing 6-7 has the configuration, including address translation, for the appliance.

Listing 6-7. The configuration object groups with ACLs

```
ciscoasa(config)# global (outside) 1 200.200.200.1
                     netmask 255.255.255.0
ciscoasa(config)# nat (inside) 1 0.0.0.0 0.0.0.0
ciscoasa(config)# static (inside,outside) 200.200.200.2 192.168.1.2
ciscoasa(config)# static (inside,outside) 200.200.200.3 192.168.1.3
ciscoasa(config)# static (inside,outside) 200.200.200.4 192.168.1.4
ciscoasa(config)# static (inside,outside) 200.200.200.5 192.168.1.5
ciscoasa(config)# static (inside,outside) 200.200.200.6 192.168.1.6
ciscoasa(config)#
ciscoasa(config)# object-group network web_servers
ciscoasa(config-network)# network-object host 200.200.200.2
ciscoasa(config-network)# network-object host 200.200.200.3
ciscoasa(config-network)# network-object host 200.200.200.4
ciscoasa(config-network)# exit
ciscoasa(config)# object-group network ftp_servers
ciscoasa(config-network)# network-object host 200.200.200.4
ciscoasa(config-network)# network-object host 200.200.200.5
ciscoasa(config-network)# network-object host 200.200.200.6
ciscoasa(config-network)# exit
ciscoasa(config)# access-list PERMIT_IN permit tcp
                     any object-group web_servers eq 80
ciscoasa(config)# access-list PERMIT_IN permit tcp
                     any object-group ftp_servers eq 21
ciscoasa(config)# access-list PERMIT_IN deny ip any any
ciscoasa(config)# access-group PERMIT_IN in interface outside
```

Two network object groups are here, one for web servers and one for FTP servers. Two ACL statements allow access to these web servers and FTP servers, but deny everything else. If you didn't use object groups, you would need six statements for the servers and then the **deny ip any any** if you wanted to view the hit counts of all dropped packets.

ICMP FILTERING

Many people understand how IOS routers deal with ACLs and apply this knowledge to the appliances, expecting them to behave the same way as the routers; however, this is not correct. I'll deal with two issues concerning ICMP in this chapter: ICMP traffic passing *through* the appliance and ICMP traffic directed *at* the appliance.

ICMP Traffic Through the Appliances

As I mentioned in Chapter 5, ICMP traffic is *not* stateful by default on the appliances. ICMP messages by default are permitted when traveling from a higher-security-level interface to a lower-level one. However, ICMP traffic is denied by default from a lower-security-level interface to a higher-level one, even if it is an ICMP message response to a user's ICMP query.

Typically you should allow the following ICMP message types into your network to help provide some basic management and troubleshooting abilities for your internal devices: echo reply, source quench, unreachable, and time exceeded. For external devices to test connectivity to your network, you might also want to permit the ICMP echo message, but I would definitely restrict what ICMP messages Internet users can generate and what destinations in your network can receive these messages.

To allow ICMP traffic to travel from a lower-level to a higher-level interface, you need to enable one of two things:

▼ Stateful processing of ICMP

▲ An ACL entry or entries for the ICMP messages

NOTE If address translation is required, you also need a matching translation policy for the ICMP traffic.

Starting in version 7.0 of the OS, you can enable stateful processing of ICMP traffic using the Cisco Modular Policy Framework (MPF), discussed in Chapters 10 and 11. However, as you will see in these chapters, enabling stateful processing of ICMP traffic has its own set of problems. And stateful processing of ICMP is only new as of version 7.0 of the appliances; in prior versions, you had to use the second option: ACLs.

I'll use the network shown previously in Figure 6-3 to illustrate what an ACL to allow returning ICMP traffic to your users would look like. I'll build upon the Listing 6-7 example that I covered in the previous section. Here's an example of the configuration to allow returning ICMP traffic:

```
ciscoasa(config)# object-group icmp-type icmp_traffic
ciscoasa(config-icmp-type)# icmp-object echo-reply
ciscoasa(config-icmp-type)# icmp-object source-quench
ciscoasa(config-icmp-type)# icmp-object unreachable
ciscoasa(config-icmp-type)# icmp-object time-exceeded
ciscoasa(config-icmp-type)# exit
ciscoasa(config)# object-group network ALL_servers
ciscoasa(config-network)# group-object web_servers
ciscoasa(config-network)# group-object ftp_servers
ciscoasa(config-network)# exit
ciscoasa(config)# access-list PERMIT_IN permit tcp
                  any object-group web_servers eq 80
```

```
ciscoasa(config)# access-list PERMIT_IN permit tcp
                       any object-group ftp_servers eq 21
ciscoasa(config)# access-list PERMIT_IN permit icmp
                       any any object-group icmp_traffic
ciscoasa(config)# access-list PERMIT_IN permit icmp
                       any object-group ALL_servers echo
ciscoasa(config)# access-list PERMIT_IN deny ip any any
ciscoasa(config)# access-group PERMIT_IN in interface outside
```

I've created two additional object groups: one for allowing ICMP returning traffic, and one that puts the web and FTP servers into a network group so that you can specifically allow ICMP echo messages to them. The first two entries in the ACL are the same as in the previous section. The two ACL entries after those are new. The first one allows ICMP traffic from anywhere and to anywhere if it matches the ICMP message types in the ICMP `icmp_traffic` object group. The entry after this allows any echoes from anywhere if they are destined to the devices specified in the `ALL_servers` object group.

ICMP Traffic Directed at the Appliances

Until version 5.2.1 of the OS, any ICMP traffic destined for any of the interfaces of the appliances would be allowed, and the appliances would automatically respond. One unfortunate drawback of this process is that an attacker could use ICMP to learn that a security appliance existed, and possibly learn some basic information about it. Up until version 5.2.1, you could not disable this function and make the appliance invisible to other devices. Starting with version 5.2.1, you now have the option of making the appliance *stealthy*—you can control how the appliance itself will respond to ICMP messages, or prevent them altogether.

Until version 8.0, you only had one option for controlling this, ICMP filtering. Starting in version 8.0, you have a second option with the use of an ACL applied to the appliance itself (not an interface), referred to as *control plane filtering*. With the former, you can control what ICMP messages the appliance will process when directed to one of its interfaces; with the latter, you can control any type of traffic that the appliance will process when directed to itself. With the second option, you create your ACL and apply it to the appliance with the **access-group** command, using the **control-plane** parameter (instead of applying it to an interface).

NOTE The ACL option gives you more flexibility in controlling what the appliance will process on an interface; however, the ICMP filtering option is much easier to set up, especially if you're only interested in controlling the ICMP traffic directed at the appliance. As discussed in Chapter 3, and later in Chapter 27, you can control what devices can remotely access the appliance using the **telnet**, **ssh**, and **http** commands. (Remote access is denied by default and must be enabled for each interface, and the host or hosts must be allowed to access the appliance on the specified interfaces.)

Restricting ICMP Traffic Directed at the Appliance

The remainder of this section will focus on using the ICMP filtering feature. To control ICMP messages destined to an interface on the appliance, use the **icmp** command:

```
ciscoasa(config)# icmp {permit | deny}
                       src_IP_address src_subnet_mask
                       [ICMP_message_type] logical_if_name
```

You must specify a source IP address and a subnet mask. Unlike with an extended ACL, there is no destination IP address, because the security appliance, itself, is the destination.

You can qualify which ICMP messages are allowed or denied by entering a value for the *ICMP_message_type* parameter. The message types can be entered as either a name or a number. If you omit the message type, the appliance will assume that you want to allow or deny all ICMP messages. The last parameter is the name of the interface for which you want to restrict ICMP messages.

The appliance processes the **icmp** commands top-down for an interface. In other words, when the appliance receives an ICMP packet destined to one of its interfaces, it checks to see if any **icmp** commands are associated with the interface. If none is defined for the interface, the appliance processes the ICMP message and responds with the appropriate ICMP response. If an ICMP filter is on the interface, the appliance processes the **icmp** commands based on the order in which you entered them. If the appliance goes through the entire list and doesn't find a match, the appliance drops the ICMP message; this is like the implicit deny statement at the end of an ACL.

To remove a specific **icmp** command, preface it with the **no** parameter. To delete all the **icmp** commands that you have configured, use the **clear configure icmp** command.

> **NOTE**   As with ACLs, an implicit deny is at the end of the **icmp** command list. Therefore, if you use the **icmp** command, you should at least specify one **permit** statement per interface, unless you want your appliance to be completely invisible from ICMP traffic on the specified interface.

ICMP Filtering Example

Now let's take a look at an example on how to use the **icmp** command to restrict ICMP messages directed at an appliance interface. In this example, you want to be able to test connectivity from the appliance to other destinations on the Internet, and you want the appliance to process only certain ICMP packets to aid in connectivity testing—all other ICMP messages should be dropped. Here's an example of how to accomplish this:

```
ciscoasa(config)# icmp permit any conversion-error outside
ciscoasa(config)# icmp permit any echo-reply outside
ciscoasa(config)# icmp permit any parameter-problem outside
ciscoasa(config)# icmp permit any source-quench outside
ciscoasa(config)# icmp permit any time-exceeded outside
ciscoasa(config)# icmp permit any unreachable outside
ciscoasa(config)# icmp deny any outside
```

As you can see, only certain items are permitted—basically ICMP replies to ICMP messages that the appliance generates, as well as to any error messages.

CONNECTION TROUBLESHOOTING

To round off this chapter, I'll discuss connection troubleshooting features. A problem many administrators will face when setting up an appliance is troubleshooting connection problems where connections break when trying to go through the appliance. In other words, you're not sure why packets are not flowing through the appliance. Traditionally, you basically had to use these appliance commands to troubleshoot problems:

▼ `show access-list`   Look at the hit count on ACL statements.

■ `show xlate`   Look at the translations in the translation table.

■ `show conn`   Look at the connections in the state table.

▲ `debug`   Examine events and traffic.

The problem with using these commands is that it is not always easy to pinpoint the problem that causes a connection to break. Therefore, Cisco introduced two new features to help administrators with connection problems through the appliance:

▼ Packet tracer (version 7.2)

▲ Packet capture (version 6.2)

The remainder of this chapter will discuss these two features.

Packet Tracer Feature

Packet tracer is a one of the unique features from Cisco that I *wish* were available on every one of their products: routers, switches, and so on; unfortunately, it is only available on the appliances starting in version 7.2. Packet tracer allows you to create a "pretend" packet and have the appliance compare the pretend packet with the policies you've configured on your appliance to see what is causing the real packets to be dropped (or allowed). Packet tracer is supported from the CLI as well as ASDM.

Packet Tracer from the CLI

From the CLI, use the following commands to create a pretend packet and have the appliance compare the packet with its policies:

```
ciscoasa(config)# packet-tracer input src_if_name protocol
                  src_addr [src_port] dest_addr [dest_port]
                  [detailed] [xml]
ciscoasa(config)# packet-tracer input src_if_name icmp
                  src_addr ICMP_message ICMP_code
                  ICMP_identifier dest_addr [detailed] [xml]
```

The *src_if_name* parameter specifies the logical source interface for the packet trace—the interface the packet is received on. The *protocol* parameter specifies the protocol type for the packet trace; supported protocols include **icmp**, **rawip**, **tcp**, or **udp**. (The **rawip** parameter should be used for protocols other than TCP, UDP, and ICMP.) Following this is the source IP address. The type of protocol will affect the information that follows. For TCP or UDP, you enter a source port number; for ICMP, you need to enter an ICMP message type, an ICMP message code, and an ICMP identifier (sequence number). After this information is the destination IP address; and if the protocol is TCP or UDP, the destination port number as well. The **detailed** parameter provides detailed information in the packet trace, and the **xml** parameter displays the trace output in an XML format.

NOTE　For ICMP types and codes, examine RFC 792 at http://www.ietf.org/rfc/rfc0792.txt.

Packet Trace Example

Let's look at an example of using packet trace. In this example, I'll assume that an external user (192.168.1.11) is trying to access an internal FTP server with a global address of 192.168.2.11. Here's the syntax to do the packet trace:

```
bciscoasa# packet-tracer input outside tcp 192.168.1.11 1025
                    192.168.2.11 21 detail
Phase: 1
Type: FLOW-LOOKUP
Subtype:
Result: ALLOW
Config:
Additional Information:
Found no matching flow, creating a new flow

Phase: 2
Type: UN-NAT
Subtype: static
Result: ALLOW
Config:
static (inside,outside) 192.168.2.11 10.0.2.11 netmask 255.255.255.255
nat-control
  match ip inside host 10.0.2.11 outside any
    static translation to 192.168.2.11
    translate_hits = 7, untranslate_hits = 2
Additional Information:
NAT divert to egress interface inside
Untranslate 192.168.2.11/0 to 10.0.2.11/0 using netmask 255.255.255.255
```

```
Phase: 3
Type: ACCESS-LIST
Subtype: log
Result: DROP
Config:
access-group ACLOUT in interface outside
access-list ACLOUT extended deny ip any any
Additional Information:
 Forward Flow based lookup yields rule:
 in id=0x3fde388, priority=12, domain=permit, deny=true
        hits=0, user_data=0x3fde348, cs_id=0x0, flags=0x0, protocol=0
        src ip=0.0.0.0, mask=0.0.0.0, port=0
        dst ip=0.0.0.0, mask=0.0.0.0, port=0

Result:
input-interface: outside
input-status: up
input-line-status: up
output-interface: inside
output-status: up
output-line-status: up
Action: drop
Drop-reason: (acl-drop) Flow is denied by configured rule
```

NOTE For TCP and UDP connections, typically the source port number you enter is something above 1,023. Also, the output you see in the preceding example will differ based on the protocol you are testing, whether the packet matches an entry in the conn table, whether the address translation is enabled, whether the connection is outbound versus inbound and if ACLs are used, and so on.

In phase 1, the appliance sees if an entry for this connection is already in the state table: in this example, no entry is in the conn table, so the appliance assumes it's a new connection. In phase 2, the appliance is doing an xlate lookup to find the local address (the real address) of the destination. Notice that **nat-control** is enabled, and the **stat-ic** command the packet matches on. In phase 3, the packet is compared with the ACL on the outside interface—notice that the ACL is called "ACLOUT" and that the pretend packet matched on the **deny ip any any** statement. In the last part, the result, a summary is displayed about the policy issue: what the action was for the packet (drop) and why the action was taken (match on a configured ACL rule).

NOTE You can find another good example of packet tracing on this web site: http://www .networkblueprints.com/troubleshooting/cisco-asa-troubleshooting-tool-kit.

Packet Capture Feature

The packet capture feature was added in version 6.2 and allows you to capture *real* packets on interfaces. Packet capture supports multiple, simultaneous capture processes; however, packet capture can affect the performance of the appliance, so disable it when you are finished troubleshooting your problem. When capturing packets, you can control what is captured by using various filters, like an ACL. Once packets are captured, you can view them from the CLI or save them to a file in a libpcap format file, which can then be viewed by a protocol analyzer like WireShark (which is a free protocol analyzer).

Creating a Packet Capture Process

To configure a packet capture process, use the following syntax, where Table 6-3 covers the parameters in the **capture** command:

```
ciscoasa# capture capture_name [type {asp-drop [drop_code] |
                    raw-data | isakmp | webvpn user webvpn_user
                    [url url]}] [access-list ACL_ID] [buffer buffer_size]
                    [ethernet-type type] [interface logical_if_name]
                    [packet-length bytes] [circular-buffer]
                    [trace trace_count]
```

Parameter	Explanation
capture_name	Specifies the name of the packet capture. You can use the same name on multiple **capture** commands to capture multiple types of traffic in one captured process.
type	Optionally lets you specify the type of data captured.
asp-drop	Optionally captures packets dropped by the accelerated security path. The *drop_code* specifies the type of traffic that is dropped by the accelerated security path. Use the **show asp drop frame** command for a list of drop codes. Note that if you do not enter a drop code, then all dropped packets are captured.
raw-data	Optionally captures inbound and outbound packets on one or more interfaces—this is the default setting.
isakmp	Optionally captures IPSec ISAKMP traffic.
webvpn	Optionally captures WebVPN data for a specific WebVPN connection.

Table 6-3. Packet Capture Parameters

Parameter	Explanation
`url`	Optionally specifies a URL prefix to match for data capture—typically this is done for WebVPN users. Use this kind of syntax for the URL: `http://`*server/path* or `https://`*server/path* to capture traffic to a web server.
`access-list`	Optionally captures traffic that matches only on **permit** statements in the ACL.
`buffer`	Optionally defines the buffer size used to store the packet in bytes; once the byte buffer is full, the packet capture process stops.
`ethernet-type`	Optionally selects an Ethernet type to capture, where the default is IP packets. An exception occurs, however, with the 802.1Q or VLAN type. The 802.1Q tag is automatically skipped, and the inner Ethernet type is used for matching.
`interface`	Optionally defines the logical name of the interface on which to enable packet capture. Note that you must configure an interface for any packets to be captured; however, you can configure multiple interfaces using multiple **capture** commands with the same *capture_name*. If you want to capture packets on the data plane of an ASA, use the **interface** keyword with **asa_dataplane** as the name of the interface. (This is used to capture packets from the optional IPS and CSC cards in the ASA.)
`packet-length`	Optionally sets the maximum number of bytes of each packet to store in the capture buffer.
`circular-buffer`	Optionally overwrites the buffer, starting from the beginning, when the packet capture buffer is full.
`trace`	Optionally captures packet trace information and the number of packets to capture. This is used with an ACL to insert trace packets into the data path when troubleshooting connection problems with the **packet-tracer** command.

Table 6-3. Packet Capture Parameters (*Continued*)

Here's an example that illustrates the use of packet capturing:

```
ciscoasa# access-list httpACL permit tcp any host 192.168.1.10 eq 80
ciscoasa# capture httpcap access-list httpACL packet-length 250
              interface outside
```

In the preceding example, the first 250 bytes of packets sent to 192.168.1.10, on TCP port 80, are captured as they enter the outside interface.

TIP To make it easier to troubleshoot connections, associate an ACL to the packet capture process to limit the information you're capturing to the specific problem a connection is having.

Viewing Captured Packets

To view the packets in a packet capture file, use the **show capture** command:

```
ciscoasa# show capture [capture_name] [access-list ACL_ID]
                       [count number] [decode] [detail] [dump]
                  [packet-number number]
```

The *capture_name* parameter specifies the name of the packet capture that you want to view. The **access-list** parameter filters out the packet information in the packet capture based on the **permit** statements in the ACL. The **count** parameter displays the first *x* number of packets specified in the capture. The **decode** parameter is used for VPN tunnels terminated on the appliance: ISAKMP data flowing through that interface will be captured after decryption and shown with more information after decoding the fields. The **detail** parameter displays additional protocol information for each packet. The **dump** parameter displays a hexadecimal dump of the packets. The **packet-number** parameter starts displaying the packets at the specified packet number.

NOTE Without any parameters, only your current capture configuration is shown—not the actual captured packets.

Here is an example that displays the capture processes enabled on the appliance:

```
ciscoasa# show capture
capture arp ethernet-type arp interface dmz
```

Here's an example that displays packets captured by the capture process called *arp*:

```
ciscoasa# show capture arp
2 packets captured
19:12:23.478429 arp who-has 172.16.1.2 tell 172.16.1.1
19:12:26.784294 arp who-has 172.16.1.2 tell 172.16.1.1
2 packets shown
```

In this example, the packets captured are two ARP packets.

NOTE Visit this web site for a good overview and example of packet capturing on the appliances: http://security-planet.de/2005/07/26/cisco-pix-capturing-traffic/.

Copying Captured Packets

If you want to save the packets you've captured for a capture process, use the **copy cap-ture** command to copy the information to a file in flash or to an external server:

```
ciscoasa# copy [/noconfirm] [/pcap] capture:capture_name URL
```

The **noconfirm** parameter copies the file without a confirmation prompt. The **pcap** parameter copies the packet capture as raw data for a protocol analyzer. The *capture_name* parameter specifies the capture process that you wish to copy. The *URL* parameter specifies the location you wish to copy the packets to. You need to include the destination type (**disk0** or **flash, disk1, ftp, http, https,** or **tftp**), possibly the directory, and the filename the packets will be stored in.

Managing Packet Capturing

To keep a packet capture process, but to clear the packets in the appliance buffer, use the **clear capture** command:

```
ciscoasa# clear capture capture_name
```

Once you are done with a packet capture process, you should remove it with the following command:

```
ciscoasa# no capture capture_name [access-list ACL_ID]
                [circular-buffer] [interface logical_if_name]
```

TIP Remember that packet capturing is very CPU- and memory-intensive for the appliances, so disable the packet capturing process(es) when you have completed your troubleshooting. However, the packet tracer tool requires few resources. Typically I'll use packet tracer first to get an idea as to what a problem is; if this isn't helpful, then I'll use the packet capture tool.

CHAPTER 7

Web Content

In Chapter 6, I talked about some of the advanced filtering abilities of the appliances, including ACLs. One limitation of ACLs is that they can only filter on the network and transport layers of the OSI Reference Model—they cannot filter on content information (information found in the payload). For instance, one type of attack that hackers like to use is to create malicious Java or ActiveX applets that users will download and run. This traffic is downloaded using HTTP port 80. The problem with ACLs is that an ACL can either permit or deny port TCP 80 traffic, which includes the applets embedded within the connection—ACLs cannot filter just the applets themselves.

Likewise, ACLs have issues when dealing with the filtering of web content. Imagine that you have a security policy that prohibits the downloading of pornographic material. Because web information changes all the time, you would have to continually find these sites and add them to your ACL configuration, which is an unmanageable process.

On top of the security problems, an issue with downloading web content is that the process can be bandwidth-intensive, especially if multiple users are going to the same sites and downloading the same content.

The appliances have three solutions to these problems. The first solution is the ability of the appliances to filter on Java and ActiveX scripts that are embedded in HTTP connections. The second solution for filtering content allows the appliances to work with third-party content filtering software to filter HTTP and FTP traffic. The third solution is the included support for the Web Cache Communications Protocol (WCCP), which allows the appliances to redirect web requests to an external web cache server to download the content.

The topics included in this chapter are as follows:

▼   Java and ActiveX filtering

■   Web content filtering

▲   Web caching

JAVA AND ACTIVEX FILTERING

Most web sites today use Java applets and ActiveX scripts to add functionality to their web services. These mechanisms can take the form of animated pictures, dynamic content, multimedia presentations, and many other types of web effects. Although these tools provide many advantages to web developers, in the wrong hands they can be used to gather information about a computer, or to damage the contents on a computer.

Java and ActiveX Issues

One solution to this problem is to use the filtering abilities built into a user's web browser. Almost every web browser includes these filtering abilities, like current versions of Mozilla Firefox, Netscape Navigator and Communicator, and Microsoft Internet Explorer. This type of filtering typically has two problems, however. First, you must ensure that every user's desktop configuration is the same and stays the same, which means that you'll have to place some type of software on each user's PC to lock down these settings and prohibit the user from changing them. Second, the configuration settings for filtering in most browsers are not a simple matter. For example, I use Firefox, and their controls are fairly simple, but not for the uneducated Java user; Internet Explorer 6.0 has almost a dozen different settings for Java and ActiveX. For the novice and intermediate user, an incorrect web browser setting might open a user's desktop to attack by Java and ActiveX.

Java and ActiveX Filtering Solutions

The appliances can filter on both embedded Java applets and ActiveX scripts without any additional software or hardware components. Basically the appliances look for embedded HTML <object> commands and replace them with comments. Some of these <object> commands include <APPLET>, <OBJECT>, and <OBJECT CLASSID>.

This filtering feature allows you to prevent the downloading of malicious applets and scripts to your users' desktops while still allowing users to download web content. One advantage of using the appliances is that they provide a central point for your filtering policies. However, the filtering can only be done based on a web server's IP address. Therefore, you do not have some of the filtering abilities that a browser or content filtering engine has, but you can use the appliance in combination with other tools, like secure browser settings and a content filtering engine, to provide the maximum security for your network. The following two sections discuss how to filter Java applets and ActiveX scripts on your appliances.

SECURITY ALERT!   When the appliances are filtering Java applets and ActiveX scripts, if the HTML object tags are split across multiple IP packets, the appliances will be unable to filter the applet or script.

Configuring Java Filters

You basically have only one method of filtering Java applets directly on your appliance: the **filter java** command. The syntax of this command is shown here:

```
ciscoasa(config)# filter java port_name_or_#[-port_name_or_#]
                          internal_IP_address subnet_mask
                          external_IP_address subnet_mask
```

One thing that you'll notice is that you do not need to activate the filter on an interface, as in the case of ACLs. The **filter java** command is automatically applied to traffic entering any interface on the appliance. The first parameter you enter is the port name or number that web traffic runs on; obviously one port you would include would be 80. You can enter a range of ports, or if they are noncontiguous, you can enter them with separate **filter java** commands.

Following the port information are two IP addresses and subnet masks. Notice that this is not the syntax an ACL uses, which specifies a source and destination address. The format of addressing in the `filter java` command has you configure the IP addressing information connected to the higher-security-level interface first, and then you configure the IP addressing information of the lower interface.

For example, if you wanted to filter all Java applets for HTTP connections, you would use the following syntax:

```
ciscoasa(config)# filter java 80 0.0.0.0 0.0.0.0 0.0.0.0 0.0.0.0
                          -or-
ciscoasa(config)# filter java http 0 0 0 0
```

NOTE Remember that you can abbreviate 0.0.0.0 as a single 0.

If you wanted to filter Java applets for the 192.1.1.0/24 external network for all your internal users, the configuration would look like this:

```
ciscoasa(config)# filter java 80 0 0 192.1.1.0 255.255.255.0
```

Configuring ActiveX Filters

In addition to being able to filter Java applets, you can also filter ActiveX scripts using the `filter activex` command. Here is the syntax of this command:

```
ciscoasa(config)# filter activex port_name_or_#[-port_name_or_#]
                          internal_IP_address subnet_mask
                          external_IP_address subnet_mask
```

The syntax of the `filter activex` command is basically the same as the `filter java` command and behaves in the same manner. If you want to filter all ActiveX scripts, use this example:

```
ciscoasa(config)# filter activex 80 0 0 0 0
                          -or-
ciscoasa(config)# filter activex http 0 0 0 0
```

As you can see, filtering ActiveX scripts is no different from filtering Java applets—both are easy to set up.

WEB CONTENT FILTERING

One major concern of many companies connected to the Internet is the type of information that their employees are downloading to their desktops. Quite a few studies have been done, and, on average, 30–40 percent of a company's Internet traffic is nonbusiness in nature (I'm actually surprised that the statistic isn't higher). In some instances, the information that employees download can be offensive to other employees. This information can range from pornography to political and religious content. A lot of the downloaded content like stock quotes and audio and video streaming is inoffensive, but can use up expensive bandwidth.

The appliances have limited and nonscalable abilities when filtering web content (I discuss this in Chapter 12). A much more scalable solution is to have the appliances work with third-party products to provide comprehensive web filtering features. The following sections cover how the appliances and web filtering products interact, the third-party web filtering products that the appliances support, and web filtering configuration on the appliances.

Web Filtering Process

To implement web content filtering, sometimes referred to as *web filtering,* two components are involved:

▼   Policies must be defined that specify what is or isn't allowed by users.

▲   The policies must be enforced.

Two methods that perform these processes are commonly deployed in networks:

▼   Application proxy

▲   Modified proxy

The following two sections will discuss these approaches.

Application Proxy

With an application proxy, both components—definition and enforcement of policies— are performed on one server. Either users' web browsers are configured to point to the proxy, or their traffic is redirected to the proxy.

With an application proxy, the following steps occur when a user wants to download web content:

1.   The user opens a web page.

2.   All connections are redirected to the application proxy server, which might require the user to authenticate before external access is allowed.

3.   The application proxy examines the connection(s) attempt and compares it with the list of configured policies.

4.   If the connection is not allowed, the user is typically shown a web page about the policy violation.

5.   If the connection is allowed, the proxy opens the necessary connections to download the content. The content is then passed back across the user's original connections and is displayed in the user's web browser.

Application proxies work quite well in small environments that have a small number of simultaneous web requests. Remember that downloading each element on a web page, like graphics, applets, and so on, requires a separate connection for each element. Therefore, the more pages that multiple users request, the less throughput occurs through the proxy—it must handle twice the number of connections: from the user to the proxy, and from the proxy to the external web servers. This process can quickly become a bottleneck on the proxy, being CPU- and memory-intensive. And if the proxy is caching information, the process can become disk-intensive.

Modified Proxy

A modified proxy splits out the two policy components: an external server has the list of policies, and a network device implements the policies as web traffic flows through it. The appliances support the modified proxy approach: to filter web content, the appliances must interoperate with an external web content server.

Figure 7-1 shows the actual interaction between the users, the appliance, the policy server, and the external web server. In this example, a user sends an HTML request to an external web server (step 1). The appliance then does two things in step 2:

▼   Forwards the HTML request (the URL information only) to the web content policy server

▲   Forwards the HTML request to the actual web server

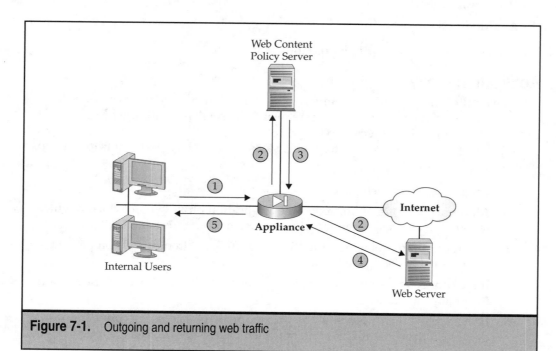

Figure 7-1.   Outgoing and returning web traffic

In step 3, the web content policy server compares the URL request with its internal policies and sends back the action to the appliance. The appliance then enforces the action on the *returning* traffic (step 4). If the web content policy server says to deny the traffic, the appliance drops the returning web traffic. If, however, the web content policy server says to permit the traffic, the appliance forwards the traffic to the internal user (step 5).

As you can see from this explanation, the appliance doesn't actually filter the *outbound* connection. This process basically allows enough time for the web content policy server to send back an action to the appliance before the external web server replies to the user, thereby introducing little if any delay in the user's traffic stream. Unlike with an application proxy, the appliances are not proxying the connections: they're allowing them outbound and enforcing the policies on the returning traffic. This is much more CPU- and memory-friendly than using a true application proxy. However, if the web content policy server is handling thousands of requests, your users may experience delay in their traffic stream. Cisco does support a limited form of load balancing to split policy lookups across multiple web content policy servers.

TIP   Because the policies are defined externally to the appliance, I recommend that the web content policy server be located close to the appliance. For two reasons, I commonly place the policy server either in a public, or more commonly, a semiprivate, DMZ that is directly connected to the appliance. First, it minimizes delay in getting a policy response from the server, which means the appliance shouldn't have to buffer connection replies from external web servers. Second, companies commonly purchase a subscription with the web content policy server so that they can get weekly updates about new sites and their classification, like an updated list of pornographic sites, so that administrators don't have to manually update or define these classifications themselves.

URL Filtering Server

Web content filtering on the appliances allows you to filter web information for users accessing web resources on the outside of your network. Cisco supports two web content policy/filtering products: Websense and Secure Computing's SmartFilter (formerly N2H2's Sentian product). The products have the capability of interacting with an external device, like the appliances, in a modified proxy role, or can function as application proxies. These products support policies for HTTP, HTTPS, and FTP URLs.

You must configure two things on the appliance to interact with the web content filtering server:

▼   Identify the web content filtering server.

▲   Specify the traffic to be filtered.

You can complete other configuration tasks optionally. The following sections cover the web content filtering commands of the appliances.

Server Identification

The first thing that you need to configure is the identity of the web content filtering server that the appliance will use. This is accomplished with the **url-server** command. Your product type will determine the parameters available.

Here is the syntax to configure the appliance interaction with a Websense server:

```
ciscoasa(config)# url-server [logical_if_name] [vendor websense]
                   host server_IP_address [timeout seconds]
                   [protocol {tcp | udp}] [connections #_of_conns]
                   [version {1 | 4}]
```

If you omit the name of the interface, it defaults to *inside.* If you omit the **vendor** parameter, it defaults to Websense. The timeout value defaults to 5 seconds—if the appliance doesn't get a reply within 5 seconds from the Websense server, it will contact a second Websense server, if you have configured one. You might want to increase this timeout period if the Websense server is located at a remote site from the appliance. The default protocol is TCP, but can be configured for UDP if you are running version 4 of Websense. The default version is 1. The **connections** parameter allows you to limit the number of lookups to a server, so that you can split lookups across multiple servers.

If you are connecting to a SmartFilter server, the syntax is as follows:

```
ciscoasa(config)# url-server [interface_name] vendor smartfilter
                   host server_IP_address [port port_number]
                   [timeout seconds] [protocol {tcp | udp}]
                   [connections #_of_conns]
```

The configuration of SmartFilter is very similar to that of Websense. One difference is that you can specify a port number for the TCP or UDP connection. The default port number is 4005.

NOTE You can configure multiple policy servers by executing the **url-server** command multiple times (up to 16 servers). However, you can only use Websense *or* SmartFilter—you cannot use both of these on the same appliance.

Traffic Filtering Policies

Once you have identified the web content policy server or servers that your appliance will use, you must now identify which content traffic (URLs) the appliance will forward to the policy servers. The command to identify the traffic to be filtered is the **filter** command. The command has three variations, depending on the protocol you want to process:

▼ Clear-text URLs

■ FTP URLs

▲ HTTPS URLs

These are discussed in the following sections.

Clear-Text URL Processing   With the `filter url` command, you are defining the clear-text HTTP URLs you want to forward to an external web content policy server:

```
ciscoasa(config)# filter url {port_#[-port_#] | except}
                    internal_IP_addr subnet_mask
                    external_IP_addr subnet_mask
                    [allow] [proxy-block] [longurl-truncate |
                    longurl-deny] [cgi-truncate]
```

You must specify either the name (`http`) or the port number(s) to have the appliance examine and copy them to the external server. The default port number for web traffic is 80. I recommend that you put in all common port numbers, including 8080, used by web servers. Next you enter your internal and external IP addresses and subnet masks that you want to perform filtering on. To examine all clear-text web traffic, enter `0.0.0.0` `0.0.0.0` `0.0.0.0` `0.0.0.0`, or 0 0 0 0.

> **NOTE**   Remember that you are not entering a source and destination address in the `filter url` command, but an internal and external address, where the internal address can represent users and/or web servers, and *likewise* for external addresses.

Some optional parameters are at the end of the `filter url` command. The `allow` parameter affects how the appliance will react if it doesn't get a reply from the policy server. By default, if the appliance doesn't get a reply, it denies the user access to the external web server. You can override this by specifying the `allow` parameter. When you configure this parameter, the appliance waits for a response from the web content policy server—if it doesn't get a reply, the appliance allows the web traffic. This allows your users to still access the Internet in the event that the web content policy server is down or unreachable. The `proxy-block` parameter causes the appliance to drop all web requests to proxy servers.

One problem that the PIX had in version 6.1 and earlier dealt with long URL names. If a URL was 1,160 characters or longer, the PIX wouldn't process it—in effect, allowing the connection. This sounds like it wouldn't be a problem, because most URLs are fewer than 80 characters. However, many CGI-BIN scripts and backend programs have information embedded in a URL passed to them—this information, in certain cases, might be very long, which creates a problem with the PIX. As of version 6.2, this limit has been increased to 4,000 characters. However, you might not want to send all of these extra characters to the content policy server, or you might even want to deny users access to these long URLs. The `longurl-truncate` parameter tells the appliance to send a portion of the URL to the content policy server for evaluation. The `longurl-deny` command has the appliance deny the user's web connection if the URL is longer than the maximum defined. The `cgi-truncate` parameter behaves the same as the `longurl-truncate` parameter with the exception that this parameter only applies to CGI-BIN script requests embedded in a URL.

FTP URL Processing   With the `filter ftp` command, you are defining the FTP URLs you want to forward to an external content policy server:

```
ciscoasa(config)# filter ftp {[port_#[-port+#] | except}
                    internal_IP_addr subnet_mask
                    external_IP_addr subnet_mask
                    [allow] [interact-block]
```

The syntax of this command is similar to the `filter url` command. With FTP filtering, the `interact-block` parameter prevents users from using an interactive FTP client to connect to an FTP server.

HTTPS URL Processing   For filtering of HTTP URLs using SSL, use the following command:

```
ciscoasa(config)# filter https {[port_#[-port+#] | except}
                    internal_IP_addr subnet_mask
                    external_IP_addr subnet_mask [allow]
```

The syntax of this command is similar to the `filter url` command.

Policy Exceptions   You can override your filtering policies by using the following command:

```
ciscoasa(config)# filter {url | ftp | https} except
                    internal_IP_address subnet_mask
                    external_IP_address external_subnet_mask
```

Instead of a port number or name as in the previous example, you can use the `except` parameter. This creates an exception to your appliance filtering function. For instance, you might want to filter on all traffic except your public web server. In this case, you would specify something like this:

```
ciscoasa(config)# filter url 80 0 0 0 0
ciscoasa(config)# filter url except 192.168.1.1 255.255.255.255 0 0
ciscoasa(config)# filter url except 0 0 192.168.1.1 255.255.255.255
```

In this example, all web traffic will be filtered by the web content filtering server with the exception of 192.168.1.1. Notice that I have two `filter url except` commands, since I want to make exceptions to the public server for inbound *and* outbound connections.

Caching URL Information

One of the issues of using a web content policy server, as I pointed out earlier, is that it can introduce a delay in the user's web traffic stream as the appliance and policy server interact to enforce your web access policies. You can have the appliance cache the information received by a filtering server so that the next time a user accesses the same server, the appliance can use its local cache to perform the filtering policy instead of forwarding the request to the policy server. The advantage of this approach is that your users' throughput will increase. The downside of this approach is that the web content policy server is not seeing the traffic and therefore cannot log it. If you are gathering information about a user's web habits, then you would not be able to log all of a user's connection information. Plus, you are taking away RAM resources on the appliance from other processes.

Caching, by default, is disabled on the appliance and is only supported for Websense servers. To enable it, use the following command:

```
ciscoasa(config)# url-cache {dst | src_dst} size cache_size
```

You have two choices on how to cache information. If you specify the **dst** parameter, the appliance caches information based only on the destination web server address—you should only choose this option if *all* your internal users have the same access policies. If your internal users have different access policies, specify the **src_dst** parameter—this causes the appliance to cache both the source and destination addresses. The cache size can range from 1KB to 128KB.

Buffering Web Server Replies to Users

As I mentioned at the beginning of this section, when an appliance receives a user's web request, it simultaneously copies the URL to the content policy server as well as forwarding the connection to the external web server. One problem that might occur is that the external web server reply to the user's request might come back to the appliance *before* the content policy server action that the appliance should take. If this should occur, the appliance automatically would drop the user's web request.

To prevent this from happening, you can buffer the external web server reply or replies until the appliance receives the action from the policy server. By default, this feature is disabled. To enable it, use the following command:

```
ciscoasa(config)# url-block block block_buffer_limit
```

This command limits the number of memory blocks URLs can use. The limit is specified in number of blocks, which can be from 1 to 128 blocks. A block is 1,550 bytes in size.

To configure the amount of memory available for buffering long or pending URLs, use the following command:

```
ciscoasa(config)# url-block url-mempool memory_size
```

The memory can be specified as a value from 2KB to 10,240KB.

As I mentioned earlier, in version 6.2 you can increase the size of URLs forwarded to the policy servers before they are truncated—however, the default is 1,159 characters. To increase the size for URLs, use the following command:

```
ciscoasa(config)# url-block url-size URL_characters
```

You can enter a value of up to 4,096 characters.

URL Filtering Verification

Once you have set up your web content filtering configuration, you can use various **show** commands to verify your configuration. To view the web content filtering servers that you have configured with the **url-server** command, use the **show run url-server** command:

```
ciscoasa# show run url-server
url-server (outside) vendor smartfilter host 10.1.1.5 port 4005
     timeout 5 protocol TCP connections 1500
url-server (outside) vendor smartfilter host 10.1.2.5 port 4005
     timeout 5 protocol TCP
```

In this example, two SmartFilter filtering servers have been configured on this appliance. You can see server connection statistics with the following command:

```
ciscoasa(config)# show url-server stats
Global Statistics:
------------------
URLs total/allowed/denied 993487/156548/837839
URLs allowed by cache/server 70843/85165
URLs denied by cache/server 801920/36819
HTTPSs total/allowed/denied 994387/156548/837839
HTTPs allowed by cache/server 70843/81565
HTTPs denied by cache/server 801920/36819
FTPs total/allowed/denied 994387/155648/838739
FTPs allowed by cache/server 70483/85165
FTPs denied by cache/server 801920/36819
Requests dropped 28715
Server timeouts/retries 567/1350
Processed rate average 60s/300s 1524/1344 requests/second
Denied rate average 60s/300s 35648/33022 requests/second
Dropped rate average 60s/300s 156/189 requests/second
URL Server Statistics:
----------------------
192.168.2.1 UP
Vendor websense
Port 17035
Requests total/allowed/denied 365412/254595/110547
Server timeouts/retries 567/1350
Responses received 365952
Response time average 60s/300s 2/1 seconds/request
192.168.2.2 DOWN
Vendor websense
Port 17035
```

```
Requests total/allowed/denied 0/0/0
Server timeouts/retries 0/0
Responses received 0
Response time average 60s/300s 0/0 seconds/request
<--output omitted-->
```

This example has two Websense servers, where the second is currently down. For the first server, you can see that 365,412 requests were sent to the server, of which 254,595 policy-allow and 110,547 policy-deny actions were received.

If you have enabled caching of URL information on your appliance that it received from the content filtering server, you can view the caching statistics with the **show url-cache stats** command:

```
ciscoasa(config)# show url-cache stats
URL Filter Cache Stats
----------------------
    Size :        1KB
 Entries :         36
  In Use :         22
 Lookups :        241
    Hits :        207
```

In this example, the cache size has been set to 1KB. The `Entries` item specifies the total number of cached entries that can fit in the cache based on the configured size. In this example, only 36 entries can be cached. The `In Use` item specifies the number of entries that are currently cached (22). The `Lookups` entry specifies the number of times the appliance has looked in the cache for a match, and the `Hits` entry shows the number of times the appliance found a match in the cache.

To view statistics about URL information received from external web servers that is being temporarily buffered by the appliance, use this command:

```
ciscoasa(config)# show url-block block stat
URL Pending Packet Buffer Stats with max block    1
---------------------------------------------------
Cumulative number of packets held:          53
Maximum number of packets held (per URL):    1
Current number of packets held (global):     0
Packets dropped due to exceeding url-block buffer limit:   78
Packets dropped due to
| exceeding url-block buffer limit: | 78
| HTTP server retransmission: | 0
Number of packets released back to client: | 0
```

As you can see in this example, 53 packets were held up because the appliance was waiting for a response from the web content filtering server. You will want to keep tabs on the number of packets being dropped because they exceeded the buffer limit—if this is continually increasing, you will want to increase the block size for buffering. To clear the statistics, use the **clear url-block block** command.

The **show perfmon** command shows you performance information for many important components of the appliance, including web content filtering performance. Here is an example:

```
ciscoasa(config)# show perfmon
PERFMON STATS:      Current        Average
Xlates              0/s            0/s
Connections         0/s            2/s
TCP Conns           0/s            2/s
UDP Conns           0/s            0/s
URL Access          0/s            2/s
URL Server Req      0/s            2/s
<--output omitted-->
```

With this command, you should focus on the URL Server Req entry, which displays the number of lookups the appliance forwarded to the web content policy server.

URL Filtering Example

To help illustrate the configuration example, I'll use the network shown in Figure 7-2. This example uses Websense for a web content filtering solution.

Listing 7-1 focuses only on the filtering commands for this setup.

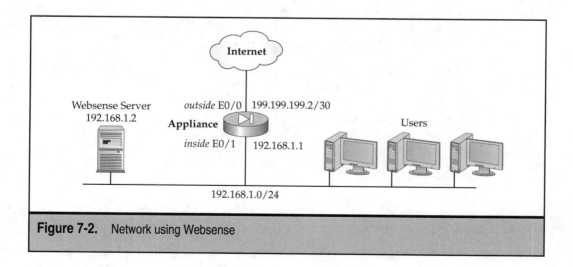

Figure 7-2.   Network using Websense

Listing 7-1. Example of a Websense setup

```
ciscoasa(config)# url-server (inside) vendor websense
                            host 192.168.1.2 protocol tcp version 4
ciscoasa(config)# filter url 80 0 0 0 0
ciscoasa(config)# filter url 8080-8099 0 0 0 0
ciscoasa(config)# url-cache dst 128
```

In this example, the **url-server** command specifies that the server is a Websense server and that the connection is using TCP. Any web traffic on port 80 or port 8080 through 8099 will be examined for filtering. The appliance can cache information returned by the Websense server using 128KB of memory. As you can see from this example, the setup of web filtering on the appliances is easy.

WEB CACHING

Web caching is used to reduce latency and the amount of traffic when downloading web content. Assuming a web cache server is deployed, when a user accesses a web site, the content that is downloaded is cached on the cache server. Subsequent access to the same content is then delivered from the local cache server versus downloading the content from the original server.

The Web Cache Communications Protocol (WCCP) allows the security appliances to interact with external web cache and/or filtering servers.

WCCP Process

To understand the benefits that WCCP provides, I'll go through the process that the appliance goes through when using WCCP:

1. The user opens a web page, where the connection (or connections) makes its way to the appliance.

2. The appliance intercepts the web connection request, encapsulates it in a Generic Routing Encapsulation (GRE) packet to prevent modification by intermediate devices, and forwards it to the web cache server.

3. If the content is cached in the server, it responds to the user directly with the content.

4. If the content is not cached in the server, a response is sent to the appliance, and the appliance allows the user's connection to proceed to the original web server.

For step 3 during the redirection process, the appliance doesn't add the connection to the state table and therefore doesn't perform any TCP state tracking, doesn't random-ize the TCP sequence number in the TCP header, doesn't perform Cut-through Proxy authorization, doesn't perform URL filtering, doesn't process the packet using IPS, and doesn't perform address translation. However, if the web cache server doesn't have the content, as in step 4, then these things are performed by the appliance.

Some of the benefits of WCCP include

▼ Users don't have to change their web browser settings.

■ The web caching server can perform optional content filtering.

■ Bandwidth is optimized if the content the user is requesting has been previously cached on the web cache server.

▲ The web cache server can log and report web requests by your users.

Cisco created the protocol, and it has two versions: 1 and 2. Some enhancements of WCCPv2 include support for other protocols besides HTTP, multicasting of requests to the web cache servers, multiple cache servers, load distribution among multiple cache servers, MD5 authentication of information between the redirector and the web cache server, and many others. Of the two versions, the appliances support only WCCPv2; however, some features are not supported by the appliances, like multicast WCCP.

WCCP Configuration

WCCP support is new in version 7.2 of the appliances' OS. Enabling WCCP redirection of users' web requests is a two-step process:

▼ Defining a WCCP server group

▲ Enabling WCCP on an interface

The following two sections will discuss the configuration of these two steps.

Defining a WCCP Server Group

To define the WCCP server group (the web cache servers), use the following command:

```
ciscoasa(config)# wccp {web-cache | service_number}
                      [redirect-list ACL_ID] [group-list ACL_ID]
                      [password password]
```

The **web-cache** parameter causes the appliance to intercept TCP port 80 connections and to redirect the traffic to the web cache servers. You can redirect other protocols, like FTP, by specifying a service number, which ranges from 0 to 254. For example, service 60 represents FTP. The **redirect-list** parameter controls what traffic is redirected to the service group (defined in an ACL), and the **group-list** command specifies the IP addresses of the web cache servers (defined in a standard ACL). The **password** parameter specifies the MD5 key used to create and validate the MD5 authentication signatures used by the web cache servers.

Enabling WCCP Redirection on an Interface

The second step is to enable WCCP redirection on the interface connected to the users and web cache server(s):

```
ciscoasa(config)# wccp interface logical_if_name
                      {web-cache | service_number} redirect in
```

This command needs to be executed for each service number.

NOTE WCCP web redirection is only supported inbound on an interface. Likewise, the users and web cache server(s) must be behind the *same* interface—the appliance won't take a user's web request on one interface and redirect to a web cache server on a different interface.

WCCP Verification

To verify the operation of WCCP, use the following command:

```
ciscoasa# show wccp {web-cache | service_number} [detail] [view]
```

The **detail** parameter displays information about all the router/web server caches; the **view** parameter displays other members of a particular server group that have or haven't been detected.

```
ciscoasa# show wccp
Global WCCP information:
  Router information:
    Router Identifier: -not yet determined-
    Protocol Version: 2.0
  Service Identifier: web-cache
    Number of Cache Engines: 0
    Number of routers: 0
    Total Packets Redirected: 0
    Redirect access-list: web-traffic-list
    Total Connections Denied Redirect: 0
    Total Packets Unassigned: 0
    Group access-list: server-list
    Total Messages Denied to Group: 0
    Total Authentication failures: 0
    Total Bypassed Packets Received: 0
```

WCCP Configuration Example

To see an illustration of the configuration and use of WCCP, examine the network in Figure 7-3. Notice that the users and the web cache server are located off the same interface on the appliance. Here's the appliance configuration for WCCP:

```
ciscoasa(config)# wccp web-cache password myMD5password
ciscoasa(config)# wccp interface inside web-cache redirect in
```

As you can see, the configuration is very simple.

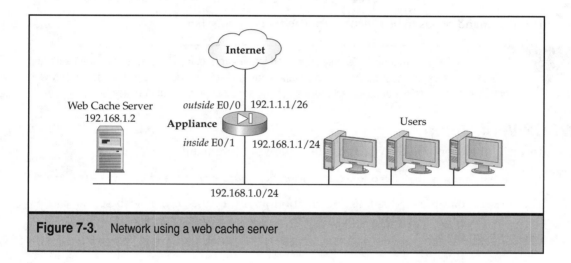

Figure 7-3.   Network using a web cache server

CHAPTER 8

CTP

In the last chapter, I talked about filtering web content on your appliance. This chapter builds upon the traffic controlling and filtering features that I have so far discussed. In this chapter, I'll explain how you can authenticate and authorize connections going through your appliance by using a feature called *Cut-through Proxy* (CTP). CTP adds an additional level of security over ACLs (discussed in Chapter 6). The topics discussed in this chapter include

▼ An overview of authentication, authorization, and accounting (AAA)

■ Configuration of AAA servers and protocols

■ Authentication of connections using CTP

■ Authorization of connections using CTP

▲ Accounting of connections using CTP

AAA OVERVIEW

One of the major problems you face when designing your network is the management of security. In large networks, you can easily have over 1,000 networking devices to manage, including routers, switches, security appliances, file servers, and many others. Each of these devices has its own local authentication method. For instance, an appliance firewall has a local telnet/SSH password and a Privilege EXEC password. Imagine if you had to periodically change these passwords on 1,000 devices to ensure a secure environment. Obviously, this would not be easy, and definitely not scalable.

AAA Components

AAA helps you centralize your security checks and is broken into three areas: *authentication* (who), *authorization* (what), and *accounting* (when). Together, all three of these areas are referred to as *AAA*.

Authentication is responsible for checking a user's identity to determine if she is allowed access to a networking device. A user must enter a username and password to validate. Once she has gained access to the networking device, authorization determines what the user can do—what commands she can execute and what privilege levels she has access to. For example, you could allow a person Privilege EXEC access to a router, but not allow her access to Configuration mode. And last, you can keep a record of a user's actions, like what commands she executed and when she executed them, with the accounting function.

AAA Example

As an example, I worked with a company that had about 1,200 routers. This company had a dozen networking administrators, as well as many networking contractors working for them; on average, they had about 50 to 60 contractors working there each week.

They basically had three job levels within their networking division: tier 1, tier 2, and tier 3. Tier 1 and 2 administrators were granted User EXEC access to the routers, and tier 3 workers were allowed Privilege EXEC access. This sounds simple enough, but the company had a major dilemma. They would never hire a tier 3 contractor, because contractors would come and go on a weekly basis, and this would mean that with each contractor departure, they would have to change all of the Privilege EXEC passwords on all of their 1,200 routers. Instead, they gave their own network administrators tier 3 access, and these individuals were responsible for performing Privilege EXEC functions. As you can imagine, these dozen employees were completely swamped with work trying to maintain the 1,200 routers.

A better solution to this problem would be to hire contractors at a tier 3 level and to give them Privilege EXEC access, offloading a lot of the work from the company's network administrators. Of course, you wouldn't want to change passwords on 1,200 routers every time a tier 3 contractor left the company. To solve this problem, you would use a centralized security solution. Instead of having the routers and other networking devices perform authentication locally, you could have them forward the authentication requests to a centralized security server or servers, which would validate the user's identity and pass the results back to the networking devices. This allows you to maintain user accounts at one location, making it easy to add and remove accounts. When a tier 3 contractor is hired, you would add that person to the security server, with the appropriate security access, and when the contract is terminated, you would simply delete the account from a single security server.

Additionally, a good security product should also offer authorization and accounting features. With authorization, you might want to control what, exactly, a tier 3 contractor could do while in Privilege EXEC mode (what commands he can execute); and with accounting, you might want a record of who logged into which networking device, what they did, and when they did it. Cisco actually sells a product, called *Cisco Secure ACS* (CSACS), which performs the functions of a security or AAA server: it allows you to centralize the security for your networking devices, like routers, switches, security appliances, and other networking equipment.

NOTE CSACS is only briefly covered in this book—enough to implement the features discussed here. For a better overview of CSACS, read *Cisco Access Control Security: AAA Administration Services* by Brandon James Carroll (Cisco Press, 2004).

AAA Protocols

To implement AAA, you need a secure protocol to transport security information between the networking device and the security (AAA) server. Three security protocols commonly are used to implement AAA:

▼ Kerberos

■ Remote Access Dial-In User Service (RADIUS)

▲ Terminal Access Controller Access Control System (TACACS+)

Some Cisco networking devices support all three protocols; however, Cisco only supports the last two on its security appliances. The next three sections provide a brief overview of these security protocols.

Kerberos

Kerberos was developed at the Massachusetts Institute of Technology (MIT) and uses DES (40- or 56-bit keys) for encrypting information between the networking device and the security server, referred to as a Key Distribution Center (KDC). Kerberos is an open standard; however, it functions at only the application layer. This means that you need to make changes to the actual application to use Kerberos. On IOS-based routers, Cisco has included Kerberos authentication for telnet, RSH, RLOGIN, and RCP. Cisco doesn't support Kerberos on the security appliances.

RADIUS

RADIUS was developed by the Livingston Corporation, which is now owned by Lucent. It is currently an open standard, defined in RFCs 2138 and 2139. However, many extensions have been added by various companies for their networking devices, making it a somewhat open standard. RADIUS supports UDP for the connection between the networking device and AAA server; it only encrypts the user's password used for authentication, nothing else, making it less secure (more susceptible to eavesdropping attacks) than Kerberos or TACACS+. For example, if a user were trying to log into a router, the router would forward the authentication information (user's access method—console, VTY, or other means—and the username) in clear text, but would encrypt the user's password. Probably RADIUS' biggest advantage over the other two security protocols is that, because it was developed for dialup and networks like ISPs, it has a very robust accounting system: keeping track of when a user connected, how long he was connected, and how many bytes were transmitted to and from the user.

NOTE   RADIUS is most commonly used on the appliances for connections going through it, like CTP and remote access VPNs. RADIUS is actually required for some security features, like 802.1*x* and LEAP. RADIUS uses one UDP connection for authentication and authorization, and a second connection for accounting. Depending on implementation of RADIUS, the port numbers for authentication/authorization and accounting are either 1645 and 1646, or 1812 and 1813, respectively.

TACACS+

TACACS was originally developed for the U. S. Defense Department and has been updated over the years by Cisco, resulting in an enhanced version called *TACACS+*. Because of the many changes Cisco has made to the protocol, TACACS+ is proprietary. Unlike RADIUS, TACACS+ uses TCP (port 49) for the connection to the AAA server and encrypts the entire payload contents in the security packets, making it more reliable and more secure than RADIUS. TACACS+ also supports a single connection feature—the networking device opens a single TCP connection to the AAA server and uses this single connection for all AAA functions. This feature provides faster response times than with RADIUS, because RADIUS uses a separate UDP connection for *each* AAA request, like each username lookup, or each command executed on the networking device.

NOTE TACACS+ is most commonly used on the appliances for controlling administrative access to the appliance itself. Note that you can use both RADIUS and TACACS+ simultaneously on your appliance. For example, you could use TACACS+ to control access to the appliance, but use RADIUS for CTP. Controlling access to the appliance using AAA is discussed in Chapter 26.

AAA SERVERS

The security appliances support AAA functionality. Normally, AAA is used to control access to the command-line interface shell of a networking device. The appliances support this function of AAA, but also use AAA for network access *through* them, allowing users to authenticate to the appliance before their connection or connections are allowed through. Some examples of these AAA appliance features are CTP and remote access VPNs, like IPSec and WebVPN.

AAA Server Configuration

One of the first items you need to configure for AAA is the connection used between your appliance and your security server: TACACS+ and/or RADIUS. Minimally, you'll need to configure the protocol that is used, the encryption key, and the remote server the appliance is connecting to. The following sections contain an overview of how to configure an AAA server and protocol on your appliance.

Appliance AAA Server Configuration

On your security appliance, the first thing you need to configure is the security protocol or protocols you'll be using between the appliance and your AAA server(s) and who the server(s) are. Both tasks are configured using the **aaa-server** command:

```
ciscoasa(config)# aaa-server group_tag protocol {tacacs+ | radius}
ciscoasa(config)# aaa-server group_tag (logical_if_name)
                    host AAA_server_IP_address AAA_encryption_key
                    [timeout value_in_seconds]
ciscoasa(config-aaa-server-host)# server-port port_number
ciscoasa(config-aaa-server-host)# key encryption_key
ciscoasa(config-aaa-server-host)# timeout seconds
```

The first command specifies which security protocol you'll use when your appliance accesses the AAA server: TACACS+ or RADIUS. The *group_tag* parameter is used to group your policy information, because you might have one set of security servers for authenticating command-line access and another set for authenticating CTP. In other words, the group tag determines where to direct AAA traffic (what protocol and server). The group tag is basically a string of characters, and the tag value must be different from other group tags.

NOTE   Cisco's AAA server, CSACS, supports both RADIUS and TACACS+. Most other vendors only support RADIUS.

Next you must specify the AAA server that your appliance will use. You must specify the name of the interface where the security is located; if you omit it, the logical name defaults to *inside*. Following this is the **host** parameter and the IP address of the AAA server. The *AAA_key* parameter specifies the encryption key used to secure the connection between the appliance and the AAA server—this key must also be configured on the AAA server and is case-sensitive. You can configure up to 256 different security servers, where each AAA server has its own configuration command.

When trying to connect to the AAA server, the appliance will wait for a reply for 5 seconds by default. It will try to contact an AAA server up to four times. If the appliance can't reach the AAA server, it will try the second AAA server that you've configured (if you have configured another one); therefore the order of the server statements is important. You can change the timeout value with the optional **timeout** parameter. The timeout can be increased up to 30 seconds.

When executing the **aaa-server** command, you are taken into a subcommand mode. Here you can optionally change the port number used for the connection (applicable to RADIUS only). You can also enter the encryption key and timeout values if you omitted this from the **aaa-server** command.

Here's an example of defining a protocol and server:

```
ciscoasa(config)# aaa-server RADIUS_SERVER protocol radius
ciscoasa(config)# aaa-server RADIUS_SERVER (inside) host 10.0.1.11
ciscoasa(config-aaa-server-host)# key cisco123
```

CSACS Configuration

Once you've logged into CSACS, you'll need to individually add each of your appliances under CSACS's Network Configuration section.

NOTE   If your appliance needs to use both TACACS+ and RADIUS to CSACS, you'll need to add the appliance *twice* to CSACS, using a different hostname for each instance in CSACS.

Follow these steps to add your appliance:

1. Click the Network Configuration button on the left side of the window.
2. Under the AAA Clients section, click the Add Entry button.

3. On the Add AAA Client screen, enter the following information:

   a. *AAA Client Hostname*   A locally descriptive name of the appliance.

   b. *AAA Client IP Address*   The IP address or addresses the appliance will use to initiate connections to CSACS.

   c. *Shared Secret*   This is the encryption key to encrypt the passwords for RADIUS or the payload of TACACS packets.

   d. *Authenticate Using*   The drop-down selector that lets you choose the AAA protocol, which can be either "TACACS+" or "RADIUS (Cisco VPN 3000/ ASA/PIX 7.x+)" for the appliances.

   e. All the other parameters are optional.

4. On the Add AAA Client window, click either the Submit or Submit+Apply button.

NOTE   The difference between the Submit and Submit+Apply buttons is that the Submit button saves your change, and Submit+Apply saves and activates your change(s). The problem of activating changes in CSACS is that the CSACS processes must be restarted, causing a small amount of disruption; therefore, it is best to save all your changes and restart the processes once. You can also restart the processes within the System Configuration section.

CTP AUTHENTICATION

In some circumstances, you may want to authenticate connections through the appliance itself. You might have a situation where using an ACL doesn't provide enough security. Remember that ACLs, discussed in Chapter 6, can only look at the layer 3 and 4 information, which can easily be spoofed. As an added security measure, you can use the appliance CTP feature, which provides application-layer authentication.

For example, you might have accounting users in a VLAN acquiring their addressing information via DHCP. In the data center across the campus reside the accounting servers in their own VLAN. If all you cared about was to restrict access from the accounting users to the accounting servers, you could easily accommodate this with an ACL. However, suppose one restricted accounting server in the server farm should be accessed by only a handful of accounting users. Since all the accounting users acquire their addressing information via DHCP, you really don't know what source IP address or addresses to allow to the restricted server.

To overcome this problem, you could statically assign the small set of users a range of addresses that are allowed, but that means you would have to manage static addresses. On top of this, these addresses could be spoofed, allowing unauthorized people to access the restricted server. Another solution would be to control access on the accounting server itself, which, in most cases, is what administrators do. However, in some cases this might not be feasible, based on what the application on the server supports. A third option is to use the appliance CTP feature, which can authenticate a user's connection attempt before allowing the user to reach the restricted server or servers. The next section will discuss how CTP works.

CTP Overview

With CTP, the appliance receives a new connection request from a user. Before accepting the connection, the appliance can first authenticate it by prompting the user with a username and password prompt. The user must enter a username and password, which are sent to the appliance. The appliance will then forward the username and password to an AAA server to have the information validated. If the user is permitted, the appliance security algorithm opens a small hole in the appliance to permit the authenticated connection.

NOTE CTP is processed after any ACL checks—so the user's initial connection attempt must be allowed by an ACL on the inbound interface. Assuming the CTP authentication is successful, the connection is added to the conn table, allowing subsequent packets for the connection.

One important item to point out is that CTP can authenticate both inbound *and* outbound connections. Currently Cisco only supports CTP connections for the following applications: HTTP, HTTPS, telnet, and FTP. As you will see in later sections, you have other methods for dealing with other applications that don't support these protocols.

Figure 8-1 shows the CTP process with an AAA server: In step 1, an external user attempts to access an internal web server. If the inbound ACL drops the packet, CTP is not performed; so when using CTP, make sure the inbound ACL allows the connection. In step 2, the appliance sends a username and password prompt to the user. The user then enters the AAA username and password.

One nice feature for this prompt is that the user can use the following nomenclature when entering the username and password (FTP and HTTP connections only):

```
AAA_username@internal_host_username
AAA_password@internal_host_password
```

The AAA username can be up to 127 characters in length, and the password can be 64 characters long. The first username and password are for CTP authentication; the second username and password are for the actual server itself. Remember that the appliances are performing a modified proxy when performing authentication.

NOTE Without the double username/password option, where only one username and password were entered, the single username and password would be used for both CTP and the internal server authentication. And if the internal server were using a different username and password than that configured on the AAA server, authentication would fail.

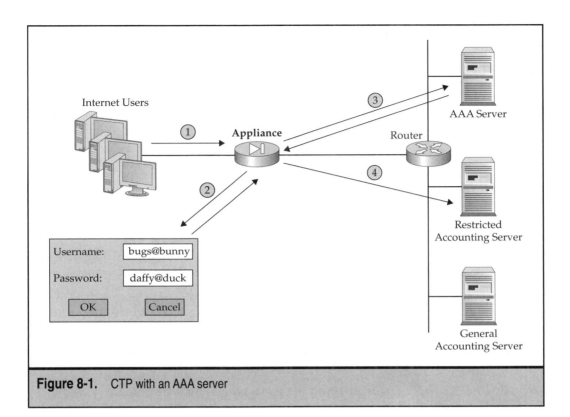

Figure 8-1.   CTP with an AAA server

The appliance then takes the AAA username and password only and forwards them to the AAA server (step 3) for validation. If the AAA server can validate the user, the server tells the appliance to permit the connection. Otherwise, it tells the appliance to deny the connection. If the connection is permitted and added to the conn table and you used the correct nomenclature, the appliance will take the supplied username and password and forward these to the internal server (step 4). This alleviates the user from having to enter a username and password on the server.

Appliance Configuration of CTP Authentication

The following sections will discuss how to set up CTP authentication on your appliance. I'll show you how to change some of the authentication parameters and how to have the appliance intercept and authenticate the connections before allowing them through.

Changing Authentication Parameters

You might want to configure some optional parameters for CTP authentication. Some optional things that you can configure are

▼ Limiting the number of proxy connections per user

■ Changing the authentication prompt presented by the appliance

▲ Changing the timeouts for authenticated connections

The following three sections cover the use and configuration of these parameters.

Limiting Proxy Connections   You can limit the number of concurrent proxy connections that a user is allowed to establish with the **aaa proxy-limit** command:

```
ciscoasa(config)# aaa proxy-limit {#_of_connections | disable}
```

For the *#_of_connections* parameter, you can specify a value from 1 to 128—the default is 16. The **disable** parameter disables the concurrent proxy connections.

Authentication Prompts   The appliance allows you to modify the prompts used during the authentication process; you can modify what the appliance sends to the user with the following command:

```
ciscoasa(config)# auth-prompt {accept | reject | prompt}
                     prompt_string
```

Actually three prompts can be involved in the password checking process:

▼ **prompt**   This text is displayed before the username and password prompt.

■ **accept**   This text is displayed once a user has successfully authenticated.

▲ **reject**   This text is displayed once a user has failed authentication.

The length of the prompt is limited based on the application the user is accessing:

▼ *FTP and telnet*   235 characters

■ *Microsoft Internet Explorer*   37 characters

▲ *Netscape Navigator*   120 characters

I recommend that you keep your prompts short so that you'll be able to support any type of application. For the actual prompt, you should not use any special characters; however, you are permitted to use spaces and punctuation marks.

Here is a simple example of setting the prompts:

```
ciscoasa(config)# auth-prompt prompt Full body cavity search
                     before proceeding!
ciscoasa(config)# auth-prompt accept Greetings Earthling!
ciscoasa(config)# auth-prompt reject Um...nice try, but you're not
                     even close!
```

Once you have configured these prompts and your AAA configuration, you can test it. Here is an example of a user performing a telnet that has been intercepted by the appliance configured for CTP:

```
Full body cavity search before proceeding!
Username: Monkey
Password: *****
Um...nice try, but you're not even close!

Full body cavity search before proceeding!
Username: Monkey
Password: *******
Greetings Earthling!
```

Authentication Timeouts   The appliance supports two different timeouts for AAA authenticated connections (which include CTP): idle and absolute. These timeouts affect when the appliance will terminate an AAA connection that a user has open (remove them from the conn table). By default, the appliance caches this information for an idle period of 5 minutes before disconnecting the user. To set these timeouts, use the `timeout` command:

```
ciscoasa(config)# timeout uauth hh:mm:ss [absolute | inactivity]
```

The `absolute` timeout affects the duration of a user's connection whether the user is active or idle on the connection. The `inactivity` timeout tells the appliance when to tear down idle connections associated with an authenticated user. To examine your timeout values, use the `show run timeout` command.

Controlling Authentication

To configure CTP authentication, you'll need to set up your `aaa authentication` commands on your appliance as well as configure your AAA server with usernames and passwords. Here is the syntax of the two authentication commands on the appliances:

```
ciscoasa(config)# aaa authentication {include | exclude}
                  application_name
                  {inbound | outbound | interface_name}
                  internal_IP_address internal_subnet_mask
                  external_IP_address external_subnet_mask
                  group_tag
ciscoasa(config)# aaa authentication match ACL_ID logical_if_name
                  group_tag
```

For the first `aaa authentication` command, the first thing you must specify is either the `include` or `exclude` parameter, which tells the appliance which applications will be intercepted and authenticated and which ones won't. After this you must specify the application name that you'll authenticate. These include **http**, **https**, **ftp**, **telnet**, or **any** (for all four applications). Next you must specify the direction or interface where CTP will be performed:

- ▼ **inbound** From a lower to a higher security level interface
- ■ **outbound** From a higher to a lower security level interface
- ▲ *logical_if_name* Inbound on this interface

Following the direction are the inside and outside addresses that authentication should be performed for. If you want to authenticate all connections, use 0.0.0.0 0.0.0.0 0.0.0.0 0.0.0.0 or 0 0 0 0—this will cause the appliance to use CTP for all of the applications that you specified for all connections. If you want to authenticate connections only to a specific web server, then list that web server as the internal address and everyone for the external address. Finally, you need to specify the *group_tag* value, which tells the appliance which security server should perform the authentication.

NOTE The first address(es) in the **aaa authentication include/exclude** command represent devices off the higher-level interface, and the second address(es) represent devices off the lower-level interface.

Your second option with the **aaa authentication** command is to use an ACL name with the **match** parameter to specify the traffic to be authenticated. When you do this, the ACL can only match on HTTP, HTTPS, FTP, and telnet traffic. This option was introduced in FOS 5.2. ACL statements with **permit** parameters specify that the matching traffic must be authenticated; statements with **deny** parameters specify that the matching traffic is exempt from authentication.

If you want to use HTTPS authentication for CTP, note that the preceding **aaa authentication** commands do not use SSL to encrypt the usernames and passwords—the SSL function doesn't take place until the user authenticates successfully to the appliance/AAA server and the connection proceeds to the destination server. If you want to use SSL to protect the username and password sent from the user to the appliance, use the following command:

```
ciscoasa(config)# aaa authentication secure-http-client
```

Here is a simple example of a CTP configuration:

```
ciscoasa(config)# aaa-server TACSRV protocol tacacs+
ciscoasa(config)# aaa-server TACSRV (inside)
                  host 192.168.1.10 thisisasecret
ciscoasa(config)# aaa authentication include http outside
                  192.168.1.12 255.255.255.255 0 0 TACSRV
```

In this example, the appliance is using TACACS+ to communicate to the security server (192.168.1.10). CTP authentication is being performed for only HTTP traffic destined to 192.168.1.12 when it enters the *outside* interface. Remember that this connection must be allowed in the ACL check. All other types of traffic will only have the ACL on the outside interface determining if the packets are allowed.

NOTE   Remember that web browsers can cache usernames and passwords. Therefore, if you have configured timeouts for HTTP connections, which will cause the appliance to re-authenticate the user, the web browser might send the same information to the appliance, which will be forwarded to the AAA server. This can cause a problem if you are using token cards for authentication; therefore, have the user close their web browser connection and re-open it—this is true if a user fails authentication and is trying to authenticate again.

Controlling Access for Nonsupported Applications

As I mentioned in the previous section, one limitation of CTP is that it can only be used to authenticate HTTP, HTTPS, FTP, and telnet connections. If you have other applications that you need to authenticate, the CTP feature will be unable to handle the authentication. However, you do have three other options available:

▼   Use authentication on the application server the user is trying to access.

■   Use the Virtual Telnet feature on the appliance—this is used when the destination server doesn't support HTTP, HTTPS, FTP, or telnet.

▲   Use the Virtual HTTP feature on the appliance—this is used when the appliance and destination web server don't use the same AAA server for authentication; in this situation, the user must perform two separate authentications…one to the appliance and one to the web server.

One problem with having the application server perform the authentication is that your authentication mechanism isn't centralized—you need to set up authentication on every server where you need user authentication. Virtual Telnet and Virtual HTTP provide a more scalable solution, as you will see in the following sections, and can authenticate and authorize connections in both the inbound and outbound directions.

Using Virtual Telnet   Typically, you'll use Virtual Telnet when you need to authenticate connections *other* than HTTP, FTP, or telnet. With Virtual Telnet, the user telnets to a virtual telnet address on the appliance and then supplies a username and password for authentication. Once authenticated, the appliance terminates the telnet session and allows the user to open her data connection. In other words, the Virtual Telnet address on the appliance cannot be used to access an EXEC shell on it. One annoyance with Virtual Telnet is that it is a two-step process for a user to connect to a resource—the user telnets into the appliance to authenticate, and then the user opens the application connection to the actual service.

Let's look at a simple example where you can use Virtual Telnet. You have an internal TFTP server (UDP 69). Obviously, CTP can't authenticate this connection. You can authenticate this connection using Virtual Telnet, however. To accomplish this, the user first telnets to a virtual IP address on the appliance—this address must be a reachable address (on the Internet, this has to be a public address). Actually the virtual IP address is similar to a loopback address on an IOS-based router. The Virtual Telnet connection must be permitted in the ACL of the interface the user's traffic is entering. For inbound users, whether or not NAT control is enabled, you must include the Virtual Telnet address in a **static** command. (An identity NAT command is commonly used, where the Virtual Telnet address is translated to itself.) The **static** command is not required for outbound Virtual Telnet. The appliance then prompts the user for a username and password, and then authenticates this information via an AAA server. If the authentication is successful, the user can now successfully access other services listed in the **aaa authentication include** or listed as **permit** statements in the ACL referenced in the **aaa authentication match** commands.

If a user wants to gracefully log out of his CTP authenticated session set up with Virtual Telnet, he only needs to re-telnet to the virtual address and re-authenticate. This second authentication process will unauthenticate the user.

To set up Virtual Telnet on your appliance, add the following command to your CTP authentication setup:

```
ciscoasa(config)# virtual telnet global_IP_address
```

The IP address must be a public-reachable address—treat this address as a loopback address on the appliance: it is an unused address associated with the appliance. For inbound users, this will typically be a public IP address; for outbound users, it can be either a public or a private IP address. After configuring this command, you must still configure your other AAA commands discussed in previous sections.

To help illustrate the use of Virtual Telnet, I'll use the network in Figure 8-2. Here is the code to set up Virtual Telnet for this network:

```
ciscoasa(config)# virtual telnet 200.200.200.2
ciscoasa(config)# aaa-server TACSRV protocol tacacs+
ciscoasa(config)# aaa-server TACSRV (inside)
                  host 192.168.1.2 thisisasecret
ciscoasa(config)# access-list INBOUND permit tcp any 200.200.200.2
                  eq 23
ciscoasa(config)# access-list INBOUND permit udp any 200.200.200.3
                  eq 69
ciscoasa(config)# access-list INBOUND permit udp any 200.200.200.4
                  eq 80
ciscoasa(config)# access-group INBOUND in interface outside
ciscoasa(config)# access-list CTP_AUTH permit tcp any 200.200.200.2
                  eq 23
ciscoasa(config)# access-list CTP_AUTH permit udp any 200.200.200.3
                  eq 69
```

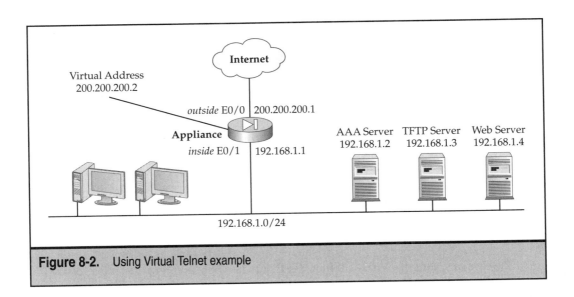

Figure 8-2. Using Virtual Telnet example

```
ciscoasa(config)# aaa authentication match CTP_AUTH outside TACSRV
ciscoasa(config)# nat-control
ciscoasa(config)# static (inside,outside) 200.200.200.2
                  200.200.200.2 netmask 255.255.255.255
ciscoasa(config)# static (inside,outside) 200.200.200.3
                  192.168.1.3 netmask 255.255.255.255
ciscoasa(config)# static (inside,outside) 200.200.200.4
                  192.168.1.4 netmask 255.255.255.255
```

In this example, the Virtual Telnet address is 200.200.200.2, which is internal to the appliance itself: notice the **static** command that translates 200.200.200.2 to 200.200.200.2, which is the identity NAT translation for the Virtual Telnet address. The AAA server is 192.168.1.2. The INBOUND ACL allows the Virtual Telnet and TFTP connections. However, the **aaa authentication** command specifies that telnet (the Virtual Telnet address), and TFTP traffic should be authenticated via the **permit** statements in the CTP_AUTH ACL.

NOTE One other important thing about this example: the INBOUND ACL also permits traffic to the web server. However, this is not included in the CTP_AUTH ACL. Therefore, external users are allowed to access the web server and are exempted from CTP authentication.

Using Virtual HTTP Virtual HTTP is used when CTP and the internal web server use different usernames and passwords for authentication because they are not using the same AAA server. In this situation, you must use the Virtual HTTP feature. Otherwise the username and password that the user enters for the appliance are passed through to the web server, where the authentication fails with the server, and thus the connection is broken.

Virtual HTTP works by having the appliance mimic a web server. The user attempts to open a connection to an internal web server, and the appliance intercepts the connection, as in CTP. The virtual web server on the appliance authenticates the user and then performs a redirect to the user's web browser—this tells the web browser that a new connection is being built (even though it's to the same IP address), but the web browser won't use the AAA username and password in its cache from the CTP authentication session. From the user's perspective, the interaction appears to be with the internal web server and not the virtual web server, making the virtual web server on the appliance seem transparent.

To set up a Virtual HTTP server on the security appliances, add the following command to your AAA configuration:

```
ciscoasa(config)#  virtual http global_IP_address [warning]
```

As in the case of setting up Virtual Telnet, the IP address here is internal to the appliance—use a public address for external users accessing internal resources, or a private or public address for internal users accessing external resources. The **warning** parameter is only applicable to text-based browsers where the redirection process cannot happen automatically. Please note that you need to set up an ACL for inbound traffic to allow the user's connection to the virtual web server address (TCP 80).

The configuration of the Virtual HTTP feature is basically the same as Virtual Telnet. Using the example in the "Using Virtual Telnet" section, the only thing that you would need to change would be to remove the **virtual telnet** command and to replace it with **virtual http**. Also you would need to change your ACL to reflect port 80 instead of 23.

Verifying CTP Authentication

Now that you have configured CTP authentication on your appliance, you will want to verify its operation. You can use many troubleshooting commands, discussed in the following two sections.

Verifying Server Interaction

To display your AAA server configuration and status, use the **show aaa-server** command:

```
ciscoasa# show aaa-server [LOCAL | group_tag [host server_IP_addr] |
                          protocol protocol]
```

You can qualify the output by specifying what servers to display with a *group_tag* parameter (and a server within the *group_tag*), by the protocol being used between the appliance and server, or local authentication (**LOCAL** parameter). Local authentication is discussed in Chapter 26.

Here's an example of the use of the preceding command:

```
ciscoasa(config)# show aaa-server
Server Group: RADGROUP
Server Protocol: RADIUS
Server Address: 192.168.1.1
Server port: 1645
Server status: ACTIVE. Last transaction (success) at
                        11:23:05 UTC Fri Nov 1
Number of pending requests 20
Average round trip time 4ms
Number of authentication requests 25
Number of authorization requests 0
Number of accounting requests 0
Number of retransmissions 1
Number of accepts 20
Number of rejects 5
Number of challenges 5
<--output omitted-->
```

In this example, 25 authentication requests were forwarded to the AAA server, where 20 were successful authentications and 5 failed the authentication process.

NOTE If you are experiencing problems with authentication using CTP, you can use the **debug aaa authentication** command, which displays the authentication interaction between the appliance and the AAA server. When you are done troubleshooting, disable the **debug** command by preceding it with the **no** parameter, or disable all debug functions with the **no debug all** or **undebug all** commands.

Viewing Authenticated Users

To see which users have authenticated via CTP on the appliance, use the **show uauth** command:

```
ciscoasa# show uauth [username]
```

Optionally, you can qualify the output by just listing one user. Here is an example of the **show uauth** command:

```
ciscoasa# show uauth
                        Current        Most Seen
 Authenticated Users      3             3
 Authen In Progress       0             3
user 'monkey' from 199.199.199.8 authenticated
user 'cow' from 199.199.199.22 authorized to:
port 192.168.1.8/telnet 192.168.1.10/http
```

```
user 'chicken' from 205.205.205.89 authorized to:
port 192.168.1.10/http 192.168.1.11/http
```

In this example, three users have been authenticated. The first user has been authenticated only, and the second two users have been authenticated and authorized. You can see the source address of the user as well as the resource that she has been authorized to access. CTP authorization is discussed in the next section.

If you want to force an authenticated user to re-authenticate, use the following **clear** command:

```
ciscoasa# clear uauth [username]
```

Omitting a username will unauthenticate all users.

CTP AUTHORIZATION

There are two main problems with CTP authentication:

▼ Users need to access multiple internal devices, but with CTP authentication, the user would have to authenticate to *each* individual device.

▲ CTP authentication is global: once a user authenticates, he can access the requested service; in other words, you can't control *who* accesses *what* service.

The following sections will discuss how CTP with authorization can solve these problems.

SECURITY ALERT!   If an authenticated user is behind a PAT translation device, all users that are mapped to the same address are authenticated. In this situation, I would highly recommend that you keep the idle timer to a small value, and also configure an absolute timer, forcing the user to periodically re-authenticate.

Users Accessing Multiple Services

Let's deal with the first problem I introduced in the last section. For example, let's assume you have a semiprivate DMZ with three web servers on it. If you only configured CTP authentication, and a user wanted to access all three servers, the appliance would intercept each separate server connection and authenticate the user. In this example, the user would have to authenticate three times: one for each of the semiprivate web servers. The more servers you have, the more confusing and aggravating this becomes for your users. With CTP authorization, the user authenticates once, and an authorization list, stored on the AAA server, determines what connections the user is allowed to open. I'll discuss the authorization list options in the next section.

Controlling Authenticated Access to Multiple Services

Now I'll deal with the second problem introduced in the last section. Another issue with CTP is that authentication only controls access based on a username and password. However, you might have a situation where you have two groups of servers that you want to control access to. With the first group of servers, only the programmers should be able to access them; and with the second group of servers, only the database people should be able to access them. In other words, you don't want programmers accessing the database servers, or the database personnel accessing the programmers' servers. CTP authentication can't solve this problem—it can only authenticate people. However, CTP with authorization can control this: you can set up an authorization list on the AAA server for the two different groups of people to restrict what they can access once they have authenticated.

NOTE If you want to use authorization, you must use authentication—authentication is done first by the appliance; however, you can use authentication without authorization. Another way of looking at this is that CTP must authenticate the user first; authorization can then control what the user is allowed to access.

CTP Authorization Options

Cisco supports two methods for authorization:

▼ Classic method

▲ Downloadable ACLs

The following two sections will discuss these options.

NOTE Of the two methods—classic and downloadable ACLs—Cisco is pushing the latter as the preferred method.

Classic Method for Authorization

In the classic method, the allowed connections are listed on the AAA server, like TCP port 80 connections to a particular server or servers. Once a user authenticates, every time she opens a connection, including the initial connection, her connection information is passed to the AAA server, which compares it with a list of authorized connections. The AAA server passes back the authorization response—allow or deny—and the appliance enforces the policy. The main disadvantage of this approach is that each connection the authenticated user opens will incur an initial delay while the policy lookup occurs; the advantage of this solution, however, is that any policy change on the AAA server is in immediate effect, since the appliance must look up each connection to determine the policy.

Downloadable ACL Authorization Method

Downloadable ACLs are new in version 6.2. Assuming your AAA server supports downloadable ACLs, you define the ACL on the AAA server for the user or the group the user belongs to. When the user authenticates, the ACL is downloaded to the appliance, and the appliance uses the ACL to determine what the authenticated user can access. Here are the basic steps that occur when you're using downloadable ACLs:

1. The appliance receives the username and password from the user and forwards this information to the AAA server.

2. The AAA server authenticates the user; if the user has successfully authenticated, the AAA server sends the name of the downloaded ACL that should be used.

3. The appliance checks to see if the ACL was already downloaded.

    a. If the ACL has already been downloaded (from another user who was authenticated and associated with the same ACL), the already downloaded ACL is used.

    b. If the ACL hasn't been downloaded, the appliance requests the ACL from the AAA server, and the server downloads it to the appliance.

4. The appliance uses the downloaded ACL to enforce authorization: the ACL is used to determine what the user can access.

5. Once the `uauth` timer expires or you execute the `clear uauth` command, the downloaded ACL is removed and the user unauthenticated.

One important point about the preceding process is that, assuming you set CTP authorization with downloadable ACLs correctly, the downloaded ACL is used to filter the authenticated user's traffic—the interface ACL is ignored for the authenticated user. By default, there is no limit to the number of downloaded ACLs you can define on an AAA server.

Classic Authorization Configuration

With classic authorization, you must define an authorization profile on your AAA server and enable authorization on your appliance with the `aaa authorization` command(s). Please note that you must first configure AAA authentication on your appliance before you can proceed with the authorization configuration. In addition to this, the appliances only support TACACS+ for the classic authorization method. The following two sections will discuss the configuration of classic authorization on CSACS and the appliances.

CSACS Classic Authorization Configuration

Before you configure authorization on your appliance, it is recommended to set up authorization on your AAA server first. Here are the steps if you are using CSACS:

1. Click the Group Setup button on the left side of the window.

2. Choose the appropriate group name from the pull-down menu, and click the Edit Settings button.

3. Go to the Shell Command Authorization Set section.

4. Under the Unmatched Cisco IOS Commands heading, click the Deny radio button.

5. Click the check box to the left of the "Command" reference, and enter the connection type allowed to the right of the reference: this can be the name of the connection, like `telnet`, `http`, or `ftp`, or it can include the protocol and port reference (*protocol_name_or_#/port_name_or_#*). An example of a protocol and port reference for TFTP would be `udp/69`.

6. If you want to restrict access to certain destinations, enter the IP addresses in the text box below the Arguments heading, and click the Permit radio button below this. To allow all destinations, don't enter IP addresses in this box, and then click the Permit radio button.

7. Click the Submit button at the bottom of the page.

8. Repeat steps 1 through 6 for each additional application.

9. Click the Submit+Restart button at the bottom of the page once you have added all the connections for the group.

Appliance Authorization Configuration

To set up CTP authorization on your appliance, use one of the two following configurations:

```
ciscoasa(config)# aaa authorization {include | exclude}
                    application_name
                    {inbound | outbound | interface_name}
                    internal_IP_address internal_subnet_mask
                    external_IP_address external_subnet_mask
                    group_tag
-or-
ciscoasa(config)# aaa authorization match ACL_ID logical_if_name
                    group_tag
```

As you can see, the syntax of these commands is almost the same as the **aaa authentication** commands.

A couple of items need to be pointed out concerning authorization. First, the appliance only supports TACACS+ for the classic CTP authorization method. Second, if the appliance doesn't find a match in any of its authorization statements, it will implicitly permit the user's connection, assuming an ACL entry doesn't deny it. Third, besides specifying an application name (**any**, **http**, **ftp**, or **telnet**), you can also list an IP protocol number or name as well as a port number or range. When you specify a range, separate the beginning and ending port numbers by a hyphen. For example, your web servers might not be running on port 80, but on ports 8080–8081. To catch this port number, use the following syntax for the *application_name* parameter: **tcp/8080-8081**.

With the `aaa authorization match` command, you list all the connections that must be looked up for authenticated users in the specified ACL before they are allowed through the appliance. Anything that matches a `deny` or implicit deny statement is exempted from authorization and is implicitly allowed.

Downloadable ACL Configuration

The configuration of downloadable ACLs is done on the AAA server. However, to make sure that they are used, you must configure at least one command on the appliance. The following two sections will discuss these items.

CSACS Downloadable ACL Configuration

Configuring and using downloadable ACLs on CSACS is a three-step process: enabling them, creating them, and referencing them for a group or user. The following three sections will discuss these steps.

Enabling Downloadable ACLs on CSACS   Downloadable ACLs are not enabled, by default, within CSACS. To enable them, go to Interface Configuration | Advanced Options. Click one or both of the following check boxes:

- ▼ User-Level Downloadable ACLs
- ▲ Group-Level Downloadable ACLs

The first option enables downloadable ACLs on a per-user basis. The second option enables them on a per-group basis. When you're done, click the Submit button.

Creating Downloadable ACLs on CSACS   Once downloadable ACLs have been enabled, you need to create them. To create a named downloadable ACL for a user or group, go to Shared Profile Components | Downloadable IP ACLs and click the Add button. In the Downloadable ACL section, you'll see a list of any named ACLs already created. Give a name to the description of ACLs.

To add an ACL, click the Add button. You are then taken to a screen where you can assign a name to your ACL and enter the actual ACL statements. Make sure you use the keyword **any** for the source address—when this is downloaded to the appliance, the appliance will use the actual IP address of the authenticated user(s) as the source IP address in the downloaded ACL. Here's the general syntax for an ACL statement in CSACS:

```
{permit | deny} protocol_name_or_# any dst_IP_addr subnet_mask
                    [protocol_info] [log]
{permit | deny} protocol_name_or_# any host dst_IP_addr
                    [protocol_info] [log]
```

As you can see from the preceding syntax, this is similar to creating ACLs on the appliance itself. When you're done creating the ACL, click the Submit button.

Here's a simple example of a configured downloadable ACL in CSACS:

```
permit tcp any host 192.168.1.1 eq 25
permit tcp any host 192.168.1.2 eq 21
```

In this example, once the user has authenticated and the ACL has been downloaded, the user can access the e-mail and FTP server listed—everything else is denied for the user.

Referencing Downloadable ACLs in Users and Groups   To apply a downloadable ACL to a user or group in CSACS, go to the Group Setup or User Setup section (in the left window pane, click the Group Setup or User Setup buttons respectively). Select a group or user to edit, and then in the Downloadable ACLs section, click the Assign IP ACL check box, and use the drop-down selector to choose the named ACL to be applied to the group or user. When done, click the Submit+Restart button.

Appliance Downloadable ACL Configuration and Verification

Once you have set up your downloadable ACLs in CSACS, when a user authenticates, on the appliance, the default is to ignore the downloaded ACL and use the one on the inbound interface. To override this behavior, reapply the existing ACL to the appliance interface, but add the **per-user-override** parameter, like this:

```
ciscoasa(config)# access-group ACL_ID in interface logical_if_name
                    per-user-override
```

Executing this command is the only requirement on the appliance. Once you have done this, any downloaded ACLs are then applied to the user's traffic on the inbound interface instead of using the ACL applied to the interface.

To see what ACL an authenticated user will use, execute the **show uauth** command discussed earlier in the "Viewing Authenticated Users" section. Here's an example:

```
ciscoasa# show uauth
                      Current     Most Seen
Authenticated Users      1            1
Authen In Progress       1            1
user 'MasterChief' at 192.168.2.1, authenticated
    access-list #ACSACL#-IP-DATABASEACL-438d7411 (*)
    absolute    timeout: 0:05:00
    inactivity timeout: 0:00:00
```

In this example, the MasterChief user has a downloaded ACL associated with him. Notice the ACL name: #ACSACL#-IP-DATABASEACL-438d7411. The "#ACSACL#" part indicates the ACL was downloaded from CSACS. The "IP" part indicates that this is an IP ACL. The "DATABASEACL" is the name you gave the ACL when creating it in ACS. The "438d7411" part is a version identifier and helps the appliance determine if any changes were made to the ACL since it was last downloaded. Every time you update the ACL in ACS, this value changes. This helps the appliance determine when a previously downloaded ACL has changed, and there is an updated version that should be downloaded instead of using the one that was previously downloaded.

To view the actual ACL that was downloaded, use the **show access-list** command. Here's an example:

```
ciscoasa# show access-list
<--output omitted-->
access-list #ACSACL#-IP-APPLIANCEACL-438d7411; 4 elements (dynamic)
access-list #ACSACL#-IP-APPLIANCEACL-438d7411 line 1 extended
    permit tcp any host 192.168.100.253 eq telnet (hitcnt=1)
access-list #ACSACL#-IP-APPLIANCEACL-438d7411 line 2 extended
    permit tcp any host 192.168.100.253 eq www (hitcnt=0)
access-list #ACSACL#-IP-APPLIANCEACL-438d7411 line 3 extended
    permit tcp any host 192.168.100.253 eq ftp (hitcnt=0)
access-list #ACSACL#-IP-APPLIANCEACL-438d7411 line 4 extended
    deny ip any any (hitcnt=0)
```

As you can see in the preceding example, the downloaded ACL has four statements, including the hit counts on the statements.

NOTE Any downloaded ACL is not saved to flash when you execute the **write memory** command.

CTP ACCOUNTING

The last function of AAA is accounting. Accounting allows you to keep a record of the actions of your users, like when they successfully or unsuccessfully authenticate, what services they are accessing, or what commands they are executing. To use AAA accounting for CTP, you need an AAA server—syslog is not supported.

Appliance Configuration for Accounting

The commands for configuring AAA accounting on the appliance are **aaa accounting**:

```
ciscoasa(config)# aaa accounting {include | exclude} accounting_service
                  {inbound | outbound | logical_if_name
                   internal_IP_address internal_subnet_mask
                   external_IP_address external_subnet_mask
                   group_tag
-or-
ciscoasa(config)# aaa accounting match ACL_ID logical_if_name
                   group_tag
```

The layout of this command is almost the same as the **aaa authentication** and **aaa authorization** commands. In the first statement, the **include** parameter specifies what connections accounting will be enabled for—if the connection isn't included, the appliance will not capture accounting information for it. The *accounting_service* parameter specifies the type of connection, like **any**, **ftp**, **http**, **telnet**, or even by protocol and port, like **udp/69**. For the latter syntax, you can specify a range of ports by separating the beginning and ending port numbers with a hyphen (**tcp/8080-8090**). You can optionally use an ACL with the **match** parameter to specify the connections to gather information from.

Here is an example where all connections will have accounting enabled for them:

```
ciscoasa(config)# aaa accounting include any inbound
                  0 0 0 0 TACSRV
ciscoasa(config)# aaa accounting include any outbound
                  0 0 0 0 TACSRV
```

Once you have set up accounting, make sure that your security server is receiving the accounting information from the appliance.

Cisco Secure ACS Reports

It is important to point out some items concerning accounting on the appliance and using an AAA server. First, when using authentication, accounting will record who was authenticated and when they became unauthenticated, so you can see how long they were logged in. Second, when you are using AAA authorization, only the classic method of authorization will keep a record of what connections the user opened that matched the **aaa authorization** command(s) and whether the CSACS server allowed them. To see these reports, in the left window pane of CSACS, click the Reports And Activity button.

If you are using downloadable ACLs instead of the classic method of authorization, any matches on the ACL statements are *not* sent to the AAA server. If you want a record of what connections were opened by a user with downloadable ACLs, you'll need to add the **log** keyword to your downloadable ACL statements on your AAA server. Then you'll need to forward these log messages either to an external syslog server or to an SNMP management station. This process is discussed in Chapter 26.

CHAPTER 9

IPv6

This chapter will introduce you to the TCP/IP version 6 (IPv6) capabilities of the appliances. IPv6 is a fairly new feature to the appliances, introduced in version 7 with the addition of the ASA security appliances. Because IPv6 is new to the appliances, its IPv6 capabilities are limited; however, Cisco will be greatly expanding them in future operating system releases. The topics covered in this chapter include

▼ IPv6 introduction and the appliance IPv6 features

■ IPv6 addresses on interfaces

■ Routing IPv6 traffic

■ Neighbor and router solicitation and advertisement messages

▲ IPv6 traffic filtering

IPv6 OVERVIEW

IPv6 will eventually replace IPv4, which is the most common networking protocol deployed today. Because of the poor scalability and the deficiencies found in IPv4, IPv6 was created. IPv6 addresses the rapid growth of companies, of technology in countries like India and China, and of the Internet. Basically, IPv6 quadruples the size of bits in IP addresses from 32 bits in IPv4 to 128 bits in IPv6: this gives us approximately 3.4×10^{38} addressable nodes, which provides more than enough globally unique IP addresses for every network device on the planet.

The following two sections will discuss the IPv6 capabilities of the appliances and their limitations when it comes to IPv6. Subsequent sections will briefly cover how to configure IPv6 on the appliances.

IPv6 Capabilities of the Appliances

The security appliances have some support for passing IPv6 traffic between interfaces; however, they are not full-functioning IPv6 devices. The appliances support a basic IPv6 configuration:

▼ Assigning IPv6 addresses to interfaces

■ Filtering IPv6 traffic with ACLs

▲ Basic routing capabilities for IPv6 via static routes

Some of the appliances' management and troubleshooting commands also support IPv6:

▼ **copy** Copying information to/from the appliance using IPv6

■ **ping** Testing connectivity

■ **ssh** Restricting remote access to the appliance using SSH

- ■ `telnet` Restricting remote access to the appliance using SSH
- ■ `debug` Troubleshooting connectivity problems
- ▲ `icmp` Restricting ICMP traffic to an appliance interface (`ipv6 icmp` command)

There are many other commands, but the preceding are the most common management and troubleshooting commands configured or executed on the appliance.

When executing a command that includes an IPv6 address, use the standard nomenclature for IPv6 addresses. For example, if you want to ping a device with an IPv6 address, the `ping` command would look something like this:

```
ciscoasa# ping fe80::2e11:eeff:aaaa:13cd
```

When using the `copy` command or when needing to reference the port number along with the address, you'll need to enclose the IPv6 address in brackets ("[]") and separate the address and following information with a colon (:). For example, if you wanted to back up the running-config file to an FTP server using IPv6 addresses, the `copy` command would look something like this:

```
ciscoasa# copy running-config
            ftp://[fe80::2e11:eeff:aaaa:13cd]:/directory/backup.cfg
```

NOTE My book *CCNA Cisco Certified Network Associate Study Guide (Exam 640-802)* (The McGraw-Hill Companies, 2008) introduces IPv6, the addressing used, and a basic configuration of Cisco routers.

The appliances also have the ability to examine the payload information (the application layer) of certain types of IPv6 packets: FTP, HTTP, ICMP, SIP, SMTP, TCP, and UDP. Other applications and protocols are not currently supported. Application inspection of payload information is discussed in more depth in Part III.

IPv6 Limitations of the Appliances

Understand that as of today, the IPv6 support included with the security appliances is very limited. Basically you can assign IPv6 addresses to interfaces, set up static IPv6 routes, filter IPv6 traffic with ACLs, and add IPv6 connections to the state table.

Many, many features are lacking, but I would expect at least the following to be added in the near future:

- ▼ Translating between IPv6 and IPv4 addresses and vice versa, as well as IPv6 to IPv6 addresses
- ■ Dynamically routing IPv6 traffic
- ■ Inspecting the same application layer payloads that IPv4 supports
- ■ Failover support with IPv6 (currently only IPv4 is supported)
- ▲ IPv6 anycast addresses

IPv6 INTERFACE CONFIGURATION

When setting up processing of IPv6 addresses, each interface that will handle IPv6 traffic minimally needs a link-local address; optionally you can add a global address on the interface. The following three sections cover the three methods of assigning an IPv6 address to an interface: autoconfiguration of IPv6 addresses, manual link-local IPv6 addresses, and manual global IPv6 addresses.

> **NOTE** The security appliances support dual-stacking: you can have both IPv6 and IPv4 addressing configured on the same interface. Note that you'll need routing configured for *both* protocols to reach subnets and networks the appliance is not connected to.

Stateless Autoconfiguration

Stateless autoconfiguration of IPv6 addresses on an interface allows the appliance to learn the 64-bit prefix address from a router advertisement message and to use the EUI-64 method to obtain the last 64 bits of the address, which include the MAC address of the interface in the EUI-64 portion. Autoconfiguration creates a link-local address on the specified interface. To use the autoconfiguration method on an interface, use the following configuration:

```
ciscoasa(config)# interface physical_if_name
ciscoasa(config-if)# ipv6 address autoconfig
```

> **NOTE** Autoconfiguration is the simplest method of assigning an IPv6 address on an appliance interface.

Duplicate IPv6 Address Detection

When using stateless autoconfiguration, the appliances have the ability to detect duplicate IPv6 addresses: an address that is configured on the appliance interface conflicts with another device connected to the same interface. During the duplicate-address-detection process, any configured IPv6 address on the interface is placed in a tentative state. The appliance will first verify any link-local address configured on an interface; then any other IPv6 addresses on the interface, like global addresses, are verified. When being verified, an IPv6 address is marked as "TENTATIVE" until verified.

If the appliance detects a duplicate address, the address is not used, and you'll see the following log message displayed:

```
%PIX|ASA-4-325002: Duplicate address IPv6_address/MAC_address
    on interface
```

When an interface IPv6 address is seen as a duplicate, it is placed in a "DUPLICATE" state. If the same link-local address is seen connected to the same interface, processing of all IPv6 packets on the interface is disabled. However, if the same global address is seen connected to the same interface, the configured global address is not used, but other IPv6 addresses on the interface are used, and processing of IPv6 packets is allowed.

The appliance uses neighbor solicitation messages to detect a duplicate address. (Neighbor solicitation messages are discussed later in the "IPv6 Neighbors" section.) By default the duplicate address check is only performed once when the interface goes active (is brought up). You can change the number of times with the following configuration:

```
ciscoasa(config)# interface physical_if_name
ciscoasa(config-if)# ipv6 nd dad attempts #_of_attempts
ciscoasa(config-if)# ipv6 nd ns-interval #_of_milliseconds
```

The number of attempts can be 0 to 600 in the **ipv6 nd dad attempts** command; setting it to 0 disables duplicate address detection on the specified interface. The **ipv6 nd ns-interval** command specifies the interval in which the duplicate address probes are generated—by default this is 1,000 milliseconds if omitted. This value can range from 1,000 to 3,600,000 milliseconds.

NOTE The **ipv6 nd ns-interval** command changes the interval for not just duplicate address checks, but for all neighbor solicitation messages on the interface.

Link-Local Address Configuration

Besides using stateless autoconfiguration, you can manually assign an IPv6 link-local address using the following configuration:

```
ciscoasa(config)# interface physical_if_name
ciscoasa(config-if)# ipv6 address IPv6_address link-local
```

A hexadecimal format is used when entering the IPv6 address.

Global Address Configuration

Global IPv6 addresses are the equivalent of a public IPv4 address. Normally you are not assigning global addresses to the appliance unless the appliance is directly connected to the Internet, which is unlikely. To assign a global address, use the following configuration:

```
ciscoasa(config)# interface physical_if_name
ciscoasa(config-if)# ipv6 address IPv6_address/prefix_length [eui-64]
```

You must enter the hexadecimal address, along with the prefix length. The **eui-64** parameter allows you to specify the network prefix only for the IPv6 address and have the appliance generate the lower 64 bits of the address automatically, using the interface MAC address as part of this address. When you assign a global address to the interface, the appliance automatically creates a link-local address also.

NOTE When you're enabling IPv6 on an interface, the `ipv6 address` command enables IPv6, alleviating the need to execute the `ipv6 enable` command on the interface. Also, the interface needs a link-local address; however, you can have both a link-local and global address on the same interface.

IPv6 Interface Configuration Verification

Once you have configured the IPv6 addressing on your appliance, you can verify your configuration with the following command:

```
ciscoasa# show ipv6 interface [brief] [logical_if_name]
```

NOTE If you want to see IPv4 addresses assigned to interfaces, use the `show ip address` or `show interface` commands.

Listing 9-1 shows an example of using the `show ipv6 interface` command.

Listing 9-1. IPv6 interface information

```
ciscoasa# show ipv6 interface
ipv6interface is down, line protocol is down
IPv6 is enabled, link-local address is fe80::20d:88ff:feee:abde
    [TENTATIVE]
No global unicast address is configured
Joined group address(es):
ff02::1
ff02::1:ffee:6a82
ICMP error messages limited to one every 100 milliseconds
ICMP redirects are enabled
ND DAD is enabled, number of DAD attempts: 1
ND reachable time is 30000 milliseconds
```

In this example, you can see the name and status of the interface, the link-local address (`fe80::20d:88ff:feee:abde`), that a global address hasn't been assigned, the multicast addresses the interface belongs to (two in the preceding example), and the neighbor discovery information. Also notice that the address is in a `TENTATIVE` state.

IPv6 ROUTING

Without IPv6 routing enabled, the security appliances will switch IPv6 traffic between directly connected IPv6 hosts on interfaces that have IPv6 addresses. Currently the appliances do not support any IPv6 dynamic routing protocols, unlike IPv4: to reach subnets and networks beyond the connected routes of the appliance, you'll need to set up static IPv6 routing. You can configure static and default IPv6 routes on the appliance with the following command:

```
ciscoasa(config)# ipv6 route logical_if_name
                        destination_IPv6_network/prefix
                        next_hop_IPv6_addr [admin_distance]
```

You must first enter the logical name of the interface that the IPv6 network resides off of. This is followed by the IPv6 destination network, including the *prefix* (the number of bits in the network number). For a default route, use `::/0` as the address and prefix. After the destination network is the next-hop IPv6 address of the neighboring router the IPv6 packets should be routed to. Last, you can optionally change the administrative distance of the static route. The administrative distance is used when there are two paths to the same destination, but you prefer one path over another—the lower the value, the more preferred the route.

To view the IPv6 routing table on the appliance, use the **show ipv6 route** command. Here's an example of this command:

```
ciscoasa# show ipv6 route
IPv6 Routing Table - 7 entries
Codes: C - Connected, L - Local, S – Static
L fe80::/10 [0/0]
via ::, inside
L fec0::a:0:0:a0a:a70/128 [0/0]
via ::, inside
C fec0:0:0:a::/64 [0/0]
via ::, inside
L ff00::/8 [0/0]
via ::, inside
<--output omitted-->
```

At the top of the listing, you can see the number of entries in the table, along with a code table that explains the letters found in the left column of the routes. For example, L is a local route and C is a connected route. To the right of the network/route are two numbers in brackets: the left number is the metric of the route, and the right number is the administrative distance. After the `via` tag is the next-hop router address (this will be null for local and connected routes), followed by the local interface the appliance will use to reach the IPv6 destination.

IPv6 NEIGHBORS

With IPv6, the appliance uses ICMPv6 messages with a solicited node multicast address to discover IPv6 neighbors: the link-layer address of neighbors on the same local link, the reachability of the neighbors, and the tracking of the neighbors. This section will discuss two kinds of messages shared with IPv6 neighbors: neighbor solicitation and router advertisement messages.

Neighbor Solicitation Messages

The appliance uses neighbor solicitation messages, via ICMPv6, on local links (connected networks) to discover the link-layer (data link layer) addresses, like MAC addresses, of other neighbors on the same local link. These are sent to the solicited node multicast address, where all neighbors on the local link will respond with a neighbor advertisement message, via ICMPv6. This is a unicast response that contains the source address of the neighbor and a destination address of the appliance interface. The payload contains the responder link-layer address. Once the appliance receives the response, it can contact the neighbor directly. This process is similar to what IPv4 does by using ARP, except that IPv6 is using ICMPv6 for this process. You can use the **clear ipv6 neighbors** command to remove the dynamically learned neighbor information.

Besides being used to discover a neighbor, neighbor solicitation messages are used for these two reasons:

▼   They verify the reachability of an existing neighbor.

▲   They are sent when a link-layer address on a device, like a MAC address, changes. The messages are used to update the IPv6-to-link-layer address tables on all the connected neighbors on the local link.

Neighbor Solicitation Message Tuning

On the appliance, you can change the interval that the appliance uses to send out the neighbor solicitation messages and can change how long to wait to consider a neighbor dead when solicitation messages are no longer seen from a neighbor. Use the following commands to configure these parameters on an appliance interface:

```
ciscoasa(config)# interface physical_if_name
ciscoasa(config-if)# ipv6 nd ns-interval milliseconds
ciscoasa(config-if)# ipv6 nd reachable-time milliseconds
```

The **ipv6 nd ns-interval** command specifies, in milliseconds, the amount of time between the transmission of neighbor solicitation messages on the interface. If you don't change the value, the default is 1,000 milliseconds (1 second). This value can range from 1,000 to 3,600,000 milliseconds. The **ipv6 nd reachable-time** command specifies the dead interval period—if a neighbor's solicitation message isn't seen during this period, the neighbor is considered dead. This value can range from 0 to 3,600,000 milliseconds, where 0 is the default. When set to 0, it is left up to the receiving device to set and track the dead period. To see what this value is on the appliances, use the **show ipv6 interface** command. In Listing 9-1, the reachable time is 30,000 milliseconds (the last line of the output).

NOTE   Don't define short dead intervals to discover dead neighbors, since too short a time might cause the appliance to incorrectly assume that a neighbor is dead.

Static Neighbor Definition

For security purposes, you can statically define your IPv6 neighbors' IPv6 addresses to MAC addresses instead of having the appliance dynamically learn this via neighbor solicitation messages. To define a static neighbor's mapping, use the following command:

```
ciscoasa(config)# ipv6 neighbor IPv6_address logical_if_name
                         MAC_address
```

When creating a static definition, you must define the neighbor's IPv6 address, the logical interface the neighbor is connected to, and the MAC address of the neighbor. Static definitions override any information learned via neighbor solicitation messages. If you execute the `clear ipv6 neighbors` command, static entries are not removed—only dynamically learned ones from neighbor solicitation messages. However, you can remove a static entry by prefacing the `ipv6 neighbor` command with the `no` parameter.

Router Advertisement Messages

Router solicitation messages are sent by IPv6 clients during an interface initialization that is configured for autoconfiguration. These are sent using ICMPv6 to the all-nodes multicast address. A router, like the appliance, can respond with a router advertisement (RA) message. These messages contain the following information:

▼ IPv6 prefix or prefixes of the local link

■ The lifetime of the prefixes

■ The type of autoconfiguration that can be used (stateless or stateful)

■ The default router address

■ The neighbor discovery transmission and reachable interval values

▲ The MTU size of the local link and the maximum hop count allowed

RA Suppression

Normally, IPv6 routers generate periodic RA messages that an IPv6 client can listen to and then use to generate its link local address with stateless autoconfiguration; however, when the IPv6 client is booting up, waiting for the RA might take awhile. In this situation, the client will generate a router solicitation message, asking the IPv6 router to reply with an RA so the client can generate its interface address. Basically the client is requesting the first 64 bits of the 128-bit IPv6 address.

By default, when a client that is connected to an IPv6 interface on the appliance generates an IPv6 router advertisement message, the appliance will act as a router and respond with an RA message that includes the first 64 bits of the IPv6 address. You might want to disable this function and let a real router handle this; or, if the appliance is directly connected to the Internet, you will probably want to disable the RA process on the external interface. Suppressing RA messages on the appliance is done on an interface-by-interface basis by using the following configuration:

```
ciscoasa(config)# interface physical_if_name
ciscoasa(config-if)# ipv6 nd suppress-ra
```

RA Parameters

If you want the appliance to respond to router solicitation messages, you can define some commands to control the process, shown here:

```
ciscoasa(config)# interface physical_if_name
ciscoasa(config-if)# ipv6 nd ra-interval [msec] seconds
ciscoasa(config-if)# ipv6 nd ra-lifetime seconds
ciscoasa(config-if)# ipv6 nd prefix IPv6_prefix/prefix_length
```

These commands are configured on an interface-by-interface basis. The `ipv6 nd ra-interval` command specifies the number of seconds (or milliseconds—`msec`) between RA messages. The default is 200 seconds, but can range from 3 to 1,800 seconds or 500 to 1,800,000 milliseconds. Note that this interval should be shorter than the one defined with the `ipv6 nd ra-lifetime` command. The latter command specifies how long clients on the local link should assume that the appliance is the default router on the local link. This defaults to 1,800 seconds, but can range from 0 to 9,000 seconds. The `ipv6 nd prefix` command configures the prefix that is included in the RA messages; you can configure more than one prefix to include. Note that for stateless autoconfiguration to work for clients, the define prefix must be 64 bits in length.

IPv6 ACLs

Besides being able to filter IPv4 traffic, the appliances can also filter IPv6 packets. Actually you can simultaneously filter both types of traffic on the appliance, on the same interfaces. The following two sections will discuss the configuration of IPv6 ACLs and an example configuration.

IPv6 ACL Configuration

Configuring an IPv6 ACL is very similar to configuring an IPv4 ACL. You can use two basic commands: one for ICMPv6 traffic and one for all other types of IPv6 traffic.

Filtering ICMPv6 Packets

The following ACL command is used to filter ICMPv6 traffic:

```
ciscoasa(config)# ipv6 access-list ACL_ID [line line_#]
                    {deny | permit} icmp6
                    {src_IPv6_prefix/prefix_length | any | host
```

```
                          src_IPv6_addr | object-group
                          network_obj_grp_id}
                      {dst_IPv6_prefix/prefix_length | any | host
                          dst_IPv6_addr | object-group
                          network_obj_grp_id}
                      [icmp_type | object-group
                          icmp_type_obj_grp_id]
                      [log [[level] [interval seconds] | disable |
                          default]]
```

As you can see, the syntax is very similar to an IPv4 ACL. Notice that you can use object groups with your IPv6 ACLs. The main difference is the addressing used: there is no address and subnet mask format. Instead, you can specify the keyword **any**, the keyword **host** followed by an IPv6 address (all 128-bits), an object group, or a network prefix and the prefix length (in bits).

For ICMPv6 message types, you can enter either the name or number of the message type. Current ICMPv6 message names include the following: **destination-unreachable**, **echo-reply**, **echo-request**, **membership-query**, **membership-reduction**, **membership-report**, **neighbor-advertisement**, **neighbor-redirect**, **neighbor-solicitation**, **packet-too-big**, **parameter-problem**, **router-advertisement**, **router-renumbering**, **router-solicitation**, and **time-exceeded**.

NOTE   Refer to Chapter 6 for an overview of IPv4 ACLs and their syntax.

Filtering Other Types of IPv6 Packets

To filter other types of IPv6 packets, use the following ACL command:

```
ciscoasa(config)# ipv6 access-list ACL_ID [line line_#]
                      {deny | permit} {protocol_name_or_# |
                          object-group protocol_obj_grp_id}
                      {src_IPv6_prefix/prefix_length | any | host
                          src_IPv6_addr | object-group
                          network_obj_grp_id} [operator
                              {port [port] |
                          object-group service_obj_grp_id}]
                      {dst_IPv6_prefix/prefix_length | any | host
                          dst_IPv6_addr | object-group
                          network_obj_grp_id} [{operator
                              port [port] |
                          object-group service_obj_grp_id}]
                      [log [[level_#] [interval seconds] |
                          disable | default]]
```

As you can see from the preceding syntax, the configuration of an IPv6 ACL command is almost the same as that of an IPv4 command, with the exception of matching on a range of IPv6 addresses with an IPv6 prefix and prefix length.

Activating and Verifying IPv6 ACLs

Activating an IPv6 ACL is the same as activating an IPv4 ACL: you use the **access-group** command. Here's the syntax:

```
ciscoasa(config)# access-group ACL_ID {in | out} interface
                        logical_if_name
```

Once you have created and activated your ACLs, you can use the **show ipv6 access-list** command to see your statements, along with the hit counts for the statements. Here's the full syntax of the command:

```
ciscoasa# show ipv6 access-list [ACL_ID
                [src_IPv6_prefix/prefix_length |
                any | host src_IPv6_addr]]
```

Without any parameters, the appliance will display all the ACLs: you can qualify the output by providing additional parameters.

IPv6 ACL Example

Now that you have a basic understanding of configuring IPv6 ACLs, let's look at a simple example to help illustrate the use of the commands. Here's a short configuration:

```
ciscoasa(config)# ipv6 access-list acl_out permit tcp any
                        host 3001:1::213:A12F:FAB6:126D eq 80
ciscoasa(config)# ipv6 access-list acl_out deny tcp any
                        host 3001:1::213:A12F:FAB6:126D eq 21
ciscoasa(config)# access-group acl_out in interface outside
```

In this example, outside web and FTP IPv6 connections are allowed to an internal server (3001:1::213:A12F:FAB6:126D).

PART III

Policy Implementation

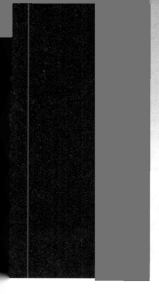

CHAPTER 10

Modular Policy Framework

This chapter will introduce you to the Cisco Modular Policy Framework (MPF) feature on the security appliances. MPF was actually ported from the Cisco IOS routers and switches and added to version 7.0 of the appliances. Obviously many similarities exist in the operation and use of MPF on both platforms; however, there are differences: MPF is primarily used to implement security functions on the appliance. The topics included in this chapter are

▼ An introduction to MPF on the appliances

■ How class maps are used to classify traffic

■ How policy maps are used to associate policies to class maps

▲ How service policies are used to activate policy maps

This chapter focuses on an overview of MPF and on generally how MPF is implemented. Subsequent chapters in Part III will focus on the particulars of how MPF is implemented for different protocols and applications and on some of the enhanced security capabilities that MPF provides you.

MPF OVERVIEW

MPF is a feature ported from the IOS to make it easier to implement consistent and flexible policies on the security appliances. One or more policies can be applied to traffic flowing through the appliance. The following two sections will discuss the policies the appliances support and the components used to implement MPF.

MPF Policies

MPF allows you to assign one or more policies to a class of traffic. The policies you can apply to traffic include the following:

▼ **Inspection of connections**   You can control what traffic is added to the state table to allow returning traffic back to the source, as well as examine the payloads of inspected applications for connection, translation, and security issues.

■ **Connection restrictions**   You can limit the number of completed and half-open (embryonic) connections on a per-group, per-user, or per-host basis; control the idle timeouts for connections in the state table; and control other parameters for connections.

■ **Traffic prioritization**   You can implement low-latency queuing (LLQ) to prioritize delay-sensitive and high-priority traffic, like voice, over normal data traffic.

■ **Traffic policing**   You can rate-limit traffic in both the inbound and outbound directions on an interface to ensure that excessive bandwidth needs of one type of traffic or application doesn't affect other traffic flowing through the appliance.

- **Intrusion prevention system (IPS)** If you have the AIP-SSM card installed in an ASA, you can define policies to copy packets to or to redirect packets into the AIP-SSM card to look for and prevent attacks.

- **Anti-X** If you have the CSC-SSM card installed in an ASA, you can define policies to have traffic redirected through the card to look for viruses, malware, spyware, phishing, and other types of issues with web, FTP, and e-mail applications.

Why MPF Is Necessary

You have already seen many reasons in the last section why you might want to use MPF. However, I need to expand on one of these items, application inspection, to see some of the more hidden advantages that MPF provides. The following three sections will discuss problems that certain applications and/or protocols might have and what MPF can do with application inspection to solve these problems. The remainder of Part III will delve into many of the applications and protocols that Cisco can perform inspection on; the next sections will focus only on some simple examples.

TIP I'm always asked when consulting or teaching Cisco security classes what's the difference between buying a SOHO firewall like a Linksys, Belkin, or D-Link compared with a security appliance like an ASA 5505. Low-end firewall products don't perform application inspection, and therefore they don't necessarily adequately protect the resources that sit behind them. I've always said that in networking, you typically get what you pay for: spending little money gets you little in the feature department.

Security Weaknesses in Applications

Many applications have become famous for their security weaknesses. E-mail and web applications are some of the more well-known ones, like Microsoft Exchange and IIS, Apache web server, and Sendmail. Sendmail and Exchange use the SMTP protocol to implement TCP/IP e-mail solutions. Many of the security weaknesses related to e-mail have to do with the supported commands used by SMTP to interact between devices. You'll want to either configure your SMTP-based e-mail package to remove unnecessary commands, or use an alternative, more centralized solution, like the security appliances, to filter out unnecessary and undesirable commands and behaviors. Some e-mail commands that are undesirable are **debug** and **wiz**. Likewise, even legitimate commands can pose problems for e-mail—for example, you wouldn't want someone using legitimate e-mail commands to harvest your e-mail directory and then to use the learned addresses for a spam attack.

Applications with Multiple Connections

Many applications, especially those related to multimedia, have issues with how they deal with port numbers. As an example, a standard application like telnet uses a well-known destination port number for communications: 23. Anytime a device wants to connect to a telnet server, it opens an unused port above 1023 as the source port and uses 23 as the destination port.

Other applications, however, might use more than one connection to transmit data. A multimedia application, for instance, might have the client open a control connection on a well-known port number, but additional connections might be opened on a range of dynamic port numbers to deliver the actual multimedia content. This process makes secure filtering a more complicated task. For example, if the data connections use completely random ports, how would the firewall device know what connections to allow? Figure 10-1 illustrates this issue.

Basically you could use two solutions to solve this problem:

▼ You could configure very promiscuous ACLs to allow a large range of ports through your firewall. This, of course, isn't very desirable since whether or not someone is using the application, the ACL would always allow the connections.

▲ You could use an intelligent firewall that examines the control connection of the application to determine when the additional connection or connections are needed and the port numbers negotiated between the user and server; then you could have the firewall add this information to its state table to allow the connections and remove them when they are done.

Obviously, of the two solutions, the latter is the preferred approach. Cisco supports this feature for many applications that flow through the appliance. This application inspection process is enabled by default for many applications; however, for others you must manually enable application inspection.

Connections with Embedded Addressing Information

Another problem with some applications is that they may embed IP addresses, and possibly port numbers, in the actual payload and expect the remote peer to use this

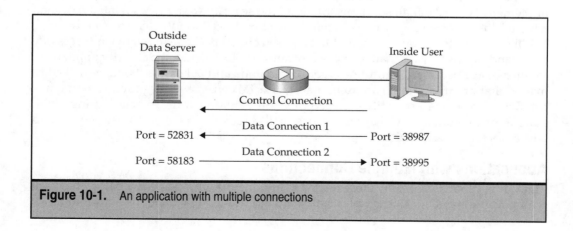

Figure 10-1.   An application with multiple connections

information for an additional connection that should be established. This can create problems with address translation devices, where they are only performing address translation at the network and transport layer, not at the session/application layer. The addressing or port information requested might conflict with what is already in the address translation table.

Look at Figure 10-2, which illustrates this problem. On the control connection, UserB notifies the data server to connect to port 38995 for the data connection; however, port 38995 is already used by another user (UserA) in the translation table.

You have two solutions to this problem: Assuming you could control what source port number the user was going to send to the server, you could define different ports for different users, and then set up a static PAT translation for each user. Obviously this isn't scalable, and on top of this issue, the application might not let you specify the port number the user sends to the server.

A better solution would have the translation device examine the application payloads of control connections to find any embedded addressing information and perform address translation on the layer 3 and layer 4 headers as well as the embedded addresses in the application-layer payloads. Again, Cisco security appliances can deal with many applications that embed addressing information in the application-layer payload and can perform address translation on this embedded information.

NOTE   Cisco doesn't support application-layer inspection for all applications—only the ones more commonly used by a company network. However, the list is quite extensive. The remaining chapters in Part III will cover many of the applications that the appliances support for the application inspection process.

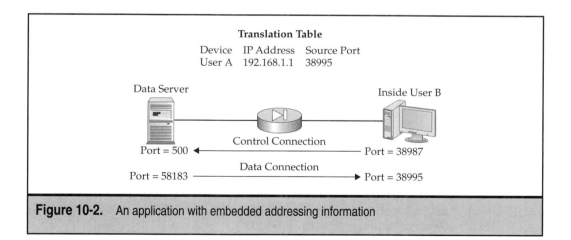

Figure 10-2.   An application with embedded addressing information

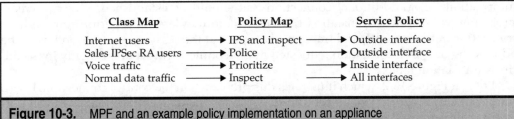

Figure 10-3.   MPF and an example policy implementation on an appliance

MPF Components

Now that you understand some of the policies that MPF can implement and why MPF is needed, let's discuss the components that comprise MPF. Implementing MPF has three components:

▼ **Class maps**   Classify and/or identify traffic that you want to associate one or more policies to

■ **Policy maps**   Associate one or more policies to a class of traffic in your class maps

▲ **Service policies**   Activate the policies in your policy maps either on a specific interface or on all interfaces of the appliance

To help understand the MPF components and how they interact with each other, examine Figure 10-3. In this example, four policies were implemented. First, all Internet traffic entering the outside interface of the appliance will have the IPS card process it and, assuming the IPS card doesn't drop it, the traffic comes back out of the card, and the appliance performs application-layer inspection on it—for valid connections; these will be added to the state table. Second, the Sales IPSec remote access (RA) users will have rate-limiting (policing) applied to their traffic on the outside interface. Third, voice traffic will be prioritized and forwarded out the inside interface before other types of traffic. Fourth, normal data traffic will be inspected on all interfaces and added to the state table as necessary.

CLASS MAPS

Class maps identify the traffic that you want to assign one or more policies to. Cisco supports different kinds of class maps:

▼ **Layer 3/4**   You classify traffic based on information the appliance sees in the layer 3 and/or layer 4 packet headers, like web traffic (TCP port 80) sent to a DMZ web server with an IP address of 192.1.1.1.

■ **Inspection (layer 7)**   You classify traffic based on information in the application payload of a packet, like someone executing the **put** command on an FTP control connection, or a URL that exceeds a certain size on a web connection: these kinds of classifications require the appliance to examine the payload information in depth.

■ **Regular expressions** You classify traffic based on regular expression strings found in the layer 7 application payloads of packets. For example, you might want to look for a URL that begins with "http://" and contains ".cisco.com/".

▲ **Management** Where the other class map types are used for identifying user traffic flowing through the appliance, the management class map is used to classify management traffic to or from the appliance.

When using class maps, you are required to use a layer 3/4 class map to identify the devices and or services, like a particular FTP server. Optionally, you can qualify your traffic by using other class maps, like an inspection class map to also look in the payload for a particular regular expression string of a filename or for an FTP command that is being executed.

NOTE This chapter will primarily focus on layer 3/4 class and policy maps. Inspection class maps will be discussed in more depth in subsequent chapters where the various applications are covered with MPF.

Layer 3/4 Class Maps

Here is the syntax to create a layer 3/4 class map:

```
ciscoasa(config)# class-map class_map_name
ciscoasa(config-cmap)# description class_map_description
ciscoasa(config-cmap)# match any
ciscoasa(config-cmap)# match access-list ACL_ID
ciscoasa(config-cmap)# match port {tcp | udp} {eq port_# |
                              range port_# port_#}
ciscoasa(config-cmap)# match default-inspection-traffic
ciscoasa(config-cmap)# match dscp value1 [value2] [...] [value8]
ciscoasa(config-cmap)# match precedence value1 [value2] [...] [value8]
ciscoasa(config-cmap)# match rtp start_port_# end_port_#
ciscoasa(config-cmap)# match tunnel-group tunnel_group_name
ciscoasa(config-cmap)# match flow ip destination-address
ciscoasa# show run class-map [class_map_name]
```

Use the **class-map** command to assign a unique name to the class map. The **match** command specifies the traffic to include in the class map, where Table 10-1 explains the parameters for this command.

Match Parameter	Description
`any`	Includes all traffic.
`access-list`	Includes any traffic that matches the `permit` parameters in the specified ACL.
`port`	Includes any traffic that matches the specified port number(s).
`default-inspection-traffic`	Includes all default application inspection traffic, which is about a dozen-and-a-half protocols.
`dscp`	Matches on the specified DSCP values in the IP header used for QoS.
`precedence`	Matches on the specified TOS values in the IP header used for QoS.
`rtp`	Matches on the range of port numbers used by RTP, which is a protocol commonly used in multimedia applications like Cisco IP/TV and SIP.
`tunnel-group`	Matches on a particular site-to-site connection or on a WebVPN or IPSec remote access group.
`flow`	Further qualifies the matching process when the configured policy is policing: for example, when you're rate-limiting remote access users, without this command, all traffic associated with the user would be rate-limited with the defined policy; with this command, the policy is applied to a user on a *per-destination* basis.

Table 10-1. The `match` Command Parameters

NOTE When you're looking for a match, most `match` commands are XOR (*Or*ed), so if any traffic matches a `match` command in a class map, it is included in the classification. However, in certain cases, it uses an XAND (*And*ed) process, like `match dscp` and `match tunnel-group` would allow you to look for different QoS settings for a particular VPN tunnel in a single class map.

Default Class Map

When you boot up an appliance with no configuration, you will find certain default configurations on it. One default configuration is for MPF, where a default class map is already configured, shown here:

```
ciscoasa# show run class-map
class-map inspection_default
 match default-inspection-traffic
```

Table 10-2 lists the default inspection protocols/applications, protocols, and source and destination ports the appliance is expecting and inspecting them on. *N/A* indicates any port. For example, by default the appliance is expecting the FTP control connection to be

Application/Protocol	Protocol	Source Port	Destination Port
CTIQBE	TCP	N/A	1748
DCERPC	TCP	N/A	135
DNS	UDP	53	53
FTP	TCP	N/A	21
GTP	UDP	2123 and 3386	2123 and 3386
H323 H225	TCP	N/A	1720
H323 RAS	UDP	N/A	1718 and 1719
HTTP	TCP	N/A	80
ICMP	ICMP	N/A	N/A
ILS	TCP	N/A	389
IM	TCP	N/A	1–65539
IPSec Pass-Thru	UDP	N/A	500
NetBIOS	UDP	137–138	N/A
RPC	UDP	111	111
RSH	TCP	N/A	514
RTSP	TCP	N/A	554
SIP	TCP/UDP	N/A	5060
Skinny (SCCP)	TCP	N/A	2000
SMTP	TCP	N/A	25
SQL*Net	TCP	N/A	1521
TFTP	UDP	N/A	69
XDMCP	UDP	177	177

Table 10-2. Default Traffic Inspection for the `match default-traffic-inspection` Command

using TCP where the destination server port is 21. Cisco created a predefined list for the most commonly used applications. If you have an FTP server using a different destination port, like 2121, the appliance doesn't know this by default—you would either have to create a specific layer 3/4 class map and include this information, or add this information to the default class map.

Class Map Configuration Example

To help illustrate the use of layer 3/4 class maps, let's look at the following configuration example:

```
ciscoasa(config)# access-list DMZ_Server_ACL permit tcp any
                       host 192.168.1.1 eq 8080
ciscoasa(config)# class-map DMZ_Web_Server
ciscoasa(config-cmap)# match access-list DMZ_Server_ACL
ciscoasa(config)# class-map L2L_Orlando
ciscoasa(config-cmap)# match tunnel-group L2L_Orlando_VPN
ciscoasa(config-cmap)# match dscp cs5
```

The first class map, DMZ_Web_Server, includes the DMZ web server listening on port 8080. I could easily have used the `match port tcp 8080` command instead of using an ACL; however, the problem with the `match port` command is that it includes all port 8080 connections. In this example, I might have a web server running on TCP port 8080, but a different server might have a different application running on port 8080. Using ACLs, I can be very specific about what traffic I'm classifying and identifying.

The second class map includes voice traffic (DSCP code CS5) on a particular IPSec site-to-site (LAN-to-LAN or L2L) connection. L2L connections are defined using a tunnel group (this is discussed in Chapter 15), where this tunnel group specifies the Orlando L2L connection.

Application Layer Class Maps

Application layer class maps are used to look for certain things in the application-layer payload; they can be used to qualify a layer 3/4 class map, which identifies the layer 3 addresses, the protocol, and possibly the port numbers of the application involved. Application layer class maps fall under two categories: regular expressions and inspection class maps. The following two sections will discuss what these are, how they are used, and introduce how they are configured.

Regular Expressions and Class Maps

Regular expressions are used to match on a string of characters or variations of characters, like looking for "richard" in either lowercase, uppercase, or mixed case. Special characters can be used to create wildcard patterns, look for information in certain parts of a string, and for many other uses. Actually, Cisco didn't invent its own special characters for regular expression pattern matching; instead, it uses the same ones that many UNIX programs use, like *grep*, *awk*, and *sed*.

Regular expressions can be used in layer 7 class and layer 7 policy maps for information embedded in the payload of a connection. For example, a layer 3/4 class map allows you to look for an FTP connection to the server at 192.1.1.1. However, a regular expression allows you to qualify this information, like looking for a particular user account the user uses to log into the server, or a particular filename or directory the user accesses on the server. The following sections will discuss how to create regular expressions, how to test them, and how to group them (using a regular expression class map) on the appliance.

Creating a Regular Expression   Creating a regular expression is done with the `regex` command:

```
ciscoasa(config)# regex regex_name regular_expression
```

First, you must give the regular expression a name that describes what you are matching on. Following this is the regular expression pattern you want to search for in a string. Table 10-3 has a list of regular expression special characters you can use to match on a string of text.

Special Character	Explanation
.	The "." matches any single character. For example, "d.g" matches "dog", "dig", "dug", and any word that contains those characters, like "daggonnit".
(exp)	The "()" segregates characters from the surrounding characters, so that you can use other metacharacters on the subexpression. For example, "d(o|i)g" matches "dog" and "dig", but "do|ig" matches "do" and "ig". A subexpression can also be used with repeated quantifiers to differentiate the characters meant for repetition. For example, "12(34){3}5" matches "123434345".
|	The "|" matches either expression it separates. For example, "dog|cat" matches "dog" or "cat".
?	The "?" indicates that there are 0 or 1 of the previous character. For example, "ra?ise" matches on "raise" or "rise". Note that you must enter **Ctrl+V** and then the question mark, or else the ASA CLI help function is performed instead.
*	The "*" indicates that there are 0, 1, or any number of the previous character. For example, "mo*se" matches on "mse", "mose", "moose", and so on.

Continues...

Table 10-3.   Regular Expression Special Characters

Special Character	Explanation
+	The "+" indicates that there is at least 1 of the previous character. For example, "mo+se" matches on "mose" and "moose", but not "mse".
{x} or {x,}	The "{}", with a number between the braces, indicates the previous expression is repeated at least "x" times. For example, "ab(fd){2,}e" matches "abfdfde", "abfdfdfde", and so on.
[abc]	The "[]" matches any character in the brackets. For example, "[Rr]" matches on "R" or "r".
[^abc]	The "[^]" matches a single character that is *not* contained within the brackets. For example, "[^abc]" matches any character other than "a", "b", or "c"; or "[^A-Z]" matches any single character that is not an uppercase letter.
[a-c]	The "[-]" matches any character in the range. For example, "[A-Z]" matches any uppercase letter. You can also mix characters and ranges: "[abcq-z]" matches "a", "b", "c", and "q" through "z". You could also write this as "[a-cq-z]".
" abc"	The """" preserves trailing or leading spaces in the string. For example, " secret" preserves the leading space when it looks for a match.
^	The "^" specifies the beginning of a line.
\	The "\", when used with a regular expression metacharacter, matches a literal character. For example, "\." matches a period ("."). This is used when you want to match on a character that is itself a metacharacter.
\r	The "\r" matches on a carriage return.
\n	The "\n" matches on a new line.
\t	The "\t" matches on a tab.
\f	The "\f" matches on a form feed (new page).
\xNN	The "\x" matches on an ASCII character specified by the two hexadecimal digits (NN).
\NNN	The "\" matches on any ASCII character specified as octal (the three digits listed).

Table 10-3. Regular Expression Special Characters (*Continued*)

To help you with creating regular expressions, here are two examples:

```
ciscoasa(config)# regex My_string1 [Rr]ichard@abc.com
ciscoasa(config)# regex My_string2 ".+\.[Jj][Pp][Gg]"
```

The `My_string1` regular expression matches on either "Richard@abc.com" or "richard@abc.com". The `My_string2` regular expression matches on any string that has at least one character before ".jpg" in any case (upper-, lower-, or mixed case). For example, this would include "a.jpg", "B.JPG", and "anyfile.JpG", but not ".jpg".

Testing Regular Expressions   If you are unsure how to create a regular expression, Cisco supports a **test** command that you can use to test a string of input against a regular expression:

```
ciscoasa# test regex input_text regular_expression
```

Here are some examples and the resulting output of the test:

```
ciscoasa# test regex dog "[Dd][Oo][Gg]"
INFO: Regular expression match succeeded.
ciscoasa# test regex cat "[Dd][Oo][Gg]"
INFO: Regular expression match failed.
ciscoasa# test regex filename.gif ".+\. [Jj][Pp][Gg]"
INFO: Regular expression match failed.
ciscoasa# test regex filename.jpg ".+\. [Jj][Pp][Gg]"
INFO: Regular expression match succeeded.
ciscoasa# test regex .jpg ".+\.[Jj][Pp][Gg]"
INFO: Regular expression match failed.
```

Grouping Regular Expressions   You can group regular expressions together in a regular expression class map. For example, you might want to look for a handful of regular expressions in the payload of a packet. Regular expression class maps can be used for this. Here is the syntax to group your regular expressions together into a set:

```
ciscoasa(config)# class-map type regex match-any class_map_name
ciscoasa(config-cmap)# match regex regex_name
```

Here is an example of configuring regular expressions and including them in a regular expression class map:

```
ciscoasa(config)# regex My_string1 [Rr]ichard@abc.com
ciscoasa(config)# regex My_string2 [Aa]lina@abc.com
ciscoasa(config)# class-map type regex match-any Email_Class
ciscoasa(config-cmap)# match regex My_string1
ciscoasa(config-cmap)# match regex My_string2
```

In the preceding example, a regular expression class map includes the two e-mail addresses, where the names of the e-mail addresses can begin with either a lower- or uppercase character.

> *NOTE*   If you are only interested in looking for one regular expression, then you usually don't need to create a regular expression class map. The regular expression class maps are typically only needed when you want to look for multiple regular expressions in a packet payload.

Inspection Class Maps

Cisco supports a handful of class maps that can be used to qualify what, in the application layer payload, you want to look for and then apply a policy to. These class maps are commonly referred to as *inspect* or *inspection* class maps. The general syntax of creating an inspection class map is as follows:

```
ciscoasa(config)# class-map type inspect application
                        [match-all | match-any] class_map_name
ciscoasa(config-cmap)#
```

For the *application* parameter, the following applications are currently supported: **dns**, **ftp**, **h323**, **http**, **im**, and **sip**. The **match-all** parameter specifies that all the **match** commands must be matched on in order to classify the traffic and associate a policy to it; the **match-any** parameter specifies that only one **match** command has to be matched on to associate a policy to the traffic; if you omit it, the parameter defaults to **match-any**.

Once you create the inspection class map, you are taken into a subcommand mode. Some of the **match** commands are the same between different application types, but many of them are different. These commands will be discussed with the applications in the remaining chapters in Part III. Just to give you an idea what an inspection class map looks like, here's an example for web traffic:

```
ciscoasa(config)# class-map type inspect http match-any
                        examine-put-and-post
ciscoasa(config-cmap)# match request method put
ciscoasa(config-cmap)# match request method post
```

In this example, if the user's web browser sends a **put** or **post** command (notice the **match-any** parameter for the class map), then this would qualify as a match.

POLICY MAPS

Policy maps are used to implement policies for traffic that matches **match** commands in class maps. There are two kinds of policy maps:

▼ **Layer 3/4 policy map**   Specifies policies for layer 3/4 class maps, which are basically traffic flows based on IP addresses and protocol information; an example layer 3/4 policy would be where you want the IPS card in an ASA to process TCP port 80 traffic as it comes into the outside interface.

▲   **Layer 7 policy map**   Specifies policies for data found in the packet payload, like a URL a web browser sends to a web server. An example layer 7 policy would be performing a TCP reset on an FTP connection when someone executes the **put** command on the FTP control connection. Layer 7 policies are sometimes referred to as *application* or *inspection* policies.

To implement policies, you must minimally use a layer 3/4 policy map. Optionally you can qualify the layer 3/4 policy with a layer 7 policy. The following sections will discuss the use and configuration of these two policy maps.

Layer 3/4 Policy Map

Layer 3/4 policy maps associate one or more policies to traffic that matches a **match** command in a layer 3/4 class map. When more than one policy is associated with the class map, the policies are enforced in the order listed next:

1. Connection limits, connection timeouts, and TCP sequence number randomization
2. CSC card
3. Stateful and application inspection
4. IPS card
5. Input policing
6. Output policing
7. Priority queuing

The following sections will discuss how to create layer 3/4 policy maps and how to associate policies with layer 3/4 class maps.

General Layer 3/4 Policy Map Syntax

Creating a layer 3/4 policy map is done with the **policy-map** command:

```
ciscoasa(config)# policy-map policy_map_name
ciscoasa(config-pmap)# class class_map_name
ciscoasa(config-pmap-c)#
```

The **policy-map** command takes you into a subcommand mode where you reference your layer-3/4 class map name or names with the **class** command. When referencing a class map, you are taken into a second subcommand mode. In this second mode, you reference the actual policies for the class of traffic. Note that you can specify more than one policy for a class of traffic. The following sections will discuss how to set up the specific policies.

Connection Limits

Connection limits are commonly used to prevent connection and flood attacks. You can have different connection policies for different applications, servers, users, or a combination of the three. These can include number of connections, timeouts, and randomization of TCP sequence numbers. The following two sections show you how to configure a connection limit policy.

TIP I've used connection limits to prevent users from spawning hundreds of connections from their bit-torrent and peer-to-peer clients. In one case, three problem users had over 500 UDP connections each, all transferring data via bit torrent. Connection limits can also prevent network hardware from being overwhelmed with attack traffic if a new worm should hit the network. I always tell my customers to implement some type of limitation, between 1 connection and below the point where the appliance conn table fills up or its CPU becomes pegged at 100 percent. Remember that by default a single user can create an unlimited number of connections and that the appliances have a finite number of connections that they can support; therefore put some connection limitation in place. Ask yourself, should a user have 500 UDP sessions at once? No? How about 100? No? How about 50? Not sure? Then 50 might be a nice place to start instead of "until the firewall chokes" because of a flood of connections.

Connection Limit Configuration   The following configuration allows you to define connection limits as well as enabling or disabling the randomization of TCP sequence numbers:

```
ciscoasa(config)# policy-map policy_map_name
ciscoasa(config-pmap)# class class_map_name
ciscoasa(config-pmap-c)# set connection conn-max max_#_conns
ciscoasa(config-pmap-c)# set connection per-client-max max_#_user_conns
ciscoasa(config-pmap-c)# set connection embyronic-conn-max
                          max_#_embryonic_conns
ciscoasa(config-pmap-c)# set connection per-client-embryonic-max
                          max_#_user_embryonic_conns
ciscoasa(config-pmap-c)# set connection random-sequence-number
                          {enable | disable}
ciscoasa(config-pmap-c)# set connection timeout tcp HH:MM:SS [reset]
ciscoasa(config-pmap-c)# set connection timeout embryonic HH:MM:SS
ciscoasa(config-pmap-c)# set connection timeout half-close HH:MM:SS
ciscoasa(config-pmap-c)# set connection timeout dcd retry_interval
                          [max_tries]
```

The **conn-max** parameter limits the maximum number of simultaneous connections for all traffic that matches the class map. The **per-client-max** parameter limits the maximum number of connections (open) for each user within the class map. The **embyronic-conn-max** parameter limits the maximum number of embryonic connections (half-open) for all traffic that matches the class map. The **per-client-embryonic-max** parameter limits the maximum number of embryonic connections (half-open) for each user within the class map.

NOTE   If you don't define any connection limits, whatever the appliance can fit in its state table (the licensed limit) is what the appliance will allow.

The `random-sequence-number` parameter enables or disables the randomization of TCP sequence numbers for traffic that matches the class map. By default this is enabled. You should only disable it if some other device is already doing this process (like a second appliance), or if a TCP application is using some type of signature process, like MD5, where the randomization feature would corrupt the signature. For example, if you have BGP routers using MD5 on different sides of the appliance, you will need to disable the TCP sequence number randomization for the two routers.

The remaining commands allow you to define timeouts for connections in the conn table. Limits you can specify are for idle TCP connections. The `timeout tcp` parameter specifies a timeout for idle TCP sessions (this defaults to 1 hour). The `reset` parameter in this command specifies that when you're removing the idle TCP connection from the conn table, you also send a TCP RST (reset) to both the source and destination devices. The `timeout embryonic` parameter specifies the timeout for half-open (embryonic TCP) connections (this defaults to 30 seconds). The `timeout half-close` parameter specifies the timeout for connections that are closing—going through the FIN/FIN-ACK (this defaults to 5 seconds). The `timeout dcd` parameter specifies that when a TCP session times out from the `set connection timeout tcp` command, the appliance should send a Dead Connection Detection (DCD) probe on the connection to both devices associated with the connection to determine if the connection is valid. If one of the end devices doesn't respond after the maximum number of tries (defaults to 5), the appliance removes the connection. If both end devices respond to the probe, the connection is considered valid, and the appliance resets the idle timer. Between each probe the appliance waits 15 seconds by default.

Connection Limit Example   To understand the use of connection limits, examine the following example configuration:

```
ciscoasa(config)# access-list DMZ_web permit tcp any
                     host 192.168.1.10 eq 80
ciscoasa(config)# access-list DMZ_web permit tcp any
                     host 192.1.1.1 eq 80
ciscoasa(config)# class-map DMZ_web_server_class
ciscoasa(config-cmap)# match access-list DMZ_web
ciscoasa(config)# policy-map outside_policy
ciscoasa(config-pmap)# class DMZ_web_server_class
ciscoasa(config-pmap-c)# set connection conn-max 2000
ciscoasa(config-pmap-c)# set connection embyronic-conn-max 1000
ciscoasa(config-pmap-c)# set connection per-client-max 150
ciscoasa(config-pmap-c)# set connection per-client-embryonic-max 100
ciscoasa(config-pmap-c)# set connection timeout tcp 00:00:30 reset
ciscoasa(config-pmap-c)# set connection timeout embryonic 00:00:10
```

In this example, connection limits are placed on the DMZ web server. The server is listed twice in the ACL: once with its local address and once for its global address. This is necessary if you want to apply a policy for both internal and external users. For this policy, no more than 2,000 total web connections to the web server are allowed, or 150 per user; of these connections, no more than 1,000 of these can be in a half-open state, with a limit of 100 half-open connections per user. The TCP idle timeout was changed from 1 hour to 30 seconds, and the embryonic timeout from 30 to 10 seconds.

NOTE Remember that you can also define connection limits and disable TCP sequence number randomization in your address translation commands: `static` and `nat`. This was discussed in Chapter 5. If you've configured both, the MPF configuration takes precedence over the address translation commands.

CSC-SSM Card

The CSC-SSM card, commonly called the *Anti-X* card, can look for a variety of attacks as well as set up many policies that apply to FTP, web, and e-mail traffic. However, by default no traffic is forwarded to the card: you must set up a policy to have traffic processed by the card. For traffic that should be processed by the CSC-SSM card, the traffic is forwarded from the backplane of the ASA into the CSC card, processed by the card, and then forwarded back to the backplane of the ASA for further processing (assuming that the traffic isn't dropped by the CSC card because of a policy violation). You can see the traffic flow in Figure 10-4. Traffic that the card can process includes FTP, HTTP, HTTPS, SMTP, and POP3. It is not recommended to forward other types of traffic, because the card will probably drop these. The following two sections will discuss how to set up a policy to have the CSC-SSM card process traffic.

CSC-SSM Configuration After you've identified what traffic you want the card to process with a layer 3/4 class map, you can associate the CSC-SSM policy to it with the following configuration:

```
ciscoasa(config)# policy-map policy_map_name
ciscoasa(config-pmap)# class class_map_name
ciscoasa(config-pmap-c)# csc {fail-open | fail-close}
```

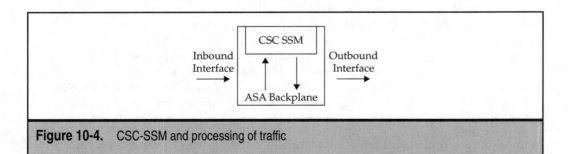

Figure 10-4. CSC-SSM and processing of traffic

The `csc` command specifies that the specified traffic should be forwarded to the CSC-SSM card for further processing. Options for traffic that should be processed by the card include

▼ `fail-open` If card is not operational, traffic bypasses the policy.

▲ `fail-close` If card is not operational, traffic is dropped.

NOTE The CSC-SSM card might not be operational because it is dead, missing its operating system, or is in the process of booting up or rebooting.

CSC-SSM Example Here's a simple example that will redirect traffic to the CSC-SSM card:

```
ciscoasa(config)# access-list CSCACL permit tcp any any eq 80
ciscoasa(config)# access-list CSCACL permit tcp any any eq 443
ciscoasa(config)# access-list CSCACL permit tcp any any eq 25
ciscoasa(config)# access-list CSCACL permit tcp any any eq 110
ciscoasa(config)# class-map CSC_map
ciscoasa(config-cmap)# match access-list CSCACL
ciscoasa(config)# policy-map inside_user_policy
ciscoasa(config-pmap)# class CSC_map
ciscoasa(config-pmap-c)# csc fail-open
```

In the preceding example, all web (HTTP and HTTPS), SMTP, and POP3 traffic will be processed by the CSC-SSM card. If the card is not operational, the traffic in the ACL is allowed to bypass the policy until the card becomes operational again, at which point the card will process the traffic. This policy allows the users to access the Internet and e-mail when the card is booting up or rebooting—your security policy will determine if you use fail-open or fail-close as your card policy.

NOTE Typically the Anti-X card is used to protect the end-users, while the IPS card is best used to protect the networks themselves and servers, like those on a DMZ segment.

AIP-SSM Card

The AIP-SSM card, commonly called the *IPS* card, can look for a variety of attacks against applications, protocols, operating systems, and networks. However, by default no traffic is processed by the card: you must set up a policy first. For traffic that should be processed by the AIP-SSM card, you can configure inline or promiscuous modes. These are shown in Figure 10-5. With inline mode, a matching packet for a policy is forwarded *into* the card, processed by the card, and returned to the backplane of the ASA for further processing. When the policy is in inline mode, the IPS card can drop packets itself. In promiscuous mode, a packet matching an IPS policy is *copied* to the card: the original

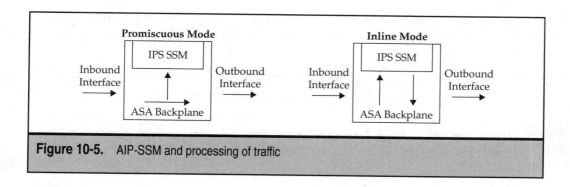

Figure 10-5. AIP-SSM and processing of traffic

packet stays on the backplane of the ASA and is processed further by the ASA. When the policy is in promiscuous mode, the IPS card itself cannot drop attacks; however, it can reset TCP connections, and it can log into the ASA and set up a shun (commonly called a *block*) to block offending traffic.

Inline mode has the card be proactive, allowing it to drop offending packets, while promiscuous mode has the card be reactive, where it can't drop the initial offending packets. Both have advantages and disadvantages. While traffic matching a policy is in inline mode, the traffic must go through the card, causing delay; plus if traffic is sent to the card that exceeds its processing capabilities, the card can be overwhelmed and drop packets. The upside of promiscuous mode is that if the card is overwhelmed, it doesn't affect traffic because the original packets stay on the backplane of the ASA. Plus, you'll get a higher Mbps performance rate by using promiscuous mode. However, the problem with promiscuous mode is that it can't effectively deal with atomic (single-packet) or Trojan horse attacks, since its reaction to the attack would typically be too little, too late.

AIP-SSM Configuration After you've identified what traffic you want the card to process with a layer 3/4 class map, you can associate the AIP-SSM policy to it with the following configuration:

```
ciscoasa(config)# policy-map policy_map_name
ciscoasa(config-pmap)# class class_map_name
ciscoasa(config-pmap-c)# ips {promiscuous | inline}
                             {fail-open | fail-close}
```

First, with the **ips** command, you must specify the mode of operation—**promiscuous** or **inline**—for the class of traffic. And as with the CSC-SSM card, you can choose from two options to configure that you can have the ASA perform if the IPS card is not operational: **fail-open** or **fail-close**.

NOTE The AIP-SSM card can simultaneously do inline and promiscuous modes: for one class of traffic, you can use promiscuous mode, and for another class of traffic, inline mode.

AIP-SSM Example   Here's a simple example that uses an AIP-SSM policy:

```
ciscoasa(config)# access-list IPSACL1 permit tcp any any
ciscoasa(config)# access-list IDSACL2 permit udp any any
ciscoasa(config)# class-map IPS_map1
ciscoasa(config-cmap)# match access-list IPSACL1
ciscoasa(config)# class-map IDS_map2
ciscoasa(config-cmap)# match access-list IDSACL2
ciscoasa(config)# policy-map outside_policy
ciscoasa(config-pmap)# class IPS_map1
ciscoasa(config-pmap-c)# ips inline fail-open
ciscoasa(config-pmap-c)# exit
ciscoasa(config-pmap)# class IDS_map2
ciscoasa(config-pmap-c)# ips promiscuous fail-open
ciscoasa(config-pmap-c)# exit
```

In the preceding example, two AIP-SSM policies are configured: TCP traffic is processed by the IPS card using inline mode, and all UDP traffic is processed using promiscuous mode.

Rate Limiting: Policing

A rate-limiting policy, commonly called a *policing* policy, can be configured to affect traffic as it enters (ingress) and/or leaves (egress) an interface. The parameters used to enforce the policy are similar to how CIR (committed information rate) and B_C (committed burst rate) are used in frame relay, using the leaky bucket algorithm to handle small bursts of traffic. The following two sections will discuss how to configure a policing policy.

Policing Configuration   After you've identified what traffic you want the card to process with a layer 3/4 class map, you can associate the rate-limiting policy to it with the following configuration:

```
ciscoasa(config)# policy-map policy_map_name
ciscoasa(config-pmap)# class class_map_name
ciscoasa(config-pmap-c)# police {input | output}
                            conform-rate-bps [burst-size-bytes |
                            conform-action {drop | transmit} |
                            exceed-action {drop | transmit} ]
```

The **police** command assigns a rate-limiting policy to the associate class map. The **input** parameter is used to set up a rate-limiting traffic policy as traffic enters the interface, and **output** is used as traffic leaves the interface. The conforming rate, in bits per second (bps), is similar to a frame relay CIR value—when traffic runs at this rate or slower, it is considered conforming. The burst size, in bytes, allows the first x bytes above the conforming rate before it is considered nonconforming. The ASA uses the leaky bucket algorithm to implement this function: once the number of bytes specified above the conforming rate has been sent, the bucket is empty and traffic continuing to be sent above this rate is nonconforming. The bucket can be filled back up by traffic going slower than the conforming rate. So basically the burst size is to allow for small bursts in data traffic. The last part of the command is where you specify the policy when the traffic is conforming or exceeding the configured policing rate: **drop** or **transmit**.

Policing Example   Here's a simple example that uses a policing policy:

```
ciscoasa(config)# class-map Remote_Access_Users
ciscoasa(config-cmap)# match tunnel-group sales
ciscoasa(config-cmap)# match tunnel-group humanresources
ciscoasa(config)# policy-map outside_policy
ciscoasa(config-pmap)# class Remote_Access_Users
ciscoasa(config-pmap-c)# police input 56000 10800
                         conform-action transmit exceed-action drop
ciscoasa(config-pmap-c)# police output 56000 10800
                         conform-action transmit exceed-action drop
```

The preceding example sets up a rate-limiting policy for two IPSec remote access user groups—each user is allowed a traffic rate of 56 Kbps with a burst of about 10 Kbps in either direction on an interface. IPSec remote access tunnel groups are discussed in Chapter 17.

Prioritization and Queuing

Packet prioritization is used on the egress of an interface to prioritize traffic—before traffic exits an interface. Prioritization is normally used for delay-sensitive traffic, like voice, or possibly video. Currently only low-latency queuing (LLQ) is supported for prioritization. The following two sections will discuss how to configure prioritization for your delay-sensitive traffic.

NOTE   You can find a very good overview of LLQ at this web site: http://www.netqos.com/resourceroom/articles/06_bandwidth_sharing.html.

Priority Configuration   To implement a prioritization policy, you must do two things: configure a policy that contains prioritization, and enable LLQ on an egress interface. Here is the syntax to accomplish both:

```
ciscoasa(config)# policy-map policy_map_name
ciscoasa(config-pmap)# class class_map_name
ciscoasa(config-pmap-c)# priority
ciscoasa(config-pmap-c)# exit
ciscoasa(config)# priority-queue logical_if_name
```

First, prioritization must be enabled within a layer 3/4 policy map with the **priority** command. Second, on each egress interface where you want to use prioritization, you must enable LLQ with the **priority-queue** command.

Priority Example   Here's a simple example that uses a prioritization policy:

```
ciscoasa(config)# class-map L2L_Orlando_Tunnel
ciscoasa(config-cmap)# match tunnel-group L2L_Orlando_Tunnel
ciscoasa(config-cmap)# match dscp cs5
ciscoasa(config)# policy-map outside_policy
ciscoasa(config-pmap)# class L2L_Orlando_Tunnel
ciscoasa(config-pmap-c)# priority
ciscoasa(config-pmap-c)# exit
ciscoasa(config)# priority-queue outside
```

In the preceding example, the site-to-site IPSec tunnel connection to Orlando has its voice traffic (**dscp code cs5**) prioritized over other types of IPSec tunnel traffic on the outside interface. In other words, the voice traffic has priority over the data traffic that is sent across the IPSec tunnel.

Traffic Inspection

The appliances perform stateful functions by default on all TCP and UDP traffic that is allowed between interfaces. In other words, assuming that TCP and UDP connections are allowed through the appliance via ACLs, the connections are added to the state table so that their returning traffic can come back through the appliance.

If you want to perform application layer inspection (examining the payloads of connections), this needs to be enabled on the appliance. Quite a few applications are enabled by default for application layer inspection, which is discussed in the "Default Layer 3/4 Policy Map" section later in the chapter. However, additional inspection policies are disabled for most protocols and applications—you have to enable them by creating a policy. The following two sections will discuss how to configure inspection policies for your appliances.

Traffic Inspection Configuration   To have the appliances perform application payload inspection or to inspect ICMP traffic, you need to create a layer 3/4 inspection policy. Here is the syntax to accomplish this:

```
ciscoasa(config)# policy-map policy_map_name
ciscoasa(config-pmap)# class class_map_name
ciscoasa(config-pmap-c)# inspect application_or_protocol [parameters]
```

The **inspect** command sets up an inspection policy for a class of traffic in a policy map. Protocols and applications you reference will have the appliance look at a limited number of things in the application layer payload based on code Cisco has written. Applications and protocols you can specify include the following: **ctiqbe, dcerpc, dns, esmtp, ftp, gtp, h323, http, icmp, icmp error, ils, im, ipsec-pass-thru, mgcp, netbios, pptp, radius-accounting, rsh, rtsp, sip, skinny, sqlnet, snmp, sqlnet, sunrpc, tftp,** and **xdmcp**. Which application or protocol is used will affect whether additional parameters can be configured for the **inspect** command. The additional parameters are discussed in the remaining chapters of Part III where I discuss the specific protocols and applications listed earlier.

When inspection is enabled for a protocol, besides adding the associated connections to the conn table, the appliance can do the following:

▼   Look for additional data connections that might be opened via the control connection, and add these to the conn table.

■   When performing address translation, look for embedded addressing information and add this to the xlate table, and fix any addressing conflicts with existing translations in the xlate table.

▲   Depending on the application or protocol, look for common security issues and prevent them.

Optionally you can sometimes qualify a layer 3/4 policy with a layer 7 (application) policy, where you can specify policies on many things found in the payload, creating much more specific and flexible policies. For example, you could define a policy for FTP traffic that limits what FTP commands can be executed on the control connection. The layer 7 policy topic is introduced in the "Layer 7 Policy Map" section later in the chapter.

Traffic Inspection Example   Here's a simple example that uses an inspection policy:

```
ciscoasa(config)# access-list INS1 permit tcp any
                          host 192.168.1.10 eq ftp
ciscoasa(config)# class-map FTP_server
ciscoasa(config-cmap)# match access-list INS1
ciscoasa(config)# policy-map outside_policy
ciscoasa(config-pmap)# class FTP_Server
ciscoasa(config-pmap-c)# inspect ftp
ciscoasa(config-pmap-c)# exit
```

In the preceding example, a minimal amount of application layer inspection is performed for the FTP server. Besides adding the control connection to the conn table, the appliance looks for additional data connections being negotiated on the control connection and adds these to the conn table, as well as adding and fixing embedded addressing information and adding this to the xlate table (if translation is configured). The topic of FTP inspection will be discussed in more depth in Chapter 12.

Default Layer 3/4 Policy Map

The appliance has a default policy configuration when the appliance boots up with cleared configuration. You can view this with the **show run policy-map** command:

```
ciscoasa# show run policy-map
policy-map type inspect dns preset_dns_map
 parameters
  message-length maximum 512
```

```
policy-map global_policy
 class inspection_default
  inspect dns preset_dns_map
  inspect ftp
  inspect h323 h225
  inspect h323 ras
  inspect rsh
  inspect rtsp
  inspect esmtp
  inspect sqlnet
  inspect skinny
  inspect sunrpc
  inspect xdmcp
  inspect sip
  inspect netbios
  inspect tftp
```

The `preset_dns_map` is a layer 7 policy map, discussed in the next section. The default layer 3/4 policy map is called `global_policy` and has inspection enabled for over a dozen applications and protocols.

NOTE You can modify the policies in the default policy map by referencing layer 7 policy maps for an application, adding additional inspection rules, or by removing an inspection rule by prefacing it with the **no** command.

Layer 7 Policy Map

If you want to perform additional inspections at the application layer, you can associate a layer 7 policy with your layer 3/4 policy map configuration. Not all applications support layer 7 policies, but Cisco does support quite a few. This section will briefly cover an overview of layer 7 policy maps and how they are used. However, the remainder chapters in Part III will discuss many of these applications and their application-layer inspection features in much more depth.

Configuring a Layer 7 Policy Map

Many applications support layer 7 policy maps, commonly called *inspection* policy maps. These maps allow you to define policies you want the appliance to enforce based on what's inside the payload of certain packets. To create a layer 7 policy map, use the **policy-map type inspect** command, shown here:

```
ciscoasa(config)# policy-map type inspect application policy_map_name
ciscoasa(config-pmap)#
```

The application names you can specify include the following: **dcerpc, dns, esmtp, ftp, gtp, h323, http, im, mgcp, netbios, radius-accounting, rtsp, sip, skinny,** and **snmp.** The policy map name can be up to 40 characters, but cannot begin with "_internal" or "_default", which are reserved names.

When executing the **policy-map type inspect** command, you are taken into a subcommand mode, where you can configure your policies. The basic commands you can include here are as follows:

▼ **match**   This command specifies matching criteria for what you want to examine in the payload and apply a policy to. You can match on regular expression strings and/or regular expression class maps, commands, and many other things. For example, you could match on specific FTP commands or on a particular HTTP URL. The policies you can assign are **drop, log,** and **reset** (the latter applies only to TCP connections).

■ **class**   This command identifies a layer 7 class map (**class-map type inspect**) and the policies that should be associated with the class map. The difference between a **match** command and a class map in a layer 7 policy map is that a class map can include multiple matches, and class maps can be used multiple times in different policies, simplifying your configuration. However, not all applications that support layer 7 policy maps support layer 7 class maps.

▲ **parameter**   This command affects how the inspection engine works; the parameters that you configure depend on the application you're setting up the policy for.

By default the **match** and **class** commands are processed in the order that you enter them in the layer 7 policy map. If an action is to drop the packet/connection or reset the connection, then no further processing of the policy map takes place. If an action is to log the transaction, further **match** commands or class maps can be processed in the layer 7 policy map. If a **match** command has more than one action defined, like **log** and **reset**, both are performed. Here's a simple example that illustrates this process:

```
ciscsoasa(config-pmap)# match request header length gt 500
ciscoasa(config-pmap-c)# log
ciscoasa(config-pmap-c)# exit
ciscoasa(config-pmap)# match request header length gt 1000
ciscoasa(config-pmap-c)# reset
```

Don't be concerned about the actual syntax of the preceding commands, since I'll be covering these commands in more depth in the other chapters in Part III. The preceding example applies to HTTP connections. If an HTTP request header were 1,100 bytes long, it would match both of the preceding **match** commands. In this situation, since the commands are processed in order, the appliance would both log and reset the connection. However, if you were to reverse the order of the two commands, only the reset would be performed.

TIP Based on the processing of `match` and `class` commands in a layer 7 policy map, your log policies should appear before your drop and reset policies.

The remainder chapters in this part will cover these components in much more depth for each of the applications that supported advanced protocol inspection.

Using a Layer 7 Policy Map

To use a layer 7 policy map, you must reference it in your inspection rule that's defined in a layer 3/4 policy map, like this:

```
ciscoasa(config)# policy-map layer_3/4_policy_map_name
ciscoasa(config-pmap)# class layer_3/4_class_map_name
ciscoasa(config-pmap-c)# inspect application_name
                         layer_7_policy_map_name
```

Layer 7 Policy Map Example

To give you a basic idea how layer 7 and layer 3/4 policy maps are used, examine the following example:

```
ciscoasa(config)# regex url_cisco1 cisco1\.com
ciscoasa(config)# regex url_cisco2 cisco2\.com
ciscoasa(config)# class-map type regex match-any MYURLs
ciscoasa(config-cmap)# match regex cisco1
ciscoasa(config-cmap)# match regex cisco2
ciscoasa(config-cmap)# exit
ciscoasa(config)# class-map type inspect http match-all L7-http-class
ciscoasa(config-cmap)# match req-resp content-type mismatch
ciscoasa(config-cmap)# match request body length gt 1100
ciscoasa(config-cmap)# match not request uri regex class MYURLs
ciscoasa(config-cmap)# exit
ciscoasa(config)# policy-map type inspect http L7-http-map
ciscoasa(config-pmap)# class L7-http-class
ciscoasa(config-pmap-c)# drop-connection log
ciscoasa(config-pmap-c)# exit
ciscoasa(config-pmap)# match req-resp content-type mismatch
ciscoasa(config-pmap-c)# reset log
ciscoasa(config-pmap-c)# exit
ciscoasa(config-pmap)# parameters
ciscoasa(config-pmap-p)# protocol-violation action log
ciscoasa(config-pmap-p)# exit
ciscoasa(config-pmap)# exit
ciscoasa(config)# access-list Web_Server_ACL permit tcp any
                         host 192.1.1.1 eq 80
```

```
ciscoasa(config)# class-map L3_Web_Server
ciscoasa(config-cmap)# match access-list Web_Server_ACL
ciscoasa(config-cmap)# exit
ciscoasa(config)# policy-map L3-web-policy-map
ciscoasa(config-pmap)# class L3_Web_Server
ciscoasa(config-pmap-c)# inspect http L7-http-map
```

Again, I don't want to focus on the complete preceding configuration and all the specific commands, since many of these are discussed in Chapter 12 for layer 7 policies. Instead I want to focus on how all class and policy maps work together and how they're referenced. In this example, it is probably easier to work through the example in *reverse*, starting at the bottom. I've highlighted the map names and how they are referenced to make it a little bit easier to understand how all these components work together.

A layer 3/4 policy map called L3-web-policy-map includes a layer 3/4 class map called L3_Web_Server, which includes TCP port 80 traffic being sent to the web server (192.1.1.1). Notice that the policy for this traffic is to perform application layer inspection for HTTP, but the inspection rule is qualified with a layer 7 policy map, L7-http-map.

This layer 7 policy map includes a layer 7 class map called L7-http-class, which is looking for certain things in the payload, that, if seen, will drop and log the connections. Notice that the class map references a regular expression class map, MYURLs, which includes two regular expressions (a URL that contains "cisco1.com" or "cisco2.com"). An additional **match** and **parameter** command defines more policies for information found in the payload of HTTP connections.

TIP   As you can see from this example, configuring policies can be a very complex process. If you are a novice with the appliances, I recommend that you do not use the CLI to configure policies. Instead use ASDM, since it has a wizard-driven process to set this up. You can then look at the commands the appliance creates to help you learn how it is configured from the CLI. ASDM is discussed in Chapter 27.

SERVICE POLICIES

A service policy is basically the activation of your layer 3/4 policy maps. The following sections will show you how to activate and verify the policies on your appliance.

Activating a Layer 3/4 Policy Map

You can activate a layer 3/4 policy map globally (all interfaces) or on a specific interface; however, you can only have one policy map applied per location. In the case where there is a global policy and an interface policy, the interface policy overrides the global policy settings.

Here is the syntax to activate a layer 3/4 policy map:

```
ciscoasa(config)# service-policy layer_3/4_policy_map_name
                  {global | interface logical_if_name}
```

The default policy, `global_policy` (discussed previously in the "Default Layer 3/4 Policy Map" section), has already been activated globally. You can verify this with the **show run** command:

```
ciscoasa(config)# show run service-policy
service-policy global_policy global
```

Only one policy map can be activated globally; however, you can add to, change, or remove the default policies. Likewise, you can only have one layer 3/4 policy map applied to an interface. However, this can include all the policies you need (class maps, and so on) to affect traffic on the specified interface.

Service Policy Verification

To verify that your policies are being enforced, use the **show service-policy** command:

```
ciscoasa# show service-policy [global | interface logical_if_name]
```

Here is an abbreviated example of the use of this command:

```
ciscoasa# show service-policy
Global policy:
  Service-policy: global_policy
    Class-map:  inspection_default
        Inspect: dns preset_dns_map, packet 0, drop 0, reset-drop 0
        Inspect: ftp, packet 0, drop 0, reset-drop 0
<--output omitted-->
Interface outside:
  Service-policy: Outside_Interface_Policy
    Class-map: Traffic_From_Internet
        IPS: card-status Up, mode inline fail-close
          packet input 0, packet output 0, drop 0, reset-drop 0
<--output omitted-->
```

The preceding example has two layer 3/4 policies: the global policy (`global_policy`) and the one for the outside interface (`Outside_Interface_Policy`). For the global policy, notice that application layer inspection for DNS and FTP is enabled, as well as others that are not shown. For each application, notice that there is a packet, drop, and reset-drop count—as packets match on the policy and the actions for the policy, you can see these counters increment. The outside interface policy includes a layer 3/4 class map called `Traffic_From_Internet` that has an IPS policy associated with it, where the traffic that matches the class map will be redirected into the AIP-SSM card. Again, you can see counters for the policy to verify that it is functioning. For the IPS policy, there is an input and output packet count—you can see the number of packets that enter the card and leave the card to return to the ASA backplane.

CHAPTER 11

Protocols and Policies

This chapter will primarily focus on inspection of protocols on the appliance, building upon the MPF topics discussed in Chapter 10. Chapters 12, 13, and 14 will focus on different applications and how the appliance performs application inspection for them. The topics in this chapter include inspection of the following protocols:

▼   ICMP

■   DCE/RPCs

■   Sun RPCs

■   ILS and LDAP

■   NetBIOS

■   IPSec Pass-Thru

■   PPTP

▲   XDMCP

NOTE   General Packet Radio Service (GPRS) Tunneling Protocol (GTP) is not discussed in this book because it is used in very few networks: GTP is used to bridge cellular data networks and traditional networks, and thus is typically found only in carrier networks. The appliances support GTP inspection; however, GTP requires a special license. RADIUS accounting inspection is also not discussed, since this feature goes hand-in-hand with GTP to prevent overbilling attacks against carrier customers.

ICMP INSPECTION POLICIES

ICMP is used in IP to provide feedback about communication problems and information related to IP connectivity. It uses IP as a transport and is designated with a protocol number of 1 in the protocol field of the IP header. In version 6 and earlier, the PIXs had limited abilities in inspecting ICMP traffic, basically fixing embedded addressing information in payloads for translation purposes. Starting in version 7, the appliances can do much more since stateful tracking of ICMP is supported. The following two sections will discuss both of these features, where both ICMPv4 and ICMPv6 inspections are supported.

ICMP Issues

One of the issues with ICMP is that it embeds addressing information in the packet payload. It copies the first part of the IP header and embeds this information in the ICMP payload. This process can cause problems with address translation devices where these devices are typically looking at just the IP header when performing translation.

To deal with this problem, an address translation device will have to look into the ICMP payload for this addressing information and translate it as well as the addresses in the IP packet header. The appliances application inspection will perform this function for ICMP packets—this has been around since version 6 of the OS. The appliances support both NAT and PAT, where the ICMP sequence numbers are used instead of TCP/UDP port numbers to differentiate between different ICMP connections. Application inspection will ensure that the following information is changed to support a transparent address translation process:

▼ IP address and checksum in the IP header

■ ICMP header checksum

▲ IP address and checksum embedded in the ICMP payload

In version 6 and earlier of ICMP, application inspection was automatically enabled on the PIX, and there was no way to disable it. Starting in version 7, ICMP inspection is disabled by default. To enable the equivalent of what was done automatically in version 6, you need to enable ICMP error inspection, which examines ICMP reply messages and performs its fix-up of addressing issues in ICMP error messages.

Starting in version 7, the appliances can add ICMP connections to the conn table as well as fix embedded addressing information in ICMP echo messages. The appliances keep track of ICMP connections in the conn table by examining the source and destination IP addresses as well as the ICMP sequence number in the ICMP header: each ICMP echo request is considered a *separate* connection. By default, state tracking of ICMP is disabled, but can be easily enabled with an inspection policy.

SECURITY ALERT! Care should be taken, however, to ensure that a flood of spoofed ICMP messages doesn't unnecessarily fill up the state table when ICMP state tracking is enabled. In other words, use ACLs with your layer 3/4 class maps to control for which devices ICMP state tracking should be enabled. I also highly recommend that you not use ACLs on interfaces to allow ICMP returning traffic (you had no choice in version 6), since ICMP traffic is very easily spoofed, and this can create bandwidth issues in your network and CPU issues on your appliances.

ICMP Inspection Configuration

To enable ICMP inspection of traffic, you need to create a layer 3/4 inspection policy:

```
ciscoasa(config)# policy-map policy_map_name
ciscoasa(config-pmap)# class class_map_name
ciscoasa(config-pmap-c)# inspect icmp error
ciscoasa(config-pmap-c)# inspect icmp
```

The **inspect icmp error** command fixes and translates (if necessary) embedded addressing information in ICMP error messages. The **inspect icmp** command allows ICMP connections to be added to the conn table and fixes embedded addressing information in the payloads of ICMP echo messages. Both these commands apply to IPv4 and IPv6 ICMP traffic.

Here's a configuration example that enables ICMP inspection on the inside interface of an appliance:

```
ciscoasa(config)# class-map icmp-class-map
ciscoasa(config-cmap)# match default-inspection-traffic
ciscoasa(config-cmap)# exit
ciscoasa(config)# policy-map icmp_policy_map
ciscoasa(config-pmap)# class icmp-class-map
ciscoasa(config-pmap-c)# inspect icmp
ciscoasa(config-pmap-c)# inspect icmp error
ciscoasa(config-pmap-c)# exit
ciscoasa(config)# service-policy icmp_policy_map interface inside
```

Again, in real life, I would control for which internal devices ICMP inspection was enabled by using an ACL with the layer 3/4 class map and denying ICMP traffic for all other devices.

DCE/RPC INSPECTION POLICIES

Distributed Computing Environment/Remote Procedure Calls (DCE/RPC) is a protocol that allows software to work across multiple computers, making it appear as if the software were on a single computer. This allows programmers to create distributed code without having to worry about the underlying network the computers are connected to. Microsoft is an example of a company that commonly uses DCE/RPCs to implement distributed client/server applications...allowing local users to easily access application resources on remote servers.

DCE/RPCs involve a client sending a query to an Endpoint Mapper (EPM) program/ service that listens on a well-known port number. The client uses this connection to learn and access the dynamically allocated network information of the application or service. Based on the information negotiated for the DCE/RPC connection or connections, the appliance, using its inspection feature for DCE/RPC, can add the dynamic connections to the conn table and perform address translation, fixing any embedded addressing information that conflicts with an existing entry in the xlate table. For Microsoft, the users connect using TCP to port 135 on the EPM service.

DCE/RPC Policy Configuration

By default, DCE/RPC inspection is disabled on the appliances; you must create an inspection policy to enable it. You are required to create an inspection policy in a layer 3/4 policy map; optionally you can qualify your policy with a layer 7 policy map. Here are the commands to set up an inspection for a DCE/RPC policy:

```
ciscoasa(config)# policy-map type inspect dcerpc L7_policy_map_name
ciscoasa(config-pmap)# description string
ciscoasa(config-pmap)# parameters
```

The `sunrpc-server` command defines the port mapper server and the interface the server is connected to on the appliance. With this command you can control the RPC program numbers the appliance will perform inspection for and add to the conn table. The protocol and port are the connection used to initially connect to the port mapper program on the server: in most instances this is TCP port 111. The `timeout` parameter controls how long to keep the additional connections added in the conn table, commonly called *pinhole* connections.

NOTE   To determine the Sun RPC program numbers, on the UNIX box use the `sunrpcinfo` command, which will list the program numbers registered in the port mapper service.

To display the Sun RPC pinhole connections added to the conn table, use the `show sunrpc-server active` command. Here's an example of the use of this command:

```
ciscoasa# show sunrpc-server active
LOCAL                  FOREIGN               SERVICE   TIMEOUT
--------------------------------------------------------------
1 192.168.200.25/0 192.168.150.3/2049  100003    0:30:00
2 192.168.200.25/0 192.168.150.3/2049  100003    0:30:00
3 192.168.200.25/0 192.168.150.3/647   100006    0:30:00
4 192.168.200.25/0 192.168.150.3/650   100006    0:30:00
```

In this example, the client (192.168.200.25) is connecting to the server (192.168.150.3) for two RPC programs (100003 and 100006).

To remove the pinhole connections from the conn table, use the `clear sunrpc-server active` command. Note that you cannot control which Sun RPC connections are removed: they are all removed from the conn table.

Sun RPC Example Configuration

Here's a simple example showing you how to set up a Sun RPC inspection policy:

```
ciscoasa(config)# sunrpc-server inside 192.168.150.3 255.255.255.255
                  service 100003 protocol tcp 111
                  timeout 30:00:00
ciscoasa(config)# sunrpc-server inside 192.168.150.3 255.255.255.255
                  service 100006 protocol tcp 111
                  timeout 30:00:00
ciscoasa(config)# class-map L3_sunrpc
ciscoasa(config-cmap)# match port tcp eq 111
ciscoasa(config)# policy-map global-policy
ciscoasa(config-pmap)# class L3_sunrpc
ciscoasa(config-pmap-c)# inspect sunrpc
ciscoasa(config)# service-policy global-policy global
```

In this example, inspection of Sun RPC services is enabled globally; however, I've controlled the inspection process to only include the one port mapper server (192.168.150.3) on the inside interface for the two RPC programs (100003 and 100006). Note that the class map for Sun RPCs isn't necessary in this example, since the appliance expects Sun RPC port mapper connections to be using TCP 111—however, if this is different, you would need to use a class map to indicate the port mapper connection parameters.

ILS/LDAP INSPECTION POLICIES

The Internet Locator Service (ILS) was developed by Microsoft to be used by their Active Directory, NetMeeting, and SiteServer products. ILS is based on the Lightweight Directory Access Protocol (LDAP). Basically ILS allows a user to find the information that is necessary to connect to another computer. The information that ILS can store includes IP addresses of devices, e-mail addresses of individuals, and usernames of accounts.

ILS allows the Microsoft SiteServer product to create a dynamic directory of NetMeeting users. This information is then used by NetMeeting users to initiate calls and to set up meetings via the directory server. Users create a connection to the ILS server and register their addressing information. The use of ILS simplifies issues where clients may be using DHCP to acquire their addresses, where their IP address may be different each time they boot up.

Mechanics of ILS/LDAP Connections

Before I begin talking about how the appliance application inspection feature deals with connectivity issues between clients and an ILS server, let's first take a look at how connections get set up between these two sets of devices. ILS/LDAP uses a client/server model with sessions being handled over a single TCP connection: A client opens a TCP connection to the ILS server at port 389. On this connection, the client will register its addressing information. Once the connection is established, the client can learn the IP addresses of peers that it might want to communicate with via NetMeeting or another H.323 application. As you can see, the setup of this connection is straightforward.

The only issues with ILS connections that the appliance deals with are embedded addressing information in the payloads of packets. The main function of the application inspection feature for ILS is to locate embedded addresses in the TCP 389 connection and fix them; PAT is not supported since LDAP only stores IP addresses. ILS inspection does have some additional limitations:

▼ ILS inspection cannot handle referral requests by the client and the corresponding responses from the ILS server.

■ ILS inspection cannot deal with users listed in multiple directories.

▲ A user cannot have multiple identities in multiple directories—if they do, ILS inspection will not function properly.

TIP If you are not using address translation, or if the addresses involved with ILS connections are using NAT 0, then ILS inspection is unneeded and should not be used, in order to improve the performance of the appliance.

ILS/LDAP Policy Configuration

Inspection of ILS was added in version 6.2 of the OS. To create an ILS/LDAP inspection policy, use the following configuration:

```
ciscoasa(config)# policy-map L3/4_policy_map_name
ciscoasa(config-pmap)# class L3/4_class_map_name
ciscoasa(config-pmap-p)# inspect ils
```

The inspection process on the appliance doesn't support layer 7 class and policy maps for ILS/LDAP.

ILS/LDAP Example Configuration

Here's a simple example showing you how to set up an ILS/LDAP inspection policy:

```
ciscoasa(config)# class-map L3_ilsldap
ciscoasa(config-cmap)# match port tcp eq 389
ciscoasa(config)# policy-map global-policy
ciscoasa(config-pmap)# class L3_ilsldap
ciscoasa(config-pmap-c)# inspect ils
ciscoasa(config)# service-policy global-policy global
```

Note that the class map for ILS/LDAP is unnecessary in this example, since the appliance expects ILS/LDAP connections to be using TCP 389—however, if this were different, you would need to use a class map to indicate the correct connection parameters.

NetBIOS INSPECTION POLICIES

NetBIOS (Network Basic Input/Output System) is a session layer protocol used in older operating systems to resolve names to addresses in small networks. It can use many protocols to transport its information, including TCP/IP and IPX/SPX. Users can statically define a resolution table using the LMHOSTS file, or use a WINS server for registering names and addresses as well as performing name lookups. For TCP/IP, NetBIOS can use either TCP or UDP, but every implementation I've seen uses UDP, and the destination port number of the WINS server is 137.

The appliance inspection role with NetBIOS is twofold:

▼ The appliance can look for embedded IP addresses and fix them if they conflict with current translations in the xlate table. (This won't work with PAT, since NetBIOS is based on IP addresses.)

▲ The appliance can look for NetBIOS protocol violations and drop and/or log them.

The following two sections will discuss how to configure NetBIOS inspection on the appliance.

NetBIOS Policy Configuration

NetBIOS inspection is enabled by default in the global policy of the appliance for all interfaces. However, this inspection only looks for and fixes embedded IP addresses in the payloads of NetBIOS packets. You can optionally have the appliance look for NetBIOS protocol violations by creating a layer 7 policy map. Here's the configuration for inspection of NetBIOS traffic:

```
ciscoasa(config)# policy-map type inspect netbios L7_policy_map_name
ciscoasa(config-pmap)# description string
ciscoasa(config-pmap)# parameters
ciscoasa(config-pmap-p)# protocol violation action
                            {drop [log] | log}
ciscoasa(config)# policy-map L3/4_policy_map_name
ciscoasa(config-pmap)# class L3/4_class_map_name
ciscoasa(config-pmap-p)# inspect netbios [L7_policy_map_name]
```

There's only two policies you can define in the layer 7 policy map for NetBIOS: drop and log or just log protocol violations. Without a layer 7 policy map, the appliance will only look for and fix embedded addressing information.

NetBIOS Example Configuration

Here's a simple example showing you how to set up a NetBIOS inspection policy:

```
ciscoasa(config)# policy-map type inspect netbios L7_netbios
ciscoasa(config-pmap)# parameters
ciscoasa(config-pmap-p)# protocol violation action drop log
ciscoasa(config)# class-map L3_netbios
ciscoasa(config-cmap)# match port udp eq 137
ciscoasa(config)# policy-map global-policy
ciscoasa(config-pmap)# class L3_netbios
ciscoasa(config-pmap-c)# inspect netbios L7_netbios
ciscoasa(config)# service-policy global-policy global
```

Note that the class map for NetBIOS is unnecessary in this example, since the appliance expects NetBIOS connections to be using UDP 137—however, if this were different, you would need to use a class map to indicate the correct connection parameters. I've also added inspection for protocol violations in NetBIOS packets.

TIP NetBIOS has been supplanted primarily by DNS. Only if you have older applications that require the use of NetBIOS, then you should leave it enabled; otherwise, if all your applications use DNS, then disable NetBIOS inspection in the global policy map.

IPSec PASS-THRU INSPECTION POLICIES

IPSec Pass-Thru is a feature Cisco added to the appliances in version 7 and is really meant for SOHO networks. As you will see in Part IV, an IPSec tunnel or session involves three connections:

 ▼   A management connection uses UDP port 500. This connection is used to exchange IPSec-related information.

 ▲   Two data connections use the ESP and/or AH protocols.

The issue is when you have an IPSec remote access client or site-to-site router behind the appliance and want it to be able to establish an IPSec tunnel to a corporate IPSec server. Assuming the client doesn't support NAT-T (see Chapter 15), the user will experience a few issues with Cisco appliances:

 ▼   ESP and AH connections are not added to the conn table of the appliance: the IPSec Pass-Thru inspection feature automatically allows these connections, assuming the corresponding UDP 500 management connection has been established. This greatly reduces your ACL configuration, since you don't need to configure ACL entries for the ESP or AH connections.

 ▲   If the end-user device is using ESP for encapsulating data and the appliance is performing PAT, the first end-user device that goes out can have the ESP connections redirected to it; however, subsequent devices won't be able to get around this problem unless they use NAT-T. In other words, the first user's ESP connection works, and subsequent users' ESP connections won't.

AH breaks when using any type of address translation. Because of this, most IPSec VPNs use ESP.

IPSec Pass-Thru Policy Configuration

Remember that since the IPSec connections are protected and encrypted, only minimal inspection is supported for IPSec: basically, besides the preceding bullet points, you can limit the number of connections allowed by a client and what their timeout is. By default, IPSec Pass-Thru inspection is disabled. Here are the commands to enable it:

```
ciscoasa(config)# policy-map type inspect ipsec-pass-thru
                     L7_policy_map_name
ciscoasa(config-pmap)# description string
```

```
ciscoasa(config-pmap)# parameters
ciscoasa(config-pmap-p)# {esp | ah} {[per-client-max #_of_conns]
                                     [timeout hh:mm:ss]}
ciscoasa(config)# policy-map L3/4_policy_map_name
ciscoasa(config-pmap)# class L3/4_class_map_name
ciscoasa(config-pmap-p)# inspect ipsec-pass-thru [L7_policy_map_name]
```

The use of AH is very uncommon with IPSec implementations; so if you're going to implement a layer 7 policy for IPSec, you'll probably be specifying **esp** as the protocol parameter. You can place a limit on the number of data connections for a device, like a user's PC, as well as place a timeout for the ESP/AH connections associated with the allowed UDP 500 management connection.

IPSec Pass-Thru Example Configuration

Here's a simple example showing you how to set up an IPSec Pass-Thru inspection policy:

```
ciscoasa(config)# policy-map type inspect ipsec-pass-thru L7_passmap
ciscoasa(config-pmap)# parameters
ciscoasa(config-pmap-p)# esp per-client-max 5 timeout 0:15:00
ciscoasa(config)# access-list passthru_ACL permit udp any any eq 500
ciscoasa(config)# class-map L3-passthru-map
ciscoasa(config-cmap)# match access-list passthru_ACL
ciscoasa(config)# policy-map outside_policy
ciscoasa(config-pmap)# class L3-passthru-map
ciscoasa(config-pmap-c)# inspect ipsec-pass-thru L7_passmap
ciscoasa(config)# service-policy outside_policy interface outside
```

In this example, I've limited the number of VPN sessions to 5, where the timeout for the ESP connections is 15 minutes.

PPTP INSPECTION POLICIES

PPTP is one of the VPN remote access solutions developed originally by Microsoft; however, it is an open standard. PPTP uses a TCP control channel (TCP port 1723) and typically two PPTP GRE tunnels for transmitting data. The control connection is used to negotiate and manage the data connections. To protect the data, it is encrypted and placed in a PPP packet, which an outer GRE header is added to, and then placed in an outer IP header. GRE is an IP protocol.

The appliance inspection feature is basically used to deal with address translation and connection issues. When inspection is enabled, only PPTP version 1 is inspected on the TCP control channel. The appliance keeps track of the outgoing call request and reply sequences, and adds xlates and connections as necessary for the data connections. NAT works without any issues; however, if you want to use PAT, the PPTP devices must support a modified version of GRE defined in RFC 2637, and the PPTP devices must negotiate this over the TCP control connection. If this occurs, then the appliance can fix embedded addressing information for PAT translations. If the modified version of GRE is not supported by the devices or is not negotiated, then the appliance cannot perform PAT inspection.

PPTP Policy Configuration

PPTP inspection is disabled by default on the appliances. To enable it, use the following configuration:

```
ciscoasa(config)# policy-map L3/4_policy_map_name
ciscoasa(config-pmap)# class L3/4_class_map_name
ciscoasa(config-pmap-p)# inspect pptp
```

Please note that layer 7 class and policy maps are not supported for PPTP inspection.

PPTP Example Configuration

Here's a simple example showing you how to set up a PPTP inspection policy:

```
ciscoasa(config)# class-map L3_pptp_ports
ciscoasa(config-cmap)# match port tcp eq 1723
ciscoasa(config)# policy-map L3_pptp_policy
ciscoasa(config-pmap)# class L3_pptp_ports
ciscoasa(config-pmap-c)# inspect pptp
ciscoasa(config)# service-policy L3_pptp_policy interface inside
```

To enable PPTP inspection for all interfaces, enable the policy in the default global policy on the appliance.

XDMCP INSPECTION POLICIES

XDMCP (X Display Manager Control Protocol) is a protocol that provides authenticated access for remote X-windows clients requesting display services from an X-windows server. X-windows is a desktop solution that has been around for more than two decades. One of the issues in the mid-1980s was the cost of desktops. In the UNIX world, a solution was developed to reduce the cost of the desktop: X-windows. Basically, X-windows allows a desktop to only need a LAN NIC, a boot flash, a graphics card, a keyboard and mouse, and a monitor. As you can see, this is a far cry from today's PCs. However, cost being an issue, the X-windows client was stripped of every possible item. The X-windows client would dynamically acquire an IP address and then set up a session with an X-windows server where it would get a graphical display to access and use resources on the X-windows server. Basically, an X-windows client is a diskless client in its simplest form.

Mechanics of XDMCP Connections

To help illustrate how XDMCP connections are established between an X-windows client and an X-windows server, I'll use the example shown in Figure 11-1. When setting up an XDCMP connection (which uses UDP), the client device will choose a port number greater than 1023 that is not currently being used by another network application. The destination port number is the well-known port 177. This connection is a *management* connection and is used to perform authentication as well as to negotiate the port parameter to use for the *display* connection.

Once the management connection is established, the X-windows client will acquire a port number from the X-windows server to set up the display connection. This connection, which uses TCP, is the pipe that the server uses to send all display information to the client as well as any interaction of the client with this display to be sent to the server. Since the X-windows server might have many X-windows clients connecting to it, the X-windows server will typically start at port 6000, assign that to the first X-windows client, and then work its way up from 6000 for each successive client; however, an administrator can control the range of ports used. Once the server assigns the port number to the client, the client then sets up the TCP display connection to this port. As you can see from the setup of these two XDMCP connections, this process is very similar to passive mode FTP, discussed in Chapter 12.

Client on the Inside of the Appliance

When the client is on the inside of the network and initiates an X-windows connection to an X-windows server on the outside of the network, the appliance will by default allow the UDP connection, since the connection is traveling from a higher security level interface to a lower one. This is *also* true for the display connection. Therefore, both of these connections will be able to be established unless you are filtering with ACLs.

Client on the Outside of the Appliance

Let's assume that the client in this example is actually on the outside of your network, and the X-windows server is on the inside. For the initial client connection to work, you'll need to configure an ACL entry that will allow traffic heading to the X-windows server for UDP port 177—without this, no type of X-windows connection can be made.

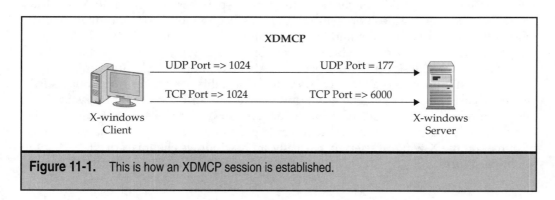

XDMCP

UDP Port => 1024   UDP Port = 177

TCP Port => 1024   TCP Port => 6000

X-windows Client   X-windows Server

Figure 11-1.   This is how an XDMCP session is established.

Once the management connection has been established, the client attempts to set up the display connection using the assigned TCP port number from the X-windows server (6000 and higher). One thing that application inspection on the appliances *won't* do with XDMCP is dynamically add the second connection coming inbound from the client. Assuming that application inspection is enabled for XDMCP, the appliance will automatically be looking at the XDMCP management connection for the negotiated ports of the display connection and will perform any address translation that is necessary, but won't add the second TCP connection—you'll need to use the `established` command to allow this. (This is not the same thing as the `established` parameter in an ACL statement on an IOS device like a router.) Please note that the appliance can fix embedded IP addresses in the payload, but not port numbers; therefore, XDMCP will break for connections that the appliance has a PAT policy configured for. The following sections will cover how to set up application inspection of XDMCP on the appliance.

SECURITY ALERT! As a word of warning, it is highly advised *not* to allow X-windows connections through a perimeter appliance, since X-windows has been known to have been exploited in the past and is not a secure protocol. If you must have external X-windows connections, it is preferred that they be transmitted through a VPN.

XDMCP Policy Configuration

XDMCP application inspection is enabled by default on the appliances in the global policy; you might want to disable it globally and then enable it for only certain interfaces. To enable or disable XDMCP inspection, use the following configuration:

```
ciscoasa(config)# policy-map L3/4_policy_map_name
ciscoasa(config-pmap)# class L3/4_class_map_name
ciscoasa(config-pmap-p)# [no] inspect xdmcp
```

Please note that layer 7 class and policy maps are not supported for XDMCP inspection.

TIP Remember that XDMCP inspection is only needed for connections going from a lower to a higher security level interface by default; you only need it for outbound connections if you have an ACL restricting outbound traffic.

Established Command Configuration

As I mentioned in the introduction of XDMCP, the `inspect xdmcp` command has the appliance examine the XDMCP management connection (UDP 177) for the negotiated ports of the display connection and will perform any address translation that is necessary. However, this command doesn't add the second TCP connection (the display connection) to the conn table. To solve this problem, you'll need to use the `established` command.

The **established** command was originally designed for oddball applications that opened multiple connections for which the PIXs originally didn't support application inspection. XDMCP is one of the applications that must use this process. With XDMCP, when application inspection is enabled in a policy and the appliance sees a management connection being established that matches the policy, the appliance compares this connection with the configured **established** commands, which will determine what additional connections are allowed to and/or from the user.

You can almost look at the **established** command as a poor man's implementation of a stateful firewall: if connection A is seen, then automatically allow connection B, and possibly additional connections like C and D. The additional connections are automatically added to the conn table once the corresponding management connection is seen. Given this behavior, you can use the **established** command for other applications or protocols that open multiple connections through the appliance, but where Cisco doesn't have application inspection that will look for the additional connections and automatically add them to the state table.

The trick with the **established** command configuration is that you have to understand how an application works and the port number or numbers it uses for additional connections in order to configure the established command correctly. The syntax of the **established** command is as follows:

```
ciscoasa(config)# established {tcp | udp} dst_port [src_port]
                   [permitto protocol port[-port]]
                   [permitfrom protocol port[-port]]
```

You must first specify the name of the protocol for the established connection. In the case of XDMCP, this is the management connection, which uses UDP. Following this you need to specify the destination and source port (note that the order is *reversed*) for the established connection. Entering a **0** indicates any port. For XDMCP, the destination port would be 177 and the source port 0 (any port). Actually, you can omit the source port, since it is optional.

NOTE The **established** command doesn't work with connections that will have PAT performed on them.

The **permitto** parameter specifies the source information of the additional connection(s) that should be allowed. For example, with XDMCP, the protocol would be tcp and the port 6000 and higher, depending on the number of displays a user needs to support. You can find the configured number in the server configuration file. Just look for this line of code in the file, where *n* represents the connection number:

```
setenv DISPLAY Xserver:n
```

For XDMCP, the destination port number would be 6000 + *n*.

The **permitfrom** parameter specifies the destination information of the additional connections. For XDMCP, the client opens the TCP connection with a port number greater than 1023, so the range of ports you would specify would be from 1024 to 65535.

Basically the established command is controlling or limiting what additional connections are allowed. First, the appliance must see the initial connection, and then connections that match the **permitfrom** for the source port and **permitto** for the destination port of the specified protocol are allowed. You can have multiple **established** commands based on the range of ports you need to dynamically add to the conn table for a specific application.

TIP Please remember that the **established** command can be used for other applications that open additional connections where the appliances don't currently support application inspection for the additional connections.

XDMCP Example Configuration

Here's an example of setting up a global inspection policy for XDMCP and using the **established** command to allow the display connections:

```
ciscoasa(config)# class-map inspection_default
ciscoasa(config-cmap)# match default-inspection-traffic
ciscoasa(config)# policy-map global_policy
ciscoasa(config-pmap)# class inspection_default
ciscoasa(config-pmap-c)# inspect xdmcp
ciscoasa(config)#  established udp 177 0
                        permitto tcp 6000 permitfrom tcp 1024-65535
```

In this example, XDMCP inspection is enabled globally. With the **established** command, if a UDP connection has been established from the external client to port 177 on the X-windows server, a subsequent display connection from this external client is allowed for TCP if the source port is from 1024 to 65,535 and the destination is port 6000.

CHAPTER 12

Data Applications
and Policies

This chapter will introduce you to the inspection capabilities of the appliances as inspection relates to commonly used data applications. The application inspections covered include

▼ DNS

■ SMTP and ESMTP

■ FTP

■ TFTP

■ HTTP

■ Instant messaging (IM)

■ RSH

■ SNMP

▲ SQL*Net

DNS INSPECTION

DNS inspection, commonly called *DNS Doctoring*, has been supported on the appliances for a long time. The following sections will discuss the application layer inspection capabilities of the appliances for DNS traffic, as well as how to configure inspection policies for DNS.

DNS Inspection Features

Cisco currently supports four inspection features for DNS:

▼ DNS Guard

■ DNS packet length verification

■ DNS A-record translation

▲ DNS application layer policies

The following sections will discuss these features in more depth.

DNS Guard

DNS Guard ensures that only a single DNS response to a DNS query is permitted back into your network. When a DNS client generates a DNS query, it uses UDP. The DNS server uses UDP to reply. When some attackers are eavesdropping and see the DNS request or reply, they generate their own DNS reply to send back to the client, possibly with a bogus address or a misdirected address. If the attackers have given one of their own addresses in the reply, the attackers can easily hijack the session that the client will try to establish. DNS Guard also prevents DNS DoS attacks, stopping a flood of DNS replies from coming back into your network, since a flood of UDP traffic on the connection will keep it in the conn table.

With DNS Guard the appliance adds an entry in the conn table when it sees the client DNS query, which is used to permit the DNS reply from the server. As soon as the appliance sees the *first* DNS reply for the session, it immediately removes the conn table entry, preventing any other replies from coming in. DNS uses an application ID (app ID) in the payload to track the DNS queries and responses. If the client generates three requests, the appliance will allow three replies, since these are seen as three connections.

> **NOTE** DNS Guard is the exception to using an idle timer for UDP connections to determine if they are done. Also, in version 6 and earlier, you could not disable DNS Guard. In version 7, it is enabled by default, but you can disable it.

DNS Packet Length Verification

Starting in version 7 of the OS, the appliances check to make sure that the DNS packet length doesn't exceed 512 bytes by default. According to the RFC, 512 bytes should be the maximum. If packets were larger than this, then they might be non-DNS packets, and the appliance would drop them by default. However, some DNS implementations bend the rules and can have packet sizes greater than 512—if you run into this situation, you can increase the maximum packet size for DNS on the appliance.

Some other checks the appliance performs by default:

▼ Makes sure the domain name length doesn't exceed 255 bytes and the label 63 bytes

■ Verifies the integrity of a domain name if it is referenced by a compression pointer

▲ Verifies if a compression pointer loop exists, which would cause an infinite number of lookups on the DNS server

DNS A-Record Translation

If your appliance is performing translation, you might have issues with DNS A-record responses from DNS servers with incorrect addressing information. I'll use Figure 12-1 to illustrate the problem and solutions. In this example, if Internet users want to access www.abc.com, the external DNS server replies back with 192.1.1.1, which the appliance then translates to 10.0.1.12 when the connection enters the network, allowing the Internet users to access the server. However, if an internal user tries to do the same thing, the DNS server responds back with 192.1.1.1, but the internal user needs the local IP address of the server: 10.0.1.12.

This problem has three solutions:

▼ Have the user use IP addresses instead of fully qualified domain names.

■ Set up a split scope on the DNS server—for internal users, send back the local address, and for external users, send back the global address.

▲ Use the appliance A-record translation feature.

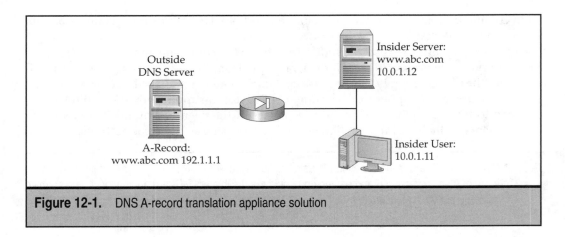

Figure 12-1. DNS A-record translation appliance solution

The problem with the first solution is that it is not scalable or manageable—names are easier to deal with than addresses. The second solution is a viable option if you control the DNS server—if it's the ISP, you're probably out of luck. The third solution, the A-record translation feature (DNS Doctoring) allows the appliance to "doctor" the DNS reply being sent back to the internal user. Configuring this is easy: all you need to do is to add the **dns** parameter to the **static** command for the server. This parameter is also available with the **nat** command if you are implementing dynamic DNS. Given the network in Figure 12-1, here is the corresponding **static** command to use DNS Doctoring:

```
ciscoasa(config)# static (inside,outside) 192.1.1.1 10.0.1.12 dns
```

The syntax of this command was discussed in Chapter 5. You can disable the DNS Doctoring feature with the **no nat-rewrite** application layer policy discussed later in the "DNS Policy Configuration" section.

NOTE In version 6.1 and earlier, the **alias** command was used to implement DNS Doctoring. The **dns** parameter for the **static** and **nat** commands was introduced in version 6.2. The latter approach is the preferred solution today.

DNS Application Layer Policies

Starting in version 7, the appliances support many DNS application layer policies you can implement, including

▼ Protect against DNS spoofing and cache poisoning.

■ Filter packets based on DNS header information, domain names, resource record types, and record classes.

■ Mask the Recursion Desired (RD) and Recursion Available (RA) flags in the DNS header to protect a server if it supports one or more internal zones.

- Look for and prevent a mismatch in the number of DNS responses when compared with queries, which could indicate a cache poisoning attack.

▲ Ensure that a Transaction Signature (TS) is included in all DNS messages.

The next section will discuss these in more depth.

DNS Policy Configuration

The following sections will discuss the configuration of DNS inspection. For in-depth inspection policies, you might need to create a layer 7 policy map and, possibly, a layer 7 class map. The following sections will discuss how to create these, as well as how to enable DNS inspection in a layer 3/4 policy map.

DNS Layer 7 Class Maps

Here are the commands to create a layer 7 class map for DNS inspection:

```
ciscoasa(config)# class-map type inspect dns [match-all]
                      L7_class_map_name
ciscoasa(config-cmap)# match [not] dns-class {eq | range}
                          {0-65535 | IN}
ciscoasa(config-cmap)# match [not] dns-type {eq | range} {0-65535 | A |
                          AXFR | CNAME | IXFR | NS | SOA | TSIG}
ciscoasa(config-cmap)# match [not] domain-name regex {class
                          regex_classmap_name | regex_name}
ciscoasa(config-cmap)# match [not] header-flag {0x0-0xffff | AA | QR |
                          RA | RD | TC}
ciscoasa(config-cmap)# match [not] question
ciscoasa(config-cmap)# match [not] resource-record {additional |
                          answer | authority}
```

The **dns-class** parameter allows you to match a DNS query or resource record class. The **not** parameter negates the corresponding match result. The **dns-type** parameter allows you to match a DNS query or resource record type. The **domain-name** parameter allows you to match a domain name or names from a DNS query or resource record. (You need to reference a regular expression or a regular expression class map that contains the actual domain names.) The **header-flag** allows you to match a particular DNS flag in a header. The **question** parameter matches a DNS question (query). The **resource-record** parameter matches the specified DNS resource record.

DNS Layer 7 Policy Maps

Here are the commands to create a layer 7 policy map for DNS inspection:

```
ciscoasa(config)# policy-map type inspect dns L7_policy_map_name
ciscoasa(config-pmap)# parameters
ciscoasa(config-pmap-p)# dns-guard
```

```
ciscoasa(config-pmap-p)# id-mismatch [count #_of_times]
                          [duration seconds] [action log]
ciscoasa(config-pmap-p)# id-randomization
ciscoasa(config-pmap-p)# message-length maximum {[client | server]
                          {auto | 512-65535}}
ciscoasa(config-pmap-p)# nat-rewrite
ciscoasa(config-pmap-p)# protocol-enforcement
ciscoasa(config-pmap-p)# tsig enforced {action [drop] [log]}
ciscoasa(config-pmap-p)# exit
ciscoasa(config-pmap)# match L7_class_map_parameters
ciscoasa(config-pmap-c)# [enforce-tsig] {[drop | drop-connection]}
                          [log]
ciscoasa(config-pmap-c)# exit
ciscoasa(config-pmap)# class L7_class_map_name
ciscoasa(config-pmap-c)# [enforce-tsig] {[drop [send-protocol-error]] |
                          drop-connection [send-protocol-error]] |
                          [reset]} | [rate-limit #_of_messages] |
                          [mask]} [log]
```

The following are the commands you can configure under the subcommand mode for **parameters**. The **dns-guard** command enforces one DNS response per query, implementing DNS Guard (enabled by default). Preface this or other commands with the **no** parameter to negate or disable them. The **id-mismatch** command reports excessive instances of DNS identifier mismatches. The **id-randomization** command randomizes the DNS identifier (app ID) in DNS query messages. The **message-length** command defines the maximum DNS message length allowed (by default this is 512 bytes). The **nat-rewrite** command translates DNS Doctoring (enabled by default). The **protocol-enforcement** command checks the format of DNS messages. The **tsig** parameter validates the TSIG resource record information.

In the preceding list of commands, you have two options on specifying what you need to match on in order to implement policies: you can use individual **match** commands or reference a layer 7 DNS class map with the **class** command. In either case, you are taken into a second subcommand mode where you specify the policy for the application layer information: drop the packet (**drop**, with the option of sending a protocol error message to the source), drop the connection (**drop-connection**), generate a log message (**log**), require TSIG resource records in a DNS message (**enforce-tsig**), send a TCP reset (**reset**), or mask out matching portions of the DNS payload (**mask**).

DNS Layer 3/4 Policy Configuration

If all you are interested in is implementing DNS Doctoring, DNS Guard, and/or preventing excessive DNS replies to corresponding DNS queries, then you do not need to implement a layer 7 policy for DNS inspection. However, if you need to implement a layer 7 DNS policy, you must have a corresponding layer 3/4 policy map that references it:

```
ciscoasa(config)# policy-map L3/4_policy_map_name
ciscoasa(config-pmap)# class L3/4_class_map_name
ciscoasa(config-pmap-c)# inspect dns [L7_policy_map_name]
```

Default DNS Inspection Configuration

Here is the default DNS inspection policy enabled on the appliances:

```
ciscoasa# show run policy-map
policy-map type inspect dns preset_dns_map
 parameters
  message-length maximum 512
policy-map global_policy
 class inspection_default
  inspect dns preset_dns_map
<--output omitted-->
```

In this configuration, DNS is globally enabled, where messages bigger than 512 bytes will be dropped, and DNS Doctoring and DNS Guard are enabled.

DNS Example Configuration

Let's look at a configuration example that implements DNS inspection:

```
ciscoasa(config)# regex DOMAIN1 abc\.com
ciscoasa(config)# regex DOMAIN2 def\.com
ciscoasa(config)# class-map type regex match-any PERMITTED_DOMAINS
ciscoasa(config-cmap)# match regex DOMAIN1
ciscoasa(config-cmap)# match regex DOMAIN2
ciscoasa(config)# class-map type inspect dns match-all L7_BAD_DNS_CLASS
ciscoasa(config-cmap)# match not header-flag QR
ciscoasa(config-cmap)# match question
ciscoasa(config-cmap)# match not domain-name regex
                        class PERMITTED_DOMAINS
ciscoasa(config)# policy-map type inspect dns L7_DNS_POLICY
ciscoasa(config-pmap)# match header-flag RD
ciscoasa(config-pmap-c)# mask log
ciscoasa(config-pmap-c)# exit
ciscoasa(config-pmap)# class L7_BAD_DNS_CLASS
ciscoasa(config-pmap-c)# drop log
ciscoasa(config)# access-list DNS permit udp any any eq 53
```

```
ciscoasa(config)# class-map L3_dns_class_map
ciscoasa(config-cmap)# match access-list DNS
ciscoasa(config)# policy-map L3_outside_policy
ciscoasa(config-pmap)# class L3_dns_class_map
ciscoasa(config-pmap-c)# inspect dns L7_DNS_POLICY
ciscoasa(config)# service-policy L3_outside_policy interface outside
```

The preceding example prevents DNS cache poisoning for any domain name with the exception of the two domains "abc.com" and "def.com." Working backwards in this example, the layer 3 policy is applied to traffic entering the outside interface. This includes all DNS traffic. The inspection rule (`inspect dns`) references a layer 7 policy map. If the DNS header contains the RD flag, it is masked out and logged. Based on the layer 7 class map and regular expression class map, if the domain names being queried are not "abc .com" and "def.com" and the DNS header doesn't contain the QR flag, then these packets are dropped and logged.

SMTP AND ESMTP INSPECTION

Internet-based e-mail systems have been widely known to be an easy way of hacking into your network. The reason is that these e-mail systems are based on SMTP (Simple Mail Transport Protocol) and ESMTP (extended SMTP), which are well documented. However, many extensions have been added, including proprietary extensions by certain vendors. Sendmail is one of the more popular UNIX SMTP e-mail systems, and its source code is open to the public, which means that hackers have spent a lot of time figuring out the weaknesses in this application.

SMTP and ESMTP Inspection Features

To prevent e-mail attacks, appliances implement ESMTP inspection by default. Prior to version 7, only the SMTP protocol was supported. Staring in version 7, ESMTP was added. This feature only allows certain SMTP commands or messages, defined in RFC 821, section .4.5.1, and certain ESMTP commands on an e-mail connection. All other commands in SMTP connections are changed to Xs, which the internal e-mail server will reject. Supported SMTP commands include DATA, HELO, MAIL, NOOP, QUIT, RCPT, and RSET. Supported ESMTP commands include AUTH, EHLO, ETRN, HELP, SAML, SEND, SOML, and VRFY.

Other security features are also implemented to protect the e-mail server, including the following:

▼ Mask the e-mail server banner to asterisks ("*") to hide/obfuscate the banner, which might give information to the hacker about the type of e-mail server you are using.

■ Monitor e-mail commands and responses and the sequence they occur in to make sure that the e-mail connection is acting according to the RFCs.

■ Look for a pipe ("|") in a MAIL or RCPT command and close the e-mail session. (This was a bug in some e-mail implementations that allowed hackers to have the e-mail server execute programs and redirect the output.)

▲ Create an audit trail of specified actions against the e-mail.

NOTE SMTP and ESMTP inspection only applies to inbound (lower to higher level) traffic.

SMTP and ESMTP Policy Configuration

Layer 7 policy maps allow you to define policies about what you want to allow for e-mail connections based on what is in the SMTP and/or ESTMP payload. Layer 7 class maps are unsupported for further classification. When creating a layer 7 policy map for e-mail inspection, you have the following commands available to you:

```
ciscoasa(config)#policy-map type inspect esmtp L7_policy_map_name
ciscoasa(config-pmap)# parameters
ciscoasa(config-pmap-p)# mail-relay domain_name action
                             [drop-connection] [log]
ciscoasa(config-pmap-p)# mask-banner
ciscoasa(config-pmap-p)# exit
ciscoasa(config-pmap)# match body length gt bytes
ciscoasa(config-pmap-c)# [drop-connection | reset] [log]
ciscoasa(config-pmap)# match body line length gt bytes
ciscoasa(config-pmap-c)# [drop-connection | reset] [log]
ciscoasa(config-pmap)# match cmd RCPT count gt #_of_recipients
ciscoasa(config-pmap-c)# [drop-connection | reset] [log]
ciscoasa(config-pmap)# match cmd line length gt bytes
ciscoasa(config-pmap-c)# [drop-connection | reset] [log]
ciscoasa(config-pmap)# match cmd verb command1 [...commandX]
ciscoasa(config-pmap-c)# [rate-limit #_per_second |
                              drop-connection | reset] [log]
ciscoasa(config-pmap)# match ehlo-reply-parameter parameter
ciscoasa(config-pmap-c)# [drop-connection | reset] [log]
ciscoasa(config-pmap)# match header length gt bytes
ciscoasa(config-pmap-c)# [drop-connection | reset] [log]
ciscoasa(config-pmap)# match header line length gt bytes
ciscoasa(config-pmap-c)# [drop-connection | reset] [log]
ciscoasa(config-pmap)# match header to-fields count gt #_of_recipients
ciscoasa(config-pmap-c)# [drop-connection | reset] [log]
ciscoasa(config-pmap)# match invalid-recipients count
                             gt #_of_recipients
ciscoasa(config-pmap-c)# [drop-connection | reset] [log]
ciscoasa(config-pmap)# match [not] mime encoding type
```

```
ciscoasa(config-pmap-c)# [drop-connection | reset] [log]
ciscoasa(config-pmap)# match [not] mime filename length gt bytes
 ciscoasa(config-pmap)# match [not] mime filetype regex
                           {class regex_class_name | regex_name}
ciscoasa(config-pmap-c)# [drop-connection | reset] [log]
ciscoasa(config-pmap)# match sender-address length gt bytes
ciscoasa(config-pmap-c)# [drop-connection | reset] [log]
ciscoasa(config-pmap)# match [not] sender-address regex
                           class regex_class_name
ciscoasa(config-pmap-c)# [drop-connection | reset] [log]
```

Two options are under the **parameters** subcommand mode. The **mail-relay** command allows you to restrict what domain name you'll allow for your e-mail servers—this is used to prevent relaying of mail via a rogue server. The **mask-banner** command obfuscates (changes) the server e-mail banner, thereby making it harder for an attacker to learn information about your server.

The remaining policies are configured with the **match** command. When executing this command, you are taken into a second subcommand mode where you can specify your policy: drop the connection, log the match, reset the TCP connection, and, with certain **match** commands, rate-limit the e-mail commands sent on the connection. Table 12-1 has a summary of what each of these commands looks for in an e-mail message.

match Command	Description
match body length gt	Specifies the length of the body of a message
match body line length gt	Specifies the length of a line in the body of a message
match cmd RCPT count gt	Specifies the number of recipients
match cmd line length gt	Specifies the length of a command line
match cmd verb	Specifies the e-mail command to match on
match ehlo-reply-parameter	Specifies the EHLO reply parameter to look for, like AUTH
match header length gt	Specifies the length of the header of a message
match header line length	Specifies the length of a line in the header of a message

Table 12-1. E-mail Policy Parameters for the `match` Command

`match` Command	Description
`match header to-fields count gt`	Specifies the number of "To:" fields to match on
`match invalid-recipients count gt`	Specifies the number of invalid e-mail recipients (nonexistent e-mail addresses) to match on
`match [not] mime encoding`	Specifies the encoding scheme to match on for attached files (`7bit`, `8bit`, `base64`, `binary`, `others`, `quoted-printable`)
`match [not] mime filename length`	Specifies the number of bytes to match on for an attached file
`match [not] mime filetype regex`	Specifies a regular expression to use to match on an attached filename or extension
`match sender-address length gt`	Specifies the length of an e-mail sender's address to match on
`match [not] sender-address regex`	Specifies a regular expression or regular expression class map to use to match on an e-mail sender's address

Table 12-1.   E-mail Policy Parameters for the `match` Command (*Continued*)

Once you are done with your layer 7 policies, you must associate them with an **inspect esmtp** command in a layer 3/4 policy map:

```
ciscoasa(config)# policy-map L3/4_policy_map_name
ciscoasa(config-pmap)# class L3/4_class_map_name
ciscoasa(config-pmap-c)# inspect esmtp [L7_policy_map_name]
```

SMTP and ESMTP Example Configuration

Let's look at an example to illustrate how to use layer 7 policy maps with e-mail inspection. I'll use the following example:

```
ciscoasa(config)# regex BAD_SENDER1 @abc\.com
ciscoasa(config)# class-map type regex match-any BAD_SENDERS
ciscoasa(config-cmap)# match regex BAD_SENDER1
ciscoasa(config)# policy-map type inspect esmtp L7_EMAIL_MAP
```

```
ciscoasa(config-pmap)# match body length gt 35000
ciscoasa(config-pmap-c)# drop-connection log
ciscoasa(config-pmap)# match sender-address regex class BAD_SENDERS
ciscoasa(config-pmap-c)# drop-connection
ciscoasa(config)# access-list email permit tcp any any eq 25
ciscoasa(config)# class-map L3_email_class_map
ciscoasa(config-cmap)# match access-list email
ciscoasa(config)# policy-map L3_outside_policy
ciscoasa(config-pmap)# class L3_email_class_map
ciscoasa(config-pmap-c)# inspect esmtp L7_EMAIL_MAP
ciscoasa(config)# service-policy L3_outside_policy interface outside
```

In this example, a regular expression ("abc.com") is referenced in a regular expression class map. The layer 7 ESMTP policy map (L7_EMAIL_MAP) will drop any e-mails that have a body greater than 35,000 characters *or* an e-mail coming from "abc.com." A layer 3/4 class map (L3_email_class_map) was created that looks for any inbound TCP port 25 connection. A layer 3/4 policy map (L3_outside_policy) is created to do inspection of ESMTP, qualifying it with the layer 7 policy map. This is activated on the outside interface of the appliance.

FTP INSPECTION

FTP is one of the oldest TCP/IP applications and was designed to move files between different networked computers. The following sections will discuss how FTP connections are built between computers, why application inspection is necessary for FTP, the inspection features for FTP, and how to configure application layer inspection for FTP.

FTP Operation

FTP, interestingly enough, is unlike normal connections such as telnet and e-mail. FTP actually uses two connections—one is a command connection (sometimes called a *control* connection) that the user uses to access the server and enter FTP commands, and the other connection is used for the actual transfer of data, including files. FTP supports two different modes—*standard* (or active) and *passive*—and based on the mode, the setup of two connections and transfer of data is slightly different. The next two sections explain these two FTP modes.

Standard Mode

To better help you understand how connections are set up with standard FTP, let's use the top part of Figure 12-2. When a user wants to initiate an FTP connection, the user sets up a *control* connection first. The user uses the control connection to execute commands, like **get** and **put**. When the user device opens a control connection, it chooses a free source port number greater than 1023 and uses a destination port number of 21.

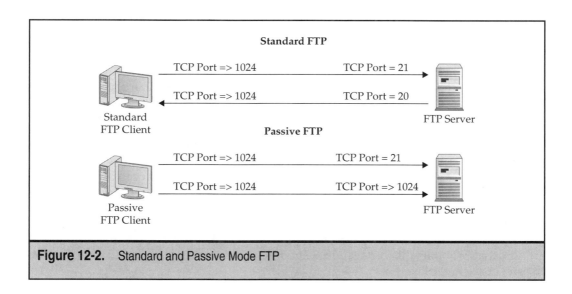

Figure 12-2. Standard and Passive Mode FTP

Whenever the user executes a command on the control connection, the FTP server opens a second connection, called a *data* connection, which is used for the transfer of information, like uploading or downloading a file. From the client (via the control connection), the server gets a port number greater than 1023 that is not being used on the client, and the server uses that port as the destination and a source port of 20.

To better help you understand some of the issues with standard-mode FTP, let's take a look at situations where a security appliance is between the client and FTP server. The next two sections explain the connectivity issues when the client is on the inside of the network versus the outside of the network.

Client on the Inside of the Appliance   When the client is on the inside of the network and initiates an FTP connection to an FTP server on the outside of the network, the appliance allows the control connection by default because the connection is traveling from a higher-level interface to a lower-level one. A problem exists, however, when the client executes an FTP command and the server tries to initiate a data connection back to the inside client.

With the application inspection feature, the appliance expects this data connection to be built and looks for an FTP command with the associated client source port number within the control connection. When the appliance sees the command, it dynamically adds the connection entry in the conn table with the appropriate information—this includes the client port number that it shared with the FTP server. Therefore, you don't have to worry about the inbound connection coming from the FTP server.

Without the application inspection feature, you would have to configure an ACL to specifically allow this second connection. The problem with this is that you don't really know which client, or possibly even which server to allow—you would basically have to permit traffic from any device (the FTP server) heading to anywhere (the clients), if the source port number is 20. Obviously, this opens a fairly large hole in your appliance. If you disable application inspection for FTP, you'll have to manually configure this type of ACL entry to allow standard mode FTP connections. Of course, disabling application inspection for FTP would prevent data transfers for internal users where standard mode was employed.

Client on the Outside of the Appliance   In this example, let's assume that the client is on the outside of your network and that the FTP server is on the inside. For the initial client connection to work, you need to configure an ACL that will allow traffic heading to the FTP server for TCP port 21—without this, no type of FTP connection can be made. Once the control connection has been established, when the client executes a command, the server initiates the data connection back to the client.

In this situation, because the data connection is coming from a higher-level interface and is exiting a lower-level interface, the appliance permits it by default, unless you have an ACL that prohibits this connection. Therefore, in this example, application inspection doesn't come into play.

Passive Mode

Just as in standard mode for FTP, *passive mode* has two connections: control and data. The bottom part of Figure 12-2 shows an example of the setup of these two connections. The control connection in passive mode is established in the same manner as standard FTP: the user device chooses an open port greater than 1023 as a source port and uses a destination port of 21. Whenever a data connection is needed, the user establishes the connection to the server—this is the opposite of standard-mode FTP. For this data connection, the user device again chooses an open port number greater than 1023 as a source port, but acquires from the FTP server what port number to use for the destination port, a number greater than 1023. This number is negotiated on the control connection.

Client on the Inside of the Appliance   When the client is on the inside of the network and initiates an FTP connection to an FTP server on the outside of the network, the appliance allows the connection by default because the connection is traveling from a higher-level interface to a lower-level one. This is also true for the data connection. Therefore, both connections can be established unless you are filtering with ACLs.

Client on the Outside of the Appliance   In this example, assume that the client is on the outside of your network and that the FTP server is on the inside. For the initial client connection to work, you need to configure an ACL that will allow traffic heading to the FTP server for TCP port 21—without this, no type of FTP connection is possible.

Once the command connection has been established, when the client attempts to retrieve or send a file, the client will attempt to establish a data connection to the server. Assuming that application inspection is enabled for FTP, the appliance automatically looks at the FTP commands that the user is entering on the command connection, as well as the connection information being negotiated, and dynamically creates an entry in the connection table for the data connection. However, if you've disabled application inspection for FTP, you will have to manually add an ACL to allow traffic to your FTP server at TCP ports greater than 1023 as well as the first filter statement for port 21 that I already mentioned.

FTP Inspection Features

As you saw in the last handful of sections, one application inspection feature is to add the additional TCP data connection dynamically to the conn table as needed. Another issue the appliance will handle is if the appliance is performing address translation on the embedded addressing information if it conflicts with an existing PAT entry in the xlate table—if this is the case, the appliance will change the embedded port information in the payload and create a new translation entry in the xlate table for the connection. The appliances have supported both features for many years.

New in version 7 is in-depth application layer inspection of FTP, where you can set up additional policies about what commands can be executed on the control connection, along with the user accounts used and the directories and files accessed, among many other things.

FTP Policy Configuration

The following sections will discuss how to configure layer 7 class and policy maps and how to associate these with a layer 3/4 inspection policy for FTP.

FTP Layer 7 Class Maps

Layer 7 class maps for FTP allow you to match on additional criteria found in FTP payloads, like the servers that users are logging into, the user accounts logged into, the files (and their types) being accessed, and the commands being executed. These can then be referenced in a layer 7 policy map where you can define your application layer policies. Here is the syntax for setting up a layer 7 class map for FTP:

```
ciscoasa(config)# class-map type inspect ftp [match-all]
                        L7_class_map_name
ciscoasa(config-cmap)# match [not] filename regex {class
                        regex_class_map_name | regex_name}
ciscoasa(config-cmap)# match [not] filetype regex {class
                        regex_class_map_name | regex_name}
ciscoasa(config-cmap)# match [not] request-command FTP_command
                        [...FTP_command]
ciscoasa(config-cmap)# match [not] server regex {class
                        regex_class_map_name | regex_name}
ciscoasa(config-cmap)# match [not] username regex {class
                        regex_class_map_name | regex_name}
```

The `filename` parameter allows you to match on a filename for FTP access—you can specify a particular regular expression or a regular expression class map. This is also true of most of the `match` commands for an FTP class map when matching on a regular expression(s). The `filetype` parameter matches on a file type for FTP transfer. The `request-command` parameter matches on a FTP request command or list of commands (separated by spaces). The commands you can match on include the following: `appe` (append to a file), `cdup` (change to the parent of the current directory), `dele` (delete a file), `get` (download a file), `help` (display help information on the server), `mkd` (create a directory), `put` (upload a file), `rmd` (delete a directory), `rnfr` (rename a file from), `rnto` (rename a file to), `site` (specify server-specific command), and `stou` (store a file with a unique name). The `server` parameter matches on one or more FTPs. The `username` parameter matches on an FTP username or names.

FTP Layer 7 Policy Maps

The following is the syntax for creating a layer 7 policy map for FTP:

```
ciscoasa(config)#policy-map type inspect ftp L7_policy_map_name
ciscoasa(config-pmap)# match L7_class_map_parameters
ciscoasa(config-pmap-c)# [reset] [log]
ciscoasa(config-pmap-c)# exit
ciscoasa(config-pmap)# class L7_class_map_name
ciscoasa(config-pmap-c)# [reset] [log]
ciscoasa(config-pmap-c)# exit
ciscoasa(config-pmap)# parameters
ciscoasa(config-pmap-p)# mask-banner
ciscoasa(config-pmap-p)# mask-syst-reply
```

Instead of creating an application layer class map, you can also reference these values within the layer 7 policy map with the `match` command. The advantage of using layer 7 class maps is that you can apply different policies to different classes (class maps). You can have the appliance reset the connection, log the match, or do both for a matching class map or `match` command. Within the `parameters` section in a layer 7 policy map, you can mask the greeting banner the FTP server sends during login (the `mask-banner` command) and also mask the server reply to the `syst` command (the `mask-syst-reply` command).

FTP Layer 3/4 Policy Maps

To enable inspection of FTP, you need to reference it in a layer 3/4 policy map:

```
ciscoasa(config)# policy-map L3/4_policy_map_name
ciscoasa(config-pmap)# class L3/4_class_map_name
ciscoasa(config-pmap-c)# inspect ftp [strict] [L7_policy_map_name]
```

FTP inspection supports a `strict` option when enabling FTP inspection in a layer 3/4 policy map. This option performs the following functions:

▼ Tracks the FTP command and response sequences for invalid behavior

■ Stops web browsers from sending embedded FTP commands

■ Drops connections with embedded FTP commands

■ Requires acknowledgment of an FTP command before a new one can be sent

▲ Checks to see if the 227 and `port` commands don't appear in an error string

You can also perform in-depth application layer inspection of FTP traffic by creating and then referencing a layer 7 policy map with the `inspect ftp` command.

NOTE By default FTP inspection is enabled in the global policy on the appliance on all interfaces; you can change this policy or set up interface-specific policies that override the global policy.

FTP Example Configuration

To help illustrate how to configure FTP inspection with layer 7 policies, examine the following configuration:

```
ciscoasa(config)# regex FTP_USER "admin"
ciscoasa(config)# regex FTP_DIR "\/private"
ciscoasa(config)# class-map type inspect ftp L7_CLASS_MAP
ciscoasa(config-cmap)# match not username regex FTP_USER
ciscoasa(config-cmap)# match filename regex FTP_DIR
ciscoasa(config)# policy-map type inspect ftp L7_POLICY_MAP
ciscoasa(config-pmap)# class L7_CLASS_MAP
ciscoasa(config-pmap-c)# reset log
ciscoasa(config)# class-map L3_FTP_TRAFFIC
ciscoasa(config-cmap)# match port tcp eq ftp
ciscoasa(config)# policy-map L3_OUTSIDE_POLICY
ciscoasa(config-pmap)# class L3_FTP_TRAFFIC
ciscoasa(config-pmap-c)# inspect ftp strict L7_POLICY_MAP
ciscoasa(config)# service-policy L3_OUTSIDE_POLICY interface outside
```

At the top, two regular expression strings are created: one for a user account and one for a directory name. These are then referenced in the FTP application layer class map (`L7_CLASS_MAP`), where the class map is basically looking for someone other than "admin" accessing the "/private" directory. The layer 7 policy map (`L7_POLICY_MAP`) then sets up the policy for this kind of access: reset and log the connection. The layer 3/4 class map (`L3_FTP_TRAFIC`) is matching on any port 21 connection. The layer 3/4 policy map (`L3_OUTSIDE_POLICY`) references this class map and enables inspection with the strict option for FTP. Additionally the layer 7 policy map is associated with the layer 3/4 inspection policy. This policy is then activated on the outside interface.

TFTP INSPECTION

Like FTP, TFTP can be used for sharing files; however, it uses a much simpler interactive process that lacks authentication. The following two sections will discuss the operation of a TFTP session and how to configure an inspection policy for TFTP.

TFTP Operation

TFTP is defined in RFC 1350 and uses UDP as a transport. The server listens on port 69 for client connections. You can't list files in a directory, move around directories, delete files, or even rename files: the only two operations that TFTP supports are reading and writing of files. (The RFC standard also supports mail functions, but no server product has yet implemented this feature.)

TFTP is a little bit similar to passive mode FTP. When the client connects to the TFTP server, it chooses a random source port above 1023 and sends its first message to UDP port 69 on the server. The server then replies with a destination port, typically above 1023, that the client will use. All subsequent packets are then sent using the client original port number and the destination newly assigned port number. One side of the connection is the receiver and the other the sender, where the role depends upon whether a file is being read on the server or copied to the server. Data is sent in blocks of 512 bytes, where a packet that is smaller than 512 bytes indicates the termination of the connection. Also, every packet sent is acknowledged—if an acknowledgment times out, the source resends the missing packet. A special error message can be any of the following:

▼ The request cannot be satisfied (like the file cannot be found, or an access violation occurs when trying to access the file).

■ Receiving a duplicated packet or an incorrectly formatted packet.

▲ The resource is no longer available (like the disk drive was filled up on the server, or the file permissions were changed during transfer and the user no longer has access to the file).

Errors are not acknowledged and will automatically terminate the connection. The one exception to this rule is if the source port number in the received packet is incorrect: in this case, an error packet is sent back to the sender.

If the user is on a higher-level interface and the server is on a lower-level interface, inspection for the server port number change is not required unless you have an ACL restricting traffic. However, for inbound TFTP connections, you'll need to use TFTP inspection to allow the second connection (subsequent packets between the client and server).

When performing inspection, if the appliance is also performing address translation, any embedded addressing information that conflicts with an entry in the xlate table will be changed in the payload and appropriately updated in the xlate table.

TFTP Policy Configuration

TFTP inspection is enabled by default in the global policy applied to all interfaces of the appliance. You can disable it globally and enable it on an interface-by-interface basis, or you can control for which server(s) inspection should be performed. To enable inspection of TFTP, you need to reference it in a layer 3/4 policy map:

```
ciscoasa(config)# policy-map L3/4_policy_map_name
ciscoasa(config-pmap)# class L3/4_class_map_name
ciscoasa(config-pmap-c)# [no] inspect tftp
```

TFTP only supports layer 3/4 inspection.

The following example modifies the global policy to control when inspection for TFTP is done (only the specified server in the ACL, 192.168.1.1):

```
ciscoasa(config)# access-list tftp permit udp any
                          host 192.168.1.1 eq 69
ciscoasa(config)# class-map L3_tftp_class_map
ciscoasa(config-cmap)# match access-list tftp
ciscoasa(config)# policy-map global_policy
ciscoasa(config-pmap)# class inspection_default
ciscoasa(config-pmap-c)# no inspect tftp
ciscoasa(config-pmap)# class L3_tftp_class_map
ciscoasa(config-pmap-c)# inspect tftp
ciscoasa(config)# service-policy global_policy global
```

HTTP INSPECTION

HTTP is one of the most common Internet protocols used today and is used to display elements in a web browser window. The following sections will discuss the inspection features for HTTP and how to configure application layer inspection for HTTP.

HTTP Inspection Features

In version 6 and earlier of the operating system, the application inspection features for HTTP were very minimal. Basically you could copy URLs to Websense or SmartFilter to filter returning web traffic, or you could filter HTTP connections that accessed Java or ActiveX content (see Chapter 7 on these topics). Starting in version 7, Cisco greatly enhanced the application layer inspection features for HTTP. Besides the items I just mentioned, the appliances support these additional inspection features for HTTP, among many others that will be discussed in the next section:

▼ Can look for and prevent tunneled traffic on web connections, like peer-to-peer (P2P), instant messaging (IM), and others

■ Can look for and prevent HTTP RFC methods and extensions (commands) that are sent

- ■ Can filter on information found in the URL
- ■ Can spoof the HTTP server heading response from the web server to hide the server's identity (like the kind of product being used and its version)
- ■ Can specify size and count limits for the HTTP elements in user requests and server responses
- ■ Can look for and filter specific MIME types
- ▲ Can look for and filter on non-ASCII characters in requests and responses

HTTP Policy Configuration

The following sections will discuss how to configure layer 7 class and policy maps and how to associate these with a layer 3/4 inspection policy for HTTP.

HTTP Layer 7 Class Maps

Layer 7 class maps for HTTP allow you to match on additional criteria found in HTTP payloads, like the requests sent by the users and the responses from the servers, the URLs being accessed, the size and contents of the body of the message, and many other things. These can then be referenced in a layer 7 policy map where you can define your application layer policies. Here is the syntax for setting up a layer 7 class map for HTTP:

```
ciscoasa(config)# class-map type inspect http [match-all]
                     L7_class_map_name
ciscoasa(config-cmap)# match [not] req-resp content-type mismatch
ciscoasa(config-cmap)# match [not] request args regex {class
                     regex_class_name | regex_name}
ciscoasa(config-cmap)# match [not] request body length gt bytes
ciscoasa(config-cmap)# match [not] request body regex {class
                     regex_class_name | regex_name}
ciscoasa(config-cmap)# match [not] request header header_options
ciscoasa(config-cmap)# match [not] request method methods
ciscoasa(config-cmap)# match [not] request uri length gt bytes
ciscoasa(config-cmap)# match [not] request uri regex {class
                     regex_class_name | regex_name}
ciscoasa(config-cmap)# match [not] response body active-x
ciscoasa(config-cmap)# match [not] response body java-applet
ciscoasa(config-cmap)# match [not] response body length gt bytes
ciscoasa(config-cmap)# match [not] response body regex {class
                     regex_class_name | regex_name}
ciscoasa(config-cmap)# match [not] response header header_options
ciscoasa(config-cmap)# match [not] response status-line regex {class
                     regex_class_name | regex_name}
```

Table 12-2 explains the different match commands you can include in your HTTP class map. Requests are from users and responses are from web servers.

`match` Command	Description
`match req-resp content-type mismatch`	Checks the header content type value against a list of supported content types for a mismatch, verifies that the header content type matches the content in the body (data), and that the content type field in the response matches the accept field value in the request message
`match request args regex`	Looks for a match with a regular expression(s) in the arguments of a request
`match request body length gt`	Looks for a body size that exceeds this number of bytes in a request message
`match request body regex`	Looks for a match with regular expression(s) in the body of a request
`match request header`	Looks for the specified field in the header of a request (see the preceding paragraph about header options you can specify)
`match request method`	Looks for the specified RFC or extended method in a request message (see the preceding paragraph about methods you can specify)
`match request uri length gt`	Looks for the URI portion of a request that exceeds the specified number of bytes (basically a long URL)
`match request uri regex`	Looks for a regular expression(s) in the URI portion of a request message
`match response body active-x`	Looks for an ActiveX script tag in the body of a response
`match response body java-applet`	Looks for a Java script tag in the body of a response
`match response body length gt`	Looks for the response body that exceeds this number of bytes
`match response body regex`	Looks for a regular expression(s) in the body of a response
`match response header`	Looks for the specified field in the header of a request (see the preceding paragraph about header options you can specify)
`match response status-line regex`	Looks for a regular expression(s) in the status line of a response message

Table 12-2. HTTP Policy Parameters for the `match` Command

HTTP header options you can match on include `accept`, `accept-charset`, `accept-encoding`, `accept-language`, `allow`, `authorization`, `cache-control`, `connection`, `content-encodng`, `content-language`, `content-length`, `content-location`, `content-md5`, `content-range`, `content-type`, `cookie`, `count`, `date`, `expect`, `expires`, `from`, `host`, `if-match`, `if-modified-since`, `if-none-match`, `if-range`, `if-unmodified-since`, `last-modified`, `length`, `max-forwards`, `non-ascii`, `pragma`, `proxy-authorization`, `range`, `referer`, `regex`, `te`, `trailer`, `transfer-encoding`, `upgrade`, `user-agent`, `via`, and `warning`.

HTTP request methods (both those defined in the RFC and the extended ones) include the following: `bcopy`, `bdelete`, `bmove`, `bpropfind`, `bproppatch`, `connect`, `copy`, `delete`, `edit`, `get`, `getattribute`, `getattributenames`, `getproperties`, `head`, `index`, `lock`, `mkcol`, `mkdir`, `move`, `notify`, `options`, `poll`, `post`, `propfind`, `proppatch`, `put`, `regex`, `revadd`, `revlabel`, `revlog`, `revnum`, `save`, `setattribute`, `startrev`, `stoprev`, `subscribe`, `trace`, `unedit`, `unlock`, and `unsubscribe`.

HTTP Layer 7 Policy Maps

The following is the syntax for creating a layer 7 policy map for HTTP:

```
ciscoasa(config)# policy-map type inspect http L7_policy_map_name
ciscoasa(config-pmap)# match L7_class_map_parameters
ciscoasa(config-pmap-c)# {log | drop-connection [log] | reset [log]}
ciscoasa(config-pmap)# class L7_class_map_name
ciscoasa(config-pmap-c)# {log | drop-connection [log] | reset [log]}
ciscoasa(config-pmap)# parameters
ciscoasa(config-pmap-p)# protocol-violation action {[{drop-connection |
                              reset}] [log]}
ciscoasa(config-pmap-p)# spoof-server server_message
```

Instead of creating an application layer class map, you can also reference these values within the layer 7 policy map with the `match` command. The advantage of using layer 7 class maps is that you can apply different policies to different classes (class maps). You can have the appliance reset and/or log the connection or drop and/or log the connection for a matching class map or a `match` command. Within the `parameters` section in a layer 7 policy map, the `protocol-violation` command looks and defines actions for protocol violations in HTTP requests and responses. The `spoof-server` command replaces the server information in the HTTP header with the message you define—it can be up to 82 characters in length.

TIP I recommend using a list of asterisks ("*") for the header or creating a fake header that incorrectly defines the type and version of product that you are using—this makes it a little bit more difficult for an attacker to identify what you are using and then to home-in on specific vulnerabilities that a web server might have.

HTTP Layer 3/4 Policy Maps

To enable inspection of HTTP, you need to reference it in a layer 3/4 policy map:

```
ciscoasa(config)# policy-map L3/4_policy_map_name
ciscoasa(config-pmap)# class L3/4_class_map_name
ciscoasa(config-pmap-c)# inspect http [L7_policy_map_name]
```

You can also perform in-depth application layer inspection of HTTP traffic by creating and then referencing a layer 7 policy map with the **inspect http** command.

NOTE   By default HTTP inspection is enabled in the global policy on the appliance on all interfaces; you can change this policy or set up interface-specific policies that override the global policy.

HTTP Example Configuration

To help illustrate how to configure HTTP inspection with layer 7 policies, examine the following configuration:

```
ciscoasa(config)# regex url_example1 abc1\.com
ciscoasa(config)# regex url_example2 abc2\.com
ciscoasa(config)# class-map type regex match-any URL_List
ciscoasa(config-cmap)# match regex example1
ciscoasa(config-cmap)# match regex example2
ciscoasa(config)# class-map type inspect http match-all L7_HTTP_class
ciscoasa(config-cmap)# match req-resp content-type mismatch
ciscoasa(config-cmap)# match request body length gt 1000
ciscoasa(config-cmap)# match not request uri regex class URL_List
ciscoasa(config)# policy-map type inspect http L7_HTTP_policy
ciscoasa(config-pmap)# match req-resp content-type mismatch
ciscoasa(config-pmap-c)# reset log
ciscoasa(config-pmap-c)# exit
ciscoasa(config-pmap)# class L7_HTTP_class
ciscoasa(config-pmap-c)# drop-connection log
ciscoasa(config-pmap-c)# exit
ciscoasa(config-pmap)# parameters
ciscoasa(config-pmap-p)# protocol-violation action log
ciscoasa(config-pmap-p)# spoof-server **************
ciscoasa(config)# class-map L3_HTTP_TRAFFIC
ciscoasa(config-cmap)# match port tcp eq 80
ciscoasa(config)# policy-map L3_outside_policy
ciscoasa(config-pmap)# class L3_HTTP_TRAFFIC
ciscoasa(config-pmap-c)# inspect http L7_HTTP_policy
ciscoasa(config)# service-policy L3_outside_policy
                        interface outside
```

In the preceding example, a regular expression class map includes two regular expressions: "abc1.com" and "abc2.com". I'll assume that these are my company domain names. Following this is a layer 7 class map (`L7_HTTP_class`) for HTTP that is looking for *all* of the following:

▼   In either a request or a response, a content type mismatch in a request or a response message (like a tag that says <IMG> but the file referenced doesn't end in an extension associated with a picture/image).

■   A request body length is greater than 1,000 bytes.

▲   A URI part of the request *doesn't* contain the two regular expressions.

Below the layer 7 class map, a layer 7 policy map (`L7_HTTP_policy`) is configured for HTTP. A global policy is defined for content type mismatches (**match req-resp content-type mismatch**): reset and log the connection. For information matching in the layer-7 class map, the connections are dropped and logged. Protocol violations are logged, but allowed. Likewise, I'm spoofing the server information in response messages, replacing the server information with a list of asterisks.

A layer 3/4 class map (`L3_HTTP_TRAFFIC`) is created that includes port 80 traffic. A layer 3/4 policy map (`L3_outside_policy`) is created that references the layer 3/4 class map and performs application layer inspection of HTTP traffic, qualifying the inspection by using the layer-7 policy map policies.

INSTANT MESSAGING INSPECTION

Users can take advantage of the multifunction capabilities of instant messaging (IM) applications: chatting, video, voice, games, file transfers, and others. Many or all of these can create productivity problems and security issues in the workplace. Inspection of IM became available in version 7, allowing you to control these functions.

Inspection features currently support Yahoo Messenger and MSN Messenger IM clients on their native ports. With these IM clients, you can control what usernames the users use to log in, the user and server addresses allowed to communicate with each other, the services the clients can use within the IM client, and many other things. The following sections will discuss how to configure an IM inspection policy.

IM Policy Configuration

The following sections will discuss how to configure layer 7 class and policy maps and how to associate these with a layer 3/4 inspection policy for IM traffic.

IM Layer 7 Class Maps

Layer 7 class maps for IM allow you to match on additional criteria found in IM connections, like the type of client being used, the services the user is using within the client, the IP addresses involved in the connection, and many other things. Here is the syntax for setting up a layer 7 class map for IM:

```
ciscoasa(config)# class-map type inspect im [match-all]
                           L7_class_map_name
ciscoasa(config-cmap)# match [not] protocol {[msn-im] [yahoo-im]}
ciscoasa(config-cmap)# match [not] service {[chat] [conference]
                           [file-transfer] [games] [voice-chat]
                           [webcam]}
ciscoasa(config-cmap)# match [not] filename regex {class
                           regex_class_name | regex_name}
ciscoasa(config-cmap)# match [not] ip-address IP_address [subnet_mask]
ciscoasa(config-cmap)# match [not] peer-ip-address IP_address
                           [subnet_mask]
ciscoasa(config-cmap)# match [not] login-name regex {class
                           regex_class_name | regex_name}
ciscoasa(config-cmap)# match [not] peer-login-name regex {class
                           regex_class_name | regex_name}
ciscoasa(config-cmap)# match [not] version regex {class
                           regex_class_name | regex_name}
```

The **protocol** parameter allows you to match on either or both of the IM clients: MSN Messenger and/or Yahoo Messenger. The service parameter allows you to match on the type of **service** the user is attempting to use within the IM client, like playing games, running video, transferring files, and others. The **filename** parameter allows you to match on a filename listed in a regular expression or expressions that are being transferred between two clients (this is supported currently only for the Yahoo client). The **ip-address** parameter allows you to match on a client IP address (or subnet). The **peer-ip-address** parameter allows you to match on the remote peer or server IP address (or subnet). The **login-name** parameter allows you to match on the user's name initiating the connection, and the **peer-login-name** parameter allows you to match on a peer name that a user wants to connect to. The **version** parameter allows you to use a regular expression(s) to match on the version information shared between the two clients.

IM Layer 7 Policy Maps

To use the layer 7 IM class map, you must reference it in a layer 7 policy map for IM:

```
ciscoasa(config)# policy-map type inspect im L7_policy_map_name
ciscoasa(config-pmap)# match L7_class_map_parameters
ciscoasa(config-pmap-c)# {[drop-connection | reset] } [log]
ciscoasa(config-pmap)# class L7_class_map_name
ciscoasa(config-pmap-c)# {[drop-connection | reset] } [log]
```

Instead of creating an application layer class map, you can also reference these values within the layer 7 policy map with the **match** command. The advantage of using layer 7 class maps is that you can apply different policies to different classes (class maps). You can have the appliance reset and/or log the connection or drop and/or log the connection for a matching class map or **match** command.

IM Layer 3/4 Policy Maps

Inspection of IM traffic is disabled on the appliance. To enable it, create your layer 7 class and/or policy maps, and associate the layer 7 policy map with a layer 3/4 inspection policy:

```
ciscoasa(config)# policy-map L3/4_policy_map_name
ciscoasa(config-pmap)# class L3/4_class_map_name
ciscoasa(config-pmap-c)# inspect im L7_policy_map_name
```

IM Example Configuration

To help illustrate how to configure IM inspection with layer 7 policies, examine the following configuration:

```
ciscoasa(config)# class-map type inspect im match-all L7_IM_class_map
ciscoasa(config-cmap)# match not ip-address 10.0.0.0 255.0.0.0
ciscoasa(config-cmap)# match not peer-ip-address 10.0.0.0 255.0.0.0
ciscoasa(config-cmap)# match protocol not msn-im
ciscoasa(config-cmap)# match not service chat
ciscoasa(config)# policy-map type inspect im L7_IM_policy_map
ciscoasa(config-pmap)# class L7_IM_class_map
ciscoasa(config-pmap-c)# reset log
ciscoasa(config)# class-map im_inspect_class_map
ciscoasa(config-cmap)# match default-inspection-traffic
ciscoasa(config)# policy-map global_policy
ciscoasa(config-pmap)# class im_inspection_class_map
ciscoasa(config-pmap-c)# inspect im L7_IM_policy_map
ciscoasa(config)# service-policy global_policy global
```

In the preceding example, a layer 7 class map (L7_IM_class_map) is including everything *except* the internal IM clients (10.0.0.0/8), the IM peers/servers (10.0.0.0/8), chatting, and the MSN client. So if it's anything else, the layer 7 policy map (L7_IM_policy_map) will reset and log it. For example:

▼ Anyone using the Yahoo client would be reset.

■ Any MSN client accessing a server not in 10.0.0.0/8 would be reset.

▲ Any MSN client trying to use webcam would be reset.

A layer 3/4 class map (im_inspect_class_map) has been created that includes IM on its native ports. This is referenced in the global layer 3/4 policy map with application inspection of IM using the layer 7 policy map, which is applied on all interfaces of the appliance.

RSH INSPECTION

RSH (remote shell) was designed for UNIX systems to alleviate the hassles of having to authenticate every time you logged into another system. One problem with telnet is that you must always enter a username and password when accessing a remote system. With RSH, you log into one machine, and then you can remotely start up a shell process on a different machine without having to again enter a username and password. On the remote UNIX system, a ".rhosts" file contains a list of IP addresses of devices that are allowed to perform RSH. This greatly simplifies accessing remote resources.

Today most people don't use RSH because it is very insecure—all traffic going across the connection is susceptible to eavesdropping, and it is very easy to execute a spoofing attack to start up a shell on a remote system with this process enabled. Because of these inherent security problems with RSH, most people use SSH (secure shell), which I discussed in Chapter 3.

SECURITY ALERT! You should not allow RSH traffic through your appliance, because it is susceptible to spoofing attacks. If you must allow it, restrict its use with ACLs.

Mechanics of RSH Connections

To help illustrate how RSH connections are established between a client and a server, I'll use the example shown in Figure 12-3. When setting up an RSH connection (which uses TCP), the client device chooses a source port number greater than 1023 that is not currently being used. The destination port number is the well-known port 514. This connection is known as a *command* connection and is used to emulate the CLI of the shell.

Once the command connection is established, the RSH server sets up another TCP connection, called an *error* connection, back to the client. The error connection is used to transmit errors related to the shell. The server asks the client on the command connection which free port number (greater than 1023) the client is assigning to this connection for the destination port number, and the server chooses a port number greater than 1023 as a source port number. The server then builds this connection to the client. As you can see, this process is very similar to standard-mode FTP.

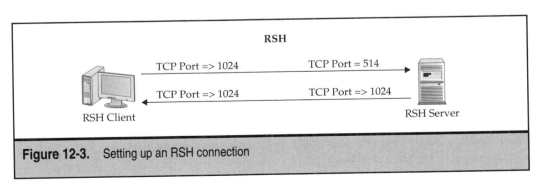

Figure 12-3. Setting up an RSH connection

The function of application inspection on the appliance is to dynamically add the error connection to the conn table as needed. Likewise if the appliance is performing address translation, and the port numbers negotiated conflict with what is already in the xlate table, the appliance will fix the numbers in the payload and add the necessary entry in the xlate table.

RSH Policy Configuration

RSH inspection is enabled by default on the appliance in the global_policy. RSH inspection doesn't support layer 7 class and policy maps. You can globally disable RSH inspection and/or enable it on an interface-by-interface basis by using the following commands:

```
ciscoasa(config)# policy-map L3/4_policy_map_name
ciscoasa(config-pmap)# class L3/4_class_map_name
ciscoasa(config-pmap-c)# [no] inspect rsh
```

SNMP INSPECTION

SNMP uses UDP connections to ports 161 and 162 to communicate between devices. Application inspection on the appliances doesn't do anything fancy, since these connections don't require any "fixing up" to function through the appliance.

SNMP versions 1, 2, and 2c have security issues, however, since they contain the community strings (the equivalent of a password) in clear text in the SNMP payload and thus are susceptible to eavesdropping and spoofing attacks. Version 3 supports encryption and HMAC functions (for digital signatures), making it more secure than the older SNMP versions. Application inspection on the appliances, therefore, is used to restrict what versions of SNMP you'll allow through the appliance.

SNMP Policy Configuration

SNMP inspection was added in version 7.0 of the appliance. Unlike with many other applications and protocols, there are no layer 7 class or policy maps. However, to define the SNMP versions you want to deny, you must create what is called an *SNMP map*:

```
ciscoasa(config)# snmp-map snmp_map_name
ciscoasa(config-snmp-map)# deny version version
```

The version number can be 1, 2, 2c, or 3. To deny multiple versions, list them in separate **deny** commands.

SNMP inspection is disabled by default. Once you've created your SNMP map, you need to reference it in a layer 3/4 policy:

```
ciscoasa(config)# policy-map L3/4_policy_map_name
ciscoasa(config-pmap)# class L3/4_class_map_name
ciscoasa(config-pmap-c)# [no] inspect snmp snmp_map_name
```

SNMP Example Configuration

To help illustrate how to configure SNMP inspection with SNMP maps, examine the following configuration:

```
ciscoasa(config)# access-list snmpACL permit tcp any any eq 161
ciscoasa(config)# access-list snmpACL permit tcp any any eq 162
ciscoasa(config)# class-map L3_snmp
ciscoasa(config-cmap)# match access-list snmpACL
ciscoasa(config)# snmp-map deny_snmp_map
ciscoasa(config-snmp-map)# deny version 1
ciscoasa(config-snmp-map)# deny version 2
ciscoasa(config-snmp-map)# deny version 2c
ciscoasa(config)# policy-map global_policy
ciscoasa(config-pmap)# class L3_SNMP
ciscoasa(config-pmap-c)# inspect snmp deny_snmp_map
ciscoasa(config)# service-policy global_policy global
```

In the preceding configuration, an SNMP policy is enabled globally, where only SNMP version 3 is allowed.

SQL*NET INSPECTION

Oracle developed a protocol called SQL*Net, which allows remote users to access an Oracle database in client/server applications. There are two version of SQL*Net: version 1 and 2. The Cisco application inspection feature is compatible with both. In the following sections, I will discuss how the application inspection feature for SQL*Net works and how to enable SQL*Net application inspection.

Mechanics of SQL*Net Connections

Before I begin talking about how the appliance application inspection feature deals with connectivity issues between Oracle clients and Oracle database server(s), let's first look at how connections get set up between these two sets of devices. Basically two different scenarios can occur when an Oracle client requests a connection to an Oracle database server:

▼   The connection will be created to the specified database server.

▲   The database server will redirect the client to a database on a *different* server.

I'll use the example shown in Figure 12-4 to assist with my explanation of the first type of connection. In this example, the Oracle client opens a TCP connection to the Oracle database server. The source port number is greater than 1023, and the destination port number is 1521. If the database server is IANA compliant, then the destination port

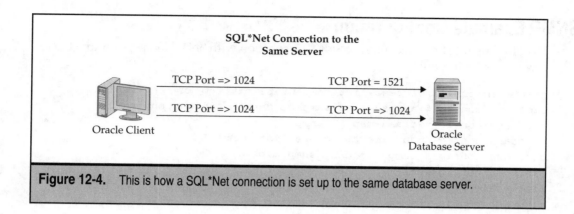

Figure 12-4. This is how a SQL*Net connection is set up to the same database server.

number should be 66. The database server, upon receiving the connection setup request, completes the connection and then notifies the client that to establish a data connection to do a table query, the client should use the TCP port number assigned by the server. The client then opens a second TCP connection to the server: the source port number is above 1023, and the destination port number is the one assigned by the Oracle server.

An interesting situation arises, however, when the actual data resources that the client wants are *not* on the same Oracle database server, or when load balancing is set up among multiple database servers. In this instance, the client connects to its configured server on TCP port 1521 (or 66), as shown in Figure 12-5. Once this connection is established,

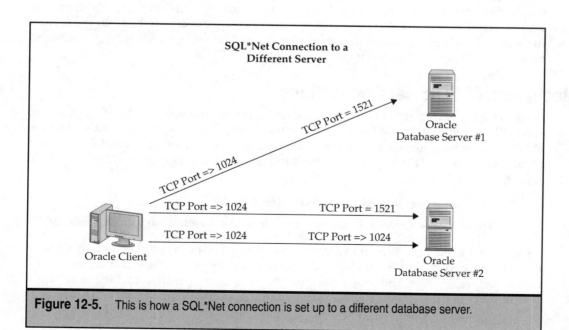

Figure 12-5. This is how a SQL*Net connection is set up to a different database server.

if this database server will not be handling the data requests, it will forward the *IP address* of another database server back to the SQL*Net client. The client will then tear down the connection to the first server and will use the IP address given to it by the first server to set up another TCP port 1521 (or 66) connection—this is the connection to the redirected database server. This second server will then negotiate the TCP port numbers for the data connection, which the client will then use to establish the data connection.

The function of application inspection on the appliance is to dynamically add these connections to the conn table as needed, including any connections to other database servers. Likewise, if the appliance is performing address translation and the port numbers (or addresses) negotiated conflict with what is already in the xlate table, the appliance will fix the numbers in the payload and add the necessary entry in the xlate table. If the port number being passed back matches a **static** command between the two interfaces, the appliance will also fix this in the payload.

SQL*Net Policy Configuration

SQL*Net application inspection is enabled, by default, in the global_policy. SQL*Net inspection doesn't support layer 7 class and policy maps. You can globally disable SQL*Net inspection and/or enable it on an interface-by-interface basis by using the following commands:

```
ciscoasa(config)# policy-map L3/4_policy_map_name
ciscoasa(config-pmap)# class L3/4_class_map_name
ciscoasa(config-pmap-c)# [no] inspect sqlnet
```

If the database server is running on a port other than 1521 or 66 (if the administrator is implementing an IANA solution), then you'll need to create a layer 3/4 class map that references the correct protocol and port (or use an ACL) and then reference the class map in a layer 3/4 policy with SQL*Net inspection.

CHAPTER 13

Voice and Policies

Τhis chapter will introduce you to the application inspection features for voice connections. Like FTP and other applications, Voice over IP (VoIP) applications use multiple connections to set up and transmit voice conversations. The topics discussed in this chapter include

▼ SIP

■ SCCP

■ CTIQBE

▲ MGCP

SIP INSPECTION

The Session Initiation Protocol (SIP), specified in RFC 2543, is used by VoIP to set up audio connections and is supported by many VoIP vendors, including Cisco. SIP is responsible for handling the sessions or the setup of the voice connections. The Session Description Protocol (SDP), specified in RFC 2327, is responsible for the assignment of the ports for the actual voice connections. The signaling for the setup of voice connections happens over a well-known connection, port 5060. The appliance will inspect this information to figure out the dynamic ports that the two sides will use for setting up the audio connection and letting the voice traffic in, by adding the necessary UDP connection(s) to the state table. The following sections will discuss how a SIP session is established, issues with SIP, the application layer inspection features of the appliances, and how to configure the inspection features.

SIP Connections and Application Inspection

The following sections will discuss how SIP connections are established between the VoIP clients (phones) and the VoIP gateway, along with the application layer inspection features of the appliances.

Setup of SIP VoIP Connections

To help illustrate how SIP connections are established between a VoIP client and a VoIP gateway, as well as setting up phone connections between SIP VoIP clients, I'll use the example shown in Figure 13-1.

When setting up the first connection (which can use either TCP *or* UDP), the client device will choose a source port number greater than 1023 that is not currently being used. The choice of protocols is based on the configuration and implementation of the VoIP solution; typically UDP is used. The destination port number is the well-known port 5060. This connection is a *signaling* connection and is used by the VoIP client to send signaling information, like a call setup or teardown request of audio phone connections, to the VoIP gateway device. The signaling connection is also used for VoIP clients to register their phone numbers and IP addresses—basically the VoIP gateway acts as a phone

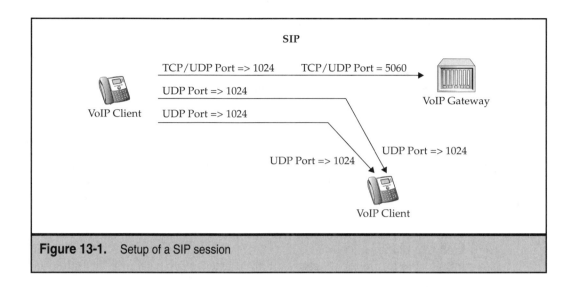

Figure 13-1. Setup of a SIP session

directory to resolve phone numbers to IP addresses and to assist clients in establishing phone connections among themselves.

Once the signaling connection is established, the VoIP client can make phone calls. When making a phone call, the client will use the signaling connection to signal the VoIP gateway of the call setup request to a destination phone. Two connections will be established to the destination VoIP phone: one for the audio and one for synchronization. Actually, the RTP protocol, discussed in the next chapter, is used to implement these connections. The source client will choose unused UDP port numbers (greater than 1023) for the *audio* and synchronization connection and will notify the gateway of its choice. The VoIP gateway will then contact the destination VoIP phone, acquire the destination UDP port numbers (greater than 1023) that are to be used for the incoming call session from the source, along with the destination IP address, and then notify the source client of this connection information so that the source can now complete the audio and synchronization connections to the destination phone.

Application Layer Inspection Features for SIP

Application inspection for SIP is new as of version 6.0 of the OS. When this feature was introduced, the appliance securely allowed the additional UDP connections by adding them to the state table and fixing embedded addressing information in the payload.

Dealing with the Additional UDP Connections for SIP   If the VoIP client establishing the voice session is connected to a lower-level interface than the VoIP gateway interface, you'll need an inbound ACL entry to allow the connection. In addition to this, if the destination VoIP client is connected to a higher-level interface than the source interface, you'll need application layer inspection enabled for SIP so the appliance can examine the signaling connection, determine that the two RTP connections are being negotiated, dynamically add these to the state table, and, if address translation is used and the new connections conflict with an existing PAT translation(s), can change the embedded port numbers in the signaling connection and create the necessary PAT translation(s) in the xlate table. If the IP addresses are being NATed, these are also fixed in the signaling connection.

The following restrictions apply to the appliance when a remote VoIP client (connected to a lower-level interface) attempts to register with a SIP gateway (connected to a higher-level interface):

▼ The client won't be able to register its IP address if the client is being PATed.

■ The additional RTP connections won't be added if the SIP proxy/gateway fails to include the port numbers in the signaling messages between the clients.

■ When setting up the UDP sessions, the appliance must be able to see the signaling connection between the client and gateway: if both of these are connected to a lower-level interface and the VoIP destination client is connected to a higher-level interface, the RTP connections will fail. Therefore, it is recommend to locate the gateway off an interface with a security level higher than all the VoIP clients.

▲ If the VoIP client has two different IP addresses, and one address appears in the owner ("o") field of the SDP portion of the packet and the other appears in the connection ("c") field, the appliance will fail to fix both addresses when address translation is enabled.

NOTE   If the VoIP client establishing the voice session is connected to a higher-level interface compared with the destination client, application inspection isn't necessary to add the two additional UDP sessions unless you are filtering traffic outbound with an ACL. However, to handle inbound calls to the higher-level client, you'll need application layer inspection of SIP.

Additional Application Layer Inspection Features for SIP   Starting in version 7, additional application inspection features were added for SIP. Besides fixing embedded addressing information in the signaling connection and adding the RTP connections to the state table, the appliances can perform the following application layer inspection functions, as well as many others:

▼ Filter phone numbers that are called

■ Inspect chat connections for the Windows Messenger RTC client

■ Restrict the duration of phone calls made

■ Look for protocol violations in the setup of phone connections

▲ Restrict the methods (commands) the VoIP client can send to the gateway

The following sections will discuss how to configure application inspection of SIP sessions.

SIP Policy Configuration

The next sections will discuss the configuration of SIP inspection. For in-depth inspection policies, you might need to create a layer 7 policy map and, possibly, a layer 7 class map. The following sections will discuss how to create these, as well as how to enable SIP inspection in a layer 3/4 policy map.

SIP Layer 7 Class Maps

Here are the commands to create a layer 7 class map for SIP inspection:

```
ciscoasa(config)# class-map type inspect sip [match-all]
                        L7_class_map_name
ciscoasa(config-cmap)# description description
ciscoasa(config-cmap)# match [not] {called-party | calling-party}
                        regex {class class_name | regex_name}
ciscoasa(config-cmap)# match [not] content length gt length
ciscoasa(config-cmap)# match [not] content type {sdp | regex
                        {class class_name | regex_name}}
ciscoasa(config-cmap)# match [not] im-subscriber regex
                        {class class_name | regex_name}
ciscoasa(config-cmap)# match [not] message-path regex
                        {class class_name | regex_name}
ciscoasa(config-cmap)# match [not] request-method method
ciscoasa(config-cmap)# match [not] third-party-registration regex
                        {class class_name | regex_name}
ciscoasa(config-cmap)# match [not] uri {sip | tel} length gt length
```

The **called-party** and **calling-party** parameters allow you to match on the phone numbers of the destination and source, respectively, using a regular expression or regular expression class map. The **content length** parameter allows you to match on the length of the SIP header, and the **content type** parameter allows you to match on whether the SIP packet contains SDP, or you can match on a regular expression(s). The **im-subscriber** parameter allows you to match on the name of the user who is using the Microsoft Messenger IM client using a regular expression(s). To match on information in the "Via" field of a SIP header, use the **message-path** parameter. The **request-method** command allows you to match on the SIP commands sent to the voice gateway in the SIP header; these include **ack**, **bye**, **cancel**, **info**, **invite**, **message**, **notify**, **options**, **prack**, **refer**, **register**, **subscribe**, **unknown**, and **update**. The **third-party-registration** parameter allows you to match a user(s) who can register other VoIP clients with a VoIP gateway or proxy (taken from the "From" field in a register message). The **uri** parameter allows you to match on the length of the SIP or TEL (telephone numbers) information in the URI portion of the header.

SIP Layer 7 Policy Maps

Here are the commands to create a layer 7 policy map for SIP inspection:

```
ciscoasa(config)# policy-map type inspect sip L7_policy_map_name
ciscoasa(config-pmap)# description string
ciscoasa(config-pmap)# match L7_class_map_parameters
ciscoasa(config-pmap-c)# {[drop [send-protocol-error] |
                          drop-connection [send-protocol-error] |
                          mask | reset] [log] |
                          rate-limit message_rate}
ciscoasa(config-pmap-c)# exit
ciscoasa(config-pmap)# class L7_class_map_name
ciscoasa(config-pmap-c)# {[drop [send-protocol-error] |
                          drop-connection [send-protocol-error] |
                          mask | reset] [log] |
                          rate-limit message_rate}
ciscoasa(config-pmap-c)# exit
ciscoasa(config-pmap)# parameters
ciscoasa(config-pmap-p)# [no] im
ciscoasa(config-pmap-p)# [no] ip-address-privacy
ciscoasa(config-pmap-p)# max-forwards-validation action [drop |
                          drop-connection | reset] [log]
ciscoasa(config-pmap-p)# rtp-conformance [enforce-payloadtype]
ciscoasa(config-pmap-p)# software-version action [mask] [log]
ciscoasa(config-pmap-p)# state-checking action [drop |
                          drop-connection | reset] [log]
ciscoasa(config-pmap-p)# strict-header-validation action [drop |
                          drop-connection | reset] [log]
ciscoasa(config-pmap-p)# [no] traffic-non-sip
ciscoasa(config-pmap-p)# uri-non-sip action [mask] [log]
```

Instead of creating an application layer class map, you can also reference these values within the layer 7 policy map with the **match** command. The advantage of using layer 7 class maps is that you can apply different policies to different classes (class maps). You can have the appliance drop the packet or connection (along with sending a protocol error), mask (obfuscate) part of the header information, reset the connection (only applicable if the signaling connection is using TCP), log the match, or rate-limit the number of SIP messages per second.

The **im** command enables or disables the use of IM via SIP—by default this is disabled. The **ip-address-privacy** command enables or disables IP address privacy—by default this is disabled. The **max-forwards-validation** command, when enabled, checks whether the "max-forwards" field in the header is set to 0, which it shouldn't be before it reaches the destination. If a violation is detected, you can drop the packet, drop the connection, reset the signaling connection (if TCP is used), and/or log the violation.

The `rtp-conformance` command checks the RTP packets that were dynamically added to the conn table for conforming to the RTP standard. The `enforce-payloadtype` enforces the payload type to be audio or video based on the signaling exchange on the signaling connection. The `software-version` command, when enabled, masks (obfuscates) the software version of the server and clients in the "server" and "user-agent" fields of the SIP header. The `state-checking` command enables state tracking, where the appliance can ensure that the requests and responses between the VoIP client and gateway appear in the correct order. The `strict-header-validation` command has the appliance validate the header fields in the SIP messages to ensure that they follow the RFC 3261 standard. The `traffic-non-sip` command, when enabled, validates the information on the SIP signaling port to determine if the traffic is SIP or something else. The `uri-non-sip` command, when enabled, identifies non-SIP URIs present in the "alert-info" and "call-info" header fields and can mask and/or log this information.

SIP Layer 3/4 Policy Maps

To enable inspection of SIP, you need to reference it in a layer 3/4 policy map:

```
ciscoasa(config)# policy-map L3/4_policy_map_name
ciscoasa(config-pmap)# class L3/4_class_map_name
ciscoasa(config-pmap-c)# inspect sip [L7_policy_map_name]
                               [tls-proxy TLS_proxy_name]
```

Without a layer 7 policy map, the appliance will only fix embedded addressing information and add the RTP voice connections to the conn table. Optionally you can enable TLS proxying with SIP. TLS proxying is where the signaling connection is encrypted between the VoIP client and the gateway, and the appliance proxies the connection between the two endpoints. This feature allows the appliance to decrypt information from one endpoint, inspect it, and re-encrypt it before sending it to the other endpoint. TLS proxying for voice connections is beyond the scope of this book.

NOTE SIP inspection is by default enabled in the global policy on the appliance. You can qualify it with a layer 7 policy map, however, or disable it globally and enable it only on a particular interface(s).

SIP Connection Timeout

By default, the following timers are used to tear down SIP connections from the conn table:

▼ A TCP signaling connection is removed from the conn table if the connection is closed, an RST is seen, or if the connection is idle for more than 1 hour by default.

▲ The RTP connections are removed from the conn table after 2 minutes of idle time have expired.

To change the idle timeout for the SIP signaling connection, use this command:

```
ciscoasa(config)# timeout sip hh:mm:ss
```

To change the idle timeout for the RTP UDP connections, use this command:

```
ciscoasa(config)# timeout sip_media hh:mm:ss
```

> **TIP** Because some compression methods don't send packets when people are quiet on the phone connection, long periods of quiet might be misconstrued by the appliance to mean that the phone conversation is over, based on the idle timer you've configured; therefore, don't set the idle timer to too low a value.

SIP Connection Verification

You can use the **show sip** and **debug sip** commands to view and troubleshoot SIP inspection issues. Here's an example of the former command:

```
ciscoasa# show sip
Total: 2
call-id c3943000-960ca-2e43-1111@10.0.1.20
state Call init, idle 0:00:01
call-id c3943000-860ca-7e1f-11f7@10.0.2.22
state Active, idle 0:00:05
```

In this example, you can see two active SIP sessions, where each `call-id` represents a separate phone session. The first session is in a `Call init` state, which indicates that the call is still being established (the caller sent the INVITE message and hasn't see the 200 OK final response). The second session is in an `active` state, which means that the call has been established (the RTP connections have been negotiated). This session has been idle for 5 seconds.

SIP Example Configuration

Here's a simple example of an inspection policy for SIP:

```
ciscoasa(config)# policy-map type inspect sip L7_sip_policy
ciscoasa(config-pmap)# parameters
ciscoasa(config-pmap-p)# no im
ciscoasa(config-pmap-p)# rtp-conformance enforce-payloadtype
ciscoasa(config-pmap-p)# software-version action mask log
ciscoasa(config-pmap-p)# state-checking action drop log
ciscoasa(config-pmap-p)# strict-header-validation action drop log
ciscoasa(config-pmap-p)# traffic-non-sip
ciscoasa(config-pmap-p)# uri-non-sip action mask log
ciscoasa(config)# policy-map global_policy
ciscoasa(config-pmap)# class inspection_default
ciscoasa(config-pmap-c)# inspect sip L7_sip_policy
ciscoasa(config)# service-policy global_policy global
```

In this example, a layer 7 policy map is configured (`L7_sip_policy`). In this policy, IM is not allowed. RTP is validated for conformance to the RFC, and the RTP connections must be voice or video, based on what was negotiated. The software version information is masked; state checking is enabled, and if there is a violation, the packet is dropped. The header information is validated, and if it doesn't follow the standard, the packet is dropped. Non-SIP traffic on the signaling connection is dropped; and the URI portion of a SIP packet, if it doesn't conform to URI information, is masked. The default layer 3/4 class map in the default layer 3/4 policy map enables stateful inspection for SIP, referencing the additional inspection processes that will be performed in the layer 7 map.

SCCP INSPECTION

SCCP (Skinny Client Control Protocol), or "Skinny" for short, is a Cisco-simplified protocol for implementing VoIP with Cisco IP Phones and the Cisco CallManager server. Skinny is interoperable with other H.323 devices (H.323 is discussed in the next chapter). Support for application inspection of Skinny was introduced in version 6.0 of the PIX software. When the appliance is performing its application inspection of Skinny, it examines Skinny signals to determine if there are embedded addresses. It changes conflicting addresses and updates the xlate table as well as looking for the call setup of audio connections, and will dynamically add these connections to the appliance conn table. Additional application layer inspection features were added in version 7.

SCCP Connections and Application Inspection

The following sections will discuss how SCCP connections are established between the VoIP clients (phones) and the VoIP gateway, along with the application layer inspection features of the appliances.

Setup of SCCP VoIP Connections

To help illustrate how SCCP connections are established between a Cisco IP Phone client and the Cisco CallManager server (VoIP gateway), as well as how connections between IP Phone clients are established, I'll use the example shown in Figure 13-2. When an IP Phone first boots up, it will use DHCP to learn its IP addressing information, which includes its IP address and subnet mask, a default gateway, a DNS server address, and a TFTP server address. With version 6.2, the appliances support DHCP options 150 and 166, which allow them to send the TFTP server address to DHCP clients, including Cisco IP Phones. I will discuss DHCP server features of the appliances in Chapter 26. The IP Phone client will use TFTP to download its configuration instructions from the TFTP server, which usually resides on the CallManager server. This will include its phone number. Normally CallManager will use the MAC address of the phone to determine the configuration file to associate with the phone.

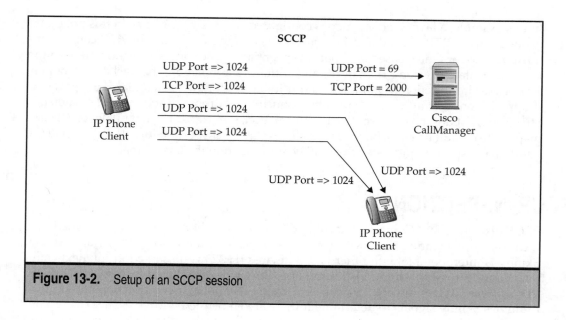

Figure 13-2. Setup of an SCCP session

NOTE If the phone is connected to a lower-level interface than CallManager, you'll need an ACL entry to allow the TFTP connection (and enable protocol inspection or TFTP). Also, if a DHCP server doesn't reside in the VLAN the phone resides in, and the appliance is not a DHCP server, you'll need to configure a DHCP relay function on the appliance to forward the DHCP request to a DHCP server on a different segment (discussed in Chapter 26).

When setting up the first connection (which uses TCP) to the CallManager server, the client device will choose a port number greater than 1023 that is not currently being used. The destination port number is the well-known port 2000. This connection is a signaling connection and is used by the client to send signaling information, like a call setup or teardown request of phone connections. Across this signaling connection, the client will indicate which UDP port it will use to handle the processing of voice packets (phone connections).

Once the signaling connection is established and the IP Phone registers its phone number and IP address, the phone can make phone calls. When making a phone call, the client will use the signaling connection to signal the CallManager server of the call setup request to a destination phone. Like SIP, RTP is used to establish the phone session to a remote phone: one UDP connection is for the audio, and the second one for synchronization of the audio (RTP is discussed in the next chapter).

The source phone will select two unused UDP port numbers (greater than 1023) for these two connections. The CallManager will then contact the destination party, acquire the destination UDP port numbers for the connections (greater than 1023) from the destination, along with the destination IP address, and then notify the source phone of the connection information so that the source can now complete the phone connection to the destination.

Application Layer Inspection Features for SCCP

Application inspection for SCCP is new as of version 6.0 of the OS. Basically the appliance securely allows the additional UDP connections by adding them to the state table and fixing embedded addressing information in the payload. Currently there are five versions of SCCP: 2.4, 3.04, 3.1.1, 3.2, and 3.3.2—the appliances support application inspection of all versions through 3.3.2.

Dealing with the Additional UDP Connections for SCCP   If the VoIP client establishing the voice session is connected to a lower-level interface compared with the VoIP gateway, you'll need an ACL to allow the signaling connection. In addition to this, if the destination VoIP client is connected to a higher-level interface compared with the source, you'll need application layer inspection enabled for SCCP in order for the appliance to examine the signaling connection, determine that the two RTP connections are being negotiated, dynamically add these to the state table, and, if address translation is used and the new connections create a conflict with an existing PAT translation(s), to change the embedded port numbers in the signaling connection and create the necessary PAT translation(s) in the xlate table. If the IP addresses are being NATed, these are also fixed in the signaling connection.

The following restrictions apply to the appliance performing application inspection of SCCP traffic:

▼ Inside NAT and PAT are supported, but outside NAT and PAT are not: therefore, if you have overlapping addresses between two networks, the IP Phones in the two networks will not be able to communicate with each other.

▲ Stateful failover (discussed in Chapter 23) is supported; however, phone calls in the middle of being established are not replicated, and the user will have to redial the number after a failover has occurred.

Additional Application Layer Inspection Features for SCCP   Starting in version 7, additional application inspection features were added for inspection of SCCP connections. Besides fixing embedded addressing information in the signaling connection and adding the RTP connections to the state table, the appliances can perform the following application layer inspection functions, as well as many others:

▼ Filter message identifiers

■ Limit the length of message identifiers

■ Require registration with CallManager before phone calls can be made

■ Look for protocol violations in the setup of phone connections

▲ Limit the size of the SCCP prefix in the header

SCCP Policy Configuration

The following sections will discuss the configuration of SCCP inspection. For in-depth inspection policies, you might need to create a layer 7 policy map; unlike SIP,

SCCP doesn't support layer 7 class maps. The following sections will discuss how to create the optional layer 7 policy map, as well as enable SCCP inspection in a layer 3/4 policy map.

SCCP Layer 7 Policy Maps

Here are the commands to create a layer 7 policy map for SIP inspection:

```
ciscoasa(config)# policy-map type inspect skinny L7_policy_map_name
ciscoasa(config-pmap)# description string
ciscoasa(config-pmap)# match [not] message id {message_ID |
                              range lower_ID_range upper_ID_range}
ciscoasa(config-pmap-c)# {drop [log]}
ciscoasa(config-pmap-c)# exit
ciscoasa(config-pmap)# parameters
ciscoasa(config-pmap-p)# enforce-registration
ciscoasa(config-pmap-p)# message-id max hex_value
ciscoasa(config-pmap-p)# rtp-conformance [enforce-payloadtype]
ciscoasa(config-pmap-p)# sccp-prefix-len {max | min} value_length
ciscoasa(config-pmap-p)# timeout {signaling | media} hh:mm:ss
```

There is currently only one **match** command supported for a layer 7 SCCP policy map: **match message id**. This command matches on one or a range of station message identifiers (specified in hexadecimal) in an SCCP message. The actions you can take when there is (or isn't) a match include dropping the packet and/or logging the match.

In the parameters section of the policy map, the **enforce-registration** command requires a VoIP phone to register to CallManager before calls can be placed. The **message-id max** command specifies the highest SCCP station message ID allowed. The **rtp-conformance** command checks the RTP packets that were dynamically added to the conn table for conforming to the RTP standard. The **enforce-payloadtype** command enforces the payload type to be audio or video based on the signaling exchange on the signaling connection. The **sccp-prefix-len** command sets the minimum or maximum SCCP prefix length allowed. The **timeout** command sets the idle timeout for the signaling and RTP audio connections. If you don't configure a timeout, the global timeouts for idle TCP and UDP connections are used.

SCCP Layer 3/4 Policy Maps

To enable inspection of SCCP, you need to reference it in a layer 3/4 policy map:

```
ciscoasa(config)# policy-map L3/4_policy_map_name
ciscoasa(config-pmap)# class L3/4_class_map_name
ciscoasa(config-pmap-c)# inspect skinny [L7_policy_map_name]
                            [tls-proxy TLS_proxy_name]
```

Without a layer 7 policy map, the appliance will only fix embedded addressing information and add the RTP voice connections to the conn table. Optionally you can enable TLS proxying with SCCP. TLS proxying is where the signaling connection is encrypted between the VoIP client and the gateway, and the appliance proxies the connection between the two endpoints. This feature allows the appliance to decrypt information from one endpoint, inspect it, and re-encrypt it before sending it to the other endpoint. TLS proxying for voice connections is beyond the scope of this book.

NOTE SCCP inspection is by default enabled in the global policy on the appliance. You can qualify it with a layer 7 policy map, however, or disable it globally and enable it only on a particular interface(s).

SCCP Connection Verification

You can use the **show skinny** command to troubleshoot problems with the SCCP inspection process. Here's an example of this command:

```
ciscoasa# show skinny
              LOCAL                FOREIGN           STATE
------------------------------------------------------------
1             10.0.1.10/51237   10.0.3.1/2000       1
      MEDIA   10.0.1.10/22948   10.0.2.21/32798
2             10.0.1.12/51231   10.0.3.1/2000       1
      MEDIA   10.0.1.12/32798   10.0.2.10/32948
```

This example has two connections from phones (10.0.1.10 and 10.0.1.12) to CallManager (10.0.3.1)—these are connections 1 and 2. Below each phone entry is a MEDIA entry, which represents a phone call using RTP. Each of the two phones has an active phone call: the first phone has a connection to 10.0.2.21 and the second phone to 10.0.2.10.

SCCP Example Configuration

Here's a simple example of an inspection policy for SIP:

```
ciscoasa(config)# policy-map type inspect skinny L7-skinny-map
ciscoasa(config-pmap)# match message-id range 0x200 0x300
ciscoasa(config-pmap-c)# drop log
ciscoasa(config-pmap)# parameters
ciscoasa(config-pmap-p)# enforce-registration
ciscoasa(config)# class-map inspection_default
ciscoasa(config-cmap)# match default-inspection-traffic
ciscoasa(config)# policy-map global_policy
ciscoasa(config-pmap)# class inspection_default
ciscoasa(config-pmap-c)# inspect skinny L7-skinny-map
ciscoasa(config)# service-policy global_policy global
```

In this example, a layer 7 SCCP policy map was used to drop and log packets that have a station message ID from 0x200 to 0x300. Registration to CallManager is required before phone calls can be placed. The default class map and global policy map are used, where the SCCP inspection has been qualified to use the layer 7 policy map.

CTIQBE INSPECTION

CTIQBE inspection allows Cisco's IP SoftPhone (software on a PC) and other Cisco Telephone Application Programming Interface (TAPI) and Java TAPI (JTAPI) PC-based applications to successfully communicate with a Cisco CallManager and other VoIP phones connected to a different interface of an appliance. The following sections will discuss how CTIQBE sessions are established, why application inspection is needed, how application inspection works, how to configure it, and how to examine CTIQBE sessions flowing through the appliance.

CTIQBE Connections and Application Inspection

The following sections will discuss how CTIQBE connections are established between the Cisco SoftPhones and CallManager, along with the application layer inspection features of the appliances.

Setup of CTIQBE VoIP Connections

To help illustrate how CTIQBE connections are established between a Cisco IP SoftPhone client and Cisco CallManager server (VoIP gateway), as well as connections between IP Phone clients, I'll use the example shown in Figure 13-3. The call setup is

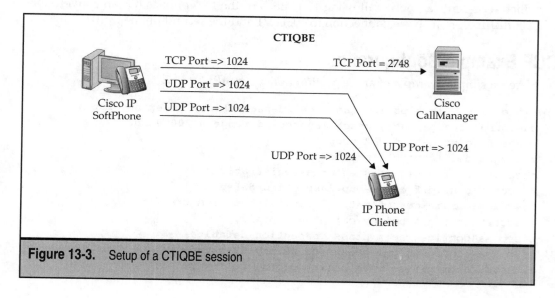

Figure 13-3. Setup of a CTIQBE session

similar to that of SIP and Skinny. When setting up the first connection (which uses TCP) to the CallManager server, the client device will choose a port number greater than 1023 that is not currently being used. The destination port number is the well-known port 2748 (this port cannot be changed on CallManager). This connection is a signaling connection and is used by the SoftPhone to send signaling information, like a call setup or teardown request of phone connections. Across this signaling connection, the client will indicate which UDP ports it will use to handle the processing of voice packets (phone connections).

Once the signaling connection is established and the SoftPhone registers its phone number and IP address, the SoftPhone can make phone calls. When making a phone call, the client will use the signaling connection to signal the CallManager server of the call setup request to a destination phone. Like SIP and SCCP, RTP is used to establish the phone session to a remote phone: one UDP connection is for the audio, and the second one for synchronization of the audio (RTP is discussed in the next chapter).

The source phone will select two unused UDP port numbers (greater than 1023) for these two connections. The CallManager will then contact the destination party, acquire the destination UDP port numbers for the connections (greater than 1023) from the destination, along with the destination IP address, and then notify the source phone of the connection information so that the source can now complete the phone connection to the destination.

Application Layer Inspection Features for CTIQBE

Application inspection for CTIQBE is new as of version 6.3 of the OS. Basically, the appliance securely allows the additional UDP connections by adding them to the state table and fixes embedded addressing information in the payload if it conflicts with any existing translations in the xlate table. Beyond this, no additional application layer inspection is performed on CTIQBE connections. The appliance does have the following limitations and restrictions when performing CTIQBE inspection:

▼ Phone calls made using CTIQBE are not replicated to a redundant appliance when stateful failover is configured. (CTIQBE phone calls are lost when failover occurs.)

■ If different SoftPhones are registered to different CallManagers, which are connected to different appliance interfaces, calls between the SoftPhones of different CallManagers will fail.

▲ Static NAT must be used when CallManager is located on a higher-level interface and NAT control is enabled. Also, the inbound control connection (port 2748) would have to be allowed with an ACL.

CTIQBE Policy Configuration

The following sections will discuss the configuration inspection of CTIQBE traffic. Unlike SIP, CTIQBE doesn't support layer 7 class and policy maps for in-depth inspection: only layer 3/4 policies are supported.

CTIQBE Layer 3/4 Policy Maps

To enable inspection of CTIQBE, you need to reference it in a layer 3/4 policy map:

```
ciscoasa(config)# policy-map L3/4_policy_map_name
ciscoasa(config-pmap)# class L3/4_class_map_name
ciscoasa(config-pmap-c)# inspect ctiqbe
```

No layer 7 class or policy maps for CTIQBE exist. By default, CTIQBE inspection is disabled in the global policy on the appliance. You can enable the inspection policy for an interface(s) or globally. Note that CallManager doesn't support a port other than 2748, so using the default class map is sufficient when setting up a layer 3/4 policy for CTIQBE.

CTIQBE Connection Verification

You can use the **show ctiqbe** command to troubleshoot problems with the setup of CTIQBE sessions. Here's an example of this command:

```
ciscoasa# show ctiqbe
Total: 1
    LOCAL FOREIGN STATE HEARTBEAT
---------------------------------------------------------------
1   10.0.1.97/1117 172.30.1.1/2748 1 120
------------------------------------------------
    RTP/RTCP: PAT xlates: mapped to 172.30.1.97(1028 - 1029)
------------------------------------------------
    MEDIA: Device ID 27 Call ID 0
           Foreign 172.30.1.97 (1028 - 1029)
           Local 172.30.1.88 (26822 - 26823)
------------------------------------------------
```

Currently only one active CTIQBE session is established to CallManager: a SoftPhone with an IP address of 10.0.1.97 is connected to CallManager at 172.30.1.1. The SoftPhone IP address is being translated to 172.30.1.97 via PAT, where one phone connection is established to 172.30.1.88. The two UDP connections for RTP are using source and destination port numbers of 1028/26822 for the audio connection and 1029/26823 for the synchronization connection.

MGCP INSPECTION

The Media Gateway Control Protocol (MGCP) is used in VoIP networks to bridge the traditional analog and digital phone services connected to PBXs and other types of traditional voice devices to a VoIP gateway like Cisco CallManager. MGCP supports both H.323 and SIP. Three devices can participate in MGCP:

▼ **Call agent** Provides call control intelligence for phone devices that have IP addresses, like the Cisco CallManager VoIP gateway product

- ■ **Media gateway**   Converts signals between circuits (digital and/or analog) to packets (this is traditionally a PBX with a VoIP card)
- ▲ **Signaling gateway**   Connects to the PSTN (Public Switched Telephone Network), which can be a media gateway or a call agent, depending on the network design

NOTE   Traditionally, the media and signaling gateway functions are found in the same physical device.

The following sections will discuss how MGCP connections are established between gateways and call agents, why application inspection is needed, and how to configure application inspection on the security appliances.

MGCP Connections and Application Inspection

MGCP is used to send messages between the gateways and call agents. Interaction between the gateways and call agents is needed when phones behind the respective devices need to establish phone calls, which use RTP. Messages are made up of commands and a mandatory response. There are two UDP connections: one from the gateway to the call agent, connecting to port 2727, and one from the call agent to the gateway, connecting to port 2427. You can see an example of this in Figure 13-4.

Application inspection is needed when the gateway(s) and call agent(s) reside off of *different* interfaces on the appliance where the security levels are different. Inspection isn't really necessary for the port 2727 and 2427 connections, since these are easily allowed using ACLs; however, the RTP UDP audio and synchronization connections, which use dynamic port numbers, are almost impossible to deal with unless application inspection is used. The RTP port numbers are sent across the UDP connections between the gateway and call agent, which the appliance examines and then dynamically adds the RTP connections to the conn table. If address translation is being performed, and the addressing information in the MGCP payload conflicts with entries already in the xlate table, these are fixed in the payload and added to the xlate table.

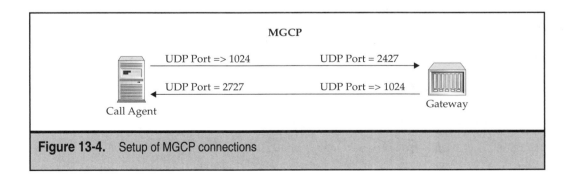

Figure 13-4.   Setup of MGCP connections

> **NOTE**   For inspection to function correctly, the IP address of the MGCP signaling connection must be the same as the RTP addresses—Cisco recommends using a loopback or virtual address to ensure that the same address is always seen for a gateway.

MGCP Policy Configuration

The following sections will discuss the configuration of MGCP inspection. To control what call agents and gateways can interact with each other, you can create a layer 7 policy map; MGCP inspection doesn't support layer 7 class maps. The following sections will discuss how to create the optional layer 7 policy map, as well as how to enable MGCP inspection in a layer 3/4 policy map.

MGCP Layer 7 Policy Maps

If you want to control which gateways and call agents interact with each other in setting up the connections between phones, create a layer 7 MGCP policy map. Here are the commands to create a layer 7 policy map for MGCP inspection:

```
ciscoasa(config)# policy-map type inspect mgcp L7_policy_map_name
ciscoasa(config-pmap)# description string
ciscoasa(config-pmap)# parameters
ciscoasa(config-pmap-p)# call-agent IP_address group_ID
ciscoasa(config-pmap-p)# gateway IP_address group_ID
ciscoasa(config-pmap-p)# command-queue #_of_commands
```

Unlike with other layer 7 policy maps, you cannot reference any layer 7 class maps or **match** commands for action policies.

In the **parameters** subcommand mode, however, you can restrict which devices can communicate with each other, and establish RTP connections for associated phones. The **call-agent** command restricts the call agents, based on their IP addresses, that will be associated with other call agents and gateways—this is accomplished by specifying a group identifier number, which allows agents and gateways with the same number to interact with each other. The group identifier can range from 0 to 4294967295. The **gateway** command specifies the gateway that will be included in a particular group identifier. A gateway can only belong to one group; however, call agents can belong to multiple groups.

The **command-queue** command restricts the number of MGCP commands that are queued up while waiting for an appropriate response. The default is 200 commands.

MGCP Layer 3/4 Policy Maps

By default MGCP inspection is disabled on the appliance. To enable inspection of MGCP, you need to reference it in a layer 3/4 policy map:

```
ciscoasa(config)# policy-map L3/4_policy_map_name
ciscoasa(config-pmap)# class L3/4_class_map_name
ciscoasa(config-pmap-c)# inspect mgcp [L7_policy_map_name]
```

If you want to control which gateways and call agents interact with each other in setting up the connections between phones, reference a layer 7 MGCP policy map in your `inspect mgcp` command.

MGCP Timeouts

You can configure two timeouts for MGCP connections:

```
ciscoasa(config)# timeout mgcp hh:mm:ss
ciscoasa(config)# timeout mgcp-pat hh:mm:ss
```

The `timeout mgcp` command specifies an idle interval, which if exceeded, causes the MGCP media connection to close (the default is 5 minutes). The `timeout mgcp-pat` command specifies an idle interval for PAT xlates associated with RTP connection established via the MGCP signaling connections (the default is 30 seconds).

MGCP Verification

To view information concerning the configuration of MGCP and MGCP session information, use the `show mgcp` command:

```
ciscoasa# show mgcp {commands | sessions} [detail]
```

The `commands` parameter lists the number of MGCP commands in the command queue. The `sessions` parameter lists the number of existing MGCP sessions. The optional `detail` parameter lists additional information about each command or session in the display output.

Here's an example of viewing the MGCP sessions:

```
ciscoasa# show mgcp sessions detail
1 in use, 1 most used
Session active 0:00:14
Gateway IP gateway-1
Call ID 0123456789fedcba
Connection ID 6789fa459c
Endpoint name bbln/1
Media lcl port 6168
Media rmt IP 192.168.1.71
Media rmt port 6059
```

MGCP Example Configuration

Here's a simple example of an inspection policy for MGCP:

```
ciscoasa(config)# policy-map type inspect mgcp L7_mgcp_map
ciscoasa(config-pmap)# parameters
ciscoasa(config-pmap-p)# call-agent 10.0.21.31 1
```

```
ciscoasa(config-pmap-p)# call-agent 10.0.21.32 1
ciscoasa(config-pmap-p)# gateway 10.0.20.101 1
ciscoasa(config-pmap-p)# call-agent 10.0.21.33 2
ciscoasa(config-pmap-p)# call-agent 10.0.21.34 2
ciscoasa(config-pmap-p)# gateway 10.0.20.102 2
ciscoasa(config-pmap-p)# gateway 10.0.20.103 2
ciscoasa(config)# policy-map global_policy
ciscoasa(config-pmap)# class inspection_default
ciscoasa(config-pmap-c)# inspect mgcp L7_mgcp_map
ciscoasa(config)# service-policy global_policy global
```

In this configuration, the layer 7 policy map (L7_mgcp_map) creates two different groups. Group 1 has two call agents (10.0.21.31 and 10.0.21.32) and one gateway (10.0.20.101). Group 2 has two call agents and two gateways. Because two groups were set up, the appliance is controlling what phone connections can be made between call agents and gateways interacting through the appliance. This is enabled in the default global policy, using the default layer 3/4 class map. The default class map already associates the two UDP connections (2427 and 2727) to MGCP.

CHAPTER 14

Multimedia and Policies

T his chapter will introduce you to the application inspection features for multimedia applications. Like FTP, VoIP, and other applications, multimedia applications use multiple connections to set up and transmit video streams, voice connections, and/or multimedia capabilities. Most multimedia applications follow either the RTSP or H.323 standards. The topics discussed in this chapter include

▼ An overview of multimedia applications

■ RTSP

▲ H.323

MULTIMEDIA OVERVIEW

Multimedia applications pose many of the same problems for firewalls and security appliances that I have so far discussed in Part III. One of the main reasons that multimedia applications are difficult to deal with is that no single unifying standard defines how they should be implemented. Each vendor, instead, has developed its own implementation method for its multimedia applications with a handful of existing standards.

Common Problems with Multimedia Applications and Firewalls

The following are some of the problems that you have to deal with concerning multimedia applications and stateful firewalls:

▼ Some multimedia applications embed IP addresses and sometimes port numbers in the payload, which can cause problems with environments that have deployed NAT and/or PAT.

■ Some multimedia applications use the same port number for both the source and destination, which makes it more difficult to determine who is initiating a session.

■ Some multimedia applications use TCP for connections while others use UDP, or some applications use a combination of protocols for their connections.

▲ Some multimedia applications use dynamic port numbers for their additional connections, which creates filtering problems since the actual port numbers can come from a very large range of numbers.

Firewall Solutions for Multimedia Applications

As you can see from the preceding list of problems, dealing with multimedia applications in a firewall environment is not an easy task. The best solution to use in dealing with multimedia applications is the Cisco application inspection feature for their security appliances. The application inspection feature of the appliances will handle the translation of embedded addressing information as well as add entries in the conn table for just the specific connections between the clients and servers—no more and no fewer.

Two main standards are commonly used for multimedia applications: the Real-Time Streaming Protocol (RTSP) and H.323. Both standards (especially the latter) define the framework for implementing multimedia applications, which might use voice, video, and or data. The problem with both standards is that they don't cover all aspects of what a vendor might want to provide for in an application. Therefore, when dealing with the application inspection feature of the appliances, even though a vendor application is using RTSP or H.323, that does not mean that Cisco supports it for application inspection. Cisco has a list of applications that it officially supports for each protocol; other multimedia applications may or may not work with the appliances, depending on their implementation. The following sections will further discuss the two protocols and the application inspection features supported by the appliances.

TIP   For nonsupported applications, you can always use ACL entries, GRE tunnels, or, more preferably, the `established` command (discussed in Chapter 11), to allow this traffic through the appliance.

RTSP INSPECTION

Many applications use RTSP to implement the communication infrastructure to transmit information between multimedia devices. RTSP is defined in RFC 2326. RTSP is used by many multimedia applications to control the delivery of information, which includes video, audio, as well as data in a real-time fashion. It supports both TCP and UDP for control and information streaming processes.

The security appliance application inspection feature will not work with every multimedia application. If you recall from the last section, not every vendor implements these multimedia applications in the same manner. Currently Cisco officially supports the following multimedia applications for RTSP:

▼ Apple QuickTime

■ Cisco IP/TV

▲ RealNetworks RealAudio, RealPlayer, and RealServer

Besides the multimedia applications in the preceding list, other multimedia applications may work, depending on how the vendor implemented them. A workaround for those applications not supported by the application inspection feature would be to use ACL entries, GRE tunnels (tunnel the multimedia connections through a single unicast GRE connection), or the `established` command to open the necessary holes in your appliance to allow connectivity. As you will see in the next few sections, the holes that you need to open on the appliance might be very large—the advantage of the application inspection feature for supported multimedia applications is that the appliance only opens holes for the connections requested between the communicating devices and maintains these connections in the conn table until they're completed.

RTSP Connections and Application Inspection

The following sections will discuss the connection used in establishing an RTSP session as well as why application inspection is needed.

Types of RTSP Connections

Typically three connections are established between a client and a server when RTSP is used:

▼ *Control* **connection**　This channel, which is bi-directional, allows the client and server to communicate with each other concerning the setting up and tearing down of multimedia connections. RTSP defines the mechanics as to how this connection is set up and the messages that traverse it. In most instances, the connection uses TCP and connects to port 554 or 8554 on the server.

■ *Multimedia* **connection(s)**　This is a unidirectional connection from the server to the client. The actual content information, like audio or video, is sent across this connection to the client. In almost all cases this is a UDP connection. One problem with this connection is that no real standards exist as far as how port numbers should be chosen. Two protocols define the setup and delivery of information across this connection: RTP (Real-Time Transport Protocol) and RDT (Real Data Transport) protocol. RTP is based on a standard and RDT was developed by RealNetworks. I'll discuss these protocols in a few moments.

▲ *Error* **connection**　This is a UDP connection that can be unidirectional or bi-directional. It is used by the client to request the resending of missing information to the server. Sometimes it is also used for synchronization purposes to ensure that video and audio streams don't experience jitter problems.

Depending on whether you are using RTP or RDT for the multimedia connection(s), the connection setup process is different. Therefore, I've included the next two sections to help describe the connection setup process for each. As I mentioned under the "Multimedia connection(s)" bulleted item in the preceding list, the use of UDP port numbers is application-specific.

Standard RTP Mode

In this section, I will use an example to show you how RTSP, using RTP, sets up connections between a client and a multimedia server. I'll use the illustration shown in Figure 14-1 to illustrate our example; the top part shows an example of RTP. The first connection that is set up between the client and server is the control connection. Every multimedia application that I've dealt with that uses RTSP uses TCP for the control connection, even though RFC 2326 supports both TCP and UDP. This control connection allows the client and server to communicate with each other and establish parameters for the multimedia connections—no actual multimedia traffic traverses this connection.

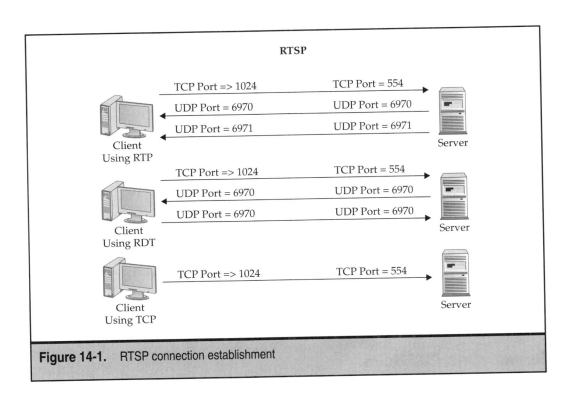

Figure 14-1. RTSP connection establishment

The client chooses an unused port number greater than 1023, and the server listens on 554 (defined in RFC 2326).

When the client requests a multimedia stream, the server and client will negotiate the port numbers for this multimedia UDP connection. For example, in a RealPlayer configuration, the default port numbers range from 6970 to 7170; however, you can easily change this in the client configuration. RTP places two restrictions on this source port number:

▼ The port number must be an even (not odd) number, like 6002, 6004, and so on.

▲ The port number cannot be a well-known port number—it must be greater than 1023.

This is a unidirectional connection—only the server can send the multimedia information on this connection back to the client. The server builds this connection to the client.

The second UDP connection setup uses RTCP (Real-Time Control Protocol). This is a bi-directional connection that the client uses to synchronize the multimedia connection as well as to request any missing UDP segments from the multimedia server. The restriction on this port number is that it must be one number greater than that used by the RTP multimedia connection; therefore, it will always be an odd number. As with the last UDP connection, the server builds this connection to the client.

When the RTSP client is on the inside of the network and initiates a signaling connection to an RTSP server on the outside of the network, the appliance will by default allow the signaling TCP (or UDP) connection at port 554 or 8554 since the connection is traveling from a higher security level interface to a lower one.

The two RTP UDP connections are initiated by the server to the client. With the RTSP application inspection feature of the appliance, the appliance will examine the RTSP control messages on ports 554 or 8554 to determine the port numbers being used on the two sides and will dynamically add this connection to the conn table. One restriction with the application inspection feature for RTSP is that the appliance can handle neither any bi-directional NAT (inside and outside) nor PAT addressing information in the control messages of the RTSP TCP connection; only unidirectional NAT is supported, like inside NAT.

Let's assume that the RTSP client, in this example, is actually on the outside of your network, and the RTSP server is on the inside. For the initial client signaling connection to work, you'll need to configure an ACL entry that will allow traffic heading to TCP (or UDP) port 554 (or 8554)—without this, no type of RTSP connection can be made.

Since the RTSP server is setting up the RTP and RTCP UDP connections, and these connections are going from a higher to a lower security level interface, you don't need to do anything special on the appliance unless you are filtering traffic outbound—then you'll need application inspection to add the two UDP connections to the conn table.

RealNetworks RDT Mode

In this section I will use an example to show you how RTSP, using RDT, sets up connections between a RealPlayer client and a RealServer. I'll use the previously shown Figure 14-1 to illustrate our example. RDT is shown in the middle of this figure.

The first connection that is set up between the client and server is the control connection (RealNetworks clients only support TCP). This control connection allows the client and server to communicate with each other and to establish parameters for the multimedia connections—no actual multimedia traffic traverses this connection. The client chooses a port number greater than 1023, and the server is listening on 554, which is defined in RFC 2326. This connection is the same connection discussed in the last section.

When the client requests a multimedia stream, the server and client will negotiate port numbers for two simplex UDP connections. A simplex connection is a unidirectional connection—you can either send or receive, but not both. One simplex connection the server builds to the client, and the other simplex connection the client builds to the server. Even though these are two distinct connections, the same port numbers can be used for both connections (remember that they're simplex connections), or different port numbers can be used. In the example shown in Figure 14-1, I used the same port number for these simplex UDP connections.

Whether the client is on the inside and the server on the outside, or vice versa, you will need application inspection in order to add the two UDP simplex connections to the conn table. This is because the server opens the multimedia RTP UDP connection, and the client opens the UDP error connection.

TCP Mode

As you saw in the last two sections, RTP and RDT use UDP for the multimedia connections. You have an option of using TCP for the multimedia connections instead of UDP. One of the advantages of using TCP is that there is only a *single* connection used to transmit *all* data—both control information and multimedia data. Therefore, pushing this connection through a firewall or appliance is fairly simple. However, because TCP adds delay in the multimedia stream, this type of connection is not commonly used for real-time connections.

The bottom part of Figure 14-1 illustrates RTSP using TCP. The first, and only, connection that is set up between the client and server is the control/data connection. This control connection allows the client and server to communicate with each other as well as to transmit multimedia data across it—this is unlike RTP and RDT mode, where a separate connection is used for the multimedia data.

TIP Of course, using TCP is less efficient because of its larger header and the use of windowing, especially for multimedia. However, it can sometimes be used as a "fix-all" for making applications work through stateful firewalls and translation devices, which might deploy low idle timers for UDP, causing the multimedia UDP connections to time out of their tables and breaking the connections. TCP typically has higher idle timeouts on these devices and thus creates fewer connection problems … at the cost of some efficiency in the transmission of the data.

RTSP Policy Configuration

The following sections will discuss the configuration of RTSP inspection. For in-depth inspection policies, you might need to create a layer 7 policy map and, possibly, a layer 7 class map. The following sections will discuss how to create these, as well as how to enable RTSP inspection in a layer 3/4 policy map.

RTSP Layer 7 Class Maps

Here are the commands to create a layer 7 class map for RTSP inspection:

```
ciscoasa(config)# class-map type inspect rtsp [match-all]
                         L7_class_map_name
ciscoasa(config-cmap)# description string
ciscoasa(config-cmap)# match [not] request-method method_name
ciscoasa(config-cmap)# match [not] url-filter regex {class
                         regex_class_name | regex_name}
```

The **request-method** parameter allows you to match on commands seen or unseen within the signaling connection (port 554). The commands you can include are **announce**, **describe**, **get_parameter**, **options**, **pause**, **play**, **record**, **redirect**, **setup**, **set_parameter**, and **teardown**. The **url-filter** parameter allows you to match on one or more URLs in RTSP control messages.

RTSP Layer 7 Policy Maps

Here are the commands to create a layer 7 policy map for RTSP inspection:

```
ciscoasa(config)# policy-map type inspect rtsp L7_policy_map_name
ciscoasa(config-pmap)# description string
ciscoasa(config-pmap)# match L7_class_map_parameters
ciscoasa(config-pmap-c)# {[drop-connection [log] |
                              rate-limit #_of_messages}
ciscoasa(config-pmap-c)# exit
ciscoasa(config-pmap)# class L7_class_map_name
ciscoasa(config-pmap-c)# {[drop-connection [log] |
                              rate-limit #_of_messages}
ciscoasa(config-pmap-c)# exit
ciscoasa(config-pmap)# parameters
ciscoasa(config-pmap-p)# reserve-port-protect
ciscoasa(config-pmap-p)# url-length-limit length
```

Instead of creating an application layer class map, you can also reference these values within the layer 7 policy map with the **match** command. The advantage of using layer 7 class maps is that you can apply different policies to different classes (class maps). Either you can have the appliance drop the connection and/or log the match if you are matching on a URL, or you can rate-limit the RTSP commands depending upon what you are matching on in an associated class map or **match** command.

Within the **parameters** section in a layer 7 policy map, you can restrict usage on the reserve port when performing multimedia negotiations (**reserve-port-protect** command) and restrict the limit of URLs, in bytes, in RTSP control messages (**url-length-limit** command). The length can be from 0 to 6,000 bytes.

RTSP Layer 3/4 Policy Maps

If all you are interested in is dynamically adding the two UDP multimedia connections to the conn table and fixing embedded addressing information, then you do not need to implement a layer 7 policy for RTSP inspection. However, if you need to implement a layer 7 RTSP policy, you must have a corresponding layer 3/4 policy map that references it:

```
ciscoasa(config)# policy-map L3/4_policy_map_name
ciscoasa(config-pmap)# class L3/4_class_map_name
ciscoasa(config-pmap-c)# inspect rtsp [L7_policy_map_name]
```

NOTE By default RTSP inspection is enabled in the global policy, which is activated on all interfaces on the appliance.

RTSP Example Configuration

Let's look at a configuration example that implements RTSP inspection:

```
ciscoasa(config)# regex badurl_1 ".+\.[Aa][Vv][Ii]"
ciscoasa(config)# regex badurl_2 ".+\.[Rr][Mm]"
ciscoasa(config)# regex badurl_3 ".+\.[Aa][Ss][Pp]"
ciscoasa(config)# class-map type regex badurls
ciscoasa(config-cmap)# match regex badurl_1
ciscoasa(config-cmap)# match regex badurl_2
ciscoasa(config-cmap)# match regex badurl_3
ciscoasa(config)# policy-map type inspect rtsp L7-rtsp-policy
ciscoasa(config-pmap)# match url-filter regex class badurls
ciscoasa(config-pmap-p)# drop-connection log
ciscoasa(config)# policy-map global_policy
ciscoasa(config-pmap)# class inspection_default
ciscoasa(config-pmap-c)# inspect rtsp L7-rtsp-policy
ciscoasa(config)# service-policy global_policy global
```

At the top of the example, three regular expressions are looking for URLs that end in ".avi", ".rm", or ".asp", in upper- or lowercase. These are included in a regular expression class map. The layer 7 policy map (`L7-rtsp-policy`) will drop and log any RTSP connections that reference the URLs in the regular expression class map. This layer 7 policy is then referenced in the default layer 3/4 class and policy map configuration across all appliance interfaces.

H.323 INSPECTION

H.323 is an ITU-T standard for the bi-directional exchange of voice, video, and data. H.323 is somewhat of a hybrid protocol in that it supports both video and audio connections. As you will see in the following sections, H.323, like most multimedia applications, is a more difficult protocol to deal with than simple VoIP connections, or even RTSP. Unlike SIP, Skinny, RTSP, or FTP, an H.323 application can have many connections that are set up between two devices. The following sections will cover the components of H.323, how connections are set up, how the application inspection feature for H.323 on the appliances functions, and how to configure application inspection.

NOTE H.323 was actually the first VoIP protocol to use RTP (which everyone now uses). All other VoIP protocols are basically a collection of other protocols, but typically rely on RTP for the actual voice connections.

H.323 Overview

Actually, H.323 is a group of standards that defines the communication process between two H.323 endpoints. H.323 includes the following standards:

- ▼ **H.225**   Registration, admission, and status
- ■ **H.235**   Call signaling to establish phone calls
- ■ **H.245**   Control signaling, which describes the messages and procedures used to share the capabilities of the endpoints, opening and closing phone, video, and/or data connections
- ■ **Q.931**   Messaging to actually establish the phone calls
- ■ **TPKT**   Packet headers
- ▲ **ASN.1**   Describes data structures for representing, encoding, transmitting, and decoding data (including phone signaling information)

For call setup and control, two TCP connections are used; for the audio and/or video connections, UDP connections are used. As you can see, this is similar to RTSP. Unlike RTSP, H.323 uses one or more TCP connections and one or more UDP connections to transmit the actual content.

The first connection is a TCP connection to the well-known port 1720 (the signaling connection). The remaining connections use UDP and/or TCP, but the port numbers are typically random (above 1023). This obviously causes problems in environments that use firewalls and filters. H.323 also uses ASN.1 (Abstract Syntax Notation One) to encode its packets, which makes application inspection difficult when deciphering the packet information.

Supported Applications

Because each vendor adds its own mechanisms above and beyond H.323, let alone because of the complexities of H.323 itself, the security appliances do not support every H.323 multimedia application. However, here is a list of some of the more commonly used H.323 applications that the appliances do support:

- ▼ Cisco Multimedia Conference Manager and CallManager
- ■ CUseeMe Meeting Point and CUseeMe Pro
- ■ Intel Video Phone
- ■ Microsoft NetMeeting
- ▲ VocalTec Internet Phone and Gatekeeper

Types of H.323 Devices

Before I begin discussing the setup of connections with H.323, let's first discuss the two types of devices that can be involved in the setup of a connection: terminals and gatekeepers. An H.323 terminal is an endpoint in the H.323 connection. It is a client that is responsible for making connections. This can be something as simple as software running on a PC or on a dedicated hardware appliance like an IP phone or voice conferencing station. One requirement of all H.323 terminals is that they must support voice communications—other types of communications, like video or data, are optional.

An H.323 gatekeeper is a central point for all multimedia calls and provides call control services to the terminals that register with it. Its two main functions are to perform address translation (can be NAT as well as telephone number to IP address translation) and bandwidth management. Note that the gatekeeper is not necessary to set up connections directly between two terminals—if the two terminals wishing to communicate know each other's addressing information, they can set up the connection directly. This is different from Skinny and SIP.

As I just mentioned, a gatekeeper is unnecessary. However, a gatekeeper does make it easier to deploy multimedia services on a large scale. A gatekeeper is the central repository for addressing information—terminals register their addressing information with the gatekeeper, and the gatekeeper gives this information to querying terminals. In this sense, it functions something like a hybrid PBX/DNS server. H.225 defines the RAS (Registration, Admission, and Status) protocol that the terminals and gatekeepers use to communicate with each other.

H.323 Connections and Application Inspection

There are three basic ways that a connection can be made between two terminals:

▼ A terminal can contact a gatekeeper for address translation information and then set up the connection directly to the destination terminal—this requires both terminals to be registered with the gatekeeper.

■ A terminal can contact a gatekeeper and have the gatekeeper handle the call signaling and control information between the two terminals—this requires both terminals to be registered with the gatekeeper.

▲ A terminal, knowing the destination terminal address, can set up the connection directly to the destination without the assistance of a gatekeeper.

The next few sections will cover the interaction of the terminal with the gatekeeper as well as between the two terminals.

Finding and Connecting to a Gatekeeper

As I mentioned previously, a gatekeeper is unnecessary to establish a multimedia connection between two terminals; however, it does help centralize and simplify your multimedia deployment. There are two basic methods of contacting a gatekeeper:

▼ The terminal uses an autodiscovery process to find the gatekeeper.

▲ The terminal has the gatekeeper's IP address hard-coded in its local configuration.

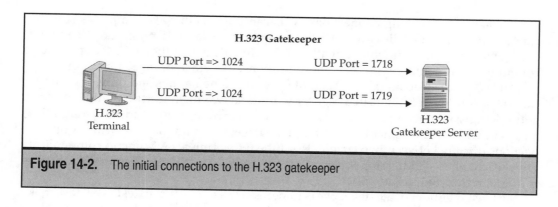

Figure 14-2. The initial connections to the H.323 gatekeeper

I'll use Figure 14-2 to demonstrate the two connections that might be used to initiate a connection to the gatekeeper.

If the terminal doesn't know the gatekeeper IP address, it will send a multicast to 224.0.1.41 (well-known multicast address). This is a UDP multicast with a destination port number of 1718. Obviously if the terminal is on one side of an appliance and the gatekeeper is on the other side, this process will fail—the appliance won't forward the multicast packets by default. Therefore, you would have to use the second solution—hard-code the IP address of the gatekeeper on the client.

Once the terminal knows the IP address of the gatekeeper, the terminal will set up a direct UDP connection to the gatekeeper—this is the second connection listed in Figure 14-2. The source port of the terminal is a random port above 1023, and the destination port is 1719. This is commonly referred to as the *RAS* connection. When this connection is established, the terminal will then register its information with the gatekeeper. This information will include the identity of the terminal (like an ID, name, E.164 phone number, or some other type of alias) as well as the IP address of the terminal. Therefore, when other terminals want to contact this terminal, they can use the destination terminal alias (which is static) to find the destination IP address in order to set up a multimedia connection(s). In this sense, the registration process is somewhat like Microsoft WINS or dynamic DNS.

NOTE If the gateway is connected to a higher-level interface on the appliance and the terminal is on a lower-level interface, you'll need an ACL to allow the UDP port 1719 connection.

Using Only Terminals to Establish Connections

Let's start out simple and examine the connection set up between two terminals without a gatekeeper involved in the process. In this situation, the source terminal must know the address of the destination terminal. I'll use the illustration shown in Figure 14-3 as an example.

The source terminal will first open a TCP connection where its source port number is greater than 1023 and the destination port number is 1720. This connection is used

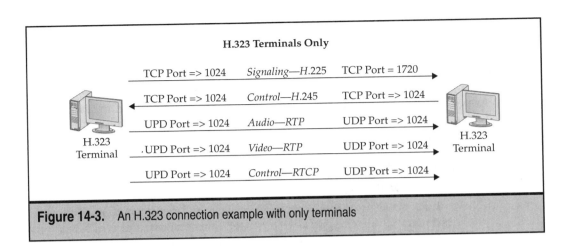

Figure 14-3. An H.323 connection example with only terminals

for call setup and signaling between the two terminals (this is defined in the H.225 and H.235 standards). This connection, called the *signaling* connection, is used to negotiate the setting up of the multimedia connections between the two terminals. The Q.931 ITU-T standard is used to implement the signaling of setting up and tearing down connections on this connection (also used by ISDN). On the signaling connection the two parties will negotiate the port numbers to use for the second TCP connection.

The called party (destination terminal) will initiate a second TCP connection back to the source. Both of the port numbers for this connection are dynamically chosen above 1023 by both parties. This connection is called the *call control* connection, and its mechanics are defined in H.245. This connection handles the multimedia connections that will be established, including which audio and video compressor-decompressors (CODECs) will be used.

Up to three UDP connections will be established from the source terminal to the destination, assuming that this is a video-conference call:

▼ Audio using RTP

■ Video using RTP

▲ Control using RTCP

The source terminal opens all three of these UDP connections—the actual port numbers are negotiated between the two sides across the signaling connection. These port numbers are random numbers greater than 1023. The source then sets up these connections to the destination. Note that the protocols used for these UDP connections are the same ones that RTSP supports in standard RTP mode.

NOTE The preceding example only applies to video conferencing. Additional UDP connections and TCP connections can be set up between the multimedia devices—each application is unique in this regard.

As you can see from Figure 14-3, the setup of a multimedia session between two terminals is not a simple process. Whether or not the source is connected to a lower- or higher-level interface on the appliance, you'll need application inspection to securely add the necessary connections to the conn table and to fix embedded addressing information in the signaling connection. If the source is connected to the higher-level interface, application inspection is necessary to dynamically add the H.245 control connection. If the source is connected to a lower-level interface, you'll need an ACL to allow the TCP port 1720 connection and application inspection to deal with the UDP connections.

Using a Gatekeeper for Address Translation Only for Terminal Connections

Let's complicate the process by throwing a gatekeeper into a network scenario. In this situation, the terminals will use the gatekeeper for registration only and will set up any other connections directly between themselves. This process is commonly referred to as *Direct mode*. I'll use Figure 14-4 as an example.

Each terminal will set up a direct UDP connection to the gatekeeper—this is the first connection listed in Figure 14-4. The source port of the terminal is a random port above 1023, and the destination port is 1719. When this connection is established, the terminal will then register its information with the gatekeeper. The terminals will use this connection to perform address translation (resolving aliases to IP addresses). In this situation, the source terminal only needs to know the alias of the destination terminal in order to build a connection to it.

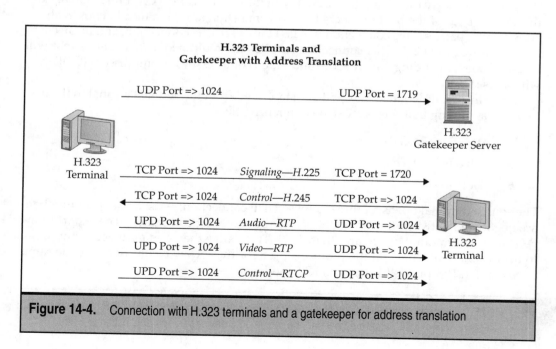

Figure 14-4.   Connection with H.323 terminals and a gatekeeper for address translation

The source terminal will then open a TCP connection to the destination terminal (not the gatekeeper) where the source terminal source port number is greater than 1023 and the destination port number is 1720. This connection is used for call setup and signaling between the two terminals (this is defined in standard H.225). On this connection the two parties will negotiate the port numbers to use for the second TCP connection. This connection is the *signaling* connection and is used to set up multimedia connections between two terminals.

The rest of the connections are established in exactly the same manner as described in the last section on building connections directly between two terminals. All of the issues mentioned in the "Finding and Connecting to a Gatekeeper" and "Using Only Terminals to Establish Connections" sections apply to the connections being set up in this section.

Using a Gatekeeper for Address Translation and Signaling and Control for Terminal Connections

The last mode that can be used for setting up multimedia connections between terminals involves a gatekeeper, as in the last section; but in this instance, the gatekeeper plays a more involved role. In this configuration, both the signaling (H.225) and control (H.245) from the terminals are set up between the terminals and the gatekeeper—not between the terminals themselves. This scenario is often referred to as *Routing mode* and is somewhat similar to the process SIP and Skinny use. I'll use Figure 14-5 to help with the explanation of the setting up of the connections.

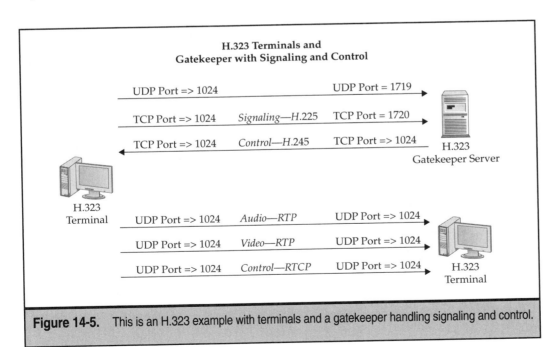

Figure 14-5.   This is an H.323 example with terminals and a gatekeeper handling signaling and control.

Each terminal will set up a direct UDP connection to the gatekeeper—this is the first connection listed in Figure 14-5. The source port of the terminal is a random port above 1023, and the destination port is 1719. When this connection is established, the terminal will then register its information with the gatekeeper. The terminals will use this connection to perform address translation (resolving aliases to IP addresses). In this situation, the source terminal only needs to know the alias of the destination terminal in order to build a connection to it.

Each terminal will then open a TCP connection to the gatekeeper (not the destination terminal) where the source terminal source port number is greater than 1023 and the destination port number is 1720. This connection is used for call setup and signaling—the gatekeeper will act as a go-between (this is defined in standard H.225). On this connection each terminal/gateway pair will negotiate the port numbers for the H.245 control connection. The *gatekeeper* will then build this TCP connection back to the terminal. Remember that the source and destination port numbers for this are random numbers above 1023 for the H.245 control connection.

Once these connections have been established between the two respective H.323 terminals and the gatekeeper, the terminals can now request connections to be set up. These UDP multimedia connections, unlike the last two TCP connections, will *not* be built to the gatekeeper, but instead will be built directly between the terminals themselves. This port information is negotiated on the TCP connections via the gatekeeper, and then the UDP connections are created from the calling party (source terminal) to the called party (destination terminal).

H.323 Application Inspection Features of the Appliances

As you can see from the preceding description, the setup of these connections is *not* a simple process. And depending on where all of these devices are relative to the appliance, application inspection is not a simple process for Cisco to implement in its security appliances. There are also four versions of H.323—v1, v2, v3, and v4; the appliances support all four versions. I'm just glad that I'm not responsible for writing the H.323 application inspection code for Cisco for their appliances!

As an example, if the source terminal were on the inside of the appliance and the gateway and destination terminal on the outside, here is what would happen with application inspection enabled:

1. The two initial connections to the gatekeeper are permitted (1719 and 1720) since they originated on the inside.

2. The H.245 TCP connection from the gatekeeper is allowed via application inspection—the appliance examines the TCP 1720 signaling connection for the port numbers and dynamically adds this connection to the connection table.

3. The UDP multimedia connections are permitted since they originate from the inside of the network.

If the source terminal is on the outside of the network and the gatekeeper and destination terminal are on the inside of the network, here is what would happen with application inspection enabled:

1. You will need an ACL to allow the UDP 1719 and TCP 1720 connections since these connections originate on the outside.

2. The H.245 TCP connection from the gatekeeper to the outside terminal is allowed by default.

3. Application inspection would examine the signaling connection to determine that a call is being set up between the outside and inside terminals, and would dynamically add the UDP connections to the connection table.

I could cover many more scenarios here, but I think that you now understand this is not a simple process the appliances are handling when dealing with application inspection for H.323. Table 14-1 summarizes the connection types and port numbers used by H.323 applications.

As a summary, remember that the appliances application inspection for H.323 provides the following two main functions:

▼   Handling any embedded addresses and ports in the H.225 TCP signaling connection that conflict with current entries in the xlate table.

▲   Dynamically adding H.245 TCP, RTP UDP, and RTCP UDP connections based on inspection of the H.225 TCP signaling connection.

Protocol	Port(s)	Description
UDP	1718	Multicast to discover the gatekeepers on a segment
TCP	1719	RAS connection used to register terminal information with the gatekeeper
TCP	1720	H.225 signaling connection used to set up and tear down connections
TCP	1024–65535	H.245 control connection
UDP	1024–65535	RTP audio connection
UDP	1024–65535	RTP video connection
UDP	1024–65535	RTCP synchronization connection

Table 14-1.   Connections Used by H.323

Here are some limitations of application inspection for H.323 on the appliances:

▼ You might experience problems with static PAT translations.

■ Fixing translation issues is unsupported on same-security-level interfaces.

▲ You might have issues with net statics if they overlap the addresses used by the terminals or gateways.

TIP If you have an H.323 application that Cisco doesn't support with application inspection, I would first try using the `established` command (see Chapter 11) to get traffic flowing between the two endpoints through the appliance. If this didn't work, I would then place a Cisco router at both locations and use a GRE tunnel to tunnel the H.323 traffic—since GRE is not stateful on the appliances, you would need an ACL entry on the lower-level interface to permit it.

H.323 Policy Configuration

The following sections will discuss the configuration of H.323 inspection. For in-depth inspection policies, you might need to create a layer 7 policy map and, possibly, a layer 7 class map. The following sections will discuss how to create these, as well as how to enable H.323 inspection in a layer 3/4 policy map.

H.323 Layer 7 Class Maps

Here are the commands to create a layer 7 class map for H.323 inspection:

```
ciscoasa(config)# class-map type inspect h323 [match-all]
                           L7_class_map_name
ciscoasa(config-cmap)# description string
ciscoasa(config-cmap)# match [not] called-party regex
                              {class class_name | regex_name}
ciscoasa(config-cmap)# match [not] calling-party regex
                              {class class_name | regex_name}
ciscoasa(config-cmap)# match [not] media-type {audio | data | video}
```

The `called-party` and `calling-party` parameters allow you to match on phone number(s) someone is dialing or on the phone number of the source of the call respectively. The `media-type` parameter allows you match on a particular type of session that is being established.

H.323 Layer 7 Policy Maps

Here are the commands to create a layer 7 policy map for H.323 inspection:

```
ciscoasa(config)# policy-map type inspect h323 L7_policy_map_name
ciscoasa(config-pmap)# description string
ciscoasa(config-pmap)# match L7_class_map_parameters
ciscoasa(config-pmap-c)# {[drop [send-protocol-error] |
```

```
                              drop-connection [send-protocol-error] |
                              | reset] [log]}
ciscoasa(config-pmap-c)# exit
ciscoasa(config-pmap)# class L7_class_map_name
ciscoasa(config-pmap-c)# {[drop | drop-connection |
                         | reset] [log]}
ciscoasa(config-pmap-c)# exit
ciscoasa(config-pmap)# parameters
ciscoasa(config-pmap-p)# call-duration-limit hh:mm:ss
ciscoasa(config-pmap-p)# call-party-numbers
ciscoasa(config-pmap-p)# h245-tunnel-block action
                         {drop-connection | log}
ciscoasa(config-pmap-p)# hsi-group group_id
ciscoasa(config-h225-map-hsi-grp)# hsi IP_address
ciscoasa(config-h225-map-hsi-grp)# endpoint IP_address logical_if_name
ciscoasa(config-h225-map-hsi-grp)# exit
ciscoasa(config-pmap-p)# rtp-conformance [enforce-payloadtype]
ciscoasa(config-pmap-p)# state-checking {h225 | ras}
```

Instead of creating an application layer class map, you can also reference these values within the layer 7 policy map with the **match** command. The advantage of using layer 7 class maps is that you can apply different policies to different classes (class maps). You can have the appliance drop the packet or connection, reset the TCP connection, and/or log the connection depending upon what you are matching on in an associated class map or **match** command.

Within the **parameters** section in a layer 7 policy map, you have many options you can define for policies. The **call-duration-limit** command allows you to place time limits on the RTP connections—by default there are no time limits. To require the sending of call party numbers during an H.323 call setup, use the **call-party-numbers** command. H245 tunneling allows endpoints to only use a single TCP connection for both H.225/235 and H.245. If you want to require the use of two TCP connections (or to log violations), use the **h245-tunnel-block** command.

H.323 signaling interface (HSI) provides the interface between the H.323 and PSTN networks. You can set up restrictions of the devices allowed to connect to the HSI by creating an HSI group with the **hsi-group** command—the group identifier can range from 0 to 2147483647. This will take you into a subcommand mode. The **hsi** command specifies the IP address of the device bridging the H.323 and PSTN networks—you can define up to five HSI devices. The **endpoint** command specifies the devices that are allowed to interact with the HSI (normally these are gateways). You can specify up to ten endpoints per group.

The **rtp-conformance** command checks the RTP UDP connections that were dynamically added to the conn table for conforming to the RTP standard. The **state-checking** command has the appliance ensure that the signaling (**h225**) and/or RAS (**ras**) connections follow the standard in the way that messages are exchanged between devices.

H.323 Layer 3/4 Policy Maps

If all you are interested in is dynamically adding the TCP control and the two or more UDP multimedia connections to the conn table and fixing embedded addressing information, then you do not need to implement a layer 7 policy for H.323 inspection. However, if you need to implement a layer 7 H.323 policy, you must have a corresponding layer 3/4 policy map that references it:

```
ciscoasa(config)# policy-map L3/4_policy_map_name
ciscoasa(config-pmap)# class L3/4_class_map_name
ciscoasa(config-pmap-c)# inspect h323 [L7_policy_map_name]
```

NOTE By default, H.323 inspection is enabled in the global policy, which is activated on all interfaces on the appliance.

H.323 and H.225 Timeouts

To configure idle timeouts for H.323 connections, use the following commands:

```
ciscoasa(config)# timeout h225 hh:mm:ss
ciscoasa(config)# timeout h323 hh:mm:ss
```

The **h225** parameter specifies an idle timeout for the TCP signaling connection (by default this is 1 hour). The **h323** parameter specifies an idle timeout for the H.245 and the media connections (by default this is 5 minutes).

H.323 Monitoring and Verification

To monitor and verify your H.323 connections, you have various **show** and **debug** commands you can use:

▼   **show h225**   View the H.225 signaling connections established through the appliance.

■   **show h245**   View the H.245 control connections established through the appliance.

■   **show h323-ras**   View the RAS connections established through the appliance.

▲   **debug h323 {h225 | h245 | ras} event**   Troubleshoot problems with the establishment of H.323 sessions.

H.323 Example Configuration

Let's look at a configuration example that implements H.323 inspection:

```
ciscoasa(config)# regex phone1 "5551237890"
ciscoasa(config)# regex phone2 "5554561234"
```

```
ciscoasa(config)# class-map type inspect h323 match-all L7_h323_class
ciscoasa(config-pmap-c)# match calling-party regex phone1
ciscoasa(config-pmap-c)# match called-party regex phone2
ciscoasa(config)# policy-map type inspect h323 L7_h323_policy
ciscoasa(config-pmap)# class L7_h323_class
ciscoasa(config-pmap-c)# drop-connection
ciscoasa(config)# policy-map global_policy
ciscoasa(config-pmap)# class inspection_default
ciscoasa(config-pmap-c)# inspect h323 L7_h323_policy
ciscoasa(config)# service-policy global_policy global
```

In the preceding example, if phone1 were to attempt to call phone2, the connection would be dropped; however, a phone call from phone2 to phone1 would be allowed. If you don't want any phone calls between the two parties, you also would need to specify phone1 as a called party and phone2 as a calling party.

PART IV

Virtual Private Networks (VPNs)

CHAPTER 15

IPSec Phase 1

This chapter will introduce you to using IPSec on your appliance, focusing on the configuration of IPSec Phase 1 and its components. The information in this chapter applies to both site-to-site (Chapter 16) and remote access IPSec sessions (Chapters 17 and 18) and lays the foundation for configuring IPSec site-to-site and remote access connections. The topics included in this chapter are

- ▼   IPSec introduction
- ■   ISAKMP configuration
- ■   Tunnel groups
- ▲   Certificate authorities

These topics will reappear in subsequent chapters on IPSec.

NOTE   Because of space constraints, this chapter will not provide you an overview of VPNs, IPSec, its components, and how they work together, like my previous book did on the PIXs. For a more thorough discussion of VPNs, please read my book *The Complete Cisco VPN Configuration Guide* (Cisco Press, 2005)—the whole first part of the book (170 pages!) discusses VPNs.

IPSec INTRODUCTION

The VPNs supported by the appliances include IPSec, SSL (called *WebVPN*), PPTP, and L2TP. For IPSec, the appliances support both site-to-site and remote access VPNs. With IPSec site-to-site connections, you can connect your appliance to other appliances and firewalls, other routers, and VPN concentrators or gateways. For remote access, Cisco supports the Cisco VPN client, but other software and hardware clients are supported, including for mobile devices. If the device you want to connect to your appliance is IPSec-compliant, then it shouldn't be an issue getting a VPN up and running. Chapter 16 focuses on site-to-site IPSec connections, commonly called LAN-to-LAN (L2L) connections; Chapters 17 and 18 discuss IPSec remote access, and Chapters 19 and 20 WebVPN.

IPSec Preparations

You'll perform six basic tasks to set up an IPSec connection to a remote IPSec peer:

1. Handle design and policy issues.
2. Allow inbound IPSec traffic.
3. Configure the policies for ISAKMP/IKE Phase 1.
4. Configure the policies for ISAKMP/IKE Phase 2.
5. Verify your configuration.
6. Check the IPSec connection.

The preceding steps detail the tasks that you'll have to complete to successfully set up your IPSec connection.

Same Interface Traffic

One main limitation of the appliance was that it could not be the hub device in a hub-and-spoke VPN topology through version 6 of the OS. The reason is that the appliance will not allow traffic to travel between interfaces of the same security level by default. For example, assume you have a PIX connected to two spokes, PeerA and PeerB. PeerA sends traffic across the VPN connection to the PIX, which in turn needs to forward it to PeerB. The PIX would not allow this (in version 6) since the original traffic came from the outside interface and then needed to be forwarded back out of the outside interface. Recall that since this is the same interface, the security levels of the entry and exit interfaces are the same, and the appliance denies this traffic. Therefore, if you had a hub-and-spoke design, you couldn't use the PIX as the hub in version 6 and earlier. The Cisco solution to this problem in version 6 and earlier is to use a router as the hub in the hub-and-spoke design.

In version 7, the **same-security-traffic** command is used to allow VPN traffic coming into and out of the same interface (physical or logical):

```
ciscoasa(config)# same-security-traffic permit intra-interface
```

By default this feature is disabled.

ISAKMP CONFIGURATION

The ISAKMP and IKE protocols define how to establish an IPSec session between two peers. Three connections make up the session: one management and two data connections. The connections are built across two phases: in Phase 1, the management connection is built, and in Phase 2, the data connections are built. The management connection is used to share IPSec-related information between the peers. The data connections are used to protect actual user traffic between the peers. The data connections are unidirectional, which is why there are two, and are protected with either the AH and/or ESP protocols. Of the two, ESP is by far the most common one used for an IPSec session.

The remainder of this chapter will focus on global and Phase 1 properties that you can or need to configure on your security appliance. Most of the commands to configure IPSec on an appliance are very similar to those used on Cisco IOS routers. Some, especially those relating to tunnel groups, are very different, though. Some of the commands introduced here will be more thoroughly covered in subsequent chapters.

Global ISAKMP Properties

This section will discuss the use and configuration of global properties for ISAKMP and IKE, like how to enable them, specify the identity type, send disconnect notices, and configure the mode to use.

Enabling ISAKMP

ISAKMP and IKE are disabled by default on the appliance in 7.2 and later—they need to be enabled on each interface you'll terminate IPSec tunnels on. Use the following command to enable them:

```
ciscoasa(config)# [no] crypto isakmp enable logical_if_name
```

NOTE You need at least a DES encryption key to set up VPNs on your appliance.

ISAKMP Identity

The ISAKMP identity type is used with IPSec L2L sessions and defines how you will refer to remote peers: based on their IP address or their name. The identity type is controlled by the **crypto isakmp identity** command:

```
ciscoasa(config)# crypto isakmp identity {address | hostname |
                        key string | auto }
```

The configuration of this command will affect the syntax of other IPSec commands on the appliance. By default the identity type is **address** for peers, which is the IP address of the peers. The **hostname** parameter specifies that the fully qualified domain name will be used to identify remote peers. The **key** parameter specifies a custom *string* value to uniquely identify peers. The **auto** parameter specifies that IP addresses identify peers that use pre-shared keys for authentication and that fully qualified domain names identify peers that use digital certificates.

Phase 1 Modes: Aggressive and Main

ISAKMP and IKE go through two phases in setting up an IPSec session. During Phase 1, the management connection is built. Two modes can be used to establish the management connection: aggressive and main. Aggressive mode is faster in the setup process, but less secure; main mode is slower, but more secure. The authentication method chosen will depend on the mode used. By default aggressive mode is used when pre-shared keys are configured for authentication, and main mode is used when certificates are configured. The following command disables aggressive mode and forces the appliance to use main mode for the Phase 1 connection:

```
ciscoasa(config)# crypto isakmp am-disable
```

Disconnect Notice

When tearing down IPSec tunnels, you can have the appliance send a disconnect notification with the following command:

```
ciscoasa(config)# crypto isakmp disconnect-notify
```

ISAKMP Policies

Phase 1 policies define how the management connection can be protected. During Phase 1, the policies are shared between the two peers, where a matching policy must be found in order for the two peers to continue building the management connection. The negotiated policies are then used to secure the management connection.

The configuration of a Phase 1 policy on the appliance is the same as on an IOS router:

```
ciscoasa(config)# crypto isakmp policy policy_number
ciscoasa(config-isakmp-policy)# authentication {pre-share | rsa-sig |
                                crack}
ciscoasa(config-isakmp-policy)# encryption {3des | aes | aes-192 |
                                aes-256 | des}
ciscoasa(config-isakmp-policy)# group {1 | 2 | 5 | 7}
ciscoasa(config-isakmp-policy)# hash {md5 | sha}
ciscoasa(config-isakmp-policy)# lifetime {seconds | none}
```

When setting up a policy, if you don't specify a command in the policy, the appliance will use a default: pre-shared keys for authentication, 3DES for encryption, Diffie-Hellman (DH) group 2 keys, SHA HMAC function, and a lifetime of one day (86,400 seconds).

The policy number ranks the policies on the appliance: you might need more than one policy if you have different peers with different capabilities. The policy with the lowest number (1) is the highest-priority policy, and the policy with the highest number (65,535) is the lowest-priority policy. You can choose from three authentication methods: pre-shared keys, certificates (RSA signatures), and the Challenge/Response for Authenticated Cryptographic Keys (CRACK). CRACK is commonly used with mobile and smart phone devices. If you will be using DH group 5, you must use AES as an encryption algorithm. The `lifetime` command specifies how long the parameters should be used for the negotiated management connection before either they should be changed or the management connection torn down; if you specify `none` for the lifetime, the management connection will never time out, and thus won't be rekeyed. To view your ISAKMP policies, use the `show run crypto isakmp policy` command.

NAT Traversal and IPSec over TCP

The management connection, which is protected by the negotiated policy, is encapsulated in UDP and sent to port 500. The two data connections in Phase 2 use ESP and/or AH to encapsulate the data for users. These latter protocols, however, pose problems when going through address translation or stateful firewall devices.

AH and ESP Issues

When going through an address translation device, AH breaks, since the input for the digital signature it creates includes the source and destination IP addresses in the outer IP header. On top of this, AH is a layer 3 protocol and thus lacks ports needed when PAT is performed. Therefore, AH is unsupported when going through any type of address translation. Also, I know of no stateful firewall that supports AH—for example, with Cisco appliances, you must use an ACL to allow returning AH traffic.

ESP also supports digital signatures, but excludes the outer IP header when generating its digital signature; therefore, ESP doesn't break when NAT is performed. However, like AH, ESP is also a layer 3 protocol and thus is not supported by PAT or most stateful firewall products. The following two sections discuss two solutions to this problem for ESP—there are no solutions for AH.

> **TIP** If the management and data connections are established, but data can't be successfully transmitted between the two peers, a translation or stateful firewall device might be causing the problem. Remember that during Phase 2, even though the data connection parameters can be successfully negotiated, this does not mean that the devices can successfully transmit data across these connections.

NAT Traversal

NAT Traversal, sometimes called *NAT Transparency* (or NAT-T for short), is an IPSec standard that inserts a UDP header between the outer IP header and the ESP header. The destination port for NAT-T is 4500. Intelligence is used with NAT-T: a discovery phase takes place during Phase 1 to determine if the two peers support NAT-T, and if they do support it, whether inserting a UDP header is necessary for the data connections to be successful in protecting and transmitting data. This is a dynamic process: if inserting a UDP header is needed, then it is done; if it is unneeded, then it is not inserted (inserting a UDP adds an additional 8 bytes of overhead).

NAT-T is globally enabled by default. One of its features is that keepalives are sent across the data connections to ensure that address translation or stateful firewall devices don't remove any idle data connections. The default idle period is 20 seconds. To change the keepalive timer interval, use the following command:

```
ciscoasa(config)# crypto isakmp nat-traversal [seconds]
```

The period can range from 10 to 3600 seconds.

IPSec over TCP

There are two problems with NAT-T, however:

▼ It uses UDP, which typically has a much smaller idle timeout than TCP connections for translation and stateful firewall devices.

▲ You are forced into using destination UDP port 4500 (it cannot be changed), which might be filtered by an intermediate device.

Cisco created a proprietary encapsulation method, called IPSec over TCP, to overcome these two problems. With IPSec over TCP, a TCP header is inserted between the outer IP header and the ESP header. IPSec over TCP is disabled, but can be enabled with the following command:

```
ciscoasa(config)# crypto isakmp ipsec-over-tcp {[port prt_#]...[prt_#]}
```

One advantage that IPSec over TCP has over NAT-T is that you can control what port or ports (up to 10) can be used; by default port 10000 is used.

NOTE   There are two problems with IPSec over TCP: it is Cisco-proprietary, which means the endpoints must be Cisco devices, and IPSec over TCP inserts a 20-byte header, almost three times as much as NAT-T inserts. Also, NAT-T and IPSec over TCP are commonly used for remote access connections, where intermediate firewalls and translation devices are more likely to be encountered.

VPN Traffic and ACLs

The following two sections will discuss how to deal with IPSec traffic flowing to or through the appliance.

IPSec Sessions Terminated on the Appliance

If your appliance has IPSec sessions terminated on it, you have two options to allow the traffic to flow from a lower- to higher-level interface:

▼   ACLs

▲   ACL bypass feature

For the first option, you'll need to add ACL statements for the *decrypted* IPSec traffic on the external interface ACL: once the traffic is decrypted, it is passed through the external interface ACL and must match a **permit** statement, or it is dropped.

The second option exempts the decrypted VPN traffic from being processed by the external interface ACL, assuming that the VPN session is terminated on the appliance. To configure the ACL bypass feature, use this command:

```
ciscoasa(config)# sysopt connection permit-vpn
```

The problem with this command is that any traffic coming out of the VPN tunnel is permitted; as you will see in subsequent chapters, you can control which traffic uses the VPN tunnel.

IPSec Sessions Terminated Behind the Appliance

If IPSec sessions are terminated on devices behind the appliance, you'll need ACL entries on your external interface to allow the management and data connections through the appliance to the internal IPSec endpoint:

```
ciscoasa(config)# access-list ACL_ID permit udp src_IP src_mask
                       dst_IP dst_mask eq isakmp
```

```
ciscoasa(config)# access-list ACL_ID permit esp src_IP src_mask
                         dst_IP dst_mask
ciscoasa(config)# access-list ACL_ID permit udp src_IP src_mask
                         dst_IP dst_mask eq non-isakmp

ciscoasa(config)# access-list ACL_ID permit tcp src_IP src_mask
                         dst_IP dst_mask eq IPSec_over_TCP_port
```

The first command allows the management connection. The following three connections allow the data connections: the second allows the ESP protocol, the third allows NAT-T, and the fourth allows IPSec over TCP. You'll need to configure the entries appropriate for your network and its configuration.

TUNNEL GROUPS

Tunnel groups were introduced in version 7 of the appliance and are unique to Cisco appliances—Cisco routers and concentrators don't support this type of functionality. Tunnel groups are used to identify information that should be used for a particular VPN type and peer, like an IPSec L2L connection or an IPSec or WebVPN remote access group of users.

Tunnel groups have two basic attributes:

▼ General
▲ VPN-specific

General attributes are non-VPN-specific and can specify things like the AAA servers to use, where the policies are stored (local to the appliance or on an AAA server), where to find the usernames and passwords to authenticate remote access users, and other information. VPN-specific attributes define properties for the tunnel group that are specific to a particular VPN type, like a pre-shared key or digital certificate to use for an IPSec L2L connection, the use of Dead Peer Detection (DPD) for IPSec connections, or what the home page looks like for clientless WebVPN sessions.

The following sections will introduce you to tunnel groups: how to create them, and how general and VPN-specific properties are associated with tunnel groups. Subsequent chapters in Part IV will discuss tunnel groups in much more depth, covering the commands and parameters that apply to a particular VPN type.

Tunnel Group Creation

A tunnel group, as I mentioned in the last section, represents a particular IPSec L2L connection or a remote access group. To create a tunnel group, use the following command:

```
ciscoasa(config)# tunnel-group tunnel_group_ID type vpn_type
```

The *tunnel_group_ID* uniquely identifies the tunnel group. For example, if the identity for L2L connections were "address," then the tunnel group ID would be the IP address of the peer; if the identity type were "hostname," then the group ID would be the fully qualified domain name of the peer. For IPSec and WebVPN remote access users, the tunnel group ID represents the name of the group, like "sales", "engineers", or "programmers".

Following the tunnel group ID is the type of VPN that represents the group. In version 8, you can specify only two parameters:

▼ `ipsec-l2l`   The "l2l" part is really "L-2-L," not "one-two-one": this represents IPSec site-to-site or L2L connections.

▲ `remote-access`   This represents IPSec and WebVPN remote access user groupings.

NOTE In prior appliance versions, instead of `remote-access`, you had `ipsec-ra` and `webvpn-ra`, where these two VPN types were represented by different groups. In version 8, these are no longer supported (they've been deprecated): both types are represented by the `remote-access` type.

General Tunnel Group Attributes

As I mentioned previously in the introduction to tunnel groups section, general tunnel group attributes are parameters associated with a tunnel group that have no bearing on the type of VPN that is being used. For example, if you had a remote access tunnel group called "engineers," general properties for the group would include whether an AAA server was used, where the user accounts were located for user authentication, and where the VPN-specific attributes of the group were found.

Once you've created your tunnel group, you can assign the general attributes to the tunnel group with the following configuration:

```
ciscoasa(config)# tunnel-group tunnel_group_ID general-attributes
ciscoasa(config-tunnel-general)# ?
group_policy configuration commands:
  accounting-server-group      Enter name of the accounting server
                               group
  address-pool                 Enter a list of address pools to assign
                               addresses from
  annotation                   Specify annotation text - to be used by
                               ASDM only
  authentication-server-group  Enter name of the authentication server
                               group
  authorization-dn-attributes  The DN of the peer certificate used as
                               username for authorization
```

`authorization-required`	Require users to authorize successfully in order to connect
`authorization-server-group`	Enter name of the authorization server group
`default-group-policy`	Enter name of the default group policy
`dhcp-server`	Enter IP address or name of the DHCP server
`exit`	Exit from tunnel-group general attribute configuration mode
`help`	Help for tunnel group configuration commands
`ipv6-address-pool`	Enter a list of IPv6 address pools to assign addresses from
`no`	Remove an attribute value pair
`override-account-disable`	Override account disabled from AAA server
`password-management`	Enable password management
`strip-group`	Enable strip-group processing
`strip-realm`	Enable strip-realm processing

Notice that you are taken into a subcommand mode where you can configure your general attributes. I'll be discussing these attributes in subsequent chapters of Part IV.

VPN-Specific Tunnel Group Attributes

Once you've created your tunnel group, to associate VPN-specific attributes to it, use the following command:

```
ciscoasa(config)# tunnel-group tunnel_group_ID
                        {ipsec-attributes | webvpn-attributes}
ciscoasa(config-tunnel-{ipsec|webvpn})#
```

You have two options for the type of attributes, depending on the type of tunnel group: IPSec attributes or WebVPN attributes. You'll be taken into a subcommand mode where you can specify the VPN-specific attributes. I'll be discussing these attributes in subsequent chapters of Part IV.

CERTIFICATE AUTHORITIES

Certificates are the most scalable solution to perform device authentication with VPNs. Certificates must be created by a neutral third-party, called a certificate authority (CA). The appliances support many CAs, including RSA, VeriSign, Netscape, Baltimore, Microsoft, Entrust, Cisco IOS routers, and the security appliances themselves (not discussed in this book). The remainder of this chapter will introduce the use of certificates, how to obtain certificates for appliances, and how to use certificates to authenticate devices for IPSec sessions.

Introducing Certificates

There are two types of certificates: root and identity. Every device participating in the certificate process must have a certificate, including the CA itself. The certificate for the CA is called a *root* certificate, and certificates for other devices are called *identity* certificates. Obtaining an identity certificate can be done either out-of-band using the file-based approach or in-band using the Simple Certificate Enrollment Protocol (SCEP), which uses HTTP.

To use certificates, the peers must have an ISAKMP Phase 1 policy that supports certificates (RSA signatures). During authentication, two items are checked, and a third is optional. For the two required items, the peers validate the digital signature on the certificate and then make sure the certificate hasn't expired. With the third item, an option exists for checking if a peer certificate has been revoked: the use of Certificate Revocation Lists (CRLs) or Online Certificate Status Protocol (OCSP) is supported. A CRL contains a list of all the certificates that have been revoked. CRLs can be downloaded when they are needed, which can be bandwidth-intensive and introduce delay in the VPN setup process, or they can be downloaded periodically and cached, which can create problems of not having the most up-to-date list when authenticating a peer. OCSP, on the other hand, has the device perform a query, with the remote peer serial number on the identity certificate, to the OCSP server in order to determine if the certificate has been revoked. Using OCSP is the preferred method.

Obtaining Certificates

The following sections will discuss how to obtain the root certificate of the CA and how to generate the certificate information, defined by the Public Key Cryptography Standards (PKCS) #10 standard, which the CA needs to create an identity certificate for the appliance.

Identity Information on the Certificate

When generating your PKCS #10 certificate information, by default the appliance associates a common name (CN) of the appliance hostname and domain name configured on the appliance. You can override this behavior and assign your own key label when generating the key pair, as you'll see in the "Basic Trustpoint Configuration" section.

To assign a name and domain name to your appliance, use the following configuration:

```
ciscoasa(config)# hostname name_of_your_appliance
ciscoasa(config)# domain-name your_appliance's_domain_name
```

These commands were discussed in Chapter 3.

Key Pairs

Cisco supports both the RSA and DSA algorithms for generating public/private keys; these are used to sign the PKCS #10 information. DSA is quicker in generating its keys, but is less secure; and not all CA products support DSA. Because of these limitations, this book only focuses on the use of RSA keys.

Generating RSA keys was discussed in Chapter 3; however, then I didn't discuss all the options available with the command. Here's the full syntax of the command:

```
ciscoasa(config)# crypto key generate rsa [usage-keys | general-keys]
                        [label key_pair_label] [modulus key_size]
                        [noconfirm]
```

The **usage-keys** parameter generates two sets of keys, while the **general-keys** parameter generates one key pair; the default is **general-keys** if you omit it, which is what you need for certificate purposes. Use **usage-keys** if you need two identity certificates from the same CA, which is uncommon. If you don't specify a label for the key pair, it defaults to "Default-RSA-Key." If you don't specify a modulus (the size of the keys, in bits), it defaults to 1024: other valid sizes include 512, 768, and 2048. The **noconfirm** parameter, when configured, will execute the command without any interaction on your part—the default is to prompt you for verification. Use the **show crypto key mypub key** command to view the public keys on your appliance.

TIP You might want more than one RSA key pair. SSH uses the default key pair label; but you might want to use a different key pair (with a different modulus) for certificates.

Here's an example of generating an RSA key pair:

```
ciscoasa(config)# crypto key generate rsa label mykeys
INFO: The name for the keys will be: mykeys
Keypair generation process
ciscoasa(config)#
```

In this example, a key pair label of "mykeys" is used to name the key pair.

NOTE If the RSA key pair already exists, you are prompted to overwrite the existing key pair. Also, to delete an RSA key pair, use the **crypto key zeroize rsa** [label key_pair_label] command.

Date and Time

Items validated on the certificate are two dates: when the certificate becomes valid and when it is no longer valid. The device will compare its local date and time with the dates and times that appear on the certificate, ensuring that the device time falls between the two periods. You can hard-code the date and time on the appliance with the **clock set** command:

```
ciscoasa# clock set hh:mm:ss {month day | day month} year
```

This is the same command used on Cisco IOS devices.

NOTE   I recommend using NTP to synchronize the time on your devices. The appliances support NTP, which I discuss in Chapter 26.

Basic Trustpoint Configuration

The CA, commonly called a *trustpoint*, configuration on the appliance defines the properties used to interact with a CA as well as to obtain certificates—root and identity. You must configure the trustpoint properties on the appliance before you can obtain the two certificates. This section will discuss some basic trustpoint configuration commands, and subsequent sections will cover how to obtain certificates and CRLs (Certificate Revocation Lists).

Here are the basic trustpoint configuration commands:

```
ciscoasa(config)# crypto ca trustpoint trustpoint_name
ciscoasa(config-ca-trustpoint)# subject-name X.500_info
ciscoasa(config-ca-trustpoint)# email email_address
ciscoasa(config-ca-trustpoint)# fqdn fully_qualified_domain_name
ciscoasa(config-ca-trustpoint)# ip-address IP_address
ciscoasa(config-ca-trustpoint)# serial-number
ciscoasa(config-ca-trustpoint)# keypair key_pair_label
ciscoasa(config-ca-trustpoint)# keysize {512 | 768 | 1024 | 2048}
ciscoasa(config-ca-trustpoint)# id-usage ssl-ipsec
ciscoasa(config-ca-trustpoint)# client-types {ipsec | ssl}
ciscoasa(config-ca-trustpoint)# accept-subordinates
```

Setting up a trustpoint is similar to how it's done on a Cisco IOS router. First, you specify the name of the trustpoint, which takes you into a subcommand mode. The name of the CA is a locally significant name and doesn't have to match the actual name of the server unless specified by the administrator of the CA.

NOTE   With Cisco IOS routers and Microsoft servers as CAs, I've never had to match up the names of the servers with the name in the `crypt ca trustpoint` command.

Optionally you can specify the X.500 information that will appear on the requested X.509v3 identity certificate with the **subject-name** command. If you don't configure this value, the common name (CN) defaults to the fully qualified domain name (FQDN) of the appliance. If you want to change it, you have to know the field values to use for the certificate information. Here's an example:

```
ciscoasa(config-ca-trustpoint)# subject-name
                cn=asa1.cisco.com,ou=mydepartment,o=cisco
```

In this example, the identity name on the certificate is "asa1.cisco.com", the organizational unit (OU) or department value is "mydepartment", and the organizational value (O) is "cisco".

Optionally you can have the CA include an e-mail address in the Subject Alternative Name (SAN) extension field of the certificate with the `email` command; however, this is not required. Instead of an e-mail address, you can include an FQDN of your choice in the SAN field with the `fqdn` command. The last two options you have for information that appears on the certificate are to include an IP address (associated with the appliance) with the `ip-address` command and/or the appliance serial number with the `serial-number` command.

The `key-pair` command specifies either an existing key-pair label to use or the name of one that will be created. The `key-size` command specifies the length of the keys to create when they don't exist. These two commands, when used together, will generate a new key pair when obtaining an identity certificate versus using an existing key pair on the appliance.

The `id-usage` command specifies how the identity certificate associated with the trustpoint can be used. With the `ssl-ipsec` parameter, the identity certificate can be used for SSL VPN and IPSec VPN authentication when the appliance is acting as the server/gateway, which is the default behavior. You can disable this by prefacing the command with the `no` parameter. The `client-type` command controls what type of VPN remote clients the certificate can be used for. There is no default value.

The `accept-subordinates` command specifies whether subordinate CA certificates (in a CA hierarchical implementation) are accepted by a peer during ISAKMP/IKE Phase 1 authentication when the local appliance currently doesn't have these certificates installed. The default is that this command is enabled.

NOTE All of the commands discussed in this section are optional.

Network Enrollment: SCEP

There are two methods to obtain the CA (root) certificate and the appliance identity certificate:

▼ Network enrollment using the Simple Certificate Enrollment Protocol (SCEP)

▲ File enrollment using an out-of-band approach

This section will discuss the former, and the next section will discuss the latter.

NOTE Network enrollment is most commonly used in environments where you are setting up your own CA. SCEP uses HTTP to access certificate information on the CA. File enrollment is most commonly used in environments where you are either using a public CA, like VeriSign, or an external CA from a different company. Of the two, I much prefer the former, since network enrollment is easier and much quicker at deploying certificates on a larger number of devices.

Configuring SCEP Enrollment Parameters To configure network enrollment using SCEP, the following commands (and possibly the commands discussed in the last section) are used:

```
ciscoasa(config)# crypto ca trustpoint trustpoint_name
ciscoasa(config-ca-trustpoint)# enrollment url URL
ciscoasa(config-ca-trustpoint)# password challenge_password
ciscoasa(config-ca-trustpoint)# enrollment retry count #_of_attempts
ciscoasa(config-ca-trustpoint)# enrollment retry period #_of_minutes
```

You have to first define the name of the trustpoint, which was discussed in the last section. This takes you into the trustpoint subcommand mode. You then specify how you'll obtain a certificate: the **enrollment url** command specifies the use of SCEP. The URL is HTTP-based, and the actual syntax depends on the CA product you'll interface with. Here's an example using a Microsoft CA:

```
ciscoasa(config)# crypto ca trustpoint caserver
ciscoasa(config-ca-trustpoint)# enrollment url
                  http://172.26.26.151:80/certsrv/mscep/mscep.dll
```

NOTE When using a Cisco IOS router as a CA, your local ASA needs to use this URL: `http://IP_address_of_Cisco_IOS_router`.

The **password** command specifies the challenge password to use during the certificate request process. The password is hashed with the certificate information, which is validated by the CA using the same password. If you are using challenge passwords, which I highly recommend, the CA administrator will have to create one for you. Depending on the administrator's setup of the CA, the password might be time-sensitive (only valid for a specific amount of time).

The **enrollment retry count** specifies a maximum number of permitted retries for SCEP enrollment before giving up. The **enrollment retry period** command specifies a retry period, in minutes, between SCEP enrollment requests when the CA is unreachable.

NOTE Of the four trustpoint commands just listed, only the **enrollment url** command is required for SCEP.

Obtaining Certificates Using SCEP Once you have specified your CA and your **enrollment** command(s), you need to first download the CA root certificate and validate it with the **crypto ca authenticate** command:

```
ciscoasa(config)# crypto ca authenticate trustpoint_name
```

When you get the fingerprint back from the CA on the root certificate—this is the self-signed signature the CA placed on its own certificate—verify the fingerprint by calling the CA administrator and manually comparing the two values. This is the only part of the certificate process that is susceptible to a man-in-the-middle attack.

Here's an example of obtaining the CA root certificate:

```
ciscoasa(config)# crypto ca authenticate caserver
INFO: Certificate has the following attributes:
Fingerprint: 3736ffc2 243ecf05 0c40f2fa 26820675
Do you accept this certificate? [yes/no]: yes
Trustpoint 'caserver' is a subordinate CA and holds a non self signed
    cert.
Trustpoint CA certificate accepted.
```

Make sure you validate the fingerprint/signature that is on the root certificate, since this certificate is used to validate any other certificate associated with this CA.

Once you have the root certificate, you can obtain your identity certificate with the following command:

```
ciscoasa(config)# crypto ca enroll trustpoint_name

ciscoasa(config)# crypto ca enroll caserver
% Start certificate enrollment ..
% Create a challenge password. You will need to verbally provide this
% password to the CA Administrator in order to revoke your certificate.
% For security reasons your password will not be saved in the
% configuration.
% Please make a note of it.
Password: abc123
Re-enter password: abc123
% The subject name in the certificate will be: asa.example.com
% The fully-qualified domain name in the certificate will be:
                                        securityappliance.example.com
% Include the device serial number in the subject name? [yes/no]: no
Request certificate from CA [yes/no]: yes
% Certificate request sent to Certificate authority.
The certificate has been granted by CA!
```

As you can see in the preceding example, you are prompted for a challenge password—you must enter something here even if the CA is not using challenge passwords. You have the option of including the serial number of the appliance on the certificate, and then the appliance requests the certificate.

File Enrollment: Manual

Once you have configured the basic trustpoint commands from the "Basic Trustpoint Configuration" section, you can use the **enrollment terminal** command in the trustpoint subcommand mode to enable the file-based approach to obtain certificates:

```
ciscoasa(config)# crypto ca trustpoint trustpoint_name
ciscoasa(config-ca-trustpoint)# enrollment terminal
```

The **enrollment terminal** command enables file-based enrollment.

Once you have configured the trustpoint, you can then generate your PKCS #10 certificate information for the CA with the **crypto ca enroll** command, discussed in the last section. Here's an example:

```
ciscoasa(config)# crypto ca enroll caserver
% Start certificate enrollment ..
% The fully-qualified domain name in the certificate will be: asa5505-1
% Include the device serial number in the subject name? [yes/no]: no
Display Certificate Request to terminal? [yes/no]: yes
Certificate Request follows:
MIIBjTCB9wIBADAaMRgwFgYJKoZIhvcNAQkCFglhc2E1NTA1LTEwgZ8wDQYJKoZI
hvcNAQEBBQADgY0AMIGJAoGBAK04Czj3ZY9GJlo4m5wDWdYwvGOSbr1gRp782k8H
<--output omitted-->
---End - This line not part of the certificate request---
Redisplay enrollment request? [yes/no]: no
```

Make sure the certificate information between the "Certificate Request follows" and "--End - This line" lines is included—copy and paste this into a file, and give the file to the CA administrator.

The CA administrator will then use this information to create an identity certificate for the appliance. The administrator will then send back two files: one contains the root certificate, and one contains the identity certificate. You'll need to load these onto the appliance in the listed order.

Use the **crypto ca authenticate** command to import the CA root certificate. Here's an example:

```
ciscoasa(config)# crypto ca authenticate caserver
Enter the base 64 encoded CA certificate.
End with a blank line or the word "quit" on a line by itself
<--paste in the CA's root certificate-->
quit
INFO: Certificate has the following attributes:
Fingerprint: 24b81433 409b3fd5 e5431699 8d490d34
Do you accept this certificate? [yes/no]: yes
Trustpoint CA certificate accepted.
% Certificate successfully imported
ciscoasa(config)#
```

You need to type the word **quit** upon entering the CA certificate information—this must be on a separate, blank line. Then you must accept the root certificate.

Once you have manually imported the root certificate, you can then import the appliance identity certificate with the **crypto ca import** command. Here's an example:

```
ciscoasa(config)# crypto ca import caserver certificate
% The fully-qualified domain name in the certificate will be:
    ciscoasa.cisco.com
Enter the base 64 encoded certificate.
End with a blank line or the word "quit" on a line by itself
<--paste in your certificate-->
quit
INFO: Certificate successfully imported
```

NOTE To properly import the root and identity certificates, the appliances must receive the certificates in a PEM (privacy enhanced mail) format.

Certificate Revocation Lists

A Certificate Revocation List (CRL) is a list of certificate serial numbers that have been revoked by the CA. Certificates can be revoked because they have expired, the device associated with a certificate has become compromised, the device is no longer being used, or a change in the security policy requires new certificates (like requiring longer key lengths).

The use of CRLs is controlled by the following trustpoint configuration:

```
ciscoasa(config)# crypto ca trustpoint trustpoint_name
ciscoasa(config-ca-trustpoint)# revocation-check crl [none]
ciscoasa(config-ca-trustpoint)# revocation-check ocsp [none]
ciscoasa(config-ca-trustpoint)# revocation-check none
```

The **revocation-check** command specifies how and if CRLs are used. The **crl** parameter specifies that a CRL is downloaded using HTTP, SCEP, or LDAP from a specified location and cached locally; adding the **none** parameter specifies that if the CRL cannot be found, then it is not used (CRLs are optional). The **ocsp** specifies that the Online Certificate Status Protocol (OCSP) is used instead of CRLs to determine if a certificate has been revoked; adding the **none** parameter specifies that if the OCSP server cannot be found, then it is not used (OCSP is optional). The **none** parameter, by itself, specifies that CRLs and OCSP are not used during device authentication.

NOTE If when using CRLs or OCSP you don't add the optional **none** parameter, and the CRL or OSCP server cannot be accessed, authentication of the peer device will fail.

CRL Usage   When using CRLs to determine if a certificate has been revoked, the appliance will periodically download and cache the CRL list. To tune this process, you can use the following configuration:

```
ciscoasa(config)# crypto ca trustpoint trustpoint_name
ciscoasa(config-ca-trustpoint)# crl configure
ciscoasa(config-ca-crl)# policy {cdp | static | both}
ciscoasa(config-ca-crl)# url number URL
ciscoasa(config-ca-crl)# protocol {http | ldap | scep}
ciscoasa(config-ca-crl)# cache-time minutes
ciscoasa(config-ca-crl)# enforcenextupdate
ciscoasa(config-ca-crl)# ldap-defaults server_name_or_IP [port_#]
ciscoasa(config-ca-crl)# ldap-dn directory_path password
```

To configure parameters for CRL usage, in the trustpoint configuration execute the **crl configure** command—this will take you into a second subcommand mode. The **policy** command specifies where to find the CRL list. The **cdp** parameter, which is the default, specifies that the CRL location will be found by examining the CA root or an RA (Registration Authority) identity certificate. The **static** parameter specifies that you will configure a static entry or entries on the appliance as to where to find the CRL. The **both** parameter specifies that the appliance will attempt to use the location on the CA/RA certificate to find the CRL, but if this is unsuccessful, then a static entry on the appliance will be used.

To configure a static entry, use the **url** command. The number following the command ranks the entry in the order that it should be used. You can create up to five entries, where the number ranges from 1 to 5. Following the number is the actual URL, like "http://172.26.26.151/crldir/caserver.crl". The **protocol** command specifies the protocol that will be used to retrieve and process the CRL list. All three protocols are allowed by default; you can use the **no** parameter to disable a particular protocol if necessary. The **cache-time** command specifies how long the CRL list is cached locally on the appliance before the CRL list is downloaded again. The default is 60 minutes and can be as large as 1440 minutes. The **enforcenextupdate** command specifies that the "NextUpdate" field in the CRL must not have expired in order for the CRL itself to be considered valid. By default this is enabled; to disable it, preface the command with the **no** parameter.

If the CRL is located on an LDAP server and the appliance needs to use the LDAP protocol to access it, you'll have to define how the appliance should interface with the LDAP server. The **ldap-defaults** command specifies the LDAP server the CRL is located on. You can either specify the name or IP address of the server; with the former, you must be able to dynamically or statically resolve this to an IP address. If you don't configure an LDAP port number, it defaults to 389. If the LDAP server requires authentication to access the CRL, use the **ldap-dn** command to specify the login credentials. The directory path is basically the X.500 information to access the CRL. Here's a simple example: **cn=crl,ou=certs,o=caserver,c=US**. This field cannot exceed 128 characters. The directory path is then followed by the LDAP password, which also cannot exceed 128 characters.

OCSP Usage There are a couple of problems with CRLs. First, the list can be quite long and must be downloaded and stored locally on a device, which can take up space like RAM, flash, or disk space. Second, once the CRL is downloaded, if certificates are revoked by the CA, a device with a cached CRL won't know this until its cache timer expires and the updated CRL is downloaded—so there is a chance that a revoked certificate would appear as valid to some devices in the network.

OCSP was created to solve these two problems. Instead of downloading a long list and caching the information, OCSP uses a query process: when a device needs to determine if a certificate has or hasn't been revoked, it sends a query to an OCSP server, which responds with the status of the queried serial number. If you have a large installed base of devices using certificates, OCSP scales much better than using CRLs.

To use OCSP, implement the following configuration:

```
ciscoasa(config)# crypto ca trustpoint trustpoint_name
ciscoasa(config-ca-trustpoint)# revocation-check ocsp [none]
ciscoasa(config-ca-trustpoint)# ocsp url URL
ciscoasa(config-ca-trustpoint)# match certificate map_name
                    override ocsp [trustpoint trustpoint_name]
                    sequence_num url URL
ciscoasa(config-ca-trustpoint)# ocsp disable-nonce
```

The **revocation-check** command was discussed earlier in the section. The **oscp url** command specifies how the appliance should contact the OCSP server. HTTP is the protocol used, so an example URL might look like this: "http://172.26.26.151". If you need to validate certain certificates using a different OCSP server, you can create a certificate map, which matches on one or more certificates, and associate this with the appropriate OCSP server (certificate maps and matching are discussed later in the "Certificate Group Matching" section).

OCSP requests sent by a device to the OCSP server include a *nonce extension* (basically a signature). The OCSP server should use this information in crafting its response, also creating a nonce extension—basically the nonce extension is used to bind the request and response in order to defeat replay attacks. However, some OCSP server implementations don't dynamically create the nonce extension; instead, they use a pre-generated response. In this situation, the appliance would see the response as invalid, reject it, and thus authentication of a peer certificate would fail. To disable the use of the nonce extension, use the **ocsp disable-nonce** command.

Certificate Management

The following sections will discuss how to manage certificates on your appliance: how to save them, how to view them, and how to troubleshoot problems with them.

Saving Certificates Prior to version 7.0, the **ca save all** command was used to save certificate and keying information on the PIXs. Starting in version 7.0, this command was deprecated. Now to save the certificate and keying information on the appliances, just use the **write memory** command.

Viewing Certificates   To view the certificates (root and identity) on your appliance, use the following command:

```
ciscoasa# show crypto ca certificates [trustpoint_name]
```

Here's an example of viewing a certificate:

```
ciscoasa(config)# show crypto ca certificates
CA Certificate
Status: Available
Certificate Serial Number 2957A3FF296EF854FD0D6732FE25123
Certificate Usage: Signature
Issuer:
CN = caserver
OU = rootou
O = dealgroup
L = oviedo
ST - florida
C = US
EA = admin@dealgroup.com
Subject:
CN = caserver
OU = rootou
O = dealgroup
<--output omitted-->
```

Notice that the certificate has a serial number at the top, which was assigned by the CA. Below this is who issued the certificate (`Issuer` section) and whom the certificate is for (`Subject` section). In the preceding example, the Issuer and Subject information is the same, meaning that this is the certificate of the CA.

Troubleshooting Certificate Problems   One of the most common problems of obtaining and using certificates involves the date and time. When validating a certificate, two things are required, and a third thing is optional. The first two things are comparing the device current time with the beginning and ending time on the certificate (if the device current time falls between these two, then the first authentication step passes), and validating the signature on the certificate. Optionally the device can check to see if the certificate has been revoked by using CRLs or OCSP.

Since the date and time are important in validating certificates, I highly recommend that you don't statically define the date and time, but use the Network Time Protocol (NTP) to make sure your CA and devices acquiring and using certificates are in synch with each other. The configuration of NTP on the appliances is discussed in Chapter 26.

To troubleshoot all other problems related to obtaining and/or using certificates, use the following command:

```
ciscoasa# debug crypto ca [messages | transactions] [level_#]
```

The **messages** parameter displays only debug messages for PKI input and output messages. The **transactions** parameter displays debug messages for PKI transactions. Not specifying either will include both in the debug output. Optionally you can include a level number in the **debug** command, which qualifies the amount of output displayed. This can range from 1 to 255. Level 1, the default, displays error messages; level 2 displays warnings; level 3 displays informational messages; and level 4 and higher display additional troubleshooting information.

Using Certificates

The following sections will discuss how to use certificates on your appliance—specifically, how you specify which identity certificate, when more than one is on the appliance, should be used for a particular peer.

Tunnel Groups and Certificates

Tunnel groups were briefly introduced earlier in the "Tunnel Groups" section. Their use will be discussed in much more depth in Chapters 16 and 17. This section will discuss how certificates are used with tunnel groups.

Once you have created a tunnel group, to associate a certificate to it for IPSec VPNs, you must go into the tunnel group IPSec attributes:

```
ciscoasa(config)# tunnel-group peer_IP_addr ipsec-attributes
ciscoasa(config-tunnel-ipsec)# peer-id-validate {cert | nocheck | req}
ciscoasa(config-tunnel-ipsec)# pre-shared-key key
ciscoasa(config-tunnel-ipsec)# trust-point trustpoint_name
```

The **peer-ip-validate** command specifies the use of certificates. The **cert** parameter specifies that certificates will be used if both peers have certificates and if during the ISAKMP Phase 1 policy negotiation they agreed that certificates should be used. The **nocheck** parameter specifies that certificates will not be used (pre-shared keys will be used instead with the **pre-shared-key** command). The **req** parameter specifies that certificates must be used with the remote peer, or a tunnel won't be built. The default setting for this command is **req**, unless you configure a pre-shared key.

The **trust-point** command specifies the name of the trustpoint (and the corresponding identity certificate) that should be used with the remote peer. If you only have one CA the appliance is using, then this command isn't necessary: the appliance will use the single root and identity certificates that it has. However, if you have more than one CA, and thus more than one identity certificate on your appliance, you'll have to tell the appliance which set of certificates should be used with which remote peer by configuring the **trust-point** command.

Certificate Group Matching

When your appliance is an Easy VPN server for IPSec VPNs (see Chapter 17) and remote access devices are using certificates for authentication, the appliances assume that the OU (Organizational Unit, sometimes called the Department) field contains the name of the tunnel group the user should be associated with. In turn, this tunnel group name tells the appliance which policies should be associated with the connecting user. If this is incorrect, you'll need to create certificate matching rules to correctly match up the user to the correct tunnel group.

By default the OU field is used in the certificate to match a user to a tunnel group. Therefore, I highly recommend that when users request their certificates, you make sure they configure their tunnel group name correctly (which is case-sensitive!) in their certificate request—otherwise you'll either have to have them reperform the request with the correct group name, or create a certificate matching rule to match the certificate to the correct group.

You can override the default lookup method with the **tunnel-group-map** command:

```
ciscoasa(config)# tunnel-group-map enable {ou | peer-ip | rules}
```

The **ou** parameter in the first command specifies that the OU field should be used (this is the default). The **peer-ip** parameter specifies that the IP address of the peer should be used. And the **rules** parameter indicates that the rules in the **crypto ca certificate map** command should be used—this command is discussed next.

The **crypto ca certificate map** command creates a single certificate matching rule, where you must specify a rule number from 1 to 65535:

```
ciscoasa(config)# crypto ca certificate map map_name rule_#
ciscoasa(config-ca-cert-map)# subject-name attr ser eq serial_#
ciscoasa(config-ca-cert-map)# subject-name attr cn eq common_name
```

This command takes you into a subcommand mode where you specify the attributes on the peer identity certificate to match on. You can match on any field within the certificate; however, the two most common ones are the serial number (which is unique within a CA domain) and/or the common name (the name of the user or device). You can match on other fields, but I've only listed the two I mentioned earlier; of these two, the most common one to match on is the serial number on the certificate.

The **tunnel-group-map** command associates the matching rule with the group this user or users should belong to:

```
ciscoasa(config)# tunnel-group-map default-group tunnel_group_name
ciscoasa(config)# tunnel-group-map map_name rule_# tunnel_group_name
```

The **default-group** parameter specifies what group a user should be associated with if it cannot be determined what tunnel group the user should be in. The default group is set to *DefaultRAGroup*. The second **tunnel-group-map** command allows you to match a particular certificate matching rule to a particular tunnel group.

Here's a simple example that places a certificate with a common name of "Richard Deal" in the tunnel group called "engineers":

```
ciscoasa(config)# crypto ca certificate map mymap 1
ciscoasa(config-ca-cert-map)# subject-name attr cn eq Richard Deal
ciscoasa(config)# tunnel-group-map mymap 1 engineers
```

NOTE Normally I prefer the former method for matching users to groups. I typically use certificate matching rules when users move from one group to another because of a change in their job function—instead of creating a new certificate with the correct group name in the OU field, I'll use certificate matching rules to correctly associate the users to their new tunnel group.

CHAPTER 16

IPSec Site-to-Site

This chapter will show you how to set up an IPSec site-to-site connection with your appliance. The topics covered previously in Chapter 15 on ISAKMP Phase 1 apply to this chapter, since site-to-site, commonly called LAN-to-LAN (L2L), connections must first establish a management connection. The topics covered in this chapter include

▼ Preparing for your site-to-site connections

■ Configuring ISAKMP Phase 2, including crypto ACLs, transform sets, and crypto maps

■ Verifying site-to-site connectivity

▲ A site-to-site configuration example

SITE-TO-SITE PREPARATION

Cisco security appliances have supported IPSec L2L connections since version 5 of the operating system. Before you begin setting up L2L connections on your appliances, you should first go through some basic preparation by determining the following:

▼ How the management connection should be protected

■ The identity type of the peer: address or name

■ The authentication method used: pre-shared keys or certificates

■ Whether address translation is needed because of overlapping addresses

■ What data traffic should be protected and how it should be protected

▲ What interface(s) L2L connections will terminate on

One thing you'll need to do is exempt the IPSec traffic flowing from a lower- to higher-security-level interface:

```
ciscoasa(config)# sysopt connection permit-vpn
```

TIP If you forget this command, you can still terminate connections on the appliance; however, traffic will be unable to flow inbound without either this command or an ACL configuration on the interface the tunnel is terminated on that allows the inbound *decrypted* traffic.

The remaining subsections in this section will review what was covered in Chapter 15, focusing on what you'll need for ISAKMP/IKE Phase 1 for L2L connections.

NOTE For a large number of L2L connections, I recommend that you use Cisco routers. Cisco routers support GRE tunnels and dynamic multipoint VPNs (DMVPNs): the combination of these two features provides a much more scalable solution than the appliances offer. I typically use appliances for L2L connections when I have a small number of sites that I don't anticipate expanding on.

ISAKMP Phase 1 Configuration

Here is a quick synopsis of the ISAKMP Phase 1 commands you need to configure for L2L connections:

```
ciscoasa(config)# crypto isakmp enable logical_if_name
ciscoasa(config)# crypto isakmp identity {address | hostname |
                    key string | auto }
ciscoasa(config)# crypto isakmp policy policy_number
ciscoasa(config-isakmp-policy)# authentication {pre-share | rsa-sig |
                    crack}
ciscoasa(config-isakmp-policy)# encryption {3des | aes | aes-192 |
                    aes-256 | des}
ciscoasa(config-isakmp-policy)# group {1 | 2 | 5 | 7}
ciscoasa(config-isakmp-policy)# hash {md5 | sha}
ciscoasa(config-isakmp-policy)# lifetime {seconds | none}
```

These commands were discussed in Chapter 15. IPSec is typically enabled on the outside interface (connected to the Internet) with the `crypto isakmp enable` command. Normally the identity type is the IP address of the remote peer, which means that you don't have to configure the `crypto isakmp address` command (unless this is not the case).

You'll need at least one matching ISAKMP policy with the remote peer. Remember that the policy number is important: this is the order that the appliance sends the policies to the remote peer during the Phase 1 negotiation. Therefore, make sure the lowest-numbered policy has the most secure parameters (like RSA signatures, AES encryption, SHA HMAC function, Diffie-Hellman key group 5, and a lifetime of 1 hour) and that the highest-numbered policy has the least-secure parameters (like pre-shared keys, DES encryption, MD5 HMAC function, Diffie-Hellman key group 1, and a lifetime of 1 day).

NOTE Normally, site-to-site connections do not travel through translation or firewall devices, and thus NAT-T and/or IPSec over TCP is not needed. However, if this is not the case, you'll need to configure these options on the appliance.

Tunnel Group Configuration

For a site-to-site connection, the tunnel group type must be "ipsec-l2l", where the "l2l" part is "L-2-L", not "one-two-one." Here's the syntax to create the tunnel group:

```
ciscoasa(config)# tunnel-group tunnel_group_ID type ipsec-l2l
```

Based on the identity type for ISAKMP Phase 1, you'll need to configure an appropriate tunnel group identifier. For example, if the identity type is "address," then the tunnel group identifier is the publicly reachable IP address of the remote peer; if the identity type is "hostname," then the group identifier is the fully qualified domain name of the remote peer, where this must be resolvable by either a static DNS entry (**name** command) or a DNS server.

No general attributes apply to L2L tunnel groups; however, there are IPSec-specific ones. Here's the syntax to configure the IPSec-specific tunnel group attributes for L2L connections:

```
ciscoasa(config)# tunnel-group peer_IP_addr ipsec-attributes
ciscoasa(config-tunnel-ipsec)# pre-shared-key key
ciscoasa(config-tunnel-ipsec)# peer-id-validate {cert | nocheck | req}
ciscoasa(config-tunnel-ipsec)# trust-point name_of_CA
ciscoasa(config-tunnel-ipsec)# isakmp keepalive threshold seconds
                               retry seconds
```

If you'll be using a pre-shared key, configure it in the tunnel group with the **pre-shared-key** command: the maximum length of the key is 128 characters. If you are using certificates, use the **peer-id-validate** command to specify their usage:

▼ **cert** If both peers support certificates and the use of certificates is negotiated during Phase 1, then certificates will be used; otherwise pre-shared keys will be used.

■ **nocheck** Certificates are not used with this tunnel group.

▲ **req** Certificates must be used with this tunnel group or the L2L tunnel will fail.

The **trust-point** command specifies the name of the CA to use—it indicates what identity certificate to use if more than one CA and identity certificate are installed on the appliance. The name specified here needs to match the name configured with the **crypto ca trust-point** command discussed in Chapter 15; however, this command is unnecessary if the appliance has only one root and identity certificate, since it will use these by default.

To enable Dead Peer Detection (DPD), use the **isakmp keepalive** command. The first threshold is the number of seconds between keepalives (10 to 3600), and the retry interval is how long the appliance should wait after the first keepalive is missed and the second one should be sent (2–10 seconds). DPD is disabled by default.

NOTE DPD sends keepalives across the management connection, allowing the appliance to detect a dead management connection. Because this is Cisco-proprietary, it should only be enabled for a tunnel group that has Cisco devices for remote peers.

VPN Traffic and Address Translation

If your appliance is performing address translation on addresses as traffic goes to the public network or you have the **nat-control** command configured, requiring address translation, you will probably want to exempt translation for the traffic traversing the

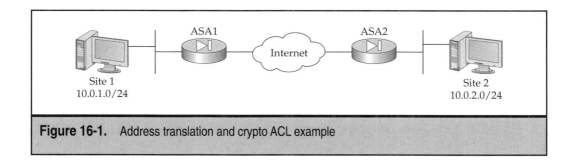

Figure 16-1. Address translation and crypto ACL example

site-to-site VPN; if you recall from Chapter 5, this is referred to as Identity NAT. The exception to this is an extranet L2L where there might be overlapping addresses between the two companies.

Use the following syntax to implement identity NAT for your intranet L2L traffic:

```
ciscoasa(config)# nat 0 access-list ACL_ID
```

In the ACL, use **permit** statements to exempt the site-to-site traffic—include both the source and destination addresses/networks.

As an example, examine the network shown in Figure 16-1. In this network, an Intranet IPSec L2L tunnel is being used, and address translation is not needed when traffic goes between the two sites. Here's the Identity NAT configuration for asa1 to exempt the traffic from translation:

```
asa1(config)# access-list ACLnonat permit ip 10.0.1.0 255.255.255.0
                                            10.0.2.0 255.255.255.0
asa1(config)# nat (inside) 0 access-list ACLnonat
```

ISAKMP PHASE 2 CONFIGURATION

This next section will focus on configuring the appliance so that the data connections, commonly called *security associations* (SAs), for an L2L connection can be built to a remote IPSec peer. You must complete three tasks:

▼ Configure a crypto ACL, which determines what data traffic is to be protected.

■ Create a transform set, which determines how the data traffic is to be protected.

▲ Create a crypto map entry for the remote peer, which brings all the parameters together for the associated peer.

The following sections will cover these required configurations, as well as optional ones.

NOTE   If you've configured these items on a Cisco IOS router before, then the syntax used by the appliances is either the same or very similar, making it easy to build IPSec L2L tunnels.

Crypto ACLs

Crypto ACLs are used to define what data traffic should be protected by the IPSec tunnel. Crypto ACLs are also used on Cisco IOS routers. Unlike a normal ACL, a crypto ACL doesn't filter traffic: it defines what data traffic (Phase 2) is or isn't protected by the IPSec tunnel. A `permit` statement in an ACL entry specifies traffic to be protected, and a `deny` statement (or the implicit deny) specifies traffic that should *not* be protected. You need to be as specific as possible when specifying the traffic that is to be protected…in other words, you definitely do not want to specify a source address and mask of `0.0.0.0` `0.0.0.0` (or `0  0` for short), because this means that *all* traffic coming into the IPSec interface on the appliance is expected to be protected. The appliance, in this situation, will drop all traffic that is not supposed to be protected, but based on your configuration, is expected to be protected, like Internet users' web traffic for your DMZ web server.

NOTE   For each remote site, you'll need a *separate* crypto ACL.

Crypto ACLs should be mirrored or symmetrical between the two peers. For example, if you have two networks, network A and network B, on the network A side the crypto ACL would be to protect traffic from A to B; however, on the network B side, the crypto ACL would be to protect traffic from B to A. Going back to Figure 16-1, here's the asa1 crypto ACL statement:

```
asa1(config)# access-list 102 permit ip 10.0.1.0 255.255.255.0
                                        10.0.2.0 255.255.255.0
```

And here's the asa2 crypto ACL statement:

```
asa2(config)# access-list 201 permit ip 10.0.2.0 255.255.255.0
                                        10.0.1.0 255.255.255.0
```

Notice that the network numbers are reversed in the two crypto ACLs.

TIP   If the crypto ACLs aren't mirrored between the two peers, you typically see a mismatched proxy condition in your logs or debug output. This indicates you have nonsymmetrical crypto ACLs on the two peers.

Transform Sets

A transform set defines the properties (transforms) as to how a data connection can be protected. A transform set has three parameters: two transforms and a mode. Here are the commands to create a transform set:

```
ciscoasa(config)# crypto ipsec transform-set set_name [{esp-3des |
                   esp-aes | esp-aes-192 | esp-aes-256 |
                   esp-des | esp-null}] [{esp-md5-hmac |
                   esp-sha-hmac | esp-none}]
ciscoasa(config)# crypto ipsec transform-set set_name mode
                   {tunnel | transport}
```

The first command defines how the data traffic is to be protected. You must give the transform set a locally significant name; in other words, the name you give the set doesn't have to match what is configured on the remote peer. The transform set name is followed by an encryption algorithm and/or an HMAC function, commonly called the *transforms*. The order that you enter the transforms doesn't matter. Notice that you don't have to use an encryption algorithm (**esp-null**) or an HMAC function (**esp-none**).

NOTE   You can have multiple transform sets for different peers—this is necessary if you have different peers with different capabilities. For example, you might have one peer that supports AES 256, but another that only supports 3DES. In this situation, you would need two transform sets for the two respective peers.

The second command defines the mode for the data connections. Data connections support two modes: tunnel and transport. Tunnel mode is used for L2L and remote access connections, and transport mode for point-to-point connections, like the appliance sending a syslog message to a syslog server. If you don't configure this second command, the mode defaults to **tunnel** for the data connections using this transform set. If you are using a point-to-point connection, then you would specify **transport** as the mode in the second command.

Connection Lifetimes

Optionally you can globally change the timeout values for your data SAs. (You can also override the global timeout on a peer-by-peer basis in a crypto map entry, discussed in the next section.) Once these timeouts are reached, the appliance will either rekey them or tear them down and rebuild the SAs.

Here's the syntax to change the global SA timers:

```
ciscoasa(config)# crypto ipsec security-association
                   lifetime seconds seconds
ciscoasa(config)# crypto ipsec security-association lifetime
                   kilobytes kilobytes
```

The default lifetimes are 3600 seconds (one hour) and 4,608,000KB of traffic sent across the SA. Changing the timeout values with the preceding commands affects only newly built SAs; existing SAs will use the timeout values that previously existed when the SAs were built.

Crypto Maps

A crypto map defines the parameters to build tunnels to peers. Each peer you want to build a tunnel to needs to be referenced as a separate entry in the crypto map. The entry binds together all of the necessary components to form an SA with a remote peer.

Crypto maps come in two varieties: *static* and *dynamic*. Static crypto maps are used when you know who you are connecting to, what traffic needs protecting, and how it should be protected. Static crypto maps are commonly used in L2L connections. Dynamic crypto maps are used when you don't know all three of these things. Dynamic crypto maps are most commonly used on a VPN gateway accepting IPSec remote access connections (I discuss this in Chapter 17).

An entry in a static crypto map must include the following information:

▼ The crypto ACL that defines which traffic is to be protected (encrypted/authenticated)

■ Which site you are connecting to (the identity of the peer at the remote site)

▲ What transform set should be used to protect your traffic to the remote peer

Other information can be configured in a crypto map, like the lifetime values of the data SAs and perfect forward secrecy (PFS), but these other configurations are optional.

Crypto Map Entries

This chapter only focuses on static crypto maps. To create an entry in a static crypto map, use the **crypto map** command. Typically you will only have one map that you will activate on the interface connected to the public network. However, if you have different divisions or companies that you are connecting with the appliance, you might need to create multiple maps, one for each interface. To distinguish one map from another, you give it a unique name. Crypto map names are locally significant and don't have to match between peers.

Here is the syntax for creating an entry in a static crypto map:

```
ciscoasa(config)# crypto map map_name entry_# match address ACL_ID
ciscoasa(config)# crypto map map_name entry_# set
                     transform-set set_name
ciscoasa(config)# crypto map map_name entry_# set
                     peer IP_address_or_name
ciscoasa(config)# crypto map map_name entry_# set
                     pfs {group1 | group2 | group5 | group7}
ciscoasa(config)# crypto map map_name entry_# set phase1-mode
                     {main | aggressive}
ciscoasa(config)# crypto map map_name entry_# set trustpoint
                     trustpoint_name
ciscoasa(config)# crypto map map_name entry_# set security-association
                     {seconds seconds | kilobytes kilobytes}
ciscoasa(config)# crypto map map_name entry_# set connection-type
                     {answer-only | bidirectional | originate-only}
```

A crypto map is made up of one or more entries. If you have more than one location you are connecting to, you'll need an entry for each location within the crypto map. For example, if you had three sites you were connecting to off the same interface, you would have three entries for the crypto map used on that interface. Each entry in a crypto map needs a unique *entry_#* or *priority number* (or what Cisco often refers to as a *sequence number*). This number is used to group together the parameters that will be used to negotiate an SA with a remote peer. If your crypto map has multiple entries, when the appliance is performing its negotiation, it always looks for the highest priority match between the policy information of each peer. The lower the number for the entry, the higher the priority, where 1 has the highest priority.

NOTE The configuration of crypto maps is slightly different on an appliance compared with an IOS router. On an appliance, all the `crypto map` commands are configured in global configuration mode. On IOS routers, each entry you create in the crypto map takes you into a subcommand mode where you complete the configuration for the associated peer. To activate the crypto map on a router, you perform this from interface subcommand mode.

You must specify the identity of the remote peer. Based on the configuration of the `crypto isakmp identity` command, you'll either enter the IP address or hostname of the remote peer with the `set peer` parameter. If you have two peers at a remote location, a primary and a backup, configure this command twice, where the first `set peer` parameter specifies the primary and the second the backup.

NOTE If you put both remote peers at a location in *separate* crypto map entries, the appliance can actually build two tunnels (one to each peer), instead of one.

Second, you must also specify which traffic is protected by referencing the crypto ACL that you previously created with the `match address` parameter in a crypto map entry. And third, you must reference the name of a transform set (or sets) in the `set transform-set` parameter in a crypto map entry. You can specify up to nine transform set names in one command—just list them one right after the other. You might need to reference more than one transform set name if you are unsure how the remote peer is configured for a transform set.

The rest of the parameters in a crypto map entry are optional. Optionally you can specify the use of Perfect Forward Secrecy (PFS). By default the keying information for the data connections (the keys for the encryption and HMAC functions) are shared across the existing protected management connection. PFS performs Diffie-Hellman (DH) a second time for the keying information for the data connections. If you want to use PFS for a peer, configure the `set pfs` parameter in a crypto map entry. When configuring this parameter, you need to specify the DH key group that will be used, which must match what the remote peer has configured.

NOTE The advantage of PFS is that it is more secure than the management connection; the disadvantage of PFS is that it slows the building of the data connections.

The optional **set phase1-mode** parameter specifies what mode should be used (aggressive or main) during ISAKMP Phase 1 when building the management connection to the peer. If you don't configure this value, main mode is used if certificates are used for authentication, and aggressive mode is used if pre-shared keys are used.

The optional **set trustpoint** parameter specifies the name of the CA trustpoint, and thus the identity certificate, to use if certificates are used during Phase 1 for authentication. Starting in version 7.0, the preferred method is to configure this within a tunnel group.

Optionally you can change the lifetimes for the data connections associated with this peer by configuring the **set security-association** parameter. The defaults are based on the configuration of the global timeout commands configured with the **crypto ipsec security-association lifetime**, discussed earlier.

The connection type, defined by the **set connection-type** parameter, allows you to control who initiates the tunnel—the default is bi-directional, where either peer can bring up the tunnel. The **answer-only** parameter forces the remote peer to establish the tunnel, and **originate-only** forces the local appliance to establish the tunnel.

NOTE If you change the parameters in a crypto map entry, the changes don't affect any existing data SAs—you must tear down the existing ones (or wait till they expire) before the changes take effect.

Crypto Map Activation

Once you have created your crypto map and its entries, you need to apply the crypto map to an interface on the appliance. This is accomplished with the **crypto map interface** command:

```
ciscoasa(config)# crypto map map_name interface logical_if_name
```

Typically the crypto map will be applied to the interface connected to the public network, like the **outside** interface. Once you apply the crypto map, the appliance will begin building tunnels and processing IPSec traffic. Also, you can only apply one crypto map to an interface. To view your crypto map commands, use the **show run crypto map** command.

NOTE Tunnels will not be built until traffic needs to be sent to a remote site that matches a crypto ACL associated with a crypto map entry.

SITE-TO-SITE VERIFICATION

Once you've configured your Phase 1 and Phase 2 commands, and traffic matches a crypto ACL entry destined for the remote peer, a tunnel is built, barring any misconfiguration or other issues. This section will show you how to view, tear down, and troubleshoot your

IPSec connections. Please note that these commands apply to all IPSec connections: L2L and remote access.

> **TIP**   One common entry to include in a crypto ACL is ICMP traffic associated with the two peers. This way performing a ping from one of the peers will attempt to bring the tunnel up.

Viewing and Clearing Connections

This section discusses how to view and tear down the Phase 1 management and Phase 2 data connections.

ISAKMP Phase 1: Management Connections

To view the Phase 1 management connections that you have established to remote peers, use the **show crypto isakmp sa** command:

```
ciscoasa# show [crypto] isakmp sa [detail]
```

Here is an example of viewing the management connections:

```
ciscoasa# show crypto isakmp sa
   Active SA: 1
   Rekey SA: 0 (A tunnel will report 1 Active and 1 Rekey SA during
         rekey)
Total IKE SA: 1
1   IKE Peer: 192.1.1.40
    Type    : L2L          Role    : responder
    Rekey   : no           State   : MM_ACTIVE
```

The State should be MM_ACTIVE (main mode) or AG_ACTIVE (aggressive mode) if the management connection is successfully built.

To tear down management connections, use the **clear crypto isakmp sa** command:

```
ciscoasa# clear [crypto] isakmp sa
```

ISAKMP Phase 2: Data Connections

To view all the IPSec data SAs that you have established to peers, use the **show crypto ipsec sa** command:

```
ciscoasa# show crypto ipsec sa [entry | identity | map map_name |
                    peer peer_IP_addr] [detail]
```

Here's an example of the use of this command:

```
ciscoasa# show crypto ipsec sa
interface: outside
```

```
Crypto map tag: mymap, local addr: 192.1.1.100
  local ident (addr/mask/prot/port): (192.168.2.0/255.255.255.0/0/0)
  remote ident (addr/mask/prot/port): (192.168.0.0/255.255.255.0/0/0)
  current_peer: 192.1.1.40

 #pkts encaps: 4, #pkts encrypt: 4, #pkts digest: 4
 #pkts decaps: 4, #pkts decrypt: 4, #pkts verify: 4
 #pkts compressed: 0, #pkts decompressed: 0
 #pkts not compressed: 4, #pkts comp failed: 0, #pkts decomp
     failed: 0
 #send errors: 0, #recv errors: 0

 local crypto endpt.: 192.1.1.100, remote crypto endpt.: 192.1.1.40
 path mtu 1500, ipsec overhead 76, media mtu 1500
 current outbound spi: 2ED644AD

inbound esp sas:
  spi: 0x76DFE868 (1994385512)
     transform: esp-aes esp-sha-hmac
     in use settings ={L2L, Tunnel, }
     slot: 0, conn_id: 1, crypto-map: mymap
     sa timing: remaining key lifetime (kB/sec): (4274999/3586)
     IV size: 16 bytes
     replay detection support: Y
outbound esp sas:
  spi: 0x2ED644AD (785794221)
     transform: esp-aes esp-sha-hmac
     in use settings ={L2L, Tunnel, }
     slot: 0, conn_id: 1, crypto-map: mymap
     sa timing: remaining key lifetime (kB/sec): (4274999/3584)
     IV size: 16 bytes
     replay detection support: Y
```

Every time you execute this command, if you see pkts information incrementing, then you have traffic traversing the tunnel. At the bottom, you see two sections—inbound and outbound esp sas. These are the two data connections built during Phase 2.

To tear down the data SA(s), use the **clear crypto ipsec sa** command:

```
ciscoasa# clear [crypto] ipsec sa [counters |
                  entry {hostname | ip_address} {esp spi |
                  map map_name | peer {hostname | ip_address}]
```

Troubleshooting Connections

For detailed troubleshooting of ISAKMP/IKE interaction with a remote peer, use the **debug crypto isakmp** command. This command displays the building of the Phase 1 and 2 connections:

```
ciscoasa# debug crypto isakmp [1-255]
```

If you omit the number at the end of the command, it defaults to "1," which displays a single message about the success or failure of the building of the tunnel. Specifying 255 is a complete hex dump of the packets. Specifying a number in the range of 100–150 gives you similar output to what you would find with this command on an IOS router. For troubleshooting of just the Phase 2 processes on the appliance, use the **debug crypto ipsec** command.

SITE-TO-SITE EXAMPLE

To help understand the configuration of L2L connections, let's look at an example. I'll use the network shown in Figure 16-2. I've broken the configuration into different parts to make it easier to understand. Here's the Phase 1 configuration for asa1 in this network:

```
asa1(config)# sysopt connection permit-vpn
asa1(config)# crypto isakmp policy 100
asa1(config-isakmp-policy)# authentication pre-share
asa1(config-isakmp-policy)# encryption aes
asa1(config-isakmp-policy)# group 2
asa1(config-isakmp-policy)# hash md5
asa1(config)# tunnel-group 201.201.201.1 type ipsec-l2l
asa1(config)# tunnel-group 201.201.201.1 ipsec-attributes
asa1(config-tunnel-ipsec)# pre-shared-key ASA2KEY
```

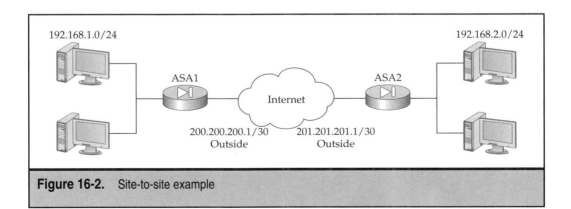

Figure 16-2. Site-to-site example

The first command exempts inbound IPSec traffic, once verified and decrypted, from ACL processing. The ISAKMP policy specifies the use of pre-shared keys, where the pre-shared key is configured in the tunnel group (case-sensitive). The tunnel group identifier is the IP address of the remote peer (asa2)—remember that the identity type defaults to "address."

The following is the Phase 2 configuration for asa1:

```
asa1(config)# access-list MATCH permit ip 192.168.1.0 255.255.255.0
                                          192.168.2.0 255.255.255.0
asa1(config)# nat (inside) 0 access-list MATCH
asa1(config)# crypto ipsec transform-set asa2transform
                      esp-sha-hmac esp-3des
asa1(config)# crypto map IPSECMAP 100 set peer 201.201.201.1
asa1(config)# crypto map IPSECMAP 100 match address MATCH
asa1(config)# crypto map IPSECMAP 100 set transform-set asa2transform
asa1(config)# crypto map IPSECMAP interface outside
```

The first part defines an ACL that is used for identity NAT as well as the crypto ACL. The second part creates a transform set. The third part creates and applies a crypto map. Notice that the crypto map entry specifies asa2 as the remote peer, the crypto ACL, and the transform set.

TIP If asa1 has connections to two sites, like asa2 and asa3, and you want traffic to flow from asa2, through asa1, to asa3, then you'll need to configure the **same-security-traffic permit intra-interface** command on asa1 to allow traffic to flow into and out of the same interface.

CHAPTER 17

IPSec Remote Access Server

Τhis chapter will show you how to set up an IPSec remote access server on an appliance using the Cisco Easy VPN feature. "Easy VPN" is a marketing term coined by Cisco that describes the setup process for remote access users: it's a fairly easy and simple process for a user to get a remote access IPSec tunnel up and running. The topics covered previously in Chapter 15 on ISAKMP Phase 1 apply to this chapter, as do some of the topics covered on site-to-site connections in Chapter 16. The topics covered in this chapter include

▼   Preparing your appliance as an Easy VPN server to allow IPSec remote access traffic

■   Configuring parameters for the ISAKMP Phase 1 management connection, including Phase 1 policies, group policies, and tunnel groups

■   Configuring parameters for the ISAKMP Phase 2 data connections, including dynamic and static crypto maps

■   Verifying your remote access connectivity

■   Viewing an example configuration of an Easy VPN server

▲   Load balancing remote access user connections by setting up a cluster of Easy VPN servers

EASY VPN OVERVIEW

Cisco security appliances have supported Easy VPN IPSec remote access connections since version 6 of the operating system. "Easy VPN" describes the deployment of IPSec remote access VPNs.

I'll use Figure 17-1 to illustrate the components of Easy VPN. With Easy VPN connections, a remote access client, commonly called an *Easy VPN remote* (the PC in this example), is assigned an internal IP address so that it appears the remote is located on the internal network at the corporate site. A tunnel is between 64.1.1.1 and 201.201.201.1 (the Easy VPN server), and the remote uses ESP tunnel mode to encapsulate IP packets to the corporate network. For the ESP connection, the actual IP addresses of the two Easy VPN devices (remote and server) are used. However, for communications between the client and the internal resources, the client creates an IP packet with the internal addressing for the source and destination—this will be encapsulated and protected in the ESP packet between the remote and the server.

NOTE   The premise behind IPSec remote access is to make it look like the remote/client is a logical extension of the corporate network. If you notice in Figure 17-1, the physical IP address (64.1.1.1) of the remote is assigned by the ISP, but when the remote needs to communicate with corporate devices, the remote uses its internal address in a packet that is tunneled to the Easy VPN server. For example, the first IP packet created by the user will have a source address of 172.16.254.1, which is protected by ESP with an outer IP header that has an address of 64.1.1.1. Once this is received by the Easy VPN server, the outer header is stripped off. The corporate office sees the remote as 172.16.254.1—part of the corporate office network.

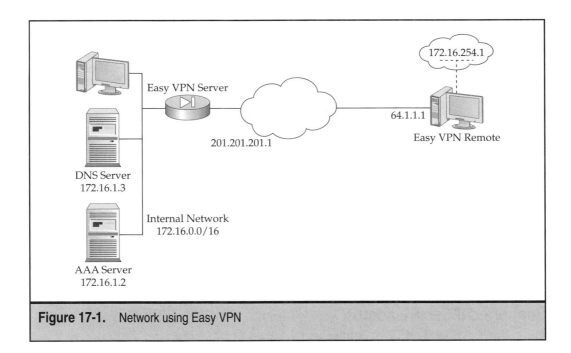

Figure 17-1.   Network using Easy VPN

According to the IPSec standard, only two components are defined for remote access:

▼   Performing a second level of authentication, called XAUTH or user authentication

▲   Assigning an internal address to the remote access client

The Cisco Easy VPN server can authenticate the remote via XAUTH by using either a local database or an AAA server. Plus, the server can assign policy information to the client, like addressing information, firewall policies, split tunneling policies, and many, many other policies (this is discussed later in the "Group Policy Configuration" section).

NOTE   You'll notice that the list of policies an Easy VPN server can assign to a remote goes beyond what the IPSec standard supports. Therefore, Cisco remote clients are only compatible with Cisco Easy VPN server products. This is also true of each vendor's IPSec remote access product, since they all add their own proprietary policy information.

Easy VPN Products

Easy VPN is a Cisco solution that provides for consistent policy and key management for your remote access devices. It accomplishes this by centralizing the administration of your IPSec remote access solution by configuring policies on the server and pushing these to the remotes during the tunnel establishment process. If you use centralized policies, your changes to policies only have to be made on the servers, simplifying your administration. The two components of Easy VPN are

▼   **Servers**   These devices have policies defined on them that are pushed to clients during tunnel establishment. Cisco servers can be ASAs and PIXs, IOS routers, and 3000 concentrators.

▲   **Remotes**   These devices build IPSec remote access connections to servers. Cisco supports software and hardware remotes. Software remotes can be installed on Windows, Linux, Solaris, and the Mac OS X operating systems. Cisco also supports third-party software clients for hand-held devices like smart phones. Hardware clients include the VPN 3002, the PIX 501 and 506E, the ASA 5505, and the 800 through 3800 series IOS routers.

Easy VPN Features

Even though Easy VPN supports the IPSec standards, Cisco has added many of its own features, and it places restrictions on the IPSec standards that are supported. The following two sections will discuss these items.

Supported IPSec Standards

The following are items Cisco supports that are part of the IPSec standard:

▼   **Encryption algorithms**   DES, 3DES, and AES (NULL is supported for data connections)

■   **HMAC functions**   MD5 and SHA

■   **Device authentication methods**   RSA signatures (certificates) and pre-shared keys

■   **Diffie-Hellman (DH) key groups**   2, 5, and 7

■   **Data connections**   ESP in tunnel mode, LZS compression, and PFS

■   **User authentication**   XAUTHv6

▲   **IKE Mode Config v6**   Assigning internal IP addresses to remotes

As you can see from the preceding list, not all IPSec standards are supported—AH, transport mode, and the DH key group 1, to name a few.

Cisco Additional Features

Cisco has added many, many features to enhance the security, administration, and flexibility of IPSec remote access. Some of the features of Easy VPN include the following:

▼   **Centralized policies**   Policies are pushed to remotes, ensuring a uniform security policy that users can't override.

■   **Group policy control**   You control what attributes are assigned to a user or group of users, like IP addresses, DNS and WINS server addresses, and split tunneling policies.

- **Control of split tunneling** Split tunneling controls what traffic is or isn't protected by the tunnel. By default the Easy VPN server forces the client to tunnel all user traffic to the server; you can ease this restriction and define split tunneling policies for your users, which your server downloads to the remote and which the remote enforces.

- **Dead Peer Detection (DPD)** DPD allows the servers and remotes to detect when the other peer is no longer there, like when a remote has its dialup connection disconnected or is rebooted. This allows the Easy VPN devices to remove the tunnel and, for remotes, try a backup server.

- **Initial contact** If a remote becomes unexpectedly disconnected from a server and attempts to reestablish a connection to the server, the server will remove the old tunnel and allow a new one to be built.

These are just some of the features of Easy VPN. This and the next chapter will expand upon these features.

Easy VPN Connectivity

Unlike site-to-site connections that go through three steps in Phase 1 to build a management connection (negotiate the policies, DH, and device authentication), with Easy VPN, peers can go through a total of seven steps. Here are the seven steps Easy VPN can take when setting up the management connection during Phase 1:

- **Step 1** The remote initiates the connection. During this initiation, the remote is configured for either pre-shared keys or certificates for authentication. If pre-shared keys are used, then Phase 1 will use aggressive mode; if certificates are used, then Phase 1 will use main mode.

- **Step 2** The remote sends a list of preconfigured Phase 1 policies. These are defined in the Easy VPN remote software by Cisco, which the user and administrator have no control over. This information includes which DH key group, authentication method (pre-shared or certificates), HMAC functions, and encryption algorithms to use. This process reduces the configuration on the remote since users don't have to worry about the policies; however, on the server, you must have at least one policy that matches. The server compares them in the order sent with the numerical order configured on the appliance. Therefore, the most secure policy on the appliance should have the lowest priority number assigned to it.

- **Step 3** Diffie-Hellman (DH) is performed. The remote generates the keys for the encryption and HMAC function, protects them, and sends them to the server.

- **Step 4** The two devices authenticate each other based on the authentication method configured/negotiated—pre-shared keys or certificates.

- **Step 5**   The Easy VPN server performs XAUTH (user authentication). This is a second level of authentication, since the pre-shared key or certificate is stored on the remote, which can present a security issue. This step is optional, but highly recommended—if someone steals a user's laptop, for instance, the thief couldn't bring up the tunnel unless he knew the user's username and password. The Easy VPN server can authenticate the user by using the server's local database or can forward the authentication information to an AAA server for authentication.

- **Step 6**   The server uses IKE Client or Mode Config to download policy and configuration information to the remote. The IPSec standard only defines how to assign addressing information to the remote. Cisco supports many other policy and configuration parameters that you can optionally assign to the remote.

- **Step 7**   In the last step of Phase 1, the Reverse Route Injection (RRI) process can optionally take place. This is a Cisco-proprietary feature. With RRI, the server creates a static route for the internal IP address (a host route) that was assigned to the remote. This can be advertised by the server to internal routers and devices so that they know which Easy VPN server a particular remote is connected to.

NOTE   Phase 2 for Easy VPN goes through the same basic setup process as Phase 2 for site-to-site connections. Also, for a better understanding of the Easy VPN process, you can check my book *The Complete Cisco VPN Configuration Guide* (Cisco Press, 2005), which covers the Easy VPN process in-depth.

REMOTE ACCESS PREPARATION

Before you begin setting up an Easy VPN server on your appliance, you should first go through some basic preparation by determining the following:

- ▼ How the management connection should be protected for the remotes
- ■ The authentication method used: pre-shared keys or certificates
- ■ What groups you'll need to create and what policies should be associated with each group
- ■ How the data connections will be protected
- ▲ What interface(s) Easy VPN connections will terminate on

TIP   If you'll be using certificates for authentication, make sure that the Organizational Unit (OU) or Department field on the remote identity certificate contains the name of the user's group, which is case-sensitive. If you don't do this, you'll have to use certificate matching, discussed in Chapter 15, to individually map each user to a specific group, which is neither an administrator-friendly, nor scalable, process.

VPN Traffic

As I mentioned in Chapter 16 with site-to-site connections, if you want to allow the IPSec data traffic to traverse from a lower- to a higher-level interface, you'll either need to have ACL entries within the external ACL to allow the data traffic, or exempt all VPN traffic from ACL processing with the **sysopt connection** command:

```
ciscoasa(config)# sysopt connection permit-vpn
```

Also, if you have split tunneling disabled (the default), this means that all remote access traffic has to come to the appliance first, before it goes anywhere else, including the Internet. In this case, the appliance by default drops traffic that enters and leaves the same interface. To allow this behavior, configure this command:

```
ciscoasa(config)# same-security-traffic permit intra-interface
```

This command was discussed in Chapter 3.

VPN Traffic and Address Translation

If your appliance is performing address translation on addresses as traffic goes to the public network, or you have the **nat-control** command configured, requiring address translation, you will probably want to exempt the internal addresses assigned to users from translation. If you recall from Chapter 5, this is referred to as Identity NAT.

Use the following syntax to implement Identity NAT for your remote internal addresses:

```
ciscoasa(config)# nat 0 access-list ACL_ID
```

In the ACL, use **permit** statements to exempt the remote access traffic. The source addressing information in the ACL should be the corporate office networks behind the appliance and the destination addressing information the internal addresses assigned to the user.

As an example, examine the network shown previously in Figure 17-1. In this network, I'll assume an internal address pool of 172.16.254.0/24 is being used for the remotes. Here's the Identity NAT configuration for Easy VPN server to exempt the traffic from translation:

```
server(config)# access-list ACLnonat permit ip
                       172.16.0.0 255.255.0.0
                       172.16.254.0 255.255.255.0
server(config)# nat (inside) 0 access-list ACLnonat
```

Tunnel Limits

Even though your appliance might support thousands of VPN tunnels, you might want to set up restrictions to ensure that other types of traffic are not adversely affected based on a large number of IPSec tunnels terminated on the appliance. To see the VPN limits on your appliance, use the **show version** command:

```
ciscoasa# show version
Cisco Adaptive Security Appliance Software Version 7.1(0)182
<--output omitted-->
VPN Peers : 750
WebVPN Peers : 500
<--output omitted-->
```

In the preceding example, the appliance is an ASA 5520 with the VPN Plus license, which supports 750 IPSec tunnels (L2L and remote access).

To limit the number of VPN sessions (tunnels), use the following command:

```
ciscoasa(config)# vpn-sessiondb max-session-limit number_of_sessions
```

NOTE The **vpn-sessiondb max-session-limit** command applies to both L2L and remote access tunnels, but is used more often to limit the number of remote access connections, since they are dynamic in nature.

ISAKMP PHASE 1 CONFIGURATION

Unlike with site-to-site connections, you need to configure a lot more for Phase 1 for Easy VPN connections. The following sections will cover the basic ISAKMP Phase 1 commands, the group policy commands, and the tunnel group commands for Easy VPN.

TIP My recommendation is that the first few times you need to set up an Easy VPN server, you use ASDM instead of the CLI. ASDM supports a wizard that greatly simplifies the setup of the Easy VPN server. ASDM is discussed in Chapter 27.

ISAKMP Phase 1 Commands

Here is a quick synopsis of the ISAKMP Phase 1 commands you need to build the management connection for remote access users:

```
ciscoasa(config)# crypto isakmp enable logical_if_name
ciscoasa(config)# crypto isakmp policy policy_number
ciscoasa(config-isakmp-policy)# authentication {pre-share | rsa-sig |
                                crack}
ciscoasa(config-isakmp-policy)# encryption {3des | aes | aes-192 |
                                aes-256 | des}
ciscoasa(config-isakmp-policy)# group {2 | 5 | 7}
ciscoasa(config-isakmp-policy)# hash {md5 | sha}
ciscoasa(config-isakmp-policy)# lifetime {seconds | none}
```

These commands were discussed in Chapters 15 and 16. IPSec is typically enabled on the outside interface (connected to the Internet) with the `crypto isakmp enable` command. You'll need at least one matching ISAKMP policy with the Easy VPN remotes. Remember that the policy number is important: this is the order in which the appliance processes the policies for the remote peer during the Phase 1 negotiation. Therefore, make sure the lowest-numbered policy has the most-secure parameters and the highest-numbered policy has the least-secure parameters. A couple things to point out about a policy for remotes:

▼ You can't use DH key group 1—Cisco doesn't support it for Easy VPN. The default DH group is 2.

▲ DH key group 7 is commonly used for hand-held devices like smart phones and PDAs.

Unlike L2L connections, with remote access, the remote might actually be located behind an address translation and/or firewall device. Thus, the remotes might need to use NAT-T or IPSec over TCP, which are implemented with the following two commands (discussed in Chapter 15):

```
ciscoasa(config)# crypto isakmp nat-traversal [seconds]
ciscoasa(config)# crypto isakmp ipsec-over-tcp {[port prt_#]...[prt_#]}
```

Group Policy Configuration

Group policies are used on the appliances to associate specific policies to remote access tunnel groups: IPSec and/or WebVPN. A policy can be shared among multiple tunnel groups if certain groups have similar policies. Policies can be defined locally on the appliance or on an external AAA server using the RADIUS communications protocol. Typically local authentication is used if you have a very small number of appliances. However, if you are using the load balancing feature (discussed in the "VPN Load Balancing" section later), the group policies are typically centralized on an AAA RADIUS server(s).

A default policy called *DfltGrpPolicy* has default policy values associated with it. You can use this policy (and edit it) and/or create your own policies. Some examples of policies you can define in a policy group include the domain name of the group, split tunneling, DNS and WINS server addresses, idle and session timeouts, where the internal addresses for the remotes are chosen, and many, many others.

Group Policy Location

Group policies can be defined locally on the appliance (internal) or on an AAA server (external). For local policies, you can inherit policies from an existing group policy on the appliance to initially establish the parameters for a new group policy and then change the policies as needed within the new group policy.

External Group Policies   When defining an external group policy, you must set up the AAA server and AAA communications protocol and reference the server tag, along with the server password (encryption key):

```
ciscoasa(config)# aaa-server group_tag protocol {tacacs+ | radius}
ciscoasa(config)# aaa-server group_tag (logical_if_name)
                      host AAA_server_IP_address AAA_encryption_key
                      [timeout value_in_seconds]
ciscoasa(config-aaa-server-host)# server-port port_number
ciscoasa(config-aaa-server-host)# key encryption_key
ciscoasa(config-aaa-server-host)# timeout seconds
```

The AAA server commands were discussed previously in Chapter 8.

To specify that a particular group policy is located on an AAA server, use the following command:

```
ciscoasa(config)# group-policy policy_name external
                      server-group group_tag
```

To the external AAA server, the external group-policy name (*policy_name*) is a user with an associated password on the AAA server. Also, the *group_tag* you specify here has to match a *group_tag* in an **aaa-server** command.

NOTE   The configuration of IPSec group policies on an AAA server is beyond the scope of this book.

Local Group Policies   For a very small number of appliances, like one or two, I would more likely define the group policies on the appliance itself. To create a group policy on the appliance, use the following command:

```
ciscoasa(config)# group-policy policy_name internal
                      [from group_policy_name]
```

Optionally you can inherit the policy attributes from another group policy that already exists on the appliance.

TIP   If two policies are very similar, after creating the first one, use the **from** option in the preceding command to inherit the policy attributes from the first group policy to the second. Then go in and modify the second group policy attributes as needed.

Group Policy Attributes

Assuming you are creating local group policies, once you define the policy name with the **group-policy** *policy_name* **internal** command, you can then associate the policies, commonly called *attributes,* to your new policy. Here are the commands to configure a policy attribute for an internal group:

```
ciscoasa(config)# ip local pool pool_name
                      beginning_IP_addr-ending_IP_addr
                      [mask subnet_mask]
ciscoasa(config)# group-policy policy_name attributes
ciscoasa(config-group-policy)# address-pools value pool_name1
                      [...pool_name6]
ciscoasa(config-group-policy)# dhcp-network-scope subnet_number
ciscoasa(config-group-policy)# default-domain value domain_name
ciscoasa(config-group-policy)# dns-server value IP_addr1 [IP_addr2]
ciscoasa(config-group-policy)# wins-server value IP_addr1 [IP_addr2]
ciscoasa(config-group-policy)# backup-servers {[IP_addr1]
                      [...IP_addr10] | clear-client-config
                      | keep-client-config}
ciscoasa(config-group-policy)# banner {exec | login | motd} message
ciscoasa(config-group-policy)# client-access-rule rule_#
                      {permit | deny}
                      type client_type version version_info
ciscoasa(config-group-policy)# client-firewall {none |
                      opt firewall_name
                      | req firewall_name}
ciscoasa(config-group-policy)# group-lock value tunnel_group_name
ciscoasa(config-group-policy)# intercept-dhcp [subnet_mask] enable
ciscoasa(config-group-policy)# ip-comp {enable | disable}
ciscoasa(config-group-policy)# ip-phone-bypass {enable | disable}
ciscoasa(config-group-policy)# ipsec-udp {enable | disable}
ciscoasa(config-group-policy)# ipsec-udp-port port_#
ciscoasa(config-group-policy)# leap-bypass {enable | disable}
ciscoasa(config-group-policy)# msie-proxy method {auto-detect |
                      no-modify | no-proxy | use-server}
ciscoasa(config-group-policy)# msie-proxy server value name_or_IP
ciscoasa(config-group-policy)# msie-proxy except-list value
                      IP_address/name [...IP_address/name]
ciscoasa(config-group-policy)# msie-proxy local-bypass
                      {enable | disable}
ciscoasa(config-group-policy)# nac {enable | disable}
ciscoasa(config-group-policy)# nac-default-acl value ACL_ID
ciscoasa(config-group-policy)# nac-reval-period seconds
ciscoasa(config-group-policy)# nac-sq-period seconds
ciscoasa(config-group-policy)# nem {enable | disable}
ciscoasa(config-group-policy)# password-storage {enable | disable}
ciscoasa(config-group-policy)# secure-unit-authentication
                      {enable | disable}
```

```
ciscoasa(config-group-policy)# user-authentication {enable | disable}
ciscoasa(config-group-policy)# user-authentication-idle-timeout minutes
ciscoasa(config-group-policy)# pfs {enable | disable}
ciscoasa(config-group-policy)# re-xauth {enable | disable}
ciscoasa(config-group-policy)# split-tunnel-policy {excludespecified |
                                  tunnelall | tunnelspecified}
ciscoasa(config-group-policy)# split-tunnel-network-list value ACL_ID
ciscoasa(config-group-policy)# split-dns value domain_name
                                  [domain_name...]
ciscoasa(config-group-policy)# vpn-access-hours value time_range_name
ciscoasa(config-group-policy)# vpn-filter value ACL_ID
ciscoasa(config-group-policy)# vpn-idle-timeout minutes
ciscoasa(config-group-policy)# vpn-session-timeout {none | minutes}
ciscoasa(config-group-policy)# vpn-simultaneous-logins #_of_sessions
ciscoasa(config-group-policy)# vpn-tunnel-protocol {[ipsec]
                                  [l2tp-ipsec] [webvpn]}
```

As you can see from the preceding listing, you can assign quite a few policy attributes to a group policy. The following paragraphs will briefly cover these attributes.

Cisco Easy VPN remotes can get their internal addresses from either a local address pool on the appliance or from a DHCP server (via the appliance). Creating a local pool of addresses is done with the `ip local pool` command, which is then referenced in the group policy with the `address-pools` command. A policy can have up to six pools of addresses associated with it.

If you are not using a local pool of addresses, you need to assign internal addresses from a DHCP server. The actual DHCP server is defined in the tunnel group (see the "General Tunnel Group Attributes" section later in the chapter). The network number that is sent to the DHCP server is defined in the group policy with the `dhcp-network-scope` command. This helps the DHCP server to determine which pool of addresses it should use when picking an unused one for a remote access user.

You can assign a default domain name to the remote access user with the `default-domain` command. This overrides any domain name currently assigned to the user's TCP/IP protocols stack until the tunnel is terminated.

You can assign up to two DNS server addresses to connecting clients with the `dns-server` command. This overrides any DNS server settings currently assigned to the user's TCP/IP protocols stack until the tunnel is terminated.

If you are using WINS for Windows name resolution, you can override the WINS server settings on the remote when the tunnel is up with the `wins-server` command. This overrides any WINS server settings currently assigned to the user's TCP/IP protocols stack until the tunnel is terminated.

By default an Easy VPN remote only needs to understand one Easy VPN server to connect to; once the remote is connected, you can have the server push down other server addresses for redundancy. You can assign up to ten additional Easy VPN server addresses as backups with the `backup-servers` command. You can also clear any existing backup server list on the remote (`clear-client-config` parameter), or keep any existing list on the remote (`keep-client-config` parameter).

You can define a login banner for the Easy VPN remotes with the `banner` command. The banner cannot exceed 256 characters.

The `client-access-rule` command restricts what client versions are allowed when connecting to the Easy VPN Server. The type and version information are strings that must match exactly in their appearance in the output of the `show vpn-sessiondb` command; you can, however, use the asterisk character ("*") as a wildcard.

For Windows remotes, you can define firewall policies that the user must meet. This feature is a precursor to network access control (NAC), but is still commonly used if you don't want to purchase an AAA server or a NAC appliance to set up NAC. With a firewall policy in the `client-firewall` command, you can specify that no firewall is necessary (`none`), a firewall is optional (`opt`), or a firewall is required (`req`); for the latter two options, you need to specify the firewall that is to be used on the user's Windows computer. This feature is called *Are You There* (AYT). With this feature, the Windows IPSec software remote checks every 30 seconds to see if the firewall is installed and operational. When `req` is chosen and the firewall is not there and operational, the IPSec client tears down the VPN tunnel, and the user sees a notification message. If you configure the `opt` parameter, the tunnel is allowed to remain up, but the user sees a notification message about the recommended firewall. Table 17-1 has a list of supported firewalls and their parameters.

You can restrict what group a user connects to with the `group-lock` command.

Firewall Parameter	Firewall
`cisco-integrated`	Cisco Integrated Client Firewall (this is a DLL that ships with the client)
`cisco-security-agent`	Cisco Security Agent
`custom`	Custom Firewall
`networkice-blackice`	Network ICE BlackICE Defender
`sygate-personal`	Sygate Personal Firewall
`sygate-personal-pro`	Sygate Personal Firewall Pro
`sygate-security-agent`	Sygate Security Agent
`zonelabs-integrity`	Zone Labs Integrity
`zonelabs-zonealarm`	Zone Labs ZoneAlarm
`zonelabs-zonealarmorpro`	Zone Labs ZoneAlarm or ZoneAlarm Pro
`zonelabs-zonealarmpro`	Zone Labs ZoneAlarm Pro

Table 17-1. Supported Firewalls and Their Parameters

The `intercept-dhcp` command is used by Microsoft L2TP/IPSec clients and allows the appliance to intercept the DHCP requests from these clients and forward them to a DHCP server.

You can enable LZS software compression of tunneled data traffic with the `ip-comp` command. You should only enable this feature for remote access groups that use dialup modems. The Easy VPN remote also has to enable LZS compression before compression can be performed.

The `ip-phone-bypass` command is used when user authentication is enabled for users behind hardware remotes, like the ASA 5505 (discussed in Chapter 18). When user authentication is enabled for users behind a hardware client, each user must authenticate to use the tunnel. Some devices, like IP phones, can't. Configuring this command allows Cisco IP phones to be exempt from the user authentication process. When this feature is enabled, the hardware client looks at the source MAC address to determine if it is a Cisco IP phone.

SECURITY ALERT! The problem with the IP phone bypass feature is that since the range of MAC addresses used by Cisco IP phones is well known, attackers could change their MAC address to fall in this range and bypass authentication.

You can enable Cisco proprietary IPSec over UDP (`ipsec-udp` and `ipsec-udp-port`), a precursor to NAT-T, to allow users associated with this policy to always encapsulate ESP packets in a UDP payload. IPSec over UDP was the first Cisco commercially available solution to tunnel ESP traffic in UDP payloads, getting around issues with address translation and firewall devices. If you enable this feature for a policy, the default UDP port number used is 10000, which you can change to a port number from 4001 to 49151, except for 4500, which is reserved for NAT-T.

TIP It is recommended to use NAT-T rather than IPSec over UDP since NAT-T uses a discovery process to determine if the UDP encapsulation of ESP is necessary.

The LEAP bypass feature, configured with the `leap-bypass` command, is used only by hardware clients implementing user authentication when wireless devices, using LEAP to pass EAP information to an AAA RADIUS server, need to pass through the hardware client. Since user authentication is being performed, and LEAP must occur before this process, this command exempts LEAP devices from user authentication. Actually, 802.1x (which is implementing LEAP) is in the process of performing user authentication, and the EAP information needs to be forwarded across the tunnel to the AAA server. So even though this command is exempting user authentication with the hardware client, it is still being done via 802.1x to an AAA server.

The `msie-proxy` commands allow you to have the Windows IPSec software remote modify the proxy setting for Microsoft Internet Explorer. You can autodetect a proxy, use the user's current configuration, or specify a server that should be used. You can even have certain web traffic bypass the proxy.

Starting in version 7, the appliances support NAC. NAC policies define criteria a user's computer must meet to connect to the network, like the user must be running a certain vendor's firewall and/or antivirus software, with a minimal version of each. NAC policies are defined on an AAA server or NAC appliance. With IPSec remote access, NAC is configured in a group policy with the `nac` command. You can enable NAC for a group policy (`nac enable`), specify an ACL to use for NAC users (`nac-default-acl`), how often the user device has to be reevaluated via NAC (300 to 86,400 seconds, where 3600 is the default in the `nac-reval-period` command), and the status query timer (300 to 1800 seconds, where 300 is the default in the `nac-sq-period` command).

Hardware remotes have two modes they can use to connect to an Easy VPN server: client and network extension modes (these are discussed in more depth in Chapter 18). Network extension mode (NEM) is disabled by default. For hardware remotes that need to use NEM, the group policy associated with their tunnel group must have this feature enabled. This is accomplished with the `nem enable` command.

By default XAUTH user passwords cannot be stored on remotes unless you allow it with a policy on the appliance. This feature prevents someone from stealing or hacking into a corporate computer and then bringing up a tunnel without providing any additional authentication credentials. If you want to override this behavior and allow XAUTH usernames and passwords to be stored locally on a remote, then configure the `password-storage` command. This command is necessary for hardware clients when using default unit authentication (discussed in Chapter 18); however, I highly recommend that you *not* enable this feature for software remotes.

For hardware clients, if you enable secure unit authentication (SUA) with the `secure-unit-authentication` command, the username's password for XAUTH is erased on the hardware client, and someone behind the hardware client must provide the XAUTH information in order to bring up the tunnel. SUA is discussed in Chapter 18.

For hardware remotes, you can enable user authentication, which requires each user *behind* the hardware remote to authenticate in order to use the tunnel. This feature is enabled with the `user-authentication` command. The default idle timeout for authenticated users is 30 minutes, but can range from 1 to 35,791,394 minutes (`user-authentication-idle-timeout`). User authentication is discussed in more depth in Chapter 18.

By default, perfect forward secrecy (PFS), which performs DH again during Phase 2, is not used by Easy VPN remotes. You can allow its use by configuring the `pfs` command. The advantages and disadvantages of PFS were discussed in Chapter 16.

When the data connection lifetime expires (the ESP connections), rekeying occurs by default, but not re-authentication of the remote. You can force re-authentication with the `re-xauth` command.

Split tunneling defines what traffic from the user must go across the tunnel and what traffic can leave the client in clear text. Split tunneling policies are defined with the `split-tunnel-policy` command. The default split-tunneling policy is `tunnelall`, which means that, with the exception of DHCP and ARP packets, all traffic from the remote must go across the tunnel. You can exclude networks from being tunneled (`excludespecified` parameter) or include networks that should only be tunneled (`tunnelspecified` parameter). When overriding the default split tunneling policy, you must use the `split-tunnel-network-list` command to specify what destination networks are (`tunnelspecified`) or are not tunneled (**excludespecified**). These are defined in an extended or standard ACL. For a standard ACL, the addresses or networks you enter are addresses that the remote is trying to reach (destination addresses). For an extended ACL, the addresses off of the higher-level interface of the appliance (corporate office networks) are the source addresses in an ACL statement, and the destination addresses are the internal addresses of the remotes.

TIP   If you allow split tunneling, then I recommend that you set up a firewall or NAC policy and require the remote to have a firewall installed to protect the user from clear-text traffic.

When split tunneling is enabled, you can enable split DNS. The domain names listed after the **split-dns** command, separated by spaces, will be resolved by the DNS server listed in the group policy configuration. Any other domain name will be resolved by the DNS server locally configured or dynamically acquired by the user's computer.

You can set up quite a few access restrictions for Easy VPN remotes in a group policy. The **vpn-access-hours** command references a time range that controls when remotes can connect to the appliance (time ranges were discussed in Chapter 6). The **vpn-filter** command specifies an ACL that restricts traffic coming from the user, out of the tunnel, and through the appliance—the appliance uses the ACL to determine what traffic it will allow from the remote. The **vpn-idle-timeout** command specifies how long a user's data connections can be idle before the tunnel is terminated (30 minutes by default). You can also control how long a user can remain connected (idle or not) with the **vpn-session-timeout** command; by default there is no limit unless an idle timer is used. The **vpn-simultaneous-logins** command limits the number of VPN sessions allowed for a user account. The **vpn-tunnel-protocol** command controls the type of remote access VPN(s) a user can set up to the appliance; by default there are no restrictions. So as you can see from this long list of policies, you are provided with many options.

User Accounts and Attributes

User accounts used for XAUTH are typically found in one of three locations:

- ▼   Locally on the appliance
- ■   On an AAA server
- ▲   On another device associated with an AAA server, like an Active Directory, NDS, or token card server, to name a few

In medium to larger networks, it is more common to define the user accounts using the latter two options just listed. Only for small networks are locally defined users on the appliance implemented.

Local User Accounts   If you will be defining user accounts on the appliance itself that should be used when performing XAUTH, then you'll need to create the accounts with the **username** command:

```
ciscoasa(config)# username name password password privilege 0
```

This command is discussed in more depth in Chapter 26.

SECURITY ALERT! For non-administrator appliance accounts, make sure the privilege level is 0, which ensures that remote access users can't access the appliance itself!

Local User Attributes For certain users, you might want to override some of the group policies that they inherit from the tunnel group they are associated with. This can be done locally on the appliance by creating user attributes with the following commands:

```
ciscoasa(config)# username name attributes
ciscoasa(config-username)# vpn-access-hours value time_range_name
ciscoasa(config-username)# vpn-filter value ACL_ID
ciscoasa(config-username)# vpn-idle-timeout minutes
ciscoasa(config-username)# vpn-session-timeout {none | minutes}
ciscoasa(config-username)# vpn-simultaneous-logins #_of_sessions
ciscoasa(config-username)# vpn-tunnel-protocol {[ipsec] [l2tp-ipsec]
                                [webvpn]}
ciscoasa(config-username)# password-storage {enable | disable}
ciscoasa(config-username)# vpn-group-policy policy_name
ciscoasa(config-username)# vpn-framed-ip-address IP_addr subnet_mask
```

All of the commands, except the last two, were discussed in the "Group Policy Attributes" section previously in this chapter. The **vpn-group-policy** command allows you to override the tunnel group policy with a different group policy for the user—this is not commonly done. The **vpn-framed-ip-address** command is used to assign an internal address to the remote. This is normally used for hardware remotes, like the ASA 5505, where you always want to assign the same internal IP address to the remote so that you can manage the hardware remote through the tunnel. In other words, since you're always assigning the same IP address, you know what IP address to connect to when using telnet, SSH, and/or ASDM.

Tunnel Group Configuration

As I mention in Chapter 15, tunnel groups are used to classify L2L and remote access traffic so that policies can be more easily applied and administered. To create an IPSec remote access tunnel group on the appliance, use the following command:

```
ciscoasa(config)# tunnel-group group_name type remote-access
```

The name of the tunnel group is the name of the remote access group. If users are using pre-shared keys for authentication, they'll need to configure this case-sensitive name in their remote software. If users will be using certificates, then this name should appear in the OU/Department field of their identity certificate, since this is what the appliance looks at by default when matching a user to a group when certificates are used. If you didn't match the OU name with the tunnel group name, you can use certificate matching to associate the user to the correct group. This was discussed in Chapter 15.

The type of the group must be **remote-access**, for IPSec remote access. The next two sections will discuss the general and IPSec-specific attributes you can associate with your IPSec remote access group.

General Tunnel Group Attributes

General tunnel group attributes are attributes that having nothing to do with the VPN technology itself. These include attributes like where users and their password for the group are found, where the policies for the group are found, what internal addresses should be used to assign to remote access users, and other non-IPSec attributes.

Once you've created the remote access tunnel group (see the preceding section), you can then assign general attributes to it using the following configuration:

```
ciscoasa(config)# tunnel-group group_name general-attributes
ciscoasa(config-tunnel-general)# authentication-server-group
                        [(logical_if_name)] [server_tag]
                        [LOCAL]
ciscoasa(config-tunnel-general)# override-account-disable
ciscoasa(config-tunnel-general)# authorization-server-group
                        [(logical_if_name)] server_tag
ciscoasa(config-tunnel-general)# accounting-server-group server_tag
ciscoasa(config-tunnel-general)# authorization-required
ciscoasa(config-tunnel-general)# default-group-policy policy_name
ciscoasa(config-tunnel-general)# address-pool [(if_name)]
                        pool_name1 [...pool_name6]
ciscoasa(config-tunnel-general)# dhcp-server IP_addr1 [...IP_addr10]
ciscoasa(config-tunnel-general)# nac-authentication-server-group
                        server_tag
ciscoasa(config-tunnel-general)# password-management
                        [password-expire-in-days days]
ciscoasa(config-tunnel-general)# strip-group
ciscoasa(config-tunnel-general)# strip-realm
```

If the user accounts that are to be authenticated during XAUTH are on an AAA server, you'll have to define the AAA server and protocol with a server tag and reference the server tag in the remote access tunnel group with the **authentication-server-group** command. The **LOCAL** keyword tells the appliance to look for the user accounts locally, defined by the **username** command. If you don't specify the method of authentication, local authentication is used.

The **override-account-disable** command is applicable only if the tunnel group is using AAA authentication: if the AAA server says the account is disabled, you can override that setting on the appliance and still use that account for XAUTH authentication.

If the group policies are defined on an AAA RADIUS server, use the **authorization-server-group** command to reference the correct AAA server tag. In this and the latter command, you can control when these commands are used based on the interface the VPNs are terminated on. For example, on one interface you could use one server tag, but on a different interface a different server tag, and thus possibly a different AAA server.

The `accounting-server-group` command allows you to forward AAA accounting records to an AAA server—this is only applicable if at least AAA authentication is being performed for the tunnel group.

The `authorization-required` command is only applicable if an AAA server is being used. When this feature is enabled, the user must be allowed remote access/dialup access on the AAA server, otherwise the user won't be able to build tunnels to the appliance.

NOTE   To use authorization and/or accounting, you must have the AAA server perform authentication.

If you are defining the group policies on the appliance locally, use the `default-group-policy` command to reference the name of the group policy to use for the remote access users in this tunnel group. If you don't define a group policy in a tunnel group, the default group policy called *DfltGrpPolicy* is used.

There are two options for assigning internal addresses to client mode connections, including the software remotes:

▼   Using a local address pool, which can be referenced in either a group policy or a tunnel group (the latter with the `address-pool` command)

▲   Using an external DHCP server

With the latter option, you must specify the network number to be forwarded to the server in the group policy (discussed previously in the "Group Policy Attributes" section). In the tunnel group configuration, the `dhcp-server` command specifies up to ten DHCP servers to forward the network number to in order to request an internal address for the remote device.

The `nac-authentication-server-group` command specifies the AAA server to forward NAC information to from the Cisco Trust Agent on the software remote. NAC policies cannot be defined on the appliance itself, but on an AAA server or NAC appliance.

For local user accounts on the appliance itself, you can enable password management with the `password-management` command. This feature allows users to change their password configured on the appliance. Optionally you can set an expiration date for the local users' password, which, once reached, forces the users to change their password. This period can range from 0 to 180 days, where 0 says never to expire.

The `strip-group` and `strip-realm` commands are needed for user authentications by the Microsoft L2TP/IPSec client, where the username and group are sent together, like john@doe. In this situation, the "@doe" part would be stripped off, and only the "john" part would be used for XAUTH user authentication. As you can see from this list of general attributes, none of these apply to site-to-site connections; they're all for remote access users.

IPSec Tunnel Group Attributes

IPSec-specific attributes for a tunnel group only apply to the IPSec process itself. These are configured using the following commands:

```
ciscoasa(config)# tunnel-group group_name ipsec-attributes
ciscoasa(config-tunnel-ipsec)# pre-shared-key key
ciscoasa(config-tunnel-ipsec)# peer-id-validate {cert | nocheck | req}
ciscoasa(config-tunnel-ipsec)# trust-point name_of_CA
ciscoasa(config-tunnel-ipsec)# isakmp keepalive threshold seconds
                                   retry seconds
ciscoasa(config-tunnel-ipsec)# isakmp ikev1-user-authentication
                                   {none | xauth | hybrid}
```

The configuration of the IPSec attributes for a remote access group is basically the same as that for an L2L connection, discussed in Chapter 16. If you don't put in a pre-shared key for the group, the assumption is that certificates are being used for authentication. The one difference between L2L and remote access is the last command. By default, XAUTH authentication is assumed. You can disable XAUTH authentication by using the **none** parameter in the **isakmp ikev1-user-authentication** command (not recommended). The **hybrid** parameter implements hybrid authentication: the user uses a tunnel group name and pre-shared key to authenticate, while the appliance uses a certificate to authenticate.

Auto Update

Auto update is a Cisco-proprietary feature that ensures that Easy VPN remotes have the most recent software installed. Auto update is a policy defined on your Easy VPN server that is pushed down in ISAKMP Phase 1 during Mode Config, telling the remotes what version or versions of software they should be running, and if they are not running the correct version, where to download and install it from. The Windows, Linux, and MAC software clients as well as the ASA 5505 and VPN 3002 hardware clients support auto update.

Auto Update Configuration

Enabling client updates is a two-step process:

1. Turn the feature on.
2. Define where the software is located and the recommended version(s) the client should be running.

To enable the auto update feature, execute the **client-update enable** command:

```
ciscoasa(config)# client-update enable
```

Then use the **client-update** command to specify the clients, the version(s) of software that they should be running, and the URL that the most current software release can be downloaded from:

```
ciscoasa(config)# client-update {component {asdm | image} |
                    device-id dev_string | family family_name |
                    type type} url url-string rev-nums rev-nums}
```

or

```
ciscoasa(config)# tunnel-group group_name ipsec-attributes
ciscoasa(config-tunnel-ipsec)# client-update ...
```

The **client-update** command can be configured globally (affects all remotes) or for a particular IPSec remote access tunnel group (overrides the global setting). Table 17-2 shows the parameters for the command.

Parameter	Description
component {asdm | image}	The software component on the client that should be upgraded.
device-id	If the auto update client is configured to identify itself with a unique string, you can specify the string that the client uses.
family	If the auto update client is configured to identify itself by a device family, you can specify the device family that the client uses, like "asa" or a text string up to 7 characters in length.
type	Specifies the operating systems of the Easy VPN remotes. Some examples include **asa5505**, **linux**, **mac**, **windows**, **win9x** (95, 98, ME), **winnt** (Windows NT 4.0, Windows 2000, and Windows XP platforms), and **vpn3002**.
rev-nums	Specifies the software or firmware images for the specified client. For Windows, Win9x, WinNT, and VPN 3002 clients, enter up to four revision numbers, in any order, separated by commas. For the 5505, only one revision number is allowed.
url	Specifies the URL for the software/firmware image update; this is typically HTTP or HTTPS and cannot exceed 255 characters in length; the exception is the 3002—it uses TFTP. The server location can be across the IPSec tunnel, which is the preferred location.

Table 17-2. Parameters for the `client-update` Command

When clients connect, they'll get the auto update information during Mode Config. You can notify currently connected clients with the `client-update` command, sending a notice to all connected clients or to a particular tunnel group.

```
ciscoasa(config)# client-update {all | group_name}
```

Auto Update Example

To help illustrate how to configure auto update, here's a simple configuration example:

```
ciscoasa(config)# client-update enable
ciscoasa(config)# tunnel-group engineering ipsec-attributes
ciscoasa(config-tunnel-ipsec)# client-update type windows url
                    https://10.0.1.10/support/updates/vpnclient.exe
                    rev-nums 4.6.1
ciscoasa(config-tunnel-ipsec)# exit
ciscoasa(config)# tunnel-group hwclients ipsec-attributes
ciscoasa(config-tunnel-ipsec)# client-update type asa5505 component
                    asdm url
                    http://10.0.1.10/support/updates/asdm601.bin
                    rev-nums 6.0(1)
```

The preceding example shows two auto update policies: one for the engineering group for the Windows Cisco VPN Client and one for the ASA5505 for its ASDM image.

ISAKMP PHASE 2 CONFIGURATION

The configuration of Phase 2 to allow the setup of the data connections is much simpler than what I just described for Phase 1. You'll need to configure three components: transform sets, a dynamic crypto map entry, and a static crypto map. The following two sections cover these three components.

Dynamic Crypto Maps

With static crypto map entries, you have to define a transform set, who the peer is, and a crypto ACL. Unfortunately that won't work with remote access, since remotes commonly acquire their addresses dynamically, and you don't know what traffic should be protected until you learn what tunnel group and what group split-tunneling policy the user is associated with.

Because of these limitations, Cisco created dynamic crypto maps. Dynamic crypto maps are used when you don't know those three items; that is, used most commonly on an Easy VPN server. Like static maps, dynamic crypto maps have entries in them; however, for remote access, you typically need only one entry to accommodate all your remote access users. When creating a dynamic crypto map entry, you only need to configure one item: a transform set.

First, you need to create a transform set with the `crypto ipsec transform-set` command:

```
ciscoasa(config)# crypto ipsec transform-set set_name [{esp-3des |
                  esp-aes | esp-aes-192 | esp-aes-256 |
                  esp-des | esp-null}] [{esp-md5-hmac |
                  esp-sha-hmac | esp-none}]
```

I discussed this command in Chapter 16.

Second, you need to create a dynamic crypto map. This is done with the `crypto dynamic-map` command:

```
ciscoasa(config)# crypto dynamic-map dynamic_map_name seq_#
                  set transform-set transform_set_name1
                  [...transform_set_name6]
ciscoasa(config)# crypto dynamic-map dynamic_map_name seq_#
                  set reverse-route
```

You must give the dynamic crypto map a name that is unique among all dynamic crypto maps—the name is locally significant. The map needs at least one entry in it, which is associated with a sequence number. All commands in the map that have the same sequence number are associated with the same entry.

Since I'm focusing on IPSec remote access, I'll only cover two of the parameters you can configure for an entry. The `set transform-set` parameter specifies up to six transform sets that can be used to protect the Phase 2 data connections: at least one of these has to match the string of transform sets the remote will be sending to the appliance.

To enable RRI, use the `set reverse-route` parameter. This will place the remote internal addresses as static routes in the appliance routing table. Optionally you can redistribute these to internal devices via RIP, OSPF, or EIGRP. Redistribution was discussed in Chapter 4.

 NOTE Redistribution is necessary when you are doing load balancing (discussed later in the "VPN Load Balancing" section). Otherwise, if you only have one appliance, use static routes on the internal devices, and point them to the appliance to reach the remote internal addresses.

Static Crypto Maps

To activate a dynamic crypto map, you need to embed it as an *entry* within a static crypto map:

```
ciscoasa(config)# crypto map static_map_name high_seq_#
                  ipsec-isakmp dynamic dynamic_map_name
ciscoasa(config)# crypto map static_map_name interface logical_if_name
```

Make sure you give the entry a sequence number higher than all the L2L connections—you don't want an L2L connection inadvertently using the dynamic map reference. The static map is then applied to the interface of the appliance.

Note that when remote access users connect and match on the dynamic crypto map entry in the static map, a dynamic, temporary entry is created in the static crypto map with the IPSec information related to that particular user. So if you had ten L2L tunnels up, and five remote access users connected, you would have a total of 15 entries in your static map (5 of which were dynamically built). If a remote user disconnects, the temporary entry for the specified remote user is then removed.

REMOTE ACCESS VERIFICATION

This section will discuss how to verify remote access connectivity to your appliance when it is acting as an Easy VPN Server. The commands I discussed in Chapter 16 also apply here (**show crypto isakmp sa, show crypto ipsec sa, debug crypto isakmp,** and so on); however, I'll cover some additional ones in this chapter.

Viewing Remote Access Connections

To view the remote access connections terminated on your appliance, use the following commands:

```
ciscoasa# show vpn-sessiondb summary
ciscoasa# show vpn-sessiondb [detail] [full] {remote | l2l |
            index indexnumber | webvpn | email-proxy}
            [filter {name username | ipaddress IP_addr |
            a-ipaddress IP_addr | p-ipaddress IP_addr |
            tunnel-group group_name | protocol protocol_name |
            encryption encryption_algorithm}] [sort {name |
            ipaddress | a-ipaddress | p-ipaddress |
            tunnel-group | protocol | encryption}]
```

These commands can be used for all remote access connections: IPSec, L2TP/IPSec, and WebVPN. With the second command, you can narrow down what connections you want to see, making it easier to find a particular connection.

Here is an example of the session summary output from the preceding command:

```
ciscoasa# show vpn-sessiondb summary
Active Sessions:                 Session Information:
IPSec LAN-to-LAN : 0             Peak Concurrent : 0
IPSec Remote Access : 0          IPSec Limit : 750
WebVPN : 0                       WebVPN Limit : 500
SSL VPN Client (SVC) : 0         Cumulative Sessions : 0
Email Proxy : 0
```

```
Total Active Sessions : 0     Percent Session Load : 0%
                              VPN LB Mgmt Sessions : 0

<--output omitted-->
```

In the preceding example, you can see that there are no active sessions as well as see the total VPN connection limits on the appliance.

Here's an example of displaying one connection:

```
ciscoasa# show vpn-sessiondb detail index 1
Session Type: Remote Detailed
Username    : dealr
Index            : 1
Assigned IP      : 172.16.254.5   Public IP      : 201.1.1.1
Protocol   : IPSec            Encryption  : AES128
Hashing    : SHA1
Bytes Tx   : 0                Bytes Rx   : 604533
Client Type      : WinNT         Client Ver  : 4.6.00.0049
Tunnel Group      : administrator
Login Time  : 15:22:46 EDT Tue May 10 2005
Duration    : 7h:02m:03s
Filter Name       :
NAC Result  : Accepted
Posture Token: Healthy
VM Result   : Static
VLAN  : 10
IKE Sessions: 1 IPSec Sessions: 1 NAC Sessions: 1
IKE:
Session ID  : 1
UDP Src Port: 500 UDP Dst Port : 500
IKE Neg Mode: Aggressive    Auth Mode   : preSharedKeysXauth
Encryption  : 3DES             Hashing    : MD5
Rekey Int (T): 86400  Seconds Rekey Left(T): 61078 Seconds
D/H Group   : 2
IPSec:
Session ID  : 2
Local Addr  : 0.0.0.0
Remote Addr : 172.16.254.5
Encryption  : AES128             Hashing: SHA1
Encapsulation: Tunnel     Rekey Int (T): 28800
Seconds Rekey Left(T): 26531 Seconds
Bytes Tx    : 0            Bytes Rx : 604533
Pkts Tx     : 0            Pkts Rx  : 8126
<--output omitted-->
```

In the preceding example, the `dealr` user from the `administrator` tunnel group has an IPSec connection established. This user is using the Windows 4.6 software client. Notice that NAC has been enabled and that this user has passed the NAC posture tests. Pre-shared keys were used for authentication, and the Phase 1 connection is protected with 3DES and MD5. The user was assigned an internal address of 172.16.254.5. The data connections are protected with AES-128 and SHA-1.

Disconnecting Remote Access Users

To disconnect a remote access user, use the following command:

```
ciscoasa# vpn-sessiondb logoff {remote | l2l | webvpn | email-proxy
            protocol protocol_name | name username |
            ipaddress IP_addr | tunnel-group group_name |
            index index_number | all}
```

You can disconnect all users from a particular type of access, a particular user based on username or index number (see the output of the **show vpn-sessiondb** command), a user's IP address, all users in a particular tunnel group, or all the users.

IPSEC REMOTE ACCESS SERVER EXAMPLE

To help illustrate how to configure an appliance as an Easy VPN server, I'll use the network shown in Figure 17-2. One tunnel group will be set up with local authentication. A local address pool is used for the internal addresses of the group, with addresses ranging from 10.0.1.224 to 10.0.1.254. I'll break up the configuration into separate parts to make it easier to read and explain.

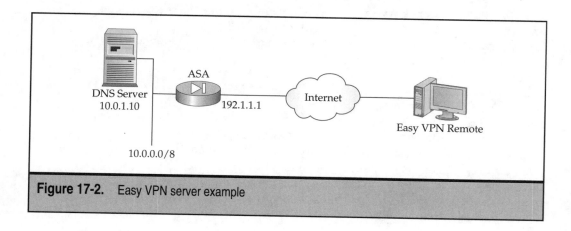

Figure 17-2. Easy VPN server example

Here's the first part of the Easy VPN server configuration:

```
ciscoasa(config)# sysopt connection permit-vpn
ciscoasa(config)# crypto isakmp enable outside
ciscoasa(config)# crypto isakmp nat-traversal 30
ciscoasa(config)# crypto isakmp policy 10
ciscoasa(config-isakmp-policy)# authentication pre-share
ciscoasa(config-isakmp-policy)# encryption 3des
ciscoasa(config-isakmp-policy)# group 2
ciscoasa(config-isakmp-policy)# hash sha
ciscoasa(config-isakmp-policy)# lifetime 3600
```

The ACL bypass feature is enabled with the **sysopt** command. I've enabled ISAKMP on the outside interface of the appliance. NAT-T is enabled with the **crypto isakmp nat-traversal** command, using a keepalive interval of 30 seconds on the data connections. ISAKMP/IKE policy 10 defines how the management connection is protected, where pre-shared keys will be used for authentication.

Here's the group policy configuration for the Easy VPN server:

```
ciscoasa(config)# group-policy eng_policy internal
ciscoasa(config)# group-policy eng_policy attributes
ciscoasa(config-group-policy)# default-domain value cisco.com
ciscoasa(config-group-policy)# dns-server value 10.0.1.10
ciscoasa(config-group-policy)# vpn-idle-timeout 15
ciscoasa(config-group-policy)# exit
```

The policy is called *eng_policy* and has a domain name and DNS server assigned with an idle timeout of 15 minutes for user inactivity.

Here's the tunnel group configuration for the Easy VPN server:

```
ciscoasa(config)# ip local pool eng_pool 10.0.1.224-10.0.1.254
                     mask 255.255.255.0
ciscoasa(config)# access-list ACLnonat permit ip 10.0.0.0 255.0.0.0
                     10.0.1.224 255.255.255.224
ciscoasa(config)# nat (inside) 0 access-list ACLnonat
ciscoasa(config)# tunnel-group engineers type ipsec-ra
ciscoasa(config)# tunnel-group engineers type general-attributes
ciscoasa(config-tunnel-general)# authentication-server-group LOCAL
ciscoasa(config-tunnel-general)# default-group-policy eng_policy
ciscoasa(config-tunnel-general)# address-pool eng_pool
ciscoasa(config)# tunnel-group engineers ipsec-attributes
ciscoasa(config-tunnel-ipsec)# pre-shared-key thisISaSECRET
ciscoasa(config-tunnel-ipsec)# isakmp keepalive threshold 30 retry 5
ciscoasa(config-tunnel-ipsec)# exit
ciscoasa(config)# username richard password mysecret privilege 0
```

I've created a local address pool and exempted it from address translation. The tunnel group, "engineers," is a remote access tunnel group. The general attributes specify that authentication is done locally (the user account is defined at the bottom of the list), the policy to use ("eng_policy"), and the addresses to use for the remote internal addresses ("eng_pool"). The IPSec attributes for the tunnel group define the pre-shared key to use for authentication and enable DPD with a keepalive interval of 30 seconds.

The following is the Phase 2 configuration for the Easy VPN server:

```
ciscoasa(config)# crypto ipsec transform-set eng_trans
                     esp-3des esp-md5-hmac
ciscoasa(config)# crypto dynamic-map dyn_map 1 set
                     transform-set eng_trans
ciscoasa(config)# crypto dynamic-map dyn_map 1 set reverse-route
ciscoasa(config)# crypto map stat_map 10000 ipsec-isakmp
                     dynamic dyn_map
ciscoasa(config)# crypto map stat_map interface outside
```

A transform set has been created, called *eng_trans,* and it's referenced in a dynamic crypto map ("dyn_map") entry, along with RRI. The dynamic crypto map is then embedded in a static crypto map ("stat_map"), and the static map is activated on the appliance *outside* interface.

NOTE   Based on the number of commands and the chance of missing something in the configuration, most administrators prefer using ASDM to at least initially set up an Easy VPN server on the appliance, and then use the CLI to change and manage it.

VPN LOAD BALANCING

Load balancing is a Cisco-proprietary feature that allows a cluster of Easy VPN servers to logically appear as one server to all the remotes. Load balancing is done on a connection-by-connection basis, not on a traffic or packet-by-packet basis. In other words, as remotes request VPN connections, these connections are spread across multiple members of the cluster, where each cluster member is solely responsible for the connections assigned it. So load balancing in this sense is not a true form of load balancing, but does split the remote access client connections across multiple cluster members.

Not all remote access protocols, servers, and clients are supported, however. For remote access protocols, IPSec and WebVPN are supported; PPTP and L2TP are not. And within IPSec, only Easy VPN connections are supported: site-to-site connections are not. For server products, the ASA 5510s and higher, as well as the 3000 concentrators, support load balancing; IOS routers and the PIX appliances do not. The Cisco VPN software client for IPSec and the AnyConnect Client v2.0 and higher for WebVPN are supported, as well as the VPN 3002, PIX 501 and 506E, and the ASA 5505 hardware clients.

Clustering Overview

There are four components to load balancing VPN connections:

▼ Cluster

■ Master

■ Client or remote

▲ Load calculation

A cluster is a group of ASA security appliances and/or 3000 VPN concentrators. The cluster is identified by a single virtual IP address, shown in Figure 17-3. When clients make a connection to the cluster, they connect to the virtual IP address, which would be 192.1.1.4 in Figure 17-3. The virtual IP address must be an unused address in the subnet the external interfaces of the cluster members are connected to. One cluster member is elected as the master of the cluster, and it will handle the inbound remote access IPSec and WebVPN AnyConnect connection requests.

For ISAKMP Phase 1 connections, the client makes the initial connection to the virtual IP address, and the master will process the initial connection attempt. The master will look at the load of each cluster member and choose the one that has the least load. Load is calculated by taking the number of active VPN sessions on a member and dividing it by the total that the member supports. Given this formula, load is not a true calculation of load, like the amount of traffic or CPU utilization of a member. However, given this formula, members that support more connections will end up with more connections, and members that support fewer connections will end up with fewer connections, so the connections are distributed based on the capabilities of the members.

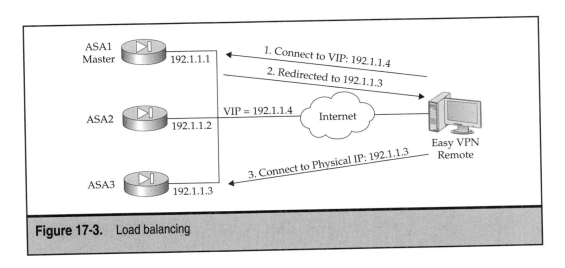

Figure 17-3. Load balancing

NOTE To elect a master and to share load information, the cluster members need to communicate with each other. Cisco uses a proprietary protocol called the *Virtual Cluster Agent* (VCA) that uses UDP and connects to port 9023 by default. This protocol is also used as a keepalive mechanism to discover new and dead members.

The master will then redirect the connecting client to the physical IP address of the cluster member with the least load. Physical addresses are IP addresses assigned to the cluster members on their external interfaces; in Figure 17-3, the physical addresses are 192.1.1.1, 192.1.1.2, or 192.1.1.3. Note that during the redirection process, if the master has the least load, the redirection will take place to the master's physical IP address. Because the redirection process in Phase 1 is proprietary to Cisco, only Cisco clients will understand it.

TIP For unsupported clients like Microsoft L2TP/IPSec or IPSec L2L peers, point them to a physical IP address of one of the members—not the virtual address of the cluster. By using this approach, you can take advantage of the features of clustering for Cisco IPSec remote access and AnyConnect clients while still being able to support other devices.

One of the main advantages of clustering is load balancing, as I previously mentioned; however, clustering does have other advantages. Since the cluster is represented by a single IP address, the clients only need to know the virtual address to establish a tunnel to the corporate site. And assuming that you are using DPD, which allows clients to discover dead servers, a client can reconnect to the master and redirect the client to an active cluster member with the least load.

Clustering Configuration

Configuring load balancing is straightforward. Here are the commands to configure load balancing:

```
ciscoasa(config)# vpn load-balancing
ciscoasa(config-load-balancing)# interface lbpublic logical_if_name
ciscoasa(config-load-balancing)# interface lbprivate logical_if_name
ciscoasa(config-load-balancing)# cluster ip address virtual_IP_address
ciscoasa(config-load-balancing)# priority number
ciscoasa(config-load-balancing)# nat IP_address
ciscoasa(config-load-balancing)# cluster port port_number
ciscoasa(config-load-balancing)# cluster encryption
ciscoasa(config-load-balancing)# cluster key shared_secret_key
ciscoasa(config-load-balancing)# participate
```

The **vpn load-balancing** command takes you into a subcommand mode to set up clustering. The **interface lbpublic** command specifies the logical name of the external interface, and the **interface lbprivate** command specifies the internal interface (required). These two interfaces will generate VCA messages periodically as a discovery and keepalive mechanism. The **cluster ip address** command specifies the virtual

IP address of the cluster (required). The virtual IP address must be an unused IP address in the subnet of the *lbpublic* interface.

The `priority` affects who becomes the master. The priority can range from 1 to 10. The member with the highest priority becomes the master. If no priority is configured, it defaults to 1 on the ASAs. This is untrue on the VPN 3000 concentrators: the lower-end models have a smaller priority, and the higher-end models have a higher priority. Because of how the VPN 3000 concentrators calculate load, they calculate it incorrectly for ASAs running 7.1 and higher. Therefore, it is recommended to have an ASA as the master in this situation.

If the addresses on the public interfaces of the cluster members are RFC 1918 addresses, including the virtual IP address, you'll need to set up static translations on a layer 3 device in front of the cluster members for each of the physical IP addresses as well as the virtual IP address. Whatever public address is used as the virtual IP address in this situation, it must be denoted as a translated address with the `nat` command.

If you don't change the port number for VCA communications, it defaults to UDP 9023. This can be changed with the `cluster port` command. However, if you change the port number on one member, you must make the same change on every member of the cluster.

TIP If you want to set up two clusters in the same subnet, changing the port number in one set logically separates the two clusters. Clients then need to know a virtual IP address in either of the clusters to connect, and then load balancing will occur within the connected cluster.

Optionally you can encrypt the VCA messages by configuring an encryption key. This is done with the `cluster key` command. Encryption is disabled by default. If you enable encryption, the key you use must be the same on each cluster member.

The last command just listed, `participate`, enables load balancing on the ASA. Once enabled, it will generate VCA messages on the *lpublic* and *lprivate* interfaces to discover other cluster members and to participate in load balancing.

Clustering Example

I'll use the network shown previously in Figure 17-3 to illustrate how `cluster` is configured. In the following example, I'm setting up the master, which is ASA1:

```
ciscoasa(config)# vpn load-balancing
ciscoasa(config-load-balancing)# interface lbpublic outside
ciscoasa(config-load-balancing)# interface lbprivate inside
ciscoasa(config-load-balancing)# cluster ip address 192.1.1.4
ciscoasa(config-load-balancing)# priority 10
ciscoasa(config-load-balancing)# cluster encryption
ciscoasa(config-load-balancing)# cluster key VCAsecretKEY
ciscoasa(config-load-balancing)# participate
```

For other cluster members, probably the only difference in their configuration will be the priority that you configure, which should be smaller than the master priority.

CHAPTER 18

IPSec Remote Access Client

This chapter rounds out the discussion on IPSec, focusing on Easy VPN remote access clients. The topics discussed in this chapter include

▼ Connection modes that Easy VPN remotes use

■ ASA 5505 remote client use and configuration

▲ An easy VPN configuration example using the 5505 as a hardware client

 NOTE Because of space constraints in this book, I cannot cover the Cisco Easy VPN software client—the Cisco VPN Client; however, my book *The Complete Cisco VPN Configuration Guide* (Cisco Press, 2005) covers this client in-depth.

CONNECTION MODES

Easy VPN uses connection modes for Easy VPN remotes to establish tunnels to an Easy VPN server. Easy VPN supports three client mode connections:

▼ Client mode

■ Network extension mode

▲ Network extension plus mode

The connection modes are illustrated in Figure 18-1. The latter two modes are proprietary to Cisco. The following three sections will discuss each of these modes in more depth.

 NOTE One restriction with remote access connections is that the remote can have only one tunnel up at a time.

Client Mode

In client mode, when the Easy VPN remote connects to the server during Phase 1 Mode Config process, an internal address is assigned to the remote. When the remote wants to send traffic through the tunnel to the corporate office, it will create an IP packet with the internal address as the source and with a destination IP address of a corporate office device behind the Easy VPN server. This packet is encapsulated and protected by ESP (Encapsulation Security Protocol). An outer header is added, with a source IP address of the client public interface (NIC) and a destination address of the Easy VPN server.

Software clients like the Cisco VPN Client only support client mode. However, hardware remotes (like the ASA 5505) support all three modes. When you are using client mode on a hardware remote, the hardware remote is still assigned an internal IP address. However, the problem this creates is that devices connected to the private interface(s) of

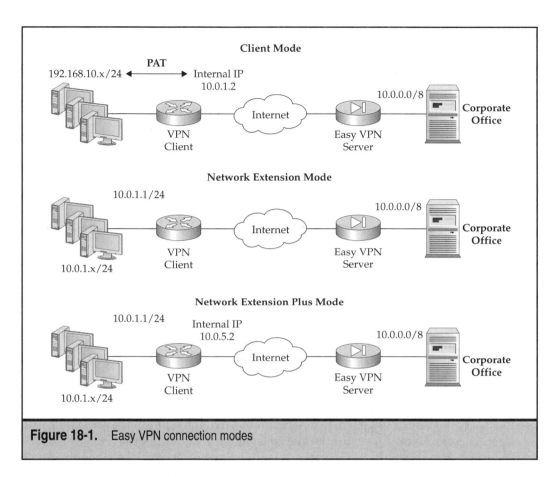

Figure 18-1.   Easy VPN connection modes

the hardware remote need to get traffic across the tunnel, not the hardware remote (at least not typically).

To solve this problem, a hardware remote like the ASA 5505 will PAT the source addresses of the private interface devices to the internal address assigned to it by the Easy VPN server. This is illustrated in the top part of Figure 18-1. The internal devices have addresses in the 192.168.10.0/24 subnet, and the internal IP address assigned to the hardware remote is 10.0.1.2. The hardware remote will PAT the 192.168.10.0/24 addresses to the 10.0.1.2 address. One nice feature of this process, and why Cisco refers to this as Easy VPN, is that you don't have to configure the PAT or ACL rules on the hardware remote to allow this process to occur: if you enable Easy VPN with client mode, the hardware remote automatically configures these rules! From the corporate office perspective, all the remote office traffic looks like it's coming from a single IP address (10.0.1.2).

NOTE   With client mode connections, the hardware remote will only bring up the tunnel to the corporate office when traffic needs to leave its public interface; it will then bring up the tunnel to determine the split tunneling policy of the group the hardware remote belongs to.

Here are some important things you should be aware of concerning client mode connections for hardware remotes. First, and this is a big advantage, every site can use the same subnet for their addressing, which conserves address space. This is possible since the addresses of the internal devices are being translated using PAT to a unique internal IP address. Second, and this is the main downside of client mode, the remote office devices must initiate connections to the corporate office. Corporate office devices, on the other hand, can't initiate connections to the remote office devices behind the hardware remote, since all the remote office devices are represented by a single internal IP address.

NOTE   Client mode is typically used when you're short of address space or you don't need corporate office devices initiating connections to remote office devices. For example, if you have a VoIP implementation, client mode would not work since phones at the corporate office wouldn't be able to establish connections to the remote office phones.

Network Extension Mode

If you recall from the last section, when a hardware remote uses client mode, it is assigned an internal IP address and PATs private interface traffic to the internal address before protecting the packets and forwarding them to the corporate office through the IPSec tunnel. With network extension mode, an internal address is not assigned to the hardware remote and PAT doesn't take place. An example of network extension is shown in the middle of Figure 18-1.

Given this scenario, each location that uses network extension mode must have a unique network number assigned to devices connected to the hardware remote private interface. Therefore, you'll need to take into consideration the additional IP address space needed for each remote office. However, the advantage of network extension mode is that since all devices—corporate and remote office—have unique IP addresses, connections can be set up in *both* directions.

One minor problem this poses is that the hardware remote might be acquiring its addressing dynamically, so the Easy VPN server wouldn't know what address to connect to in order to reach a site if a corporate office device needed to connect to a remote office device. To solve this problem, the Easy VPN remote will bring up the tunnel once its public interface acquires an IP address and is operational. For that matter, if the remote were ever to lose the tunnel to the Easy VPN server, it would continually try to bring up the tunnel until it succeeded.

If you have more than one Easy VPN server, for either redundancy or load balancing, the corporate office users won't know which server to send their traffic to so that it gets to the correct remote office. To solve this problem, you'll need to enable RRI on the server, which was discussed in Chapter 17. With RRI enabled, at the end of Phase 1 the hardware remote will take the network number or numbers associated with its internal/private interface(s) and share these with the server. By default the server will place these as static routes in its local routing table. You can then set up redistribution to redistribute the static routes via a local routing protocol (OSPF or EIGRP), solving your corporate office reachability dilemma.

 NOTE Network extension mode is commonly used when corporate office devices, like VoIP phones or management stations, need to access remote office devices.

Network Extension Plus Mode

Network extension plus mode, shown in the bottom part of Figure 18-1, is basically the same as network extension mode, except that the Easy VPN server *does* assign an internal address to the remote; however, this address is not used to perform PAT for internal addresses. Internal addresses (the remote inside network numbers) are sent natively across the tunnel; so, just as with network extension mode, each remote office needs a unique network number.

The purpose of assigning an internal address to the hardware remote is to be able to remotely manage the remote through the tunnel by using tools like ping, telnet, SSH, and ASDM (if it's a 5505). This is necessary when the hardware remote uses a dynamic method to acquire an IP address for its external interface. For management purposes, you'd typically not know what the address of the remote is unless someone were to log into it at the remote office and tell you what the remote public address is (assuming that it is a public address). Because you want to be able to always use the same internal IP address for the remote, you'll want to set up an AAA or local user account with an associated internal IP address that should always be used for the specific remote when it authenticates (this was discussed in Chapter 17).

 NOTE Because you are typically using private IP addresses in your addressing scheme at remote offices and you probably have the need to manage the hardware remote through the tunnel from the corporate site, most companies use network extension mode plus for hardware remotes.

ASA 5505 REMOTE CLIENT

ASA 5505s support hardware remote functionality for Easy VPN. Other supported hardware remotes include the PIX 501 and 506E, the VPN 3002, and the 800 to 3800 series routers. The following sections will discuss authentication options for your appliance acting as a hardware remote, as well as the basic configuration and management of the Easy VPN remote functionality.

Hardware Client XAUTH Authentication Methods

All authentication policies are controlled and defined on the Easy VPN server and pushed down to the hardware remote during IKE Mode Config (Phase 1). The default XAUTH authentication for a hardware remote is referred to as *default* or *unit* authentication.

With unit authentication, the XAUTH username and password are stored locally on the hardware remote in flash memory along with the rest of the remote configuration. The problem with unit authentication is that if the hardware remote were stored in an insecure location at a remote office, it could be stolen; the thief could then bring up a tunnel with the authentication credentials stored on the hardware remote.

Secure unit authentication (SUA), previously called Interactive Unit Authentication (IUA), solves this security problem. SUA is a group policy defined on an Easy VPN server with the group policy **secure-unit-authentication enable** command (see Chapter 17). When enabled, the policy is passed from the server to the remote during Phase 1 Mode Config. Upon receiving the policy, if the hardware remote was originally using unit authentication, it will automatically erase the username and password used for XAUTH.

Since the XAUTH username and password are erased, someone behind the hardware remote will have to supply this information to bring up the tunnel. Only a web browser is supported for SUA. The easiest way to accomplish this is to have a user open a web browser connection to something beyond the external interface of the hardware remote. The hardware remote will intercept the web connection and redirect it to a local login page on the remote itself. The user then supplies the username and password for XAUTH in order to bring up the tunnel. Once authenticated, the user is redirected back to the URL that he was originally trying to reach.

One problem with this approach is that when all the users at the remote office come into work in the morning and power up their PCs and laptops, no one will know if the tunnel is up. I recommend putting their web browser in the Windows Startup folder with a default home page of a web server at the corporate office behind the Easy VPN server. Therefore, one of the users will see the login page and will authenticate, which will bring up the tunnel for everyone. Also, you'll probably want to give the users different usernames and passwords, but put them in the same tunnel group.

NOTE Even though network extension mode automatically brings up a tunnel, the tunnel will fail to come up if you have an SUA policy defined—someone at the remote office will have to supply the XAUTH username and password; SUA and network extension mode combined gives you secure access to the corporate LAN and also gives corporate office access to and management of the remote office LAN devices.

User Authentication

The problem with unit authentication and SUA is that once the tunnel is up, anyone connected to the remote office hardware remote can send traffic across the tunnel. This can be an issue in remote offices that are not as secure, perhaps because they are using wireless or because the office is a shared workspace.

User authentication is used in environments where you can't control what devices are connected behind the hardware remote. Sometimes this feature is called "individual user authentication," but Cisco commonly calls it *user authentication*. With user authentication, once the tunnel comes up (device and XAUTH authentication have occurred), *each* device behind the hardware remote that wants to send traffic across the tunnel must first authenticate. User authentication is enabled on the Easy VPN server and passed down to the hardware remote during the Phase 1 Mode Config step. To enable user authentication on the Easy VPN server, you configure the **user-authentication enable** command in the group policy associated with the hardware remote (see Chapter 17). The default idle timeout for a user is 30 minutes, after which the user will have to re-authenticate to use the tunnel again. This timeout can be changed on the Easy VPN server with the **user-authentication-idle-timeout** command in the related group policy (see Chapter 17).

As with SUA, users must use a web browser to authenticate; again, I recommend putting their web browser in the Windows Startup folder with a default home page of a web server behind the Easy VPN server. This way they will see the login page when they boot up their computer and log in, and can immediately start using the tunnel to access corporate resources. Once authenticated, the hardware remote keeps track of authenticated devices based on their IP/MAC address pairs, so if a device changes its IP or MAC address, it will have to re-authenticate to use the tunnel.

One problem with user authentication is that a web browser is required to perform the authentication; certain devices, like wireless devices performing LEAP, IP phones, and network printers, don't have a web browser, can't authenticate, and thus can't use the tunnel. As I mentioned in Chapter 17, you can exempt Cisco IP phones and wireless devices performing LEAP authentication by using the **ip-phone-bypass enable** and **leap-bypass enable** commands, respectively, in the hardware remote group policy.

Basic Client Configuration

Configuring the ASA 5505 as a hardware remote is a much easier process than configuring it as an Easy VPN server. Here are the commands to configure the appliance as a hardware remote:

```
ciscoasa(config)# vpnclient enable
ciscoasa(config)# vpnclient server IP_primary [IP_secondary_1 ...
                     IP_secondary10]
ciscoasa(config)# vpnclient vpngroup group_name password preshared_key
ciscoasa(config)# vpnclient trustpoint CA_name [chain]
ciscoasa(config)# vpnclient username XAUTH_username password password
ciscoasa(config)# vpnclient mode {client-mode | network-extension-mode}
ciscoasa(config)# vpnclient nem-st-autoconnect
ciscoasa(config)# vpnclient ipsec-over-tcp [port tcp_port_#]
ciscoasa(config)# crypto ipsec df-bit clear-df if_name
ciscoasa(config)# vpnclient mac-exempt mac_addr1 mac_mask1
                     [mac_addr2 mac_mask2...mac_addrX mac_maskX]
ciscoasa(config)# vpnclient {connect | disconnect}
```

To enable the ASA 5505 as a hardware remote, use the **vpnclient enable** command. The **vpnclient server** command specifies the Easy VPN Server to connect to.

When connecting to a load balancing cluster (see Chapter 17), enter the virtual IP address that represents the cluster. If you are using pre-shared keys for group authentication, then use the **vpnclient vpngroup** command to configure the tunnel group name that the 5505 belongs to and the pre-shared key associated with the tunnel group. If you omit this command, the 5505 assumes certificates are being used for device authentication. If the 5505 has more than one certificate, you can specify which identity certificate to use with the **vpnclient trustpoint** command. The **chain** parameter is used in a CA hierarchical implementation: the root and all subordinate CA certificates, along with the identity certificate, are shared with the Easy VPN server during device authentication. Obtaining certificates on appliances was discussed in Chapter 15.

If you are using unit (default) authentication, the XAUTH username and password need to be defined with the **vpnclient username** command. If you don't specify the connection mode with the **vpnclient mode** command, it defaults to client mode. To configure the 5505 to automatically initiate IPSec data tunnels when NEM and split tunneling are configured, use the **vpnclient nem-st-autoconnect** command.

If you'll need to use IPSec over TCP, enable it with the **vpnclient ipsec-over-tcp** command on the 5505—the port defaults to 10000, but can be changed. You'll also need to enable IPSec over TCP on the Easy VPN server and match the port number. For large TCP segments from the user, make sure that the DF (don't fragment) bit is cleared in the TCP segment header for large packets on the external interface with the **crypto ipsec df-bit clear-df** command.

If user authentication is employed, you can use the **vpnclient mac-exempt** command to exclude certain devices, like file and print servers, from authenticating in order to use the tunnel. The MAC address mask is the network mask for the corresponding MAC address. A MAC mask of ffff.ff00.0000 matches all devices made by the same manufacturer. A MAC mask of 0000.0000.0000 matches a single device.

TIP   As you can see from the preceding configuration, you don't have to configure any ISAKMP policies, tunnel groups or policies, transform sets, or crypto maps. Actually most of these components are configured, but *you* don't have to do it: the appliance will do this automatically for you! So you can see why Cisco uses the term "Easy VPN" to describe their IPSec remote access solution.

Tunnel Maintenance

When using client mode on the ASA 5505, you can execute the **vpnclient connect** command to bring up a tunnel or the **vpnclient disconnect** command to tear down a tunnel. When you're using network extension mode, the **vpnclient connect** command really doesn't do anything, since the 5505 will automatically bring up the tunnel and keep on trying if it can't. Likewise the **vpnclient disconnect** command will tear down a tunnel, but if the 5505 is using network extension mode, the tunnel will automatically be rebuilt.

EASY VPN CONFIGURATION EXAMPLE WITH A HARDWARE REMOTE

To help illustrate how to configure an ASA 5505 as a hardware remote and have it build a tunnel to an Easy VPN server (also a security appliance), the following two sections will cover the configuration of these two devices.

ASA 5505 Configuration Example

The following configuration example shows how simple it is to set up a network extension mode connection on a 5505 using pre-shared keys:

```
client(config)# vpnclient enable
client(config)# vpnclient server 192.1.1.1
client(config)# vpnclient vpngroup hwclients password group_secret
client(config)# vpnclient username asa5505-1 password asa_secret
client(config)# vpnclient mode network-extension-mode
```

As you can see from this configuration, the setup is very easy.

Example Easy VPN Server Configuration

Here's the Easy VPN server configuration for an appliance that will accept tunnel connections from the ASA 5505 hardware remotes:

```
ciscoasa(config)# sysopt connection permit-vpn
ciscoasa(config)# crypto isakmp enable outside
ciscoasa(config)# crypto isakmp nat-traversal 30
ciscoasa(config)# crypto isakmp policy 10
ciscoasa(config-isakmp-policy)# authentication pre-share
ciscoasa(config-isakmp-policy)# encryption 3des
ciscoasa(config-isakmp-policy)# group 2
ciscoasa(config-isakmp-policy)# hash sha
ciscoasa(config-isakmp-policy)# lifetime 3600
ciscoasa(config)# group-policy hw_policy internal
ciscoasa(config)# group-policy hw_policy attributes
ciscoasa(config-group-policy)# vpn-idle-timeout 15
ciscoasa(config-group-policy)# nem enable
ciscoasa(config-group-policy)# exit
ciscoasa(config)# tunnel-group hwclients type ipsec-ra
ciscoasa(config)# tunnel-group hwclients type general-attributes
ciscoasa(config-tunnel-general)# authentication-server-group LOCAL
ciscoasa(config-tunnel-general)# default-group-policy hw_policy
ciscoasa(config)# tunnel-group hwclients ipsec-attributes
ciscoasa(config-tunnel-ipsec)# pre-shared-key group_secret
```

```
ciscoasa(config-tunnel-ipsec)# isakmp keepalive threshold 30 retry 5
ciscoasa(config-tunnel-ipsec)# exit
ciscoasa(config)# username asa5505-1 password asa_secret privilege 0
ciscoasa(config)# username asa5505-1 attributes
ciscoasa(config-username)# password-storage enable
ciscoasa(config-username)# vpn-framed-ip-address
                               10.0.1.223 255.255.255.0
ciscoasa(config-username)# exit
ciscoasa(config)# access-list ACLnonat permit ip 10.0.0.0 255.0.0.0
                      10.0.1.223 255.255.255.255
ciscoasa(config)# nat (inside) 0 access-list ACLnonat
ciscoasa(config)# crypto ipsec transform-set hw_trans
                      esp-3des esp-md5-hmac
ciscoasa(config)# crypto dynamic-map dyn_map 1
                      set transform-set hw_trans
ciscoasa(config)# crypto dynamic-map dyn_map 1 set reverse-route
ciscoasa(config)# crypto map stat_map 10000 ipsec-isakmp
                      dynamic dyn_map
ciscoasa(config)# crypto map stat_map interface outside
```

This example is similar to the one shown and discussed previously in Chapter 17, so I'll skip most of the commands and focus on the parts that are important for the 5505 hardware remote. First, notice that the group policy has network extension mode enabled (**nem enable** command). Second, a tunnel group was created with a pre-shared key, and DPD was enabled (automatically done on the ASA 5505 hardware remote). Third, a local user account was created for the 5505; its attributes allow the XAUTH information to be stored on the 5505 (overrides the default); and a static address is assigned for network extension plus mode. Last, Identity NAT was configured to exempt the internally assigned address from address translation on the Easy VPN server.

CHAPTER 19

SSL VPNs: Clientless

Tis chapter will introduce the concepts of SSL VPNs. Cisco refers to their SSL VPN implementation as *WebVPN*. Cisco supports three implementations of WebVPN: clientless, thin client, and network or tunnel client. This chapter will focus on the former two and the next chapter on the latter implementation. The topics discussed in this chapter include

▼ Introducing SSL VPNs and the different access methods

■ Configuring basic WebVPN components for clientless access

■ Defining group policies for WebVPN clientless users

■ Creating tunnel groups for WebVPN users

■ Becoming familiar with the clientless and thin client home page

■ Supporting non-web traffic using port forwarding, plug-ins, and smart tunnels

▲ Verifying and troubleshooting clientless and thin client access

NOTE   Cisco Secure Desktop, a feature that complements WebVPN sessions, will be covered in Chapter 27. Also, the ASAs can be an SSL certificate authority (CA), giving out SSL identity certificates to user devices. The configuration of an ASA as an SSL CA is beyond the scope of this book.

INTRODUCTION TO SSL VPNs

"WebVPN" is the Cisco marketing term that describes the use of SSL to provide a VPN remote access solution. Some vendors also support LAN-to-LAN (L2L) connections, but the only current Cisco L2L technology is using IPSec. SSL VPNs are becoming more popular as a VPN solution. Common uses for SSL VPNs include accessing web-based and e-mail applications, accessing company resources from noncompany computers, and accessing a small number of non-web-based applications.

SSL was originally designed to protect data between a user's web browser and a web server, typically for financial and security transactions. However, many networking vendors have taken this standard and adapted it to a VPN role. When using SSL, TCP is used as a transport to carry the data between the user's desktop and the SSL gateway. SSL provides the following protection features:

▼ **Confidentiality**   RC-4, DES, 3DES, and AES encryption algorithms

■ **Authentication**   Digital certificates and/or a username and password

▲ **Packet integrity**   MD5 and SHA-1

Compared with other VPN implementations, SSL VPNs don't require a specialized client to be installed on the user's desktop to set up a VPN; however, most vendor SSL VPN implementations lack anti-replay protection.

Connection Modes

Cisco's SSL implementation supports three SSL VPN access modes:

▼   Clientless mode

■   Thin client mode

▲   Network client or tunnel mode

The following sections will cover the access modes in more depth.

Clientless Mode

"Clientless" is a misnomer for the first access method, since a web browser is used as a "client"; however, Cisco and other vendors use this term to describe a special client that doesn't need to be installed on the user's desktop: the assumption is that a web browser is already there. Cisco clientless implementation supports Windows 2000, XP, and Vista, as well as Linux and the Mac OS, where language localization can be easily integrated into the access. With clientless mode, only web-based applications are protected, with no protection for most non-web-based applications. In clientless mode, the SSL gateway acts as a *proxy* for the user when accessing resources behind the SSL gateway. The Cisco implementation supports proxying for HTTP, HTTPS, IFS Windows file share (CIFS, or Common Internet File Services), and e-mail (POP3S, SMTPS, and IMAP4S).

Thin Client Mode

The main limitation of clientless mode is that it doesn't support non-web-based applications. Thin client mode was created to add support for some, but not all, of these applications. In thin client mode, the SSL gateway acts as a TCP proxy, proxying TCP connections from the user to resources beyond the gateway. Cisco supports three thin client implementations: port forwarding, plug-ins, and smart tunnels. All require that a web browser and Java 1.5 or later be installed on the user's desktop to operate correctly.

With the thin client function, the user logs into the SSL gateway via clientless mode and then starts the thin client function; optionally you can have the thin client process start up automatically once the user logs in. Some modification of the supported applications may be necessary to successfully protect them across the SSL tunnel. Currently Cisco does not support all non-web-based applications using the thin client mode. Some common supported applications include telnet, SSH, e-mail, Citrix, VNC, Windows Terminal Services, and many others.

Tunnel Mode

The main problems of thin client mode include

▼   Only a small number of TCP applications can be proxied.

▲   Users might have to reconfigure their application to have it successfully tunneled across the SSL VPN.

Tunnel mode implementation was created by Cisco to deal with these problems. Tunnel mode function is more similar to how the IPSec remote access client (Easy VPN remote) functions, where most IP protocols and applications function across the tunnel without any user changes. The users use their applications as they normally would without a VPN in place. Tunnel mode requires a special Java-based client to be installed on the user's desktop. The Cisco original tunnel mode client was called the SSL VPN Client (SVC); this has now been replaced by the AnyConnect client and is similar to the IPSec client in functionality and features. The SVC client is supported in version 7.0 through 7.2 of the ASAs and the AnyConnect client in version 8.0.

The tunnel mode client advantages over the IPSec client are that it is more user-friendly and can be automatically installed over a WebVPN clientless connection (optionally you have to send it to the user in a stand-alone install package and have the user install it manually). The tunnel mode client is only around 3 MB in size and doesn't require a reboot after installation. However, its disadvantage is that it cannot provide the same kind of protection as the IPSec client—it lacks anti-replay capabilities.

WebVPN Restrictions

WebVPN is not supported on the PIXs, unfortunately. Cisco's current products that support WebVPN include the ASAs, the 3000 concentrators, and the IOS routers. Cisco no longer develops code for the 3000 concentrators since they are end-of-sale (EOS). Today all initial WebVPN development is done on the ASAs and eventually ported to the routers.

TIP Currently the routers are about 6 to 12 months behind the ASAs in their WebVPN capabilities. So if you want the latest and greatest for WebVPN, use the ASAs.

Here are the current restrictions when using clientless or thin client mode for WebVPN:

▼ Web browser cookies must be enabled—otherwise after authenticating, the user will be asked to authenticate again (the authentication credentials are stored in cookies).

■ Port forwarding doesn't work if CA identity certificates are used: Java doesn't have the ability to access the client SSL certificate in the web browser key store.

■ Microsoft Outlook MAPI is unsupported for clientless and thin client; it is supported for tunnel mode connections.

■ Contexts are unsupported for any type of VPN: SSL, IPSec, PPTP, and L2TP.

■ A user cannot connect to sites that have expired certificates: the appliance will drop the connection. (Remember that the ASA is proxying the connections, and it, not the user, is the one that will reject the expired certificate.)

■ You cannot apply address translation policies to the clientless and thin client connections; however, you can for tunnel mode connections.

▲   The following Modular Policy Framework (MPF) features are unsupported for clientless and thin client connections: application inspection, QoS and traffic policing, and connection limits; however, tunnel mode connections are supported.

NOTE   By default an ASA only supports a license for two WebVPN sessions—you need to purchase the appropriate license for the number of simultaneous WebVPN sessions you'll need to support.

BASIC WebVPN CONFIGURATION

The remainder of this chapter will focus on setting up an ASA as an SSL VPN gateway for clientless and thin client connections. Chapter 20 will cover tunnel mode connections. In this section, I'll cover some basic concepts on setting up WebVPN on the ASAs, including defining SSL connection policies, enabling WebVPN, allowing for both WebVPN and ASDM on the same interface, using DNS to resolve names to addresses, having an external web proxy to proxy the traffic instead of the ASA, and defining general WebVPN access properties.

Implementing SSL Policies

The following two sections will discuss how to exempt WebVPN inbound connections from ACL checks and controlling the encryption algorithm(s) the user can use for the SSL traffic.

Allowing WebVPN Traffic

By default WebVPN traffic is not exempted from ACL checks when going from a lower- to higher-level interface; once the traffic is decrypted, it is run through the inbound ACL on the lower-level interface. You must either include **permit** statements for the decrypted traffic in the ACL, or implement the ACL bypass feature, which I covered in Chapter 15. To implement the ACL bypass feature, execute the following command:

```
ciscoasa(config)# sysopt connection permit-vpn
```

This command exempts all decrypted VPN traffic, including SSL VPNs, from being processed by the ACL on the inbound interface.

Controlling SSL Encryption Algorithms Used

One problem with SSL is that even though many encryption algorithms are supported, the user's web browser ultimately controls what algorithm to use, the weakest of which is RC-4. You can restrict what encryption algorithms and SSL versions are used with the following configuration:

```
ciscoasa(config)# ssl encryption {3des-sha1 | aes128-sha1 |
                  aes256-sha1 | des-sha1 | rc4-md5 |
```

```
                              rc4-sha1 | null-sha1}
ciscoasa(config)# ssl server-version {any | sslv3 | sslv3-only |
                              tlsv1 | tlsv1-only}
```

The defaults are to allow any encryption algorithm and any SSL version. The **ssl encryption** command is used to restrict the encryption algorithm(s) and HMAC functions that can be used by the user's web browser. The **ssl server-version** is used to restrict the SSL version the user's web browser is allowed to use. By default all versions are allowed; the most secure is SSL version 3.

Enabling WebVPN

Enabling WebVPN is an easy proposition. Most WebVPN commands are executed in the WebVPN subcommand mode (**webvpn** command):

```
ciscoasa(config)# webvpn
ciscoasa(config-webvpn)# enable logical_if_name
ciscoasa(config-webvpn)# port port_#
```

First, you must enable WebVPN with the **enable** command, specifying the logical name of the interface it will be enabled on, like *outside*. Optionally you can change the SSL port number used for HTTPS connections with the **port** command; if you omit this, it defaults to 443.

I would highly recommend that you configure port redirection: most users forget to type in **"https://"** when accessing the ASA, and instead enter **"http://"**. You can set up port redirection, where, if the user connects to port 80 on the ASA, the ASA will automatically redirect the web browser to port 443. This is accomplished with the **http redirect** command:

```
ciscoasa(config)# http redirect logical_if_name port_#
```

Here's an example:

```
ciscoasa(config)# http redirect outside 80
```

This command will redirect port 80 connections to the HTTPS port (443 by default).

TIP Using port redirection will greatly cut down on the number of phone calls from forgetful users trying to connect by using clientless or thin client mode to the ASA when they forget to type in `https://` in the address bar of their web browser.

Supporting Both WebVPN and ASDM

ASDM, discussed in Chapter 27, is a GUI interface used to manage the appliance. ASDM uses SSL to protect the interaction between the administrator's PC and the appliance.

WebVPN and ASDM can coexist on the same interface; however, they both can't use port 443 for their SSL connections, which is the default for both if not overridden. In WebVPN, you can change the port number with the **port** command in the WebVPN sub-command mode, but then users have to remember what port to use for their SSL tunnels. Instead, I recommend that you change the port number for ASDM. Here's the syntax for specifying the ASDM port:

```
ciscoasa(config)# http server enable port_#
```

Here's an example that listens for ASDM on port 444:

```
ciscoasa(config)# http server enable 444
ciscoasa(config)# http 192.168.3.0 255.255.255.0 outside
```

To access ASDM, use **https://**IP_address**:444**, as an example. ASDM is discussed in Chapter 27.

Performing DNS Lookups

When acting as a proxy for WebVPN, the ASA must be able to resolve names (found in URLs) to IP addresses using DNS. By default DNS lookups are not configured on the ASAs. Here's the basic configuration to enable DNS lookups and to specify a DNS server(s) to use:

```
ciscoasa(config)# dns lookup logical_if_name
ciscoasa(config)# dns name-server IP_address  [...IP_address6]
ciscoasa(config)# dns server-group DNS_server_group_name
ciscoasa(config-dns-server-group)# domain-name domain_name_for_group
ciscoasa(config-dns-server-group)# name-server IP_address
ciscoasa(config-dns-server-group)# retries #_of_retries
ciscoasa(config-dns-server-group)# timeout seconds
```

To allow DNS lookups to occur on a particular interface, use the **dns lookup** command; this specifies the interface a DNS server is connected to. To globally define DNS servers to use, configure the **dns name-server** command—you can list up to six DNS server addresses.

Optionally you can create different groupings of DNS servers to be used by different tunnel groups (different groups of users), which override the global DNS server configuration. To create a DNS server group, use the **dns server-group** command. The name you enter here must be referenced in the tunnel group configuration (discussed later in the chapter). The **domain-name** specifies for what domains the configured servers of the group will resolve addresses. When doing a DNS lookup, the default number of retries is 2 and the default timeout is 2 seconds—these can be changed globally or overridden in the DNS server group configuration with the **retries** and **timeout** commands respectively.

To see the DNS host table of resolved hostnames, use the **show dns-hosts** command:

```
ciscoasa# show dns-hosts
Host Flags Age Type Address(es)
a1.dealgroup.com (temp, OK) 0 IP 10.0.1.11
a2.dealgroup.com (temp, OK) 0 IP 10.0.1.12
server.dealgroup.com (temp, OK) 0 IP 10.0.1.99
```

Implementing Web Proxying

For clientless connections, you have two approaches to performing the proxy process for the web connections: have the appliance perform the proxying, or use an external web proxy. The next section will discuss how to use an external web proxy. If the ASA is performing the proxy process, you might want to enable web caching to speed up the download process—this is discussed in the second section.

Defining External Web Proxies

Instead of having the ASA proxy the web connections, you can have an external proxy server perform this function, thereby offloading this process-intensive process to a different device. The **http-proxy** and **https-proxy** commands perform this function:

```
ciscoasa(config)# webvpn
ciscoasa(config-webvpn)# {http-proxy | https-proxy} host_IP [port]
                         [exclude url] [username username
                         {password password}]
ciscoasa(config-webvpn)# {http-proxy | https-proxy}
                                  pac URL_for_pacfile}
```

The *host_IP* is the proxy server; you can optionally change the port number the proxy server is listening on.

Here's a simple example of configuring an external proxy:

```
ciscoasa(config)# webvpn
ciscoasa(config-webvpn)# http-proxy 10.0.1.15
```

Optionally you can exclude URLs that are forwarded to the proxy, using these additional special expressions:

▼　　*　To match any string, including slashes (/) and periods (.). You must accompany this wildcard with a character string, like "*.cisco.com".

■　　?　To match any single character, including slashes and periods.

■　　[x-y]　To match any single character in the range of *x* and *y*, where *x* represents one character and *y* represents another character in the character set.

▲　　[!x-y]　To match any single character that is not in the range.

Here's an example that excludes all URLs for "mycompany.com" for the 10.1.1.1 proxy to handle:

```
ciscoasa(config-webvpn)# http-proxy 10.1.1.1 port 80
                                exclude *.mycompany.com
```

If the proxy requires a username and password, you can provide this information. Here's an example:

```
ciscoasa(config-webvpn)# http-proxy 10.0.1.15 username proxyuser
                        password myhiddenpassword
```

The **pac** parameter identifies a proxy autoconfiguration file (using a URL) to download to the user's web browser. Once it is downloaded, the PAC file uses a JavaScript function to identify a proxy for each URL the user tries to access. This allows you to use different proxies for different web connections. Here's an example:

```
ciscoasa(config-webvpn)# http-proxy pac http://www.example.com/pac
```

Implementing Web Caching Policies

You can have the appliance cache web information when it acts as a proxy and control the cache process with a group policy configuration. Here are the commands to control the caching process:

```
ciscoasa(config)# webvpn
ciscoasa(config-webvpn)# cache-fs limit size_in_MB
ciscoasa(config-webvpn)# cache
ciscoasa(config-webvpn-cache)# cache-static-content enable
ciscoasa(config-webvpn-cache)# disable
ciscoasa(config-webvpn-cache)# expiry-time minutes
ciscoasa(config-webvpn-cache)# lmfactor value
ciscoasa(config-webvpn-cache)# min-object-size size_in_KB
ciscoasa(config-webvpn-cache)# max-object-size size_in_KB
```

By default 20 MB of content can be cached in flash on the ASA. This can be changed with the **cache-fs** command. The largest amount you can specify is 32 MB. The rest of the commands for caching policies are configured under the cache subcommand mode (**cache** command) in the WebVPN subcommand mode. The **cache-static-content** command automatically caches content by the ASA that is not subject to any rewriting. The **disable** command disables caching of downloaded content by the ASA. The **expiry-time** command configures an expiration time for caching objects without revalidating them. The ASA uses the value of the **lmfactor** to estimate the length of time for which it considers a cached object to be unchanged. This is referred to as the *expiration time* (**expiry-time** command). The ASA estimates the expiration time by the time elapsed since the last modification multiplied by the **lmfactor** value, which can range from 0 to 100. Setting it to 0 forces an immediate revalidation of the content, while setting it to 100 results in the longest allowable time until revalidation. The **min-object-size** and **max-object-size** commands control the size of objects that can be cached for WebVPN sessions by the ASA.

Defining General WebVPN Properties

Some general properties you can define for clientless access include the following:

```
ciscoasa(config)# webvpn
ciscoasa(config-webvpn)# default-idle-timeout seconds
ciscoasa(config-webvpn)# internal-password enable
ciscoasa(config-webvpn)# keepout "string"
ciscoasa(config-webvpn)# onscreen-keyboard {all | logon}
```

The default idle timeout for clientless WebVPN connections is 30 minutes (1800 seconds). This can be globally changed with the **default-idle-timeout** command. If the WebVPN password is different than what an internal web server uses, you can have the user supply both passwords, where the first is used by the ASA and the second by the internal server. You need to use the **internal-password enable** command to enable this feature. When you need to temporarily take WebVPN out of service, you can have a particular text string displayed on the screen instead of the login page. This is configured with the **keepout** command. If you are concerned about keystroke capturing programs during the WebVPN login process or afterward, you can have an onscreen keyboard displayed, where the users use their mouse to enter their login credentials or information after they log in. The **onscreen-keyboard** command enables this feature—this feature is disabled by default.

WebVPN GROUP POLICIES

Group policies were previously introduced in Chapter 17, where I discussed IPSec remote access. Group policies can also be used for WebVPN users. The following two sections discuss how to define group policies and how to override them on a per-user basis.

Configuring Group Policies

Group policies can be defined either locally or on an AAA RADIUS server. To define the name of the policies and where they are found, use the **group-policy** command—these commands were discussed in Chapter 17:

```
ciscoasa(config)# group-policy policy_name internal
                  [from group_policy_name]
ciscoasa(config)# group-policy policy_name external server-group
                  server_group password user_password
```

To specify the WebVPN attributes for a local policy, use the preceding configuration. Non-WebVPN policy commands were discussed in Chapter 17.

Specifying Internal Policies

Within a local group policy, you can control the VPN protocols that users of specific tunnel groups can use:

```
ciscoasa(config)# group-policy policy_name internal
ciscoasa(config)# group-policy policy_name attributes
ciscoasa(config-group-policy)# vpn-tunnel-protocol {[svc] [webvpn]
                              [ipsec] [l2tp-ipsec]}
```

Enter all the protocols allowed on a single line—if you omit this command, it defaults to IPSec only (**ipsec** parameter), so you need to include **webvpn** for clientless and **svc** for the SVC and AnyConnect client connections.

To enter the WebVPN policies for the group policy, enter the **webvpn** command, which takes you into a secondary subcommand mode:

```
ciscoasa(config)# group-policy policy_name attributes
ciscoasa(config-group-policy)# webvpn
ciscoasa(config-group-webvpn)#
```

From this second-level subcommand mode, you can control what appears on the login page for clientless and thin client connections, control what appears on the user's home page, filter web content, and define restrictions for uploading and downloading content. The following sections will discuss the configuration of these policies.

If a user successfully logs in, but the **vpn-tunnel-protocol** command doesn't allow WebVPN, you can display an appropriate message with the **deny-message value** command within the WebVPN subcommand mode for the group policy:

```
ciscoasa(config)# group-policy policy_name attributes
ciscoasa(config-group-policy)# webvpn
ciscoasa(config-group-webvpn)# deny-message value "string"
```

Controlling Home Page Elements

The home page, commonly called the *home portal*, is what authenticated users see once they log in; you can control what appears on a per-group basis. The following sections will discuss some common home page elements you might want to control.

Customization Profiles   Customization profiles affect the look and feel of the WebVPN login, logout, and home pages. Since customization profiles are no longer configured from the CLI in version 8, you must use ASDM, which is discussed in Chapter 27, or an XML editor. One nice feature of ASDM is that it supports a quasi-XML editor/ builder that allows you to build the home portal and preview it. You can use a different customization profile for different groups of users, thus giving you specific control over what each group of users can see and do from their respective home page.

If you've already created the XML file and have it on an external server, or restore one that you misconfigured with ASDM, you can pull it into flash with the **import webvpn customization** command:

```
ciscoasa# import webvpn customization profile_name URL
```

You'll have to define the name of the customization profile that the ASA will use when referencing it and the location of the external server and filename to pull it from.

Here's an example of importing an existing customization profile:

```
ciscoasa# import webvpn customization general_profile
              tftp://10.0.1.11/profiles/general_profile.xml
Accessing
tftp://10.0.1.11/customization/general_profile.xml...!!!!!!!!!!!!!!
!!!!!!!!!!!!!!!!!!!!!!!!!!!!!!!!!!!!!!!!!!!!!!!!!!!!!!
Writing file disk0:/csco_config/customization/general_profile...!!
!!!!!!!!!!!!!!!!!!!!!!!!!!!!!!!!!!!!!!!!!!!!!!!!!!!!!!
329994 bytes copied in 5.350 secs (65998 bytes/sec)
```

The customization profiles that are imported are stored in the "csco-config/customization/" directory in flash: this directory is hidden and cannot be accessed from the CLI. When the file is pulled in, a basic XML syntax check is performed on it.

Once you import the customization profile, it is not used until it is referenced in either a tunnel group or a group policy. To specify a customization profile a group policy should use, configure the **customization value** command in the group policy:

```
ciscoasa(config)# group-policy policy_name attributes
ciscoasa(config-group-policy)# webvpn
ciscoasa(config-group-webvpn)# customization value
                              {DfltCustomization | profile_name}
```

You can reference the default customization policy, or one you created with ASDM or manually imported from the CLI.

You can export a customization profile from flash to an external server with the **export** command:

```
ciscoasa# export webvpn customization profile_name URL
```

You might want to export a file if you want to copy it from one ASA to another.

NOTE Use the **revert webvpn customization** command to remove a specified imported customization profile.

Predefined URLs and URL Policies You can predefine URLs that will appear on a user's home portal. In version 8, you must use the ASDM built-in editor or an external XML editor to create these. URLs that you can define on the home portal include HTTP, HTTPS, FTP, and CIFS.

Use the `import` command to pull in an existing URL list from an external server:

```
ciscoasa# import webvpn url-list URL_list_name URL
```

Here's an example of importing a file that has a predefined list of URLs:

```
ciscoasa(config)# import webvpn url-list salesURLlist
                  ftp://192.168.1.66/SalesURLlist.xml
!!
%INFO: URL list 'salesURLlist' was successfully imported
329994 bytes copied in 5.350 secs (65998 bytes/sec)
```

The URL list is stored in the "csco-config/url-lists/" directory: this directory is hidden and cannot be viewed from the CLI. You can use the `export webvpn url-list` command to back up a URL list created from ASDM—you might want to do this if you want to copy a list from one ASA to another.

NOTE Use the `revert webvpn url-list` command to remove a specified imported URL list.

Once you have either created a URL list in ASDM or imported an external one, it is not used unless referenced in a group policy with the `url-list` command:

```
ciscoasa(config)# group-policy policy_name attributes
ciscoasa(config-group-policy)# webvpn
ciscoasa(config-group-webvpn)# url-list {value URL_list_name | none}
```

If a URL list is not specified, then no URLs are displayed on the home page by default.

The `url-entry` command controls whether an address text box is displayed on the home portal so that users can type in their own URLs that the ASA will proxy:

```
ciscoasa(config)# group-policy policy_name attributes
ciscoasa(config-group-policy)# webvpn
ciscoasa(config-group-webvpn)# url-entry {enable | disable}
```

By default an address text box is not displayed on a user's home page.

Other Home Page Elements If you don't want to create a home portal on the ASA, but want to use an internal server web page as the home page when the user logs in, configure the `homepage` command:

```
ciscoasa(config)# group-policy policy_name attributes
ciscoasa(config-group-policy)# webvpn
ciscoasa(config-group-webvpn)# homepage {none | value URL}
```

If you want to allow users to browse CIFS file shares, use the `file-browsing` command:

```
ciscoasa(config)# group-policy policy_name attributes
ciscoasa(config-group-policy)# webvpn
ciscoasa(config-group-webvpn)# file-browsing {enable | disable}
```

By default this is disabled.

Some web-based applications used ActiveX controls to launch a Microsoft Office application—to allow or disallow this behavior, use the `activex-relay` command:

```
ciscoasa(config)# group-policy policy_name attributes
ciscoasa(config-group-policy)# webvpn
ciscoasa(config-group-webvpn)# activex-relay {enable | disable}
```

By default this is disabled.

A hidden share is identified by a dollar sign ($) at the end of the share name. For example, drive C is shared as C$. With hidden shares, a shared folder is not displayed, and users are restricted from browsing or accessing these hidden resources. To control the visibility of hidden shares for CIFS files, use the `hidden-shares` command:

```
ciscoasa(config)# group-policy policy_name attributes
ciscoasa(config-group-policy)# webvpn
ciscoasa(config-group-webvpn)# hidden-shares {visible | none}
```

This policy is only applicable if you allow users CIFS file share access.

Filtering Content

One of the features of WebVPN in version 7 allows you to use ACLs to filter web content. Normally this is not something you do on the appliance, but rather on either a full-blown web proxy or a modified proxy like that discussed in Chapter 7 with web content filtering. With the latter feature, web policies are defined on a Smartfilter or Websense policy server, and the appliances implement the policies on returning web traffic. Using ACLs on the ASAs to filter web content is typically done in smaller environments where you want to allow or restrict a few locations and where it makes no economic sense to buy an extra server to perform this process.

To filter web content, you use a new type of ACL called a *webtype* ACL. With webtype ACLs, you can filter URLs or IP addresses. Here is the full syntax of the two commands you can use to filter web content:

```
ciscoasa(config)# access-list ACL_ID webtype {deny | permit}
                  url [url_string | any] [log [[disable | default] |
                  level] [interval secs] [time-range name]]
ciscoasa(config)# access-list ACL_ID webtype {deny | permit}
                  tcp [host ip_address | ip_address subnet_mask |
                  any] [oper port [port]]
```

```
                    [log [[disable | default] | level]
                    [interval secs] [time-range name]]
```

To filter on URLs, use the first command; to filter on addresses, use the second command.

To use the webtype ACL, reference it in a group policy, like this:

```
ciscoasa(config)# group-policy policy_name attributes
ciscoasa(config-group-policy)# webvpn
ciscoasa(config-group-webvpn)# filter value webvpn_ACL_ID
```

Any users associated with this policy (discussed in the "Tunnel Groups" section later in the chapter) will then have this policy applied to their proxied traffic.

The **html-content-filter** command allows you to perform general filtering: stripping out cookies, images, Java scripts, and script code from downloaded web pages. Here's the syntax to set this up for a group policy:

```
ciscoasa(config)# group-policy policy_name attributes
ciscoasa(config-group-policy)# webvpn
ciscoasa(config-group-webvpn)# html-content-filter {[cookies]
                    [images] [java] | [scripts]}
```

Restricting Downloads and Uploads

Another option you have for proxied traffic is to place limits on downloads and uploads in a group policy:

```
ciscoasa(config)# group-policy policy_name attributes
ciscoasa(config-group-policy)# webvpn
ciscoasa(config-group-webvpn)# download-max-size bytes
ciscoasa(config-group-webvpn)# post-max-size bytes
ciscoasa(config-group-webvpn)# upload-max-size bytes
```

You can restrict the maximum size of an object that can be downloaded with the **download-max-size** command; this can be used to ensure that large files, like movies or similar content, are restricted. You can also restrict the maximum object size that can be posted with the POST method (**post-max-size** command) and the maximum object size that can be uploaded (**upload-max-size** command). The default is 2,147,483,647 bytes (over 2 GB!) for all three.

Overriding Group Policies on a Per-User Basis

As I discussed in Chapter 17, you can create a local database on the appliances that contains the usernames and passwords for remote access users. The **username** command is used to create a local user account, as shown here:

```
ciscoasa(config)# username name password password privilege 0
```

The following sections will discuss some of the general and WebVPN attributes you can override on a user-by-user basis. Please note that overriding users policies based on the group they are associated with is uncommon and not very manageable.

> **SECURITY ALERT!**   For non-administrator appliance accounts, make sure the privilege level is 0, which ensures that remote access users can't access the appliance itself!

User General Attributes

You can override the group policies associated with the user on a user-by-user basis. Here are the general attributes you can override for a user accessing the ASA using WebVPN:

```
ciscoasa(config)# username username attributes
ciscoasa(config-username)# group-lock value tunnel_group_name
ciscoasa(config-username)# memberof tunnel_group_name
                          [...tunnel_group_name]
ciscoasa(config-username)# service-type {admin | nas-prompt |
                           remote-access}
ciscoasa(config-username)# vpn-access-hours value time_range_name
ciscoasa(config-username)# vpn-filter value ACL_ID
ciscoasa(config-username)# vpn-group-policy group_policy_name
ciscoasa(config-username)# vpn-idle-timeout minutes
```

You can lock a user into a particular group with the **group-lock** command. You can associate the user to multiple tunnel groups with the **memberof** command. The **service-type** command restricts the kind of access the user account has:

▼ **admin**   Access to configuration mode on the appliance

■ **nas-prompt**   Access to EXEC mode on the appliance

▲ **remote-access**   No access to EXEC mode on the appliance (used only for remote access authentication for your user/non-administrator population)

The other preceding commands were discussed in Chapter 17. Other general commands you can configure include **vpn-session-timeout**, **vpn-simultaneous-logins**, and **vpn-tunnel-protocol**.

User WebVPN Attributes

To override users' WebVPN-specific attributes based on the group they are associated with, use the following configuration:

```
ciscoasa(config)# username username attributes
ciscoasa(config-username)# webvpn
ciscoasa(config-username-webvpn)# commands
```

Here is a list of commands you can enter to override a particular user's group policy configuration (some were discussed earlier in the chapter or will be discussed in Chapter 20): `activex-relay`, `auto-signon`, `customization`, `deny-message`, `download-max-size`, `file-browsing`, `file-entry`, `filter`, `hidden-shares`, `homepage`, `html-content-filter`, `http-comp`, `http-proxy`, `keep-alive-ignore`, `timer`, `port-forward`, `auto-download`, `applet`, `post-max-size`, `smart-tunnel`, `sso-server`, `storage-key`, `storage-objects`, `svc`, `unix-auth-gid`, `upload-max-size`, `url-entry`, `url-list`, and `user-storage`.

TUNNEL GROUPS

Tunnel groups for IPSec remote access were introduced in Chapter 17, where I discussed setting up an appliance as an Easy VPN server. Tunnel groups are used to more easily assign policies and attributes to a common group of users or L2L connections. As with IPSec remote access, Cisco supports a tunnel group for WebVPN users. To create a WebVPN tunnel group, use the following command:

```
ciscoasa(config)# tunnel-group tunnel_group_name
                  type remote-access
```

The name of the tunnel group should be descriptive, describing the type of users that will be using the attributes and policies of the tunnel group. Most administrators use job functions to classify people, like "executives," "sales," "programmers," "marketing," "pctechs," and other similar functional names. The following sections will discuss the general and WebVPN-specific attributes you can assign to your tunnel groups.

Tunnel Group General Attributes

General attributes for tunnel groups are attributes not associated with a specific VPN type. General attributes include where to find the user accounts to authenticate them, where to find the group policies for the users, and where to store accounting records of a user's access. Here are the commands to configure these attributes:

```
ciscoasa(config)# tunnel-group tunnel_group_name general-attributes
ciscoasa(config-tunnel-general)# authentication-server-group
                       [(logical_if_name)] server_tag [LOCAL]
ciscoasa(config-tunnel-general)# authorization-server-group
                       [(logical_if_name)] server_tag
ciscoasa(config-tunnel-general)# default-group-policy group_policy_name
ciscoasa(config-tunnel-general)# accounting-server-group server_tag
```

All these commands were discussed in Chapter 17. If you don't specify the method of authentication, local authentication is used with the `username` commands. If you don't define a group policy, the default group policy called *DfltGrpPolicy* on the ASA is used; you can create specific policies on the appliance, or specify an AAA server to find them (`authorization-server-group` command).

Tunnel Group WebVPN Attributes

WebVPN-specific attributes for a tunnel group are configured with the following set of commands:

```
ciscoasa(config# tunnel-group tunnel_group_name webvpn-attributes
ciscoasa(config-tunnel-webvpn)# authentication {[aaa] [certificate]}
ciscoasa(config-tunnel-webvpn)# customization profile_name
ciscoasa(config-tunnel-webvpn)# dns-group dns_server_group_name
ciscoasa(config-tunnel-webvpn)# group-alias other_group_name
                                {enable | disable}
ciscoasa(config-tunnel-webvpn)# group-url URL {enable | disable}
ciscoasa(config-tunnel-webvpn)# nbns-server WINS_server_IP [master]
                                [timeout seconds] [retry retry_count]
ciscoasa(config-tunnel-webvpn)# radius-reject-message
```

In the WebVPN attributes configuration of a tunnel group, the **authentication** command specifies that AAA, digital certificates, or both are used to authenticate WebVPN users. The default is AAA if you don't configure this command. The **customization** command specifies the customization profile to use for the tunnel group—this affects the look and feel of the home page when they log in. You can also define this within the group policy in the general attributes of the tunnel group. The **dns-group** command specifies the DNS server group to use to resolve names to addresses—this overrides the global DNS server settings. DNS server groups were previously discussed in the "Performing DNS Lookups" section.

The **group-alias** command allows you to specify an additional name for the tunnel group that users might be more familiar with. This *must* be configured if you configured the **tunnel-group-list enable** command under the WebVPN subcommand mode of the **webvpn** global command:

```
ciscoasa(config)# webvpn
ciscoasa(config-webvpn)# tunnel-group-list enable
```

If you don't configure the **tunnel-group-list** command along with the **group-alias** command, then the user will be connected to the default WebVPN group called *Default-WEBVPNGroup*. For every group you want to see in the drop-down group selector on the login page, you need the **group-alias** command for the group and the **tunnel-group-list enable** command for the global WebVPN setting. Use the **show webvpn group-alias** [*tunnel_group_name*] command to view the aliases for your tunnel groups.

The **group-url** command specifies a URL that will represent the users' home page when they log in—this is an external server behind the ASA. Configure this command if another device will be proxying the connections and a home page has already been configured on this second server. (See the "Defining External Web Proxies" section earlier in the chapter.)

If you are allowing users to access CIFS file shares and are using WINS for name resolution, in the tunnel group WebVPN properties, you'll need to define the WINS server or servers with the **nbns-server** command—execute the command separately for each server. The primary server should be denoted with the **master** parameter. If you don't change the timeout or number of retries, they default to 2 seconds and 2 retries respectively.

> **NOTE** WINS for name resolution was originally used in Windows-based networks; however, most Windows-based networks today use DNS for name resolution, so you probably won't need to configure a WINS server address with the **nbns-server** command.

The **radius-reject-message** only applies to a tunnel group when RADIUS authentication is used. In this instance, if the user fails to log in successfully on the login screen, the reject message from the RADIUS server is displayed—the default is not to display this message.

Group Matching Methods

In Chapter 17, where I discussed Easy VPN remote access, users are associated to a particular tunnel group based on one of the following methods:

- ▼ **Pre-shared keys**   The group name entered by the user, along with the correct pre-shared key.
- ▲ **Digital certificates**   The group name in the Organizational Unit (OU) or Department field. (You can use certificate matching to match on other fields on the certificate.)

WebVPN has multiple methods of matching users to WebVPN groups. If you are using digital certificates, the default is to look at the Organizational Unit (OU) field (commonly called the Department field) to match a user to a group; you can override this by creating certificate group matching rules (discussed in Chapter 17). If you aren't using digital certificates, you have the following options:

- ▼ Let the user choose the group from the login page.
- ■ Define the group the user belongs to on a per-user basis (on the AAA server or locally with the username's attributes).
- ▲ Place the user in a default group.

The following sections will discuss the two common options in associating a user to a particular WebVPN tunnel group.

Tunnel Group Lists

As I mentioned earlier in the "Tunnel Group WebVPN Attributes" section, you can display a drop-down list of group names on the login screen for clientless and thin client access.

The `tunnel-group-list` command displays a drop-down selector of tunnel group names on the login screen for clientless mode that allows the users to choose what group they should be associated with. An alias for the group must be specified to see the drop-down menu (via the `group-alias` command).

Here's a simple example:

```
ciscoasa(config# tunnel-group sales-group webvpn-attributes
ciscoasa(config-tunnel-webvpn)# group-alias sales enable
ciscoasa(config-tunnel-webvpn)# exit
ciscoasa(config# tunnel-group hr-group webvpn-attributes
ciscoasa(config-tunnel-webvpn)# group-alias human_resources enable
ciscoasa(config-tunnel-webvpn)# exit
ciscoasa(config)# webvpn
ciscoasa(config-webvpn)# tunnel-group-list enable
```

NOTE   You can lock a user into a group to restrict the policies applied to the user. This can be done on an AAA server or, if local authentication is used, within the local user account attributes.

Certificate Group Matching

If you will be using certificates to authenticate WebVPN users, you can examine information on the certificate to determine which tunnel group to associate the user to. Normally this will be the OU field; you can override this mapping by creating certificate mapping rules, which I discussed in Chapter 17. With certificate mapping rules, once you create the list of rules, you need to associate them with the WebVPN process:

```
ciscoasa(config)# webvpn
ciscoasa(config-webvpn)# certificate-group-map map_name rule_#
                             tunnel_group_name
```

Notice that in the `certificate-group-map` command, you associate the rule to a particular tunnel group name.

NOTE   Certificate mapping of users to tunnel groups is not normally used to associate a large number of users to their respective groups; instead, it is more commonly used to associate a user who has changed job functions. In this instance, you don't have to create a new certificate for the user; you use a certificate mapping rule to match the user to his new group.

WebVPN CLIENTLESS HOME PORTAL

The next few sections will provide a brief overview of using the WebVPN clientless interface: what the users see when they log in, how to navigate the home portal, and the floating toolbar.

Login Screen

To access the WebVPN interface, the user must connect to the address of the interface on the ASA that WebVPN is enabled on, using HTTPS. By default the port number is 443, unless you've changed this in the global WebVPN configuration, discussed previously in the "Enabling WebVPN" section. Here's the syntax the users need to use in their web browser address text box:

https://ASA_IP_address[:port_number]

For example, if the ASA IP address for WebVPN is 192.1.1.1, then the user would enter **https://192.1.1.1** in her web browser address text box.

When you connect, you are taken to the login screen, shown in Figure 19-1. You won't see the group drop-down selector unless you set up an alias for at least one tunnel group and enabled the drop-down selector in the global WebVPN configuration; this was discussed previously in the "Tunnel Group Lists" section.

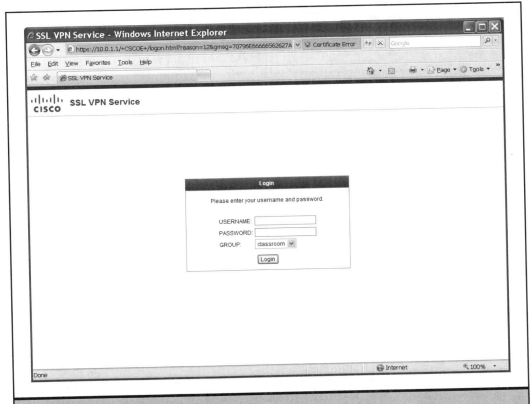

Figure 19-1.   WebVPN login screen

Home Portal Overview

Once you log in, you are taken to the home portal page, commonly called the *WebVPN home* page. This can be seen in Figure 19-2. In the top left corner, you can see the Cisco logo and the name of the page, which is "SSL VPN Service" by default (you can replace these two items with your own choices). At the top-right corner of the screen, click the Logout hyperlink or the red *X* icon to gracefully log out.

To the left is the Address bar. You won't see this if you didn't configure the `url-entry enable` command I discussed previously in the "Predefined URLs and URL Policies" section. The Address bar is broken into two components: a drop-down selector to choose the type of access (HTTP, HTTPS, FTP, and CIFS) and a text box where the users can complete the rest of the URL that they want proxied.

In the left column are icons/tabs you can click. Clicking the Home tab will take you to the screen shown in Figure 19-2. The elements you've defined for your home portal will affect what tabs you see in the left column. In Figure 19-2, I've predefined web URLs,

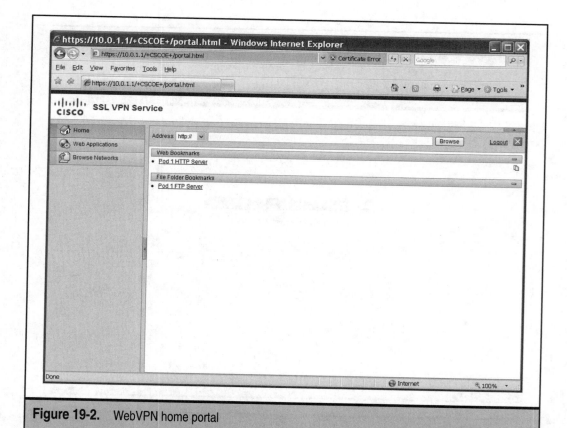

Figure 19-2. WebVPN home portal

FTP URLs, and allowed Windows file share (CIFS) access, so you see the Web Applications (web) and Browse Networks (FTP and CIFS) tabs. These items are controlled in the group policy associated with the user's tunnel group. All the URLs that are defined for this user's policy are displayed within the home page, broken into two sections: web URLs and file URLs. If you click a web hyperlink, you are proxied directly to the destination, where the contents of the remote web server page are displayed in the same window as your WebVPN access. If you examine to the right of the web URL on the home page ("Pod 1 HTTP Server"), you'll notice an icon of two pieces of paper—clicking this icon will open a proxied connection in a separate web browser window.

Home Portal Tabs

Clicking the Web Applications tab will list only the web-based URLs that you've predefined (HTTP and HTTPS). This tab can be seen in Figure 19-3. Clicking the Browse Networks tab, shown in Figure 19-4, will list only the file share URLs (CIFS and FTP).

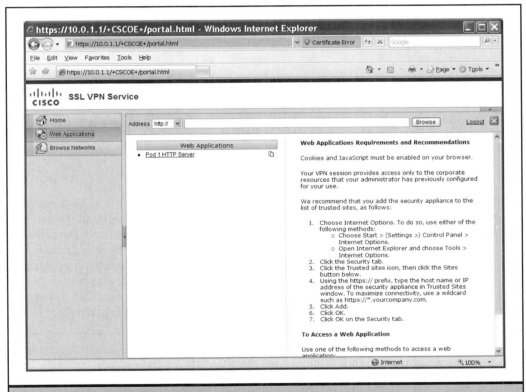

Figure 19-3. WebVPN Web Applications tab

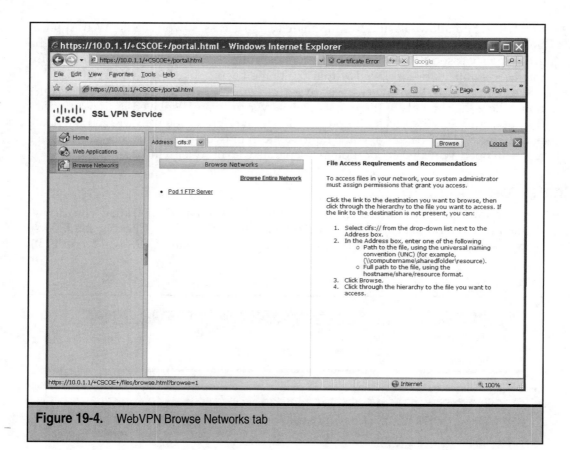

Figure 19-4.   WebVPN Browse Networks tab

You'll see the "Browse Entire Network" hyperlink if you've configured the **file-browsing enable** command for the user's group policy. When accessing a file share (CIFS or FTP), you'll see something similar to that shown in Figure 19-5. In this example, I'm interfacing with an FTP server. Notice the icons below the Address bar and the list of files below them. You can use this screen to upload, download, copy, delete, and rename files, as well as to create, delete, and rename directories (assuming you have the appropriate permissions on the file/FTP server). The GUI interface for manipulating files and directories is not the same as using Windows Explorer, but the process is somewhat similar.

NOTE   Other icons or window panes you may see within the WebVPN clientless web browser will depend upon what you've enabled for the group policy the user is associated with.

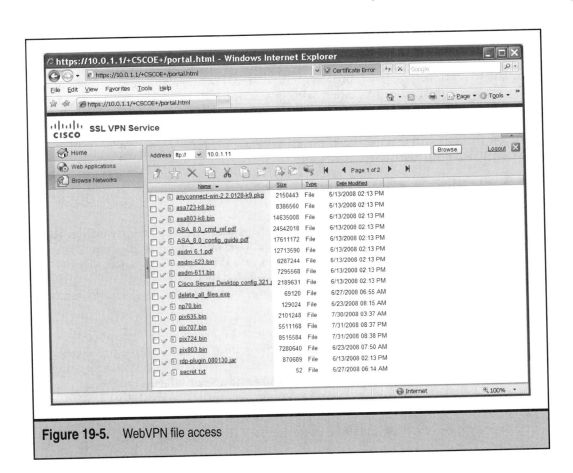

Figure 19-5.   WebVPN file access

NON-WEB TRAFFIC

For applications that don't use FTP, HTTP, or HTTPS (commonly referred to as *non-web* applications), you can still give the user access to these applications. You have two basic options: if the user is using only a web browser for WebVPN, then you can use the thin client feature for accessing non-web applications; otherwise the user must use the network client (AnyConnect), discussed in Chapter 20. This chapter will focus on the former option. The thin client feature supports three solutions for non-web applications: port forwarding, plug-ins, and/or smart tunnels. As you will see in the following sections, each has advantages and disadvantages, and you can pick and choose which ones you want to use based on your particular situation and needs.

Port Forwarding

Port forwarding was the original Cisco thin client solution to allow non-web-based applications to work across a web-browser SSL session. Port forwarding rules are created on the ASA and pushed down, along with JavaScript code, to the user. The JavaScript code then listens for local port connections based on the port forwarding rules and redirects these connections across the SSL tunnel, where the ASA will proxy them. The following sections will discuss the applications that port forwarding works with, along with how to set it up and troubleshoot it.

Port Forwarding Supported Applications, Requirements, and Restrictions

Cisco only supports a small number of TCP-based applications for port forwarding. These applications include Lotus Notes, Microsoft Outlook and Outlook Express, Perforce, Sametime, Secure FTP (FTP over SSH), SSH, Telnet, and Windows Terminal Services. Other applications may work, but haven't been officially tested by Cisco.

Port forwarding actually has many restrictions, which is why it was not commonly used by many companies when it was originally introduced by Cisco:

▼   Port forwarding requires the use of Sun Java 1.5 or later—JavaScript code must be installed on the user's desktop, which requires administrative privileges. The code can either be preinstalled or installed when the user connects using clientless mode. Because it requires administrative privileges, it cannot typically be used on public or noncompany computers, like airport kiosks.

■   Port forwarding only works with connections that use static port numbers— applications that use dynamic port numbers, like FTP, won't work.

■   The Microsoft MAPI protocol for exchange is not supported for port forwarding, along with smart tunnels: instead, a network layer client like AnyConnect or Easy VPN must be used.

▲   Port forwarding sessions are not replicated when stateful failover is implemented: users will lose their connections and have to reconnect.

Port Forwarding Configuration

Implementing port forwarding is a two-step process:

1. You must create the port forwarding rules in the WebVPN configuration mode.
2. You must associate the rules to a group policy.

Port Forwarding Lists   A port forwarding list is basically a grouping of port forwarding rules that specify the TCP connections that will be proxied by the ASA. These are configured using the **port-forward** command in the WebVPN subcommand mode:

```
ciscoasa(config)# webvpn
ciscoasa(config-webvpn)# port-forward {port_list_name local_port_#
                          remote_server remote_port_# [description]}
```

The *port list name* for the port forwarding rules groups the rules together in a set. You must specify a local port number that is unlikely to be used on the local PC. This is the port number the local application must use and that the JavaScript code is listening on. An application connecting to this port will have its traffic redirected by the JavaScript code across the SSL tunnel to the ASA, and then proxied to the actual destination. Cisco recommends using local port numbers greater than 65000, since these are not commonly used by local applications. The remote server can be the server IP address or hostname. If it is the latter, the JavaScript code will edit the "winnt/system32/drivers/etc/hosts" file and put an entry in it for local resolution, like this:

```
127.0.0.2    myremotehost.com # added by WebVpnPortForward
```

Notice that the remote server name is resolved to a loopback address. It is important that your users gracefully close down port forwarding in order for the extra added entries from the hosts file to be correctly cleaned up. I discuss this later in the "Port Forwarding and the Windows' Local Hosts File" section. The remote port number in the **port-forward** command is the actual port number the application is listening on at the remote server end. Basically the port forwarding rules tell the JavaScript code and the ASA how to perform the proxy for TCP applications.

Here's a simple example of two port forwarding rules in the same rule set:

```
ciscoasa(config)# webvpn
ciscoasa(config-webvpn)# port-forward STPorts 65025 SMTPserver 25
ciscoasa(config-webvpn)# port-forward STPorts 65023 10.0.1.100 23
```

The first rule specifies that when an e-mail connection is opened to SMTPserver on port 65025, JavaScript code will redirect it across the SSL tunnel. Remember that SMTPserver is resolved to a local loopback address based on the modification to the host file by the JavaScript code. The second command specifies that a telnet connection to port 65023 will be redirected across the tunnel; the one catch with the second method is that the user cannot telnet to the actual destination IP address of 10.0.1.100. Instead, for the JavaScript code to intercept the connection, the user must connect to port 65023 on the PC itself. In this situation, the telnet command would look something like this:

```
C:\> telnet 127.0.0.1 65023
```

NOTE The preceding process can be confusing to users, since if they are at the company office, they would type in **telnet 10.0.1.100** to connect to the server; however, for it to be redirected across the SSL tunnel and proxied by the ASA, they must use the **telnet** command just listed. If this creates too much confusion for your users, which it probably will, then you'll want to look at other alternatives, like plug-ins, smart tunnels, or the AnyConnect or Easy VPN network clients.

Enabling Port Forwarding   Once you have created your port forwarding rules, you need to associate them with a group policy in the WebVPN subcommand mode:

```
ciscoasa(config)# group-policy group_policy_name attributes
ciscoasa(config-group-policy)# webvpn
ciscoasa(config-group-webvpn)# port-forward {auto-start | enable }
                               port_list_name
```

The **auto-start** parameter will automatically download the JavaScript code and port forwarding rules when the user logs in using clientless mode; the **enable** parameter requires users to manually start port forwarding from the home portal once they log in.

Here's an example that associates the port forwarding rules in the example from the last section to a group policy:

```
ciscoasa(config)# group-policy ST_group_policy attributes
ciscoasa(config-group-policy)# webvpn
ciscoasa(config-group-webvpn)# port-forward auto-start STports
```

Using the Port Forwarding Feature

If port forwarding must be started manually by the user, the user first logs in and then clicks the Application Access tab, shown in Figure 19-6. The user then clicks the Start Applications button. A window will pop up where JavaScript will download, and the port forwarding rules will be displayed (the bottom right of Figure 19-6). The local column indicates what the user needs to use for the connection parameters to have the TCP application proxied by the ASA. This window must remain open until the user is done with the port forwarding process.

NOTE   If the autostart feature for port forwarding is enabled for the group policy, then the pop-up window will appear immediately when the user logs in.

Port Forwarding and the Windows' Local Hosts File

When a user starts the port forwarding process, the Windows local host file is copied to "hosts.webvpn" in the same directory. To ensure that the Windows local host file is returned to its original state after a user is done using port-forwarded applications, the user should close the pop-up window with the port forwarding rules. This will restore the original file and delete the file called "hosts.webvpn." If users don't follow this procedure, or they ungracefully close down the WebVPN clientless session or lose power to their PC, the next time they try to start up port forwarding, they'll receive this error message: `Backup HOSTS file.`

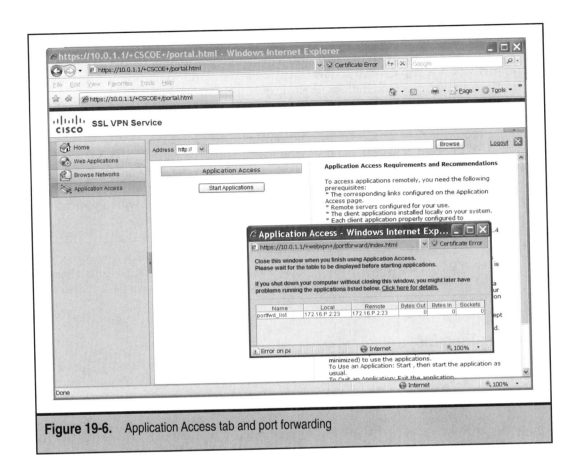

Figure 19-6.   Application Access tab and port forwarding

To recover from this problem, the user has three options to choose from to fix the problem:

▼   **Restore from backup**   The "hosts.webvpn" file is copied to the "hosts" file, and the "hosts.webvpn" file is deleted; at this point, the user can start port forwarding.

■   **Do nothing**   Choosing this option takes the users to the home page; port forwarding won't start until the problem is fixed.

▲   **Delete backup**   The "hosts.webvpn" file is deleted, where the "hosts" file has the port forwarding entries in it; port forwarding then uses the existing "hosts" file.

Web Browser Plug-Ins

Port forwarding is a legacy solution for proxying a limited number of TCP applications. Plug-ins, new in version 8.0, are an alternative to using port forwarding rules. A *plug-in* is basically Java code, located in flash on the appliance, that is downloaded and included as part of the web browser and contains the actual application: the user therefore doesn't need this application on their desktop! Plug-ins try to minimize the impact on the user by hiding the thin client process—port forwarding rules don't have to be created and downloaded. Plug-ins also perform much better than port forwarding and don't require anything to be installed on the user's PC, as is the case with port forwarding.

Cisco-supported plug-ins can be downloaded with a CCO account on the Cisco site under the ASA software section. Cisco supports plug-ins for the following applications: VNC, Citrix, SSH, telnet, Windows Terminal Services, as well as non-Cisco ones.

NOTE Plug-ins can only be used if the ASA, not an external proxy server, is proxying the connections. Also, when stateful failover is implemented, the proxied plug-in sessions are not copied from the active to standby units; therefore, when a failover occurs, plug-in sessions will fail and have to be reestablished by the user.

Importing Plug-Ins

To use a plug-in, you must load it into flash of the ASA with the **import webvpn plug-in** command:

```
ciscoasa# import webvpn plug-in protocol protocol URL
```

The protocol is the name of the application the plug-in will handle: the URL is the remote server the plug-in is located on. When importing the "ssh-plugin.jar" file, if you want both telnet and SSH to appear as connection options in the address bar of the home page, list both protocols in the **import** command separated by a comma and no spaces, like this:

```
ciscoasa# import webvpn plug-in protocol ssh,telnet
                ftp://192.168.1.66/ssh-plugin.jar
!!!!!!!!!!!!!!!!!!!!!!!!!!!!!!!!!!!!!!!!!!!!!!!!!!!!!!!!!!!!!!!!!!!
!!!!!!!!!!!!!!!!!!!!!!!!!!!!!!!!!
<--output omitted-->
```

Plug-ins are loaded to flash on the ASA and stored in the "csco-config/97/plugin" directory, which is a hidden directory.

Using Plug-Ins

Plug-ins allow the user to use the address bar on the home portal page. Once you have imported plug-ins, when you log into the ASA using the clientless approach and use the drop-down selector for the address bar, you should see the plug-ins listed. These include the following in the drop-down selector of the address bar:

- ▼ `rdp://`   Terminal services plug-in
- ■ `ssh://`   SSH plug-in
- ■ `telnet://`   SSH plug-in
- ■ `vnc://`   VNC client plug-in
- ▲ `ica://`   Citrix client plug-in

Figure 19-7 displays an example of plug-ins appearing in the Address bar. You can also define these in URL lists that appear as hyperlinks on the home page.

Smart Tunneling

Smart tunnels are new in version 8.0. A smart tunnel is a secure connection using an SSL VPN session via clientless mode between a Winsock 2 TCP-based application and a server behind the ASA. In that sense, it's something like port forwarding or plug-ins.

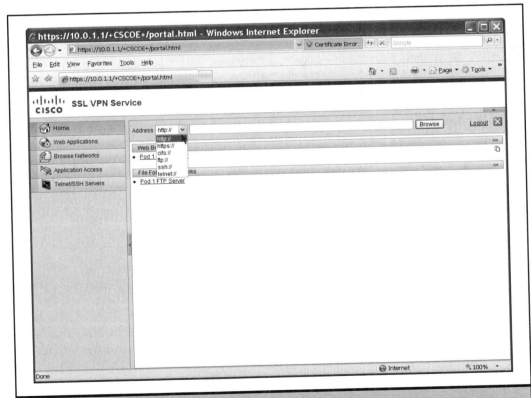

Figure 19-7.   WebVPN home page and plug-ins

With port forwarding, you must define port forwarding rules that are downloaded to the user's web browser, and Java listens on a local port number and redirects the traffic across the SSL tunnel where the ASA proxies the connection.

Plug-ins, like telnet or SSH, basically have the actual application reside on the ASA itself, so users don't need the actual application installed. Their main disadvantage, though, is that Cisco only supports a handful of them.

Smart tunnels bridge the gap between plug-ins and port forwarding. Unlike plug-ins, the application must be installed on the user's desktop. However, unlike with port forwarding, you don't have to change the user's application in order for the traffic to be tunneled. Some common applications that you can use for smart tunnels include MS Outlook and Outlook Express, Lotus Notes, and many, many others.

Smart Tunnel Requirements and Restrictions

To use smart tunnels, you must be running a 32-bit version of Microsoft Windows 2000 or XP, and your web browser must support and have enabled either Java, ActiveX, or both. (I have successfully used them on Windows 2003; however, Cisco doesn't officially support this OS.) As with plug-ins and port forwarding, stateful failover doesn't replicate these sessions between the active and standby units. As with port forwarding, Microsoft Outlook Exchange proxy (MAPI) is not supported—the AnyConnect or Easy VPN client must be used instead.

TIP So, you have three options—plug-ins, smart tunnels, and port forwarding—and you're not sure which you should use. Plug-ins don't require the actual application, like telnet, to reside on the user's desktop or additional Java software to be installed. Therefore plug-ins are the preferred solution; however, they support only a handful of applications. Smart tunnels should be used for the remainder of the applications, since they don't require users to modify how they use their applications and don't need administrative privileges to use smart tunnels. The problem with smart tunnels is that they only work on Windows 2000 and XP; for other operating systems, legacy port forwarding is your only solution, unless you want to install a full-fledged VPN client, like AnyConnect or Easy VPN remote, on the user's desktop.

Smart Tunnel Configuration

Implementing smart tunnels is similar to port forwarding, involving the same two-step process:

1. You must create smart tunnel lists in the WebVPN configuration mode.
2. You must associate a list to a group policy.

Smart Tunnel Lists   A smart tunnel application list is a list of applications that can use the smart tunnel function. The list is created in the WebVPN subcommand mode with the **smart-tunnel list** command:

```
ciscoasa(config)# webvpn
ciscoasa(config-webvpn)# smart-tunnel list st_list_name app_name
                         app_path/file_name [hash_value]
```

The list is given a name (*st_list_name*) that groups the applications. Each application that will be smart-tunneled must have a display name (*app_name*). Normally this is the name of the application itself, but you can call it whatever you want—this might be necessary if two different versions of the application with different names exist. Next you follow it with the application path and/or filename. If you don't specify the application path, but just "program.exe," that would include any file called "program.exe" on the user's drive space. You can be more specific and list a directory path. If there is the possibility of having more than one directory path for the application, list the application multiple times, giving it different *app_names*, and the different directory path and filename.

Optionally you can include a hash value of the application—this reduces the likelihood of another program "masquerading" as a valid program. To find out the hash value of an application, use the Microsoft File Checksum Integrity Verifier (FCIV) program, which is available at http://support.microsoft.com/kb/841290/. Once you've installed FCIV, place a temporary copy of the application to be hashed on a directory path that contains no spaces (for example, c:\temp\fciv.exe); then enter the following at a command-line prompt (cmd.exe):

```
fciv.exe -sha1 application
```

For example, **fciv.exe -sha1 c:\msimn.exe** will display a SHA-1 hash value for "msimn.exe." The SHA-1 hash is always 40 hexadecimal characters.

TIP Remember that if you use hash values, every time the application is updated, its hash value will change, so you'll need multiple *app_name* entries in your smart tunnel list for the application in question, where each time you'll list it with a different valid hash value. For example, if you just upgraded Outlook, you'd need an entry for the application for the old hash value and an additional entry with an updated hash value for the updated version of Outlook.

Here's a simple example of a smart tunnel list of various applications:

```
ciscoasa(config)# webvpn
ciscoasa(config-webvpn)# smart-tunnel list myapps CmdPrompt "cmd.exe"
ciscoasa(config-webvpn)# smart-tunnel list myapps telnet "telnet.exe"
ciscoasa(config-webvpn)# smart-tunnel list myapps putty "putty.exe"
ciscoasa(config-webvpn)# smart-tunnel list myapps OutlookExp "msimn.exe"
```

Enabling Smart Tunnels Once you have created your smart tunneling list, you need to associate it with a group policy in the WebVPN subcommand mode:

```
ciscoasa(config)# group-policy group_policy_name attributes
ciscoasa(config-group-policy)# webvpn
ciscoasa(config-group-webvpn)# smart-tunnel {auto-start | enable}
                               st_list_name
```

Notice that this is similar to associating a set of port forwarding rules to a group policy. The **auto-start** parameter will automatically start up the smart tunneling process when the user logs into clientless mode on the ASA; using the **enable** parameter requires users to manually start the smart tunneling process from the home portal once they log into the ASA.

Here's an example that associates the smart tunnel list from the example in the last section to a group policy:

```
ciscoasa(config)# group-policy my_group_policy attributes
ciscoasa(config-group-policy)# webvpn
ciscoasa(config-group-webvpn)# smart-tunnel auto-start myapps
```

NOTE A group or user cannot be associated with more than one list of smart tunnel applications.

Using Smart Tunnels

If smart tunneling must be started manually, the user logs in and clicks the Application Access tab. Below the Start Applications button, you can see the list of *app_names* that can be tunneled using smart tunneling—it's best to give these descriptive names to help out the users (see Figure 19-8). Click the Start Smart Tunnel button. A window will pop

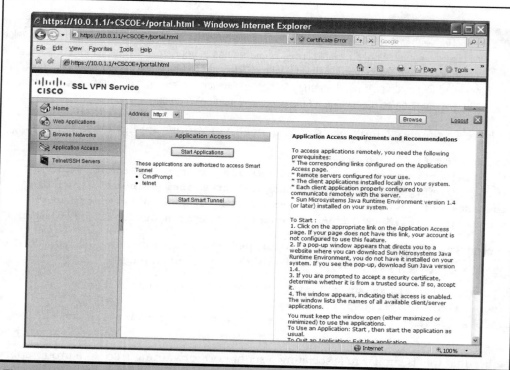

Figure 19-8. WebVPN home page and smart tunnels

up asking you to accept the self-signed applet, and another window will pop up asking you if you want to tunnel traffic (data to pass through) to the ASA: click the Yes button. If the autostart feature was enabled for the group policy, then the pop-up window would appear immediately when the user logs in.

WebVPN VERIFICATION AND TROUBLESHOOTING

Once you have set up clientless and/or thin client functionality and users are connecting to the ASA using WebVPN, you can use **show** and **debug** commands to verify and troubleshoot connectivity. The following two sections briefly cover these commands.

show Commands

To see a summary of the VPN sessions established on the appliances or the actual sessions themselves, respectively, use the following two commands:

```
ciscoasa# show vpn-sessiondb summary
ciscoasa# show vpn-sessiondb [detail] {webvpn | svc}
```

Here's an example using the **summary** parameter:

```
ciscoasa# show vpn-sessiondb summary
Active Sessions:              Session Information:
IPSec LAN-to-LAN : 0          Peak Concurrent : 0
IPSec Remote Access : 0       IPSec Limit : 750
WebVPN : 8                    WebVPN Limit : 500
SSL VPN Client (SVC) : 0      Cumulative Sessions : 0
Email Proxy : 0
Total Active Sessions : 0     Percent Session Load : 0%
                             VPN LB Mgmt Sessions : 0
<--output omitted-->
```

Notice that eight clientless/thin-client connections are established on the ASA.
You can log off a WebVPN user by using the following command:

```
ciscoasa# vpn-sessiondb logoff {remote | 121 | webvpn |
            email-proxy | protocol protocol_name |
            name username | ipaddress IP_address |
            tunnel-group group_name | index index_number | all}
```

debug Commands

You can use the debug command to troubleshoot WebVPN connectivity issues:

```
ciscoasa# debug webvpn [chunk | cifs | citrix | failover | html |
            javascript | request | response | svc |
            transformation | url | util | xml] [level]
```

Table 19-1 explains the parameters for the **debug webvpn** command.

Parameters	Description
chunk	Displays messages about memory blocks used for WebVPN connections
cifs	Displays messages about connections between WebVPN users and CIFS servers
citrix	Displays messages about connections between Citrix ICA clients and Citrix Metaframe servers over a WebVPN session
failover	Displays messages about failovers affecting WebVPN sessions
html	Displays messages about HTML pages sent over WebVPN sessions
javascript	Displays messages about JavaScript sent over WebVPN sessions
request	Displays messages about requests issued over WebVPN connections
response	Displays messages about responses issued over WebVPN connections
svc	Displays messages about connections from SSL VPN clients or AnyConnect clients
transformation	Displays messages about WebVPN content transformation
url	Displays messages about web requests issued over WebVPN sessions
util	Displays messages about the CPU utilization by WebVPN users
xml	Displays messages about JavaScript sent over WebVPN sessions
level	Sets the debug output level to display, between 1 and 255, where the default is 1

Table 19-1. The debug webvpn Parameters

CHAPTER 20

SSL VPNs: AnyConnect Client

T his chapter introduces the Cisco AnyConnect WebVPN Client. The AnyConnect client is the Cisco WebVPN tunnel mode client, which provides network layer protection of traffic between users and the ASAs using a tunnel mode (network layer) connection. This connection is protected using SSL. The topics covered in this chapter include

▼   Overview of the AnyConnect client

■   Preparing the ASA for AnyConnect client connections and installing the client

▲   Managing and troubleshooting AnyConnect client sessions

NOTE   Cisco Secure Desktop (CSD), a feature that complements WebVPN sessions, will be covered in Chapter 27.

ANYCONNECT CLIENT OVERVIEW

The Cisco AnyConnect client is an SSL client that protects traffic at the network layer and above. In this sense, it can protect the same kind of traffic that the Cisco Easy VPN IPSec remote software client can protect. Unlike the Easy VPN client, the AnyConnect client uses SSL for protection of traffic. It can use both TCP and UDP as a transport for protecting user traffic. Most people assume that SSL is TCP-based; however, a new RFC now allows UDP as a transport. (This topic is further discussed in the "DTLS as a Transport" section later in the chapter.) DTLS is commonly used to protect delay-sensitive traffic like voice and video.

WebVPN Network Clients

WebVPN has two network software clients, which are shown in Table 20-1. Cisco commonly refers to network layer protection as *tunnel mode* protection when referring to these two clients; this is similar to the tunnel mode process used by IPSec remote access clients.

Client	ASA OS	User Desktop OS
SSL VPN Client (SVC)	7.0–7.2	Windows 2000 and XP
Cisco AnyConnect Client	8.0+	Windows 2000, XP, and Vista MAC OS X (Intel and PowerPC), and Linux

Table 20-1.   WebVPN Network-Layer Clients

The SVC client was the Cisco original network-layer WebVPN client; it has been supplanted by the AnyConnect client. This book focuses only on the use of the AnyConnect client; however, the preparation performed on the ASA for either client is basically the same. The AnyConnect client requires that Java or ActiveX be preinstalled on the user's desktop.

NOTE   Cisco doesn't charge money for the client itself; instead, the number of SSL tunnels is controlled by the license installed on the ASA.

AnyConnect Client Implementation

The two operating modes for the AnyConnect client are

▼   Web launch mode

▲   Stand-alone mode

In web launch mode, the user employs a web browser and logs into the WebVPN server via clientless mode. Currently the two WebVPN server products that support the AnyConnect client are the ASAs and certain IOS-based routers. The group policy for the user must allow the use of the AnyConnect client. Assuming the correct policy has been defined, the user would click the AnyConnect tab on the left side of the screen and then click the Start AnyConnect button. The AnyConnect client is then downloaded and installed on the user's desktop. Once installed, the client automatically opens a tunnel to the WebVPN server, and an icon appears in the taskbar indicating that the tunnel is up. At the end of the session, the user has the option of keeping the client installed or having it uninstalled. Optionally instead of the users manually starting the tunnel from the WebVPN clientless session, you can automate the download for the users once they log in via clientless mode.

In stand-alone mode, the user doesn't have to log in via clientless mode to initiate the SSL tunnel; instead users start up the client manually from their desktop and provide their authentication credentials. In this mode, you can either send the users the AnyConnect software to manually install, or they can log in via clientless mode to perform the initial installation.

TIP   One handy feature of the AnyConnect client is that each time it connects, if there is a newer version of the client, the user is notified and has the option of downloading and installing the update from the WebVPN server.

AnyConnect Client Connections

Once connected, the AnyConnect client uses a transport process similar to what Easy VPN uses with IPSec. If you recall from Chapter 17, Easy VPN uses ESP in tunnel mode, encapsulating an IP packet in the ESP payload—basically tunneling IP within IP.

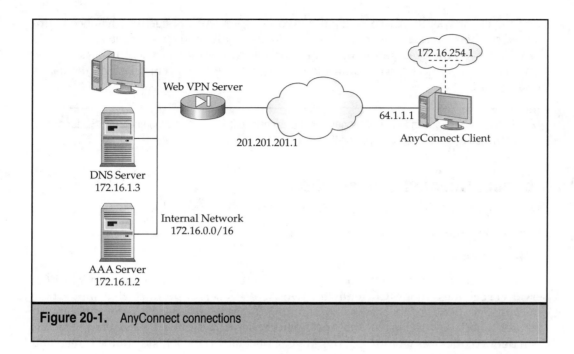

Figure 20-1. AnyConnect connections

The AnyConnect client uses a similar process, as shown in Figure 20-1. The WebVPN server must assign an internal address to the AnyConnect client. The server can obtain this address from a local pool of addresses, from a DHCP server, or from an AAA server; DHCP is the most common implementation. Whenever the AnyConnect client needs to send traffic to the corporate office, an IP packet is created with the internal address as the source and a destination address of the resource at the corporate office. This packet is then protected and either encapsulated in TCP (SSL) or UDP (DTLS). An outer IP header is then added, with a source IP address of what is assigned to the user's NIC and a destination IP address of the WebVPN server.

NOTE AnyConnect supports split tunneling. The default policy is that all traffic, except for DHCP and ARP messages, must be transported across the tunnel. As the administrator of the WebVPN server, you define the split tunneling policy on a per-group or per-user basis.

ANYCONNECT CLIENT PREPARATION AND INSTALLATION

The AnyConnect client is supported on the following user desktops: Microsoft Vista, XP, and 2000; Mac for Intel and PowerPC; and Linux. There are two client installation options: manual, where users must manually install the client on their desktop, and automatic, where the client is automatically downloaded and installed when users connect using clientless mode. With either method, users require administrative privileges to install the client.

NOTE Even though the AnyConnect client isn't officially supported on Windows 2003, I've successfully installed and used it on this operating system. However, if you have issues with the client on this operating system, you probably won't get much help from Cisco with your problem.

With the manual mode, you'll need to download the AnyConnect installation package from the Cisco site by using an authorized CCO (Cisco Connection Online) account. The software can be found under the same section as the ASA operating system files. The Windows downloaded package uses the Microsoft MSI package installer (.msi extension). Just have the user install it from an administrator account. Unlike with the Easy VPN Remote software, users don't have to reboot their PC once the installation is complete.

If you want the user to log into the ASA and download the software via clientless mode, you'll need to download from the Cisco site a different software package, which ends in a .pkg extension. This software will need to be placed in flash on the ASA, and you'll need to tell the ASA which PKG files can be used by your users. The users will then connect to the ASA via clientless mode, and the software will be downloaded and installed (which again requires administrative privileges on the user desktop).

TIP Of the two approaches, I prefer the latter, since I can automate the installation process as soon as users authenticate via their WebVPN clientless session. This feature is a plus compared with the Easy VPN IPSec client, which must be manually shipped out and installed by the users themselves (or automated via some type of login script).

ASA Preparation for the AnyConnect Client

To prepare for the use of the AnyConnect client, you must initially perform the following three steps on the ASA:

1. Copy the PKG file or files to flash on the ASA.
2. Specify which AnyConnect client(s) can be used on the ASA.
3. Enable the use of the AnyConnect client(s).

Once you have completed these steps, you can then define AnyConnect policies for your users. The following sections will cover these three steps.

Copying the PKG File to Flash

If you'll be using the automatic approach to install the AnyConnect client on the user's desktop, you'll first need to copy the PKG file you downloaded from Cisco to flash on the ASA. Here's the syntax you'll use to copy the file to flash:

```
ciscoasa# copy {tftp | ftp | scp}://IP_address/client_image.pkg
              {disk0: | disk1:}
```

Please note that there are different installation packages for the different operating systems. Windows has two versions: one, referred to as "gina," allows the AnyConnect client to start before the Windows Login process starts; the other, referred to as "win," is used for users that will log into Windows first and then bring up the AnyConnect client. Cisco does have a ZIP file that contains all the AnyConnect clients in one file. Here's an example of a Windows PKG filename: "anyconnect-win-2.2.0140-k9.pkg."

Here is an example of copying an AnyConnect client image to flash on the ASA:

```
ciscoasa# copy ftp://192.168.1.66/anyconnect-win-2.2.0128-k9.pkg disk0:
Address or name of remote host [192.168.1.66]?
Source filename [anyconnect-win-2.2.0128-k9.pkg]?
Destination filename [anyconnect-win-2.2.0128-k9.pkg]?
Accessing ftp://192.168.1.66/anyconnect-win-2.2.0128-k9.pkg...!!!!!!
<--output omitted-->
Writing file disk0:/anyconnect-win-2.2.0128-k9.pkg...
!!!!!!!!!!!!!!!!!!!!!!!!!!!!!!!!!!!!
<--output omitted-->
2150443 bytes copied in 2.270 secs (1075221 bytes/sec)
```

Specifying the Use of AnyConnect Clients

Once you have copied the PKG files to flash, they are not used by default. Instead, they must be "installed," or unpackaged, in flash of the ASA by using the **svc image** command in WebVPN subcommand mode:

```
ciscoasa(config)# webvpn
ciscoasa(config-webvpn)# svc image disk0:image_name [order]
```

The *image_name* parameter is the name of the PKG file you downloaded from an external server. You can specify more than one image name, since you might have to support multiple operating systems or multiple AnyConnect client versions. If you don't specify the order parameter, they are added sequentially.

TIP For the operating system that is most commonly used, I recommend you use a small number as the order number, since this is the image that is downloaded first to the user's desktop; if this doesn't match, then the second is downloaded. Therefore, if you are upgrading from one version to another, make sure you remove the older version from the operating system to ensure that the new one is automatically downloaded to users when they connect.

Here's an example of specifying a PKG file to use:

```
ciscoasa(config)# webvpn
ciscoasa(config-webvpn)# svc image disk0:anyconnect-win-2.2.0128-k9.pkg
```

This command is also used to install updated images on users' PCs—just make sure the newer client image has a *lower* order number than the original image.

When you install an image, the contents can be viewed with the `dir cache:stc` command; for each order number you create, you'll see a subdirectory under the main cache directory. Here's an example of entry number 1:

```
ciscoasa(config-webvpn)# dir cache:stc/1/
Directory of cache:stc/1/
0       ----  0                   07:34:01 May 19 2008  Windows
0       ----  408                 07:34:01 May 19 2008  VPNManifest.xml
0       ----  8419     07:34:01 May 19 2008  tips.htm
0       ----  3784     07:34:01 May 19 2008  strings.js
<--output omitted-->
2181120 bytes total (2144993280 bytes free)
```

Enabling AnyConnect

Once you have installed the appropriate AnyConnect images in flash, they aren't used unless you globally enable WebVPN tunnel mode in the WebVPN subcommand mode with the **svc enable** command:

```
ciscoasa(config)# webvpn
ciscoasa(config-webvpn)# svc enable
```

Use the **show webvpn svc** command to verify your configuration:

```
ciscoasa# show webvpn svc
1. disk0:/anyconnect-win-2.2.0128-k9.pkg 1 dyn-regex=/Windows NT/
   CISCO STC win2k+
   2,2,0128
   Fri 03/28/2008 15:48:45.81
1 SSL VPN Client(s) installed
```

In this example, a Windows PKG file has been installed as entry 1.

AnyConnect Policies

Many of the group policy configurations of Easy VPN discussed in Chapter 17 apply here, like assigning an internal address, split tunneling and split DNS, DNS server names, and other group policies. This chapter will only focus on the AnyConnect-specific group policy attributes defined on the ASA itself (not on an AAA server); for information on the other group policies, like split tunneling and split DNS, refer back to Chapter 17.

AnyConnect Client Usage

First, you must also allow the usage of the SVC or AnyConnect client in the group policy with the **vpn-tunnel-protocol** command:

```
ciscoasa(config)# group-policy group_policy_name internal
ciscoasa(config)# group-policy group_policy_name attributes
```

```
ciscoasa(config-group-webvpn)# vpn-tunnel-protocol {[svc] [webvpn]
                                     [ipsec] [l2tp-ipsec]}
```

The first command specifies that the group policy is defined on the ASA itself. The **vpn-tunnel-protocol** command is configured as an attribute of the group policy; use the **svc** parameter to allow users associated with the policy to use either of the two tunnel-mode clients.

Client Installation Policies

The **svc ask** command, if enabled, prompts users to download the AnyConnect client when they log into the ASA using clientless mode:

```
ciscoasa(config)# group-policy group_policy_name attributes
ciscoasa(config-group-policy)# webvpn
ciscoasa(config-group-webvpn)# svc ask {none | enable
                                  [default {webvpn | svc}
                                  timeout seconds]}
```

The default for this command is **svc ask none default webvpn**, where the ASA immediately displays the home/portal page for WebVPN clientless connections. The **default** keyword specifies what should happen if the user doesn't choose within the specified period—download the AnyConnect or SVC client (**svc**), or display the home/portal page (**webvpn**). The **timeout** parameter specifies the number of seconds the user has to accept the download; if not accepted, the user is taken to the home/portal page.

Figure 20-2 shows an example where the following configuration was used for the group policy:

```
ciscoasa(config)# group-policy anyconnect_policy
                       attributes
ciscoasa(config-group-policy)# webvpn
ciscoasa(config-group-webvpn)# svc ask enable default svc timeout 10
```

In this example, the default is the AnyConnect client (**svc**), where you can see the user has 9 more seconds (see Figure 20-2) to choose before the AnyConnect client is automatically downloaded.

Temporary or Permanent Client Installation

By default when the user logs in and downloads the AnyConnect client, the client is not permanently installed on the user's PC—once the user terminates the session, the client is automatically uninstalled. If you want to permanently install the client, use the **svc keep-installer installed** group policy command:

```
ciscoasa(config)# group-policy group_policy_name attributes
ciscoasa(config-group-policy)# webvpn
ciscoasa(config-group-webvpn)# svc keep-installer {installed | none}
```

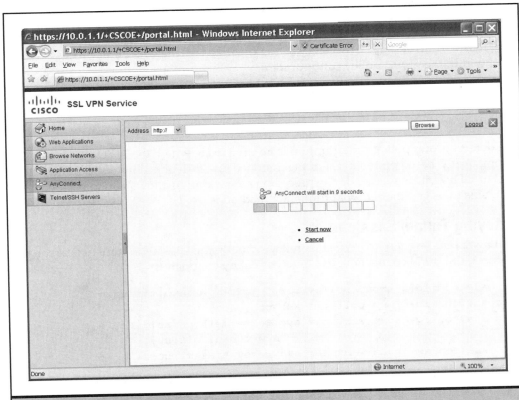

Figure 20-2.   Prompting to install the AnyConnect client

AnyConnect Modules

AnyConnect modules are add-on features that add functionality to the AnyConnect client. Valid module names can be found from the AnyConnect release notes. For example, **vpngina** is a module name that enables the "start before login" feature—the AnyConnect starts up first; then the Windows logon screen is displayed. To use this module, the user must enable this feature in the local profile (profiles are discussed later in the "Client Profiles" section) as well as the module being downloaded from the ASA. Here is the group policy command to specify the module names that are allowed to be used:

```
ciscoasa(config)# group-policy group_policy_name attributes
ciscoasa(config-group-policy)# webvpn
ciscoasa(config-group-webvpn)# svc modules value list_of_module_names
```

MTU Size Adjustment

The AnyConnect client (not the older SVC client) has the ability to adjust the MTU (Maximum Transmission Unit) size for the overhead of the tunneling process. This is done within the group policy configuration:

```
ciscoasa(config)# group-policy group_policy_name attributes
ciscoasa(config-group-policy)# webvpn
ciscoasa(config-group-webvpn)# svc mtu #_of_bytes
```

The default group policy configuration is **no svc mtu**, where the MTU size is adjusted automatically, based on the MTU of the interface that the connection uses, minus the IP, TCP, or UDP/DTLS overhead. The preceding configuration allows you to hard-code the MTU size to use no matter what tunneling method is used.

Rekeying Tunnel Sessions

To allow a remote client to perform a rekeying upon the expiration (timeout) of the tunnel-mode SSL VPN connection, use the **svc rekey** command:

```
ciscoasa(config)# group-policy group_policy_name attributes
ciscoasa(config-group-policy)# webvpn
ciscoasa(config-group-webvpn)# svc rekey method {ssl |
                                       new-tunnel | none}
ciscoasa(config-group-webvpn)# svc rekey time minutes
```

The **method** parameter specifies when rekeying of encryption/HMAC keys is done. The **none** parameter disables rekeying; the **ssl** parameter specifies that SSL renegotiation takes place during the rekeying; and the **new-tunnel** parameter specifies that the client must establish a new tunnel when rekeying is needed. The **svc rekey time** command specifies the number of minutes from the start of the session until when rekeying is needed (4 to 10,080 minutes).

DTLS as a Transport

DTLS was developed to deal with the latency involved in running real-time, voice, and multimedia applications across SSL VPN tunnels. Using TCP creates performance problems with these kinds of applications: voice, video, and multimedia. DTLS uses UDP instead. This process is defined in RFC 4347. When DTLS is enabled, two tunnels are used between the client and the server: one uses SSL with TCP port 443, and the other uses DTLS with UDP with port 443.

DTLS Configuration   When WebVPN is enabled, DTLS is automatically enabled; however, DTLS can be disabled globally or on a per-group policy basis using the following two configurations:

```
ciscoasa(config)# webvpn
ciscoasa(config-webvpn)# enable logical_if_name tls-only
```

or

```
ciscoasa(config)# group-policy group_policy_name attributes
ciscoasa(config-group-policy)# webvpn
ciscoasa(config-group-webvpn)# svc dtls {none | enable}
```

When DTLS is being used, it uses UDP with a destination port of 443. To change the port number for DTLS, use this command in the WebVPN subcommand mode:

```
ciscoasa(config)# webvpn
ciscoasa(config-webvpn)# dtls port port_#
```

Dead Peer Detection Because DTLS uses UDP, intermediate firewalls or address translation devices can create problems by timing out idle DTLS connections before they are done. Dead Peer Detection (DPD) can be used to send keepalives across the DTLS connection to ensure this doesn't happen. The DPD interval should be set two times higher than the firewall's idle threshold. The keepalive interval should be set to something less than the firewall's idle timer. For example, if the firewall has an idle timer of 30 seconds, the DPD interval should be set to 60 seconds, and the keepalive interval to 20 or 25 seconds.

This configuration is performed within the group policy:

```
ciscoasa(config)# group-policy group_policy_name attributes
ciscoasa(config-group-policy)# webvpn
ciscoasa(config-group-webvpn)# svc dpd-interval client seconds
ciscoasa(config-group-webvpn)# svc keepalive seconds
```

WebVPN Tunnel Groups

You must create a WebVPN tunnel group for the tunnel or clientless mode connections. The function of the tunnel group is to associate the group policy and other parameters that will be applied to a particular group of remote access people. The general attributes of the tunnel group are the same as those discussed in Chapters 17 and 19. WebVPN attributes were introduced in Chapter 19. In this chapter, I'll only focus on the tunnel group properties specific to AnyConnect client users.

Tunnel Group Properties

To create your tunnel group for WebVPN users (clientless, thin client, and tunnel mode client) use the following command:

```
ciscoasa(config)# tunnel-group tunnel_group_name type remote-access
```

Give the tunnel group a descriptive name.

Once you've created the tunnel group, you can then associate attributes or properties to it. General properties for remote access were discussed in Chapter 17:

```
ciscoasa(config)# tunnel-group tunnel_group_name general-attributes
ciscoasa(config-tunnel-general)# authentication-server-group
                              [(logical_if_name)] server_tag
                              [LOCAL]
```

```
ciscoasa(config-tunnel-general)# authorization-server-group
                           [(logical_if_name)] server_tag
ciscoasa(config-tunnel-general)# default-group-policy policy_name
ciscoasa(config-tunnel-general)# accounting-server-group server_tag
```

The **authentication-server-group** command specifies where to find the user credentials to authenticate the AnyConnect users: these can be on an AAA server or defined locally. The **authorization-server-group** command specifies the AAA server the group policies are located on; if the policies are defined on the ASA itself, then specify the name of the policy with the **default-group-policy** command. And if you're using AAA and want a record of who connects and how long they're connected, you can specify an AAA server to send accounting records with the **accounting-server-group** command.

Instead of authenticating users based on user accounts, you could authenticate them by using digital certificates obtained from an SSL certificate authority (CA) by configuring the following WebVPN tunnel group attribute:

```
ciscoasa(config)# tunnel-group tunnel_group_name webvpn-attributes
ciscoasa(config-tunnel-webvpn)# authentication {[aaa] [certificate]}
```

If you want to authenticate users based only on certificates, then only specify the **certificate** parameter; if you want to authenticate users based only on usernames and passwords, then specify the **aaa** parameter; and if you want to use both, specify both parameters (the order of the parameters doesn't matter).

NOTE If you'll be using certificates, both the user and the ASA will need certificates from a CA that can generate SSL identity certificates. The ASA itself can be a CA for SSL certificates; however, how to configure this on the ASA is beyond the scope of this book.

Internal Address Assignment

When using the AnyConnect client, the ASA must assign an internal address to the user. Assigning addresses was discussed in Chapter 17 (what applies there also applies here). Internal addresses can be obtained from the following sources:

▼ From an AAA server (per-user)

■ From a DHCP server

■ From a local address pool defined on the ASA

▲ From attributes of a local user account defined on the ASA

If you'll be using a local pool of addresses, use the following configuration:

```
ciscoasa(config)# ip local pool pool_name
                     beginning_IP_addr-ending_IP_addr
                     [mask subnet_mask]
```

```
ciscoasa(config)# tunnel-group tunnel_group_name general-attributes
ciscoasa(config-tunnel-general)# address-pool addr_pool_name
```

If you'll be acquiring the internal address from a DHCP server, you'll need to define the network number to send to the DHCP server in a group policy, and then define the DHCP server(s) in the general attributes of the tunnel group:

```
ciscoasa(config)# group-policy policy_name attributes
ciscoasa(config-group-policy)# dhcp-network-scope subnet_number
ciscoasa(config-group-policy)# exit
ciscoasa(config)# tunnel-group tunnel_group_name general-attributes
ciscoasa(config-tunnel-general)# dhcp-server IP_addr1 [...IP_addr10]
```

Tunnel Groups and User Association

Authentication of users was discussed in the last chapter. If you will be supporting more than one group and are not using certificates to match the user to the name of the group, then you will need to create an alias for the tunnel group name and enable the listing function for WebVPN:

```
ciscoasa(config)# webvpn
ciscoasa(config-webvpn)# tunnel-group-list enable
ciscoasa(config-webvpn)# exit
ciscoasa(config)# tunnel-group tunnel_group_name webvpn-attributes
ciscoasa(config-tunnel-webvpn)# group-alias group_name_alias enable
```

These commands were discussed in the last chapter.

Here's an example:

```
ciscoasa(config)# webvpn
ciscoasa(config-webvpn)# tunnel-group-list enable
ciscoasa(config-webvpn)# exit
ciscoasa(config)# tunnel-group salesgroup webvpn-attributes
ciscoasa(config-tunnel-webvpn)# group-alias sales enable
```

TIP   My recommendation is to use both certificates and user accounts for authentication. I primarily rely on the OU field of the certificate to match the user to the correct tunnel group (discussed in Chapters 17 and 19) and add an extra layer of protection by requiring the user to authenticate with a username and password. Most companies I've worked with use the Microsoft CA product, which is included in Windows 2000, 2003, and 2008 server products, but you could also use your ASA—just make sure you always back up the configuration, certificate, and keying information on the CA, no matter what product you use!

Client Profiles

Client profiles are XML files that control the interface and configuration of the Any-Connect client on the user's desktop, including items like who the WebVPN server is (its IP address), the start before login feature, and others. The profile is stored in a file on the user's hard drive. The client type will determine where you'll find the profile:

▼   **Windows 2000 and XP**   C:\Documents and Settings*your_username*\
Application Data\Cisco\Cisco AnyConnect VPN Client\Profile

■   **Windows Vista**   C:\ProgramData\Cisco\Cisco AnyConnect VPN Client\Profile

▲   **Linux and Mac**   /opt/cisco/vpn/profile

By default when the AnyConnect installation occurs on the user's desktop, the profile is copied from flash on the ASA to one of the preceding directories. A default template XML file can be found in the preceding directories and it is called "AnyConnectProfile.tmpl." You can use an XML editor to edit the file and then give it a descriptive name, like the name of the group that will use the configuration profile. This can then be used by users of a particular group. Place this file on an FTP, TFTP, or SCP server.

Installing the Profile on the ASA

For a user to use the profile, you'll need to first copy it to the ASA flash drive:

```
ciscoasa# copy URL_of_profile disk0:
```

After you've copied the client profile to the ASA flash, you'll need to load it into the ASA WebVPN cache with the **svc profiles** WebVPN subcommand mode:

```
ciscoasa(config)# webvpn
ciscoasa(config-webvpn)# svc profiles profile_name
                             disk0:/profile_file_name.xml
```

You can have different profiles for different groups of users, where each profile will need to be given a descriptive *profile_name*, like *salesprofile* or *engineeringprofile*. You can view the installed profiles with the **dir cache:/stc/profiles** command:

```
ciscoasa# dir cache:/stc/profiles
Directory of cache:/stc/profiles/
0       ----   6424          15:37:15 May 19 2008   profile_name.xml
2189312 bytes total (2144993280 bytes free)
```

Associating the Profile to a Group Policy

Once you've loaded a profile into the ASA WebVPN cache, you need to associate it to a group policy in order to use it:

```
ciscoasa(config)# group-policy group_policy_name attributes
ciscoasa(config-group-policy)# webvpn
ciscoasa(config-group-webvpn)# svc profiles value profile_name
```

After you have done this, the next time a user connects who is associated with this group policy, the client profile will automatically be downloaded to the user's desktop and installed in the Profile subdirectory...the next time the user connects, she'll use the newly installed profile.

TIP A quick way of testing this is to start up an AnyConnect client connection, log in, and then disconnect. Then bring up the AnyConnect client interface on the user's desktop, and verify the profile settings in the AnyConnect client GUI.

MANAGING AND TROUBLESHOOTING ANYCONNECT SESSIONS

Now that you understand how to configure the ASA to accept AnyConnect client connections, this last section in the chapter will cover how to download the client from the ASA to a user's desktop, use the client on the user's desktop, and how to manage client sessions from the ASA.

Connecting to a WebVPN Server

The next two sections discuss how to install the AnyConnect client on a user's desktop and how to use it once it is installed.

Installing the AnyConnect Client

The easiest way of installing the client is to have your users connect via WebVPN clientless mode and either have the user manually start the AnyConnect download from the home page or have this automatically done (if you've configured the **svc ask** command discussed previously in the "Client Installation Policies" section).

If you'll be using this method, first connect to the ASA using a web browser (HTTPS), enter your username and password, and select a group you belong to. Then click the Login button. In the following figures, I'll be performing the install from a Windows XP desktop. The software first performs some validation steps, shown in Figure 20-3. The install can use either ActiveX or Java: if you'll be using Java, you'll need to accept the self-signed Java code. Once the software is installed, the AnyConnect client automatically connects to your ASA. If the connection is successful, in Windows you can look at your taskbar: you should see an icon with two globes and a closed yellow lock, indicating that the tunnel is up. At this point you can close the web browser clientless mode connection.

TIP Remember to train your users to disconnect the clientless connection once the AnyConnect session has been established; otherwise both connections will count against the SSL license limit on your ASA!

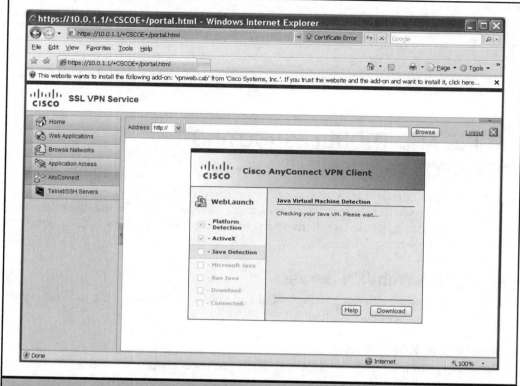

Figure 20-3.   AnyConnect client install process using clientless mode

Using the AnyConnect Client

When a session has been established, you can pull up the connection statistics or discon-nect the client by right-clicking the icon in the taskbar and choosing Open or Disconnect, respectively. The statistics window is shown in Figure 20-4. In this example, the internal address assigned to the client is 192.168.1.200, and the IP address assigned to the user's NIC is 10.0.1.11. The number of bytes sent and received will increment as traffic is sent across or received from the tunnel.

To disconnect an AnyConnect client session, perform either of the following:

▼   Right-click on the AnyConnect icon in the taskbar and choose Disconnect.

▲   In the Connection tab of the AnyConnect client GUI, click the Disconnect button.

If the client is installed on your computer, you can manually start it up, displaying the window shown in Figure 20-5. If more than one profile has been installed, you can

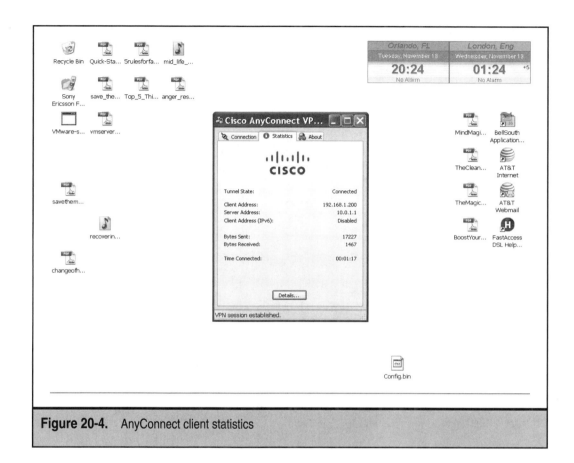

Figure 20-4. AnyConnect client statistics

select the profile in the drop-down Connect To selector—this allows the user to choose which ASA to connect to. Unlike in clientless mode where you have to access the Logon page to see the groups and enter your username and password, as soon as you choose a profile, this is done for you automatically. Select the Group name, enter your Username and Password, and click the Connect button. When done, you should see the AnyConnect icon in the taskbar with a closed yellow lock, indicating that you have successfully established a tunnel mode connection to the ASA.

TIP   If you have multiple ASAs, use the load balancing feature discussed in Chapter 17. In this instance you only need one AnyConnect profile with the virtual IP address of the cluster defined.

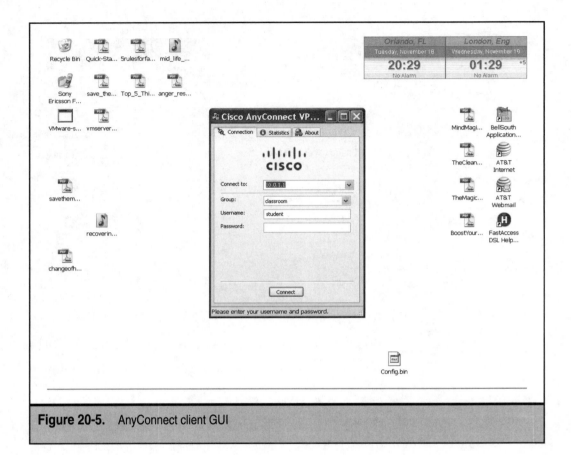

Figure 20-5. AnyConnect client GUI

Viewing and Managing Connected Users

On the ASA, you can use the **show vpn-sessiondb svc** command to view any connected AnyConnect client users using tunnel mode:

```
ciscoasa# show vpn-sessiondb svc
Session Type: SVC
Username      : student             Index        : 10
Assigned IP   : 192.168.1.200       Public IP    : 10.0.1.11
Protocol      : Clientless SSL-Tunnel DTLS-Tunnel
License       : SSL VPN
Encryption    : RC4 AES128          Hashing      : SHA1
Bytes Tx      : 1015195             Bytes Rx     : 189358
Group Policy  : webvpn_group_policy Tunnel Group : classroom
Login Time    : 00:51:04 UTC Tue Jul 1 2008
```

```
Duration      : 0h:07m:11s
NAC Result    : Unknown
VLAN Mapping  : N/A                    VLAN         : none
```

In the preceding example, you can see the username that was authenticated ("student"), the assigned IP address ("192.168.1.200"), and the group policy and tunnel group associated with the user.

To disconnect all SVC users, use the **vpn-sessiondb logoff svc** command:

```
ciscoasa# vpn-sessiondb logoff svc
```

Optionally you can disconnect particular users by their username or index number (see the output from the **show vpn-sessiondb svc** command):

```
ciscoasa# vpn-sessiondb logoff name username
ciscoasa# vpn-sessiondb logoff index index_#
```

For detailed troubleshooting of AnyConnect client sessions, use the following **debug** command:

```
ciscoasa# debug webvpn svc [1-255]
```

This command displays debug messages about connections to SSL VPN clients over WebVPN. Optionally you can qualify the level of debugging (the default is 1, which means the output is sparse).

PART V

Advanced Features of the ASA

CHAPTER 21

Transparent Firewall

This chapter will introduce you to the transparent firewall feature of the security appliances, which allows the appliances to behave similarly to layer 2 switches with firewall capabilities. The topics include

▼ Processing of layer 2 traffic versus layer 3 traffic

■ Configuring transparent mode on the appliances

▲ Implementing advanced layer 2 features on the appliances

LAYER 2 PROCESSING OF TRAFFIC

If you have your Cisco Certified Network Associate (CCNA), then the Open Systems Interconnect (OSI) Reference Model is nothing new to you. The OSI Reference Model was primarily designed as a teaching aid to help people understand how computers create, transmit, and receive data. The appliances deal with all seven layers of the OSI Reference Model. Obviously they have to deal with the two bottom layers—physical and data link—in order to accept frames on an interface. And up through version 6 of the OS, the appliances had to route traffic, so they had to deal with layer 3. With application inspection of many traffic types, the appliances can deal with all seven layers.

In version 6.0 and earlier, as I mentioned, the appliances would not process traffic on an interface unless you assigned an IP address to them. So basically the appliance was acting as a routing device: traffic would come in an interface, the appliance would compare the destination IP address to its routing table, find the corresponding destination network and the interface to exit from, apply the policies to the packet, and the appliance would forward the packet out the exit interface. Without IP addressing on the appliance, traffic wouldn't flow through it.

Routed vs. Transparent Mode

Starting in version 7 of the OS, the appliances support two modes of operation: *routed* and *transparent*. In routed mode, the appliance acts as a layer 3 device and forwards packets based on destination IP addresses. In transparent mode, the appliance acts as a layer 2 device, like a bridge or switch, and forwards Ethernet frames based on destination MAC addresses.

Figure 21-1 compares the two modes. Let's examine the routed mode example shown on the left side first. The two interfaces, whether they're physical or logical (trunked with VLANs), must be in separate VLANs (broadcast domains). Since routed mode is used and the appliance must see these as two distinct networks, two subnets are used for the layer 3 addressing. The appliance then forwards frames based on the IP addresses it sees inside the IP packet headers.

The right side of Figure 21-1 shows an example of transparent mode. Notice that the two interfaces involved in the layer 2 process are in separate VLANs (broadcast domains), but they are in the *same* layer 3 subnet (10.0.1.0). When in transparent mode, the appliance

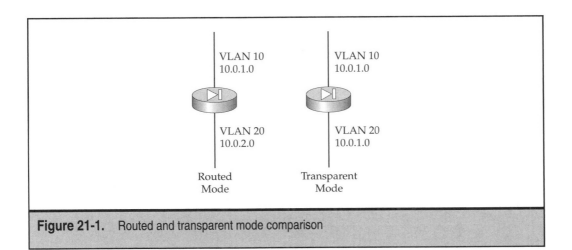

VLAN 10
10.0.1.0

VLAN 10
10.0.1.0

VLAN 20
10.0.2.0

VLAN 20
10.0.1.0

Routed
Mode

Transparent
Mode

Figure 21-1.   Routed and transparent mode comparison

behaves more like a layer 2 switch or bridge, where it switches frames between interfaces based on the MAC addresses in the Ethernet frame headers. As you will see later in the chapter, the appliances still have the capability of filtering traffic based on information in the layer 3 and layer 4 headers as well as the application layer (layer 7) payload.

One interesting point about the transparent mode process on the right side of Figure 21-1 is that the process is kind of strange when you examine it from a layer 2 device perspective. In a layer 2 network of switches, devices in the same subnet are in the same broadcast domain, and thus are in the same VLAN. So why would Cisco require you to put devices in the same subnet into *different* VLANs or broadcast domains?

Let's examine Figure 21-2 to understand why Cisco makes this requirement. Cisco assumes that all the devices that need to communicate with each other are connected to the same switch. If you were to put all the devices in the same VLAN on the switch, then the appliance couldn't control traffic between the devices, like the users and the default gateway, since the switch would allow devices in the same VLAN to communicate with each other. By placing the devices in separate VLANs, like 10 and 20 in the example shown in Figure 21-2, you are forcing the traffic to go through the appliance, where you can apply policies to the traffic.

NOTE   If the two interfaces of the appliance are connected to two different switches and the switches are not directly connected together, then you can use the same VLAN number for the interfaces of the appliance between the two switches.

Bridges vs. Transparent Mode

One thing to keep in mind about transparent mode is that even though an appliance is operating at layer 2, it does not behave exactly the same way as layer 2 switches or bridges. Yes, they are both operating at layer 2, but there are quite a few differences between how a switch and an appliance will handle traffic.

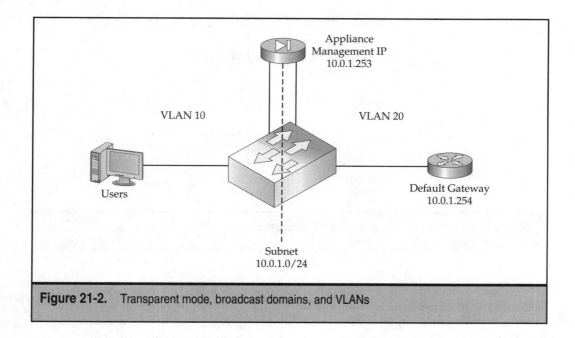

Figure 21-2. Transparent mode, broadcast domains, and VLANs

Let's examine some of the things that switches and appliances have in common as well as some of their differences. Switches perform three primary functions:

▼ Learn what MAC addresses are associated with which interfaces, and store them in a local MAC address table (sometimes called a CAM table).

■ Intelligently forward traffic using the MAC address table, but flood unknown destination unicast addresses, multicast addresses, and broadcast addresses.

▲ Use the Spanning Tree Protocol (STP) to break up layer 2 loops to ensure that only one active path exists between a source and destination.

Like switches, appliances when configured for transparent mode will perform the first bullet point: when a frame comes into an interface, the appliance compares the source MAC address in the frame and adds it to the MAC address table if it isn't already there.

The appliance will also use the MAC address table to intelligently forward frames based on the destination MAC addresses in the frame headers; however, the appliance will *not* flood destination unicast addresses that are not found in the MAC address table. The appliance will flood broadcasts and multicasts. The appliance assumes that if the devices are using TCP/IP, they'll go through the ARP process to discover destination MAC addresses that are associated with layer 3 IP addresses; through this discovery process the appliance will learn the respective source MAC addresses and the interfaces they are associated with. Therefore, if a device breaks away from this expectation and uses a hard-coded MAC address that the appliance hasn't learned (either dynamically or statically), the appliance will drop the unknown destination MAC address.

The second deviation from layer 2 devices is that the appliances do not participate in STP. Thus it is *very important* that you ensure you don't inadvertently create any layer 2 loops when setting up transparent mode. If you create a loop, you'll quickly figure this out when the CPU utilization on the appliance and switches jumps up to 100 percent.

NOTE   In the example in Figure 21-2, I would recommend that you filter BPDUs (Bridge Protocol Data Units) on the two switch interfaces connected to the appliance, or disable STP completely on these two interfaces, to alleviate any confusion the switch might have about seeing its own BPDUs on different interfaces. Again, just make sure you aren't creating any layer 2 loops when using transparent mode.

The third deviation from switches is that while switches process traffic at layers 1 and 2, the appliances can process traffic from layers 1 through 7! When an appliance is configured to operate in transparent mode, it will forward traffic based on layer 2 information, just like a switch; however, it can filter traffic on information at layers 2 through 7. Traffic filtering can be accomplished with Ether-Type ACLs, IP ACLs, and even application-specific policies created with Modular Policy Framework (MPF).

Supported and Unsupported Features

Certain features will be unavailable to you when the appliance is running in transparent mode. Here's a list of unsupported features:

▼   Only two interfaces (physical or VLAN) can be used; you can get around this issue by using contexts, which are discussed in the next chapter. (With contexts, each context can use two interfaces if it is configured in transparent mode.)

■   You cannot terminate VPNs like IPSec and WebVPN on the appliance.

■   CDP (Cisco Discovery Protocol) and IPv6 packets are dropped.

■   Ethernet frames that don't have a valid Ether-Type greater than or equal to 0x600 are dropped; however, you can make exceptions for STP BPDUs and certain non-IP protocols.

■   Through version 7, address translation was unsupported; in version 8, it is optional.

■   Quality of Service (QoS) with low-latency queuing (LLQ) is unsupported as a policy.

■   The appliance cannot act as a DHCP relay. (This isn't necessary since DHCP requests, which are broadcasts, are transmitted between interfaces.)

■   You cannot configure multicast commands. (Again, this isn't necessary since multicast traffic is flooded between the two interfaces in transparent mode.)

▲   Routing is unsupported—the appliance is operating at layer 2!

Given the list of restrictions, transparent mode does provide some distinct advantages when running in transparent, versus routed, mode. First, you can easily insert an appliance in an existing segment and control traffic between the two sides without having to re-address or reconfigure the devices! Examine Figure 21-3 as an example. This figure shows a typical campus network design—the access layer connects the user devices; the distribution layer provides layer 3 separation from the rest of the network as well as other services, like security and QoS; and the core connects the various distribution layers and the campus data center. For the access layer devices, their default gateway is the layer 3 switch IP addresses, or more than likely a virtual address from HSRP (Hot Standby Router Protocol) or VRRP (Virtual Router Redundancy Protocol). You could easily place transparent mode appliances in this design without having to change any addressing on the devices at the access or distribution layers: when Cisco uses the term "transparent," they mean it! If you put the appliances in as routed devices, you'd probably have to configure DHCP relay (see Chapter 26) to forward DHCP requests to the distribution layer; you'd have to change the default gateway address on the user devices to point to the security appliances; you'd have to create a separate subnet between the appliances and the distribution layer 3 switches; and you'd have to configure routing on the appliances.

NOTE In the design in Figure 21-3, if the distribution devices are layer 3 switches like the Catalyst 6500s, another option would be to purchase the Firewall Services Module (FWSM), which is basically a modular card running software similar to that of the PIXs and ASAs.

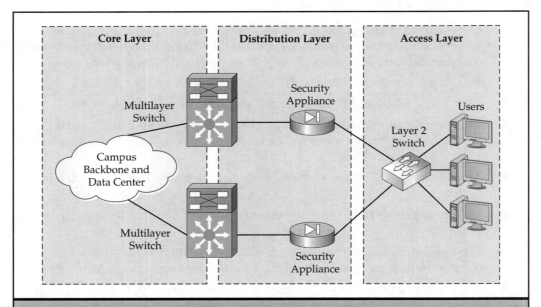

Figure 21-3. Common use for transparent mode

A second advantage of using transparent mode is that non-IP traffic can be allowed between interfaces. By default non-IP traffic is denied, like AppleTalk, IPX, STP BPDUs, and MPLS (Multiprotocol Label Switching). This traffic can be configured to go through the appliance by using an Ether-Type ACL.

A third advantage of transparent mode is that many, many features that work in routed mode also are supported in transparent mode, like address translation (in version 8), stateful filtering, standard and extended ACLs, CTP, web content filtering, MPF, and many, many others.

Traffic Flow and ACLs

Cisco still uses security levels to control traffic between interfaces when an appliance is running in transparent mode, where the same rules apply:

▼ Outbound connections are allowed by default unless restricted.

▲ Inbound connections are denied by default unless allowed.

The exception to these rules is ARP packets, which are always allowed by default since ARP is used as a discovery process to learn the MAC addresses of devices. You can restrict ARP packets, however, but this is optional.

When an appliance is at the perimeter of your network, the outside is the Internet (the non-trusted devices), and the inside is your corporate network (the trusted devices). When you are using an appliance inside your network, like that shown in Figure 21-3, the outside of your network would be the user devices at the access layer, and the inside of your network the distribution and core layers. Given this design, all traffic originated by your users would be denied by default unless you configured ACL entries to allow traffic. This creates more work on your part, but you can be much more specific about what is and isn't allowed.

TIP A more scalable approach in this situation would be to use Cut-through Proxy (CTP) with downloadable ACLs. You'd create downloadable ACLs on a per-group basis on an AAA server, and once users authenticated, the ACL would be downloaded and used. This approach is more scalable and flexible because all your filtering policies are centralized in one location, making it easier to change policies.

CONFIGURING TRANSPARENT MODE

When an appliance boots up, Cisco assumes you're running it in routed mode. Of course, when you run the setup script (see Chapter 3), that's the first question the script asks, where the answer defaults to routed mode. Changing it to transparent mode is a very simple process, as you'll see in the next section.

NOTE   When setting up transparent mode, only two interfaces, physical and/or VLAN, can be used. The devices on the two sides must be in different broadcast domains, like VLANs, but they must be in the same subnet. You can get around the two-interface limit with transparent mode: set up contexts, which are discussed in Chapter 22. A context is basically a virtual firewall. You could have some contexts in transparent mode and some in routed mode, where the contexts in transparent mode support two interfaces each.

Switching to Transparent Mode

If your appliance is currently running in routed mode, you can very easily switch it to transparent mode with the following command:

```
myappliance(config)# firewall transparent
ciscoasa(config)#
```

Because many features in routed mode are unsupported in transparent mode, the configuration on the appliance is cleared. To revert back to routed mode, use the **no firewall transparent** command.

SECURITY ALERT!   When switching from routed to transparent mode, you are not prompted to continue the process—the appliance immediately executes the command, your configuration is erased, and you're in transparent mode. So if you want to try transparent mode on an appliance with a routed mode configuration, first back up the configuration before trying it! (You would think, given that the appliance is doing something this drastic, the appliance would first display a note to you about the ramifications of executing the command and then would give you the option to abort it.)

Once you've converted the mode to transparent (or routed, for that matter), you can verify the mode with the **show firewall** command, like this:

```
ciscoasa(config)# show firewall
Firewall mode: Transparent
```

Management IP Address

You can assign an IP address to the appliance for management purposes. This IP address has to be from the subnet the two interfaces are connected to. For example, if you reexamine the right side of Figure 21-1, the management address would have to be an unused address from 10.0.1.0.

When you're assigning a management IP address to the appliance, the address must be from the subnet connected to the two interfaces on the appliance. Here's the command to configure the management address:

```
ciscoasa(config)# ip address IP_address [subnet_mask]
                      [standby IP_address]
```

Notice that the `ip address` command is a global command—you are not in an interface when configuring it. The `standby` parameter assigns a management IP address to the standby unit in a failover configuration (failover is discussed in Chapter 23). Use the `show ip address` command to verify your management IP address configuration.

NOTE The assignment of a management address is optional. Also the management address is just that: a management address. For devices in the subnet, do not point them to this address as a default gateway. Remember that the appliance is in transparent mode, acting as a layer 2 device: it is not acting as a router.

MAC Address Table and Learning

As I mentioned in the "Bridges vs. Transparent Mode" section, the appliances will build a MAC address table of source MAC addresses associated with an interface. You can view the MAC address table with the `show mac-address-table` command:

```
ciscoasa# show mac-address-table [logical_if_name | count | static]
```

Without any parameters, all the MAC addresses in the table are shown. You can limit the display to MAC addresses associated with a particular interface, to a count of the total addresses in the table, or to listing just the statically defined entries.

Here's an example of this command:

```
ciscoasa# show mac-address-table
Interface    Mac Address      Type     Time Left
-----------------------------------------------
outside      0009.7cbe.2101   static   -
inside       0010.7cbe.6102   static   -
inside       0009.7cbe.5103   dynamic  10
```

Notice that the first two entries have been statically defined (discussed later in this section) and the last dynamically learned.

Dynamically learned MAC addresses will be aged out of the table if they are idle for 5 minutes by default. This timer can be changed with the `mac-address-table aging-time` command.

```
ciscoasa(config)# mac-address-table aging-time minutes
```

If you want to hard-code a MAC address association for a logical interface, use the `mac-address-table static` command:

```
ciscoasa(config)# mac-address-table static logical_if_name mac_address
```

This is sometimes done to prevent MAC address spoofing of critical services like a default gateway or DHCP server. You can even completely disable MAC address learning on an interface with this command:

```
ciscoasa(config)# mac-learn logical_if_name disable
```

If you disable learning, then you must configure the necessary MAC address static entries for the interface, or only broadcasts and multicasts will be allowed on the interface.

And if you're having problems with the MAC address learning function or the static entries you built on the appliance, you can use the **debug mac-address-table** command to troubleshoot the problems.

ADDITIONAL LAYER 2 FEATURES

This section will discuss the configuration of a couple of enhanced layer 2 features of transparent mode: Ether-Type ACLs and ARP inspection.

Non-IP Traffic and Ether-Type ACLs

When you're operating in routed mode, the only way to get non-IP traffic to flow through the appliance is to encapsulate it in GRE and tunnel it through the appliance using this layer 3 TCP/IP protocol. The appliances do not handle non-IP traffic natively—this must be handled by a different device (typically a router). The problem with a different device handling the traffic is that it isn't very efficient: you're adding overhead to the process and introducing delay by having to encapsulate and de-encapsulate every packet.

If you're concerned about this process, you can run your appliance in transparent mode instead. Unlike TCP/IP unicast traffic, which uses security levels to determine whether a connection is allowed, *all* non-IP traffic is denied by default when running in transparent mode. To allow non-IP traffic, you must create an Ether-Type ACL (or ACLs) and apply it to each interface you want to allow the non-IP traffic on.

The syntax for creating an Ether-Type ACL is as follows:

```
ciscoasa(config)# access-list ACL_ID ethertype {deny | permit}
                  {ipx | bpdu | mpls-unicast | mpls-multicast |
                  any | hex_#_of_protocol} [log]
```

Notice that the **ethertype** parameter specifies that this is not an IP ACL. Following the **permit** or **deny** parameter, you specify the protocol that will be matched on. Optionally you can specify a hexadecimal number greater than or equal to 0x600 for the protocol (currently you cannot filter on actual MAC addresses in the Ethernet frame header). For example, TCP/IP uses a protocol number of 0x0800 and AppleTalk uses 0x809b.

Once you have created your Ether-Type ACL, you need to apply it to an interface with the **access-group** command, which was discussed in Chapter 5:

```
ciscoasa(config)# access-group ACL_ID in interface logical_if_name
```

TIP Remember that when allowing non-IP traffic, you'll need to apply an ACL (or ACLs) to *both* interfaces in order to allow traffic in both directions.

ARP Inspection

By default all ARP packets are allowed through the appliance. The source generates a broadcast ARP query to learn the IP-to-MAC address association of the destination. And since the appliance is learning the source MAC address of the requester, when the destination replies with an ARP unicast response, this is allowed (the source MAC address is in the ARP table), given that the destination MAC address is found in the MAC address table and the packet is an ARP reply.

The problem with the ARP protocol, however, is that it is very easy for an attacker to spoof responses or to generate a gratuitous ARP announcement with incorrect IP-to-MAC address information or by matching the attacker's MAC address with someone else's IP address. To somewhat limit the effectiveness of ARP spoofing, Cisco supports an ARP inspection feature on the appliances when they are running in transparent mode. The ARP inspection feature looks for mismatches between the IP address, MAC address, and the associated interface for ARP replies. If the appliance sees the wrong combination of IP-to-MAC address matching in an ARP reply, or sees an ARP reply with a source of an incorrect interface, the appliance will drop the packet. Of course the appliance has to know what the correct address matchings are; the appliance can either learn this dynamically by examining the ARP replies on its interfaces, or you can define them statically. The following sections will discuss how to configure and verify ARP inspection.

ARP Inspection Configuration

By default the ARP inspection feature is disabled, which means that when the appliance sees an ARP query, it is flooded out the opposite interface. Enabling ARP inspection is done with the **arp-inspection** command:

```
ciscoasa(config)# arp-inspection logical_if_name enable
                       [flood | no-flood]
```

ARP inspection is enabled on an interface-by-interface basis. The **flood** parameter, which is the default if omitted, will flood all ARPs received on the interface. The **no-flood** parameter will not forward an ARP reply if it doesn't match a specific static ARP entry on the appliance. Therefore, when using the **no-flood** parameter, you'll need to create static entries for the associated interface with the **arp** command:

```
ciscoasa(config)# arp logical_if_name IP_address MAC_address
```

If you don't configure this command and ARP flooding is disabled, devices will be unable to communicate with each other via IP across the associated interface.

ARP Inspection Verification

To see the status of ARP inspection and your configuration, use the **show arp-inspection** command. Here's an example:

```
ciscoasa# show arp-inspection
interface    arp-inspection    miss
----------------------------------------------------------
```

```
inside enabled flood
outside disabled
```

Once you have enabled ARP inspection, to examine the local ARP table on the appliance, use the **show arp** command. Here's an example:

```
ciscoasa# show arp
inside 10.0.1.11 0008.023b.1234
inside 10.0.1.12 0001.023a.abcd
```

If you are having issues with the ARP inspection feature, or feel that the appliance might be dropping ARP requests and replies that it shouldn't, you can use the **debug arp-inspection** command to troubleshoot the problem.

TIP　The problem with ARP inspection on the appliance is that it will not stop ARP spoofing attacks occurring off the same interface, like a hacker impersonating a user's MAC address, where both devices are connected to the same switch, which is then connected to an interface on the appliance. ARP inspection will prevent ARP spoofing attacks between interfaces on the appliance. Therefore, in production networks, I've never enabled this feature on the appliance; instead, I've enabled it on the switches. (Cisco Catalyst switches support an ARP inspection feature, as well as many other layer 2 security features.)

TRANSPARENT FIREWALL EXAMPLE CONFIGURATION

Now that I've introduced the concepts of the transparent firewall feature, let's look at an example configuration to see how it's implemented. I'll use the example shown previously in Figure 21-2 for this configuration, where I'll assume VLAN 10 is the non-trusted side and VLAN 20 is the trusted side. Also, I'll use an ASA 5510, with one physical interface connected to the switch, which will use 802.1Q trunking. The users should be allowed to open any HTTP, FTP, DNS, SMTP, or ICMP connection. ICMP won't be configured as stateful, so for ICMP traffic from the campus network, the ICMP replies will have to be allowed back through the appliance.

Here's the ASA 5510 configuration:

```
myasa# show firewall
Firewall mode: Router
myasa(config)# firewall transparent
ciscoasa(config)# show firewall
Firewall mode: Transparent
ciscoasa(config)# interface e0/0
ciscoasa(config-if)# no shutdown
ciscoasa(config-if)# exit
ciscoasa(config)# interface e0/0.10
ciscoasa(config-subif)# vlan 10
```

```
ciscoasa(config-subif)# nameif outside
ciscoasa(config-subif)# security-level 0
ciscoasa(config-subif)# exit
ciscoasa(config)# interface e0/0.20
ciscoasa(config-subif)# vlan 20
ciscoasa(config-subif)# nameif inside
ciscoasa(config-subif)# security-level 100
ciscoasa(config-subif)# exit
ciscoasa(config)# ip address 10.0.1.253 255.255.255.0
ciscoasa(config)# access-list ACLoutside permit icmp any any
ciscoasa(config)# access-list ACLoutside permit tcp any any eq 80
ciscoasa(config)# access-list ACLoutside permit tcp any any eq 21
ciscoasa(config)# access-list ACLoutside permit tcp any any eq 25
ciscoasa(config)# access-list ACLoutside permit udp any any eq 53
ciscoasa(config)# access-list ACLoutside deny ip any any
ciscoasa(config)# access-group ACLoutside in interface outside
```

In the preceding example, I enabled transparent mode. I then set up e0/0 with trunking, along with the two VLANs, 10 and 20. The management IP address I assigned was 10.0.1.253. I then set up an ACL to allow the users in VLAN 10 to access campus network resources in or beyond VLAN 20.

TIP   In real life, I would be as specific as possible about what is and isn't allowed from the users to the campus network. My recommendation in a campus situation is to primarily rely on CTP with downloadable ACLs to restrict users' access versus static ACL entries on the appliance: this gives you more flexibility and scalability when implementing your policies.

CHAPTER 22

Contexts

This chapter will introduce you to the concept of contexts and the advantages they give you in deploying a wide diversity of security policies. The topics in this chapter include

▼ Introducing contexts, including their uses and components

■ Switching to multiple mode and setting up contexts

▲ Managing your contexts

CONTEXT OVERVIEW

A context is basically a virtual firewall; however, contexts are not the same as VMware—with VMware, you can have multiple operating systems running on the same computer. With contexts, each context uses the same operating system and ASDM image. However, each context can have its own security policies and its own set of administrators to manage the context. The following sections will introduce the licensing, use, restrictions, and implementation of contexts.

Licensing

Not every security appliance supports contexts. The PIX 515 and higher and the ASA 5510 and higher support contexts. And for the appliances that do support contexts, you get two contexts for free by default; if you want more contexts, you'll have to buy the appropriate license. There are four license levels for purchasing security contexts—5, 10, 20, and 50—as well as upgrade licenses to upgrade from one number to another.

With the 5510, you need the Security Plus license to use contexts, and the 5510 supports a maximum of five contexts. The 5520 supports a maximum of 20 contexts, and the higher-end ASAs support up to 50 contexts. The PIX 515 and 515E support up to 5 contexts, and the 525 and 535 support up to 50 contexts. I discuss how to upgrade the license key on the appliances in Chapter 26.

Context Uses

Contexts can be used for a variety of situations; however, I've seen them most commonly used in these three:

▼ Active/active failover

■ ISP and co-location/hosting companies that host services requiring firewall functions

▲ Companies needing more than one firewall in the same physical location

Failover and Contexts

Failover is a Cisco-proprietary feature that allows two appliances to provide firewall redundancy for connections flowing through them. In active/standby failover, only one appliance can forward traffic at a time. In active/active failover, both appliances can simultaneously forward traffic, allowing you to implement load balancing. Active/active failover requires the use of contexts: one context for each logical flow of traffic. Failover is discussed in Chapter 23.

ISPs and Contexts

Many ISPs and hosting or co-location companies host services for companies, and one of the options they can provide and/or sell their customers is firewall services. Prior to contexts, a provider would have to purchase many firewalls to implement the policies for the companies it was hosting services for. With contexts, you can purchase one firewall and configure up to 50 contexts—50 virtual firewalls, where a virtual firewall would handle traffic for a single company! This is a much more cost-effective approach compared with purchasing a physical firewall per hosted company—this is especially true in co-location/hosting companies, where your billing is based on rack space, power consumption, heat output, and bandwidth utilization.

Companies and Contexts

Contexts can even be used within a company infrastructure. Imagine you have two departments in one building, where each department wants its own firewall because of security issues. You could purchase two firewalls, but a more economical approach would be to buy one appliance and set up two contexts, where each department could only access and manage its respective context and its security policies.

Context Restrictions

Even though contexts allow you to create more firewalls on your appliance, they do have their downside: not all appliance features are supported when using contexts. Here is a list of features unsupported on the appliances when you've implemented contexts on them:

▼   Dynamic routing protocols (unicast and multicast) are unsupported: you must use static routes.

■   No VPN type—IPSec, L2TP, or WebVPN—is supported.

▲   Threat detection is unsupported.

Other than these restrictions, all other appliance features are supported. For example, if you had the need, you could set up one context to run in routed mode and another in transparent mode; you could set up address translation in one context, and use a different address translation policy in a second context; you could have the IPS card for the ASAs process traffic for two contexts, but not a third context; you could have different filtering and inspection policies for the different contexts; and I could go on and on with the flexibility of implementing policies with contexts.

Context Implementation

By default when you receive your appliance from Cisco and boot it up, the appliance is running in single mode. In single mode, the appliance acts as a stand-alone firewall. To use contexts (assuming you have the appropriate licensing on the appliance), you have to switch to multiple mode. As you will see later in the "Switching to Multiple Mode" section, you have the option of importing the appliance stand-alone (single mode) configuration into a context.

System Area

When you boot up in multiple mode from the CLI, you are taken into the system area. The system area is used to configure the physical properties of the interfaces, create VLANs for trunking, create resource classes to restrict the context system resource usage, and initially to create the contexts themselves. You can also password-protect the system area to restrict access to it, as well as other administrative functions. In other words, the system area is where you configure system resources that affect the security appliance as a whole; however, the individual security policies are configured within the contexts themselves. The system area doesn't count as a context itself and thus doesn't affect your licensing.

Context Properties

A context must have a name, interfaces allocated to it, and a configuration file to store the security policies and configurations of the actual context itself. One context must be denoted as the administrative context. This context is used by the system area to communicate with external devices, like an FTP server, to back up the system area configuration file, to upgrade the appliance operating system or ASDM image, or to send syslog messages associated with the system area to a syslog server. Other than this special function, the administrative context can be used for normal data functions. When the appliance boots up, it automatically creates one context, called the *admin* context, which defaults to being the administrative context. Any context can be the administrative context; so if you don't like the name "admin" for the context, you can delete it and create a context with a different name that will perform the administrative context functions. However, one of the contexts on your appliance must be the administrative context.

NOTE   By default an administrator who has access to the administrative context can switch to the system area unless you restrict this. However, non-administrative contexts do not have access to the system area.

Context Chaining

The appliances support chaining, sometimes referred to as cascading, of contexts. With chaining, one context is logically connected to another, where a packet can come in one physical interface to one context, where policies are applied to the packet, and then

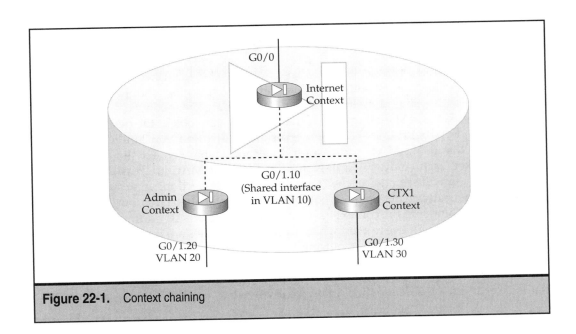

Figure 22-1. Context chaining

forwarded to a second (or more) context for more policies to be applied, before the packet physically leaves the appliance.

Figure 22-1 illustrates chaining. In this figure, the Internet context has two interfaces associated with it: G0/0 is connected to the Internet, and G0/1.10 is in VLAN 10. The Admin context has two interfaces: G0/1.10 is in VLAN 10, and G0/1.20 is in VLAN 20. The CTX1 context has two interfaces: G0/1.10 is in VLAN 10, and G0/1.30 is in VLAN 30. Notice that all three contexts share the same logical interface, which interconnects them.

NOTE When chaining contexts, a VLAN interface must be shared among the contexts. Basically you're creating the illusion that a logical segment is interconnecting the contexts. Given this, even though the same interface is being shared, each context will have to have a different MAC address for that interface, making it appear that the shared interface really appears as multiple, logical interfaces to each context that is chained. I highly recommend for security purposes that if the shared interface is physically connected to a switch, you do not place any other device in this VLAN.

Traffic Classification

One of the features of contexts, as you saw in the last section, is that multiple contexts can share the same interface—physical or VLAN subinterfaces. If you don't share interfaces across contexts, then it is very easy for the appliance to classify what context should handle an inbound packet, since only one context is associated with the respective interface.

NOTE   A packet entering an interface without a context associated with it will be dropped.

If you are sharing a physical or VLAN subinterface between two or more contexts, however, the appliance must somehow determine which context should process an inbound packet on the shared interface. When determining what context should process an inbound packet on a shared interface, the appliance can look at the destination MAC address in the Ethernet frame and/or the translation rules and translation entries in the xlate table. When using MAC addresses to determine what context should handle an inbound packet, each context will have to use a *different* MAC address for the shared interface. As you will see later in the "Creating Contexts" section, you can have the appliance automatically create unique MAC addresses for the interfaces, or you can manually do this by going into the context itself and changing the MAC address for the shared interface. Translation rules are used when the MAC addresses are duplicated across contexts. I recommend, even if you are using translation rules, that you ensure the shared interfaces have unique MAC addresses, though. The one translation policy the appliance cannot use for context matching a packet is the **nat 0** commands, since they only specify the source, and not the destination, interface involved.

NOTE   You might assume that if each context has unique IP addressing, the appliance would use the routing table to match up a packet to the correct context; however, this is not the case. Only MAC addresses and translation rules are used to match a packet to a context when interfaces are shared.

CONTEXT MODE

This section will cover how to implement contexts on your appliance: switching from single to multiple mode, creating contexts, and restricting resources the contexts can use.

Switching to Multiple Mode

The **mode multiple** command is used to switch from single to multiple mode. Here's an example of the use of this command:

```
ciscoasa# mode multiple
WARNING: This command will change the behavior of the device
WARNING: This command will initiate a Reboot
Proceed with change mode? [confirm] <ENTER>
Convert the system configuration? [confirm] <ENTER>
The old running configuration file will be written to disk0
The admin context configuration will be written to disk0
The new running configuration file was written to disk0
Security context mode: multiple
<--output omitted-->
```

To switch to multiple mode, the appliance will have to reboot itself. This process is one of the few instances where your current configuration is automatically backed up to flash in case you don't like contexts and want to switch back to single mode. The file is called "old_running.cfg." You also have the option of importing your existing configuration into the automatically created admin context; if you don't choose the import option, the appliance will reset itself to the factory defaults once it boots up. Upon rebooting, the appliance takes you into the system area automatically.

In the system area, use the **show mode** command to verify the mode in which your appliance is running. Here's an example:

```
ciscoasa# show mode
Security context mode: multiple
```

NOTE   To switch back to single mode, use the **mode single** command in the system area.

System Area Configuration

Upon rebooting from single to multiple mode, you are taken into the system area if you happen to be using the console. The system area is primarily used to manage the appliance itself, whereas contexts are used to move traffic through the appliance. From the system area you can perform the following tasks:

▼   Control management access to the system area.

■   Assign physical properties to interfaces.

■   Create logical VLAN subinterfaces.

■   Set up active/active failover.

■   Create and manage contexts.

■   Upgrade the OS and ASDM images.

▲   Create resource classes to limit the resources a context(s) uses.

When you're in the system area, there is no method of moving traffic between interfaces that are not associated with a context(s); to move traffic between interfaces, the interfaces must be associated with a context(s). Likewise, you can't set up policies for traffic; again, this is done within the contexts themselves, like setting up ACLs, translation policies, Module Policy Framework (MPF) policies, and so on.

Designating the Administrative Context

By default the appliance automatically creates a context, called *admin*, when switching to multiple mode. This context is designated as the administrative context. As I mentioned earlier, the administrative context is the context the system area uses when it needs to communicate with devices beyond the appliance. If you delete the admin context, you'll need to denote another context to perform this role. To designate a context as the administrative context, use the **admin-context** command:

```
ciscoasa(config)# admin-context context_name
```

Only one context can be the administrative context.

Creating Contexts

The following sections will discuss how you initially create your contexts so that you can set up security policies and move traffic through them.

MAC Addresses and Contexts

If you recall from the "Traffic Classification" section, when an interface is shared among multiple contexts, destination MAC addresses and translation rules are used to determine which context a packet should be processed by. Therefore, when an interface is shared, each context should use a different MAC address for the shared interface.

You can automatically have the appliance generate unique MAC addresses for an interface that is shared across multiple contexts with the **mac-address auto** command.

```
ciscoasa(config)# mac-address auto
```

This command is executed from the system area.

NOTE   You can also go into a context and associate a MAC address to the interface, but the **mac-address auto** command is the recommended approach to ensuring that shared interfaces have unique MAC addresses across the respective contexts.

Context Creation

To create a context, you must give it a name, allocate at least one interface, and specify where the configuration file for the context is stored. Here are the commands to accomplish these tasks:

```
ciscoasa(config)# context context_name
ciscoasa(confix-ctx)# allocate-interface physical_if_name[.subif]
                       [map_name] [visible | invisible]
ciscoasa(config-ctx)# config-url URL
```

Each context must have a unique name, which is case-sensitive. The names "null" and "system" are reserved and cannot be used. When you execute the **context** command, you are taken into a subcommand mode where you can set up the context's initial properties.

The **allocate-interface** command associates an interface to a context (when in the context, you can see only the interfaces allocated to it). You can assign physical as well as VLAN subinterfaces to a context. VLAN subinterfaces must first be created in the system area before you can assign them to a context. The *map_name* parameter allows you to assign a different name that will appear in the context instead of the actual physical name. The **visible** parameter allows an administrator to see both the physical and mapped interface names within a context; however the **invisible** parameter only allows the administrator to see the mapped interface names. Basically the latter parameter allows you to hide the name of the physical interface for security purposes.

Each context has its own configuration file. The **config-url** command specifies the location and name of the configuration file. Locations you can specify include **disk0** (**flash**), **disk1**, **tftp**, **ftp**, and **https**. The last can only be read from, not written to. Whenever you're in a context and execute the **write mem** command, the context configuration is stored in the specified location.

TIP If the configuration file is located on an external server and the appliance boots up and can't reach the external server, the context configuration will not be loaded, and thus the context will fail. Therefore, I recommend that a context configuration file be placed in flash on the appliance itself (flash on the motherboard or, for the ASA, on the additional compact flash card).

Once you've performed the preceding configuration steps, the context is active—you can switch to the context and set up its security policies.

Here's a simple example of setting up contexts:

```
ciscoasa(config)# interface ethernet0/1
ciscoasa(config-subif)# no shutdown
ciscoasa(config)# interface ethernet0/1.10
ciscoasa(config-subif)# vlan 10
ciscoasa(config)# interface ethernet0/1.20
ciscoasa(config-subif)# vlan 20
ciscoasa(config)# context CTX1
Creating context 'CTX1'... Done. (4)
ciscoasa(config-ctx)# allocate-interface ethernet0/1.10 inter1
ciscoasa(config-ctx)# allocate-interface ethernet0/1.20 inter2
ciscoasa(config-ctx)# config-url disk0:/CTX1.cfg
```

In this example, the e0/1 interface is activated, and two VLANs are associated with the physical interface in the system area. A context, called "CTX1," is created that includes these two interfaces (with mapped names), and the configuration file for the context is located in the appliance flash memory.

Context Verification

Use the **show context** command to verify your context configuration in the system area:

```
ciscoasa# show context [name | detail | count]
```

Here's an example of the use of this command:

```
ciscoasa# show context
Context Name    Interfaces          URL
*admin          Ethernet0/0         disk0:/admin.cfg
                Ethernet0/1
CTX1            Ethernet0/2         disk0:/CTX1.cfg
                Ethernet0/3
Total active Security Contexts: 2
```

An "*" beside a context name indicates that the context is the administrative context. In the preceding example, this is the admin context.

Managing Resources

One of the initial issues with contexts when they were introduced in version 7.0 was that you couldn't place any resource restrictions on them; therefore, one context and its behavior could easily affect the other contexts on the appliance. For example, a TCP SYN flood attack occurring in one context could fill up the conn table and adversely affect connections attempting to be built in other contexts.

Supported Resource Limits

Starting in version 7.2, you can define resource limits for a context, ensuring that one context doesn't create resource conflicts for other contexts. Resource limits you can define include the number of

▼ Management connections: ASDM, telnet, and SSH

■ Hosts

■ MAC addresses

■ Xlates in the translation table

■ Connections in the state table

■ Syslog messages/second

▲ Application inspections/second

All resources are set to unlimited for a context, unless overridden, except for the following limits, which are by default set to the maximum allowed per context:

▼ Telnet sessions: Five sessions

■ SSH sessions: Five sessions

■ IPSec sessions: Five sessions

▲ MAC addresses: 65,535 entries

Defining Resource Limits

Resource limits are defined in a resource class. All contexts get their resource restriction from a default class called *default*, by default. You can override this behavior by creating a resource class and associating it to a specific context. This is accomplished with the following configuration:

```
ciscoasa(config)# class {default | resource_class_name}
ciscoasa(config-class)# limit-resource all 0
ciscoasa(config-class)# limit-resource asdm #_of_sessions
ciscoasa(config-class)# limit-resource ssh #_of_sessions
ciscoasa(config-class)# limit-resource telnet #_of_sessions
ciscoasa(config-class)# limit-resource hosts #_of_hosts
ciscoasa(config-class)# limit-resource mac-addresses #_of_addresses
ciscoasa(config-class)# limit-resource rate
                          inspect #_of_inspects/second
ciscoasa(config-class)# limit-resource [rate] conns {#_of_conns | xx%}
ciscoasa(config-class)# limit-resource rate syslogs #_of_logs/second
ciscoasa(config-class)# limit-resource xlates #_of_xlates | xx%}
```

For some resource limits, you can specify a percentage (%), such as 20% for the number of entries in the state table, like this: `limit-resource conns 20%`.

To associate a resource class to a context, from the system area, enter the context configuration and use the **member** command, like this:

```
ciscoasa(config)# context context_name
ciscoasa(config-ctx)# member resource_class_name
```

Here's a simple example that illustrates the configuration of a resource class and associates it with the CTX1 context:

```
ciscoasa(config)# class resource-CTX1
ciscoasa(config-class)# limit-resource asdm 3
ciscoasa(config-class)# limit-resource ssh 3
ciscoasa(config-class)# limit-resource conns 50%
ciscoasa(config)# context CTX1
ciscoasa(config-ctx)# member resource-CTX1
```

In this example, no more than three ASDM and three SSH management sessions are allowed, and users sending traffic through the CTX1 context cannot use more than 50 percent of the entries in the state table.

Viewing Context Resource Allocations

You can see what resources have been allocated to a context by using the **show resource allocation** command:

```
ciscoasa# show resource allocation [detail]
```

Here's a simple example of the use of this command:

```
ciscoasa# show resource allocation
Resource          Total       % of Avail
Conns [rate]      35000       N/A
Inspects [rate]   35000       N/A
Syslogs [rate]    10500       N/A
Conns             305000      30.50%
Hosts             78842       N/A
SSH               35          35.00%
Telnet            35          35.00%
<--output omitted-->
```

You can also see what resources are being used by a context(s) with the **show resource usage** command:

```
ciscoasa# show resource usage [context context_name | top n | all |
          summary | system | detail] [resource {[rate]
          resource_name | all}] [counter counter_name
          cnt_threshold]]
```

Here's an example of the use of this command with the **summary** parameter:

```
ciscoasa# show resource usage summary
Resource          Current   Peak       Limit     Denied    Context
Syslogs [rate]    1743      2132    12000(U)         0     Summary
Conns              584       763   100000(S)         0     Summary
Xlates            8526      8966      93400          0     Summary
Host               254       254     262144          0     Summary
Conns [rate]       270       535      42200       1704     Summary
Inspects [rate]    270       535   100000(S)         0     Summary
U = Some contexts are unlimited and are not included in the total.
S = System: Combined context limits exceed the system limit;
the system limit is shown.
```

Here's an example of the use of this command for examining the admin context resource usage:

```
ciscoasa# show resource usage context admin
Resource          Current   Peak  Limit      Denied     Context
Telnet             1         1      5            0       admin
Conns              44        55    N/A           0       admin
Hosts              45        56    N/A           0       admin
```

CONTEXT MANAGEMENT

Once you have created your contexts, you can switch to them from the CLI or access them using ASDM to set up their configuration and security policies. The following sections will discuss how to switch between contexts from the CLI, how to save the configuration file of a context, and how to delete a context.

Switching Between Contexts

From the CLI, to move between the system area and a context, use the **changeto** command:

```
ciscoasa# changeto {system | context context_name}
```

When changing, depending whether an access restriction has been set up, you might have to authenticate to access the respective context or system area.

Here's an example of switching from the system area to the CTX1 context and then switching back to the system area:

```
ciscoasa# changeto context CTX1
ciscoasa/CTX1#
ciscoasa/CTX1# changeto system
ciscoasa#
```

Notice that when switching to a particular context, the name of the context shows up in the CLI prompt, preceded by a slash. The first name you see is the name of the appliance defined in the system area with the **hostname** command; the second name is the name of the context defined by the **hostname** command within that context. (By default this is the name of the context you specified in the **context** command when creating it.) You can see this in the second line of output just shown (ciscoasa/CTX1). If you only see one name (like the last line of output just shown), then you're in the system area.

Saving Configurations

When you are in the system area or in a specific context, use the **write memory** (**copy running-config startup-config**) command to save that specific location configuration file. The problem with this command is that you might want to reboot the appliance, but not be sure if all the configuration files of all the contexts and the system area have been saved. And it would be a real hassle to access each location and execute the **write memory** command to ensure this.

As a shortcut, from the system area, you can execute the following command:

```
ciscoasa# write memory all
```

This command performs the equivalent of a **write memory** command in *each* context and the system area. The only restriction with this command is that it must be executed from the system area.

Removing Contexts

If you no longer need a context, or really messed it up and want to start from scratch, you can easily delete it from the system area by using the following command:

```
ciscoasa(config)# no context context_name
```

This command deletes the entire context. If you want to delete all the contexts on the appliance, use the **clear configure context** command.

 NOTE You cannot delete a context that has been flagged as the administrative context. You first have to denote another context as the administrative context, and then you can delete it.

CONTEXT EXAMPLE

To help you understand how to switch to multiple mode, create the contexts, and configure the contexts, let's look at an example. I'll use the network shown in Figure 22-2 to illustrate the configuration. The appliance is a 5510. E0/0 and E0/1 are trunk connections, where I've created two VLANs on each of these physical interfaces.

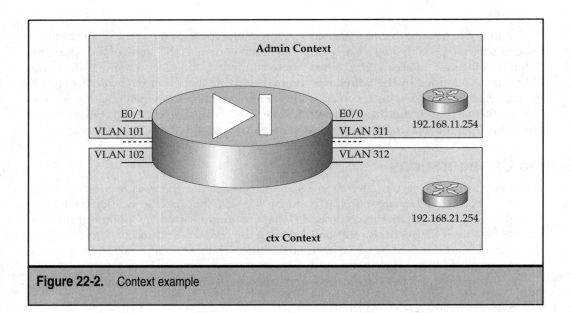

Figure 22-2. Context example

Example: Changing to Multiple Mode

To make it easier to understand the configuration, I'll break it into sections. Currently the ASA 5510 is in single mode, so the first thing I'll do is switch it to multiple mode:

```
ciscoasa(config)# mode multiple
WARNING: This command will change the behavior of the device
WARNING: This command will initiate a Reboot
Proceed with change mode? [confirm] <ENTER>
Convert the system configuration? [confirm] N
Security context mode: multiple
<--output omitted-->
ciscoasa# show mode
Security context mode: multiple
```

Notice that I'm not importing the single mode configuration to the admin context in multiple mode; once the appliance has booted up, I've verified that it is running in multiple mode.

Example: Setting Up the Interfaces

From the system area, I then set up the interfaces:

```
ciscoasa(config)# interface e0/0
ciscoasa(config-if)# no shutdown
ciscoasa(config-if)# exit
ciscoasa(config)# interface e0/1
ciscoasa(config-if)# no shutdown
ciscoasa(config-if)# exit
ciscoasa(config)# interface e0/0.1
ciscoasa(config-subif)# vlan 311
ciscoasa(config-subif)# exit
ciscoasa(config)# interface e0/0.2
ciscoasa(config-subif)# vlan 312
ciscoasa(config-subif)# exit
ciscoasa(config)# interface e0/1.1
ciscoasa(config-subif)# vlan 101
ciscoasa(config-subif)# exit
ciscoasa(config)# interface e0/1.2
ciscoasa(config-subif)# vlan 102
ciscoasa(config-subif)# exit
```

I enabled the two physical interfaces that I'm using—e0/0 and e0/1—and I've created my subinterfaces for the four VLANs. VLAN 311 and 101 will be placed in one context, and 312 and 102 in a second context.

Example: Creating the Contexts

I'll now create and set up my two contexts ("admin" and "ctx"):

```
ciscoasa(config)# admin-context admin
Creating context 'admin'... Done. (1)
ciscoasa(config)# context admin
ciscoasa(config-ctx)# allocate-interface e0/0.1
ciscoasa(config-ctx)# allocate-interface e0/1.1
ciscoasa(config-ctx)# config-url flash:/admin.cfg
WARNING: Could not fetch the URL flash:/admin.cfg
INFO: Creating context with default config
INFO: Admin context will take some time to come up .... please wait.
ciscoasa(config-ctx)# exit
ciscoasa(config)# context ctx
Creating context 'ctx'... Done. (2)
ciscoasa(config-ctx)# allocate-interface e0/0.2
ciscoasa(config-ctx)# allocate-interface e0/1.2
ciscoasa(config-ctx)# config-url flash:/ctx.cfg
WARNING: Could not fetch the URL flash:/ctx.cfg
INFO: Creating context with default config
ciscoasa(config-ctx)# exit
ciscoasa(config)# show context
Context Name  Class     Interfaces              URL
*admin        default   Ethernet0/0.1,Ethernet0/1.1 flash:/admin.cfg
 ctx          default   Ethernet0/0.2,Ethernet0/1.2 flash:/ctx.cfg
Total active Security Contexts: 2
```

Notice that I allocated my VLAN subinterfaces to the respective contexts as well as specified the location of the configuration files for the contexts.

Example: Configuring the Admin Context

Now I'll set up the configuration and policies for the admin context:

```
ciscoasa(config)# changeto context admin
ciscoasa/admin(config)#
ciscoasa/admin(config)# interface e0/0.1
ciscoasa/admin(config-if)# nameif outside
INFO: Security level for "outside" set to 0 by default.
ciscoasa/admin(config-if)# security-level 0
ciscoasa/admin(config-if)# ip address 192.168.11.1 255.255.255.0
ciscoasa/admin(config-if)# no shutdown
ciscoasa/admin(config-if)# exit
ciscoasa/admin(config)# interface e0/1.1
ciscoasa/admin(config-if)# nameif inside
```

```
INFO: Security level for "inside" set to 100 by default.
ciscoasa/admin(config-if)# security-level 100
ciscoasa/admin(config-if)# ip address 10.0.1.111 255.255.255.0
ciscoasa/admin(config-if)# no shutdown
ciscoasa/admin(config-if)# exit
ciscoasa/admin(config)# route outside 0.0.0.0 0.0.0.0 192.168.11.254
ciscoasa/admin(config)# nat-control
ciscoasa/admin(config)# nat (inside) 1 0.0.0.0 0.0.0.0
ciscoasa/admin(config)# global (outside) 1 interface
INFO: outside interface address added to PAT pool
ciscoasa/admin(config)# access-list ACLoutside permit icmp any any
ciscoasa/admin(config)# access-list ACLoutside deny ip any an
ciscoasa/admin(config)# access-group ACLoutside in interface outside
```

Notice that when I executed the **changeto** command, the prompt changed to include the name of the context. (This is what the **hostname** command defaults to within the context.) I've set up a real simple configuration: configuring the interfaces with IP addresses, logical names, and security levels, defining a static route, setting up a PAT translation policy for outbound traffic, and allowing ICMP traffic to flow inbound.

Example: Configuring the ctx Context

Next I'll switch to the ctx context and set it up:

```
ciscoasa/admin(config)# changeto context ctx
ciscoasa/ctx(config)#
ciscoasa/ctx(config)# interface e0/0.2
ciscoasa/ctx(config-if)# nameif outside
INFO: Security level for "outside" set to 0 by default.
ciscoasa/ctx(config-if)# security-level 0
ciscoasa/ctx(config-if)# ip address 192.168.12.1 255.255.255.0
ciscoasa/ctx(config-if)# no shutdown
ciscoasa/ctx(config-if)# exit
ciscoasa/ctx(config-if)# interface e0/1.2
ciscoasa/ctx(config-if)# nameif inside
INFO: Security level for "inside" set to 100 by default.
ciscoasa/ctx(config-if)# security-level 100
ciscoasa/ctx(config-if)# ip address 10.0.2.111 255.255.255.0
ciscoasa/ctx(config-if)# no shutdown
ciscoasa/ctx(config-if)# exit
ciscoasa/ctx(config)# route outside 0.0.0.0 0.0.0.0 192.168.12.254
ciscoasa/ctx(config)# nat-control
ciscoasa/ctx(config)# nat (inside) 1 0.0.0.0 0.0.0.0
ciscoasa/ctx(config)# global (outside) 1 interface
INFO: outside interface address added to PAT pool
```

```
ciscoasa/ctx(config)# access-list ACLoutside permit icmp any any
ciscoasa/ctx(config)# access-list ACLoutside deny ip any any
ciscoasa/ctx(config)# access-group ACLoutside in interface outside
```

This configuration is similar to the admin context configuration.

Example: Saving the Appliance Configuration

Last, I'll switch to the system area and save the configuration of everything on the appliance:

```
ciscoasa/ctx(config)# changeto system
ciscoasa(config)#
ciscoasa(config)# write memory all
Building configuration...
Saving context :            system : (000/002 Contexts saved)
Cryptochecksum: 470df27f 7c312655 ba32399a fe96cb77
996 bytes copied in 0.820 secs
Saving context :            admin : (001/002 Contexts saved)
Cryptochecksum: 83a9938b ec06cf12 7d579f12 e7808459
1350 bytes copied in 0.840 secs
Saving context :            ctx : (002/002 Contexts saved)
Cryptochecksum: 0dac15dc 927b7011 a126adc6 00d45ab4
1348 bytes copied in 0.860 secs
[OK]
```

NOTE Because no interfaces were shared between contexts, the MAC addresses on the subinterfaces could be the same or different; however, if an interface were shared between contexts, make sure you execute the `mac-address auto` command in the appliance system area.

CHAPTER 23

Failover

This chapter will introduce one of the advanced features that has been supported on the appliances for quite some time: failover. Failover provides redundancy between appliances, so if one appliance fails, you can have a redundant appliance take over for the failed one. The topics discussed in this chapter include

▼ An introduction to failover, including the failover types, hardware, software, and license requirements, failover restrictions, and software upgrades

■ The two implementations of failover: active/standby and active/active

■ Cabling the appliances that will participate in failover

■ How appliances communicate with each other about failover, how they detect problems, and when failover can occur

■ Configuring active/standby failover

▲ Configuring active/active failover

FAILOVER INTRODUCTION

Failover is a Cisco-proprietary feature unique to the security appliances. Failover provides redundancy between paired appliances: one appliance backs up another appliance. This redundancy provides resiliency in your network. And depending on the failover type you use and how you implement failover, the failover process can be, in most situations, transparent to your users and hosts.

This section will introduce failover concepts. I'll discuss the two types of failover (hardware and stateful), the requirements you must meet to set up failover, the restrictions you'll face when implementing failover, and how to handle software upgrades for appliances paired together in a failover configuration.

Failover Types

There are two failover types: hardware failover (sometimes called chassis or stateless failover) and stateful failover. Of the two, when failover was originally introduced, only hardware failover was available. Starting in version 6, stateful failover was introduced.

Hardware failover only provides for hardware redundancy—in other words, a physical failover of one of the appliances. The configurations between the appliances are synchronized, but nothing else. So, for example, if a connection were being handled by one appliance and it failed, the other appliance could take over the traffic forwarding for the failed appliance. But since the original connection wasn't replicated to the second appliance, the connection fails: all active connections will be lost and must be rebuilt through the second appliance. For hardware failover, a failover link is required between the appliances, which is discussed later in the "Failover Cabling" section.

Stateful failover provides both hardware and stateful redundancy. Besides the configuration of the appliances being synchronized, other information is also synchronized.

This additional information includes the conn table, the xlate table, the current date and time, the layer 2 MAC address table (if the appliances are in transparent mode), SIP signaling sessions, and VPN connections. The latter is new in version 7.0, but only if implementing active/standby failover (see the "Failover Implementations" section). When implementing stateful failover, you'll need two links between the appliances: a failover link and a stateful link (discussed in more depth in the "Failover Cabling" section).

Failover Requirements

To implement failover, you have to have the correct appliances and the appropriate licensing, and to match up the hardware and software on the units. The following sections will discuss these items in more depth.

Supported Models

Not all appliances support failover. All the ASAs support failover; however, the ASA 5505 doesn't support active/active failover (see the "Failover Implementations" section). Of the PIXs, only the 515s and higher support failover. The Firewall Services Module (FWSM) also supports failover.

NOTE   The FWSM is a card for the Catalyst 6500 and the router 7600 chassis. Its operating system is based on the same operating system used by the appliances. Unlike the appliances, it has no physical interfaces. Instead, all its interaction is with its connected switch or router via trunked VLANs. Most of the configuration is very similar to the appliances, but some, like the initial setup of the logical/ VLAN interfaces, is different. A discussion on using and configuring the FWSM is beyond this book.

Hardware, Software, and Configuration Requirements

For the hardware between the two appliances, the only thing that doesn't have to be the same is the flash memory size—all other components must be the same. For example, you could use two 5510s, but not a 5510 and a 5520. You could use two ASA 5540s, but not if one had an IPS card and the other didn't. Basically, with the exception of flash, the hardware between the two units must be identical: same models, same interfaces and cards, same amount of RAM, and so on.

If you had PIXs running version 6 or earlier, the two PIXs in failover had to be running the same OS image and the same PIX Device Manager (PDM) image. (ASDM is the replacement for PDM and is discussed in Chapter 27.) For example, if one PIX were running version 6.3(4) and the other were running 6.3(5), failover wouldn't work—they would have to be running exactly the same version of software in version 6 and earlier. Starting in version 7, Cisco slightly loosened the software requirements: the minor releases had to match up, but not subreleases within a minor release. For example, if one appliance were running 7.1(1) and the other 7.1(2), the two appliances could participate in failover; however, if one were running 7.0(4) and the other were running 7.1(2), failover would fail.

Another software requirement on the appliances is that the same licensed features must be enabled on both appliances. If one appliance only has a DES license and the other has a DES/3DES/AES license, failover won't work. Likewise, if one appliance has a 5-context license and the other has a 50-context license, again, failover won't work.

The configurations on the appliances must be basically the same, with the exception of the IP and MAC addresses and the unit type used by the two appliances. The unit types are primary and secondary, and these don't change when a failover occurs. At least you don't have to manually synchronize the configurations between the two appliances: you'll make your changes on the active appliance in the failover pair, and the configuration change will automatically be replicated to the other appliance.

License Requirements

If you have an ASA 5505 or 5510, you need the Security Plus license to implement failover. The 5520s and higher don't require any special licensing. The PIXs, on the other hand, are a bit more complicated with their licensing. The PIXs that support failover (the 515s and higher) support three kinds of general licenses: restricted (R), unrestricted (UR), and failover (FO).

A PIX restricted license restricts the amount of RAM and the number of interfaces the PIX can use, as well as failover. An unrestricted license supports the maximum amount of RAM and interfaces the PIX model supports, as well as allowing for the use of failover. Obviously there is a price difference between the two. When Cisco sold the PIXs, a 515E with a restricted license, for example, might cost $3,000 US, while the same unit with an unrestricted license would cost over $6,000 US. One complaint customers had about the licensing had to do with failover. Back in version 6 and earlier, only one implementation of failover was available: active/standby. As you'll see later in the chapter, with this implementation, the active unit processes traffic, and the other waits until the active unit fails, and then this standby unit will start processing traffic. In other words, the standby unit will only process traffic if the active unit fails ... which might be never!

To make customers happy, Cisco created a third license for the PIXs, called a *Failover* (FO) license. The FO license is meant for a standby unit, and it costs about the same, if not a little bit less, than a restricted license. An FO license has all the same features and capabilities as the UR license. One concern Cisco had about the FO license is that they didn't want customers buying a PIX with the FO license and running it as a stand-alone unit or pairing two FO licensed PIXs together—Cisco wanted their customers to buy the appropriate license based on their needs. Therefore, the PIXs won't let two FO licensed devices work with failover. Likewise if an FO licensed PIX boots up and doesn't see a failover mate with a UR license, at least once every 24 hours the FO licensed PIX will reboot itself. However, if the FO unit boots up and sees its primary mate, and the primary mate fails, the FO unit will not perform the random reboot process. This ensures that customers don't try to run the FO license in a stand-alone configuration since rebooting obviously creates disruption for company traffic.

NOTE To use active/active failover, both PIXs must have a UR license. If one has a UR license and the other an FO license, you can only implement active/standby failover.

Failover Restrictions

When using failover, certain restrictions apply. For example, the following addressing is currently unsupported on appliances participating in failover:

▼ DHCP client

■ PPPoE client

▲ IPv6 addressing

Another restriction is that if you will be implementing active/active failover, which requires the use of contexts, VPNs of any type are unsupported. And even with active/standby failover, if the failover pair involves ASA 5505s and they're configured as Easy VPN remotes, failover will not function.

Software Upgrades

Basically you can use two methods to upgrade the OS and ASDM images on your appliance when using failover: manual from the CLI or ASDM, or using the Auto Update Server (AUS), which is a component of Cisco Security Manager (CSM); CSM is the replacement of Cisco Works for Cisco security devices.

When you have appliances paired in a failover configuration and want to manually upgrade either the OS or ASDM, you must upgrade both units individually. (I discuss upgrading the appliances from the CLI in Chapter 26.) There is no synchronization of the OS or ASDM images between the appliances—only their configurations. Assuming you've upgraded the OS on both units, you'll need to manually reboot them, one at a time, to use the new OS version.

Unlike with a manual upgrade, you can define an upgrade policy on the AUS server and have the primary appliance in the failover pair periodically contact the AUS to see if an upgrade is available. This is called the auto update feature, which I discuss how to configure in Chapter 26. If an upgrade is available, the primary appliance is responsible for downloading and installing the update on itself as well as copying the image or images to the secondary unit. Once the image or images have been copied to the secondary appliance, the secondary will automatically reboot itself; after the secondary boots up, the primary appliance will reboot.

FAILOVER IMPLEMENTATIONS

In the last few sections I've mentioned the terms "active/standby" and "active/active failover." These are the two implementations that Cisco supports for failover. Through version 6 of the OS, only active/standby was supported, with active/active support being added in version 7. The following sections will discuss these two failover implementations as well as how addressing (IP and MAC) of the units is implemented in either of the two implementations.

Active/Standby Failover

The active/standby implementation of failover has two appliances: primary and secondary. By default the primary unit performs the active role, and the secondary the standby role. Only one unit, the active appliance, will process traffic between interfaces, as can be seen in the left side of Figure 23-1. With few exceptions, all configuration changes are made on the active unit and are then synchronized with the standby unit. The standby appliance serves as a hot standby or backup of the active unit. It does not pass traffic between interfaces. Its main responsibility is to monitor the active unit and promote itself to the active role if the active unit can no longer do this, as can be seen in the right side of Figure 23-1.

Addressing and Failover

Each appliance (or context) participating in failover needs unique addresses—IP and MAC—for each subnet it is connected to, which can be seen in the top-left side of Figure 23-2. If a failover occurs, the current standby unit promotes itself to the active role and changes its IP and MAC addresses to match those of the primary, as can be seen in the bottom-right side of Figure 23-2. The new active appliance then sends out frames on each interface to update any connected switch MAC address table. Note that the failed appliance will not become a standby unit unless the problem that caused the failover is fixed. When the problem is fixed, the previously active unit will come back online in a *standby* state and assume the IP and MAC addresses of the original standby unit. In active/standby failover, there is no preemption process; however, in active/active failover, preemption is optional. This somewhat makes sense because performing any kind of cutover can create disruptions for traffic.

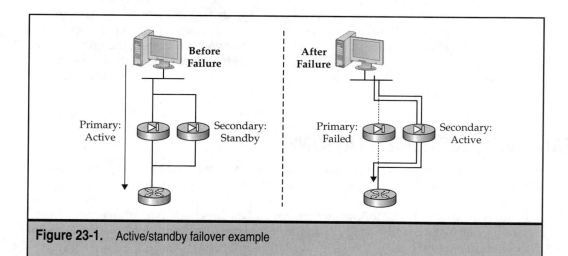

Figure 23-1. Active/standby failover example

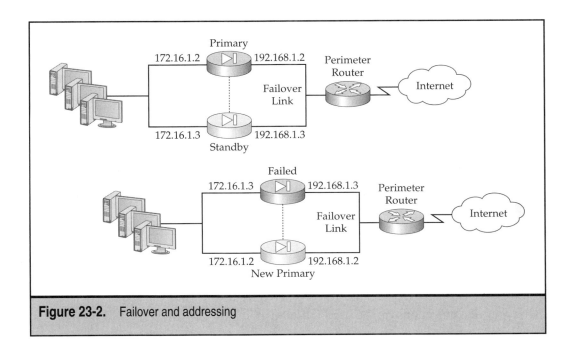

Figure 23-2. Failover and addressing

NOTE The one exception where the IP and MAC addresses don't change between the appliances when a failover occurs is when using LAN-based failover (LBF)—the LBF interface itself will keep the original IP/MAC addresses; however, the data interfaces will have their addresses swapped between the two units. LBF is discussed in the "Failover Cabling" section.

Active/Active Failover

In the active/active implementation of failover, both appliances in the failover pair process traffic. To accomplish this, two contexts are needed, as is depicted in the right side of Figure 23-3. On the left appliance, CTX1 performs the active role and CTX2 the standby role—the roles are reversed for the two contexts on the other appliance. Then, static routes on the connected routers are used to load-balance traffic between the two contexts, assuming they are running in routed mode. If the contexts are running in transparent mode, then the connected routers could use a dynamic routing protocol to learn of the two equal-cost paths through the contexts to the routers on the other side.

NOTE Failover can occur if a context fails (context based) or if the entire appliance fails (unit based).

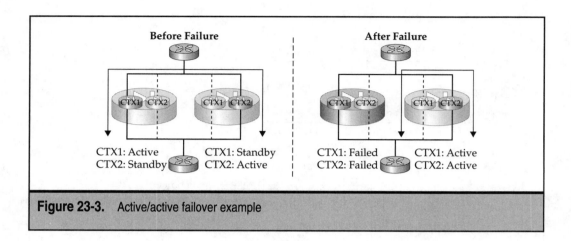

Figure 23-3.   Active/active failover example

FAILOVER CABLING

Two types of connections can be used for failover:

▼   Failover cable or link

▲   Stateful cable or link

The following sections will discuss the differences between these two types of cables or links, as well as how to cable up the appliances.

Failover Link

The failover link is used to replicate appliance commands and to share information about the status of failover between the failover pair. This link must be a dedicated connection between the two appliances, where no user traffic is allowed. There are two kinds of failover links:

▼   Serial

▲   LAN-based failover (LBF)

Serial Cable

The serial cable method of connecting the appliances is only supported on the PIXs. The serial cable is a Cisco proprietary RS-232 cable, clocked at 115 Kbps, with DB-15 connectors. The PIX 515s and higher come with this serial interface installed. One end of the cable is marked "primary," which connects to the primary unit, and the other is marked "secondary." If you purchased the PIXs in a failover bundle, where one has a UR and the other an FO license, the UR-licensed appliance needs to be connected to the primary end of the cable, and the FO-licensed appliance to the secondary end.

The maximum length of the cable is 2–3 meters, so one main disadvantage of using this cabling method is that the two appliances must be physically close to each other. The main advantage of using the serial cable, however, compared with LBF, is that one of the pin-outs on the serial cable is power. If one of the units loses power, the other will immediately notice this.

LAN-Based Failover Cable

LBF was introduced in version 6.2. LBF uses one of the Ethernet interfaces on the appliance to communicate with its mate. Cisco uses a proprietary IP protocol for the communications, where both appliances will need IP addresses on the LBF interface to communicate with each other. This interface must be dedicated to failover—it cannot be used for data functions; however, you could easily set up a trunk connection on an interface, where one VLAN would be dedicated to failover communications and other VLANs for data communications.

Cisco originally designed LBF for companies that do not want to place the paired appliances physically close to each other. For example, if you have a campus network and the building the appliances are in loses power, failover doesn't do you any good; however, if you could place the appliances in *different* buildings, when one building loses power, you still have an appliance in the second building that can process traffic. And since you can use fiber to connect the appliances in the two buildings (this would require a copper-to-fiber transceiver for RJ-45 Ethernet interfaces), the buildings could be separated by a few kilometers.

Given its advantages, LBF does have two limitations: first, unlike the serial cable, LBF cannot directly detect that a mated pair has lost power—it must use keepalives to detect this (which is discussed later in the "Failover Operation" section). Therefore, failover will take a little bit longer to occur in this situation. Second, certain kinds of failures cannot be detected if a crossover cable is used to connect the two appliances. For example, when you're using a crossover cable and directly connecting the two appliances together, if an interface failure occurs on the failover link, the two appliances will be unable to determine which of the two interfaces is causing the problem. Actually, in version 6, you couldn't use a crossover cable; this has been added in version 7. Cisco recommends that you connect the appliances together either via a switch, where the failover connection is in its own VLAN, or via a hub.

Stateful Link

The stateful link, if stateful failover is enabled, is used to replicate state information between the appliances, like the conn and xlate tables, among other things. The state link must be an Ethernet interface; on the PIXs, you can't use the serial interface. Because of the amount of information that might have to be replicated, Cisco recommends that you don't use a data interface for this function. Either use a dedicated interface or, if you are using LBF, have both LBF and the state information run on the same interface.

TIP Because replicating state information between appliances is resource intensive, Cisco recommends that you don't enable it on a PIX 515, even though this product supports stateful failover. Enabling stateful failover on a 515 will create performance issues if a lot of state information must be replicated between the two 515s in the failover pair.

PIX Cabling

Now that you understand the two kinds of links—failover and state—let's discuss how you cable up the appliances. I'll start with the PIXs first, which is illustrated in Figure 23-4. As you can see, you have a lot of options. Without a stateful link, only hardware or chassis redundancy is provided. For PIXs located close to each other, I would recommend using the serial cable for the failover link. For units that are more than 3 meters apart, and if you also need to implement stateful failover, I would use the option listed on the right side of Figure 23-4, where both the failover and stateful links share the same interface.

NOTE For the PIX, the serial cable has the two ends marked "primary" and "secondary"—the primary end should be plugged into the PIX that will be performing the active role, and the secondary end should be plugged into the PIX that will be performing the standby role.

ASA Cabling

Because the ASAs don't have a serial interface, only Ethernet connections can be used, which means that you must use LBF. So as you can see in Figure 23-5, you have fewer options than with the PIXs. As with the PIXs, though, if you are also implementing stateful failover, I recommend that you use the same Ethernet interface for each.

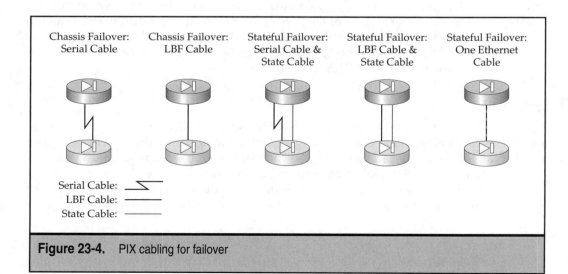

Figure 23-4. PIX cabling for failover

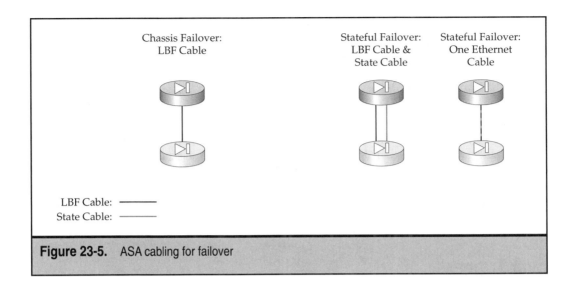

Figure 23-5. ASA cabling for failover

FAILOVER OPERATION

Now that you understand how to cable up the appliances, let's talk about how failover works: how the appliances communicate with each other, how they discover problems, and when failover occurs.

Failover Communications

As I mentioned earlier in the "Failover Cabling" section, the failover link is either the serial cable used on the PIXs or an Ethernet cable with LBF. The failover link is used to communicate the following information between the paired appliances:

▼ The state of the appliances: active or standby

■ If the appliances are PIXs, their power status

■ Failover hello messages

■ Network link status of the appliances interfaces

■ Exchange of MAC addresses used on the appliance interfaces

▲ Configuration of the active unit synchronized with the standby unit

When implementing stateful failover, the following information is transferred across the stateful link from the active to the standby unit: xlate table, conn table, VPN sessions (only in active/standby failover), MAC address table (when running in transparent mode), SIP signaling information, and the current date and time. As you can see, not all state information is replicated across the state link. This includes the uauth table used by Cut-through Proxy (CTP), HTTP sessions (by default), the local routing table, the ARP table, DHCP server addresses that are currently leased, SSM card information, and certain WebVPN components (AnyConnect client sessions, clientless sessions, Citrix authentication, and so on).

TIP HTTP connections in the conn table of the active unit are not by default replicated to the standby unit. Cisco set this as the default since downloading a web page can involve many connections that typically are very short-lived. If most of your traffic is web based, this can create a huge processing burden to replicate all these changes. You have the option of enabling HTTP connection replication, but I typically don't recommend it. If a failover occurs in the middle of someone opening a web page, the easiest way to fix this problem is to have the users click their refresh button within their web browser application.

Failover Triggers

Many things can trigger failover on an appliance: loss of power, one or more interfaces failing, a card failing, a software problem like memory exhaustion, or someone forcing failover with the `failover active` command on the standby unit. Based on the amount of time it takes to detect a problem, cutover to the standby unit might not be immediate. Table 23-1 shows the cutover times for ASAs, and Table 23-2 for PIXs.

Failover Condition	Default Time	Minimum Time	Maximum Time
Active unit loses power or stops normal operation	15 seconds	800 ms	45 seconds
Active unit motherboard interface is down	5 seconds	500 ms	15 seconds
Active unit 4-GE card interface is down	5 seconds	2 seconds	15 seconds
Active unit IPS or CSC card fails	2 seconds	2 seconds	2 seconds
Active unit interface is up, but has connection problems that cause interface testing	25 seconds	5 seconds	75 seconds

Table 23-1. ASA Failover Times

Failover Condition	Default Time	Minimum Time	Maximum Time
Active unit loses power or stops normal operation	15 seconds	800 ms	45 seconds
Active unit interface is up, but has connection problems that cause interface testing	25 seconds	5 seconds	75 seconds

Table 23-2.   PIX Failover Times

Failover Link Monitoring

Basically two types of interfaces are monitored by the failover pair: failover link and data interfaces. This section will discuss what monitoring on the failover link is, and the next section will discuss monitoring of the data interfaces.

Failover hello messages are generated on the failover link every 15 seconds by default. (I'll show you how to change this later in the chapter.) If three consecutive hello messages are missed from a failover mate, an ARP is generated on all the appliance interfaces. If no response is received from the mate on any of the interfaces, failover will take place, with the unit promoting itself to an active state, assuming that it was in a standby state. If no response to the ARP is seen on the failover link, but a response is seen on one of the other interfaces (stateful link or data interfaces), then failover will not occur. In this situation, the failover link is marked as "failed."

Interface Monitoring

Interface monitoring is used to monitor the status of any of the data or stateful link interfaces on the appliance. Failover hello messages are generated on all active interfaces. These are the same messages used on the failover link connection. Up to 250 interfaces can be monitored per appliance. If a hello message from a mate is not seen on a monitored interface for one-half the hold-down period, the appliance will run interface tests on the suspect interface to determine what, if any, problem exists.

The purpose of the interface tests is to determine which unit, if any, has had a failure. Before each test begins, the received packet count statistic is cleared on the interface. At the conclusion of each test, each appliance checks to see if any valid frames/packets were received; and if so, the interface is considered operational. If no traffic is seen for a particular test, then the appliance proceeds to the next test. The four interface tests that the appliance may run include the following:

▼   **Link up/down test**   The suspect interface is disabled and re-enabled, where normal interface hardware diagnostics are run.

■   **Network activity test**   The appliance looks for valid frames coming into the interface for up to 5 seconds.

- ■ **ARP test**   The appliance generates ARP queries for the two most recent entries in the ARP table, where the appliance is looking for *any* valid frame (not just an ARP reply) coming into the interface for up to 5 seconds.

- ▲ **Broadcast ping test**   The appliance generates a broadcast ping, where again, the appliance is looking for *any* valid frame (not just an ICMP echo reply) coming into the interface for up to 5 seconds.

Table 23-3 lists the possible results that can occur and what will occur based on the results.

Switch Connections

Normally the appliances are connected to switches for layer 2 connectivity. Based on the fact that the appliances generate failover messages on all their active interfaces by default, it is important that nothing disrupts this process, causing inadvertent failovers, or, in a worst-case situation, temporarily having both appliances in an active state.

To greatly reduce the likelihood of unattended failovers, you should make sure that the paired interfaces on the mates can see each other's hello messages. Therefore, on the switch, you need to make sure that the interfaces are in the same VLAN. (If this is impossible, you can disable monitoring for the unconnected interface, which I discuss later in the chapter.) Next make sure that any disruptions that STP might create won't cause the appliance interfaces to be placed into a nonforwarding state, like blocking. For Cisco Catalyst switches, you should enable the PortFast feature, which keeps the ports in a forwarding state when changes in STP are occurring. If you forget to do this and your switches are not using rapid STP (RSTP), but are using IEEE's original implementation (802.1d), then STP recalculations, which could take anywhere from 30 to 45 seconds, will probably cause the appliances to miss three hello messages and cause possible failover problems.

Failover Result	Failover Response
Both appliances see no valid frames on the interface being tested.	No failover takes place.
Both appliances see a valid frame on the interface being tested.	No failover takes place.
The active unit sees a valid frame on the interface being tested, but the standby unit doesn't.	No failover takes place.
The active unit doesn't see a valid frame on the interface being tested, but the standby unit does.	Failover takes place.

Table 23-3.   Failover Results and Responses

ACTIVE/STANDBY CONFIGURATION

The last two sections in this chapter will discuss how to configure failover on the appliances. This section discusses how to set up active/standby failover by using the serial cable on the PIXs or by using LBF. The second section discusses how to set up active/active failover on the appliances.

Active/Standby: PIXs and the Serial Cable

Of all the failover configurations to set up, setting up active/standby on two PIXs using the serial cable for the failover link is definitely the easiest. This and the next few pages will discuss how to set up failover on PIXs using the serial cable. To make it more readable, I've broken up the configuration into easily understood steps.

Active/Standby Using the Serial Cable: Step 1

In the first step, make sure the secondary appliance is not connected to the network. If the secondary appliance has any configuration on it, erase it:

```
secondary# write erase
```

Then turn the secondary appliance off.

Active/Standby Using the Serial Cable: Step 2

Once the secondary unit is turned off, cable up the appliances, making sure you plug the primary end of the serial cable into the primary appliance, and the secondary end of the cable into the secondary appliance. Also connect the data interface to your switches and the stateful link connection if you'll be enabling stateful failover.

NOTE When cabling up the appliances, if e0 on a PIX or e0/1 on an ASA is connected to the outside on the primary, you must also cable it up this way on the secondary. The cabling of the interfaces of the two appliances must match.

Active/Standby Using the Serial Cable: Step 3

After you have connected the two appliances to the network, you're ready to begin the configuration of the primary appliance. First, you'll configure the IP addresses on the data interfaces. This is slightly different than what was discussed in Chapter 3, where each interface had a single IP address. With failover, the interface will have two IP addresses: one address will be used by the active appliance, and the second address by the standby appliance.

Here's the command to configure the IP addressing on the data interfaces:

```
primary(config)# interface phy_if_name
primary(config-if)# ip address active_IP_addr net_mask
                    standby standby_IP_addr
```

Active/Standby Using the Serial Cable: Step 4

After configuring the IP addresses on the data interfaces, you're ready to enable failover on the primary/active appliance with the failover command:

```
primary(config)# failover
```

This command enables failover on the appliance; and since the secondary unit is turned off, you're guaranteeing that this appliance will take over the active role.

> **NOTE** Either before or after this step, you can enable optional `failover` commands, discussed later in the "Active/Standby: Optional Commands" section.

Active/Standby Using the Serial Cable: Step 5

After enabling failover on the primary appliance, verify the failover process with the **show failover** command. Here's an example of verifying failover on the primary appliance when the secondary hasn't been turned on yet:

```
primary# show failover
Failover On
Failover unit Primary
Failover LAN Interface: N/A - Serial-based failover enabled
Unit Poll frequency 500 milliseconds, holdtime 6 seconds
Interface Poll frequency 600 milliseconds, holdtime 15 seconds
Interface Policy 1
Monitored Interfaces 2 of 250 maximum
Version: Ours 7.2(1), Mate Unknown
Last Failover at: 13:21:38 UTC Dec 10 2006
        This host: Primary - Active
                Active time: 200 (sec)
                Interface outside (192.168.1.2): Normal (Waiting)
                Interface inside (10.0.1.1): Normal (Waiting)
        Other host: Secondary - Not detected
                Active time: 0 (sec)
                Interface outside (192.168.1.7): Unknown (Waiting)
                Interface inside (10.0.1.7): Unknown (Waiting)

Stateful Failover Logical Update Statistics
        Link : Unconfigured
```

Notice that at the top of the preceding example, this appliance is using serial-based failover, with the primary end of the cable plugged into it. At the bottom of the example, notice that this appliance is in an active role, and the secondary appliance hasn't been detected yet (because it is turned off). Also notice at the very bottom of the example that stateful failover hasn't been configured.

Active/Standby Using the Serial Cable: Step 6

Now that the primary appliance is ready, turn on the secondary appliance. If you happen to be at the console of the primary when the secondary finishes booting up, you see the following message displayed on the primary:

```
Detected an active mate
Beginning configuration replication to mate.
End configuration replication to mate.
```

This message indicates that the primary appliance configuration has been successfully replicated to the secondary. If you happen to be on the secondary console when it finishes booting up, the message will read from mate instead of to mate.

Active/Standby Using the Serial Cable: Step 7

Once you have turned on the secondary appliance and the configuration replication takes place, use the **show failover** command on the primary (or secondary) to verify the operation of failover. Here's an example of the use of this command on the primary appliance:

```
primary# show failover
Failover On
Failover unit Primary
Failover LAN Interface: N/A - Serial-based failover enabled
Unit Poll frequency 500 milliseconds, holdtime 6 seconds
Interface Poll frequency 600 milliseconds, holdtime 15 seconds
Interface Policy 1
Monitored Interfaces 3 of 250 maximum
Version: Ours 7.2(1), Mate 7.2(1)
Last Failover at: 13:21:38 UTC Dec 10 2006
        This host: Primary - Active
                Active time: 320 (sec)
                Interface outside (192.168.1.2): Normal
                Interface inside (10.0.1.1): Normal
    Other host: Secondary - Standby Ready
                Active time: 0 (sec)
                Interface outside (192.168.1.7): Normal
                Interface inside (10.0.1.7): Normal
Stateful Failover Logical Update Statistics
        Link : Unconfigured
```

At the bottom of the display, notice that this appliance is the primary and is performing the active role; the secondary has been detected and is performing the standby role. Two interfaces were configured on the primary, where the configuration was replicated to the secondary: you can see the logical names and IP addresses each is using on its data interfaces, as well as the status of these interfaces.

Active/Standby Using the Serial Cable: Step 8

The last step, which is optional, but highly recommended, is to test your failover configuration. You could turn off the primary appliance, or, if you are at the console of the secondary appliance, execute the **failover active** command:

```
secondary(config)# failover active
```

Then use the **show failover** on the secondary appliance to make sure it is performing the active role and the primary appliance (assuming it is up) is performing the standby role.

Active/Standby: LBF

In this section I'll discuss how to implement active/standby failover using LAN-based failover (LBF). The PIXs support this, as well as serial cabling; however, the ASAs support only this approach. In active/standby failover for a PIX or ASA using the LBF cable, the first three steps are the same as those for using a serial failover cable on the PIXs. After this, the configuration is radically different.

Active/Standby Using LBF: Step 1

In the first step, make sure the secondary appliance is not connected to the network. If the secondary appliance has any configuration on it, erase it:

```
secondary# write erase
```

Then turn the secondary appliance off. This is the same as Step 1 of a PIX using a serial cable.

Active/Standby Using LBF: Step 2

Once the secondary unit is turned off, then cable up the appliances' Ethernet interfaces: the data interfaces, the LBF interface, and the stateful interface (if used and if different from the LBF interface). Again this is basically the same as Step 2 of a PIX using a serial cable.

Active/Standby Using LBF: Step 3

After you have connected the two appliances to the network, you're ready to begin the configuration of the primary appliance. First, you'll configure the IP addresses on the data interfaces, which was discussed previously in Step 3 of a PIX using a serial cable:

```
primary(config)# interface phy_if_name
primary(config-if)# ip address active_IP_addr net_mask
                    standby standby_IP_addr
```

Active/Standby Using LBF: Step 4

The configuration of LBF at this point greatly differs from the PIXs using a serial failover cable. First, you'll need to determine which interface you'll be using on the appliances for the failover link—this must be exactly the same on both appliances. Then you need to enable the interface for LBF: this can be a physical interface or a logical subinterface associated with a particular VLAN:

```
primary(config)# interface physical_LBF_if_name
primary(config-if)# no shutdown
```

In either case, the failover link *cannot* be a data interface with a security level (**security-level** command), logical name (**nameif** command), or IP address (**ip address** command).

After you've enabled the LBF interface on the primary appliance, you're ready to configure failover:

```
primary(config)# failover lan enable
primary(config)# failover lan unit primary
primary(config)# failover lan interface logical_LBF_if_name
                 physical_LBF_if_name
primary(config)# failover interface ip logical_LBF_if_name
                 primary_IP_addr subnet_mask
                 standby secondary_IP_addr
primary(config)# failover key encryption_key
primary(config)# failover
primary# show failover
```

The **failover lan enable** command is only applicable to the *PIXs*: it disables the use of the serial cable interface (this command doesn't exist on the ASAs). The **failover lan unit primary** command specifies the role the appliance should perform; in this case the appliance is the primary. The **failover lan interface** command assigns a logical name of the LBF interface. The **failover interface ip** command assigns the primary and secondary IP addresses to the LBF connection. When failover occurs, these addresses are not changed on the appliances. Optionally you can encrypt the LBF messages using the **failover key** command. If you want to encrypt messages, the primary and secondary units must use the same key. Finally, the **failover** command enables failover on the primary; at this point you should verify the status of the primary appliance with the **show failover** command.

Active/Standby Using LBF: Step 5

Once the primary has been configured, you are ready to configure the secondary. Unlike serial failover where all you had to do was cable up the secondary and turn it on for the synchronization to take place, LBF communicates with IP, so you'll need a minimal configuration on the secondary appliance. Actually the configuration done in Step 4 for the primary is almost the same configuration you'll execute on the secondary … with one exception: the secondary appliance must have a role of "secondary" so that it knows to use the second IP address in the **failover interface ip** command. This is accomplished by using the `failover lan unit secondary` (instead of the `failover lan unit primary`) command:

```
secondary(config)# failover lan unit secondary
```

Active/Standby Using LBF: Step 6

Now you're ready to verify your failover operation with the `show failover` command on the paired appliances. Here's an example of the status of failover of a secondary appliance after Step 5 has been completed:

```
secondary(config)# show failover
Failover On
Failover unit Secondary
Failover LAN Interface: LANFAIL GigabitEthernet0/2 (up)
Unit Poll frequency 500 milliseconds, holdtime 6 seconds
Interface Poll frequency 600 milliseconds, holdtime 15 seconds
Interface Policy 1
Monitored Interfaces 3 of 250 maximum
Version: Ours 7.2(1), Mate 7.2(1)
Last Failover at: 18:03:38 UTC Dec 12 2006
  This host: Secondary - Standby Ready
    Active time: 0 (sec)
      slot 0: ASA5520 hw/sw rev (1.0/7.2(1)) status (Up Sys)
          Interface outside (192.168.1.7): Normal (Waiting)
          Interface inside (10.0.1.7): Normal (Waiting)
      slot 1: ASA-SSM-10 hw/sw rev (1.0/5.0(2)S152.0) status
              (Up/Up)IPS, 5.0(2)S152.0 Up
 Other host: Primary - Active
   Active time: 3795 (sec)
        slot 0: ASA5520 hw/sw rev (1.0/7.2(1)) status (Up Sys)
          Interface outside (192.168.1.2): Normal (Waiting)
<--output omitted-->
```

Notice that in the preceding example this unit is the secondary, and the other unit, the primary, is performing the active role.

Active/Standby: Optional Commands

Other optional commands you can configure to tune your active/standby configuration are

```
ciscoasa(config)# failover link logical_if_name
ciscoasa(config)# failover replication http
ciscoasa(config)# [no] monitor-interface logical_if_name
ciscoasa(config)# failover polltime [unit | interface] [msec] time
                      [holdtime time]
```

```
ciscoasa(config)# failover interface-policy number[%]
ciscoasa(config)# failover mac address phy_if active_MAC_addr
                    standby_MAC_addr
```

To enable stateful failover, use the `failover link` command. If you are using LBF, the logical name for stateful failover can be the LBF logical name. By default HTTP connections are not replicated when you enable stateful failover. If you want to replicate HTTP connections, use the `failover replication http` command.

Monitoring of physical interfaces is enabled by default: the appliance generates failover keepalives on all active physical interfaces; monitoring of logical interfaces (subinterfaces) is disabled by default. With trunk connections the keepalives are sent in the native VLAN (untagged). You can change this behavior with the `monitor-interface` command and specify the logical name of the subinterface, causing the appliance to generate keepalives on the VLAN subinterfaces as well. Likewise if two appliances have a monitored interface that is not in the same broadcast domain, you can disable the keepalive function on the respective interface with the `no monitor-interface` command.

The `failover polltime` command determines how often failover hello messages (keepalives) are generated on interfaces—LBF, stateful, and data interfaces. By default this is 15 seconds. The `unit` parameter applies the keepalive interval to all interfaces, including LBF or the serial, whereas the `interface` parameter specifies the keepalive interval is for the data interfaces. Valid values for the `failover polltime` command are from 1 to 15 seconds or, if the `msec` keyword is used, from 500 to 999 milliseconds. The hold time determines how long it takes from the time a hello packet is missed to when the interface is marked as failed, where valid values are from 2 to 75 seconds. You cannot enter a hold time that is more than five times greater than the poll time interval.

By default a single interface failure will cause a failover. You can increase this value to affect the number of interfaces (or percentage of interfaces) that have to fail before a failover will occur. This is configured with the `failover interface-policy` command.

When in active/standby mode, the MAC addresses for the primary unit are *always* associated with the active IP addresses. However, if the secondary unit boots up first and thus assumes the active role, it uses its own burned-in (MAC) addresses (BIAs) for its interfaces. Thus, when the primary unit comes online and when it assumes the active role, the secondary unit will automatically obtain the MAC addresses from the primary unit and change its MAC addresses. Obviously this change can disrupt your user's traffic, since the active unit MAC addresses changed from the secondary ones to the primary ones. You can configure virtual MAC addresses for each interface with the exception of the failover (LBF) and stateful links, since these don't change during a failover. To configure virtual MAC addresses, use the `failover mac address` command.

Active/Standby: Example Configuration

To help you better understand how to configure active/standby on the appliances, let's look at an example. I'll use the network shown in Figure 23-6. I'll use two ASA 5510s, which require LBF for the failover LAN link. In this example, I'll primarily focus on the

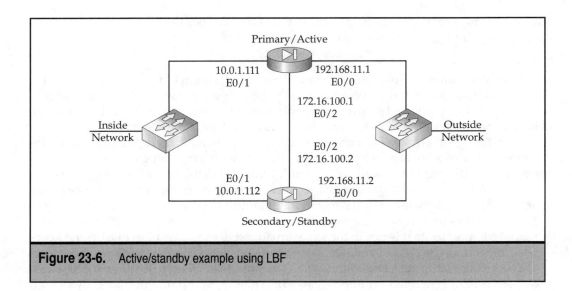

Figure 23-6. Active/standby example using LBF

failover configuration of the two appliances. To make the example more readable, I've broken it into different sections.

Active/Standby Example: Primary Data Interfaces

I'll first set up the data interfaces on the primary, which are e0/0 and e0/1:

```
primary(config)# interface e0/0
primary(config-if)# no shutdown
primary(config-if)# ip address 192.168.11.1 255.255.255.0
                    standby 192.168.11.2
primary(config-if)# nameif outside
primary(config-if)# security-level 0
primary(config-subif)# exit
primary(config)# interface e0/1
primary(config-if)# no shutdown
primary(config-if)# ip address 10.0.1.111 255.255.255.0
                    standby 10.0.1.112
primary(config-if)# nameif inside
primary(config-if)# security-level 100
primary(config-if)# exit
```

NOTE For an existing appliance, you would only have to change the IP addresses on the existing interfaces for failover, specifying the standby unit address for each interface you are using.

Active/Standby Example: Primary Failover Configuration

Next I'll set up the LBF interface (e0/2) on the primary and enable failover:

```
primary(config)# interface e0/2
primary(config-if)# no shutdown
primary(config-if)# exit
primary(config)# failover lan unit primary
primary(config)# failover lan interface lanfail e0/2
INFO: Non-failover interface config is cleared on Ethernet0/2
and its sub-interfaces
primary(config)# failover interface ip lanfail
                       172.16.100.1 255.255.255.0 standby 172.16.100.2
primary(config)# failover
```

Now I'll verify the failover operation and configuration on the primary:

```
primary(config)# show failover
Failover On
Cable status: N/A - LAN-based failover enabled
Failover unit Primary
Failover LAN Interface: lanfail Ethernet0/2 (up)
Unit Poll frequency 15 seconds, holdtime 45 seconds
Interface Poll frequency 5 seconds, holdtime 25 seconds
Interface Policy 1
Monitored Interfaces 0 of 250 maximum
Version: Ours 8.0(3), Mate Unknown
Last Failover at: 00:25:08 UTC Jan 1 1993
        This host: Primary - Active
                Active time: 465 (sec)
                    Interface outside (192.168.11.1): Normal
                    Interface inside (10.0.1.111): Normal
        Other host: Secondary - Not Detected
                Active time: 0 (sec)
                    Interface outside (192.168.11.2): Unknown
                    Interface inside (10.0.1.112): Unknown

Stateful Failover Logical Update Statistics
        Link : Unconfigured.
```

In the preceding output, notice that LBF is enabled, this unit is the primary and is performing the active role, and the LBF interface is called *lanfail* and is operational. Also notice that the secondary appliance hasn't been detected (we haven't configured it yet).

Active/Standby Example: Secondary Failover Configuration

Now that the primary has been configured, I'll set up the secondary. Before you begin, make sure you have cleared the configuration on the secondary. Here's the configuration of the secondary appliance:

```
secondary(config)# interface e0/2
secondary(config-if)# no shutdown
secondary(config-if)# exit
secondary(config)# failover lan unit secondary
secondary(config)# failover lan interface lanfail e0/2
INFO: Non-failover interface config is cleared on Ethernet0/2 and
      its sub-interfaces
secondary(config)# failover interface ip lanfail
                      172.16.100.1 255.255.255.0  standby 172.16.100.2
secondary(config)# failover
Detected an Active mate
Beginning configuration replication from mate.
End configuration replication from mate.
primary(config)#
```

As you can see, the only difference between this and the primary configuration is the **failover lan unit** command. One other item to point out is the bottom of the configuration: notice that once the replication from the primary is complete, the prompt on the secondary appliance changed from "secondary" to "primary." This occurred because the primary replicated its entire configuration, including the **hostname** command, which the secondary automatically executes.

Let's go ahead and verify the operation of failover on the secondary appliance:

```
primary(config)# show failover
Failover On
Cable status: N/A - LAN-based failover enabled
Failover unit Secondary
Failover LAN Interface: lanfail Ethernet0/2 (up)
Unit Poll frequency 15 seconds, holdtime 45 seconds
Interface Poll frequency 5 seconds, holdtime 25 seconds
Interface Policy 1
Monitored Interfaces 0 of 250 maximum
Version: Ours 8.0(3), Mate 8.0(3)
Last Failover at: 20:37:30 UTC Jul 2 2008
        This host: Secondary - Standby Ready
              Active time: 0 (sec)
                  Interface outside (192.168.11.2): Normal
                  Interface inside (10.0.1.112): Normal
        Other host: Primary - Active
              Active time: 1545 (sec)
```

```
                    Interface outside (192.168.11.1): Normal
                    Interface inside (10.0.1.111): Normal

Stateful Failover Logical Update Statistics
        Link : Unconfigured.
```

In the preceding output, notice that the appliance is configured as the secondary and is performing the standby role.

Active/Standby Example: Optional Commands

Once failover is operational, I decide to tune it by enabling stateful failover and changing the hello interval with the following commands:

```
primary(config)# failover link lanfail
primary(config)# failover polltime msec 500
INFO: Failover unit holdtime is set to 2 seconds
```

In this example, I'm using the LBF link for both failover communications and replication of the state table.

NOTE With few exceptions, all commands must be executed on the active appliance and are then replicated across the failover link to the standby appliance.

I'll verify my failover configuration with the **show failover** command on the primary/active unit:

```
primary(config)# show failover
Failover On
Cable status: N/A - LAN-based failover enabled
Failover unit Secondary
Failover LAN Interface: lanfail Ethernet0/2 (up)
Unit Poll frequency 500 milliseconds, holdtime 2 seconds
Interface Poll frequency 5 seconds, holdtime 25 seconds
Interface Policy 1
Monitored Interfaces 0 of 250 maximum
Version: Ours 8.0(3), Mate 8.0(3)
Last Failover at: 21:42:26 UTC Jul 2 2008
        This host: Primary - Active
                Active time: 452 (sec)
                    Interface outside (192.168.11.1): Normal
                    Interface inside (10.0.1.111): Normal
        Other host: Secondary - Standby Ready
                Active time: 0 (sec)
                    Interface outside (192.168.11.2): Normal
                    Interface inside (10.0.1.112): Normal
```

```
Stateful Failover Logical Update Statistics
        Link : lanfail Ethernet2 (up)
        Stateful Obj    xmit        xerr        rcv         rerr
        General         17          0           15          0
        sys cmd         15          0           15          0
        up time         0           0           0           0
        RPC services    0           0           0           0
        TCP conn        0           0           0           0
        UDP conn        0           0           0           0
<--output omitted-->
```

Notice that the bottom of the display has changed. You can see that the stateful link is "lanfail," as well as see the count of the different types of information replicated to the standby appliance. Now that you have failover up and running, you can go ahead and complete the configuration on the active appliance, like configuring translation rules, ACLs, MPF, and so on.

ACTIVE/ACTIVE CONFIGURATION

Active/active failover configuration requires that you place the appliances in multiple mode to set up contexts. You'll need two contexts, as previously described in Figure 23-3. The following sections will lead you through the process of setting up active/active failover, followed by an example.

Active/Active: LBF Configuration

Even though active/active is supported on the PIXs using the serial cable, this part of the chapter will only discuss the use of LBF. Some of the steps are the same as or similar to the steps performed when configuring active/standby.

Active/Active LBF Configuration: Step 1

The first three steps are basically the same as those used with active/standby LBF. In the first step, make sure the secondary appliance is unconnected to the network. If the secondary appliance has any configuration on it, erase it:

```
secondary# write erase
```

Then turn the secondary appliance off.

Active/Active LBF Configuration: Step 2

Once the secondary unit is turned off, cable up the appliances Ethernet interfaces: the data interfaces, the LBF interface, and the stateful interface (if used and if different from the LBF interface). Again this is the same as you would do if configuring active/standby.

Active/Active LBF Configuration: Step 3

Next switch the primary appliance to multiple mode (**mode multiple** command). Then enable the interfaces you will use on the primary appliance. Once this is done, create your two contexts, allocate the interfaces to them, and specify the location of their configuration files. This process was discussed in Chapter 22.

Active/Active LBF Configuration: Step 4

Once you've created the two contexts, you'll need to go *into* them (**changeto context** command) and configure the two sets of addresses (active and standby) for each data interface. The command to do this is the same used when configuring active/standby, except that you must be in a context to execute it:

```
ciscoasa(config)# interface phy_if_name
ciscoasa/context(config-if)# ip address active_IP_addr net_mask
                                  standby standby_IP_addr
```

NOTE Actually creating the contexts and assigning the IP addresses to the data interfaces can be done at any time—before or after the configuration of failover.

Active/Active LBF Configuration: Step 5

Enabling active/active failover using LBF for the failover link is similar to configuring active/standby. Failover is actually configured within the system area—not in the two contexts. In the system area, you'll need to enable the LBF interface and configure your **failover** commands:

```
primary(config)# interface physical_LBF_if_name
primary(config-if)# no shutdown
primary(config-if)# exit
primary(config)# failover lan enable
primary(config)# failover lan unit primary
primary(config)# failover lan interface logical_LBF_if_name
                    physical_LBF_if_name
primary(config)# failover interface ip logical_LBF_if_name
                    primary_IP_addr net_mask
                    standby secondary_IP_addr
primary(config)# failover key encryption_key
```

As you can see from the preceding, the commands are the same on the primary. Notice that the commands are configured in the system area, not in a particular context. And the LBF interface is assigned IP addressing in the system area—this is one exception to the rule of assigning IP addresses when using contexts. If you're using a PIX and will be using LBF, you'll need to execute the **failover lan enable** command. Also, don't enable failover at this point; you'll need to create the failover groups first, which is discussed in the next step.

Active/Active LBF Configuration: Step 6

In this step, you'll need to create two failover groups. The function of a failover group is to determine what role, primary or secondary, an appliance will perform for an associated context. For example, if you had contexts CTX1 and CTX2, you would make one context a member of failover group 1 and the other a member of group 2, splitting the roles—primary and secondary—between the two contexts. This is only done on the primary unit and will be synchronized with the secondary unit, along with whatever contexts you create, across the failover link (LBF).

> **NOTE**   The synchronization of the contexts themselves to the secondary is a great feature, since this really reduces the amount of configuration you'll have to do on the secondary appliance!

To create your failover groups, use the following configuration:

```
primary(config)# failover group 1
primary(config-fover-group)# primary
primary(config-fover-group)# exit
primary(config)# failover group 2
primary(config-fover-group)# secondary
primary(config-fover-group)# exit
```

To associate a failover group to a context, so that the appliance knows what role it should play for a context, use the following configuration:

```
primary(config)# context context_name
primary(confix-ctx)# join-failover-group {1 | 2}
primary(confix-ctx)# exit
```

Once you've associated the failover groups to the correct contexts, you can go ahead and enable failover on the primary:

```
primary(config)# failover
```

You can use the show failover command to verify your configuration:

```
primary# show failover [group group_#]
```

Optionally you can qualify the output, examining the failover information for a particular failover group (context).

Active/Active LBF Configuration: Step 7

Once the primary LBF configuration is complete, you're now ready to set up the secondary unit. If you haven't already done this, you'll need to switch the secondary to multiple mode

(`mode multiple` command). Once the secondary has switched to multiple mode, from the system area you can set up LBF. The LBF configuration on the secondary is basically the same as step 5 on the primary—the exception is the `failover lan unit` command.

```
secondary(config)# interface physical_LBF_if_name
secondary(config-if)# no shutdown
secondary(config-if)# exit
secondary(config)# failover lan enable
secondary(config)# failover lan unit secondary
secondary(config)# failover lan interface logical_LBF_if_name
                  physical_LBF_if_name
secondary(config)# failover interface ip logical_LBF_if_name
                  primary_IP_addr net_mask
                  standby secondary_IP_addr
secondary(config)# failover key encryption_key
secondary(config)# failover
```

Again note that you are in the system area when setting up LBF. Also notice that you don't have to configure failover groups or contexts—just enable failover with the `failover` command. Once you've done this, assuming you've configured everything correctly, the secondary should connect to the primary, and the two should synchronize, where the secondary will automatically get this information from the primary.

Active/Active: Optional Commands

Many of the optional configurations available in active/standby exist in active/active, as well as a few others—the main difference is where and how the commands are executed. Here are the optional commands you can configure for active/active failover:

```
standby(config)# [no] failover active group group_#
active(config)# failover link logical_LBF_if_name
active(config)# failover group {1 | 2}
active(config-fover-group)# preempt [seconds]
active(config-fover-group)# replicate http
active(config-fover-group)# polltime interface [msec] time
                           [holdtime time]
active(config-fover-group)# interface-policy number[%]
```

The `failover active group` command is executed on the standby appliance: it forces the standby to promote itself to the active role for the contexts in the specified group; and the currently active appliance will demote itself to a standby role for the group. The `failover link` command enables stateful failover on the appliance.

The remaining optional commands are configured on a per-failover group basis. Preemption allows a unit to come back online and preempt the other unit if the failed unit was originally performing the active function for a context. To enable preemption, use the `preempt` command—you can specify the number of seconds to wait before preemption occurs. To change the failover hello interval, use the **polltime** command. To change how many data interfaces have to fail before failover takes place, use the **interface-policy** command.

Active/Active: Example Configuration

To help you better understand how to configure active/active failover on the appliances, let's look at an example. I'll use the network shown in Figure 23-7. I'll use two ASA 5510s, which require LBF for the failover LAN link. In this example, I'll primarily focus on the failover configuration of the two appliances. To make the example more readable, I've broken it into different sections.

Active/Active Example: Primary Initial Configuration

First you'll need to switch the primary appliance to multiple mode and then enable the interfaces, as shown here:

```
primary(config)# mode multiple
<--output omitted-->
primary(config)# interface e0/0
primary(config-if)# no shutdown
primary(config-if)# exit
primary(config)# interface e0/1
primary(config-if)# no shutdown
primary(config-if)# exit
primary(config)# interface e0/2
primary(config-if)# no shutdown
primary(config-if)# exit
```

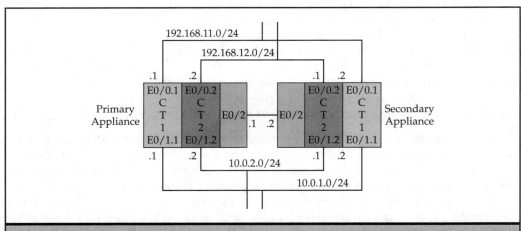

Figure 23-7. Active/active example using LBF

Next I'll create the subinterfaces that will be used for trunking on e0/0 and e0/1:

```
primary(config)# interface e0/0.1
primary(config-subif)# vlan 311
primary(config-subif)# exit
primary(config)# interface e0/0.2
primary(config-subif)# vlan 312
primary(config-subif)# exit
primary(config)# interface e0/1.1
primary(config-subif)# vlan 101
primary(config-subif)# exit
primary(config)# interface e0/1.2
primary(config-subif)# vlan 102
primary(config-subif)# exit
```

E0/0.1 and E0/1.1 will be in the ct1 context, and E0/0.2 and E0/1.2 will be in the ct2 context.

Active/Active Example: Primary Failover Configuration

Next I'll configure the failover commands for the primary, using E0/2 as the LBF interface:

```
primary(config)# failover lan interface lanfail e0/2
primary(config)# failover interface ip lanfail
                     172.16.100.1 255.255.255.0 standby 172.16.100.2
primary(config)# failover link lanfail
primary(config)# failover lan unit primary
primary(config)# failover polltime msec 500
primary(config)# failover group 1
primary(config-fover-group)# exit
primary(config)# failover group 2
primary(config-fover-group)# exit
primary(config)# failover
        Group 1 No Response from Mate, Switch to Active
        Group 2 No Response from Mate, Switch to Active
```

In the preceding, example I enabled LBF and stateful failover, changed the hello interval, and created the two failover groups.

Here's the failover status of the primary:

```
primary(config)# show failover
Failover On
Cable status: N/A - LAN-based failover enabled
Failover unit Primary
Failover LAN Interface: lanfail Ethernet0/2 (up)
```

```
Unit Poll frequency 500 milliseconds, holdtime 2 seconds
Interface Poll frequency 5 seconds, holdtime 25 seconds
Interface Policy 1
Monitored Interfaces 0 of 250 maximum
Version: Ours 8.0(3), Mate Unknown
Group 1 last failover at: 00:11:14 UTC Jan 1 1993
Group 2 last failover at: 00:11:14 UTC Jan 1 1993

   This host:      Primary
   Group 1         State:          Active
                   Active time:    103 (sec)
   Group 2         State:          Active
                   Active time:    103 (sec)


   Other host:     Secondary
   Group 1         State:          Not Detected
                   Active time:    0 (sec)
   Group 2         State:          Not Detected
                   Active time:    0 (sec)
<--output omitted-->
```

Notice that the primary is in an active state for both groups, since the secondary hasn't been configured yet.

Active/Active Example: Primary Context Configuration

After completing the failover configuration on the primary, I'll create and set up the contexts. Again, this is done on the primary appliance. Actually this step can occur before or after the failover configuration. I'll create two contexts: ct1 and ct2. Here's the configuration, which I covered in Chapter 22:

```
primary(config)# admin-context ct1
primary(config)# context ct1
primary(config-ctx)# allocate-interface e0/0.1
primary(config-ctx)# allocate-interface e0/1.2
primary(config-ctx)# config-url flash:/ct1.cfg
primary(config-ctx)# join-failover-group 1
primary(config-ctx)# exit
primary(config)# context ct2
primary(config-ctx)# allocate-interface e0/0.2
primary(config-ctx)# allocate-interface e0/1.2
primary(config-ctx)# config-url flash:/ct2.cfg
primary(config-ctx)# join-failover-group 2
primary(config-ctx)# exit
```

After creating the contexts, I'll switch to them and set up the IP addressing on their data interfaces:

```
primary(config)# changeto context ct1
primary/ct1(config)# interface e0/0.1
primary/ct1(config-if)# nameif outside
primary/ct1(config-if)# security-level 0
primary/ct1(config-if)# ip address 192.168.11.1 255.255.255.0
                                 standby 192.168.11.2
primary/ct1(config-if)# no shutdown
primary/ct1(config-if)# exit
primary/ct1(config)# interface e0/1.1
primary/ct1(config-if)# nameif inside
primary/ct1(config-if)# security-level 100
primary/ct1(config-if)# ip address 10.0.1.111 255.255.255.0
                                 standby 10.0.1.112
primary/ct1(config-if)# no shutdown
primary/ct1(config-if)# exit
primary/ct1(config)# changeto context ct2
primary/ct2(config)# interface e0/0.2
primary/ct2(config-if)# nameif outside
primary/ct2(config-if)# security-level 0
primary/ct2(config-if)# ip address 192.168.12.2 255.255.255.0
                                 standby 192.168.12.1
primary/ct2(config-if)# no shutdown
primary/ct2(config-if)# exit
primary/ct2(config)# interface e0/1.2
primary/ct2(config-if)# nameif inside
primary/ct2(config-if)# security-level 100
primary/ct2(config-if)# ip address 10.0.2.112 255.255.255.0
                                 standby 10.0.2.111
primary/ct2(config-if)# no shutdown
primary/ct2(config-if)# exit
```

NOTE I skipped the rest of the configuration for each context, like address translation, ACLs, static routing, and so on—this will still need to be completed.

Active/Active Example: Secondary Configuration

Now that the primary is finished, I'll connect to the console of the secondary appliance and set it up:

```
secondary(config)# mode multiple
<--output omitted-->
secondary(config)# interface e0/2
```

```
secondary(config-if)# no shutdown
secondary(config-if)# exit
secondary(config)# failover lan interface lanfail e0/2
secondary(config)# failover interface ip lanfail
                       172.16.100.1 255.255.255.0 standby 172.16.100.2
secondary(config)# failover lan unit secondary
secondary(config)# failover
Detected an Active mate
Beginning configuration replication from mate.
WARNING: Unable to delete ct1 context, because it doesn't exist.
INFO: Admin context is required to get the interfaces
Creating context 'ct1'... Done. (1)
WARNING: Skip fetching the URL flash:/ct1.cfg
INFO: Creating context with default config
INFO: ct1 context will take some time to come up .... please wait.
Creating context 'ct2'... Done. (2)
WARNING: Skip fetching the URL flash:/ct2.cfg
INFO: Creating context with default config
        Group 1 Detected Active mate
        Group 2 Detected Active mate
```

Notice that once failover was enabled, the secondary automatically pulled the two contexts (and their configurations) into itself.

Here's the status of the secondary appliance at this point:

```
secondary(config)# show failover
Failover On
Cable status: N/A - LAN-based failover enabled
Failover unit Secondary
Failover LAN Interface: lanfail Ethernet0/2 (up)
Unit Poll frequency 500 milliseconds, holdtime 2 seconds
Interface Poll frequency 5 seconds, holdtime 25 seconds
Interface Policy 1
Monitored Interfaces 0 of 250 maximum
Version: Ours 8.0(3), Mate 8.0(3)
Group 1 last failover at: 00:52:14 UTC Jan 1 1993
Group 2 last failover at: 00:52:14 UTC Jan 1 1993


  This host:      Secondary
  Group 1         State:          Standby Ready
                  Active time:    0 (sec)
  Group 2         State:          Standby Ready
                  Active time:    0 (sec)
<--output omitted-->
```

Notice that the secondary is in a standby state for both contexts.

Active/Active Example: Primary Preemption Configuration

Since one of the purposes of using active/active failover is to have both appliances process traffic, you'll need to configure preemption to get around the issue shown in the secondary status from the previous **show failover** command. This is done on the primary appliance:

```
primary(config)# failover group 1
primary(config-fover-group)# primary
primary(config-fover-group)# preempt
primary(config-fover-group)# exit
primary(config)# failover group 2
primary(config-fover-group)# secondary
primary(config-fover-group)# preempt
primary(config-fover-group)# exit
```

Now when I examine the status of failover on either appliance, I should see that one is active for one context, and the other appliance is active for the second context:

```
primary(config)# show failover
Failover On
Cable status: N/A - LAN-based failover enabled
Failover unit Primary
Failover LAN Interface: lanfail Ethernet0/2 (up)
Unit Poll frequency 500 milliseconds, holdtime 2 seconds
Interface Poll frequency 5 seconds, holdtime 25 seconds
Interface Policy 1
Monitored Interfaces 0 of 250 maximum
Version: Ours 8.0(3), Mate 8.0(3)
Group 1 last failover at: 01:15:13 UTC Jan 1 1993
Group 2 last failover at: 01:11:19 UTC Jan 1 1993

  This host:      Primary
  Group 1         State:          Active
                  Active time:    329 (sec)
  Group 2         State:          Standby Ready
                  Active time:    0 (sec)

      ct1 Interface outside (192.168.11.1): Normal (Not-Monitored)
      ct1 Interface inside (10.0.1.111): Normal (Not-Monitored)
      ct2 Interface outside (192.168.12.1): Normal (Not-Monitored)
      ct2 Interface inside (10.0.2.111): Normal (Not-Monitored)

  Other host:     Secondary
  Group 1         State:          Standby Ready
                  Active time:    367 (sec)
```

```
Group 2       State:          Active
              Active time:    696 (sec)

    ct1 Interface outside (192.168.11.2): Normal (Not-Monitored)
    ct1 Interface inside (10.0.1.112): Normal (Not-Monitored)
    ct2 Interface outside (192.168.12.2): Normal (Not-Monitored)
    ct2 Interface inside (10.0.2.112): Normal (Not-Monitored)

Stateful Failover Logical Update Statistics
        Link : lanfail Ethernet0/2 (up)
<--output omitted-->
```

In the preceding example, the primary appliance is active for failover group 1 (ct1 context), and the secondary appliance is active for failover group 2 (ct2 context). Also notice the status of the data interfaces: "Not-Monitored." Remember that subinterfaces by default are not included in the failover hello process—only the native VLAN on the trunk interface. You can optionally enable this feature, if needed, however.

CHAPTER 24

Network Attack
Prevention

This chapter will introduce you to the features used to detect and prevent network attacks. Some features applicable to this topic have already been discussed in earlier chapters. For example, to limit the effect of TCP SYN flood attacks, you can use the TCP Intercept feature discussed in Chapter 5. In Chapter 10 I discussed how you can limit the number of connections, randomize TCP sequence numbers, and change connection timeouts. The additional topics covered in this chapter include the following:

▼ The threat detection features of the appliances

■ Software IPS implementation supported by the appliances

▲ Miscellaneous network attack prevention features, including TCP normalization, reverse path forwarding, and placing limits on fragments

THREAT DETECTION

The first part of this chapter will introduce you to the threat detection features of the appliances. This includes basic threat detection, which allows you to monitor dropped packet rates and security events; scanning threat detection, which allows you to detect scan attacks; and compiling threat statistics, which allows you to monitor the appliance threat statistics.

Basic Threat Detection

The basic threat detection feature of the appliance is new in version 8. With this feature enabled, the appliance monitors the dropped packet rate and security events and, if it sees a threat, the appliance generates a log message with a log identifier number of 730100. The kinds of security events or dropped packet rates that the appliance monitors include

▼ Matches on deny statements in ACLs.

■ Malformed packets (for example, invalid IP header values or an incorrect header length).

■ Packets that fail application layer inspection policies defined by the Modular Policy Framework (MPF) or that inherit in the application inspection process itself. (For example, if a specified URL in a policy was seen, causing an HTTP connection to be reset, or if a `wiz` command was executed on an SMTP/ESMTP connection respectively.)

■ Defined connection limits that have been exceeded, which includes global system values as well as limits you've defined with MPF or the `static`/`nat` commands.

■ Seeing unusual ICMP packets or connections.

- Examining the combined rate of all security-related packet drops in this bulleted list.

- An interface became overloaded, causing packet drops.

- A scanning attack was detected. (For example, the TCP three-way handshake failed, or the first packet in a TCP connection was not a SYN—this is discussed in the "Scanning Threat Detection" section later in the chapter.)

▲ An incomplete connection was detected. (For example, the TCP three-way handshake failed, or UDP traffic is only seen in one direction of a connection.)

The following two sections will discuss how to configure and monitor basic threat detection.

Basic Threat Detection Configuration

Setting up basic threat detection is a simple process that involves one required step: enabling it. To enable basic threat detection, use the following command:

```
ciscoasa(config)# threat-detection basic-threat
```

NOTE Basic threat detection only affects the performance of the appliance when the appliance detects dropped packets or a potential threat. But even in this scenario, the impact of basic threat detection in the appliance is very minimal.

Once enabled, the appliance uses the default event thresholds in Table 24-1 to determine if a threat exists; these can be seen on the appliance with the **show running-config all threat-detection** command. These rates are used by the appliance to determine when a device is considered a victim or attacker. You can see two packet rates in the table: the average event rate over a time interval, as well as a burst event rate over a shorter time interval. The burst rate is 1/60th of the average rate or 10 seconds, whichever value is higher. When events are detected by the appliance, they are tallied over the various intervals and compared with the respective thresholds. If only one threshold—average or burst—is exceeded for a security event, then only one log message is generated. However, if both thresholds are exceeded, then the appliance will generate two log messages—one for each event. If the threshold is exceeded multiple times during the time interval of a security event, only one message is generated for the threshold (otherwise you'd be flooded with possibly hundreds of log messages).

Optionally you can override the default thresholds of the events in Table 24-1 with the **threat-detection rate** command, shown here:

```
ciscoasa(config)# threat-detection rate {acl-drop | bad-packet-drop |
                    conn-limit-drop | dos-drop | fw-drop |
                    icmp-drop | inspect-drop | interface-drop |
                    scanning-threat | syn-attack}
                    rate-interval rate_interval
                    average-rate average_rate burst-rate burst_rate
```

Security Event	Average Rate	Burst Rate
DoS attack, malformed packet, connection limits exceeded, and unusual ICMP packets/connections	100 drops per second over the last 600 seconds or 80 drops per second over the last 3,600 seconds	400 drops per second over the last 10 seconds or 320 drops per second over the last 60 seconds
Scanning attack	5 drops per second over the last 600 seconds or 4 drops per second over the last 3,600 seconds	10 drops per second over the last 10 seconds or 8 drops per second over the last 60 seconds
Incomplete sessions	100 drops per second over the last 600 seconds or 80 drops per second over the last 3,600 seconds	200 drops per second over the last 10 seconds or 160 drops per second over the last 60 seconds
Packets dropped by ACLs	400 drops per second over the last 600 seconds or 320 drops per second over the last 3,600 seconds	1,600 drops per second over the last 10 seconds or 1,220 drops per second over the last 60 seconds
All security-related (firewall) packet drops and failed packet inspections	400 drops per second over the last 600 seconds or 320 drops per second over the last 3,600 seconds	800 drops per second over the last 10 seconds or 640 drops per second over the last 60 seconds
Interface overload	2,000 drops per second over the last 600 seconds or 1,600 drops per second over the last 3,600 seconds	8,000 drops per second over the last 10 seconds or 6,400 drops per second over the last 60 seconds

Table 24-1. Basic Threat Detection Thresholds

The `rate-interval` parameter specifies the number of seconds in the sampled interval for the average rate, which can range from 600 to 2,592,000 seconds (or 30 days). The burst rate interval is calculated from this value, basically dividing the average rate interval by 60 seconds. If the computed value for the burst rate interval is less than 10 seconds, it is rounded up to 10 seconds. The `average-rate` and `burst-rate` parameters specify the drop threshold (number of packet drops), which can range from 0 to 2,147,483,647.

NOTE When defining your thresholds, you can define up to three different rate intervals for each event type. If you have three average rate thresholds for dropped packets matching against ACL deny statements, and all three are exceeded, the appliance will only generate one log message for these events. However, if you have three average and three burst rate thresholds, and all six are exceeded, one log message is generated for all of the average threshold for the event and one for the burst threshold.

Basic Threat Detection Verification

To view the statistics for basic threat detection, use the **show threat-detection rate** command:

```
ciscoasa# show threat-detection rate [min-display-rate
            min_display_rate] [acl-drop | bad-packet-drop |
            conn-limit-drop | dos-drop | fw-drop | icmp-drop |
            inspect-drop | interface-drop | scanning-threat |
            syn-attack]
```

The **min-display-rate** parameter limits the displayed statistics to those that exceed the one specified by this parameter (in events per second). This value can range from 0 to 2,147,483,647 seconds.

Here is an example of the use of this command:

```
ciscoasa# show threat-detection rate
                  Average(eps)  Current(eps)  Trigger  Total events
10-min ACL drop:            0             0        0            33
1-hour ACL drop:            0             0        0           122
1-hour SYN attck:           6             0        3         24318
10-min Scanning:            0             0       31           243
1-hour Scanning:          115             0       15        348667
1-hour Bad pkts:           84             0        3        247609
10-min Firewall:            0             0        4            34
1-hour Firewall:           84             0        3        269411
10-min DoS attck:           0             0        0             8
1-hour DoS attck:           0             0        0            44
10-min Interface:           0             0        0           194
1-hour Interface:          92             0        0        321333
```

Five columns are in the display, where the statics are showed in events per second (eps). Each event type is shown in two intervals in the first column: the last 10 minutes and the last hour. The first statistical column is the Average rate in events per second (eps) over the specified period. This is followed by the Current burst rate in events per second over the burst interval (1/60th of the average rate interval). The Trigger column specifies the number of times that the rate was exceeded in the time interval. The last column specifies the total number of events in the period.

For the burst rate displayed, the appliance stores the tallied count at the end of each burst interval, for up to a total of 60 burst intervals; therefore, if you execute the command in the middle of the current burst interval, you won't see the statistics for the current interval; you'll only see the statistics for the previously completed interval. The exception to this rule is if the number of events in the current burst interval actually exceeds the number of events in the just previously tallied burst interval. In this case the appliance displays the current events in the yet uncompleted burst interval. This calculation process allows you to detect a large burst in events in a real-time fashion.

To clear the basic threat statistics, use the Privilege mode `clear threat-detection rate` command.

Scanning Threat Detection

Scanning threat detection was added in version 8.0 of the appliances. This feature allows the appliance to detect scanning attacks, where an attacker is scanning IP addresses of devices or scanning ports on a device or multiple devices in a subnet. Your typical IPS or IDS can easily detect fast scan attacks by comparing traffic with its signature database. Scanning signatures are basically templates that define the kinds of traffic and the thresholds that have to be reached to indicate a scanning attack. More intelligent IPS/IDS solutions will use heuristic analysis to better determine if a scanning attack is taking place, even those that are spread out over a period.

The scanning threat detection feature of the appliances falls into the latter camp in its approach to detecting scanning attacks. The appliance maintains a database in memory of host statistics and the connections and devices sources are accessing to determine if a scan attack is taking place. Basically the appliance is looking for connection anomalies that would indicate scanning, like traffic from a source, without responding traffic from a destination(s), or a source accessing a port that is closed on a destination, using the same IPID numbers in fragments that are part of the same packet (the IPID is the fragment identifier number), and many other anomalies.

When a scan is detected, the appliance automatically generates a log message about the scan with a log message ID of 730101; optionally you can have the appliance block traffic from the offender, which Cisco calls *shunning*.

TIP Enabling scanning threat detection on the appliance *will* affect its CPU and memory usage, since the appliance must build a database of devices and their connection characteristics, and then compare connections with the database. So if you enable the feature, you should carefully monitor it to ensure that the scanning threat detection feature doesn't overwhelm the appliance and cause the appliance to inadvertently drop legitimate packets.

Scanning Threat Detection Configuration

Scanning threat detection is disabled by default on the security appliances. To enable it, use the following command:

```
ciscoasa(config)# threat-detection scanning-threat [shun
                    [except {ip-address IP_address subnet_mask |
                    object-group network_object_group_ID}]]
```

Configuring the **shun** keyword will automatically drop traffic from the scanning attacker. The **except** parameter allows you to make exceptions to the shunning process, where you can make exceptions for an address or range of addresses or a group of addresses defined in a network object group (discussed in Chapter 6). Devices that you might want to create exceptions for include networking devices, like SNMP management stations that scan hosts periodically to determine their status.

Optionally you can change the scanning event thresholds as to when the appliance considers that a scanning attack is taking place. These thresholds are defined with the following command:

```
ciscoasa(config)# threat-detection rate scanning-threat
                    rate-interval rate_interval
                    average-rate average_rate
                    burst-rate burst_rate
```

The average and burst rate were described previously in the "Basic Threat Detection Configuration" section. Actually, if you have already configured the thresholds with basic threat detection, the scanning threat detection will use these configured thresholds. If you configure the rate interval in the command just shown, this applies to the average rate. The rate interval can range from 300 to 2,592,000 seconds (30 days). The burst rate interval takes this rate and divides it by 60. If the number is less than 10 seconds, it is rounded up to 10 seconds. You can configure up to three of these commands with different rate intervals.

For each event the appliance is monitoring that it considers a scanning attack, it compares it with the average and burst rate limits. If either limit is exceeded, the device is considered a target, and the security appliance generates a log message and optionally shuns the attack, depending on whether you configured the **shun** parameter in the **threat-detection scanning-threat** command.

Scanning Threat Detection Verification

To examine the devices that the appliance determines are performing scanning attacks or are the recipient of a scanning attack, use the **show threat-detection scanning-threat** command:

```
ciscoasa# show threat-detection scanning-threat [attacker | target]
```

If you don't qualify the command, both attackers and targets are listed.

Here's an example of viewing the detected attackers performing scans:

```
ciscoasa# show threat-detection scanning-threat attacker
10.1.5.7
10.1.6.6
200.135.101.215
```

The preceding command lists three scanning attackers.

Shunned Hosts

If you've enabled shunning, you can see the addresses that are shunned with the **show threat-detection shun** command. Here's an example of the use of this command:

```
ciscoasa# show threat-detection shun
Shunned Host List:
10.1.5.7
10.1.6.6
```

If a device has been shunned and it had a legitimate reason for the scanning function, you can clear the shunned status and then make an exception to it with the **threat-detection scanning-threat** command. To manually clear a shunned address or range of addresses, use the following command:

```
ciscoasa# clear threat-detection shun [IP_address [subnet_mask]]
```

If you do not specify an IP address or range of addresses, all hosts are cleared from the shun list.

You can use other methods of setting up shunning of hosts on the appliance. For example, an intrusion prevention or intrusion detection system (IPS or IDS) could see an attack, log into the appliance, and set up a temporary shun. You can also set up a manual shun on the appliance to block offending devices and their connections. To set up a manual shun, use the following command:

```
ciscoasa(config)# shun src_IP_addr [dst_IP_addr src_port dst_port
                      [protocol]] [vlan VLAN_ID]
```

If you only specify the source address, all traffic from the source is dropped. For the ports and protocol, you can specify the name or number—specifying 0 for the port includes all ports, and specifying 0 for the protocol includes all IP protocols.

Once you execute the **shun** command, from here forward the matching traffic is dropped by the appliance. Actually the **shun** commands are processed by the appliance before *any* other policies or configurations, including the comparing of the packet with the conn table. To remove a **shun** command (one that was added by you or by an IDS or IPS), use the following configuration:

```
ciscoasa(config)# no shun src_IP_addr [vlan VLAN_ID]
```

Threat Detection Statistics

The security appliances can collect detailed statistics on both permitted and dropped traffic rates. The following sections will discuss how to enable and view the appliance threat statistics.

Threat Statistics Configuration

By default, only statistics for ACLs are enabled. To enable all the threat statistics on the appliance, use the **threat-detection statistics** command:

```
ciscoasa(config)# threat-detection statistics [{access-list |
                    host | port | protocol}]
```

Without any qualifiers, all the threat statistics are enabled on the appliance; optionally you can enable threat statistics for a particular type. For host statistics, the statistics are accumulated for as long as the device is active and currently in the scanning threat database. If the device is inactive for more than 10 minutes, it is removed from the database and its statistics are cleared. If port statistics are enabled, statistics are gathered on TCP and UDP protocols. Other IP protocol statistics can be gathered by enabling the **proto-col** parameter.

 NOTE If you enable threat statistics, the performance of the appliance can suffer. Port statistics have the least impact on the appliance, and host statistics the most impact.

Threat Statistics Verification

Once threat statistics are enabled, you can view them with the **show threat-detection statistics** command. Actually the command has variations.

For example, to view the Top 10 threat detection statistics, use this command:

```
ciscoasa# show threat-detection statistics [min-display-rate
                    min_display_rate] top [{access-list | host |
                    port-protocol} [rate-1 | rate-2 | rate-3]]
```

The **min-display-rate** parameter limits the displayed output to only those statistics that exceed the minimum display rate in the events per second. If you don't qualify the output, the Top 10 statistics for all the categories are shown—ACL matches, hosts, and ports and protocols. The **rate-1**, **rate-2**, and **rate-3** parameters display the statistics for the smallest fixed-rate measurement interval, the next largest interval, and the largest interval.

To view statistics for one or more hosts, use this command:

```
ciscoasa# show threat-detection statistics [min-display-rate
                    min_display_rate] host [IP_address [mask]]
```

To view the statistics for a TCP or UDP port or range of ports, use this command:

```
ciscoasa# show threat-detection statistics [min-display-rate
                    min_display_rate] port [start_port[-end_port]]
```

To view the statistics for a specific protocol or all protocols, use this command:

```
ciscoasa# show threat-detection statistics [min-display-rate
                     min_display_rate] protocol [protocol_number |
                ah | eigrp | esp | gre | icmp | igmp | igrp |
                ip | ipinip | ipsec | nos | ospf | pcp | pim |
                pptp | snp | tcp | udp]
```

Here's an example of the host threat detection statistics:

```
ciscoasa# show threat-detection statistics host
                 Average(eps) Current(eps) Trigger Total events
Host:10.0.0.1: tot-ses:282935 act-ses:25271 fw-drop:0 insp-drop:0
null-ses:21348 bad-acc:0
1-hour Sent byte:       2942          0         0      10530808
8-hour Sent byte:        376          0         0      10530808
24-hour Sent byte:       132          0         0      10530808
1-hour Sent pkts:         28          0         0        140443
8-hour Sent pkts:          5          0         0        140443
24-hour Sent pkts:         1          0         0        140443
20-min Sent drop:          8          0         1         10581
1-hour Sent drop:          4          0         1         10581
1-hour Recv byte:       2967          0         0       9726170
8-hour Recv byte:        383          0         0       9726170
24-hour Recv byte:       121          0         0       9726170
1-hour Recv pkts:         31          0         0        108486
8-hour Recv pkts:          4          0         0        108486
24-hour Recv pkts:         2          0         0        108486
20-min Recv drop:         51          0         5         56057
1-hour Recv drop:         22          0         2         56057
<--output omitted-->
```

The `tot-ses` value displays the total number of sessions since the host was added to the threat statistics database. The `act-ses` value displays the active sessions that the associated host is currently involved with. The `fw-drop` value displays the number of firewall drops for the host, which includes dropped packets due to matched deny ACL statements, malformed packets, exceeded connection limits, suspicious ICMP packets, TCP SYN flood packets, DoS packets, and others. (This doesn't include interface overload, failed application inspections, or scanning attacks.) The `insp-drop` value displays the number of packets dropped because of application inspection policies. The `null-sess` value displays the number of TCP sessions that didn't complete the three-way handshake and the number of UDP sessions where a server didn't send a response within 3 seconds after the session has started. The `bad-acc` value displays the number of access attempts by the host to closed ports.

IP AUDIT

The appliances have supported IPS capabilities for a long time. The original IPS implementation on the appliances was software based, which was originally designed for SOHO networks. It supports over 50 signatures to detect attacks. The software implementation doesn't even begin to compare to the capabilities of the ASA AIP-SSM IPS module, which can detect over 1,500 attacks. However, if you don't have this card, you can supplement the security of your appliance with the IPS software feature, commonly called *IP audit*. The following sections will discuss the supported signatures and the configuration of IP audit.

IP Audit Signatures

IP audit signatures fall under two categories: informational and attack. Informational signatures look for connections, which could be normal traffic; attack signatures look for network attacks. Table 24-2 lists the signatures supported by IP audit that are used to look for different kinds of traffic or attacks.

Signature Number	Signature Type	Signature Description
1000	Informational	Looks for incomplete or malformed information in the IP options field of the IP header
1001	Informational	Looks for the option 7 setting (record packet route) in the IP options field of the IP header
1002	Informational	Looks for the option 4 setting (timestamp) in the IP options field of the IP header
1003	Informational	Looks for the option 2 setting (security options) in the IP options field of the IP header
1004	Informational	Looks for the option 3 setting (loose source route) in the IP options field of the IP header
1005	Informational	Looks for the option 8 setting (SATNET stream identifier) in the IP options field of the IP header
1006	Informational	Looks for the option 2 setting (strict source routing) in the IP options field of the IP header
1100	Attack	Looks for an IP packet with an offset value that is less than 5 but greater than 0 in the IP header offset field, indicating an IP fragment attack

Table 24-2. IP Audit Signatures

Signature Number	Signature Type	Signature Description
1102	Attack	Looks for an IP packet where the destination and source IP addresses are the same, indicating the Land attack
1103	Attack	Looks for overlapping fragments
2000	Informational	Looks for an ICMP echo reply message
2001	Informational	Looks for an ICMP host unreachable message
2002	Informational	Looks for an ICMP source quench message
2003	Informational	Looks for an ICMP redirect message
2004	Informational	Looks for an ICMP echo request message
2005	Informational	Looks for an ICMP time exceeded message
2006	Informational	Looks for an ICMP parameter problem message
2007	Informational	Looks for an ICMP timestamp request message
2008	Informational	Looks for an ICMP timestamp reply message
2009	Informational	Looks for an ICMP information request message
2010	Informational	Looks for an ICMP information reply message
2011	Informational	Looks for an ICMP address mask request message
2012	Informational	Looks for an ICMP address mask reply message
2150	Attack	Looks for fragmented ICMP packets
2151	Attack	Looks for ICMP packets larger than 1,024 bytes
2154	Attack	Looks for the Ping of Death attack
3040	Attack	Looks for a single TCP packet where the SYN, FIN, ACK, or RST flags are *not* set
3041	Attack	Looks for a single TCP packet where the SYN and FIN flags are set
3042	Attack	Looks for a single TCP packet with the FIN flag set that is sent to a port less than 1024
3153	Informational	Looks for a port command on an FTP control connection that is not the same as the requesting host
3154	Informational	Looks for a port command on an FTP control connection that specifies a data port less than 1024 or greater than 65535
4050	Attack	Looks for a UDP packet that has a length less than the length in the IP header length field (UDP bomb attack)

Table 24-2.   IP Audit Signatures (*Continued*)

Signature Number	Signature Type	Signature Description
4051	Attack	Looks for a UDP packet with a source port of 7, 19, or 135, indicating a Snort attack
4052	Attack	Looks for a UDP packet with a source port of 7 and a destination port of 19, indicating a Chargen DoS attack
6050	Informational	Looks for access to HINFO records on a DNS server
6051	Informational	Looks for a DNS zone transfer with a source port of 53
6052	Informational	Looks for an illegal DNS zone transfer where the source port is not 53
6053	Attack	Looks for a DNS request requesting all DNS records
6100	Informational	Looks for an attempt to register new RPC services on a host
6101	Informational	Looks for an attempt to unregister existing RPC services on a host
6102	Informational	Looks for an RPC dump request sent to a host
6103	Attack	Looks for a proxied RPC request sent to the portmapper program on a host
6150	Informational	Looks for a request to the portmapper program for the YP server daemon
6151	Informational	Looks for a request to the portmapper program for the YP bind daemon
6152	Informational	Looks for a request to the portmapper program for the YP password daemon
6153	Informational	Looks for a request to the portmapper program for the YP update daemon
6154	Informational	Looks for a request to the portmapper program for the YP transfer daemon
6155	Informational	Looks for a request to the portmapper program for the YP mount daemon
6175	Informational	Looks for a request to the portmapper program for the remote execution (rexd) daemon
6180	Informational	Looks for a request to the rexd daemon
6190	Attack	Looks for a large statd request, indicating a buffer overrun attack to gain access to system resources

Table 24-2.   IP Audit Signatures (*Continued*)

SECURITY ALERT! As you can see from the list of signatures in Table 24-2, the number of attacks that IP audit can detect is *very* minimal. A real IDS/IPS, like the AIP-SSM card for the ASAs or the 4200 series sensors, should be used if you are concerned about network attacks. The IP audit feature is something I might turn on for a SOHO ASA 5505, if even that.

IP Audit Configuration

By default IP audit is disabled on the appliances. To enable it, use the following configuration:

```
ciscoasa(config)# ip audit name audit_policy_name info
                       [action [alarm] [drop] [reset]]
ciscoasa(config)# ip audit name audit_policy_name attack
                       [action [alarm] [drop] [reset]]
ciscoasa(config)# ip audit interface logical_if_name audit_policy_name
```

The `ip audit name` command specifies which of the two signature categories you'll be enabling. The policy that you've created must then be enabled on a logical interface. If you want to enable both informational and attack signatures for an interface, use the same policy name when enabling them. You can have the appliance generate an alarm, drop the offending packet, and/or reset the connection (if it is using TCP). If you don't specify an action when there is a match on the signature, it defaults to `alarm`. The `ip audit interface` command enables the named policy on an interface in the inbound direction.

You can disable a signature listed in Table 24-2 with the following command:

```
ciscoasa(config)# ip audit signature signature_number disable
```

You might want to disable a signature when legitimate traffic matches the signature in most situations, creating false alarms; however, disabling the signature is performed at a global level, meaning that no traffic will trigger the signature (even bad traffic) when it is disabled.

ADDITIONAL FEATURES

The last part of this chapter will focus on three additional appliance features you can implement to deal with various network threats and attacks: TCP normalization, unicast reverse path forwarding (RPF), and fragmentation limits.

TCP Normalization

The TCP normalization feature on the appliance allows you to look for and prevent abnormal or unusual TCP packets. The normalization feature is actually an extension of the Modular Policy Framework (MPF) process introduced in Chapter 10. The following two sections will discuss how to look for abnormal TCP packets and the policy that should be implemented for them.

Configuring TCP Normalization Maps

The first step in setting up TCP normalization is to create a TCP normalization map. This map contains the abnormal criteria that you'll look for in TCP connections. Creating a TCP normalization map involves the following configuration:

```
ciscoasa(config)# tcp-map TCP_map_name
ciscoasa(config-tcp-map)# check-retransmission
ciscoasa(config-tcp-map)# checksum-verification
ciscoasa(config-tcp-map)# exceed-mss {allow | drop}
ciscoasa(config-tcp-map)# queue-limit number_of_packets
ciscoasa(config-tcp-map)# reserved-bits {allow | clear | drop}
ciscoasa(config-tcp-map)# syn-data {allow | drop}
ciscoasa(config-tcp-map)# tcp-options {selective-ack | timestamp |
                   window-scale} {allow | clear}
ciscoasa(config-tcp-map)# tcp-options range lower upper
                   {allow | clear | drop}
ciscoasa(config-tcp-map)# [no] ttl-evasion-protection
ciscoasa(config-tcp-map)# urgent-flag {allow | clear}
ciscoasa(config-tcp-map)# window-variation {allow | drop}
```

Each map must be given a unique name, which takes you into a subcommand mode.

The `check-retransmission` command has the appliance verify TCP retransmissions: if the data being retransmitted is different, then it should be dropped. The `checksum-verification` command causes the appliance to check if the TCP header has a checksum, and if not, to drop the TCP packet. To allow or drop the TCP packets that exceed the maximum segment size (MSS) set by the peer during the initial three-way handshake, configure the `exceed-mss` command.

The `queue-limit` command is used to control the maximum number of out-of-order packets that can be queued up for a particular TCP stream. By default packets need to be reordered if you are doing stateful inspection, IP audit, or checking the retransmissions on TCP packets. By default two packets are allowed, per flow, to be out of order. You can increase the size of the queue up to 250 packets; however, increasing the size can affect your memory, since every stream will require more RAM resources.

Configuration of the `reserved-bits` command causes the appliance to look in the TCP reserved field for bits being set. Allowing these settings through creates ambiguity for how the appliance and the end host should handle the connection, which might cause either the appliance or destination to desynchronize or tear it down. You can allow these bits through, clear them, or drop the offending TCP packet.

According to the RFC for TCP, TCP is required to accept data in the payload of a SYN packet (even though the three-way handshake is in progress). Some end-devices might not deal with this packet correctly, which might create a vulnerability for the application and lead to an access attack. To have the appliance drop SYN packets that have data, configure the **syn-data drop** command.

The **tcp-options** command can clear certain options in the TCP header. For example, the **selective-ack** parameter allows you to clear the SACK option. The **timestamp** parameter allows you to clear or allow the timestamp option, which disables PAWS (Protect Against Wrapped Sequence) numbers and RTT (round-trip time). The purpose of PAWS, which is defined in RFC 1323, is to protect a TCP connection against old, duplicate segments in the same connection. There is a possibility, however, that PAWS may discard valid reordered segments. By clearing this in the TCP header, you are removing this likelihood. The **window-scale** parameter allows you to clear the window scale mechanism used by TCP. The **range** parameter allows you to control the range of options used in the TCP header.

TTL evasion protection is enabled by default (the **ttl-evasion-protection** command). This feature looks for packets that have a shorter than normal TTL, where an attacker might be creating a short TTL that is allowed through the appliance, but dropped between it and a destination device by an intermediate router because the TTL has expired. The attacker would then send a malicious packet with a longer TTL, which might appear to the appliance as a retransmission of the first packet, and the appliance might allow it. Allowing the second, malicious packet through might enable an access or DoS attack against the destination device. TTL evasion protection should only be disabled if you have a legitimate device that is scanning the network and attempting to learn minimum and maximum hops to a destination via multiple paths; otherwise it should be left enabled for everyone else.

The URG (urgent) pointer is a flag in the TCP header indicating an offset in the TCP payload that is high priority, which the destination device should process first; however, the RFC for TCP is not very clear on exactly how the URG pointer should be used and/or implemented, which has led vendors to interpret its meaning differently. This could lead to a destination device becoming vulnerable to an attack. By default the URG pointer and its corresponding offset are cleared; if you have an application that uses it, however, you should create a TCP map with this enabled (**urgent-flag allow** command), but qualify it with a class map that only includes the application server.

Windowing is used by TCP to control the flow of the amount of data when data is dropped. What could happen is that a device could start out with a very large window size and very quickly drop it to a small size when sending little data, which is not recommended. The appliances, when detecting this condition on a TCP connection, will drop the packet with the large change in the window size. If you need to allow this, you can enable it with the **window-variation allow** command.

Using TCP Normalization Maps

Once you've created your TCP map, you need to associate it with a class map in a layer 3/4 policy map, as follows:

```
ciscoasa(config)# policy-map policy_map_name
ciscoasa(config-pmap)# class class_map_name
ciscoasa(config-pmap-c)# set connection advanced-options TCP_map_name
```

The policy map can be applied to an interface, or you could implement the policy in the global policy.

NOTE   Remember that TCP maps are only applicable for TCP connections; so make sure that the corresponding layer 3/4 class map only contains TCP connections.

Example Using TCP Normalization

To help you better understand how TCP maps are used, let's look at an example. To allow urgent flag and urgent offset packets for all traffic sent to the well-known FTP data port, enter the following commands:

```
ciscoasa(config)# tcp-map my_tcp_map
ciscoasa(config-tcp-map)# urgent-flag allow
ciscoasa(config-tcp-map)# check-retransmission
ciscoasa(config-tcp-map)# exit
ciscoasa(config)# class-map tcp_urgent_class
ciscoasa(config-cmap)# match port tcp ftp-data
ciscoasa(config-cmap)# exit
ciscoasa(config)# policy-map my_policy_map
ciscoasa(config-pmap)# class tcp_urgent_class
ciscoasa(config-pmap-c)# set connection advanced-options my_tcp_map
ciscoasa(config-pmap-c)# exit
ciscoasa(config)# service-policy my_policy_map global
```

In this example, the URG flag is allowed for the FTP data connection (port 20 when in active/ standard mode), and retransmissions of the same packet are checked and verified.

Reverse Path Forwarding

Reverse path forwarding (RPF) is used to prevent spoofing attacks, like that shown in Figure 24-1. Normally when a layer 3 device like a router receives a packet, it looks at the destination IP address, compares that with the network numbers in its routing table, and then makes a routing decision for the packet. RPF is the reverse of the process. Instead of looking at the destination address, the layer 3 device compares the *source* address in the packet with the network numbers in its routing table and verifies where it is coming *from*. If the packet is coming from a network that is not associated with the source interface, the packet is dropped. If you examine Figure 24-1, RPF would examine the inbound packet, notice the source address of 2.5.5.17, compare it with its routing table, notice that the 2.5.5.0/24 network is connected to a *different* interface (the DMZ), and drop the spoofed packet. This process is described in RFC 2267.

On the appliances, since ICMP packets do not have a session (each ICMP request has a unique sequence number), the appliance has to examine the source address of every ICMP packet. However, with TCP and UDP, which are session oriented, the appliance

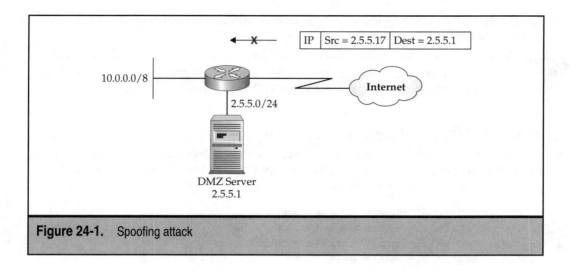

Figure 24-1. Spoofing attack

only has to validate the source address of the first packet in the session, which if allowed, is then added to the conn table. The conn table is then used to allow subsequent packets.

RPF is disabled by default and is enabled on an interface-by-interface basis with the following command:

```
ciscoasa(config)# ip verify reverse-path interface logical_if_name
```

Fragmentation Limits

Fragments are basically parts of an IP packet that has to be split into two or more packets because the original packet is larger than the supported MTU (maximum transmission unit) size for the connected segment. Fragmentation used to be a common occurrence when LAN networks used mixed topologies like Ethernet, Token Ring, and/or FDDI (Fiber Distributed Data Interface). Today fragmentation is less likely in networks; however, it can occur in certain situations. Probably the most common place where fragmentation will occur in networks today is in VPNs, since VPNs can add a lot of overhead to a packet. For example, if you're implementing IPSec over TCP for the data connections, you're adding an outer IP header, a TCP header, and an ESP header, which might cause fragmentation. (See my book *The Complete Cisco VPN Configuration Guide* (Cisco Press, 2005) for more information on this topic.) NFS, the Network File System, is another service that commonly creates fragments.

By default the appliance allows up to 24 fragments that will make up a complete IP packet, as well as up to 200 fragments that are waiting to be reassembled back into a complete packet. If you do not expect fragments in your network, then you should have the appliance drop any fragments that it receives. This is accomplished with the following command:

```
ciscoasa(config)# fragment chain 1 [logical_if_name]
```

The **chain** parameter specifies the number of fragments that can make up a complete packet; by setting it to 1, you are ensuring that your appliance won't allow fragments through it, since fragments are commonly used in DoS attacks. If you don't configure the interface name, this configuration applies to all interfaces on the appliance. So, for example, if you have legitimate reasons for seeing fragments on two or more internal interfaces, but not on the external interface, you should configure the preceding command, but reference the logical name of the external interface.

NOTE You can use the **fragment** command to control how many fragments make up a packet, the number of concurrent fragmented packets, and the period that the appliance must receive all the fragments for a given packet. The number of fragments the appliance will allow for a packet defaults to 24, where the number of concurrently fragmented packets can't exceed 200 and the timeout for reassembling fragments back to a complete packet is 5 seconds.

CHAPTER 25

SSM Cards

This chapter will provide an overview of the AIP-SSM (IPS) and CSC-SSM (Anti-X) cards. If you recall from Chapter 1, these two cards are supported by the ASA 5510 through the ASA 5540 models. In Chapter 10, I introduced the Cisco Modular Policy Framework (MPF), where two of the policies I discussed were having these cards process traffic. The topics covered in this chapter include

▼ Preparing the AIP-SSM card

■ Preparing the CSC-SSM card

▲ Managing the SSM cards

NOTE Configuring the actual cards is beyond the scope of this book...I could easily write an entire book on these topics alone. This chapter focuses on what you need to do on the ASAs to prepare them for using the cards, plus the initial access to the cards themselves.

AIP-SSM CARD

The AIP-SSM card, commonly called the *IPS* card, is basically an IPS sensor, like the Cisco 4200s, inside the chassis of the ASA 5500s: it has its own processor, RAM, flash drive, operating system, and configuration: in other words, it's a "box-in-a-box." The software the AIP-SSM card runs is basically the same software that the 4200 series sensors run. The OS is based on the Red Hat Linux operating system, with the Cisco IPS software running on top of that. The Cisco IPS software can be managed using the CLI of the AIP-SSM; however, Cisco expects you to use either ASDM or IPS Device Manager (IDM) to manage the card. If you are using ASDM, Cisco runs IDM within your ASDM session. ASDM is discussed in Chapter 27.

The card itself has only one physical interface: a gigabit Ethernet interface. This is used for out-of-band management of the card, like performing an OS recovery or accessing the card using IDM or SSH. All other access to the card is done via the backplane of the ASA, including console access (there is no physical console port). The remainder of this section will discuss the operation of the card, how to put a basic configuration on the card, and how to set up policies on the ASA to have the card process traffic.

AIP-SSM Card Modes and Failure Options

The AIP-SSM supports two card modes—inline and promiscuous—and two failure options—fail-open and fail-close. The following two sections will discuss these in more depth.

Inline and Promiscuous Modes

If you recall from Chapter 10, the AIP-SSM card supports two modes for MPF policies:

▼ **Inline mode** Traffic in a class map that is associated with an inline mode policy is *redirected into* the AIP-SSM card to be processed for attacks. If an attack is detected, one of the policies you can configure for the card is to drop the offending traffic. Assuming the traffic passes the policies of the card, it is redirected back to the backplane of the appliance.

▲ **Promiscuous mode** Traffic in a class map that is associated with a promiscuous policy is *copied* to the card for further processing, while the original traffic remains on the backplane of the appliance.

Inline mode provides the advantage where atomic-based (attacks contained in a single packet), Trojan horse, and worm attacks can be easily thwarted, since the AIP-SSM card can drop offending packets. However, the downside of inline mode is that it introduces delay in a packet stream, possibly affecting delay-sensitive traffic. Likewise, if the card becomes overwhelmed with too many packets, some packets are dropped. The advantages and disadvantages of using inline mode, however, are the reverse for promiscuous mode. In promiscuous mode, if an attack is detected, the AIP-SSM card can react to the attack by optionally logging into the ASA itself and setting up a shun function (see Chapter 24) to block the attacker. One advantage of the ASA is that you can define policies where some traffic uses inline mode with the AIP-SSM card, and other traffic uses promiscuous mode.

Fail-Open and Fail-Close

When setting up your policies for traffic to be processed by the AIP-SSM card, you must specify the failure mode: fail-open or fail-close. With a fail-open policy, if the card is not operational, traffic is allowed to bypass the matching ASA policy. Once the card is operational, the traffic is then examined by the card for attacks. A card might be non-operational if it is booting up, rebooting, or experiencing a malfunction.

With a fail-close option, if the card is non-operational, traffic is dropped by the ASA until the card becomes operational and can again process traffic. This option is used when it is absolutely critical that certain types of traffic be examined for attacks or when you shouldn't accept the packets because of the sensitive nature of the data or the importance of the server the traffic is being directed to.

Traffic and the AIP-SSM Card

As I mentioned in Chapter 10, traffic is not processed by the IPS card by default: you must set up policies either to copy packets to the card or to redirect traffic into the card. To understand how the ASAs process packets and when traffic would be processed by the card, examine the following summarized steps:

1. Traffic enters the ASA.

2. The ASA applies the firewall policies to the traffic.

3. The IPS card then processes the traffic if the traffic matches an IPS policy on the ASA.

4. When in inline mode, any traffic that passes the policies is placed back on the backplane of the ASA.

5. The ASA applies VPN policies to the traffic.

6. The traffic exits an interface on the ASA.

NOTE For a more detailed description of the traffic flow process, please review Chapter 10.

Traffic Forwarding to the AIP-SSM Card

You can use the AIP-SSM card on an ASA that is configured for single or multiple mode. In multiple mode, you can define IPS policies in individual contexts that will have the matching traffic processed by the AIP-SSM card. Assuming you are running the IPS 6.0 software or later on the AIP-SSM card, you can configure virtual sensors. A virtual sensor is similar to the concept of contexts on the appliances. With virtual sensors, you can have different sets of signatures with different policies for different classes of traffic and/or contexts, as is shown in Figure 25-1. By default, only one virtual sensor exists on the sensor, and it processes all traffic from the ASA. You can be very creative in pairing up traffic on the ASA to the IPS card:

▼ When an ASA is running in single mode, you can have different classes of traffic processed by the same virtual sensor on the IPS card.

■ When the ASA is running in single mode, you can have different classes of traffic processed by different virtual sensors on the IPS card.

■ When the ASA is running in multiple mode, you can have all contexts use the same virtual sensor on the IPS card.

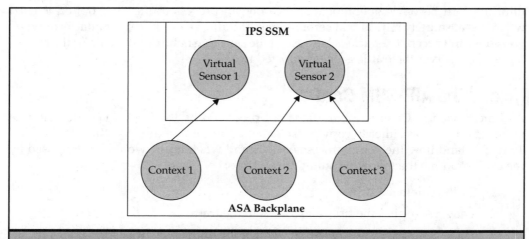

Figure 25-1. Contexts and virtual sensors

■ When the ASA is running in multiple mode, you can have multiple contexts using the same virtual sensor on the IPS card, where some contexts use one virtual sensor and others use another virtual sensor.

▲ When the ASA is running in multiple mode, you can have each context assigned to its own virtual sensor on the IPS card.

AIP-SSM Basic Configuration

The following sections discuss how to access the AIP-SSM card, how to place a basic configuration on it so that you can access it via ASDM or IDM, how to assign virtual sensors to contexts, and a brief review of creating policies of the ASA so that you can have traffic processed by the card.

Accessing the AIP-SSM CLI

To access the CLI of the IPS SSM card, you must first log into the CLI of the ASA. From the ASA's Privilege mode, use the **session 1** command—at this point you're dealing with Cisco software running on top of Red Hat Linux of the SSM card. You'll need to log in using the account name of *cisco* and a password of *cisco*—you're forced to change the password. Here's an example of the login process:

```
ciscoasa# session 1
Opening command session with slot 1.
Connected to slot 1. Escape character sequence is 'CTRL-^X'.
login: cisco
Password: cisco
You are required to change your password immediately (password aged)
Changing password for cisco
(current) UNIX password: cisco
New password: <new password>
Retype new password: <new password>
Last login: Fri Sep 2 06:21:20 from 10.0.1.1
***NOTICE***
<--output omitted-->
***LICENSE NOTICE***
There is no license key installed on the system.
Please go to http://www.cisco.com/go/license
to obtain a new license or install a license.
sensor#
```

When you're changing the password, the new password must be at least 8 characters long and cannot be in the Linux password dictionary. If you see a license notice concerning a missing license key before the EXEC prompt, then you will be unable to upgrade the signature files from updates that Cisco creates. License keys are used to track customers with paid subscriptions, which are valid for 1 year.

Using the setup Script

Once you have logged into the AIP-SSM card, you'll need to place a basic configuration on it. To put a basic configuration on the card, use the **setup** command. This command executes a script that allows you to place a basic configuration on the card, similar to that of the system configuration dialog script on the appliances and IOS devices. Here's an example:

```
sensor# setup
    --- System Configuration Dialog ---
At any point you may enter a question mark '?' for help.
User ctrl-c to abort configuration dialog at any prompt.
Default settings are in square brackets '[]'.
Current Configuration:
service host
network-settings
host-ip 10.0.1.4/24,10.0.1.2
host-name sensor
telnet-option disabled
access-list 10.0.2.0/24
<--output omitted-->
Current time: Fri Dec 21 14:33:34 2007
Setup Configuration last modified: Thu Dec 20 18:34:08 2007
Continue with configuration dialog?[yes]: yes
Enter host name[sensor1]: ips1
Enter IP interface[10.0.1.4/24,10.0.1.2]: 10.0.1.4/24,10.0.1.2
Enter telnet-server status[disabled]: <cr>
Enter web-server port[443]: <cr>
Modify current access list?[no]: yes
Current access list entries:
  [1] 10.0.2.0/24
Delete: 1
Delete:
Permit: 10.0.1.0/24
Permit:
Modify system clock settings?[no]: yes
  Use NTP?[no]: <cr>
  Modify summer time settings?[no]: <cr>
  Modify system timezone?[no]: <cr>
```

```
Modify interface/virtual sensor configuration?[no]: no
Modify default threat prevention settings?[no]: <cr>
The following configuration was entered.
service host
network-settings
host-ip 10.0.1.4/24,10.0.1.2
host-name ips1
telnet-option disabled
access-list 10.0.1.0/24
<--output omitted-->
[0] Go to the command prompt without saving this config.
[1] Return back to the setup without saving this config.
[2] Save this configuration and exit setup.
Enter your selection[2]: 2
Configuration Saved.
*14:36:29 UTC Fri Dec 21 2007
Modify system date and time?[no]: <cr>
sensor#
```

Minimally you'll need to assign an IP address to the external interface of the card and specify which IP addresses are allowed to manage the card (their source addresses). The rest of the parameters are optional. Actually once you've completed the script successfully, you can now use ASDM via the backplane of the ASA to complete the rest of the card configuration or use IDM via the external Ethernet interface of the card itself. To return to the CLI of the ASA, use <CNTRL><SHIFT>6 x, the break sequence used on IOS devices.

NOTE The use of ASDM or IDM to configure policies for the card itself is beyond the scope of this book—it would actually take a book in-and-of-itself to adequately cover this topic.

Assigning Virtual Sensors to Contexts

Starting in version 6.0 of the Cisco IPS software, you can create multiple virtual sensors, each with its own set of signature and attack policies. To run version 6.0 on the AIP-SSM card, the ASA itself must minimally be running version 8.0 software. You can create and use up to four virtual sensors on the IPS card. (This limit is true of all Cisco IPS sensor products that support virtual sensors.)

If you have multiple virtual sensors on the IPS card, you'll have to specify which contexts will use which virtual sensors. How this is accomplished depends on if the ASA is running in single versus multiple mode and if you are or are not using multiple virtual sensors. The following two sections will discuss these configurations.

Creating Traffic Policies on the ASA in Single Mode   I introduced IPS policies in Chapter 10, including how to have packets redirected or copied to the IPS card. I'll expand on that topic, since I didn't cover the capabilities of the card, specifically the feature of multiple virtual sensors, at that point. Here is the basic configuration to set up an IPS policy for traffic on an appliance running in single mode:

```
ciscoasa(config)# policy-map policy_map_name
ciscoasa(config-pmap)# class class_map_name
ciscoasa(config-pmap-c)# ips {promiscuous | inline}
                             {fail-open | fail-close}
                             [sensor virtual_sensor_name]
```

The basic syntax of this configuration was discussed in Chapter 10. If you are not using virtual sensors on the appliance, the default virtual sensor is used (vs0). If you have created virtual sensors on the AIP-SSM card, you need to specify the name of the virtual sensor on the card that should process the traffic; otherwise vs0 is used.

To see the names of the virtual sensors, use the **show ips** command:

```
ciscoasa# show ips
Sensor name
------------
vs0
vs1
```

Here's a simple example of using single mode with two virtual sensors on the IPS card:

```
ciscoasa(config)# class-map IPS_map1
ciscoasa(config-cmap)# match any
ciscoasa(config)# class-map IDS_map2
ciscoasa(config-cmap)# match any
ciscoasa(config)# policy-map dmz1_policy
ciscoasa(config-pmap)# class IPS_map1
ciscoasa(config-pmap-c)# ips inline fail-open sensor vs0
ciscoasa(config-pmap-c)# exit
ciscoasa(config-pmap)# exit
ciscoasa(config)# policy-map dmz2_policy
ciscoasa(config-pmap)# class IDS_map2
ciscoasa(config-pmap-c)# ips promiscuous fail-open sensor vs1
ciscoasa(config-pmap-c)# exit
ciscoasa(config-pmap)# exit
ciscoasa(config)# service-policy dmz1_policy interface dmz1
ciscoasa(config)# service-policy dmz2_policy interface dmz2
```

In the preceding example, two policies are defined: one for inline mode for all traffic on the dmz1 interface, and one for promiscuous mode for all traffic on the dmz2 interface. Notice that in both cases, a different virtual sensor (vs0 and vs1) is used on the IPS card.

Creating Traffic Policies on the ASA in Multiple Mode   If your ASA is running in multiple mode, when creating the contexts, you'll need to include which virtual sensors can be *used* by a context—this is similar to assigning interfaces to the context (discussed in Chapter 22). To allocate a virtual sensor to a context, use the following configuration:

```
ciscoasa(config)# context context_name
ciscoasa(config-ctx)# allocate-ips virtual_sensor_name [mapped_name]
                      [default]
```

The **allocate-ips** command associates a virtual sensor to the context. To see the virtual sensor names available on the card, use the **show ips** command discussed in the last section. If you specify a mapped name, in the actual context you'll need to reference this name for your IPS policy instead of the virtual sensor name. The **default** parameter is used in a context when you set up a policy and don't specify which virtual sensor to use—the **allocate-ips** command with the **default** parameter is used in this case. Once you have allocated the virtual sensor or sensors a context can use, switch to the context with the **changeto** command. Then set up a policy like the example in the last section that will copy packets to the card or redirect packets into the card and be processed by the appropriate virtual sensor process.

Here's an example configuration that illustrates the setup of a multiple mode appliance with an IPS card that has multiple virtual sensors:

```
ciscoasa(config)# context ctx1
ciscoasa(config-ctx)# allocate-ips vs0 ips1 default
ciscoasa(config-ctx)# allocate-ips vs1 ips2
ciscoasa(config-ctx)# exit
ciscoasa(config)# context ctx2
ciscoasa(config-ctx)# allocate-ips vs0 ips1 default
ciscoasa(config-ctx)# allocate-ips vs1 ips3
ciscoasa(config-ctx)# exit
ciscoasa(config)# changeto context ctx1
ciscoasa/ctx1(config)# class-map outside_map1
ciscoasa/ctx1(config-cmap)# match any
ciscoasa/ctx1(config)# class-map inside_map2
ciscoasa/ctx1(config-cmap)# match any
ciscoasa/ctx1(config)# policy-map outside_policy
ciscoasa/ctx1(config-pmap)# class outside_map1
ciscoasa/ctx1(config-pmap-c)# ips inline fail-open
ciscoasa/ctx1(config-pmap-c)# exit
ciscoasa/ctx1(config-pmap)# exit
ciscoasa/ctx1(config)# policy-map inside_policy
ciscoasa/ctx1(config-pmap)# class inside_map2
ciscoasa/ctx1(config-pmap-c)# ips promiscuous fail-open sensor ips2
ciscoasa/ctx1(config-pmap-c)# exit
ciscoasa/ctx1(config-pmap)# exit
```

```
ciscoasa/ctx1(config)# service-policy outside_policy interface outside
ciscoasa/ctx1(config)# service-policy inside_policy interface inside
ciscoasa/ctx1(config)# changeto context ctx2
<--output omitted-->
```

In the preceding example, four virtual sensors are on the IPS card. The top part of the configuration shows the configuration in the system area, where I'm allocating the virtual sensors to their respective contexts. In the policy for ctx1 in the outside_map1 class map, notice that since I didn't specify a virtual sensor name, the default virtual sensor is used, which is the mapped name of ips1 (mapped to vs0 in the system area). I have two policies for ctx1: traffic on the *inside* interface is processed with promiscuous mode using vs1, and *outside* interface traffic is processed in inline mode using inline mode using vs0. I've omitted the configuration of ctx2, but the command structure is basically the same.

CSC-SSM CARD

As I mentioned in Chapter 1, there are two CSC-SSM cards, the model 10 and 20. Table 25-1 summarizes the cards and the licenses. The base license only allows you to perform antivirus, antispyware, and file blocking. The plus license adds anti-phishing, antispam, URL blocking and filtering, and content control. The licenses are based on number of users, so you need to ensure that you buy the right card and license based on the number of IP addresses you want the card to process.

NOTE The CSC-SSM supports up to 120 Mbps of traffic that can flow through it before it will start dropping packets.

Traffic and the CSC Card

The CSC-SSM card was designed to examine only certain protocols to protect against viruses, spyware, spam, phishing attacks, and unwanted files and content. The protocols supported include FTP (TCP port 21), HTTP (TCP port 80), POP3 (TCP port 110), and SMTP (TCP port 25). You can scan traffic for all these protocols or a combination of them.

CSC-SSM Card	Basic License	Additional User Licenses
CSC-SSM-10	50	100, 250, and 500
CSC-SSM-20	500	750 and 1,000

Table 25-1. CSC-SSM Cards

However, because of the limited throughput of the card and its processing capabilities, you should only divert the traffic you need the card to examine. In other words, don't forward protocols like ICMP or SIP which the card can't scan.

NOTE When you define a policy for the CSC card, the policy is *bi-directional*. This means that if traffic matches the policy on either an inbound interface or an outbound interface where there is a CSC policy, the traffic will be redirected into the card for further processing.

Forwarding Traffic to the CSC-SSM Card

By default the card processes no traffic unless you set up an MPF policy to forward matching packets to the card. You must define an MPF policy containing the **csc** command to determine which traffic will be forwarded into the card. This process was discussed in Chapter 10.

Here are the commands you need:

```
ciscoasa(config)# policy-map policy_map_name
ciscoasa(config-pmap)# class class_map_name
ciscoasa(config-pmap-c)# csc {fail-open | fail-close}
```

For more information on the preceding commands, see Chapter 10.

TIP When setting up a class map for CSC traffic inspection, I recommend that you use an ACL to match on only the protocols the card supports.

To illustrate the configuration of a CSC policy for the ASAs, examine the network shown in Figure 25-2. In this example, all internal users' traffic that is HTTP, SMTP, and POP3 should be examined by the card; the exception to this is web traffic to the DMZ web server. Also, e-mail traffic sent to the e-mail server from the outside should be examined. Here's the configuration to accomplish this policy:

```
ciscoasa(config)# access-list csc_out deny tcp
                  192.168.3.0 255.255.255.0
                  host 192.168.2.6 eq 80
ciscoasa(config)# access-list csc_out permit tcp
                  192.168.3.0 255.255.255.0 any eq 80
ciscoasa(config)# access-list csc_out permit tcp
                  192.168.3.0 255.255.255.0 any eq 110
ciscoasa(config)# class-map csc_outbound_class
ciscoasa(config-cmap)# match access-list csc_out
ciscoasa(config-cmap)# exit
ciscoasa(config)# policy-map csc_out_policy
ciscoasa(config-pmap)# class csc_outbound_class
```

```
ciscoasa(config-pmap-c)# csc fail-close
ciscoasa(config-pmap-c)# exit
ciscoasa(config)# service-policy csc_out_policy interface inside
ciscoasa(config)# access-list csc_in permit tcp any
                          192.168.2.6 255.255.255.0 eq 80
ciscoasa(config)# access-list csc_in permit tcp any
                          192.168.2.5 255.255.255.0 eq 25
ciscoasa(config)# class-map csc_inbound_class
ciscoasa(config-cmap)# match access-list csc_in
ciscoasa(config)# policy-map csc_in_policy
ciscoasa(config-pmap)# class csc_inbound_class
ciscoasa(config-pmap-c)# csc fail-close
ciscoasa(config)# service-policy csc_in_policy interface outside
```

Notice that in both policies (for the users and the DMZ servers) the fail-close option is used; therefore, if the CSC card is operational, traffic that matches **permit** statements in the ACLs will be dropped until the card becomes operational.

NOTE For the CSC card to scan FTP file transfers, application inspection for FTP must be enabled either globally or for the interface FTP traffic is entering. By default FTP inspection is enabled in the global policy on the ASA.

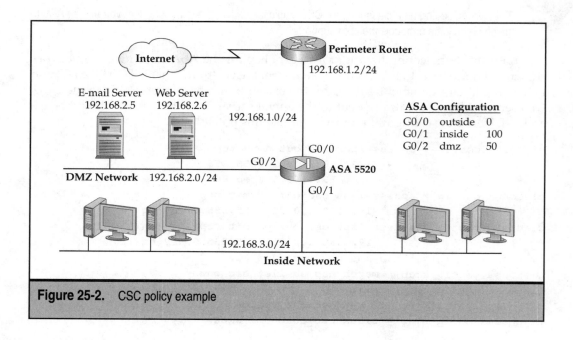

Figure 25-2. CSC policy example

Setting Up the CSC-SSM Card

To set up and verify the operation of the CSC-SSM card, you must use ASDM. Unlike the AIP-SSM card, which can be accessed via the backplane of the ASA or through the external Ethernet interface on the card, the CSC-SSM card lacks any physical interfaces: almost all access to it must be made via the backplane of the ASA using ASDM. However, you can place a basic configuration on it using a CLI so that the rest of the configuration can be accomplished using ASDM (this is somewhat similar to the AIP-SSM card).

Basically the following information needs to be configured either via the CLI or ASDM before the card can be used: a subscription activation key; a management IP address, subnet mask, and default gateway address; a DNS server address; a host and domain name; an e-mail and SMTP server address for e-mail notifications; addresses allowed to manage the card; and a new management password.

Here's an example of accessing the CLI of the card and placing a basic configuration on it:

```
hostname# session 1
Opening command session with slot 1.
Connected to slot 1. Escape character sequence is 'CTRL-^X'.
login: cisco
Password: cisco
You are required to change your password immediately (password aged)
Changing password for cisco
(current) UNIX password: cisco
New password: <new password>
Retype new password: <new password>

Trend Micro InterScan for Cisco CSC SSM Setup Wizard
-------------------------------------------------------------
To set up the SSM, the wizard prompts for the following information:
1. Network settings
2. Date/time settings verification
3. Incoming email domain name
4. Web console administrator password
5. Notification settings
6. Activation Codes
The Base License is required to activate the SSM.
Press Control-C to abort the wizard.

Press Enter to continue ... <ENTER>

Network Settings
-------------------------------------------------------------
Enter the SSM card IP address: 192.168.1.20
```

```
Enter subnet mask: 255.255.255.0
Enter host name: csc
Enter domain name: dealgroup.com
Enter primary DNS IP address: 4.2.2.1
Enter optional secondary DNS IP address: 4.2.2.2
Enter gateway IP address: 192.168.1.1
Do you use a proxy server? [y|n] n

Network Settings
----------------------------------------------------------------------
IP                192.168.1.20
Netmask           255.255.255.0
Hostname          csc
Domain name       dealgroup.com
Primary DNS       4.2.2.1
Secondary DNS     4.2.2.2
Gateway           192.168.1.1
No Proxy
Are these settings correct? [y|n] y
Applying network settings ...
Do you want to confirm the network settings using ping? [y|n] y
Enter an IP address to ping: 192.168.1.1
PING 192.168.1.1 (192.168.1.1): 56 data bytes
64 bytes from 192.168.1.1: icmp_seq=0 ttl=255 time=0.2 ms
64 bytes from 192.168.1.1: icmp_seq=1 ttl=255 time=0.1 ms
<--output omitted-->
--- 192.168.1.1 ping statistics ---
5 packets transmitted, 5 packets received, 0% packet loss
round-trip min/avg/max = 0.1/0.1/0.2 ms
Press Enter to continue ... <ENTER>

                    Date/Time Settings
-----------------------------------------------------------
SSM card date and time: 10/06/2005 18:14:14
The SSM card periodically synchronizes with the chassis
Is the time correct? [y|n] y
Incoming Domain Name
-----------------------------------------------------------
Enter the domain name that identifies incoming email messages:
(default:example.com)
Domain name of incoming email: dealgroup.com
Is the incoming domain correct? [y|n] y
```

```
Administrator/Notification Settings
---------------------------------------------------------------
The password will be hidden while you type.
Web console administrator password: cisco123
Retype Web console administrator password: cisco123
Administrator email address: richard.deal@dealgroup.com
Notification email server IP: 192.168.1.250
Notification email server port: (default:25) 25

Administrator/Notification Settings
---------------------------------------------------------------
Administrator email address: tester@example.com
Notification email server IP: 192.168.1.250
Notification email server port: 25
Are the notification settings correct? [y|n] y

                            Activation
---------------------------------------------------------------
You must activate your Base License, which enables you to update
your virus pattern file. You may also activate your Plus License.

Activation Code example: BV-43CZ-8TYY9-D4VNM-82We9-L7722-WPX41
Enter your Base License Activation Code:
     PX-ABTD-L58LB-XYZ9K-JYEUY-H5AEE-LK44N
Base License activation is successful.
(Press Enter to skip activating your Plus License.)
Enter your Plus License Activation Code:
     PX-6WGD-PSUNB-9XBA8-FKW5L-XXSHZ-2G9MN
Plus License activation is successful.

Activation Status
---------------------------------------------------------------
Your Base License is activated.
Your Plus License is activated.

Stopping services: OK
Starting services: OK
The Setup Wizard is finished.
Please use your Web browser to connect to the management console at:
https://192.168.1.20:8443
Press Enter to exit ... <ENTER>
Remote card closed command session. Press any key to continue.
Command session with slot 1 terminated.
hostname#
```

The default username and password are *cisco* and *cisco*, which you must change when logging in the first time. After the basic configuration, you can either access the CSC-SSM card via ASDM, or by directly using a web browser by entering the following in the address text bar of a web browser: **https://***management_IP_address***:8443**.

NOTE   Instead of using the CLI for the initial configuration of the CSC card, you can also use ASDM. For detailed instructions on setting up the CSC-SSM card, read the *Trend Micro InterScan for Cisco CSC SSM Administrator Guide* on the Cisco web site (http://www.cisco.com/en/US/docs/security/csc/csc60/administration/guide/csc6.html).

SSM CARD MANAGEMENT

You might have issues with the operation of the SSM cards, like the corruption of flash. This section will cover how to discover these issues and how to re-image the AIP-SSM and CSC-SSM cards.

Verifying an SSM Card Operational Status

You can display the status of a module with the **show module** command:

```
ciscoasa# show module [module_#] detail
```

If you don't qualify the module number, then module 0 and module 1 are displayed, where module 0 is the ASA itself.

Here's an example of this command where an AIP-SSM card is installed:

```
ciscoasa# show module 1
Mod Card Type                                      Model           Serial No.
--- -------------------------------------- --------------- ----------
  1 ASA 5500 SSM Module-10   ASA-SSM-10       12345678
Mod MAC Address Range                   Hw Ver  Fw Ver  Sw Ver
--- -------------------------------- ------- -------- ------------
  1 000b.fcf8.0170 to 000b.fcf8.0170  1.0     1.0(7)2  6.0(0.22)S129.0
Mod Status
--- -----------------
  1 Up
```

Notice that the version of IPS software is 6.0(0.22)S129.0 and the module is operational (Up).

Here's an example of a CSC-SSM card:

```
ciscoasa# show module 1 detail
Getting details from the Service Module, please wait...
SSM-IDS/10-K9
Model:             SSM-IDS10
```

```
Hardware version:       1.0
Serial Number:          0
Firmware version:       1.0(8)1
Software version:       CSC SSM 6.0 (Build#1345)
MAC Address Range:      000b.fcf8.0159 to 000b.fcf8.0159
App. name:              CSC SSM
App. Status:            Down
App. Status Desc:       CSC SSM scan services are not available
App. version:           6.0 (Build#1345)
Data plane Status:      Up
Status:                 Up
HTTP Service:           Down
Mail Service:           Down
FTP  Service:           Down
Activated:              No
Mgmt IP addr:           <not available>
Mgmt web port:          8443
Peer IP addr:           <not enabled>
```

Notice that in the preceding example the services are down, the license hasn't been activated, no management address is defined, and no remote management addresses are defined. Assuming you have gone through the CSC-SSM CLI initialization script, you should see the following instead:

```
ciscoasa# show module 1 detail
Getting details from the Service Module, please wait...
SSM-IDS/20-K9
Model: SSM-IDS20
Hardware version:       1.0
Serial Number:          0
Firmware version:       1.0(8)1
Software version:       CSC SSM 6.0 (Build#1177)
MAC Address Range:      000b.fcf8.0134 to 000b.fcf8.0134
App. name:              CSC SSM proxy services are not available
App. version:
App. name:              CSC SSM
App. version:           6.0 (Build#1177)
Data plane Status:      Up
Status:                 Up
HTTP Service:           Up
Mail Service:           Up
FTP  Service:           Up
Activated:              Yes
Mgmt IP addr:           192.168.1.20
Mgmt web port:          8443
Peer IP addr:           <not enabled>
```

Hardware Module Commands

When you have problems with the AIP-SSM and CSC-SSM cards, you can sometimes troubleshoot them from the CLI of the ASA. The **hw-module** command is used in these instances:

```
ciscoasa# hw-module module slot_# password-reset
ciscoasa# hw-module module slot_# reload
ciscoasa# hw-module module slot_# reset
ciscoasa# hw-module module slot_# shutdown
```

The **hw-module module** command is used to reset the password of the SSM card, as well as to perform a soft reboot, a hard reboot, or to turn it off.

Here's an example of resetting the password on the SSM card:

```
ciscoasa(config)# hw-module module 1 password-reset
Reset the password on module in slot 1? [confirm] y
```

Here's an example of performing a soft reset of the SSM card, which is equivalent to logging into the card and performing a reboot:

```
ciscoasa# hw-module module 1 reload
Reload module in slot 1? [confirm] y
Reload issued for module in slot 1
%XXX-5-505002: Module in slot 1 is reloading. Please wait...
%XXX-5-505006: Module in slot 1 is Up.
```

If there is an issue and the operating system is not responding, you can perform a hard reset, which would be similar to turning the card off and back on. Here's an example of performing a hard reset:

```
ciscoasa# hw-module module 1 reset
The module in slot 1 should be shut down before
resetting it or loss of configuration may occur.
Reset module in slot 1? [confirm] y
Reset issued for module in slot 1
%XXX-5-505001: Module in slot 1 is shutting down. Please wait...
%XXX-5-505004: Module in slot 1 shutdown is complete.
%XXX-5-505003: Module in slot 1 is resetting. Please wait...
%XXX-5-505006: Module in slot 1 is Up.
```

If you want to gracefully shut the card down, use the following command:

```
ciscoasa# hw-module module 1 shutdown
Shutdown module in slot 1? [confirm] y
Shutdown issued for module in slot 1
%XXX-5-505001: Module in slot 1 is shutting down. Please wait...
%XXX-5-505004: Module in slot 1 shutdown is complete.
```

Re-Imaging an SSM Card

If the SSM card operating system in flash becomes corrupt, you'll have to perform an image recovery. If you examine the status of the SSM card with the **show module** command, you can determine a corrupted OS problem. Here's an example where the AIP-SSM card OS image in flash is corrupted:

```
ciscoasa# show module 1 detail
Getting details from the Service Module, please wait...
Unable to read details from slot 1
ASA 5500 Series Security Services Module-10
Model:              ASA-SSM-10
Hardware version:   1.0
Serial Number:      12345678
Firmware version:   1.0(7)4
Software version:
Status:             Init
```

In the preceding example, notice that the information of the card can't be read, thus the **show module** command doesn't display the software version of the OS running on the SSM card, and that the card is in an init state. This might be the case if the card is in the process of booting up, but if it remains in this state, more than likely the OS is corrupted on the flash drive of the SSM card, and the card will have to be re-imaged from the CLI of the ASA.

You'll need to pull a new image, via the ASA CLI, from a TFTP server. The **hw-module module recover configure** command is used to define the TFTP server, the file, and the IP address on the *card's* interface. Here's an example:

```
ciscoasa(config)# hw-module module 1 recover configure
Image URL [tftp://0.0.0.0/]: tftp://10.0.1.11/AIP-SSM-K9-sys-1.1-a-
5.0-0.24.img
Port IP Address [0.0.0.0]: 10.0.1.12
VLAN ID [0]:
Gateway IP Address [0.0.0.0]:
```

You can view what you configured with the **show module 1 recover** command. The preceding command doesn't actually perform the recovery process: it defines the parameters to use during the recovery.

Once you have defined the configuration parameters for the SSM card recovery process, use the **hw-module module recover boot** command to perform the actual recovery:

```
ciscoasa(config)# hw-module 1 recover boot
The module in slot 1 will be recovered.  This may
erase all configuration and all data on that device and
attempt to download a new image for it.
```

```
Recover module in slot 1? [confirm]
Recover issued for module in slot 1
%The module in slot 1 is unresponsive.
%The module in slot 1 is recovering.
<--output omitted-->
```

When the recovery process is done, use the **show module** command to make sure the module state is Up.

NOTE   Use the **debug module** command to troubleshoot the SSM image update process. Also, any configuration information on the card is lost when re-imaging it from the ASA; therefore, make sure you periodically backup the card's configuration file.

PART VI

Management of the ASA

CHAPTER 26

Basic Management from the CLI

This chapter will cover many of the management features of the security appliances. In Chapter 3, I introduced how to access the CLI of the appliances, including remote access via telnet and SSH, and placing a basic configuration on the appliances. This chapter will expand on that content, specifically focusing on the management features and additional management tasks you would commonly need to perform on the appliances. The topics include

▼ Using DHCP services, including DHCP server and relay features

■ Implementing remote management features, including NTP, logging, and SNMP

■ Managing files in flash, including configuration files, operating system files, and ASDM images, as well as upgrading the appliance license key

■ Performing a password recovery

▲ Implementing AAA (authentication, authorization, and accounting) to lock down management access to the appliance

DHCP SERVICES

The appliances support many DHCP services, including being a DHCP server and/or client as well as relaying DHCP client requests for addressing information on one interface to a second interface that has a DHCP server connected to it. This is similar to the IOS IP Helper feature. In Chapter 3, I discussed how to configure an appliance interface to acquire addressing information dynamically from a DHCP server. This is most commonly done on a low-end appliance, like the ASA 5505, when connecting it directly to the ISP. This part of the chapter will focus on the other two DHCP features: using the appliance as a DHCP server and implementing the DHCP relay function.

DHCP Server

The appliances have supported DHCP server functions since version 6 of the operating system. I must stress that many other DHCP server products in the market offer many more features than the appliances do; however, for a SOHO environment, the appliances can easily solve address management issues.

DHCP Server Configuration

The following commands are used to configure the appliance as a DHCP server:

```
ciscoasa(config)# dhcpd address IP_address-IP_address logical_if_name
ciscoasa(config)# dhcpd domain domain_name
ciscoasa(config)# dhcpd dns dns_IP_1 [dns_IP_2]
ciscoasa(config)# dhcpd wins wins_IP_1 [wins_IP_2]
ciscoasa(config)# dhcpd lease lease_length
```

```
ciscoasa(config)# dhcpd ping_timeout milliseconds
ciscoasa(config)# dhcpd option option_number ip IP_address
ciscoasa(config)# dhcpd auto_config logical_if_name
                       [[vpnclient-wins-override]
                       interface logical_if_name]
ciscoasa(config)# dhcpd enable logical_if_name
```

Notice that all the commands begin with **dhcpd**. The **address** parameter specifies an address pool that should be used for clients connected to the specified logical interface. The **domain** parameter assigns the domain name to the clients. The **dns** parameter allows you to specify up to two DNS server addresses that should be assigned to the requesting clients, and the **wins** parameter allows you to specify up to two WINS server addresses. The default lease length of an assigned address is 3,600 seconds if not configured: you can override this with the **lease** parameter. Two pings are sent to an address to verify that it is not being used before it is assigned to a requesting client; the timeout for the echo replies can be changed with the **ping_timeout** parameter (the default is 50 milliseconds).

The **option** parameter assigns different types of IP addressing information to the requesting client. For example, the option **3** parameter assigns a default gateway address, whereas options **66** and **150** are used to assign a TFTP server address for IP phones and similar devices. The **auto_config** parameter allows the appliance to acquire some of its addressing information from an interface where the appliance is a DHCP client and then to use this information for another interface where it is a DHCP server, like the learned domain name and DNS server addresses. Optionally you can override this behavior and have the client use the addressing information assigned to it when the appliance is acting as a VPN remote/client (from the Easy VPN server), versus using the DHCP client information on the logical interface (the physical interface the appliance is connected toward the ISP where the appliance is a DHCP client). Last, the **enable** parameter enables the DHCP server for the specified interface.

DHCP Server Verification

The **show dhcpd** command displays the address bindings and statistics for the DHCP server:

```
ciscoasa# show dhcpd {binding [IP_address] | state | statistics}
```

Here's an example of the use of this command, which displays the IP addresses assigned to requesting users:

```
ciscoasa# show dhcpd binding
IP Address Hardware Address Lease Expiration Type
10.0.1.101 0100.a0d4.e834 84985 seconds automatic
```

In this example, only one address has been assigned to a client.

> **NOTE** If you are using dynamic DNS in your network, you can have the appliance update the DNS A records on the DNS server with the name and address of the requesting client. Configuring dynamic DNS is beyond the scope of this book.

DHCP Server Configuration Example

Here's a simple DHCP server configuration where the appliance is assigning itself as the default gateway (10.0.1.1) for the inside interface:

```
ciscoasa(config)# dhcpd address 10.0.1.200-10.0.1.254 inside
ciscoasa(config)# dhcpd domain dealgroup.com
ciscoasa(config)# dhcpd dns 4.2.2.2
ciscoasa(config)# dhcpd ping_timeout 500
ciscoasa(config)# dhcpd option 3 ip 10.0.1.1
ciscoasa(config)# dhcpd enable inside
```

DHCP Relay

DHCP relay allows a directly connected client to request addressing information via a broadcast and to have the appliance redirect this to a particular DHCP server or servers. This feature is necessary when the appliance isn't a DHCP server itself and the DHCP server is connected to a different appliance interface than the clients themselves.

> **NOTE** If the appliance is in multiple mode and an interface is shared between contexts, DHCP relay is unsupported. Also, DHCP relay is unnecessary if the appliance is in transparent mode since the appliance will forward broadcasts between interfaces by default.

DHCP Relay Configuration

To configure the DHCP relay functionality, use the following commands:

```
ciscoasa(config)# dhcprelay server IP_address logical_if_name
ciscoasa(config)# dhcprelay timeout seconds
ciscoasa(config)# dhcprelay setroute logical_if_name
ciscoasa(config)# dhcprelay enable logical_if_name
```

You need to specify the server or servers to redirect requests to with the **dhcprelay server** command—if you have more than one DHCP server, you can execute the command multiple times. The **timeout** parameter is used when more than one server is configured; if the first server doesn't respond within the configured time, the request is forwarded to the second server. The **setroute** parameter is used to override the default gateway address assigned by the DHCP server and to use an IP address on the appliance itself. The **enable** parameter enables the DHCP relay functionality. You can use the

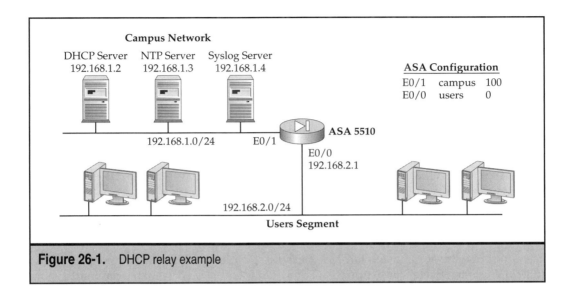

Figure 26-1.   DHCP relay example

show dhcprelay state and **show dhcprelay statistics** commands to verify the configuration and operation of the DHCP relay, respectively, on the appliance.

DHCP Relay Configuration Example

To illustrate how to configure the DHCP relay feature, I'll use the network shown in Figure 26-1. Here's the DHCP relay configuration of the appliance:

```
ciscoasa(config)# dhcprelay server 192.168.1.2 campus
ciscoasa(config)# dhcprelay setroute 192.168.2.1
ciscoasa(config)# dhcprelay enable users
```

REMOTE MANAGEMENT FEATURES

The next few sections will discuss some remote management features of the appliances: how to configure the date and time, which is important when logging information; certificate authentication, and etcetera; how to configure logging; and how to configure SNMP support.

Date and Time

You can use two methods to change the date and time on your appliance: manually with the **clock** command or dynamically by using the Network Time Protocol (NTP). The following two sections will discuss both options.

Manual Date and Time

To manually set the date and time on an appliance, use the **clock** command:

```
ciscoasa(config)# clock set hh:mm:ss [day MONTH year]
ciscoasa(config)# clock timezone zone_name hours [minutes]
ciscoasa(config)# clock summer-time zone_name recurring
                        [week weekday month hh:mm
                         week weekday month hh:mm] [offset]
```

The **clock set** command changes the date and time. The format of this command is basically the same as that used on Cisco IOS devices. The time is in a 24-hour time format: 3:00 PM would be configured as 15:00. The month is configured as a name, which can be abbreviated. If you omit the date, it defaults to today's date. Here's an example:

```
ciscoasa(config)# clock set 15:00:00 23 may 2003
```

The time zone the appliance is located in can be specified with the **timezone** parameter, followed by the offset (+ or –) from UTC time. Optionally you can enable daylight saving time with the **summer-time** parameter.

Use the **show clock** command to see the current date and time on the appliance.

TIP I recommend that all devices be configured in the same time zone, preferably UTC. By doing this, when you examine logs of devices in physically different time zones, it is easier to see a correlation of events on different devices if they are using the same time zone for their date and time. Otherwise you have to convert the times in your head to figure out if two events in different time zones are occurring at the same time, and thus might be related to each other.

Network Time Protocol

To dynamically acquire the date and time from an external NTP server, you'll need to configure your appliance to use the NTP protocol. This is accomplished using the following commands:

```
ciscoasa(config)# ntp server NTP_server_IP_address [key key_number]
                        source logical_if_name [prefer]
ciscoasa(config)# ntp trusted-key key_number
ciscoasa(config)# ntp authentication-key key_number md5 key_value
ciscoasa(config)# ntp authenticate
```

To define the NTP server, use the **ntp server** command. The **source** parameter specifies which interface to use to access the server. The **prefer** parameter is used to prefer this NTP server over other configured servers on the appliance. The optional **key** parameter specifies the authentication information to use with the NTP server (must be an NTPv3 server). The key number is required if you'll be authenticating NTP server messages using MD5, but authenticating the messages is optional unless the server requires it. The key number must match what the server is using.

To enable authentication, use the `ntp trusted-key` command to specify the number of the key that is considered "trusted" or used for a particular server. Use the `ntp authentication-key` command to specify the authentication key used to create the digital signature for the packet (MD5 is used for this process). Note that the key number must match up between the `ntp server`, `ntp trusted-key`, and `ntp authenticate-key` commands. Last, use the `ntp authenticate` command to enable authentication.

NOTE You should use different keys with different NTP servers.

Here are the **show** commands for NTP:

▼ `show ntp associations`   Displays information about the configured time servers

■ `show ntp associations detail`   Provides detailed information for the associations

▲ `show ntp status`   Displays information about the NTP clock for the associations

Going back to Figure 26-1, here's an example of setting up NTP to the campus NTP server, using authentication:

```
ciscoasa(config)# ntp server 192.168.1.3 key 1 source campus
ciscoasa(config)# ntp trusted-key 1
ciscoasa(config)# ntp authentication-key 1 md5 mySecretKey
ciscoasa(config)# ntp authenticate
```

TIP Never use a time source from the Internet to acquire your timing information, since no server that I know of will authenticate messages on the Internet, and there is a chance you might receive a spoofed message. This can create a denial of service attack when you're using certificates and/or corrupt your logging information. Always set up your own internal time source and enable NTPv3 authentication of time messages. Normally I attach a GPS to a Microsoft server and use it as my NTP time source; but many operating systems, like UNIX, can also be used.

Logging

The appliance generates log messages to document such events as denied TCP connections, translation slot depletion in the xlate table, console logins, and bytes transferred for each connection in the conn table. The appliances can log to the following destinations: the console, an internal buffer, an SNMP management station via SNMP traps, e-mail messages, and an external syslog server. The default is to log information to the console; however, Cisco highly recommends in a production network that you either log to the internal buffer of the appliance or to an external syslog server.

Log Message Contents

Here's an example of a log message:

```
November 1 2006 11:00:01 asa1: %ASA-6-302014: Teardown TCP connection
      395 for outside:192.1.1.1/50010 to 187.5.3.2/80
      duration 00:00:21 bytes 484 TCP Reset 0
```

At the beginning of the log message is the date and time, which are optional. Following this is the identifier of the device (asa1), which is also optional. The ASA-6 indicates the type of device generating the message and the logging level. The logging levels implemented on the appliances are the same ones used on Cisco IOS devices, which are summarized in Table 26-1. The lower the level number, the more severe the message. After the level number is the message number, indicating which message this is (302014): each message has its own number. Following the message number is a brief description of the log message. In the preceding example, a connection is being removed from the conn table.

NOTE To see a list of log messages for the ASA, visit Cisco's site at http://www.cisco.com/en/US/docs/security/asa/asa80/system/message/syslog.html.

Level Number	Level Name	Description
0	Emergencies	Indicates that the appliance is unusable.
1	Alerts	You need to take immediate action to fix the problem or issue.
2	Critical	A critical condition exists on the appliance.
3	Errors	The appliance experienced an error.
4	Warnings	There is a configuration or processing problem on the appliance.
5	Notifications	A normal, but important, event occurred on the appliance, like someone configuring the appliance.
6	Informational	Something has occurred on the appliance, like a match on a deny ACL entry.
7	Debugging	Displays the output of **debug** commands.

Table 26-1. Logging Levels

Logging Configuration

Configuring and controlling logging is done with the following commands:

```
ciscoasa(config)# logging enable
ciscoasa(config)# logging buffered severity_level
ciscoasa(config)# logging console severity_level
ciscoasa(config)# logging monitor severity_level
ciscoasa(config)# [no] logging message message_ID
ciscoasa(config)# logging host [(logical_if_name)]
                     syslog_IP_address [tcp|udp[/port_#]]
ciscoasa(config)# logging facility facility_number
ciscoasa(config)# logging standby
ciscoasa(config)# logging device-id {hostname | ipaddress IP_address |
                     string text}
ciscoasa(config)# logging timestamp
ciscoasa(config)# logging trap severity_level
```

By default system logging is not enabled for any logging destination. To enable it, configure the **logging enable** command. The **logging buffered** command specifies the logging level (name or number) to be sent to the internal buffer (RAM) of the appliance; by default this is disabled. You can fit 512 messages in the buffer before it fills up and new messages overwrite the oldest ones. The **logging console** command specifies the logging level for messages to be sent to the console of the appliance. The **logging monitor** command specifies the logging level for telnet and SSH sessions. Logging messages are not displayed on non-console lines by default; for the aux line on the ASAs and all telnet and SSH sessions, you need to first execute the **terminal monitor** command.

The **logging message** command specifies which messages can be logged by the appliance. By default the appliance will log all messages. You can precede this command with the **no** parameter, along with a specific message number, to disable the specified log message. The log message numbers can be viewed in the actual log message as well as in the "Syslog Message" section in the documentation for the appliance. There is only one message that you cannot disable: `%appliance-6-199002: appliance startup completed. Beginning operation.`

TIP To disable logging for a particular location, preface it with the **no** parameter; for example, to disable logging to the appliance internal buffer, use `no logging buffered`.

The **logging host** command specifies the IP address of the syslog server to send messages to; by default syslogging is disabled. You can optionally specify the interface where the syslog server is located (it defaults to **inside** if omitted). You can also specify the IP transport layer protocol, which defaults to **udp**, and the port number if you are using a different one than the standard one. Cisco offers the free Firewall Syslog server product, which supports TCP as a transport method. The **logging facility** command specifies the location of the file where syslog messages will be directed to on the syslog server.

Eight facility levels are supported: local0–local7. The default is local4, if omitted. The `logging standby` command allows a standby appliance configured for failover to log messages to a syslog server; by default, only the active failover unit will send messages to a syslog server. The `logging device-id` command specifies a unique device ID included in a log message sent to a syslog server. This can be the hostname of the appliance, an IP address of the appliance (only one IP address is used, based on what you configure), or a text string you configure. The `logging timestamp` command adds a timestamp to logging messages. The syslog server will do this automatically, but if they are using different time zones, you might want to see two timestamps in the message: the appliance one and the syslog server one. The `logging trap` command specifies the logging level for messages forwarded to a syslog server or SNMP management station (the configuration of SNMP is discussed in the "SNMP" section later in the chapter).

Logging Verification

The `show logging` command displays the configuration of logging on your appliance:

```
asa1(config)# show logging
Syslog logging: enabled
    Facility: 20
    Timestamp logging: enabled
    Standby logging: disabled
        Deny Conn when Queue Full: disabled
    Console logging: disabled
    Monitor logging: disabled
    Buffer logging: disabled
    Trap logging: level warnings, facility 20, 0 messages logged
        Logging to inside 10.0.1.11 errors: 11 dropped: 21
    History logging: disabled
    Device ID: hostname "asa1"
    Mail logging: disabled
    ASDM logging: disabled
```

If you have enabled logging to the appliance's internal buffer, these messages will display at the end of the `show logging` output. To clear the log messages from the appliance internal buffer, use the `clear logging` command.

Logging Configuration Example

Here's a simple example that will log messages from level 1 to 5 to the syslog server shown previously in Figure 26-1:

```
ciscoasa(config)# logging enable
ciscoasa(config)# logging host (campus) 192.168.1.4
ciscoasa(config)# logging device-id hostname
ciscoasa(config)# logging timestamp
ciscoasa(config)# logging trap 5
```

SNMP

The appliances have limited support for SNMP. Currently only versions 1 and 2 of SNMP are supported. Because these versions of SNMP have security issues, the management information bases (MIBs) supported by Cisco only allow read access, where access is not allowed to configure information on the appliance—only to statistical information. For example, some of the statistics you can pull from an appliance include the failover status, memory and CPU usage, changes in an interface status, the number of entries in the xlate and conn tables, and other similar types of information. Normally SNMP on the appliance is used as an alternative or a complement to using syslog, where SNMP traps are used to send log information to an SNMP management station.

Configuring SNMP support involves the following commands:

```
ciscoasa(config)# snmp-server enable
ciscoasa(config)# snmp-server host logical_if_name IP_address
                     [trap | poll] [community text] [version 1 | 2c]
                     [udp-port port]
ciscoasa(config)# snmp-server community key
ciscoasa(config)# snmp-server {contact | location} text
ciscoasa(config)# snmp-server enable traps [all | syslog |
                     snmp [trap] [...] | entity [trap] [...] |
                     ipsec [trap] [...] | remote-access [trap]]
```

To enable the SNMP service on the appliance, execute the **snmp-server enable** command. The **snmp-server host** command specifies the SNMP network management station (NMS) that is allowed to access the appliance—you can restrict the access to sending traps (**trap**) to the NMS or to getting information from the appliance (**poll**). The community string must match that configured on the NMS; if you omit this, the community string specified in the **snmp-server community** command is used. If you omit the SNMP version, it defaults to 1; and if you omit the UDP port, it defaults to 162, which is used by SNMP traps. The **snmp-server contact** and **location** commands specify information about the person responsible for the appliance and where the appliance is located—these commands are optional.

To enable the appliance to forward traps to the SNMP NMS, use the **snmp-server enable traps** command. If you don't qualify the command, all traps are forwarded (the **all** parameter). Optionally you can qualify which traps are forwarded to the NMS. Table 26-2 lists the different types of traps you can specify for the related command parameter. If you specify **syslog** in the command, use the **logging history** severity_level command to control what log messages are forwarded to the NMS, along with the **logging enable** command.

Parameter	Traps
snmp	authentication, linkup, linkdown, coldstart
entity	config-change, fru-insert, fru-remove
ipsec	start, stop
remote-access	session-threshold-exceeded

Table 26-2. SNMP Traps

FILE MANAGEMENT

This section of the chapter will focus on upgrading the images on the appliance (both the operating system and ASDM), updating the license key to add additional features, and controlling the bootup process of the appliance.

Files and Flash

Before I begin discussing the file management features of the appliance, I first need to introduce some basic concepts concerning files and the flash system used by the appliances. In version 6.0 and earlier, the following file types were stored in flash: operating system, configuration file, private data file (keying information), PIX Device Manager (PDM, which is the precursor to ASDM), and, possibly, a crash file. Only one file of each type was supported; so, for example, if you upgraded the operating system on the PIX, the PIX would overwrite the old image with the new one.

NOTE Unlike most IOS devices, the security appliances lack NVRAM. On IOS devices, NVRAM is used to store the configuration file. Security appliances store their configuration file in flash.

Starting in version 7.0, you can have multiple operating systems, ASDM images, and configuration files in flash; the latter is a requirement when you use contexts, since each context has its own configuration file (see Chapter 22). To view the contents of flash, use the **dir** or **show flash** or **show disk** commands:

```
ciscoasa# dir [/all] [/all-filesystems] [/recursive]
              [{disk0: | disk1: | flash:}] [path]
```

Note that **disk0** and **flash** both refer to the flash on the appliance motherboard. The **disk1** parameter refers the flash in the compact flash slot of an ASA.

NOTE During the upgrade from version 6 to 7, the flash file system was redone—basically the flash file system must be reformatted. During this process, the old operating system and configuration file are saved in the new file system format.

Here's an example of viewing the files in flash:

```
ciscoasa# dir
Directory of flash:/
11     -rw-  5919340     16:11:12 Apr 29 2005  asdm-611.bin
12     -rw-  5124096     16:49:07 Apr 29 2005  asa803-k8.bin
```

To delete a file in flash, use the **delete** command—you'll be prompted to erase it, ensuring that you don't inadvertently delete an important file like the operating system itself.

NOTE You can create subdirectories in flash (**mkdir**), move around to different directories in flash (**cd**), delete directories in flash (**rmdir**), and view text files in flash (**more**).

OS Upgrades

To see the operating system and ASDM image versions the appliance is using, as well as the unlocked license features on the appliance, use the **show version** command:

```
ciscoasa(config)# show version
Cisco Adaptive Security Appliance Software Version 7.2(2)
Device Manager Version 5.2(2)
Compiled on Wed 22-Nov-06 14:16 by builders
System image file is disk0:/asa722-k8.bin
Config file at boot was "startup-config"
<--output omitted-->
This platform has an ASA 5510 Security Plus license.
Serial Number: JMX0946K0FT
Running Activation Key: 0x832a225b 0x1896ad94 0xdcc211dc
    0xb85000e0 0x821ac9aa
Configuration register is 0x1
<--output omitted-->
```

In the preceding example, the OS version is 7.2(2) and the ASDM version is 5.2(2). The operating system was loaded from the "asa722-k8.bin" file in flash. The serial number is used by Cisco to unlock paid features with a license key (the running activation key). At the bottom of the display is the configuration register value, which controls the bootup process of the appliance: setting it to 0x1 causes the appliance to boot up in the default manner. (This would be equivalent to a register value of 0x2102 on a Cisco IOS device.)

The following two sections will discuss how to upgrade the software on the appliance; subsequent sections will discuss how to control the bootup process as well as entering a new license key for purchased features.

CLI Upgrade

You can use three basic methods to upgrade the appliances: use the CLI from Privilege EXEC mode, use the CLI from monitor mode, or use the auto update feature. Normally the monitor mode (ROMMON mode on an ASA) method is not used unless the OS in flash is corrupted and the appliance won't boot up.

Upgrading the appliance from the OS CLI is the same as on an IOS device and is done with the **copy** command:

```
ciscoasa# copy URL {flash | disk0 | disk1}:[/filename]
```

You can use TFTP, FTP, or SCP to copy the OS or ASDM image from the specified server to flash on a PIX or ASA, or use the PCMCIA flashcard slot for the ASAs only. For FTP or SCP, if you don't specify the username and password in the URL, you'll be prompted for it.

Here's an example where I'm pulling in an image from an FTP server:

```
ciscoasa# copy ftp://10.0.1.11/asa803-k8.bin disk0:/asa803-k8.bin
```

Auto Update

Auto update is a proprietary Cisco feature that allows appliances, as well as other types of Cisco devices, to periodically poll an Auto Update Server (AUS) to see if there are newer OS or ASDM images and updated configuration files. AUS is a component of Cisco Works and Cisco Security Manager (CSM). If there is updated information, the appliance can download and apply the updates. AUS was added to the appliances in version 6.

NOTE One limitation of auto update is that it won't work if you are running the appliance in multiple mode.

To interact with an AUS, use the following commands:

```
ciscoasa(config)# auto-update server URL [source logical_if_name]
                      [verify-certificate]
ciscoasa(config)# auto-update device-id {hardware-serial | hostname |
                      ipaddress [logical_if_name] | mac-address
                      [logical_if_name] | string text}
ciscoasa(config)# auto-update poll-period poll_period_minutes
                      [retry-count [retry_period_minutes]]
ciscoasa(config)# auto-update poll-at day_of_the_week time
                      [randomize minutes] [retry_count
                      [retry_period]]
ciscoasa(config)# auto-update timeout period_minutes
```

In the **auto-update server** command, when entering the URL for the AUS server, use this syntax: **http[s]://**[*user:password***@**]*server_ip*[*:port*]*/pathname*. You'll need to specify an account name and password used on the AUS. The device ID in the **auto-update device-id** command is used by the AUS to look up the update policy for the appliance that is contacting the AUS. Normally I use the hostname parameter, but some companies I have dealt with also use an IP address associated with the appliance. How often the appliance should poll the AUS is controlled by the **auto-update poll-period** command. The update polling period defaults to 720 minutes (12 hours), with a retry count of 0 and a retry period of 5 minutes if left unconfigured. The **auto-update poll-at** command controls when the polling period should start, where the **randomize** parameter specifies that when the period is reached, wait another *X* minutes, which is between 0 and the specified randomized minutes, before performing the next poll. This parameter is used to ensure that hundreds of devices don't perform the poll function at the same time. The **auto-update timeout** command specifies that if the AUS is not contacted within the specified period, the appliance should stop passing traffic—the default is 0, which means to never time out.

Here is an example configuration of defining an AUS:

```
ciscoasa(config)# auto-update server https://richard:deal@10.0.1.10:1742/
management/asa source inside
ciscoasa(config)# auto-update device-id hostname
ciscoasa(config)# auto-update poll-at Friday Saturday Sunday 22:00
                        randomize 60 2 10
```

To verify your configuration and operation of AUS, use the **show auto-update** command. Here's an example:

```
ciscoasa# show auto-update
Server: https://********@192.168.10.1:1742/management.cgi?1276
Certificate will be verified
Poll period: 720 minutes, retry count: 2, retry period: 5 minutes
Timeout: none
Device ID: host name [ciscoasa]
Next poll in 5.33 minutes
Last poll: 12:46:43 EST Tue Nov 1 2008
Last ASDM update: 12:48:03 EST Tue Nov 1 2008
```

Controlling the Bootup Process

By default the first image in flash for the OS and ASDM is used. Use the **boot system** command to specify a different operating system to boot from:

```
ciscoasa(config)# boot system {flash | disk0 | disk1}:/OS_image_name
```

After specifying a different OS, to use the newly specified OS, you must reboot the appliance with the **reload** command.

To control what ASDM image in flash the appliance will use, configure the **asdm image** command:

```
ciscoasa(config)# asdm image {flash | disk0 | disk1}:/ASDM_image_name
```

Unlike with an OS update, you don't have to reboot the appliance to use the newly specified ASDM image.

By default when the appliance boots up, the appliance obtains its configuration file from the startup-config file in flash. You can override this with the **boot config** command:

```
ciscoasa(config)# boot config {flash | disk0 | disk1}:/config_file
```

License Keys

License keys, commonly called activation keys, are used to control the features that you can use on your appliance. The appliance type—PIX versus ASA—and the model of the appliance will affect what a license key controls. For example, on a PIX 515E, the license key controls the number of interfaces and VLANs you can use, the amount of RAM you can use, how many contexts, if any, you can create, and whether failover is supported.

Obtaining a License Key

License keys are tied to the serial number of your appliance. The serial number is located on the motherboard and can be obtained by using the **show version** command discussed earlier in the "OS Upgrades" section. When purchasing a licensed feature on the appliance, like WebVPN sessions for an ASA, you will receive a product authorization code from your Cisco authorized reseller. You'll then need to log into the Cisco site using your CCO account and enter your appliance serial number, along with the product authorization code, to obtain a new license key. Since your serial number was used to create the key, the key can only be used on the associated appliance.

Entering a License Key

Prior to version 6.2 on the PIXs, license keys had to be entered by doing a re-imaging of the PIX operating system from monitor mode. During the re-imaging process, you were prompted for your license key. Many administrators complained of this approach since they only wanted to enter a new key, not upgrade the OS on the PIX.

Starting in version 6.2, the **activation-key** command can be used to update the license key from global Configuration mode; however, you have to reboot the appliance to have the new key value take effect. Here's the command to enter a new license key:

```
ciscoasa(config)# activation-key {activation_key_four_tuple |
                  activation_key_five_tuple}
```

If you are updating the license key on a PIX, you'll enter four sets of hexadecimal numbers; if it's an ASA, then you'll enter five sets of hexadecimal numbers. You can easily copy and paste the key from the Cisco web site or e-mail message into the appliance.

You'll see one of three messages after entering the key:

▼ `The activation key you entered is the same as the running key` You entered the same key the appliance is already using.

■ `The flash image and the running image differ` You entered a correct key—you will need to reboot the appliance to use the new key.

▲ `The activation key is not valid` You entered an incorrect key value.

The `show activation-key` command will also display the preceding output. Once you enter a new license key, remember that you must reboot the appliance for the license key change to take effect.

PASSWORD RECOVERY

If you have forgotten the password to access the appliance, as with IOS devices, you can break into it if you have console access. The following sections will discuss how to disable the password recovery process in insecure environments as well as how to perform the password recovery process on a PIX and ASA (the two use different methods).

Restricting the Password Recovery Process

The password recovery process is enabled by default, which is performed from monitor (PIX) or ROMMON (ASA) mode. You can disable the password recovery process with the following command:

```
ciscoasa(config)# no service password-recovery
WARNING: Executing "no service password-recovery" has disabled the
password recovery mechanism and disabled access to ROMMON. The only
means of recovering from lost or forgotten passwords will be for
ROMMON to erase all file systems including configuration files and
images. You should make a backup of your configuration and have a
mechanism to restore images from the ROMMON command line.
```

Disabling the password recovery process might be required by your security policy. The most common situation where I've seen this feature implemented is in a shared SOHO location, where there's a chance that someone might steal the appliance. In this situation, you can protect your appliance configuration by disabling the password recovery process.

Once you've disabled the password recovery process, in order to break into the appliance, all files in flash are erased: configuration, operating system, ASDM, crash dumps, and private files! The break-in must occur from monitor/ROMMON mode, and you'll have to TFTP an OS into flash, boot up the appliance, and reconfigure it from scratch (or pull in a saved configuration from a server).

NOTE You can re-enable the password recovery by re-executing the `service password-recovery` command without the `no` parameter.

Performing the PIX Password Recovery Process

You can use two different procedures for the password recovery process on a PIX, depending on the PIX model that you have:

▼ The 520 and older models have a floppy drive.

▲ Newer models do not have a floppy drive (like the 501 or 515).

This chapter only covers the non-floppy method, since Cisco hasn't sold a PIX with a floppy drive in many years. Note that the password recovery procedure requires console access to your PIX and erases only the passwords on the PIX, not the actual startup configuration in flash—this is different from how IOS routers perform the password recovery process, which boots up without a configuration file. The following pages will cover the non-floppy drive method. As you will see, the process is different from that used with a Cisco IOS device.

Downloading the Password Recovery File

First, you need to acquire a file from the Cisco site in order to perform the password recovery procedure for a PIX. A file called "np*xy*.bin" contains a software image that will erase the passwords configured on your PIX. The *xy* stands for the software image that is running on your PIX. If you are running version 7.0 or higher, download the "np70.bin" file. You can find this file on the Cisco web site by doing a search for "PIX password recovery"; you don't need a CCO account to download it. You will then need to take this file and place it on a TFTP server.

Configuring Monitor Mode

Next obtain console access to your PIX. Reboot your PIX and break into monitor mode—this is similar to ROMMON mode on a Cisco router. Either use the BREAK or the ESC keystroke sequence to do this. You have 10 seconds to do this when prompted.

Once you are in monitor mode, you'll need to configure your PIX to download the password recovery file. At this point the PIX hasn't loaded the operating system and is *not* running the configuration file in flash; therefore, it is *not* passing traffic between interfaces. Here are the basic commands you can execute in monitor mode to perform the password recovery process:

```
monitor> interface [number]
monitor> address PIX's_IP_address
monitor> gateway router's_IP_address
monitor> server [IP_address_of_TFTP_server]
```

```
monitor> file BIN_file_name
monitor> ping IP_address
monitor> tftp
```

The **interface** command sets the interface where the TFTP server is. Enter the number, not the name of the interface: for ethernet1, this would be 1. This defaults to the outside interface if omitted, which is 0. The **address** command sets the IP address of the PIX selected interface. Note that you don't configure a subnet mask value. The **gateway** command specifies the default gateway address—this is only needed if the TFTP server is not on the same segment as the PIX selected interface. The **server** command defines the IP address of the TFTP server—if you omit this, it defaults to 255.255.255.255. The **file** command defines the name of the BIN file on the TFTP server that will be used for the password recovery procedure. Optionally you can use the **ping** command to test connectivity. Once you've defined the connectivity parameters, executing the **tftp** command starts the download of the BIN file and the password recovery process.

NOTE   If you have a PIX 535, your TFTP server cannot be located off a Fast Ethernet port in a 64-bit slot since monitor mode doesn't recognize the cards in these slots.

Executing the Password Recovery File

After you perform the monitor mode configuration, executing the **tftp** command will perform the TFTP download of the BIN file, execute it, and erase the authentication information used for password checking. The password recovery process on the PIXs erases the Privilege EXEC **enable password** command and any **aaa authentication** commands: you'll need to reconfigure these once the appliance boots up. During the password recovery process the appliance will display the **aaa** commands that it will erase…copy these down so that it will be easy to reconfigure them upon rebooting. The rest of the configuration will be executed when the PIX boots up.

Example PIX Password Recovery

Here's an example of configuring a PIX to obtain the BIN file from its ethernet1 (inside) interface:

```
monitor> interface 1
monitor> address 10.0.1.1
monitor> server 10.0.1.11
monitor> file np70.bin
monitor> tftp
Do you wish to erase the passwords? [yn] y
Passwords have been erased.
Rebooting...
```

Performing the ASA Password Recovery Process

The ASA password recovery process is basically the same as that used on Cisco IOS devices: from ROMMON mode, you change the configuration register so that the ASA boots up *without* its configuration file, thereby bypassing any password checks. As with the password recovery on the PIXs, you need console access to perform the recovery process.

Changing the Configuration Register on the ASA

Use either the BREAK or the ESC keystroke sequence when the ASA is booting up when prompted for accessing ROMMON mode. You have 10 seconds to do this when prompted.

At the ROMMON mode prompt, use the **confreg** command to change the default bootup process:

```
rommon> confreg [config_register]
```

This is the same command used by IOS devices. Without any parameters, you are led through a script that asks you questions about the bootup process: when you get the question "disable system configuration?" answer **y** to perform the password recovery process. Here's an example of running the script:

```
rommon> confreg
Current Configuration Register: 0x00000001
Configuration Summary:
  boot default image from Flash
Do you wish to change this configuration? y/n [n]: y
enable boot to ROMMON prompt? y/n [n]:
enable TFTP netboot? y/n [n]:
enable Flash boot? y/n [n]: y
select specific Flash image index? y/n [n]:
disable system configuration? y/n [n]: y
go to ROMMON prompt if netboot fails? y/n [n]:
enable passing NVRAM file specs in auto-boot mode? y/n [n]:
disable display of BREAK or ESC key prompt during auto-boot? y/n [n]:
Current Configuration Register: 0x00000041
Configuration Summary:
  boot default image from Flash
  ignore system configuration
Update Config Register (0x41) in NVRAM...
rommon> boot
```

At the end of the script, use the **boot** command to boot the appliance into its OS.

Instead of answering questions asked by the script, you can specify the configuration register value with the **confreg** command, like this:

```
rommon> confreg 0x41
```

The default configuration register value is `0x1`; setting it to `0x41` causes the ASA to boot up in a normal fashion, but doesn't load the startup-config file in flash. Note that the configuration register values that the ASAs use are different from IOS devices.

After the ASA Password Recovery Process

Remember that once you have booted up the ASA, no configuration has been loaded. To fix your password problem, perform the following:

1. Enter Privilege mode—there's no configuration loaded, and thus no password.

2. Execute the `copy startup-config running-config` command.

3. Reconfigure the `enable password` command.

4. Change the configuration register back to 0x1: `config-register 0x1`.

5. Re-enable the data interfaces with the `no shutdown` command.

6. Save your configuration: `write memory`.

AAA

AAA was introduced in Chapter 8 when I discussed Cut-through Proxy (CTP). As a brief overview, the three *A*s in "AAA" stand for authentication, authorization, and accounting. Authentication specifies who can access a device; authorization defines what a user is allowed to do once the user is authenticated; and accounting keeps track of when someone does something and what they do. For the appliance and AAA, the appliance supports both TACACS+ and RADIUS for external authentication, as well as using a local authentication database on the appliance itself.

This section will focus on using AAA to lock down administrative access to the appliance itself. Authentication controls an administrator's initial access, including the type of access, like console or SSH. Authorization controls what the administrators can do once they are logged in (the commands they can execute). Accounting can keep a record of who logged in, how long they were logged in, and what commands they executed. Of the three *A*s, only authentication is required: authorization and/or accounting are optional.

Restricting CLI Access

Controlling access to the appliance itself is referred to as *console authentication*. The term "console" is very misleading, since this refers to access to the appliance, which includes these access methods:

▼ **Serial** Console and auxiliary ports
■ **telnet**
■ **SSH**
■ **HTTP** ASDM and CSM
▲ **Enable** Privilege EXEC mode

To control access to the appliance itself by prompting an administrator with a user-name and password, use the following command:

```
ciscoasa(config)# aaa authentication {serial | enable | telnet |
                    ssh | http} console {AAA_group_tag | [LOCAL]}
```

The *AAA_group_tag* parameter specifies which AAA security protocol and server to use (**aaa-server** commands were discussed in Chapter 8). If you are having the appliance look on an AAA server specified in the group tag value, the TACACS+ protocol is preferred over RADIUS since TACACS+ supports command authorization and RADIUS doesn't. If you want to use the usernames defined on the appliance as a backup to the AAA server(s), use the **LOCAL** keyword after the name of the group tag. If both an AAA tag and the local user accounts are defined, the local user accounts are a backup—they are only used if the AAA server(s) are unreachable.

NOTE If the AAA server is unavailable and no local accounts are defined on the appliance, you can still gain access to the appliance by using the username *pix* (on both PIXs and ASAs) and the *Privilege EXEC* password as a back door. However, if you don't know what these values are, you'll have to use the password recovery procedure to break into the appliance discussed in the previous section.

Local Authentication Database

The **username** command is used to create a local database of usernames and passwords associated with a particular privilege level:

```
ciscoasa(config)# username username {nopassword | password} password
                    [encrypted] [privilege privilege_level]
```

If you omit the privilege level, it defaults to 15. Privilege levels can range from 0 to 15. The **username** command can then be used to authenticate/authorize user access to the appliance itself. These commands are used when the group tag in the **aaa authentication** command is specified as **LOCAL**.

NOTE Please note that all passwords and keys on the appliance are automatically encrypted, unlike with Cisco IOS devices.

If you'll be using the local user database, then there is no limit, by default, as to the number of failed authentication attempts a user can make. This can be restricted with the **aaa local authentication attempts max-fail** command:

```
ciscoasa(config)# aaa local authentication attempts
                    max-fail #_attempts
```

You can specify the number of failed attempts from 1 to 16. If you configure this command and a user exceeds the limit, the user's account is locked out and can only be reactivated with the `clear aaa local user lockout` command:

```
ciscoasa(config)# clear aaa local user {fail-attempts | lockout}
                    {all | username username}
```

NOTE Please note that the lockout feature doesn't apply to (work with) administrator accounts (level 15).

Use the `show aaa local user` command to see the number of failed attempts on an account and whether it is locked:

```
ciscoasa(config)# show aaa local user
```

TIP When using Cisco Secure ACS to authenticate administrators to appliances, you must allow EXEC access for the group the administrator belongs to. Optionally you can enable this on a per-user basis. In either the group or user configuration for the administrator, select the Shell (EXEC) check box under TACACS+ Settings. If you don't do this, you'll experience authorization failure: the name and password the administrator enters can be authenticated, but without having shell access enabled, the administrator fails authorization.

AAA Authentication Example

Here's an example of securing access to the appliance itself by implementing AAA authentication:

```
ciscoasa(config)# username richard password mysecret
ciscoasa(config)# aaa-server AAATAC protocol tacacs+
ciscoasa(config)# aaa-server AAATAC (inside) host 10.0.1.11
                      key cisco123
ciscoasa(config)# aaa authentication serial console AAATAC LOCAL
ciscoasa(config)# aaa authentication enable console AAATAC LOCAL
ciscoasa(config)# aaa authentication ssh console AAATAC
ciscoasa(config)# aaa authentication http console AAATAC
ciscoasa(config)# ssh 10.0.1.0 255.255.255.0 inside
ciscoasa(config)# http 10.0.1.0 255.255.255.0 inside
```

In the preceding example, a backup account (`richard`) is defined for serial (console and auxiliary ports) and enable access, where the primary authentication method is using TACACS+ to an AAA server. Remember that for SSH, telnet, and HTTP access, you also need to specify which devices are allowed to connect with these protocols. This topic was discussed in Chapter 3.

Command Authorization

Command authorization is used to restrict what commands an authenticated user can execute. By default this is controlled based on the EXEC mode you are in: User or Privilege. Few commands are associated with level 1 (User EXEC), while most commands require level 15 access (Privilege EXEC).

You can use three types of authorization to restrict what commands an administrator executes on an appliance:

▼ Using the **enable** command and specifying a level of access and supplying the appropriate password

■ Using a locally defined username and password that are restricted to executing commands at a certain level and lower

▲ Using an AAA defined username and password that are restricted to executing commands within the group or shared profile component on an AAA server

The next sections will cover all three methods.

Enable Password Command Authorization

One method of authorization is to have the users, once they have access to User mode, type in the **enable** command followed by a privilege level of access, like this:

```
ciscoasa> enable [privilege_level]
```

If you omit the privilege level, it defaults to 15. Of course, most commands are at level 15, with a few at level 1; therefore, to take advantage of this approach, you'll need to change the privilege level of various commands and assign a password to access that privilege level.

You need to configure three commands in order to set up command authorization:

▼ **privilege** Specifies which commands are at which privilege level.

■ **aaa authentication** Specifies where to find user accounts and/or password for authentication; this is not required if using enabled passwords for Privilege EXEC access.

▲ **aaa authorization command** Enables command authorization and the use of the privileges defined in the **privilege** command.

To change the privilege levels of commands, use the **privilege** command:

```
ciscoasa(config)# privilege [show | clear | configure] level level
                 [mode enable | configure] command command
```

Three parameters follow the **privilege** command: **show**, **clear**, and **configure**, which set the privilege level for this particular command type. The **level** parameter specifies the privilege level a user must be at in order to execute the command. There are

16 privilege levels: 0–15. Level 1 is User EXEC access, and level 15 is Privilege EXEC access. After this is the optional **mode** parameter, where you can specify in which mode the command can be executed. The last part is where you specify the actual command.

Here is a simple example, where the **show access-list** command is at level 9, and the **access-list** command in Configuration mode is level 11:

```
ciscoasa(config)# privilege show level 9 command access-list
ciscoasa(config)# privilege configure level 11 command access-list
```

Of course you must first enter the passwords for each privilege level that you have created with the **privilege** commands. To do this, use the **enable password** command with the optional **level** parameter:

```
ciscoasa(config)# enable password password
                    [level privilege_level] [encrypted]
```

Last, you must enable command authorization, which specifies where to find the privilege levels for the command:

```
ciscoasa(config)# aaa authorization command {LOCAL | AAA_group_tag}
```

The **LOCAL** keyword specifies to use the privilege commands on the appliance itself; an AAA group tag specifies that the appliance should look up the answer on an AAA server (only TACACS+ is permitted).

NOTE You can create a PIX/ASA Command Authorization set in Cisco Secure ACS under the Shared Profile Components section. This is basically a list of commands that can be executed on an appliance or appliances. Enter all the commands in a set that can—or can't—be executed. Then associate the list with either a group or user that will be managing the appliance(s).

Once you have set up your privilege configuration, use the **show run privilege** command to display your **privilege** commands. The **show curpriv** command displays the user account that is logged in as well as its privilege levels.

Here are examples of these commands:

```
ciscoasa# show run privilege
privilege show level 15 command aaa
privilege clear level 15 command aaa
privilege configure level 15 command aaa
<--output omitted-->
ciscoasa# show curpriv
Username: asaguru
Current privilege level: 15
Current Mode/s: P_PRIV
```

Here's an example that sets up two Privilege EXEC passwords for level 9 and 11:

```
ciscoasa(config)# enable password secret9 level 9
ciscoasa(config)# enable password secret11 level 11
ciscoasa(config)# privilege show level 9 command access-list
ciscoasa(config)# privilege configure level 11 command access-list
ciscoasa(config)# privilege level 11 command static
ciscoasa(config)# aaa authentication enable console LOCAL
ciscoasa(config)# aaa authorization command LOCAL
```

In this example, you must be at level 9 or higher to view ACLs; however, you must be at level 11 or higher to configure an ACL or to create static translations.

Local User Database Command Authorization

The problem of using enable passwords to control what commands an administrator can execute is that if multiple administrators need the same level of access, they must use the same password, which creates accountability problems. A better solution is to use usernames and passwords. One option is to use a local database of accounts, where each account is assigned a level of access that restricts what it can do.

I've already discussed the commands necessary to accomplish this, so let's look at an example that illustrates authentication and authorization using a local database:

```
ciscoasa(config)# username admin1 password secret1 privilege 9
ciscoasa(config)# username admin2 password secret2 privilege 11
ciscoasa(config)# username admin3 password secret3 privilege 15
ciscoasa(config)# privilege show level 9 command access-list
ciscoasa(config)# privilege configure level 11 command access-list
ciscoasa(config)# privilege level 11 command static
ciscoasa(config)# aaa authentication ssh console LOCAL
ciscoasa(config)# aaa authentication console console LOCAL
ciscoasa(config)# aaa authentication enable console LOCAL
ciscoasa(config)# aaa authentication http console LOCAL
ciscoasa(config)# aaa authorization command LOCAL
```

This example uses three administrator accounts at privilege levels 9, 11, and 15. I've used the same privilege levels discussed in the last example. One difference between this and the last example is the **aaa authentication** commands: these are used to prompt a user for a username and password, based on the method of access the user might use to gain access to the appliance.

AAA Server Command Authorization

The main problem with local command authorization is scalability: if you have one appliance, you only have to create your user accounts and privilege commands once. However, if you have 30 appliances, replicating this information and keeping it in synch would be difficult. Given this scenario, I recommend that you centralize the administrator accounts and the commands they can execute on an AAA server. The one restriction, however, is that if you want to control what commands an administrator can execute, you must use the TACACS+ protocol, which reduces to less than a handful the number of products you can purchase.

I've already discussed AAA and its configuration in Chapter 7. Here's an example that employs command authorization, where both the administrative accounts and command privileges are defined on an AAA server:

```
ciscoasa(config)# username backdoor password doorback privilege 15
ciscoasa(config)# aaa-server AAATAC protocol tacacs+
ciscoasa(config)# aaa-server AAATAC (inside) host 10.0.1.11
                        key cisco123
ciscoasa(config)# aaa authentication serial console AAATAC LOCAL
ciscoasa(config)# aaa authentication enable console AAATAC LOCAL
ciscoasa(config)# aaa authentication ssh console AAATAC
ciscoasa(config)# aaa authentication http console AAATAC
ciscoasa(config)# aaa authorization command AAATAC LOCAL
```

One item to point out about the preceding configuration is that I created a backup level 15 account in case the AAA server is unreachable.

Management Accounting

If you want to have a record of who logged into the appliance and what commands they executed, you'll need to configure AAA accounting. One restriction with accounting is that you must record the accounting records on an AAA server (syslog and SNMP are unsupported); and for commands that are executed, you must be using TACACS+ as the AAA communications protocol.

Here are the commands to enable AAA accounting for administrative access to the appliances:

```
ciscoasa(config)# aaa accounting {serial | telnet | ssh | enable}
                        console AAA_server_tag
ciscoasa(config)# aaa accounting command [privilege level]
                        AAA_server_tag
```

The first command creates an accounting record when someone logs into or out of the appliance based on the access method defined. The second command creates an accounting record for each command executed at the specified level. If you have created multiple privilege levels and want to have account records created for commands executed at each level, you'll need a separate **aaa accounting command** for each privilege level.

CHAPTER 27

ASDM

This chapter will introduce you to the Adaptive Security Device Manager (ASDM), which is an alternative to the command-line interface (CLI) for configuring the security appliances. The topics covered in this chapter include

▼ Introducing ASDM requirements and restrictions

■ Preparing the security appliance to use ASDM

■ Accessing ASDM for the first time

■ Understanding the elements on the ASDM Home screen

■ Configuring the appliance with ASDM

■ Monitoring the status of the appliance using ASDM

▲ Using ASDM when the appliance is in multiple mode (contexts)

ASDM OVERVIEW

ASDM is the replacement for the PIX Device Manager (PDM). PDM is used in version 6 of the OS; ASDM is used for version 7 and later. ASDM is a Java-based GUI interface to configure and manage the appliances. All ASAs that ship today include ASDM in flash. To use ASDM, you must either run the setup script or manually enter the corresponding commands. You can use both the CLI and ASDM simultaneously, since certain functions must still be performed from the CLI, like the initial configuration of the appliance. When you're using ASDM, HTTPS (SSL) is used to protect the communications between your desktop and the configurations sent to or pulled from the appliance.

NOTE   This chapter focuses on the use of ASDM version 6.1.

ASDM Requirements

ASDM was introduced in version 7.0 of the security appliances and is supported on both the PIXs and ASAs. ASDM is Java-based code that sits in flash on the appliances. Table 27-1 displays the security appliance operating systems and their corresponding ASDM images; when upgrading from one version of the OS to another, like version 7.0 to 7.1, you will also have to upgrade your ASDM image to its corresponding version. ASDM takes about 7–8 MB of space in flash. For the ASAs, this is not an issue, since they have large amounts of flash; however, for the PIXs, only one operating system and one ASDM image will fit into flash. So upgrading a PIX will require you to first delete the older images before performing an upgrade.

Operating System Version	ASDM Version
7.0	5.0
7.1	5.2
7.2	5.2
8.0	6.0
8.0 or 8.1	6.1

Table 27-1. Security Appliance Operating Systems and ASDM Versions

ASDM is a web-based, Java-based tool. To use ASDM, you must be using one of the following operating systems on your PC:

▼ Windows 2000, 2003, XP, or Vista

■ Mac OS X

▲ Red Hat Linux

Your initial ASDM access to the appliance is via a web browser using SSL. ASDM supports Internet Explorer (IE) 6.0 and later as well as Firefox 1.5 and later. For the Java component, you'll need Sun Java 1.4(2), 5.0, or 6.0.

NOTE Not all Java versions are compatible with ASDM, so be careful when you update Java on your desktop.

ASDM Restrictions

Almost all configuration commands are supported within ASDM. When you're using ASDM, most configurations are performed in a GUI-based window. However, ASDM supports a CLI tool that allows you to type in commands and send them to the appliance (this is discussed in the "CLI Tool" section). When you're using the CLI tool, however, certain commands are unsupported, for example, `access-list`, `ipv6`, as well as any interactive command that requires administrator input, like `setup` and `crypto key generate rsa`.

Besides these restrictions, when the appliance is running in single mode, you cannot have more than five ASDM active sessions. When the appliance is running in multiple mode (using contexts), you can have no more than five ASDM sessions per context; and across all contexts, you cannot have more than a total of 32 ASDM sessions.

ASDM CONFIGURATION PREPARATIONS

With the exception of the ASA 5505, none of the ASAs or PIXs includes a base configuration that will allow ASDM access. You have two options to placing a basic configuration on the appliance to use ASDM:

▼ The **setup** script

▲ CLI commands

The following two sections will discuss both options.

Setup Script

The use of the **setup** command was discussed in Chapter 3, so I'll just briefly review its use here. This script places a basic configuration on the appliance, including the setup of the *inside* interface and specifying an administrator PC that will access ASDM on the appliance. Here's an example of executing the script, which must be done from Configuration mode:

```
ciscoasa(config)# setup
Pre-configure Firewall now through interactive prompts [yes]? <ENTER>
Firewall Mode [Routed]: <ENTER>
Enable password [<use current password>]: <ENTER>
Allow password recovery [yes]? <ENTER>
Clock (UTC): <ENTER>
  Year [1964]: <ENTER>
  Month [May]: <ENTER>
  Day [23]: <ENTER>
  Time [20:51:33]: <ENTER>
Inside IP address [0.0.0.0]: 10.0.1.1
Inside network mask [0.0.0.0]: 255.255.255.0
Host name [ciscoasa]: asa
Domain name: dealgroup.com
IP address of host running Device Manager: 10.0.1.11
<--output omitted-->
Use this configuration and write to flash? yes
```

NOTE The script only allows you to specify a single IP address for ASDM access (10.0.1.11 in the preceding example); however, you can always add more addresses after the fact from either ASDM or the CLI. Also, if running this script from Configuration mode, at least one interface needs to be configured and enabled.

Basic Configuration Commands

If you don't use the `setup` command to prepare the appliance for ASDM, you can manually enter the commands, which follow:

```
ciscoasa(config)# asdm image {disk0|disk1}:/ASDM_image_name
ciscoasa(config)# hostname name_of_your_appliance
ciscoasa(config)# domain-name your_appliance's_domain_name
ciscoasa(config)# enable password password
ciscoasa(config)# interface physical_if_name
ciscoasa(config-if)# nameif logical_if_name
ciscoasa(config-if)# ip address IP_address [subnet_mask]
ciscoasa(config-if)# security-level number
ciscoasa(config-if)# speed {10|100|1000|auto|nonegotiate}
ciscoasa(config-if)# duplex {auto|full|half}
ciscoasa(config-if)# [no] shutdown
ciscoasa(config)# http server enable [port_#]
ciscoasa(config)# http IP_address_or_network subnet_mask
                      logical_if_name
```

The `asdm image` command specifies the ASDM image to use in flash (if more than one exists). You need to configure a name and domain name for the appliance, since these are used to generate the RSA keys for SSL. You also need to set up the interface that your PC will connect to—typically this is the inside interface, which will have a security level of 100.

The `http server enable` command enables ASDM. By default the port number used is 443 (the SSL default port number); however, you can change this, as was discussed in Chapter 19, if you need to support both WebVPN and ASDM on the same interface. If this is the case, let WebVPN use port 443, and specify a different port number for ASDM. By default the `http` command specifies the address or addresses allowed to connect to the appliance using ASDM on the specified interface—you can execute this command multiple times for different administrator addresses or networks.

TIP As you can see from the preceding commands, it is actually much easier to run the `setup` command instead of typing in the individual commands.

ASDM ACCESS

Once you have put a basic configuration on your appliance to allow ASDM access, you are ready to access the appliance using a web browser, and to download and execute the Java code. The following two sections will discuss how to access and download ASDM and how to use the Startup Wizard to put an initial configuration on the appliance that will allow outbound access for users, along with allowing the corresponding returning traffic back to the users.

Web Browser Access

To access ASDM, start up a supported web browser, and type in the HTTPS URL to access your appliance, like this:

```
https://IP_address_of_the_appliance
```

A window will pop up where you'll have to accept the self-signed certificate of the appliance. After you accept the self-signed certificate, your web browser should display the screen shown in Figure 27-1. You have three options at this point:

▼ *Install ASDM Launcher and Run ASDM*   ASDM will be installed on your PC so that you don't have to use a web browser to download it again the next time you want to use it.

■ *Run ASDM*   ASDM is downloaded and executed on your PC, but is not installed on your PC.

▲ *Run Startup Wizard*   ASDM is downloaded and executed on your PC, where the Startup Wizard begins, allowing you to put a basic configuration on your appliance; ASDM is not installed locally on your PC.

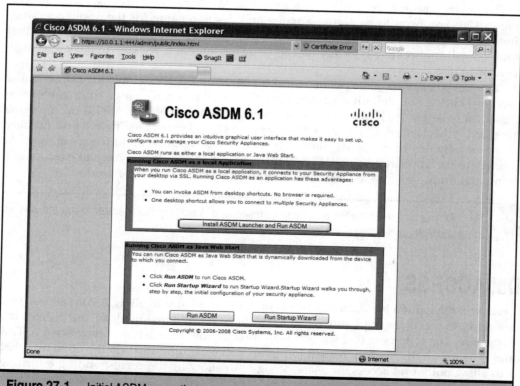

Figure 27-1.   Initial ASDM run options

Figure 27-2. ASDM login screen

NOTE In the figures where I've captured screenshots for ASDM, I've used port 444, since I am also using WebVPN on the same ASA on external interfaces.

Once you click one of the three options on the previous screen, you'll be prompted to download the JavaScript code for ASDM. You'll have to accept the JavaScript code and log into ASDM. If you have not configured AAA for HTTP access (see Chapter 26), then you'll need to enter only the Privileged mode password from the **enable password** command. (The login process is shown in Figure 27-2.) Once you have successfully logged in, you'll either be presented with the Home screen or the Home screen with a pop-up window for the Startup Wizard.

NOTE Once ASDM launches, you can close down your initial web browser window.

Startup Wizard

The Startup Wizard puts a minimal configuration on the appliance—basically to allow initial TCP and UDP connections outbound and the corresponding replies for these connections back into the network. The initial screen of the Startup Wizard is shown in Figure 27-3. You can modify the configuration you have, or start from scratch. The appliance model you are accessing will determine the number of screens the wizard will lead you through. Here is a brief description of the screens on an ASA 5505, which is not configured as an Easy VPN remote:

▼ Screen 1: Modify the existing configuration, or restore the appliance back to the factory defaults and configure it from scratch.

■ Screen 2: Assign a hostname, domain name, and a Privilege EXEC password.

■ Screen 3: Enable and configure auto update parameters.

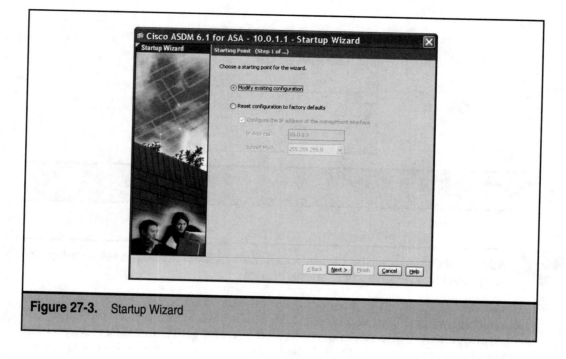

Figure 27-3. Startup Wizard

- Screen 4: On the ASA 5505, set up the VLANs.
- Screen 5: On the ASA 5505, assign the physical interfaces to VLANs.
- Screen 6: Assign IP addressing and parameters to the interfaces.
- Screen 7: Create static routes.
- Screen 8: Set up DHCP server parameters.
- Screen 9: Configure dynamic translation rules for outbound traffic, if necessary (`nat` and `global` commands).
- Screen 10: Change the administrative access for using ASDM.
- ▲ Screen 11: Displays a summary of the changes that will be made—click the Finish button to accept the changes and be returned to the Home screen.

ASDM HOME SCREEN

Figure 27-4 is the first screen you're presented with when accessing the ASDM GUI. At the top of the screen are various menu options. Below this are the toolbar buttons. And the main part of the screen has two tabs that control the elements displayed on the screen: the Device Dashboard, which is in the foreground, and the Firewall Dashboard. The following sections will discuss the elements found on the Home screen.

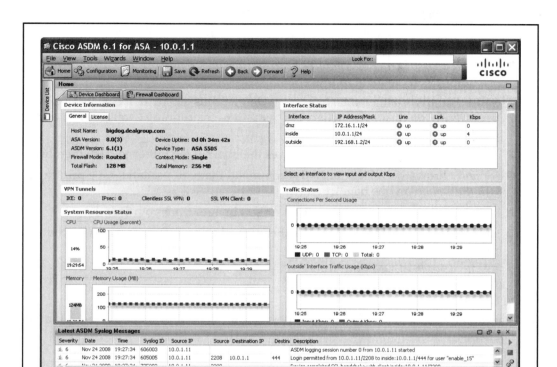

Figure 27-4. ASDM Home screen and the Device Dashboard

Menu Items

At the top of the ASDM Home screen are the menu items: File, View, Tools, Wizards, Window, and Help. The following sections will discuss these menu options.

File Menu Items

The File menu manages the appliance configurations and includes these items:

▼ *Refresh ASDM with the Running Configuration on the Device* Loads a copy of the running configuration into ASDM.

■ *Reset Device to the Factory Default Configuration* Restores the appliance configuration to the factory default.

■ *Show Running Configuration in New Window* Displays the current running configuration of the appliance in a pop-up window.

- *Save Running Configuration to Flash*   Saves a copy of the running configuration to flash memory (executes the `write memory` command on the appliance).

- *Save Running Configuration to TFTP Server*   Saves a copy of the current running configuration file on a TFTP server.

- *Save Running Configuration to Standby Unit*   Sends a copy of the running configuration file on the active failover unit to the running configuration of a failover standby unit.

- *Save Internal Log Buffer to Flash*   Saves the internal log buffer to flash memory.

- *Print*   Prints the current page (I recommend that you use landscape printing to fit the screen on one page).

- *Clear ASDM Cache*   Removes local ASDM images from your PC.

- *Clear Internal Log Buffer*   Empties the internal syslog message buffer on the appliance.

- ▲ *Exit*   Closes ASDM gracefully.

View Menu Items

The View menu controls the display functions for the ASDM GUI and includes the following items:

- ▼ *Home*   Displays the Home screen.

- *Configuration*   Displays the Configuration screen.

- *Monitoring*   Displays the Monitoring screen.

- *Device List*   Shows and hides a list of devices (contexts) in a dockable pane: contexts are accessed using this approach.

- *Navigation*   Shows and hides the display of the Navigation pane in the Configuration and Monitoring screens.

- *ASDM Assistant*   Shows and hides a pane that lets you search for information in ASDM.

- *Latest ASDM Syslog Messages*   Shows and hides the display of the Latest ASDM Syslog Messages pane at the bottom of the Home screen.

- *Addresses*   Shows and hides the display of the Addresses pane, which is only available for the Access Rules, NAT Rules, Service Policy Rules, AAA Rules, and Filter Rules panes in the Configuration screen.

- *Services*   Shows and hides the display of the Services pane, which is only available for the Access Rules, NAT Rules, Service Policy Rules, AAA Rules, and Filter Rules panes in the Configuration screen.

- *Time Ranges* Shows and hides the display of the Time Ranges pane, which is only available for the Access Rules, Service Policy Rules, AAA Rules, and Filter Rules panes in the Configuration screen.

- *Global Pools* Shows and hides the display of the Global Pools pane, which is only available for the NAT Rules pane in the Configuration screen.

- *Find in ASDM* Locates an item for which you are searching.

- *Back* Goes back to the previous screen.

- *Forward* Moves forward to a more recent screen.

- *Reset Layout* Returns the layout to the default configuration.

- ▲ *Office Look and Feel* Changes screen fonts and colors to the Microsoft Office settings.

Tools Menu Items

The third menu item in the menu bar at the top of the ASDM GUI is the Tools menu item. The Tools menu item includes the following options:

- ▼ *Command Line Interface* Provides a text-based tool for sending actual commands to the appliance and viewing the resulting output of the commands. The only commands you cannot send to the appliance are interactive commands that require user input, like `setup`.

- *Show Commands Ignored by ASDM on Device* Displays unsupported commands that are ignored by ASDM.

- *Packet Tracer* Lets you trace a packet from a specified source address and interface to a destination (the `packet-tracer` command).

- *Ping* Lets you have the appliance execute the `ping` command and display the resulting output.

- *Traceroute* Lets you have the appliance execute the `traceroute` command and display the resulting output.

- *File Management* Lets you view, move, copy, and delete files and directories stored in flash.

- *Upgrade Software from Local Computer* Lets you choose an appliance image, ASDM image, or another image on your PC, and upload the file to flash.

- *Upgrade Software from Cisco.com* Lets you upgrade the appliance operating system and ASDM images through a wizard directly from the Cisco site (requires a CCO account on the Cisco web site).

- *System Reload* Lets you reboot the appliance or schedule a reboot of the appliance.

- *Administrator Alerts to Clientless SSL VPN Users*   Lets an administrator send an alert message to clientless WebVPN users.

- *Preferences*   Changes the behavior of specified ASDM functions between administrative sessions.

- *ASDM Java Console*   Shows the ASDM Java console.

- *Backup Configurations*   Backs up configurations.

▲ *Restore Configurations*   Restores previously backed up configurations.

The following sections will expand on some of the more complex options.

Packet Tracer   To access the Packet Tracer tool, go to Tools | Packet Tracer, which will open a pop-up window where you can use the Packet Tracer tool. Enter the information at the top of the window, like the source interface, protocol, addresses, and protocol information, and click the Start button. By default the animation at the top of the window displays each component of the appliance that is processing the "pretend" packet. Green checkmarks mean the process allows the packet. A red *X* means the process denied the packet. Below the animation, you can expand the specific processes to see what is happening with the packet, especially if it is being denied. Figure 27-5

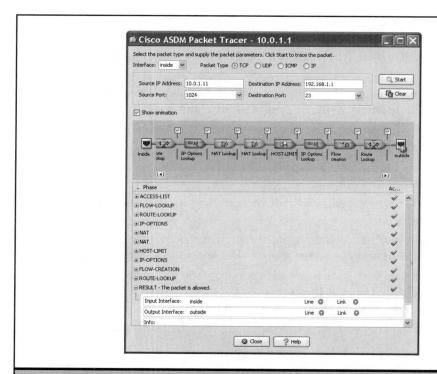

Figure 27-5.   Packet Tracer tool

shows an example of this tool, where testing a telnet connection passed and would be permitted if the packet were real. For more information on using the Packet Tracer tool, see Chapter 6.

CLI Tool One really handy feature of ASDM is that you can send actual commands to the appliance and have the results shown within ASDM with the CLI tool: Tools | Command Line Interface. You can send down a single command or multiple commands (many commands in one batch). Use the drop-down selector to choose a command, or type your own command within this text box. With only a few exceptions, you can execute any command here that you can execute from the appliance CLI. Figure 27-6 shows an example of sending the **show xlate** command to the appliance and the resulting output.

TIP You can even use the **?** in your commands in the CLI tool, which will display the help for the command you sent to the appliance.

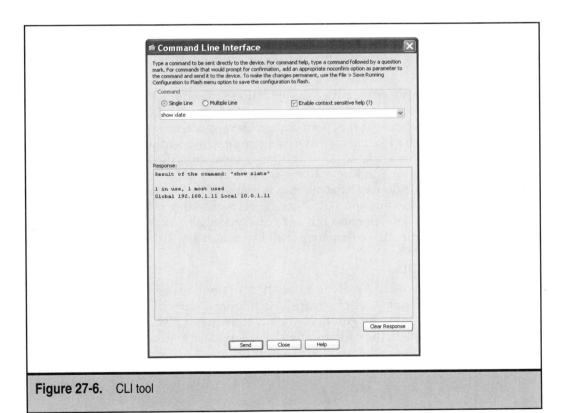

Figure 27-6. CLI tool

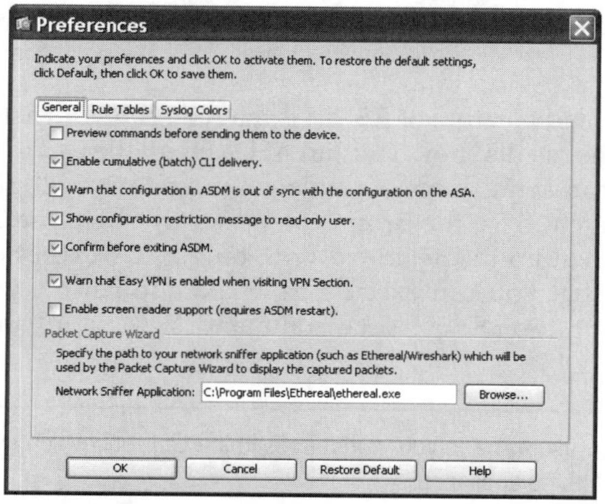

Figure 27-7. Preferences tool

Preferences Tool   You can change the GUI operation preferences for ASDM by going to Tools | Preferences. You can see the pop-up window in Figure 27-7. One nice feature in the Preferences pop-up window is the command preview option (the first check box): when this is enabled, you see a list of commands in a pop-up window that will be executed on the appliance when you click the Apply button to send an ASDM configuration to the appliance. In the pop-up window with the list of commands, click the Deliver button to send the commands down to the appliance. Without this feature, the configuration is sent to the appliance, but you don't see the corresponding commands that ASDM created based on the GUI elements you configured. Using the command preview option is a great way of learning the commands used for certain appliance features.

Wizards Menu Items

ASDM supports wizards to help you to easily configure complex appliance features. Wizards lead you through a set of screens to configure a particular feature. By using a wizard, you minimize misconfigurations—while from the CLI, you might forget a command or two to complete the configuration of a particular feature. Wizards should be used to perform the initial configuration of a feature; tuning or changing your configuration should then be done from the Configuration screen.

ASDM supports the following wizards from the Wizards menu:

▼ **Startup Wizard** This wizard walks you through a step-by-step process to place an initial configuration on your appliance.

■ **IPSec VPN Wizard** This wizard enables you to configure an IPSec VPN site-to-site or remote access (Easy Server and Remote) configuration on your appliance.

■ **SSL VPN Wizard** This wizard enables you to configure a WebVPN clientless or tunnel mode configuration.

■ **High Availability and Scalability Wizard** This wizard allows you to configure failover and VPN clustering on your appliance.

▲ **Packet Capture Wizard** This wizard allows you to configure packet captures on your appliance.

The Startup Wizard was discussed previously in the "Startup Wizard" section. The IPSec VPN, SSL VPN, and High Availability and Scalability wizards will be discussed later in the chapter. The Packet Capture Wizard allows you to capture packets on the appliance. You must specify the ingress interface, optionally the addresses and protocols involved (filtering what packets you want to capture), the egress interface, the largest packet size of a packet, and the buffer size of the total number of packets to capture. The Packet Capture feature was discussed in Chapter 6.

Other Menu Items

The other two menu items are Window and Help. The Window item is used when you have more than one ASDM window open (perhaps to multiple contexts or to complete different appliances), and it allows you to quickly change to a different appliance. The Help item allows you to display the help topics for using ASDM, the release notes for the current ASDM image, and help information about the elements on the currently displayed window.

Toolbar Buttons

Below the menu items are the toolbar buttons or icons. The toolbar buttons allow you to quickly perform a common function within ASDM. Here is a description of the toolbar buttons:

▼ **Home** Displays the Home screen, which lets you view important information about your security appliance such as the status of your interfaces, the version of code you are running, licensing information, and performance information

■ **Configuration** Displays the Configuration screen, which allows you to configure the features of the appliance

- **Monitoring** Displays the Monitor screen, which allows you to view the appliance operation and configured features
- **Save** Saves the running configuration to the startup configuration in flash (`write memory`)
- **Refresh** Refreshes ASDM with the current running configuration of the appliance
- **Back** Takes you back to the last pane of ASDM that you visited
- **Forward** Takes you forward to the more previous pane of ASDM that you visited
- **Look For** Lets you search for a feature in ASDM
- ▲ **Help** Shows context-sensitive help for the window or pane that is currently open

Home Screen Elements

Two Home screen elements control what you see in the main part of the home page: the Device Dashboard and the Firewall Dashboard. The following two sections discuss these elements.

Device Dashboard

The Device Dashboard on the Home screen (shown previously in Figure 27-4) is a tab that is in the foreground by default. Here you can see version and hardware information about the appliance (General tab), the status of the interfaces, the number of VPN tunnels that are up, the CPU and memory utilization, the quick snapshot of the traffic statistics, and log messages (bottom of the screen). Note that this screen automatically refreshes itself every 10 seconds. If you click the License tab, you can see what features are currently unlocked by your appliance activation/license key.

Firewall Dashboard

By clicking the Firewall Dashboard tab (below the toolbar buttons), you can see the following updated statistics (see Figure 27-8):

- ▼ State and xlate table entries being added/removed
- Top dropped packets by ACLs and inspection rules
- Possible scan and SYN attacks
- ▲ Top 10 statistics for services, source addresses, and destinations

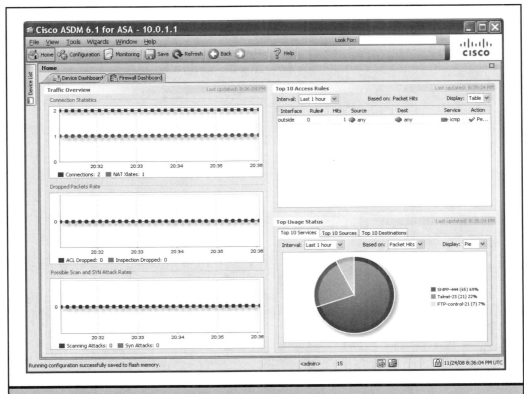

Figure 27-8. ASDM Home screen and the Firewall Dashboard

ASDM CONFIGURATION SCREENS

To access the Configuration screens, click the Configuration button in the toolbar, shown in Figure 27-9. To access the various configuration elements, click the element name in the left pane. Configuration elements include Device Setup, Firewall, Remote Access VPN, Site-to-Site VPN, and Device Management. Clicking an element will display the configuration items at the top of the left pane. The following sections will cover the Configuration screens.

Device Setup Tab

When you click the Configuration button at the top of the screen, the default view displayed is the Device Setup configuration element—you can also reach this screen within the configuration section by clicking the Device Setup tab in the left pane (shown in Figure 27-9).

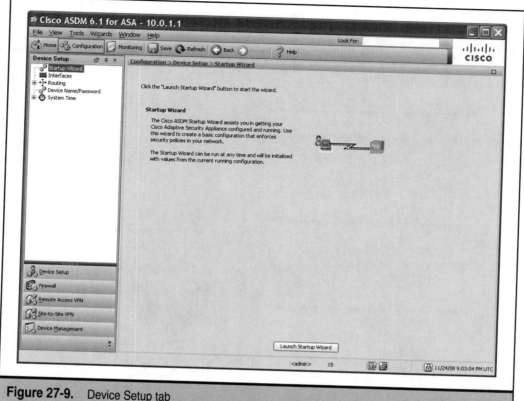

Figure 27-9. Device Setup tab

The default configuration element is the Startup Wizard (discussed previously in the "Startup Wizard" section). The Device Setup configuration section allows you to set up basic properties for the appliance, like its name, domain name, password, routing (static routes and dynamic routing protocols), the date and time, and use of the Startup Wizard.

NOTE When you are done making changes on a particular screen, click the Apply button at the bottom to send the changes to the appliance.

Firewall Tab

Clicking the Firewall tab in the left pane opens options in the pane above it. Here you can configure your appliance ACLs, dynamic and static translation rules, service policies (including class and policy maps), Cut-through Proxy (CTP) rules, URL filtering rules for Websense and SmartFilter, threat detection policies, object groups, and advanced features like antispoofing with reverse path forwarding (RPF) and others. The following sections will cover the three most commonly configured elements: access rules, NAT rules, and service policy rules.

Access Rules Element

When you click the Firewall tab, the Access Rules element is displayed by default in the middle pane. This screen can be seen in Figure 27-10. ACL policies are broken out on an interface-by-interface basis. Figure 27-10 shows three interfaces: *dmz, inside,* and *outside.* The *dmz* and *inside* interfaces have two implicit rules, while the *outside* interface has one ACL statement that allows ICMP traffic and an implicit rule that drops everything else. Notice the Enabled column that allows you to disable a particular statement. To add a statement to an existing interface ACL, select a statement in the list, and click the Add button at the top. (You can click the down arrow to the right of Add to add a statement before or after an existing ACL statement.) To edit or delete a statement, first select it and then click the corresponding button above the ACL statements. To move an ACL statement to a different position within the ACL, first select the statement and then click the up or down arrows above the list of ACL statements. You can also cut a selected ACL statement

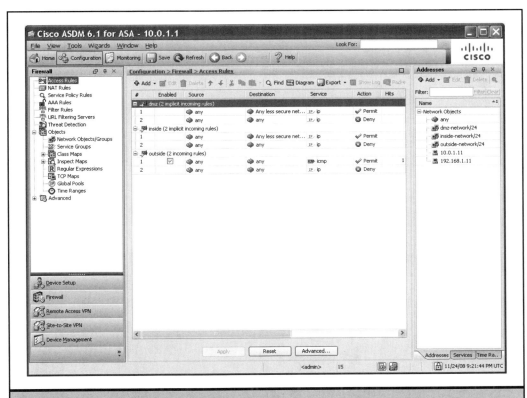

Figure 27-10. Firewall tab: Access Rules element

by clicking the scissors icon; you can then paste the statement before or after a selected ACL statement by clicking the paste icon above the list of ACL statements. The find icon (magnifying glass) allows you to search for a particular ACL statement in the list.

TIP On the far right side of each configured ACL statement is a Hits column, which displays the number of matches on a particular statement (the hit counts).

The right pane has three tabs at the bottom: Addresses (defaults to the foreground), Services, and Time Ranges. The Addresses tab allows you to create **name** statements and network object groups that you can use in your ACL statements; the Services tab allows you to create service, ICMP, and protocol object groups that you can use in your ACL statements; and the Time Ranges tab allows you to create time ranges you can then reference in your ACL statements.

NAT Rules Element

To access the NAT Rules element, go to Configuration | Firewall | NAT Rules, as shown in Figure 27-11. You can see static and dynamic access rules in the middle pane. To create

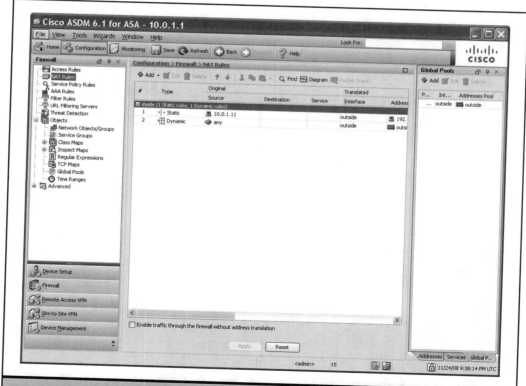

Figure 27-11. Firewall tab: NAT Rules element

a global address pool used in dynamic translations, click the Global Pools tab in the bottom of the right pane, and then click the Add button at the top of the right pane. Adding a translation rule is as easy as clicking the Add button at the top of the middle pane and choosing the type of translation rule you want to create: static rule, dynamic rule, NAT exemption rule, static policy rule, or a dynamic policy rule. See Chapter 5 for more information on translation rules.

> **TIP** If the check box at the bottom of the pane is *not* checked, then the `nat-control` command is enabled, requiring the use of address translation rules.

Service Policy Rules Element

To access the Service Policy Rules element, go to Configuration | Firewall | Service Policy Rules, shown in Figure 27-12. From here you can create and modify your service policies: QoS, policing, application inspection, IPS, and CSC. Creating your policies is done by using the Add Service Policy Rule Wizard, accessed by clicking the Add button. The wizard has three screens: selecting an interface or a global policy, creating a class

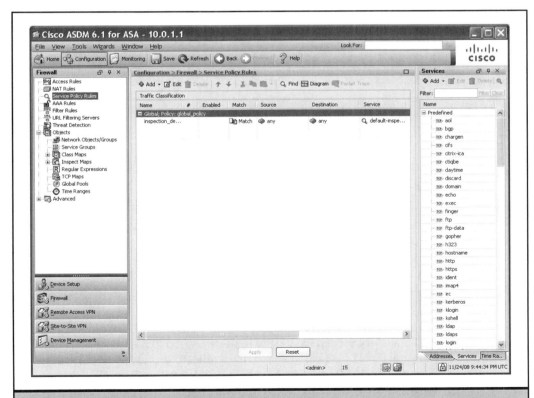

Figure 27-12. Firewall tab: Service Policy Rules element

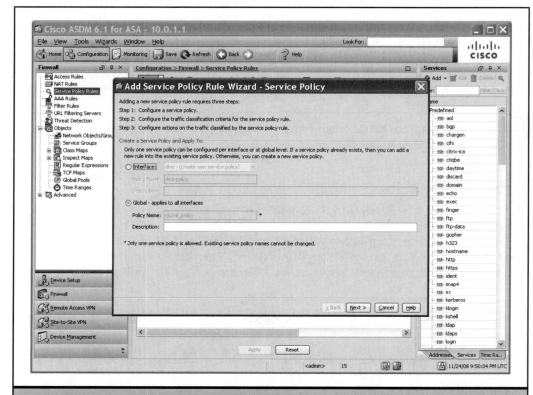

Figure 27-13. Firewall tab: Add Service Policy Rule Wizard

map, and creating a policy map with the policies for the class map. The first screen is shown in Figure 27-13.

TIP The Objects element under the Firewall tab allows you to create layer 7 class and policy maps for your service policy rules.

Remote Access VPN Tab

When you click the Remote Access VPN tab in the bottom-left corner pane of the Configuration screen, you can configure your VPN policies for WebVPN clientless and tunnel mode connections, Easy VPN Server, Easy VPN Remote (ASA 5505 only), and L2TP/IPSec connections (see Figure 27-14). You can also set up certificate services. The following sections will cover how to use ASDM to set up an Easy VPN server, a WebVPN gateway, an AnyConnect gateway, and Cisco Secure Desktop (CSD).

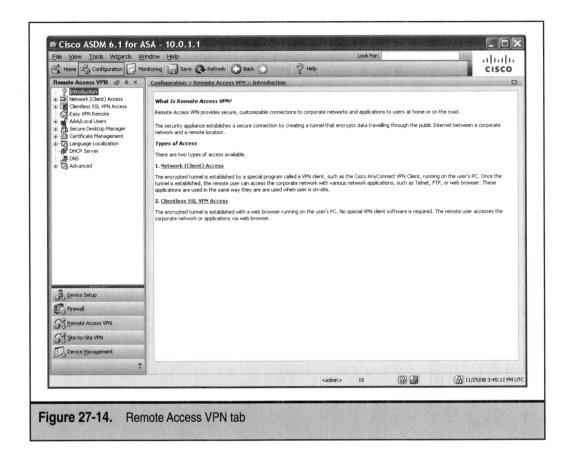

Figure 27-14. Remote Access VPN tab

Easy VPN Server

You can easily set up and manage an Easy VPN Server on your appliance when using ASDM. For the initial setup, ASDM supports a wizard for Easy VPN Server functions. Once you've used the wizard, changing Easy VPN policies is easy with the ASDM configuration screens. The following two sections will introduce you to these topics.

IPSec Wizard for Easy VPN Server To access the IPSec wizard to initialize the Easy VPN server feature, go to Wizards | IPSec VPN Wizard, shown in Figure 27-15. In the initial pop-up window, you can either create a site-to-site IPSec connection, or set up the Easy VPN Server feature. Choose the Remote Access option for the latter. You also need to choose the interface the IPSec sessions will be terminated on. Optionally choosing the check box at the bottom will configure the `sysopt connection permit-vpn` command, which allows decrypted VPN traffic to be exempted from ACL checks when going from a lower- to higher-level interface.

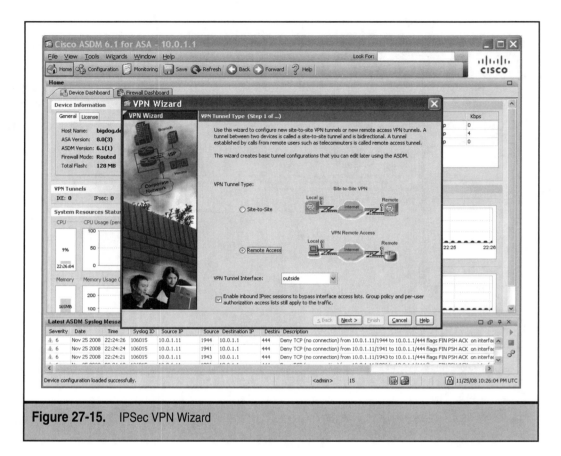

Figure 27-15. IPSec VPN Wizard

Here are the screens you'll go through when using the wizard to set up your Easy VPN Server:

▼ Screen 1: Choose the type of IPSec VPN: Site-to-Site or Remote Access (Easy VPN Server).

■ Screen 2: Select the type of clients that will be supported: Cisco VPN Client 3.*x* and higher or L2TP/IPSec.

■ Screen 3: Choose the device authentication method (pre-shared keys or certificates) and the name of the tunnel group for one group of remote access users.

■ Screen 4: Specify the location of user accounts: the local database of `username` commands or an AAA server group.

■ Screen 5: If you chose the local database option, you'll be asked to add user accounts on this screen.

- ■ Screen 6: Create or specify a local address pool that will be used to assign internal addresses to Easy VPN Remotes.

- ■ Screen 7: Specify Mode Config properties. (You can only specify DNS and WINS server addresses as well as a domain name in the wizard—other policies must be assigned from the Remote Access VPN tab after completing the wizard.)

- ■ Screen 8: Create a Phase 1 policy. (The default policy uses 3DES, SHA, and DH group 2.)

- ■ Screen 9: Create a Phase 2 transform set. (The default policy uses ESP with 3DES and SHA.)

- ■ Screen 10: Set up address translation exemption (`nat 0`) of the internal addresses to the corporate office networks as well as a split tunneling policy.

- ▲ Screen 11: Accept your configuration by clicking the Finish button.

NOTE You can add only one tunnel group and one group policy using the wizard during the wizard process; however, you can either use the wizard a second time to add an additional group, or easily add tunnel groups and group policies from the Remote Access VPN tab on the Configuration screen.

IPSec Attributes for Easy VPN Server Once you've set up at least one tunnel group and its policies for Easy VPN, you can either use the wizard to add additional groups and policies, or change any Easy VPN policy or attribute from the Remote Access VPN tab. I'll highlight some of the screens to tune your Easy VPN Server configuration.

To add or edit your group policies, go to Configuration | Remote Access VPN tab | Network (Client) Access | Group Policies. I selected the "students" group policy in Figure 27-16 and clicked the Edit button. These attributes were discussed in Chapter 17. To change general properties for IPSec remote access connections, go to Configuration | Remote Access VPN tab | Network (Client) Access | Advanced | IPSec (see Figure 27-17). From here, you can edit the crypto maps, IKE Phase 1 policies, IKE parameters (like NAT-T), Phase 2 transform sets, certificate matching rules, and specify auto update policies for software clients.

Clientless WebVPN

You can easily set up and manage clientless WebVPN sessions on your appliance when using ASDM. For the initial setup, ASDM supports a wizard for WebVPN functions. Once you've used the wizard, changing client policies like the look and feel of the home/portal page or thin client policies is easy with ASDM Configuration screens. The following two sections will introduce you to these topics.

SSL VPN Wizard for Clientless WebVPN Connections The SSL VPN Wizard allows you to set up clientless and AnyConnect/SVC client connections. To access the SSL VPN Wizard

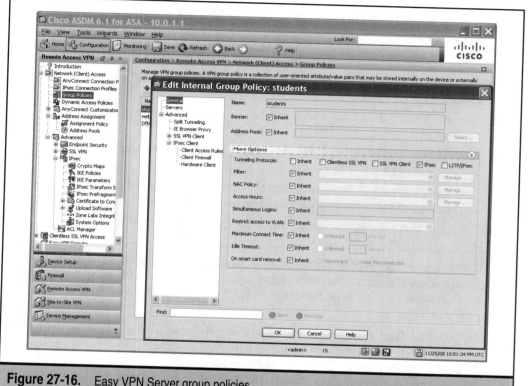

Figure 27-16. Easy VPN Server group policies

to initialize the WebVPN server feature, go to Wizards | SSL VPN Wizard, shown in Figure 27-18. In the initial pop-up window, you can create a clientless WebVPN configuration, an AnyConnect WebVPN configuration, or both.

Here are the screens you'll go through when using the wizard to set up your client-less policies:

▼ Screen 1: Choose the type of WebVPN session—clientless, AnyConnect, or both.

■ Screen 2: Define the tunnel group name, the name of the interface that users will connect to using SSL, the certificate to be used (optional), the alias name for the tunnel group, and if the list of alias names will appear on the login screen.

■ Screen 3: Specify the location of user accounts: the local database of `username` commands, or an AAA server group. If you chose the local database option, you'll be asked to add user accounts on this screen.

■ Screen 4: Choose if you want to create a new group policy or modify an existing one.

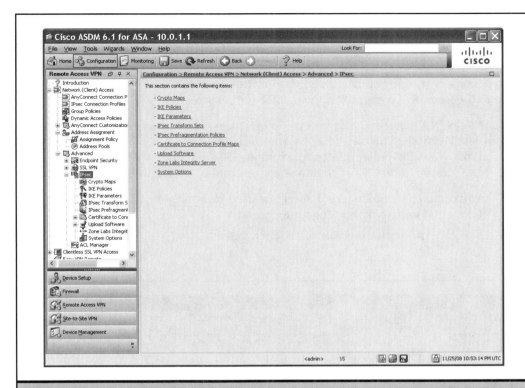

Figure 27-17.   General Easy VPN IPSec properties

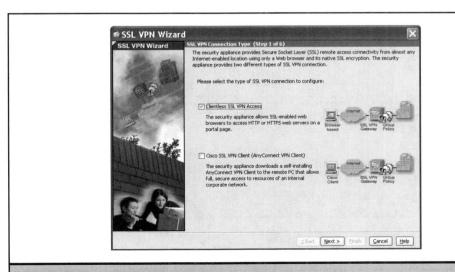

Figure 27-18.   SSL VPN Wizard

■ Screen 5: Create or reference a bookmark list (the list of URLs that will appear on the home portal/page).

▲ Screen 6: Accept your configuration by clicking the Finish button.

Other policies and configuration changes must be done after the completion of the wizard from the Remote Access tab on the Configuration screen.

Clientless WebVPN Attributes   Once you've set up at least one tunnel group and its policies for clientless WebVPN, you can either use the wizard to add additional groups, or change any clientless WebVPN policy or attribute from the Remote Access VPN tab. I'll highlight some of the screens to tune your clientless configuration, shown in Figure 27-19:

▼ You can create bookmarks that will be used by a tunnel group; bookmarks are URLs that will appear on the home portal.

■ You can install plug-ins for thin client access.

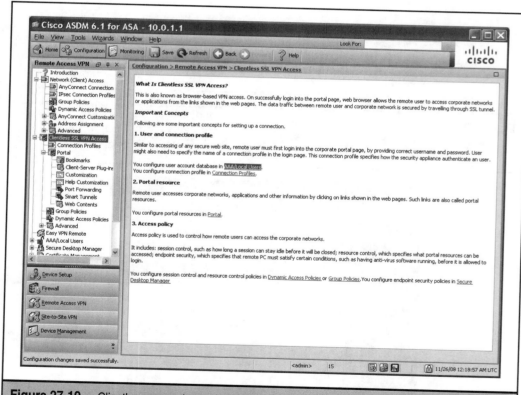

Figure 27-19.   Clientless properties

- You can create a customization profile, which controls the look and feel of the user's home portal. (This is an XML document and requires the use of a web browser to create it, similar to a WYSIWYG—what you see is what you get—GUI editor.)

- You can create a customization help profile, which allows you to specify additional languages to be used in the display of the home portal.

- You can create port forwarding rules for thin client access.

- You can specify applications for smart tunneling, which are used for thin client access.

▲ You can import web contents, like images, that will be used on the home portal.

To create a bookmark (URL list) for the home page of a clientless connection, go to Configuration | Remote Access VPN | Clientless SSL VPN Access | Portal | Bookmarks. Click the Add button. Give the bookmark list a name, and click the Add button to add the individual URLs. There are advanced options that you can expand for a URL, like including a thumbnail image for the URL.

For example, to create the look and feel of the home portal for clientless connections, go to Configuration | Remote Access VPN | Clientless SSL VPN Access | Portal | Customization, and click Add (this can also be done in the wizard). Give the profile a name, and then select it and click Apply.

To change a profile, select a profile name and click the Edit button—a web browser window will open, allowing you to change the look and feel of the home page for a clientless connection. Click the hyperlinks on the left to change the various properties. Click the Preview button on the right to see what your changes would look like. Click the Save button in the top right to save your changes to the appliance. After saving your changes, you can close the web browser window.

TIP When you're using clientless mode, the appliance acts as a web proxy; in this situation, you'll need to define DNS servers to resolve names to addresses. I'm surprised this is not part of the wizard, but it can be completed by going to Configuration | Remote Access VPN | DNS, shown in Figure 27-20.

AnyConnect Client

You can easily set up and manage AnyConnect WebVPN sessions on your appliance when using ASDM. For the initial setup, ASDM supports a wizard for AnyConnect functions. Once you've used the wizard, installing additional AnyConnect software clients or profiles, or changing AnyConnect policies, is easy with ASDM Configuration screens. The following two sections will introduce you to these topics.

SSL VPN Wizard for AnyConnect WebVPN Connections   As mentioned in the "SSL VPN Wizard for Clientless WebVPN Connections" section, the SSL VPN Wizard allows you to set up clientless and/or AnyConnect/SVC client connections. To access the SSL VPN Wizard to initialize the WebVPN server feature, go to Wizards | SSL VPN Wizard, shown

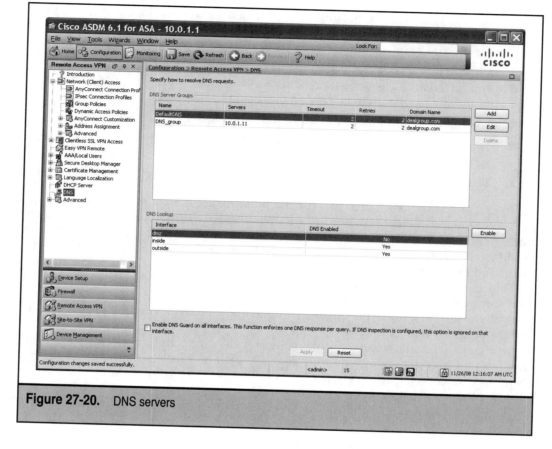

Figure 27-20. DNS servers

previously in Figure 27-18. In the initial pop-up window, you can create a clientless WebVPN configuration, an AnyConnect WebVPN configuration, or both.

Here are the screens you'll go through when using the wizard to set up your AnyConnect policies:

▼ Screen 1: Choose the type of WebVPN session—clientless, AnyConnect, or both.

■ Screen 2: Define the tunnel group name, the name of the interface that users will connect to using SSL, the certificate to be used (optional), the alias name of the tunnel group, and if the list of alias names will appear on the login screen.

■ Screen 3: Specify the location of user accounts: the local database of `username` commands or an AAA server group; if you chose the local database option, you'll be asked to add user accounts on this screen.

■ Screen 4: Choose if you want to create a new group policy or modify an existing one.

■ Screen 5: Select an existing address pool, or create a new address pool for the internal addresses, and specify the AnyConnect image in flash of the appliance.

(If one doesn't exist, you have an option to download it from Cisco using a CCO account.) Note that you'll need to manually add a `nat 0` policy configuration under the Configuration | Firewall | NAT Rules screen: you're reminded of this with a pop-up window.

▲ Screen 6: Accept your configuration by clicking the Finish button.

Other policies and configuration changes must be done after the completion of the wizard from the Remote Access tab on the Configuration screen.

AnyConnect WebVPN Attributes   Once you've set up at least one tunnel group and its policies for AnyConnect client access, you can either use the wizard to add additional groups, or change any AnyConnect policies or attributes from the Remote Access VPN tab. I'll highlight some of the screens to tune your AnyConnect configuration.

To change the policies for your AnyConnect client sessions, go to Network (Client) Access | AnyConnect Connection Profiles under the Remote Access VPN tab (shown in Figure 27-21). To add additional AnyConnect clients that exist in flash, go to Advanced | SSL VPN | Client Settings under the Remote Access VPN tab (shown in Figure 27-22).

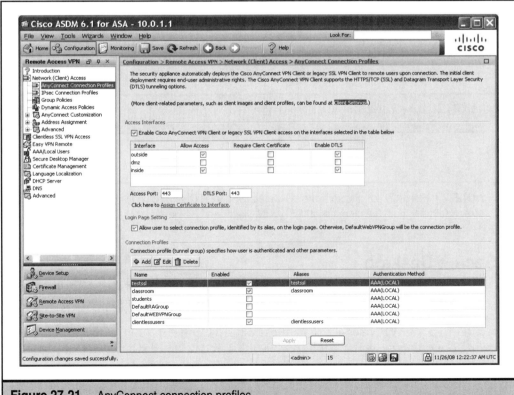

Figure 27-21. AnyConnect connection profiles

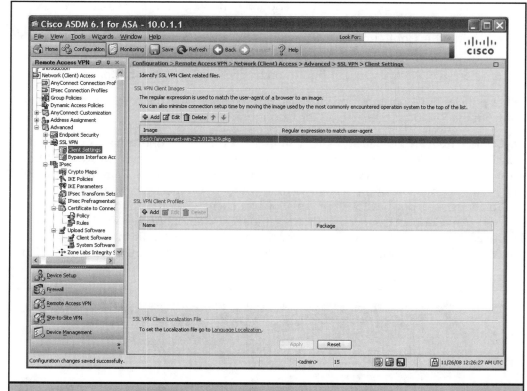

Figure 27-22. AnyConnect software images

NOTE In Figure 27-22, the software is labeled "SSL VPN Client," which is misleading, because the screen refers to both the older client (SSL VPN Client) and the newer one (AnyConnect Client).

Cisco Secure Desktop

Cisco Secure Desktop (CSD) is a WebVPN enhancement that provides additional security to your WebVPN sessions—upon logging in, during the session, and when ending the session. CSD is a stand-alone Java-based software package that provides additional protection to a WebVPN session (clientless or AnyConnect). CSD is supported on the following operating systems: Windows 2000, XP, and Vista (the latter in CSD 3.3), Mac OS X, and Linux.

NOTE CSD policies must be defined from ASDM—the CLI is unsupported.

CSD Dynamic Access Policies and Prelogin Assessment

The appliance integrates CSD features into dynamic access policies (DAPs). Depending on the appliance configuration, the security appliance uses one or more user attribute values, along with optional AAA attribute values, as conditions for assigning a DAP to a user. CSD features supported by the user attributes of DAPs include the OS of the user PC, prelogin policies, results of a Basic Host Scan, and Endpoint Assessment. The DAP then provides (or denies) network access to resources at the level that is appropriate for the end-point AAA attribute value.

DAPs you can define include host scans and prelogin assessments. You can have the CSD software perform the following:

▼ *Basic host scan* Identifies the OS and patches/service packs applied on the user PC.

■ *End-point assessment* Looks for antivirus, antispyware, firewall software, and the appropriate definition updates.

▲ *Advanced end-point assessment* With the appropriate license, CSD can update the required security software on the user's PC.

The prelogin assessment installs itself after the user connects to the appliance, but before the user logs into the appliance. The prelogin assessment can check for defined files on the user's desktop, certificates that are installed, the OS version installed on the user desktop, the IP address on the user's NIC, and MS Windows registry key values.

Protections Provided by CSD

CSD can provide four main protective services for a user's desktop:

▼ Secure Session (commonly called Secure Desktop)

■ Cache Cleaner

■ Keystroke Logger

▲ Host Emulation Detection

The secure session feature, commonly called the *Secure Desktop* or Secure Vault, is only supported on the Windows 2000, XP, and Vista desktop. The Secure Desktop encrypts data and files (located on the disk drive only—not memory) associated with or downloaded during the WebVPN session—these can be either clientless or tunnel mode (AnyConnect) connections. Basically the downloaded information is stored in a secure desktop partition that looks like a virtual PC desktop. Upon the WebVPN session termination, U.S. Department of Defense (DoD) standards are followed to safely and securely remove the partition.

Because the Secure Desktop is only supported on certain Windows systems, an alternative to the Secure Vault is the Cache Cleaner: it safely deletes the browser cache and information associated with the WebVPN session and is commonly used with clientless connections, where the user cannot install additional software on the desktop. The Cache Cleaner is supported on Windows 2000, XP, and Vista, Mac OS X, and Linux operating systems.

The Keystroke Logger Detection feature can configure a prelogin policy to have CSD scan for keystroke logging applications on the user desktop and to deny WebVPN access if this kind of application is detected. You can use an option to exempt specified applications from the examination if necessary. The Keystroke Logger Detection feature is disabled by default; if enabled, it is downloaded with Secure Desktop, Cache Cleaner, or Host Scan policies. Like the Secure Desktop feature, this feature is only supported on Windows 2000, XP, and Vista systems.

NOTE It is possible to enforce an on-screen keyboard (OSK) for key logger avoidance. A user types her username, and then an OSK pops up for her password, where she uses a mouse to click the characters in her password. That will work on any GUI OS. This feature is actually recommended for users who connect from kiosks or computers other than their own.

The Host Emulation Detection feature allows you to configure a prelogin policy to determine if Windows 2000, XP, or Vista is running within virtualization software like VMware. By default this feature is disabled; if enabled, it is downloaded with Secure Desktop, Cache Cleaner, or Host Scan policies.

Processing CSD Components

Because many policies can be configured with CSD, they are processed in the following order only when CSD is enabled for a WebVPN session:

1. The user connects using clientless or tunnel mode.

2. Prelogin dynamic assessment policies (DAPs) can check for OS type, existence of files, registry keys, certificates, the IP address used by the user, key logging programs, and so on.

3. Based on the results of the prelogin assessment, either the user will see a `Login Denied` message, or a prelogin policy name is assigned to the user, and the name is reported to the appliance.

4. If enabled, the Host Scan is downloaded and runs Secure Desktop or Cache Cleaner.

5. The user is allowed to authenticate.

6. The appliance applies a DAP to the session, based on the prelogin policy, the host scan results, and the authentication data of the user (like the user's policies or certificate information).

7. Upon logging out of the WebVPN session, the Host Scan terminates, and the Cache Cleaner or Secure Desktop performs its clean-up functions.

NOTE   If the OS on the user desktop cannot be detected, Secure Desktop is not downloaded—only Cache Cleaner can be used.

Installing CSD

To access and set up CSD, go to Configuration | Remote Access VPN | Secure Desktop Manager | Setup, shown in Figure 27-23. You can copy the CSD file ("securedesktop_ asa-X.Y.Z.aaaaa-k9.pkg") manually to flash, or download it via your ASDM session (clicking the Upload button). Once you have selected an image to install, select the Enable Secure Desktop check box, and then click the Apply button.

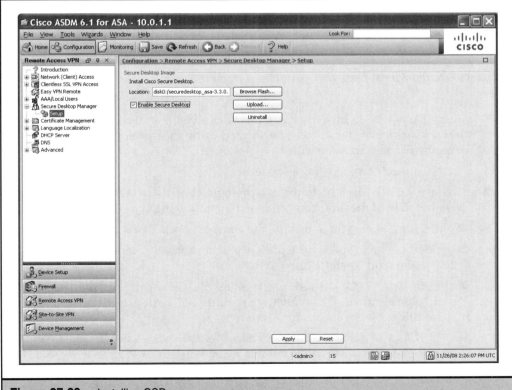

Figure 27-23.   Installing CSD

NOTE You can't just copy the CSD image to flash and use it; you must also install it. CSD information is stored in the "cache:" location on the ASA flash. To view it, execute `dir cache:/sdesktop`.

If you will be using the AnyConnect Client *and/or* CSD and you also are using the Cisco Security Agent (CSA) on the user's desktop, you'll need to perform the following additional tasks:

1. Go to the Cisco site (www.cisco.com/cgi-bin/tablebuild.pl/asa) and download the "AnyConnect-CSA.zip" and "CSD-for-CSA.zip" files to the CSA MC device.

2. Extract the EXPORT files from the ZIP package files.

3. Find the correct version of EXPORT file to import in CSA MC. (Version 5.2 EXPORT files work with CSA MC 5.2 and later.)

4. In CSA MC, go to Maintenance | Export/Import and import the EXPORT file.

5. Attach the new rule module to your VPN policy and generate your new rules.

Prelogin Policies for CSD

Once you have completed the CSD preparation from the Setup screen, you now have access to other CSD screens. When you click the Secure Desktop Manager | Prelogin Policy option in the Remote Access VPN pane, you are shown the default policy.

Explaining Prelogin Screen Elements   You can see the following information in the center pane:

▼ *Start*   Displayed in blue, this icon provides a visual indication of the beginning of the sequence of checks to be performed during the prelogin assessment. You cannot edit the start node icon.

■ *Line*   Connects two icon nodes together.

■ *Plus sign*   Click this icon to insert a prelogin check between the two icon nodes on either side of the line. You can insert the following types of prelogin checks:

   ■ *Registry*   Lets you detect the presence or absence of a registry key.

   ■ *File*   Lets you specify the presence or absence of a particular file, its version, and its checksum.

   ■ *Certificate*   Lets you specify the issuer of a certificate, and one certificate attribute and value to match. (For additional certificate attributes, create additional login checks for those.)

   ■ *OS Check*   Lets you configure checks for the user's OS: Microsoft Windows 2000, Windows XP, and Windows Vista; Win 9x (for Windows 98), Mac (for Apple Mac OS 10.4), and Linux. The editor inserts a Failure line and Login Denied end node for remote connections that fail the OS checks.

■ *IP Address*   Lets you specify an IP address range or network address and subnet mask.

▲ *Default*   This icon is displayed in green and is the end node that specifies a prelogin policy named "Default." By default CSD assigns this profile to every remote PC that attempts a VPN session, if you enable Cisco Secure Desktop. You can add prelogin checks to this policy or any other prelogin policy to specify criteria to match before CSD assigns the policy to a remote user's session.

Adding a Prelogin Policy   To add a policy, click the plus icon, the circle with a plus sign within it; you'll be presented with a drop-down selector where you can choose the type of prelogin assessment that will be performed. In the example in Figure 27-24, an OS check policy was added, where only Windows 2000, XP, and Vista are allowed. The plus icon was clicked again, where the policy chosen was IP Address Check. The Add button was clicked, displaying the range or subnet of addresses that are allowed. You can see that the IP Address Check policy was added in Figure 27-24. When you are done with your prelogin policy assessments, click the Apply All button.

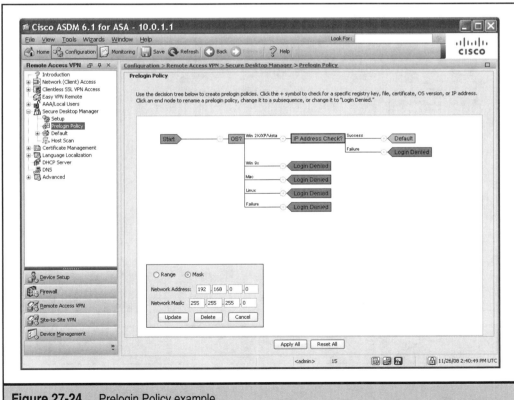

Figure 27-24.   Prelogin Policy example

Configuring Secure Desktop Features

When you click the Secure Desktop Manager | Default option in the left pane for Remote Access VPN, you can choose to install the Secure Desktop or Cache Cleaner (see Figure 27-25). The former has preference, but it if can't be installed, then Cache Cleaner is installed. (Remember that Secure Desktop is only available on Windows 2000 and later platforms.)

Configuring Keystroke Logging and Host Emulation   The keystroke logging and host emulation check are disabled by default. To enable these checks, under the Remote Access VPN tab go to Secure Desktop Manager | Default | Keystroke Logger & Safety Checks (see Figure 27-26). When you enable keystroke logging, you can define a list of programs/modules that are exempted.

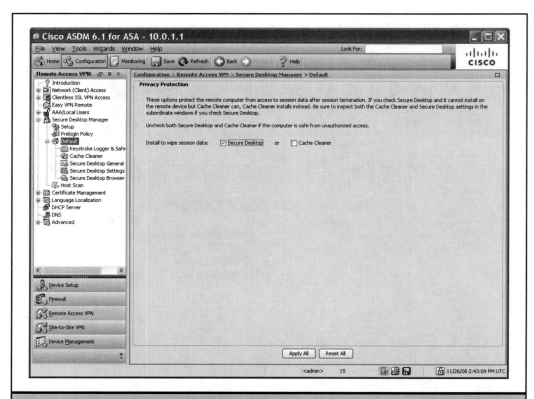

Figure 27-25.   Enabling Secure Desktop or Cache Cleaner

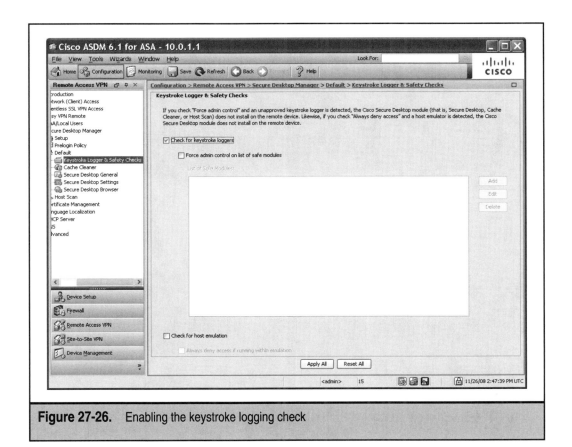

Figure 27-26. Enabling the keystroke logging check

Configuring Cache Cleaner The Cache Cleaner functionality is enabled by default. To further refine your configuration, under the Remote Access VPN tab go to Secure Desktop Manager | Default | Cache Cleaner (see Figure 27-27). This figure shows the options for configuring the Cache Cleaner feature. The Launch Hidden URL After Installation option checks for a URL for administrative purposes that is hidden from the remote user. This is used so that you know that the user has the Cache Cleaner installed. For example, you could create a cookie file on the user's PC and then later check for the presence of the installed cookie. The Secure Delete option specifies the number of passes of random writes over downloaded content (following DoD standards), ensuring that someone who tries to examine the disk space after the fact has less of a chance deciphering what was downloaded.

Configuring Secure Desktop General Attributes To configure the general attributes for the Secure Desktop, under the Remote Access VPN tab, go to Secure Desktop Manager |

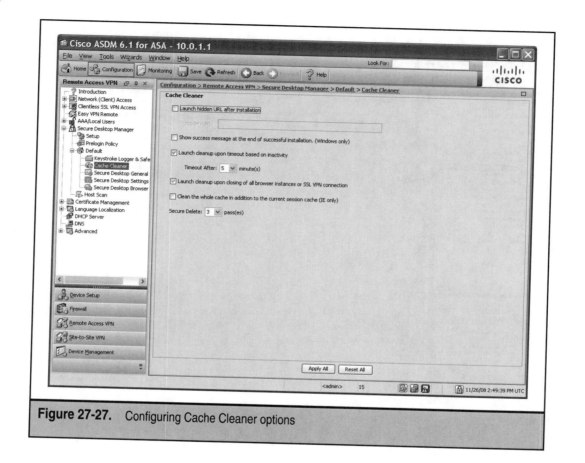

Figure 27-27. Configuring Cache Cleaner options

Default | Secure Desktop General. The following options are available on the Secure Desktop General screen, shown in Figure 27-28:

▼ *Enable switching between Secure Desktop and Local Desktop* Cisco strongly recommends that you enable this to let users switch between Secure Desktop and the untrusted desktop. This feature is called *desktop switching* and provides users with the flexibility they might need to respond to a prompt from another application requiring an okay to let Secure Session continue processing. Unchecking this option minimizes the possible risk where a user might leave traces on the untrusted desktop.

■ *Enable Vault Reuse* Checking this option allows users to close Secure Session and open it again later, sort of like a save feature. The Secure Session becomes a persistent desktop that is available from one session to the next. If you enable this option, users must enter a password to re-access and restart the Secure Session. This option is useful if users are running Secure Session on PCs that

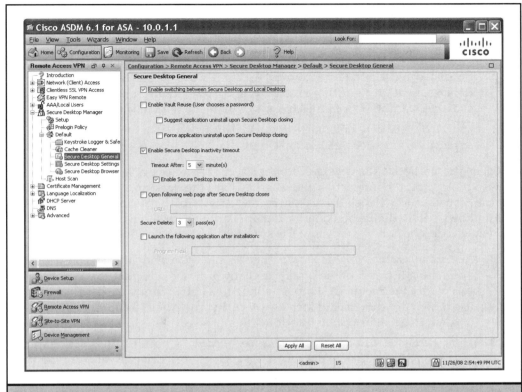

Figure 27-28. Configuring Secure Desktop General settings

are likely to be reused, like a home PC. When a user closes Secure Session, it is not deleted. If you do not enable this option, Secure Session automatically deletes itself (securely) upon termination.

■ *Suggest application uninstall upon Secure Desktop closing* Checking this option prompts the user and recommends that Secure Session be uninstalled when it closes. In contrast to the option below it, the user has the choice to refuse the uninstall.

■ *Force application uninstall upon Secure Desktop closing* Check this option if you do not want to leave Secure Session on untrusted PCs after users are done; when checked, the Secure Session uninstalls itself when the session closes.

■ *Enable Secure Desktop inactivity timeout* Checking this option closes the Secure Session automatically after a period of inactivity. Mouse movement and network traffic across the VPN restarts the idle timer.

- *Open following web page after Secure Desktop closes* Checking this box and entering a URL in the field ensures that the Secure Session automatically opens a web page when it closes.

- *Secure Delete* The Secure Session encrypts and writes itself to the remote PC disk drive. Upon termination, it executes a U.S. Department of Defense (DoD) sanitation algorithm, overwriting the session information with random characters X number of times (passes), where the default is three passes.

▲ *Launch the following application after installation* Launches the specified application after Secure Desktop closes.

Configuring Secure Desktop Settings and Browser Screens The Secure Desktop Settings screen allows you to limit the interaction the user has with the desktop, like the applications that can be used and the disk drives that can be accessed. The Secure Desktop Browser screen allows you to define bookmarks that appear in the user's web browser.

Here is a description of the Secure Desktop Settings you can configure:

▼ *Restrict application usage to the web browser only* Checking this lets only the originating browser of the session and any browser helpers that you specify run within the Secure Desktop. Enabling this option limits the user's ability to use other applications, but increases security. You can add additional programs once you select this option by adding them to a text list.

- *Disable access to network drives and network folders* Checking this prevents a user from accessing network resources and network drives while running the Secure Desktop.

- *Do not encrypt files on network drives* Checking this lets the user save files to network drives. Secure Session does not encrypt the files and leaves the files behind after the session ends. If you uncheck "Disable access to network drives and network folders" and this attribute, Secure Desktop encrypts the files the user saves to network drives, and then removes them upon Secure Session termination.

- *Disable access to removable drives and removable folders* Checking this option prevents the user from accessing portable drives, like flash drives and CDs/DVDs while running Secure Desktop. (This option only applies to the drives that Microsoft labels "Removable" in Windows Explorer.)

- *Do not encrypt files on removable drives* Checking this option lets the user save files to removable drives: the Secure Desktop does not encrypt the files and leaves the files after the session ends.

- *Disable registry modification* Checking this option prevents the user from modifying the registry from within the Secure Desktop (recommended to enable this).

- *Disable command prompt access* Checking this option prevents the user from running the DOS command prompt from within the Secure Desktop (recommended to enable this).

■ *Disable printing* Checking this option prevents the user from printing while using the Secure Desktop. When dealing with any type of sensitive data, it is recommended to check this option.

▲ *Allow email applications to work transparently* Checking this option lets the user open e-mail while within a Secure Desktop and prevent it from deleting e-mail upon terminating the session. When enabled, the Secure Desktop handles e-mail the same way the local desktop does. This feature works only with these e-mail applications: Microsoft Outlook Express, Microsoft Outlook, Eudora, and Lotus Notes. When this option is enabled, any attachments downloaded are visible within both desktops (Secure Desktop/Vault and the local desktop).

Using Secure Desktop

Figure 27-29 shows an example of the Secure Desktop/Vault, or logical desktop. Notice the buttons on the right that allow you to switch to the physical computer desktop or close down the Secure Session. Notice the lock picture in the middle of the screen. In the taskbar (not seen in the figure), you'll see a yellow icon indicating that the Secure Desktop is secure.

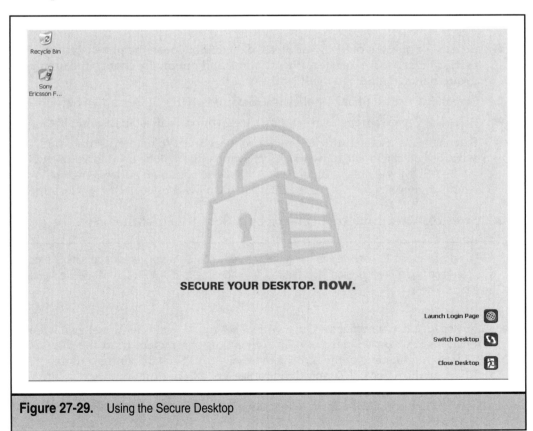

Figure 27-29. Using the Secure Desktop

Site-to-Site VPN Tab

You can easily set up and manage IPSec site-to-site (LAN-to-LAN or L2L) connections on your appliance when using ASDM. For the initial setup, ASDM supports a wizard for L2L connections. Once you've used the wizard, changing the L2L policies is easy with ASDM configuration screens. The following two sections will introduce you to these topics.

IPSec Wizard for L2L Connections   To access the IPSec wizard to set up the L2L connection, go to Wizards | IPSec VPN Wizard, shown previously in Figure 27-15. In the initial pop-up window, you can either create an IPSec L2L connection, or set up the Easy VPN Server feature. Choose the Site-to-Site radio button for the former. You also need to choose the interface the IPSec sessions will be terminated on. Optionally selecting the check box at the bottom will configure the `sysopt connection permit-vpn` command, which allows decrypted VPN traffic to be exempted from ACL checks when going from a lower- to higher-level interface.

Here are the screens you'll go through when using the wizard to set up your L2L connection:

▼ Screen 1: Choose the type of IPSec VPN: Site-to-Site or Remote Access (Easy VPN Server).

■ Screen 2: Enter the public IP address of the remote peer, the pre-shared key or certificate to use for device authentication, and optionally change the tunnel group name (defaults to the IP address of the peer).

■ Screen 3: Create a phase 1 policy (the default is 3DES, SHA, and DH group 2).

■ Screen 4: Create a transform set for phase 2 (the default is 3DES and SHA).

■ Screen 5: Specify the traffic to protect between the two networks; in the wizard, you can create network object groups that will be used in your crypto ACLs ASDM will create. By default ASDM will set up an address translation exemption policy (`nat 0`) of the internal addresses between the two locations.

▲ Screen 6: Accept your configuration by clicking the Finish button.

TIP   Add all your L2L connections using the wizard, since it's a very quick and simple process; you can modify the configuration after the fact from the Site-to-Site VPN tab on the Configuration screen.

IPSec Attributes for L2L Connections   Once you've set up at least one tunnel group for an L2L connection, you can change the L2L connection parameters from the Site-to-Site VPN tab. I'll highlight some of the screens to tune your IPSec L2L configuration.

To add or edit the IPSec L2L connection profiles, go to Configuration | Site-to-Site VPN tab | Connection Profiles, shown in Figure 27-30. You can change the general connection properties of an L2L connection from here, or even add a new one without having to use

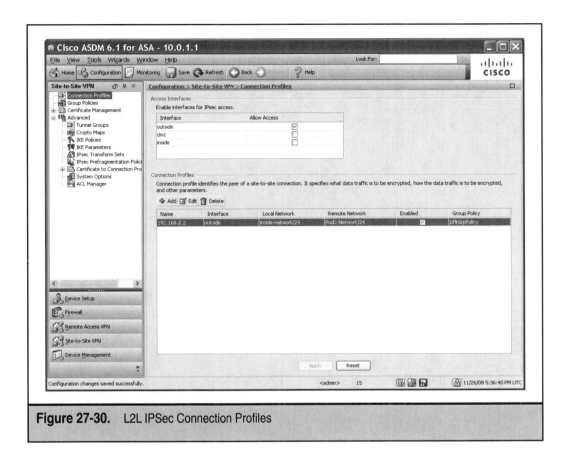

Figure 27-30. L2L IPSec Connection Profiles

the wizards. To change general properties for IPSec L2L connections, go to Configuration | Site-to-Site VPN tab | Network (Client) Access | Advanced. From here, you can edit the crypto maps, IKE Phase 1 policies, IKE parameters (like NAT-T), Phase 2 transform sets, crypto ACLs, and so on.

Device Management Tab

When you click the Device Management tab in the bottom-left corner of the Configuration pane, you can configure other properties of the appliance that didn't fall under any of the other Configuration tabs. Figure 27-31 displays the Device Management tab options. These include restricting management access to the appliance, the images to boot from or use, failover, logging, usernames and AAA, obtaining and managing certificates, DHCP settings, DNS servers and settings, and other properties.

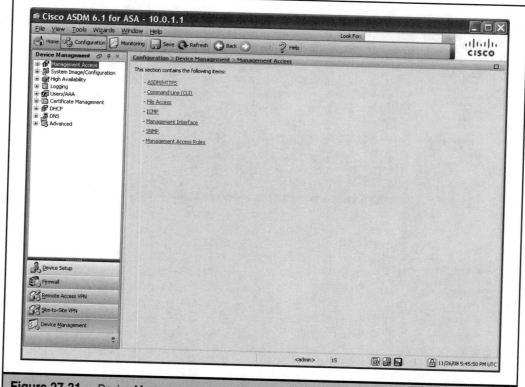

Figure 27-31. Device Management tab

ASDM MONITORING SCREENS

The Monitoring section of ASDM allows you to see information, sometimes in a near-real-time fashion, for processes running on the appliance. You can view graphs of statistical information, like interface statistics, as well as information about existing connections. You can access the monitoring screens by clicking the Monitoring button at the top of ASDM. When clicking the Monitoring button, you can see various monitoring tabs in the left pane:

▼ Interfaces

■ VPN

■ Routing

■ Properties

■   Logging

▲   IPS/CSC (if you have either of these modules installed)

The following sections will briefly discuss the monitoring screens available in ASDM.

Interfaces Tab

To access interface statistics, go to Monitoring | Interfaces. From here you can view the appliance ARP table, DHCP server statistics, interface statistics, and PPPoE client information. Figure 27-32 shows an example of the displaying Interface statistics: from the Interfaces tab, I first selected the interface (inside) in the Interface Graphs pane and then selected Bit Rates in the middle pane. I then clicked the Add button to add the information to the graph, and clicked the Show Graphs button at the bottom of the screen. A window popped up, displaying the Kbps of traffic entering and leaving the *inside* interface.

NOTE   The fastest that monitoring statistics can be updated is every 10 seconds in the pop-up window.

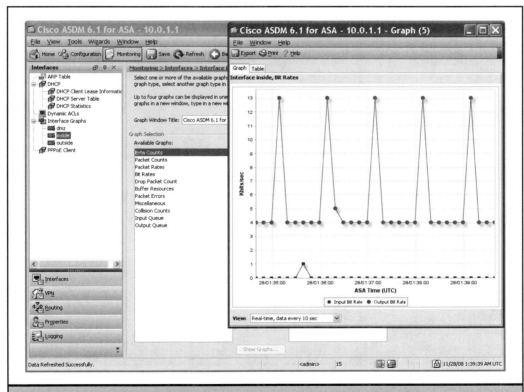

Figure 27-32.   Interface statistics

VPN Tab

When you click the VPN tab in the left pane, you can display statistics related to VPN sessions and tunnels: Easy VPN Remotes, L2L connections, L2TP sessions, and WebVPN (clientless and AnyConnect) sessions. As an example (see Figure 27-33), I went to Monitoring | VPN | VPN Statistics | Sessions. At the top is a summary of the VPN sessions connected to the appliance. In the Filter By drop-down selector in the middle pane, I qualified the output to just WebVPN clientless sessions, of which currently one session is active.

Routing Tab

When you click the Routing tab in the left pane, you can view dynamic routing information on the appliance (OSPF and/or EIGRP) and the appliance routing table. Figure 27-34 displays the appliance routing table, which was accessed by going to Monitoring | Routing | Routes. In this example, you can see multiple connected routes as well as one default (static) route.

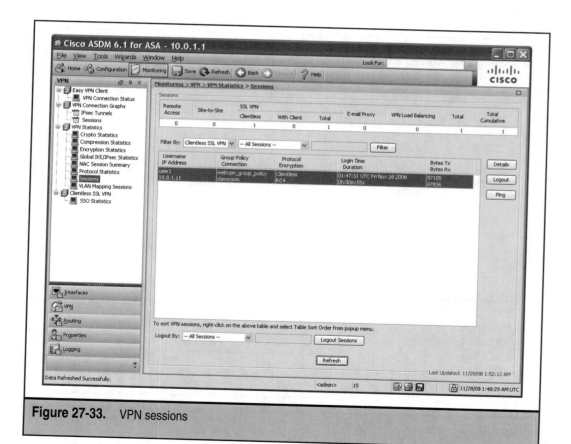

Figure 27-33. VPN sessions

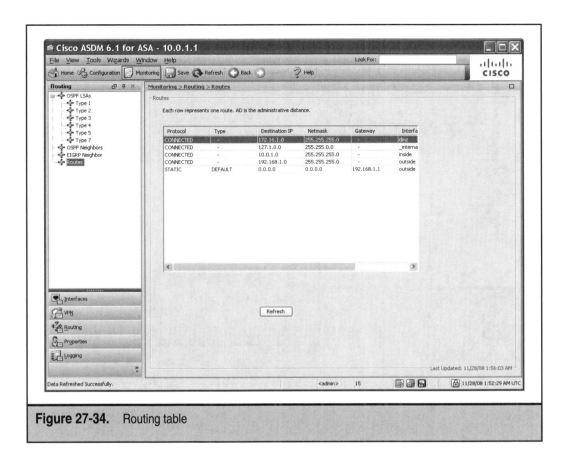

Figure 27-34. Routing table

Properties Tab

The Properties tab is sort of a catchall for the remaining statistical information on the appliance. From this tab you can view statistics on who's logged into the appliance, connections in the conn and xlate tables, failover, system resources (like CPU and memory usage), and many others. As an example (see Figure 27-35), I went to Monitoring | Properties | System Resources Graphs | CPU, clicked CPU Utilization under the Available Graphs column in the adjoining pane, clicked the Add button, and then clicked the Show Graphs button. This displays the CPU utilization of the appliance in the pop-up window on the right of Figure 27-35.

Logging Tab

You can view the logging information in the ASA buffer within ASDM—assuming you've enabled this feature. This information can be viewed from the ASDM home page or by

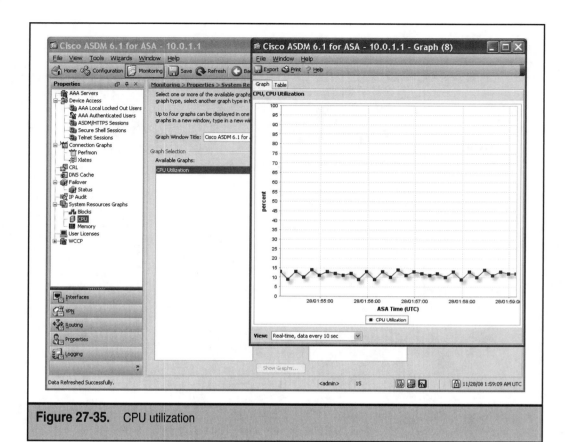

Figure 27-35. CPU utilization

going to Monitoring | Logging. The former shows a near-real-time update of log messages in the appliance memory (buffer). When going to Monitoring | Logging, you can open a separate pop-up window where you can view the information in the current buffer or in a window where you can view a near-real-time update of log messages. Figure 27-36 shows the log messages in the appliance buffer. One handy feature about logging in the pop-up window is that you can click a particular log message and see an explanation of it in the bottom pane.

TIP Another nice feature of ASDM logging is that for certain log messages that deal with ACL matches, you can select the log message, and click the Create Rule toolbar button at the top of the middle pane to create an appropriate ACL entry to permit (or deny) the traffic in question.

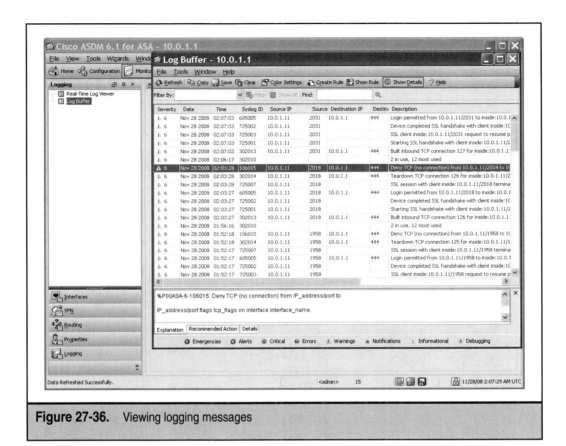

Figure 27-36.   Viewing logging messages

ASDM AND CONTEXTS

You can also use ASDM in multiple mode. First, you switch to multiple mode, create your contexts, allocate their interfaces, and configure their configuration file URLs. This was discussed in Chapter 22. Then switch to the administrative context with the **changeto context** command, and run the **setup** command from within the administrative context. Once you have done this, you can access the appliance using ASDM via the administrative context. The following sections will discuss accessing the administrative context and system as well as setting up failover.

NOTE   When using ASDM to access the system area, you must first log into the administrative context.

Initial Access and Context Manipulation

Once you've created your contexts from the system area and at least have run the `setup` command in the administrative context, you can then access the appliance using ASDM. The initial access is shown in Figure 27-37, where you can see the Device List in the left pane and the home page for the administrative context, called *admin*. The Device List allows you to switch to different contexts or to the system area, or even to different security appliances. Each context, as well as the system area, you can secure individually. When switching, you'll need to provide the appropriate authentication credentials to the appliance, context, or system area that you are accessing. There are Configuration and Monitoring buttons available for each context and system area.

To switch to the system area, double-click the System icon in the Device List. You can see the Home screen of the system area in Figure 27-38. On the system area home page,

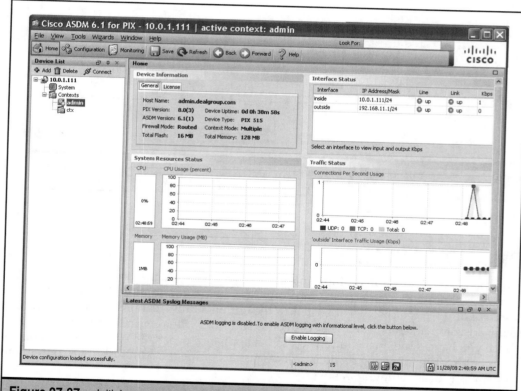

Figure 27-37. Initial access via the administrative context

Figure 27-38. System area home page

you can see the interfaces and the contexts they are associated with, the total connections across all the contexts or the connections per context, and the CPU and memory usage. Clicking the Configuration button when in the system area allows you to set up the interfaces, contexts, and system resources under the Context Management tab, seen in Figure 27-39.

TIP   When in multiple-context mode, go to File | Save All Running Configurations To Flash to save the system area and all other context configurations to flash memory.

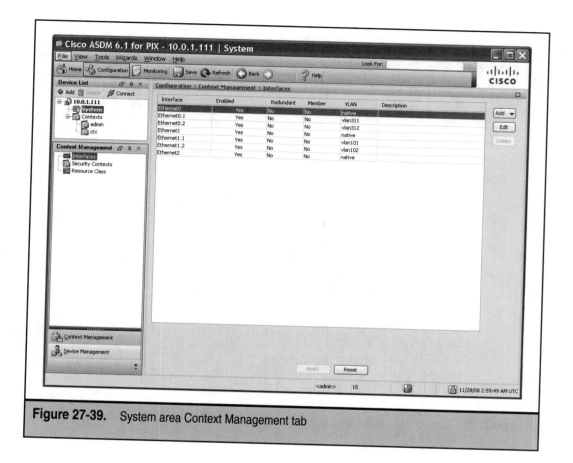

Figure 27-39. System area Context Management tab

Failover

Failover can be set up in single or multiple mode...from the CLI and/or ASDM. I'll wrap up this chapter by briefly discussing failover in multiple mode (the process is similar when the appliance is running in single mode). The High Availability and Scalability Wizard allows you to set up active/active failover, active/standby failover, and VPN clustering (the latter feature is only for the ASA 5510s and higher). The wizard can be

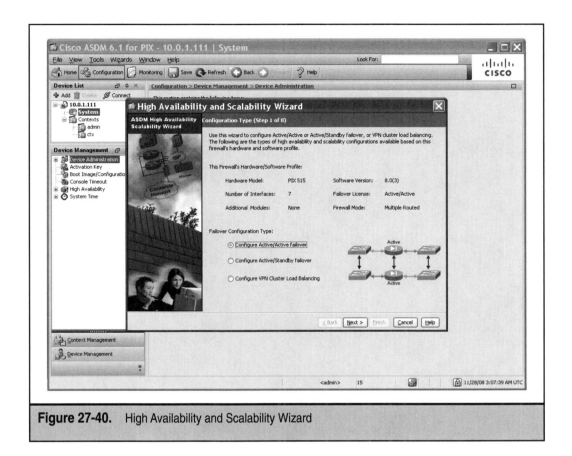

Figure 27-40. High Availability and Scalability Wizard

accessed by first accessing the system area and then going to Wizards | High Availability and Scalability Wizard. The wizard is shown in Figure 27-40. You can tune the failover process after the fact from the Configuration screens (go to Configuration | Device Management | High Availability in the system area).

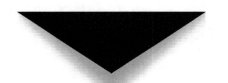

INDEX

References to figures are in italics.

4GESSM, 28

 A

AAA, 639
    authentication example, 641
    components, 208
    example, 208–209
    local authentication database,
        640–641
    overview, 208
    protocols, 209–211
    server command authorization,
        644–645
    server configuration, 211–213
access control lists. *See* ACLs

accounting. *See* AAA; CTP
ACLs, 9–10, 152
    activation, 160
    appliance and IOS router ACL
        comparison, 152–153, 154
    appliance with three interfaces,
        166–170
    appliance with two interfaces,
        163–165
    crypto ACLs, 400
    deleting, 162
    Ether-Type ACLs, 518
    extended, 156–157
    IPv6 ACLs, 242–244
    logging, 158–159
    non-IP traffic and Ether-Type
        ACLs, 518
    processing of, 153–155
    remarks, 157

ACLs (*cont.*)

    sequenced ACLs, 161

    standard ACLs, 155–156

    timed ACL entries, 153, 159–160

    and traffic flow, 515

    updating, 161–162

    using with address translation policies, 131

    verification, 160–161

    webtype ACLs, 464–465

active mode, 110

active/active failover, 17–18, 547–548

    example configuration, 570–576

    LAN-based failover (LBF), 566–569

    optional commands, 569–570

    See also failover

active/standby failover, 17, 546

    example configuration, 561–566

    LAN-based failover (LBF), 558–560

    optional commands, 560–561

    PIXs and the serial cable, 555–558

    See also failover

ActiveX, 190–191

    configuring ActiveX filters, 192

    filtering solutions, 191

Adaptive or Appliance Security Device Manager. *See* ASDM

Adaptive Security Algorithm (ASA), 7

Adaptive Security Device Manager. *See* ASDM

address resolution protocol (ARP), 70

address translation, 18–19

    advantages of, 120–121

    creating global address pools, 130–131

    disadvantages of, 121–122

    finding a matching translation policy, 141–142

    identifying local addresses for translation, 129–130

    interface PAT example, 133

    NAT and PAT example, 133

    NAT example, 123–125, 132

    needs for, 120

    PAT and Identity NAT example, 134–135

    PAT example, 125–128

    PAT example with two global pools, 134

    Policy Identity NAT example, 137–138

    Policy NAT example, 136–137

    private addresses, 119–120

    requiring address translation, 128–129

    terms and definitions, 122, 123

    three-interface NAT example, 135–136

    using ACLs with address translation policies, 131

    See also dynamic address translation

Advanced Inspection and Prevention SSM. *See* AIP-SSM

AH, issues, 375–376

AIP-SSM, 22

    modules, 29

AIP-SSM cards, 265–267, 598

    accessing the AIP-SSM CLI, 601–602

    assigning virtual sensors to contexts, 603–606

    fail-open and fail-close policies, 599

    hardware module commands, 614

    inline mode, 599

    promiscuous mode, 599

    setup script, 602–603

    traffic and, 599–600

    traffic forwarding to, 600–601

Anti-X card, 21, 264–265

AnyConnect client

    AnyConnect client usage policy, 493–494

    ASA preparation for, 491–493

    client installation policies, 494

    client profiles, 499–501

connecting to a WebVPN server, 501–504

connections, 489–490

copying the PKG file to Flash, 491–492

DTLS as a transport, 496–497

enabling, 493

implementation, 489

installing, 501

modules, 495

MTU size adjustment, 496

overview, 488, 490–491

rekeying tunnel sessions, 496

specifying the use of, 492–493

temporary or permanent client installation, 494–495

using, 502–503

viewing and managing connected clients, 504–505

WebVPN tunnel groups, 497–499

application proxy, 193–194

applications

and embedded addressing information, 111–112, 250–251

with multiple connections, 110–111, 249–250

and security issues, 112–113

security weaknesses in, 249

Are You There (AYT), 421

ARP inspection, 519

configuration, 519

verification, 519–520

ASA

cabling, 550–551

configuration example, 73–74

features, 4

management, 6–7

ASA 5505, 18, 24–25

configuration example, 449

interface configuration, 59–61

remote client, 445–448

ASA 5510, 25–26, 27

ASA 5520, 25–26, 27

ASA 5540, 25–26, 27

ASA 5550, 25–26, 27

ASA 5580, 26–28

ASA models, license limits, 114

ASDM, 7, 35

Access Rules element, 665–666

AnyConnect client, 675–678

basic configuration commands, 651

Cisco Secure Desktop, 678–679

CLI tool, 659

Clientless WebVPN, 671–675

configuration screens, 663

and contexts, 697–700

Device Dashboard, 654, 655, 662

Device Management tab, 691–692

Device Setup configuration, 663–664

Easy VPN Server setup, 669–671

failover, 700–701

File menu, 655–656

Firewall configuration, 664–665

Firewall Dashboard, 654, 662–663

Help menu, 661

High Availability and Scalability Wizard, 661, 700–701

home screen, 654–663

interface statistics, 693

IPSec VPN Wizard, 661, 669–671, 690

logging information, 695–697

monitoring screens, 692–697

NAT Rules element, 666–667

overview, 648

Packet Capture Wizard, 661

packet tracer, 658–659

Preferences tool, 660

properties, 695

Remote Access VPN configuration, 668–669

requirements, 648–649

restrictions, 649

routing information, 694–695

Service Policy Rules element, 667–668

setup script, 650

ASDM (*cont.*)
    Site-to-Site VPN tab, 690–691
    SSL VPN Wizard, 661, 671–678
    Startup Wizard, 653–654, 661
    supporting both WebVPN and, 456–457
    toolbar buttons, 661–662
    Tools menu, 657–660
    versions, 649
    View menu, 656–657
    VPN statistics, 694
    web browser access, 652–653
    Window menu, 661
    Wizards menu, 660–661
asterisks, 316
authentication. *See* AAA; CTP
authorization. *See* AAA; CTP
auto update, 428–430, 632–633

 B

banners, 54
Base and Security Plus license, 31
bi-directional PIM, 100, 101
bootup sequence, 36–37, 633–634
bridges, vs. transparent mode, 511–513
buffering web server replies to users, 199

 C

CallManager, 335–336
CAs, 380–381
    certificate group matching, 392–394
    date and time, 382
    file enrollment, 387–388
    identity certificates, 381
    identity information on the certificate, 381
    key pairs, 381–382
    network enrollment using SCEP, 384–387

    root certificates, 381
    saving certificates, 390
    troubleshooting, 391–392
    trustpoint configuration, 383–384
    and tunnel groups, 392
    viewing certificates, 391
certificate authorities. *See* CAs
certificate group matching, 470
Certificate Revocation Lists (CRLs), 381, 388–389
Check Point, 5
Cisco IOS routers, 9–10
Cisco Secure Access Control Server. *See* CSACS
Cisco Secure Desktop. *See* CSD
Cisco Secure Manager. *See* CSM
class maps
    application layer, 256–260
    configuration example, 256
    default, 254–256
    inspection (layer 7), 252–253, 260
    layer 3/4, 252, 253–254
    management, 253
    regular expressions, 253, 256–260
clear commands, 51–52
clear xlate command, 148–149
clear-text URLs, processing, 197
CLI, 7, 34, 36, 659
    ASA and router IOS CLI comparison, 41–43
    command abbreviation, 42
    Configuration mode, 39–40
    context-sensitive help, 41–42
    editing features, 43
    history recall, 42–43
    levels of access and prompts that go with them, 38
    packet tracer, 181–182
    Privilege EXEC mode, 39
    prompt, 37
    remote access, 65–68
    restricting access to, 639–641
    ROMMON mode (Monitor mode), 40–41

terminal emulation settings for appliance's console access, 35
upgrades, 632
User EXEC mode, 38–39
client-update command, 429–430
clustering, 437–439
command abbreviation, 42
command authorization, 642
enabling password command authorization, 642–644
local user database command authorization, 644
command-line interface. *See* CLI
commands
clear, 51–52
copy, 49–50
for device names, 53
for host and domain names, 52–53
write, 51
companies, and contexts, 525
conduits, 15
conn table, 7, 113, 146
clearing entries in, 148–149
connected routes, 77
connection-oriented protocols, 106
See also TCP
connections, 113
embryonic, 117
limits, 113–114, 261–264
removing, 114–115
TCP connection example, 115–118
troubleshooting, 181–187
viewing active connections, 146–147
connectivity testing
address resolution protocol (ARP), 70
ping, 68–69
traceroute, 69–70
console authentication, 639–640
contexts, 20, 31, 524
chaining, 526–527

and companies, 525
creation, 530–531
defining resource limits, 533
designating the administrative context, 529–530
examples, 536–540
and failover, 525
implementation, 526–527
and ISPs, 525
and licensing, 524
MAC addresses and, 530
properties, 526
removing, 536
restrictions, 525
saving configurations, 535
supported resource limits, 532
switching between, 535
switching to multiple mode, 528–529
system area, 526, 529
traffic classification, 527–528
uses, 524
verification, 531–532
viewing context resource allocations, 533–534
context-sensitive help, 41–42
control plane filtering, 179
copy commands, 49–50
CPU utilization, 72–73
CRACK, 375
crypto ACLs, 400
crypto maps, 402–404
dynamic crypto maps, 430–431
static crypto maps, 431–432
CSACS, 11, 209
configuration, 212–213
CSC-SSM, 21
modules, 29–30
CSC-SSM cards, 264–265, 606
forwarding traffic to, 607–609
hardware module commands, 614
setting up, 609–612
traffic and, 606–607

CSD, 678–679
 Cache Cleaner, 684, 685
 configuring general attributes, 685–689
 configuring keystroke logging and host emulation, 684–685
 dynamic access policies and prelogin assessment, 679
 installing CSD, 681–682
 prelogin policies, 682–683
 processing CSD components, 680–681
 protections provided by, 679–680
 using, 689
CSM, 7, 35
CTIQBE inspection, 340
 application layer inspection features, 341
 connection verification, 342
 layer 3/4 policy maps, 342
 setup of CTIQBE VoIP connections, 340–341
CTP, 11–13
 accounting, 230–231
 appliance authorization configuration, 227–228
 appliance configuration for accounting, 230–231
 appliance downloadable ACL configuration and verification, 229–230
 authentication, 213–224
 authorization, 224–230
 changing authentication parameters, 216–217
 classic method for authorization, 225
 controlling access for nonsupported applications, 219–222
 controlling authenticated access to multiple services, 225
 controlling authentication, 217–219
 CSACS classic authorization configuration, 226–227
CSACS downloadable ACL configuration, 228–229
 CSACS reports, 231
 downloadable ACL authorization method, 226
 overview, 214–215
 users accessing multiple services, 224
 verifying server interaction, 222–223
 viewing authenticated users, 223–224
Cut-through Proxy. *See* CTP

 D

data connections, 110
DCE/RPC
 example configuration, 281
 inspection policies, 280–281
 policy configuration, 280–281
Dead Peer Detection (DPD), 413, 497
debug commands, 485–486
default routes, 77
defined state machines, 107
dense mode (DM), 100
designated routers (DRs), 102
device names, commands, 53
DHCP, 620
 clients, 62–63
 relay, 622–623
 server configuration and verification, 620–622
DNS Doctoring. *See* DNS inspection
DNS inspection, 296
 default configuration, 301
 DNS application layer policies, 298–299
 DNS A-record translation, 297–298
 DNS Guard, 109, 296–297
 DNS packet length verification, 297
 example configuration, 301–302

layer 3/4 policy configuration,
   300–301
layer 7 class maps, 299
layer 7 policy maps, 299–300
DNS lookups, 457–458
domain names, commands, 52–53
dynamic access policies (DAPs), 679
dynamic address translation, configuring,
  129–138
dynamic addressing
    DHCP clients, 62–63
    dynamic DNS, 65
    PPP over Ethernet (PPPoE), 63–65

E

Easy VPN
    client mode, 442–444
    connection modes, *443*
    connectivity, 413–414
    Easy VPN remote, 410
    example server configuration,
      449–450
    features, 412–413
    network extension mode, 444–445
    network extension plus mode, 445
    overview, 410–411
    products, 411–412
    supported IPSec standards, 412
editing, control sequences for, 43
EIGRP, 76, 91
    authentication, 92
    basic configuration, 92
    route filtering, 94
    summarization, 93
    verification, 94
embryonic connections, 117
ESMTP inspection, 302
    example configuration, 305–306
    features, 302–303
    policy configuration, 303–305
ESP, issues, 375–376
Ether-Type ACLs, 518

F

failover, 15, 542
    active/active, 17–18, 547–548,
      566–576
    active/standby, 17, 546, 555–566
    addressing and, 546–547
    ASA cabling, 550–551
    communications, 551–552
    and contexts, 525
    failover link, 548
    hardware, 16, 542
    interface monitoring,
      553–554
    LAN-based failover
      cable, 549
    license requirements, 544
    link monitoring, 553
    PIX cabling, 550
    requirements, 543–544
    restrictions, 545
    serial cable, 548–549
    software upgrades, 545
    stateful, 16–17, 542–543
    stateful link, 549–550
    supported models, 543
    switch connections, 554
    triggers, 552–553
    types of, 542–543
Finesse Operating System
  (FOS), 5
firewall applications, 5
firewalls, 4
    for multimedia applications,
      348–349
    vs. security appliances, 249
    See also stateful firewalls;
      transparent firewalls; virtual
      firewalls
flash, 48
    files and, 630–631
    See also startup-config
fragmentation limits, 594–595

FTP inspection, 306
    control connection, 306
    data connections, 307
    example configuration, 311
    features, 309
    layer 3/4 policy maps,
      310–311
    layer 7 class maps, 309–310
    layer 7 policy maps, 310
    passive mode, 308–309
    standard mode, 306–308
FTP URL processing, 198

▼ G

Gigabit Ethernet modules, 28–29
group policies, 417
    attributes, 418–424
    configuring, 460–465
    external, 418
    filtering content, 464–465
    home page elements,
      461–464
    internal policies, 461
    local, 418
    location, 417–418
    overriding on a per-user basis,
      465–467
    restricting downloads and
      uploads, 465
    supported firewalls and their
      parameters, 421
Guard, 144

▼ H

H.323 inspection
    call control connection, 359
    connections, 357
    connections with terminals and
      a gatekeeper for address
      translation, 360–361
    connections with terminals and
      a gatekeeper for signaling and
      control, 361–362
    Direct mode, 360
    example configuration,
      366–367
    features, 362–364
    finding and connecting to
      a gatekeeper, 357–358
    H.323 and H.225 timeouts, 366
    H.323 monitoring and
      verification, 366
    layer 3/4 policy maps, 366
    layer 7 class maps, 364
    layer 7 policy maps, 364–365
    overview, 355–356
    Routing mode, 361
    signaling connection, 359, 361
    supported applications, 356
    types of devices, 356–357
    using only terminals to establish
      connections, 358–360
half-open connections, 22
hardware, 23–28
hardware failover, 16, 542–543
    See also failover
hardware modules, 28–30
    commands, 614
hardware remote, basic client
   configuration, 447–448
history recall, 42–43
home portal
    login screen, 471
    overview, 471–473
    tabs, 473–475
host names, commands, 52–53
HTTP inspection
    example configuration,
      317–318
    features, 313–314
    layer 3/4 policy maps, 317
    layer 7 class maps, 314–316
    layer 7 policy maps, 316
HTTPS URL processing, 198

▼ I

ICMP
    inspection configuration, 279–280
    inspection policies, 278–280
    issues, 278–279
    object groups, 174
    overview, 109
ICMP filtering, 177
    example, 180–181
    ICMP traffic directed at appliances, 179–181
    ICMP traffic through appliances, 178–179
    restricting ICMP traffic directed at appliances, 180
ICMPv6 packets, filtering, 242–243
Identity NAT, 129
    and PAT example, 134–135
IGMP
    interface configuration, 97–98
    limiting the IGMP proxy process, 98–99
    proxying, 96–97
ILS/LDAP
    connections, 284–285
    example configuration, 285
    inspection policies, 284–285
    policy configuration, 285
IM inspection, 318
    example configuration, 320
    layer 3/4 policy maps, 320
    layer 7 class maps, 318–319
    layer 7 policy maps, 319–320
implicit deny statements, 153
inbound connections, 56
incoming connection requests
    TCP, 107–108
    UDP, 109
inspection policies
    DCE/RPC, 280–281
    ICMP, 278–280
    ILS/LDAP, 284–285

IPSec Pass-Thru, 287–288
NetBIOS, 285–287
PPTP, 288–289
Sun RPC, 281–284
XDMCP, 289–293
instant messaging inspection. *See* IM inspection
Interactive Unit Authentication (IUA), 446
interface tests, 553–554
interfaces
    ASA 5505 interface configuration, 59–61
    logical names, 56
    physical interface configuration, 57–58
    physical names, 55–56
    security levels, 56–57
    verification, 61–62
    VLAN configuration, 58–59
Internet Control Management Protocol. *See* ICMP
Internetwork Operating System (IOS), 5
intrusion detection system (IDS), 22
intrusion prevention system (IPS), 22
IP audit, 587
    configuration, 590
    signatures, 587–590
IPS card, 265–267
IPSec
    overview, 372
    remote access server, 434–436
    same interface traffic, 373
    sessions terminated behind the appliance, 377–378
    sessions terminated on the appliance, 377
    setting up an IPSec connection to a remote IPSec peer, 372–373
IPSec over TCP, 376–377
IPSec over UDP, 422
IPSec Pass-Thru, inspection policies, 287–288

IPSec site-to-site connection
    connection lifetimes, 401
    crypto ACLs, 400
    crypto maps, 402–404
    example, 407–408
    ISAKMP Phase 1 configuration, 397
    ISAKMP Phase 2 configuration,
        399–404
    preparation, 396
    transform sets, 400–401
    troubleshooting connections, 407
    tunnel group configuration,
        397–398
    viewing and clearing connections,
        405–406
    VPN traffic and address translation,
        398–399
IPv6
    ACLs, 242–244
    capabilities of the appliances,
        234–235
    duplicate address detection,
        236–237
    filtering packets, 243–244
    global address configuration,
        237–238
    interface configuration
        verification, 238
    limitations of the appliances, 235
    link-local address
        configuration, 237
    neighbor solicitation messages, 237,
        240–241
    neighbors, 239–242
    overview, 234
    router advertisement messages,
        241–242
    routing, 238–239
    stateless autoconfiguration, 236–237
    static neighbor definition, 241
    traffic, 20
ISAKMP, 373
    aggressive mode, 374
    disconnect notice, 374

    enabling, 374
    global properties, 373–374
    identity, 374
    main mode, 374
    Phase 1 configuration, 397,
        416–417
    Phase 2 configuration, 399–404,
        430–432
    policies, 375
ISPs, and contexts, 525

J

Java, 190–191
    configuring Java filters, 191–192
    filtering solutions, 191

K

Kerberos, 210

L

L2L connections, 690–691
layer 2 processing, 510–515
LEAP, 422
license keys, 30–31, 634–635
licensing, 30–31
    and contexts, 524
    and failover, 544
    license limits of ASA models, 114
load balancing, 436–439
local host information, viewing,
    147–148
logging, 625
    configuration, 627–628
    configuration example, 628
    levels, 626
    message contents, 626
    verification, 628
login banners, 54

▼ M

MAC addresses, contexts and, 530
management accounting, 645
match command, 253, 254
    e-mail policy parameters for,
        304–305
    HTTP policy parameters
        for, 315
memory usage, 72
MGCP inspection, 342–343
    call agent, 342
    connections, 343–344
    example configuration, 345–346
    layer 3/4 policy maps, 344–345
    layer 7 policy maps, 344
    media gateway, 343
    signaling gateway, 343
    timeouts, 345
    verification, 345
modified proxy, 194–195
Modular Policy Framework. *See* MPF
monitor mode, configuring, 636–637
MPF, 248
    components, 251
    needs for, 249–251
    policies, 248–249
    See also class maps; policy maps;
        service policies
multicasting, 19–20, 95
    multicast usage, 96
    stub multicast routing (SMR),
        96–100
    traffic and appliances, 95
multimedia
    common problems, 348
    firewall solutions, 348–349

▼ N

NAT
    example, 123–125, 132
    NAT and PAT example, 133
    three-interface NAT example,
        135–136
    See also static NAT
NAT Traversal, *See* NAT-T
NAT-T 376
neighbor solicitation messages, 237,
    240–241
NetBIOS, inspection policies, 285–287
network attack prevention, 22–23
network object groups, 173
Network Time Protocol *See* NTP
not-so-stubby areas. *See* NSSAs
NSSAs, 88
NTP, 624–625

▼ O

object groups, 19, 171
    advantages of, 171
    configuration example, 176–177
    creating, 171–172
    deleting, 174–175
    descriptions, 172
    displaying, 174
    ICMP, 174
    nesting, 172–173
    network, 173
    object types for, 172
    protocol, 173
    service, 173
    using, 175–176
one-time passwords (OTPs), 13
Online Certificate Status Protocol
    (OCSP), 381, 390
operating systems, 5
    proprietary, 6
    upgrades, 631–633
OSPF, 19, 76, 84–85
    area stubs, 87–88
    authentication, 86–87
    basic configuration, 85–86
    interface parameters, 86
    not-so-stubby areas (NSSAs), 88

OSPF (*cont.*)
    route filtering, 89
    route redistribution, 89–91
    summarization, 88–89
    verification, 91
outbound connections, 56
outbound filters, 15
outgoing connection requests
    TCP, 107
    UDP, 108–109

▼ P

packet capture, 184
    copying captured packets, 187
    creating a packet capture process,
        184–186
    managing packet capturing, 187
    parameters, 184–185
    viewing captured packets, 186
packet filtering firewalls, vs. stateful
    firewalls, 9–10
packet tracer, 181–183, 658–659
passive RIP, 19
password recovery
    file, 636, 637
    performing the ASA password
        recovery process, 638–639
    performing the PIX password
        recovery process, 636–637
    restricting the process, 635–636
passwords
    Privilege EXEC password, 54
    User EXEC password, 53–54
PAT
    example, 125–128
    example with two global pools, 134
    and Identity NAT example,
        134–135
    interface PAT example, 133
    NAT and PAT example, 133
    See also static PAT
per-user licensing, 31

PIM multicast routing, 100
    dense mode (DM), 100
    sparse mode (SM), 100
PIM routing protocol, 100–101
    designated routers (DRs), 102
    and interfaces, 101
    static RPs, 101
PIM-SM, 100, 101
ping, 68–69
PIX, 18
    cabling, 550
PKCS #10, 381
plug-ins, 480
    importing, 480
    using, 480–481
policing policy, 267–268
Policy Identity NAT, example, 137–138
policy implementation, 13–15
policy maps
    activating a layer 3/4 policy map,
        274–275
    AIP-SSM card, 265–267
    connection limits, 261–264
    CSC-SSM card, 264–265
    default layer 3/4, 270–271
    layer 3/4, 260, 261–271
    layer 7, 261, 271–274
    prioritization and queuing, 268–269
    rate-limiting policy, 267–268
    syntax, 261
    traffic inspection, 269–270
    See also service policies
Policy NAT, example, 136–137
port address redirection (PAR).
    See static PAT
port forwarding, 476–479
PPP over Ethernet (PPPoE), 63–65
PPTP, inspection policies, 288–289
Preferences tool, 660
prioritization, 268–269
Private Internet Exchange. *See* PIX
Privilege EXEC password, 54
proprietary operating systems, 6
protocol object groups, 173

protocols, 110
    AAA, 209–211
    See also individual protocols
proxy ARP, 136

 Q

queuing, 268–269

 R

RA. *See* router advertisement messages
RADIUS, 210
RAM, 48
    See also running-config
rate-limiting policy, 267–268
redundancy, 15–18
regular expressions, 253, 256–257
    creating, 257–259
    grouping, 259
    special characters, 257–258
    testing, 259
re-imaging SSM cards, 615–616
remote access, 65–68
    disconnecting users, 434
    IPSec server example, 434–436
    preparation, 414–416
    verification, 432–434
    viewing connections, 432–434
remote management
    date and time, 623–624
    manual date and time, 624
    network time protocol,
        624–625
rendezvous points. *See* RPs
reverse path forwarding. *See* RPF
RFC 1918, 119
RIP, 76, 82
    configuration example, 84
    global configuration, 82
    interface configuration, 83
    verification, 83–84

routed mode, vs. transparent mode,
    510–511
router advertisement messages, 241–242
routing, 19–20
    administrative distance, 76–77
    recommendations, 76
    static routes, 77–82
RPF, 593–594
RPs, 100
    static RPs, 101
RSH inspection, 321
    connections, 321–322
    policy configuration, 322
RTCP, 351
RTSP inspection
    control connections, 350
    error connections, 350
    example configuration, 355
    layer 3/4 policy maps, 354
    layer 7 class maps, 353
    layer 7 policy maps, 354
    multimedia connections, 350
    overview, 349
    RealNetworks RDT mode, 352
    standard RTP mode, 350–352
    TCP mode, 353
running-config, 48
    viewing partial configurations, 49

 S

SAs, 399
SCCP inspection, 335
    application layer inspection
        features, 337
    connection verification, 339
    example configuration, 339–340
    layer 3/4 policy maps, 338–339
    layer 7 policy maps, 338
    setup of SCCP VoIP connections,
        335–336
SCEP, 384–387
Secure Desktop. *See* Cisco Secure Desktop

secure shell. *See* SSH
secure unit authentication (SUA), 446
security algorithm, 7
security appliances, 4
    vs. firewalls, 249
security associations. *See* SAs
Security Plus license, 31
Sequence Number Randomization.
    See SNR
sequenced ACLs, 161
service object groups, 173
service policies
    activating a layer 3/4 policy map,
      274–275
    verification, 275
setup script, 46–48
show commands, 485
show conn command, 146–147
show local-host command, 147–148
show xlate command, 144–145
shunned hosts, 584
signaling connection, 328–329
Simple Certificate Enrollment Protocol.
    See SCEP
SIP inspection, 328
    application layer inspection
      features, 329–330
    connection timeout, 333–334
    connection verification, 334
    example configuration, 334–335
    layer 3/4 policy maps, 333
    layer 7 class maps, 331
    layer 7 policy maps, 332–333
    setup of SIP VoIP connections,
      328–329
smart tunneling, 481–485
smartcard systems, 13
SmartFilter, 195
SMTP inspection, 302
    example configuration, 305–306
    features, 302–303
    policy configuration, 303–305
SNMP, 629
    traps, 630

SNMP inspection, 322
    example configuration, 323
    policy configuration, 322
SNMP maps, 322
SNR, 10–11
sparse mode (SM), 100
split tunneling, 413, 423–424
SQL*Net inspection, 323
    connections, 323–325
    policy configuration, 325
SSH, 67–68
SSL VPNs, 21
    clientless mode, 453
    overview, 452
    thin client mode, 453
    tunnel mode, 453–454
    See also AnyConnect client
SSM cards
    hardware module commands, 614
    re-imaging, 615–616
    verifying operational status,
      612–613
    See also AIP-SSM cards; CSC-SSM
      cards
startup-config, 48
    viewing, 49
stateful failover, 16–17, 542–543
    See also failover
stateful firewalls, 7–9
    and applications with multiple
      connections, 110–111
    and embedded addressing
      information, 111–112
    vs. packet filtering firewalls, 9–10
    and security issues, 112–113
static NAT
    example, 139–140
    syntax, 138–139
static PAT, 140–141
static routes, 77
    configuration example, 80
    configuration, 78–79
    route verification, 79
    tracking, 80–82

static RPs, 101
stealthy appliances, 179
stub multicast routing (SMR), 96
    configuration example, 99–100
    IGMP protocol and proxying, 96–97
    interface configuration for IGMP,
        97–98
    limiting the IGMP proxy process,
        98–99
stubs, 87–88
subnet masks, 153
Sun RPC
    configuring a layer 3/4 Sun RPC
        policy, 282
    controlling Sun RPC services,
        282–283
    example configuration, 283–284
    inspection policies, 281–284
suppressing RA messages, 241–242

▼ T

TACACS+, 210–211
TCP
    connection example, 115–118
    overview, 106–108
TCP Intercept, 143
    with SYN cookies, 143–144
TCP normalization, 22, 590–591
    configuring TCP normalization
        maps, 591–592
    example, 593
    using TCP normalization maps,
        592–593
TCP SYN flood attacks, 143–144
telnet, 66
    Virtual Telnet, 219–221
TFTP inspection, 312
    policy configuration, 313
threat detection
    basic threat detection, 578–579
    basic threat detection configuration,
        579–581

basic threat detection
    thresholds, 580
basic threat detection verification,
    581–582
scanning threat detection, 582
scanning threat detection
    configuration, 582–583
scanning threat detection
    verification, 583
shunned hosts, 584
statistics, 584–586
timed ACL entries, 153, 159–160
timed ranges, 159–160
traceroute, 69–70
Traffic Anomaly Detector, 144
traffic filtering, 19
traffic flow, and ACLs, 515
transform sets, 400–401
translations, 113, 115
    viewing active translations, 144–145
Transmission Control Protocol. See TCP
transparent firewalls, 20–21
    example configuration, 520–521
    See also transparent mode
transparent mode, 515–516
    vs. bridges, 511–513
    MAC address table and learning,
        517–518
    management IP address, 516–517
    vs. routed mode, 510–511
    supported and unsupported
        features, 513–515
    switching to, 516
    See also transparent firewalls
troubleshooting, connections, 181–187
trustpoints. See CAs
tunnel groups, 425–426
    attributes, 379–380
    and CAs, 392
    certificate group matching, 470
    configuration, 397–398
    creating, 378–379
    general attributes, 426–427, 467
    group matching methods, 469–470

tunnel groups (*cont.*)
    IPSec-specific attributes, 428
    lists, 469–470
    overview, 378
    VPN-specific attributes, 380
    for WebVPN, 467, 497–499
    WebVPN attributes, 468–469
tunnel maintenance, 448

 U

UDP, 108–109
URL filtering server, 195
    buffering web server replies to
      users, 199
    caching URL information, 198–199
    filtering example, 202–203
    policy exceptions, 198
    traffic filtering policies, 196–198
    verification, 200–202
    See also web content filtering
user authentication, 446–447
User Datagram Protocol. *See* UDP
User EXEC password, 53–54

 V

version information, 71–72
Virtual Cluster Agents (VCAs), 438
virtual firewalls, 18, 20
Virtual HTTP, 221–222
virtual private networks. *See* VPNs
virtual sensors, assigning to contexts,
    603–606
Virtual Telnet, 219–221
VLANs, configuration, 58–59
VPNs, 21
    load balancing, 436–439
    traffic and address translation,
      398–399, 415
    tunnel limits, 415–416
    See also Easy VPN; WebVPN

▼ **W**

WCCP
    configuration example, 206
    defining a WCCP server group,
      204–205
    enabling WCCP redirection on an
      interface, 205
    process, 203–204
    verification, 205
Web Cache Communications Protocol.
    See WCCP
web caching, 203–206, 459–460
web content filtering, 192
    application proxy, 193–194
    modified proxy, 194–195
    See also URL filtering server
web filtering. *See* web content filtering
web proxies, 458–460
Websense, 195
webtype ACLs, 464–465
WebVPN, 21, 452
    allowing WebVPN traffic, 455
    clientless home portal, 470–475
    controlling SSL encryption
      algorithms used, 455–456
    defining general properties, 460
    enabling, 456
    group policies, 460–467
    network clients, 488–489
    overriding group policies on
      a per-user basis, 465–467
    performing DNS lookups,
      457–458
    port forwarding, 476–479
    restrictions, 454–455
    supporting both WebVPN and
      ASDM, 456–457
    user WebVPN attributes,
      466–467
    verification and troubleshooting,
      485–486
    web caching, 459–460

web proxying, 458–460
See also AnyConnect client; SSL VPNs
write commands, 51

 X

XAUTH
    authentication methods, 445–446
    user accounts and attributes, 424–425
    user authentication, 446–447

XDMCP
    clients on the inside of the appliance, 290
    clients on the outside of the appliance, 290–291
    connections, 290
    established command configuration, 291–293
    example configuration, 293
    inspection policies, 289–293
    policy configuration, 291
xlate tables, 113
    clearing entries in, 148–149